FOURTH EDITION

Community Resources for OLDER ADULTS

I am dedicating this book to Jani Malkiewicz who, after 25 years, continues to be a steady and loving source of encouragement and support to me in all of my endeavors.

I would also like to dedicate this book to my Mother, Alta Wacker, who passed along to me her passion for education and belief in its power to change lives and communities. I am grateful to her for her lifelong support of my work in higher education, and it is my hope that you will help me celebrate her memory by carrying with you a passion for lifelong learning.

—RRW

I am dedicating this book to my husband, Steven Sheetz, for his never-ending love, support, and encouragement as I pursue the multiple facets of my career, as well as making coffee in the early morning hours when most of my writing gets done and calming candle-light dinners to end each day.

—KAR

We both dedicate this book to the people who have chosen a career in Gerontology and who work tirelessly and with compassion to provide older adults the support they need to live with the dignity they deserve in the last years of their lives – thank you.

—RRW

—KAR

FOURTH EDITION

Community Resources for OLDER ADULTS

Programs and Services in an Era of Change

Robbyn R. Wacker

University of Northern Colorado

Karen A. Roberto

Virginia Polytechnic Institute and State University

Los Angeles | London | New Delhi
Singapore | Washington DC

Los Angeles | London | New Delhi
Singapore | Washington DC

FOR INFORMATION:

SAGE Publications, Inc.
2455 Teller Road
Thousand Oaks, California 91320
E-mail: order@sagepub.com

SAGE Publications Ltd.
1 Oliver's Yard
55 City Road
London EC1Y 1SP
United Kingdom

SAGE Publications India Pvt. Ltd.
B 1/I 1 Mohan Cooperative Industrial Area
Mathura Road, New Delhi 110 044
India

SAGE Publications Asia-Pacific Pte. Ltd.
3 Church Street
#10-04 Samsung Hub
Singapore 049483

Acquisitions Editor: Kassie Graves
Associate Editor: Maggie Stanley
Editorial Assistant: Elizabeth Luizzi
Production Editor: Stephanie Palermini
Copy Editor: Matthew Sullivan
Typesetter: C&M Digitals (P) Ltd.
Proofreader: Sarah J. Duffy
Indexer: Karen Wiley
Cover Designer: Gail Buschman
Marketing Manager: Lisa Brown
Permissions Editor: Adele Hutchinson

Printed in the United States of America

Library of Congress Cataloging-in-Publication Data

Wacker, Robbyn R.

Community resources for older adults : programs and services in an era of change / Robbyn R. Wacker, University of Northern Colorado, Karen A. Roberto, Virginia Polytechnic Institute and State University. — Fourth Edition.

pages cm
Includes bibliographical references and index.

ISBN 978-1-4522-0246-4 (hbk. : alk. paper)

1. Older people—Services for—United States. 2. Community health services for older people—United States. 3. Old age assistance—United States. 4. Older volunteers in social service—United States. I. Roberto, Karen A. II. Title.

HV1461.W32 2013
362.6′30973—dc23   2012044455

This book is printed on acid-free paper.

13 14 15 16 17 10 9 8 7 6 5 4 3 2 1

Brief Contents

Detailed Contents

6 Education Programs

7   Senior Centers and Recreation   118

8   Employment Programs   143

9   Income Programs   160

10   Nutrition and Meal Programs   177

11 Health Care and Wellness   200

12 Mental Health Services   238

13   Legal Services

16 Care Management

17 Home Care Services   357

18 Respite Services   377

The Authors' Purpose

Students preparing for careers in gerontology and related areas need more than a description of existing community resources available for older adults. They need to understand how programs come to exist through federal legislation, who uses these resources, how they are delivered, and the challenges service providers face in meeting the needs of the aging baby boom cohort.

We have developed a text that gives students a basic understanding of aging policy that created the "aging network" and of theories that can be used to explain help-seeking behavior. Each chapter provides the reader with a summary of the legislation behind the development of pivotal programs and services, an in-depth review of the programs and services provided by the aging network and the private sector, current scholarship in each topic area, and international, national, and Internet resources. Students will learn to identify the challenges inherent in providing services to older adults through case studies, learning activities, and best-practice models. Instructors can use these learning activities to stimulate critical thinking about program and service delivery and to explore what changes might be needed to support future generations of individuals and families in their later years. We hope that *Community Resources for Older Adults* is a text that both students and faculty enjoy.

Robbyn R. Wacker
University of Northern Colorado

Karen A. Roberto
Virginia Polytechnic Institute and State University

Acknowledgments

As is typical of a project of this magnitude, many people have helped us along the way. Some did so willingly, others by default because they were in the right (or maybe wrong) place at a time that we needed help. We would like to take this opportunity to acknowledge those persons who made undertaking the revisions for this edition a pleasant and manageable experience. First, we thank students and staff members at the University of Northern Colorado (UNC) and at the Center for Gerontology at Virginia Polytechnic Institute and State University (Virginia Tech) for all their help in collecting articles, tracking down the latest statistics and references, and offering feedback. They include Sonja Rizzolo from UNC and Katie Barrows, Nancy Brossoie, Marya McPherson, Emma Potter, Alie Reichling, and Raven Weaver from Virginia Tech. Our administrative staff Carlene Arthur, Jane Graff, and Frances Braafhart supported us in many ways. We appreciate the assistance of Sharon Larson, Region VIII Administration on Aging, for providing so much information on the Older Americans Act and its history. Thanks to Linda Piper, former director of the Weld County Area Agency on Aging, who was our co-author for the first two editions of the text.

We are also indebted to the reviewers who offered their insights for the fourth edition: Mejai Avoseh, University of South Dakota; Susan Collins, University of Northern Colorado; Emmanuel Gale, California State University Sacramento; Phyllis Greenberg, St. Cloud State University; Martha Jacob, Dominican University; Shannon Jarrott, Virginia Polytechnic Institute and State University; Cheryl Osborne, Sacramento State University; and James Swan, University of North Texas.

A big thank you goes to Kassie Graves and her staff at Sage who, once again, aptly guided us through this revision.

Robbyn R. Wacker

Karen A. Roberto

PART I

The Social Context of Community Resource Delivery

CHAPTER 1

On the Threshold of a New Era

What will society in the United States be like in the year 2030? It is hard to know exactly how different our daily lives will be, but we do know that by the year 2030, our society will be experiencing something that none other has experienced. As we move through the twenty-first century, more Americans than ever before will be in their seventh, eighth, and ninth decades of life. Between 2011 and 2030, about 10,000 baby boomers will turn 65 each day (Cohn & Taylor, 2010). By the year 2030, the first members of the baby boom generation, born in 1946, will be 84 years of age, and the youngest members, born in 1964, will be 65. By the year 2030, there will be about 72 million people aged 65 and older—more than twice the number in 2000 (Federal Interagency Forum on Aging-Related Statistics, 2010). Demographically, the baby boom cohort is sandwiched between two smaller cohorts. As a result of its enormous size and vast racial and ethnic diversity, it has commanded attention at every stage of its life course. In the 1960s, school systems were forced to react to the soaring enrollments of the baby boom cohort; soon, social institutions that serve the older population will be challenged to respond to the baby boomers as well.

Will this graying of our population dramatically change our society? As demographers, economists, gerontologists, sociologists, and others debate this question, we can be relatively safe in predicting that, because of their unique characteristics, the aging baby boomers will cause a reexamination of current aging policies and services. Unlike the generations before them, collectively, they will be better educated, better off financially, living in the suburbs, and beneficiaries of the programs that were put in place for their grandparents. On the other hand, this giant cohort is tremendously diverse. About 77% of boomers have completed high school and 20% have a bachelor's degree or more (U.S. Census Bureau, 2011b). Although boomers' earnings are comparable with their parents' at a similar stage in life, the distribution of wealth in the United States has become more unequal in the past two decades; it is projected that 2% of boomers will live in poverty and 5% will live in near-poverty (up to 125% of the poverty line) in 2030 (K. Smith, 2003). Race and ethnicity are related to poverty in late life. About 6.8% of White elders lived below the poverty level in 2010, compared with 18.0% of Black elders, 14.6% of Asian elders, and 18.0% of Hispanic elders (Administration on Aging [AoA], 2011b).

A new Supplemental Poverty Measure (SPM) released by the U.S. Census Bureau in 2011 provides additional information about the economic profile of older Americans. In contrast to the official poverty rate, the SPM takes into account regional variations in cost of living, the impact of noncash benefits received (e.g., food stamps, low-income tax credits), and nondiscretionary expenditures including medical out-of-pocket costs. Using this measure, the number of older people living below poverty is significantly higher than the official poverty line indicates—15.9% of all individuals 65 and older are (AoA, 2011b). While not replacing the official poverty measure, the SPM sheds light on the effect of social safety-net programs and the marked impact of out-of-pocket medical expenses for older adults, raising awareness about how many older individuals are hovering dangerously close to poverty at any point in time (Tavernise & Gebeloff, 2011). In the coming decades, high rates of near-poverty and poverty will no doubt have implications for the financial well-being and quality of life of persons of all races and ethnicities in later life.

Another unique characteristic of the boomer cohort is their marriage and family patterns as compared with those of their parents and grandparents. Boomers tended to marry later, have smaller families, and have higher rates of divorce than their parents. In 2009, one in three boomers (aged 45 to 63 years) was unmarried (31% men; 37% women; Lin & Brown, 2012). This was a 50% increase in the number of unmarried individuals as compared to the same age cohort in 1980. Approximately 58% of these unmarried boomers were divorced, 32% were never married, and 10% were widowed (Lin & Brown, 2012). There is a greater tendency to never marry among younger boomers (born 1959–1964): 16.7% of men and 11.4% of women have never married, compared to 7.5% of men and 7.1% of women who comprise the older boomer population (born 1946–1951; MetLife Mature Market Institute, 2010a, 2010b). These unmarried boomers are changing the economic and social landscape of late life—they have a poverty rate almost five times higher than among married boomers; more than three times the number of unmarried boomers rely on public assistance (e.g., food stamps, SSI) than married boomers; and unmarried boomers report twice the disability rate of married boomers, but are less likely to have health insurance coverage (Lin & Brown, 2012).

Boomers also are redefining the traditional definition of "family" and thereby increasing the complexity of kin networks. Boomer families take many forms, including single-parent families, stepfamilies, cohabiting heterosexual and same-gender couples, childless families, and intergenerational families. Because families play a key role in providing instrumental and emotional support, as well as long-term care, to their older members, it is uncertain how these changes will influence family support patterns. Compared to their parent's generation, boomers are less likely to have a spouse to rely on and will have fewer adult children to serve as caregivers (L. H. Ryan, Smith, Antonucci, & Jackson, 2012). Thus, will adult children feel an obligation to care for both biological and stepparents? Will families who choose not to have children be at risk of having fewer informal resources? Will friends and families of choice be acknowledged and accepted as important sources of support and caregivers for lesbian, gay, bisexual, and transgender elders? Although the exact influence of family composition changes on the use of formal services is not known, we can anticipate that community programs and services will play a significant role in the lives of *all* older adults.

Collectively, these demographic characteristics will shape the type, amount, and nature of community resources in the future. They will increase the demand for home health care and retirement housing options. Many baby boomers will move into third, fourth, and even fifth careers and seek educational opportunities and greater flexibility in work and retirement options. The social safety net may need to be expanded for the underclass and lower class. The sheer numbers of aged boomers will challenge policy makers to rethink health care, retirement programs, and pension plans. Even now, projections—both dire and not so dire—are being made about Social Security and Medicare. Thus, demographic characteristics of the next generation of older adults will have direct implications on social policies that, in turn, support programs and services for older adults. In this next section, we discuss a few more of the salient demographic characteristics of the boomer cohort and the current populations of older adults.

GROWTH OF THE OLDER POPULATION

In 1950, 12.3 million persons (8.2% of the population) living in the United States were aged 65 and older. By 2000, the number of persons aged 65 and older had grown to 35 million (12.4% of the population). According to the 2010 Census, there are now 40.3 million (13.0% of the population) aged 65 and older (Werner, 2011). The older population will continue to grow rapidly over the next few decades as the first baby boomers turned 65 in 2011 (Exhibit 1.1). The number of older adults is expected to reach 71.5 million (19.6% of the population) by 2030 and 88.5 million (20% of the population) by 2050 (G. K. Vincent & Velkoff, 2010). Members of the older population are also aging. In 2010, 21.7 million persons were between the ages of 65 and 74, 13.1 million persons constituted the 75 to 84 age group, and 5.4 million people were 85 years of age and older, including 53,364 people 100 years of age and over (Werner, 2011). Moreover, persons 85 years of age and older represent the fastest-growing segment of the older adult population. The number of persons aged 85 and older is expected to grow to 8.7 million in 2030 and reach 19 million by 2050 (G. K. Vincent & Velkoff, 2010).

While growth in the aging population will be seen across the United States, some states and regions will be more dramatically impacted by growth in their aging populations than others. The older population lives predominantly in the most populous states (California, Florida, New York, and Texas), and largely in metropolitan areas (Colello, 2007). In 2010, 78.9% of persons 65 and older lived in metropolitan areas, with 36% of these older adults living in principal cities (AoA, 2011b). However, older adults also account for a larger proportion of the U.S. population living in nonmetropolitan rural areas than any other age group (Colello, 2007), with 20% of older adults living in rural regions (AoA, 2011b). This relatively large proportion of older adults residing in rural communities has stimulated concern among some policy makers and human services providers about their access to affordable housing, transportation, general and specialized health providers, and social services (Colello, 2007).

States and regions of the country are seeing dramatic growth in their population proportion of older adults due to migration patterns. Over the past few decades, some Southern and Western regions have seen an increase in older population because they have become popular retirement destinations, while some states in the Midwest and Northeast have seen a higher concentration of older adults largely due to out-migration of younger workers while older residents remained (Colello, 2007). Between 2000 and 2010, 13 states have seen their 65 and older population increase by 25% to 50%: Alaska (50.0%), Nevada (47.0%), Idaho (32.5%), Arizona (32.1%), Colorado (31.8%), Georgia (31.4%), Utah (31.0%), South Carolina (30.4%), New Mexico (28.5%), North Carolina (27.7%), Delaware (26.9%), Texas (26.1%), and Washington (25.3%).

What are the social implications of such an increase in the older adult population? Many writers in the popular press suggest that the increase in the number of older adults signals an impending social and fiscal crisis, and that aged persons will become a financial burden to society (e.g., Samuelson, 2005; Thompson, 2012). Others (e.g., Singer, 2011) argue that a "crisis mentality" overlooks other important demographic factors. Although it is true that the United States, along with other developed nations, will experience an increase in the older adult population, the number of older adults has steadily increased during the past

130 years. This steady increase has allowed society to adapt to the changes of an aging population, and provided new opportunities for scientific and business innovation and growth. Many scholars believe society will be able to adapt to this new cohort of older adults as well (J. H. Schulz & Binstock, 2006).

The assumption that older adults will place a burden on society is often based on the economic dependency ratio. The economic dependency ratio is the ratio of persons in the total population (including Armed Forces overseas and children) who are not in the labor force per 100 of those who are in the labor force. For every 100 persons in the 2010 labor force, about 100 persons were not. Of this group, about 43 were under the age of 16, 37 were aged 16 to 64, and 22 were 65 years of age or older (Toossi, 2012). The part of the economic dependency ratio that has been steadily increasing is the portion attributable to older persons, and with the aging of the baby boomers, the dependency ratio of the aged 65+ group is expected to increase to 26 by 2030.

The increase in the number of older adults, however, does not automatically result in a greater social burden. The aging population presents serious challenges that face all sectors of society. Meeting these challenges will require a new vision of American life that reaches beyond the immediate challenge of the aging of the boomers and promotes active engagement and a high quality of life throughout the lifespan (MacArthur Foundation Research Network on an Aging Society, 2008).

Exhibit 1.1   Actual and Projected Growth of the Population Aged 60+ (in thousands): 2010 to 2050

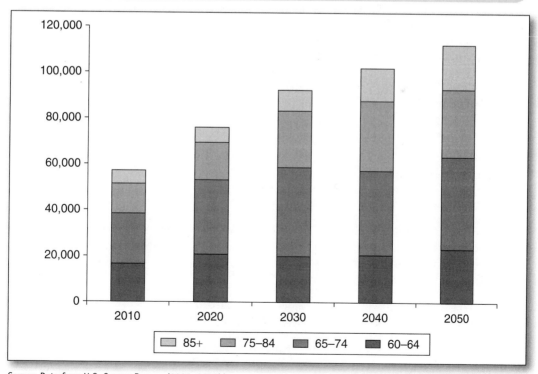

Source: Data from U.S. Census Bureau (2008; 2012b).

GROWTH OF THE OLDER POPULATION OF RACIAL AND ETHNIC MINORITIES

With the aging of the baby boomers, the older population is growing more diverse. Approximately 15% of baby boomers are from racial and ethnic minority groups: 9% are Black, 3% are Asian alone, and 3% represent all other races alone or in combination (Federal Interagency Forum on Aging-Related Statistics, 2010). Fewer than 10% of boomers are of Hispanic origin. Although non-Hispanic White older adults will still represent about 58% of those over age 65 in the year 2050 (G. K. Vincent & Velkoff, 2010), the percentages of Hispanics and of non-Hispanic Blacks and Asian Americans will increase dramatically. Exhibit 1.2 shows the percentage of older adults by race for the years 2010, 2030, and 2050 (U.S. Census Bureau, 2008; 2012b). This growing minority of the elder population brings new challenges and opportunities for providers of community programs and services (Goins, Mitchell, & Wu, 2006; Villa, Wallace, Bagdasaryan, & Aranda, 2012).

GROWTH IN THE NUMBER OF OLDER ADULTS LIVING ALONE

A final demographic characteristic with social service implications is the increase in the number of older adults who will be living alone. In 2010, 29% of all noninstitutionalized

Exhibit 1.2   Actual and Projected Distribution of Population Aged 65+ by Race: 2010, 2030, and 2050 (percentage)

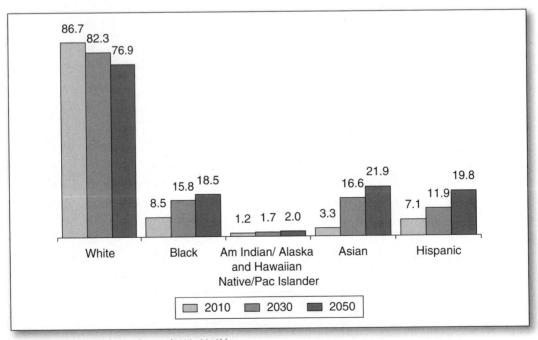

Source: Data from U.S. Census Bureau (2008, 2012b).

persons aged 65 years and older lived alone, representing 37.3% of older women and 19.1% of older men (AoA, 2011b). Living arrangements also varied by racial and ethnic status. Among both non-Hispanic White and Black women aged 65 and older, approximately 41% lived alone, compared with 22% of Asian and 27% of Hispanic older women. In contrast, 30% of Black older men live alone, compared to 18% of non-Hispanic White, 11% of Asian, and 13% of Hispanic older men (Federal Interagency Forum on Aging-Related Statistics, 2010). Moreover, the percentage of older men and women living alone increased with age. Among women aged 75 and over, for example, approximately 50% live alone compared with about 30% of women aged 65 to 74 (Federal Interagency Forum on Aging-Related Statistics, 2010). Among men aged 75 and over, approximately 22% live alone, compared to 16% of men aged 65 to 74. Differences in living arrangements of adults aged 65+ by sex, race, and Hispanic origin can be seen in Exhibit 1.3. Most notable is the generally high percentage of men who live with their spouses, compared with women and the large percentage of women living alone, across all groups. Living with other relatives and nonrelatives occurs more than twice as often with Black and Hispanic women than with White women.

Older adults who live alone are more likely to live in poverty. In 2010, approximately 16.0% of persons aged 65 and older living alone were living in poverty compared with 5.3% of older persons living with families (AoA, 2011b). Sex, race, and ethnicity further differentiate the percentage of older adults living in poverty. For example, 40.8% of older Hispanic women living alone were in poverty, compared with 12.3% of older Hispanic

Exhibit 1.3   Living Arrangements of Older Adults by Sex, Race, and Hispanic Origin, 2008

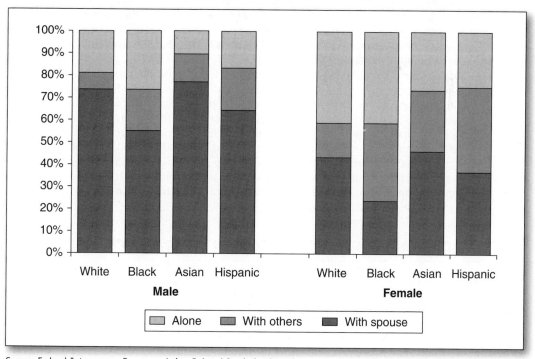

Source: Federal Interagency Forum on Aging-Related Statistics (2010).

women living with their spouses. Likewise, 30.7% of older Black women living alone lived in poverty, compared with 14.9% of their married counterparts.

IMPLICATIONS OF DEMOGRAPHIC CHARACTERISTICS FOR COMMUNITY RESOURCES

These selected demographic projections and unique characteristics have a number of implications for the delivery of community resources to older adults. The growth in the older adult population will increase the demand for all types of services. Professionals working to deliver the programs and services designed to improve the quality of life of older adults will thus be challenged to do even more with less. Because of the diverse nature of the boomer population with regard to ethnicity, income, family history, and life experience, professionals will be expected to be knowledgeable about a wide range of services and programs that serve both mainstream and disenfranchised individuals. Community programmers also must recognize and accommodate cultural diversity and remove the social and cultural barriers to service accessibility. A concerted effort needs to be made to design culturally appropriate programs and interventions that are responsive to the needs of minority communities (AoA, 2010e; Center on an Aging Society, 2004). Professionals must be visionaries in planning and developing services and programs to meet the needs of this new cohort with its diverse characteristics.

Now that we have had a chance to consider the challenges that lie ahead for services and programs that assist older adults, let's return to the present and consider more immediate issues. In every community, resources are designed to assist older adults in a variety of ways. Therefore, individuals working with older adults need to have a good understanding of these resources as well as the patterns of service use by older adults and their families. Anyone who has ever worked with older adults knows that the problems they confront tend to be complex and multifaceted.

Consider the case of Mrs. Duran, who confides that she is about to be evicted from her apartment. Further questioning reveals that she has not received her Social Security check for two months. She has limited resources for food, has received a utility shutoff notice, and has been unable to renew her insulin prescription for her diabetes. Or consider Mr. Jackson, who does not know what to do with himself since he retired. He has played golf or fished almost every day but is getting bored and disillusioned with retirement life. What community resources can be accessed to help Mrs. Duran and Mr. Jackson? Advocates who have an understanding of various programs and services assisting older adults can recommend appropriate options for both Mrs. Duran and Mr. Jackson.

A TEXT ABOUT PROGRAMS AND SERVICES IN AN ERA OF CHANGE

Because of the multiple challenges that older adults can experience and the changing demographics of the older adult population, we have created a text that provides a broad-based discussion of community resources. We believe that to effectively meet the needs of older adults who can benefit from using services and programs, professionals must understand the social and psychological dynamics of help-seeking behavior. It is not enough to know what services are available and appropriate; practitioners must also be armed with theoretical knowledge to understand *why* a daughter, despite her exhaustion, refuses to bring her father to the local adult day program, and *why* an older adult, who barely survives on a small pension, refuses to apply for additional income support that would make life a bit more bearable. In addition, we believe that practitioners must understand service use patterns and how families interact with the formal network when they need assistance in caring for their older family members. Greater understanding of these patterns can better prepare students and practitioners for understanding the dynamics of when and how families choose to use the formal network.

We also believe that simple descriptions of existing programs and services that assist older adults provide an incomplete picture. Practitioners and students should benefit from the interplay that exists between research and practice because research results have practical applications for the delivery of services and programs. In each chapter, we draw from empirical research to describe who uses and who provides such programs. We also include information about program outcomes when available.

Next, professionals need to be alerted to the infinite number of programs and services in communities that exist outside those funded through the Older Americans Act (OAA) of 1965 and subsequent amendments. Thus, we attempt to introduce readers to many programs that are both publicly and privately funded. Moreover, we discuss the different ways in which aging programs have successfully networked with one another to develop public and private partnerships in an attempt to reach more older adults.

In preparing the fourth edition of this book, we maintained the organizational structure of previous editions while updating and expanding the content to address the changes in community programs and services available to older adults throughout the United States. In addition to including the most up-to-date statistical data available, we have described important updates and additions to federal policies that provide the underlying framework for aging services. Each chapter includes reference to the latest research and highlights some programs and services throughout the United States and across the globe that serve as examples of innovative ways in which communities are meeting the needs of older adults and their families. We acknowledge the increasing diversity among members of the aging population by addressing the need for cultural competency in service delivery and by including new research findings (when available) and illustrative examples of resources and programs for older adults from different racial, ethnic, and cultural groups, as well as older persons living in rural areas, and for older adults who are gay, lesbian, bisexual, or transgender. The increasing availability of information online has allowed us to add many new web-based resources, including a specific section on international resources, for students to access further information about a particular issue, policy, program, or service.

ORGANIZATION OF THE BOOK

This book consists of three parts. In addition to this chapter, Part I has two other chapters. Chapter 2 presents a brief review of major aging policies, including Social Security, Medicare, and the OAA, the basis for the existence of many older adult programs. Chapter 3 explains the patterns of service use by older adults and the theories that can predict help-seeking behavior.

Part II of the book is based on the concept of the continuum of care. Conceptually, the *continuum of care* is a system of social, personal, financial, and medical services that supports the well-being of any older adult, regardless of the person's level of functioning. The goal, of course, is to have the appropriate services available to match the presenting needs. The continuum is often conceptualized in a linear way—older adults move from one end of the continuum (independence) to the other (dependence), and services exist at every point along the continuum to meet their social, medical, and personal needs. In addition, services impinge differently on the personal autonomy of their participants. For example, those who attend senior centers come and go as they please and make choices about their level of participation. In contrast, a nursing home is the most restrictive environment and impinges a great deal on personal autonomy and choice.

We have opted to depict the continuum of services as a more dynamic and interactive system (see Exhibit 1.4). Rather than moving in a linear fashion from independence to dependence, older adults move in and out of areas of service need as they experience changing levels of independence and dependence, health and illness, and financial stability and instability. For example, older adults just discharged from the hospital may need in-home services as well as home-delivered meals. Yet, as they become less dependent, they may access services offered at the senior center. Those who are striving to maintain their independence can access services along the continuum.

Therefore, Part II presents the variety of community resources available for older adults and is divided into three sections, based on our depiction of the continuum of services. The first section presents information about *community services*. These are services that benefit older adults with low levels of dependency and impinge little on their personal

Exhibit 1.4   Continuum of Services

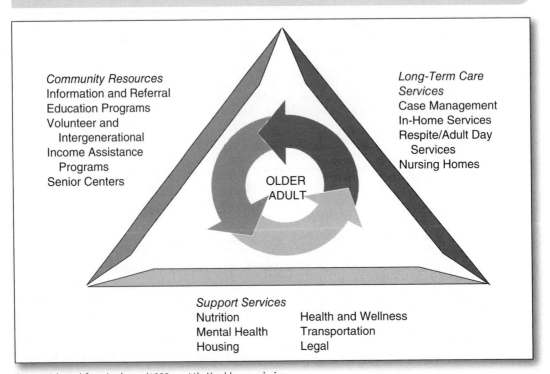

Source: Adapted from Levinson (1988, p. 44). Used by permission.

autonomy. These services offer participants opportunities to enhance personal and social well-being. Specifically, we address information and referral services (Chapter 4), volunteer and intergenerational programs (Chapter 5), education programs (Chapter 6), senior centers (Chapter 7), employment programs (Chapter 8), and income assistance programs (Chapter 9).

Support services are discussed in the second section of Part II. These services help older adults who need assistance in maintaining their level of functioning. Support services include nutrition programs (Chapter 10), health and wellness programs (Chapter 11), mental health services (Chapter 12), legal services (Chapter 13), transportation (Chapter 14), and housing (Chapter 15).

The final chapters in Part II provide information about *community-based* and *institutional long-term care services*. These are services to assist individuals who have greater dependency needs. Chapters in this section are on care management (Chapter 16), home care (Chapter 17), respite care (Chapter 18), and nursing homes (Chapter 19).

We have organized each chapter in Part II to include policy background, a description of users and programs, and future concerns. Each chapter includes case studies to help readers think critically about the service delivery issues. These cases were developed on the basis of actual experiences we have encountered (names and situations were altered to protect individuals' identity). In addition, best-practice models that highlight creative and unique programs and sources for additional information are presented. The best-practice models are representative of the programs and services that exist in various communities. Learning activities designed to expand understanding of the issues are also included. Additional resources, including the names and addresses of professional organizations and Internet resources, are located at the end of each chapter.

Part III contains the final chapter on programs and services for the future (Chapter 20). This chapter presents an in-depth look at the challenges that lie ahead for the aging network.

Accessing Updated Information

Because statistical profiles of older adults are constantly being updated, and because Congress frequently enacts legislation that affects the existence of community resources and programs, information presented in texts such as this can become quickly outdated. To keep up with these changes, we recommend regular visits to the following websites and others suggested throughout this book:

AARP International: www.aarpinternational.org

Administration on Aging: www.aoa.gov

Centers for Medicare & Medicaid Services: www.cms.hhs.gov

Data Warehouse on Trends in Health and Aging: www.cdc.gov/nchs/agingact.htm

Federal Interagency Forum on Aging-Related Statistics: www.agingstats.gov

FIRSTGOV for Seniors: www.firstgov.gov/Topics/Seniors.shtml

U.S. Census Bureau: www.census.gov

Legislative Foundations for Programs, Services, and Benefits Supporting Older Adults

It had been a busy week at the Area Agency on Aging office. Dorothy, the administrative assistant, was tidying up her desk on Friday afternoon and thinking about all the people the office had helped that week. Mrs. Wright, in her early 80s, came first to her mind. Mrs. Wright's husband had just undergone surgery for throat cancer. For the next couple of months, he would be restricted to a liquid diet for most of his meals. A low-income couple, but not at poverty level, the Wrights could not afford the full cost of a nutritional food supplement at their local grocery store. The Wrights found out about the Area Agency on Aging's food supplement program from their doctor. It had saved them nearly half the cost of the two cases a week required for Mr. Wright while he was recovering. With her many years' experience working at the agency's front desk, Dorothy knew that this couple would not have qualified for welfare assistance. She realized, yet again, how important the Older Americans Act (OAA) programs were to many people.

In countless communities across the country, local Area Agencies on Aging (AAAs) work to help older adults such as the Wrights. All Americans aged 60 and older can benefit from services provided by the "aging network" because of legislation enacted more than 45 years ago. On July 14, 1965, President Lyndon B. Johnson signed into law the OAA, thus launching milestone legislation in the evolution of the nation's public policy for older adults. The OAA is one of many laws that have been enacted to assist older adults in maintaining their physical, social, psychological, and financial well-being. This chapter will discuss some of the important laws that laid the foundation for the creation of programs, services, and benefits for older adults. We begin with a review of some of the more notable aging legislation enacted.

LEGISLATIVE FOUNDATIONS OF SOCIAL PROGRAMS AND SERVICES

Long before the enactment of the OAA, policies designed to protect older adults from the vicissitudes of old age were slowly put into place (see Exhibit 2.1). For example, in 1920, the Civil Service Retirement Act, a federal pension program, was enacted for government employees, members of Congress, and people in the uniformed and civil service. Some 15 years later, the Social Security Act (1935) was passed. Social Security—now contained under the Old-Age, Survivor, and Disability Insurance (OASDI) legislation—was created to ensure that working American families had a measure of economic security. Social Security is one of the best-known legislative policies enacted for the benefit of retirees, and later for survivors, dependents, and persons with disabilities. It was the first legislation to represent a "social contract" that was "to provide protection as a matter of right for the American worker in retirement" (Ficke, 1985, p. 115). It has proved to be one of the most popular, as well as one of the most adaptable, pieces of legislation in existence.

The Social Security Act was signed into law by President Franklin D. Roosevelt on August 14, 1935. The main provision of the act was to provide a social insurance program designed to

Exhibit 2.1   National Policy on Aging: Selected Historical Highlights

1920 THE CIVIL SERVICE RETIREMENT ACT was enacted to provide a retirement system for many government employees, including members of the U.S. Congress and those in the uniformed and civil services.	**1959** THE HOUSING ACT was amended authorizing a direct loan program of non-profit rental projects for the elderly at low interest rates. Provisions also reduced the eligible age for public low-rent housing for low-income older persons to age 62 for women and age 50 for disabled individuals.
1927 AMERICAN ASSOCIATION FOR OLD AGE SECURITY organized to further national interest in old age legislation.	**1961** First WHITE HOUSE CONFERENCE ON AGING convened in Washington, D.C.
1935 THE SOCIAL SECURITY ACT was passed and signed into law by President Roosevelt "to provide protection as a matter of right for the American worker in retirement."	SOCIAL SECURITY AMENDMENTS lowered retirement age for men from age 65 to 62, increased minimum benefits paid, broadened program to include additional categories of retired persons, increased benefits to aged widows, and liberalized the retirement test.
1937 RAILROAD RETIREMENT ACT was enacted to provide annuities pensions, for retired railroad employees, and their families.	**1962** More than 160 BILLS INTRODUCED IN CONGRESS related to the aged and aging; EIGHT WERE ENACTED.
U.S. HOUSING ACT stimulated passage of enabling legislative in majority of states, to provide low-rent public housing.	**1964** FOOD STAMP ACT provided for improved levels of nutrition among low-income households through a cooperative federal-state program of food assistance.
1950 The first NATIONAL CONFERENCE ON AGING conference in Washington, D.C., sponsored by the Federal Security Agency.	Formalizing a loose confederation of state administrators of aging program, the NATIONAL ASSOCIATION OF STATE UNITS ON AGING was officially established April 26, 1964.
SOCIAL SECURITY ACT AMENDED to establish program of aid to permanently and totally disabled and to broaden aid to dependent children to include relative with whom the child is living.	
1956 SPECIAL STAFF ON AGING was assigned coordinating responsibilities for aging within the Office of the Secretary of HEW	**1965** THE OLDER AMERICANS ACT was passed and signed into law. Major provisions

(Continued)

Exhibit 2.1 (Continued)

included establishment of the ADMINISTRATION ON AGING within the Department of Health, Education, and Welfare and grants to states for community planning, services, and training. The Act also stipulated that STATE AGENCIES ON AGING be established to administer the program.

MEDICARE health insurance program for the elderly was legislated. Financed through the social security system.

SOCIAL SECURITY AMENDMENTS established Title XIX. "Grants to States for Medical Assistance." Commonly known as Medicaid.

1967 AMENDMENTS TO THE OLDER AMERICANS ACT extended its provisions for two years and directed the Administration on Aging (AoA) to undertake a study of personnel needs in the aging field.

AGE DISCRIMINATION ACT OF 1967 was passed and signed into law by President Johnson.

1967 AMENDMENTS TO THE OLDER AMERICANS ACT extended its provisions for three years and authorized the use of Title III funds to support AREA WIDE MODEL PROJECTS.

1971 Second WHITE HOUSE CONFERENCE ON AGING convened in Washington, D.C.

1972 THE NUTRITION PROGRAM FOR THE ELDERLY ACT was passed and signed into law by President Nixon (redesignated Title VII of the Older Americans Act, as amended in 1973).

1972 SUPPLEMENTAL SECURITY INCOME is passed as a part of the Social Security Act.

1973 THE OLDER AMERICANS COMPREHENSIVE SERVICE AMENDMENTS established AREA AGENCIES ON AGING under an expanded Title III. Also authorized grants for model projects, senior centers, and multidisciplinary centers of gerontology added a new Title IX.

"Older Americans Community Service Employment Act" authorized funding for Title VII nutrition projects and extended the Act's provisions for two years.

THE DOMESTIC VOLUNTEER SERVICE ACT was passed and signed into law. Major provisions included the RSVP and Foster Grandparent programs. Title VI of the Older Americans Act, as a result, was later repealed.

1974 AMENDMENTS TO THE OLDER AMERICANS ACT added a special TRANSPORTATION program under Title III "model projects."

1974 SOCIAL SECURITY AMENDMENTS authorized TITLE XX. "Grants to States for Social Services." Among the programs which could be supported under this provision were: protective services, homemaker services, adult day care service transportation services, training, employment opportunities, information and referral, nutrition assistance, and health support.

1975 AMENDMENTS TO THE OLDER AMERICANS ACT added new language authorizing the Commissioner on Aging to make grants under Title III to INDIAN TRIBAL ORGANIZATIONS. PRIORITY SERVICES were mandated (transportation, home care, legal services, and home renovation, repair). Amendments also made minor changes in Title IX, "Community Service Employment for Older Americans."

1977 AMENDMENTS TO THE OLDER AMERICANS ACT authorized changes in the Title VII nutrition services program, primarily related to the availability of surplus commodities through the U.S. Department of Agriculture.

1978 THE COMPREHENSIVE OLDER AMERICANS ACT AMENDMENTS OF 1978 consolidated Titles Ill, V, and VII (social services, multipurpose centers, and nutrition services, respectively) into one Title III;

redesignated the previous Title IX (Community Service Employment Act) as Title V, and added a new Title VI, "Grants for Indian Tribes."

AMENDMENTS TO THE OLDER AMERICANS ACT extended the Act's programs for three years through September 30, 1984.

1984   OLDER AMERICANS ACT AMENDMENTS OF 1984 clarified the roles of State and Area Agencies on Aging in coordinating community-based services and in maintaining accountability for the funding of national priority services (legal, access, and in-home services), provided for greater flexibility in administering programs by providing for increased transfer authority between parts B and C of Title III, and added a new Title VII, "Older Americans Personal Health Education and Training Program," for funding grants to institutions of higher education to develop standardized programs of health education and training for older persons to be provided in multipurpose senior centers.

1987   Amendments to the Older Americans Act required coordination of in-home, access, and legal services with on going activities of agencies working with persons with Alzheimer's disease.

In-home support services for frail elders and disease prevention and health promotion services are now supported under Title III.

1991   The Administration on Aging becomes an independent agency that reports to the United States Department of Health and Human Services (USDHHS).

1992   Title III C authorizes school-based meals for older school volunteers and to help pay the costs of meals of older adults who volunteer in intergenerational programs.

Amendments to the OAA added Part D authorizing support for frail elders.

Amendments to the Older Americans Act added Part F to Title III titled "Disease Prevention and Health Promotion Services."

Office of Long-Term Care Ombudsman Programs is established within the Administration on Aging.

Title VII, the Vulnerable Elder Rights Protection Title enacted, combining many of the provisions under Title III.

2000   AMENDMENTS TO THE OLDER AMERICANS ACT moved Part D, in-home services, Part E, Special needs, and Part G, Supportive activities for Caretakers to Part B, Supportive Services; created Part E, National Family Caregiver Support Program; established a White House Conference on Aging in 2005.

2003   The Medicare Prescription Drug, Improvement and Modernization Act provides seniors and individuals with disabilities with a prescription drug benefit.

2006   Reauthorization of the Older Americans Act creates National Center on Senior Benefits Outreach and Enrollment and Choices for Independence initiative.

Medicare Part D Prescription Drug program went into effect.

Enactment of the Lifespan Respite Care Act (administered by AoA).

2010   Enactment of the Affordable Care Act which included the CLASS (Community Living Assistance and Supports) program to be administered by the AoA.

2012   CLASS (Community Living Assistance and Supports) program implementation is suspended.

2012   Reorganization of AoA and three other areas in USDHHS under the Administration for Community Living.

Source: Complied by the author from Ficke (1985); OAA of 1965, as amended; and AoA (2011e).

pay retired workers aged 65 or older a continuing income after retirement. The first payments began in 1937 and were made as lump sum payments averaging $58.06. Monthly payments began in January 1940. The first monthly retirement check was issued to Ida May Fuller of Ludlow, Vermont, in the amount of $22.54. Miss Fuller died in January 1975 at the age of 100. During her 35 years as a beneficiary, she received more than $20,000 in benefits (Social Security Administration, 1997). Originally, the amount received by Miss Fuller—$22.54— would be the amount she would receive for the rest of her life. Not until 1952 did Congress legislate increases in the monthly benefit. From that point, increases came only when legislated by Congress until 1972, when Congress enacted a law providing for annual cost-of-living increases, the amount to be determined by the annual increase in consumer prices.

There have been hundreds of amendments to the Social Security Act. Most have made minor adjustments to the Act; several, however, have profoundly increased the responsibility of the Act to extend benefits to previously uncovered groups (see Exhibit 2.1). One such amendment, passed by Congress in 1950, extended benefits to permanently and totally disabled workers. This was eventually broadened to cover workers under age 50 and their dependents. By 1960, some 559,000 people were receiving disability benefits, with an average benefit of $80 per month. In 2010, 8.2 million disabled workers received an average benefit of $1,067 per month (Social Security Administration, 2012a).

Another significant amendment to the Social Security Act occurred in 1972 when, at the request of President Richard M. Nixon, the joint federal–state programs of Old-Age Assistance, Aid to the Blind, and Aid to the Permanently and Totally Disabled were streamlined to create the Supplemental Security Income (SSI) program. Under the SSI program, each eligible person over the age of 65 living in his or her own household and having no other income was provided, as of 2012, with an average monthly cash payment of $414.90 (Social Security Administration, 2012b). In 2000, the Social Security Act was amended to reflect changing demographics and needs of older workers through the passage of H.R. 5, the Senior Citizens' Freedom to Work Act of 2000. Signed on April 7, 2000, by President Bill Clinton, this law amended Social Security to eliminate the Retirement Earnings Test, which required eligible retirees to have their benefits reduced if they were also working (Senior Citizens' Freedom to Work Act, Pub. L. No. 106-182 [2000]). Both Social Security and SSI are discussed in greater detail in Chapter 9.

Other early legislation benefiting older adults, enacted soon after the Social Security Act, included the Railroad Retirement Act of 1937 (providing pensions for railroad retirees) and the U.S. Housing Act of 1937 (enabling legislation for states to provide low-rent housing). Between 1940 and 1964, a number of other legislative and political activities occurred. In addition to the amendments added to the Social Security Act mentioned above, the Housing Act was amended and expanded, and the Food Stamp Act of 1964 was enacted.

The 1950s marked the emergence of another important influence on the evolution of aging policy—the White House Conferences on Aging. The first National Conference on Aging was held in Washington, DC, in 1950, and the first White House Conference on Aging was held in 1961 (Ficke, 1985); the most recent conference was held in 2005. The conference delegates—representatives of federal, state, and local governments as well as professionals in the field of gerontology and older adults—convened to develop specific recommendations for executive or legislative action on aging policy.

The next significant date in the history of aging policy is 1965, when two major laws were enacted—Medicare and the OAA. Sixteen days after President Johnson signed the OAA, he signed Medicare, the national health insurance program for older adults, into law on July 30, 1965, through amendments to the Social Security Act. The passage of both the OAA and Medicare in the same year has marked the mid-1960s as the most politically friendly period for older Americans' programs in history. The passage of Medicare was historic not only for the health benefits that it would afford millions of older Americans but also for the sheer significance of overcoming more than 30 years of political opposition, largely from the American Medical Association, to government-funded health coverage. All along, most proponents had intended for government-funded health coverage to be universal. After years of debate, a compromise was offered that adopted an incremental approach whereby older adults would be covered first, thereby pushing universal coverage into the distant future (Rich & Baum, 1984). The debate about universal health care coverage reemerged on the political scene in 2009 with the debate over and ultimate passage of the Patient Protection and Affordable Care Act of 2010 (ACA). The ACA is a comprehensive piece of legislation that expands health care access and coverage to all Americans including older Americans under Medicare. One component of the ACA was the Community Living Assistance and Supports program that was designed to establish a voluntary insurance program for American workers to help pay for long-term care services and supports that they may need in the future. The program was to be administered by the AoA, but the program was put on hold because it was uncertain whether it could meet the fiscal targets established in the law (U.S. Department of Health and Human Services [USDHHS], 2011b). Today, Medicare provides partial health coverage for 50 million Americans 65 years of age and older, as well as people of any age with permanent kidney failure and certain people with disabilities under the age of 65 (Centers for Medicare and Medicaid Services [CMS], 2012b). Specific benefits of Medicare and the recent expansion of Medicare with passage of the ACA are discussed in Chapter 11.

Although not the first major legislation addressing the needs of America's older adults, the OAA has become a landmark in the evolution of the nation's public policy for older adults (Bechill, 1992) and is largely responsible for the development of what is frequently referred to as the *aging network*. The advocacy and coordination mandates of the Act, as we will discuss later, have played a significant role in encouraging our nation's systems of human services to come together to do a better job of meeting the needs of older Americans.

In the remainder of this chapter, we discuss the history of the passage of the OAA,[1] followed by a review of each of the Act's titles and a discussion of the impact of the OAA on the lives of older adults. We conclude by presenting some of the controversial issues surrounding the OAA.

EMERGENCE OF THE AGING NETWORK

The origin of the OAA can be traced to the 1961 White House Conference on Aging. Health care coverage was the key issue that emerged from the many state aging conferences that were held prior to the White House Conference. After the White House Conference in 1961, a special committee drafted resolutions that eventually led to the 1965 enactment of both Medicare and the OAA. The OAA was the first program to focus on community-based services for older adults and the first legislation mandated to bring

---

[1]As this book goes to press, the reauthorization of the OAA, which was scheduled to be the subject of Congressional action in 2011 and implemented in 2012, was introduced in the Senate in January 2012 and referred to the congressional Committee on Health, Education, Labor, and Pensions, where it has yet to be considered. Reauthorization is not likely to occur in 2012. To track the progress of the OAA reauthorization, go to http://thomas.loc.gov.

together a fragmented and uncoordinated public and private service delivery system to meet the basic needs of elders at the community level (J. J. Lee, 1991). This visionary nature of the OAA sets it apart from other previous and subsequent legislative initiatives.

The passage of the OAA created a network of services that is unique to social programming. Much more than a collection of agencies, the aging network is a formidable structure, made up of a well-defined system that links the HHS, the AoA, 56 State Units on Aging (SUAs), 629 local AAAs, Title VI grants to 246 Indian tribes, two Native Hawaiian organizations, and some 29,000 providers delivering services to older Americans. This network is bonded together around a central role—to support the federal government in transforming a patchwork of programs for the older population into a locally coordinated service system. Relying on partnerships among the three levels of federal, state, and local government; universities; and a wide range of voluntary organizations working with older people, the aging network's emphasis on planning, coordination, and advocacy has provided an infrastructure and point of entry for other public and private initiatives that supplement OAA funding. These public–private initiatives represent an extraordinary record of achievement in making a small amount of federal money go a long way to help hundreds of thousands of older people remain living independently in the community. Today, aging network programs are supported by an array of sources in conjunction with the AoA, including Medicaid, social service block grants, state and local governments, the private sector, and individual contributions. With this combination of resources, more than 10.4 million older adults received services or participated in programs funded under the OAA in 2010 (AoA, n.d.e).

In 2012, three separate offices under the HHS—AoA, the Administration on Developmental Disabilities, and the Office on Disability—were reorganized under one office called the Administration for Community Living (ACL) and report to the ACL Administrator, which is the Assistant Secretary for Aging (see Exhibit 2.2; USDHHS, 2012b). The purpose of the reorganization was to establish a single, formal infrastructure in HHS to ensure consistency and coordination in community living policy and to focus on community living support for older adults and people with disabilities while still meeting unique needs of each population. The units under the ACL are now the AoA, Administration on Intellectual and Developmental Disabilities, Center for Disability and Aging Policy, and Center for Management and Budget. The regional offices, which were previously under the AoA and supported only OAA activities, will now directly report to the ACL Administrator and will broaden coordination activities at the regional level to include all of the programs and populations served under ACL.

The reorganization has not changed the AoA's role and function as outlined in the Titles under the OAA (explained in more detail later in the chapter); however, the AoA office has also been reorganized into five offices (USDHHS, 2012a, 2012f):

1. Office of Supportive and Caregiver Services is the focal point for supportive services programs and family caregivers programs under Titles II-B and III-E of the OAA, designed to provide information and referral services to older adults and caregivers, and to support technical assistance, outreach, and information dissemination that are culturally and linguistically appropriate to meet the needs of diverse populations of older adults.

2. Office of Nutrition and Health Promotion Programs is the focal point for the operation, administration, and assessment of the programs authorized under Titles III-C and III-D of the OAA, which are the nutrition programs and programs related to preventive health.

3. Office of Elder Rights Protection is the focal point for the operation, administration, and assessment of the elder abuse prevention, legal assistance development, and pension counseling programs under Titles II and VII of the OAA. In addition, the office administers the Senior Medicare Patrol projects and other related activities under Title IV of the OAA.

4. Office of American Indian, Alaskan Native, and Native Hawaiian Programs is the focal point for programs authorized under Title VI of the OAA and will assist in the evaluation of programs to native people under Titles III and VI. The office will also serve as the advocate within the HSS and with other departments and agencies of the federal government regarding all federal policies affecting older individuals who are Native Americans. The office will also work with state, local, and tribal governments by providing leadership and coordination of activities, services, and policies affecting American Indians, Alaskan Natives, and Native Hawaiian elders.

5. Office of Long-Term Care Ombudsman Programs is the focal point for advocacy regarding federal policies and laws that may adversely affect the health, safety, welfare, or rights of residents of long-term care facilities. The office will also work with the Office of Elder Rights to administer the Long-Term Care Ombudsman Program and the National Ombudsman Resource Center.

Best Practice: Linking Public and Private Partnerships

Many local area agencies on aging have worked to develop partnerships with the private sector to meet the needs of older adults in their communities. Here are a few examples.

- The Colorado Aging and Adult Services/SUA was a part of the Governor's Older Worker Task Force, which was an interagency group of state-level government organizations providing employment services or funding to older adults. Shortly after the group was formed, members realized that they needed private sector input and created the Private Sector Advisory Council. The council provided the Colorado SUA with knowledge, viewpoints, and information about older workers' issues. The council developed a public education project, including a brochure about the impact of Colorado's aging workforce, a conference for employers, and an award to honor employers who do an exemplary job of hiring and retaining older employees. The group also created a training curriculum for staff at employment centers who are assigned to assist older workers (http://www.doleta.gov/seniors/other_docs/training.pdf).

  For more information, contact Colorado Aging and Adult Services, phone: 303-866-5700.

- The Clearfield County (Pennsylvania) AAA's "Blizzard Box Program," launched in 1984, is a collaborative effort with the Clearfield Rotary Club and businesses such as Dairy Queen and Wal-Mart. Volunteers assemble the boxes at the local Wal-Mart distribution center and deliver Blizzard Boxes—emergency food kits—along with regular home-delivered meals during the fall. The Blizzard Boxes are to be used when bad weather prevents the delivery of regular meals.

  For more information, contact Clearfield County Area Agency on Aging, Clearfield, PA, phone: 814-765-2696.

Exhibit 2.2   Organizational Structure of the Administration on Aging and the Older Americans Act Network

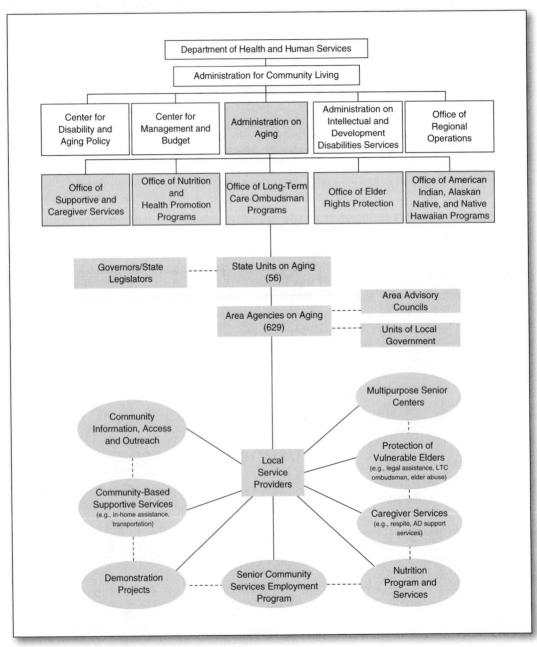

Source: Adapted from Ficke (1985) and USDHHS (2012b).

Another notable aspect of the OAA and the network of services that has evolved from the Act is that this service network is a universal program. This universal emphasis recognizes that all older persons have needs and that programs and services should be available, as a result, to them all (Bechill, 1992). Therefore, there is no means test cutoff for programs and services funded under the Act; persons are eligible for services regardless of income or assets. Using an age-based criterion, all older persons 60 years of age or older are eligible for services. Language in the Act, however, places emphasis on helping older persons with the greatest social and economic need, particularly low-income persons of color. Amendments to the OAA in 2000 and 2006 emphasized services to older adults who are frail, in addition to low-income, rural, and racial and ethnic elders, including those with limited English proficiency (see Exhibits 2.1 and 2.3). Specifically, the term *greatest social need* means the need caused by noneconomic factors, which include

(A) physical and mental disabilities;
(B) language barriers; and
(C) cultural, social, or geographical isolation, including isolation caused by racial or ethnic status, that
  (i) restricts the ability of an individual to perform normal daily tasks; or
  (ii) threatens the capacity of the individual to live independently. (OAA of 1965, as amended, §101[23]).

Exhibit 2.3   Key Changes in the Reauthorization of the Older Americans Act, 2006

- Improve access to benefits programs for seniors with limited income through creation of a National Center on Senior Benefits Outreach and Enrollment.
- Strengthen and expand long-term care options and the availability of home and community services through the Administration on Aging's Choices for Independence initiative.
- Promote evidence-based health promotion and disease-prevention programs.
- Provide broader opportunities for seniors' civic engagement.
- Establish a program of grants and technical assistance to improve transportation for seniors.
- Establish a cabinet-level interagency coordinating committee on aging.
- Expand eligibility for the National Family Caregiver Support Program, to allow participation by a relative caregiver beginning at age 55, and to allow participation by a caregiver of any age who cares for a person with Alzheimer's disease or a related neurological disorder.
- Instruct the Assistant Secretary for Aging to designate someone to coordinate elder abuse prevention and services.
- Expand the programs on elder abuse and elder justice.
- Authorize creation of Aging and Disability Resource Centers in all 50 states.
- Target services to seniors with limited English proficiency.
- Make more explicit the inclusion of mental health as a concern and target for programming under the Act.

Source: National Council on Aging (2007, p. 1).

In 2012, the AoA further clarified the above definition of greatest social need under the OAA by stating that "greatest social need does not exclude isolated populations other than racial and ethnic minorities and may include, depending on the planning and service area, religious minorities, individuals isolated due to sexual orientation or gender identity or other special populations" (AoA, 2012d).

In the 2006 reauthorization of the Act, Congress included language allowing programs to establish cost-sharing with participants in some circumstances (AoA, 2006a, 2006c). Cost-sharing is not permitted for information and assistance, outreach, benefits counseling or case management services, ombudsman, elder abuse prevention, legal services or other consumer protection services, congregate or home-delivered meals, or any service delivered through tribal agencies. Individuals with self-declared incomes at or below the federal poverty level would be exempt from cost-sharing. If a program is allowed to implement cost-sharing, a sliding scale based solely on income must be used; however, an older adult cannot be denied the service based on income or failure to make a payment. The cost-share amount is based on a confidential declaration of income made by the participant. The OAA also encourages providers of services to give participants the "opportunity" to donate toward the cost of a service, but the law strictly forbids denying anyone access to a service because of an inability to donate or pay the cost-share amount. The challenges arising from the emphasis on universality, targeting, and cost-sharing in the same legislation will be discussed in more detail later in the chapter and in Chapter 20.

TITLES OF THE OLDER AMERICANS ACT

Currently, the OAA contains seven titles. *Title I* sets forth 10 broad policy objectives aimed at improving the lives of older people with regard not only to income (the principal objective of Social Security) but also to physical and mental health, housing, employment, and community service. These broad objectives, listed below, continue to be the philosophical cornerstone of this Act:

1. An adequate income in retirement in accordance with the American standard of living

2. The best possible physical and mental health that science can make available, without regard to economic status

3. The provision and maintenance of suitable housing, independently selected, designed, and located with reference to special needs, and available at costs that older citizens can afford

4. Full restorative services for those who require institutional care, and a comprehensive array of community-based long-term care services adequate to appropriately sustain older people in their communities and in their homes, including support to family members and other persons providing voluntary care to older individuals needing long-term care services

5. Opportunity for employment with no discriminatory personnel practices because of age

6. Retirement in health, honor, and dignity after years of contribution to the economy

7. Participation in and contribution to meaningful activity within the widest range of civic, cultural, and recreational opportunities

8. Efficient community services, including access to low-cost transportation, that provide a choice in supported living arrangements and social assistance in a coordinated manner and that are readily available when needed, with emphasis on maintenance of a continuum of care for vulnerable older individuals

9. Immediate benefit from proven research knowledge that can sustain and improve health and happiness

10. Freedom, independence, and the free exercise of individual initiative for older adults in planning and managing their own lives, full participation in the planning and operation of community-based services and programs provided for their benefit, and protection against abuse, neglect, and exploitation (OAA of 1965, as amended, Title I, p. 1)

These far-reaching goals are to be carried out jointly by federal, state, tribal, and local governments to achieve an adequate offering of community-based services for older adults. With a $2 billion budget in fiscal year (FY) 2012, the programs and services funded through OAA still make the OAA one of the smallest federal programs (USDHHS, 2012c).

For Your Files: Policy and Planning for Disaster Preparedness

In 2005, Hurricane Katrina brought devastation to the Gulf Coast, and a disproportion number of older adults died in the storm and the chaos in the days after the storm. Although older adults aged 60 and over accounted for approximately 15% of the New Orleans population, 74% of the dead were 60 or older; nearly half were older than age 75 (*The Knight Ridder News Service*, cited in T. A. Glass, 2006). The emergency response that occurred afterward often resulted in inappropriate displacements and deterioration in health and functioning (AARP, 2006). Scholars have called for a reexamination of disaster preparedness policies and programs that address the unique evacuation needs of community-dwelling and institutionalized older adults, who face different risks in disasters due to physical and psychosocial limitations. The AoA responded by sending more than $1.6 million in emergency funds from its OAA FY2005 budget to aid in the reconstruction, and AoA awarded disaster assistance grants to Alabama, Mississippi, Louisiana, and Texas. The AoA entered into a Statement of Understanding with the American National Red Cross to cooperate on the preparation for and response to disasters. In addition, in 2005, the AARP convened a diverse group of government officials at federal, state, and local levels; emergency preparedness and response experts; relief organizations; and aging and disability advocates to identify lessons learned and share promising practices in protecting older persons in disasters. The report, *We Can Do Better: Lessons Learned for Protecting Older Persons in Disasters* can be obtained at http://assets.aarp.org/rgcenter/il/better.pdf. The AoA has also published a *Disaster Preparedness Manual for the Aging Network* and the *Emergency Assistance Guide 2006*, both available at http://aoa.gov/AoARoot/Preparedness/Resources_Network/index.aspx

Title II created the AoA within the Office of the Secretary of the HHS. AoA is headed by an Assistant Secretary on Aging, appointed by the President, who now also serves as the Administrator for the ACL. Through the years, there has been considerable debate about the placement of AoA within the executive branch of government. The debate has centered on whether AoA should be an independent office at the White House level, be an office of the HHS, or be placed under a department of the HHS. In 1992, President Clinton placed the AoA Assistant Secretary directly under the HHS Secretary—a move applauded by aging advocates because the Commissioner has the direct ear of the HHS Secretary and even the President when necessary. Although the AoA has a different organizational structure under the HHS, the Assistant Secretary of Aging continues to report directly to the HHS Secretary and to be the federal focal point for aging issues and program planning. The AoA has two principal roles. First, it is responsible for carrying out the planning, coordination, and provision of services to older adults. AoA promotes training, technical assistance, and regulatory direction to help the states and local AAAs carry out their mandates. Essentially, every time the Act is reauthorized and amended, AoA must interpret Congressional intent through rule making and rule interpretation. States, local AAAs, and other interested parties may comment on the rules and frequently influence the way a particular rule is written. This is often a long and drawn-out process.

Another important role of AoA is to provide leadership on national policies affecting older adults. This is done by encouraging cooperation and coordination among the major federal agencies on federal aging policies. AoA is thus a major advocate for older adults throughout the federal government. For example, the U.S. Department of Housing and Urban Development plans and implements programs to address housing needs of *all* low-income population groups. The Federal Transit Administration helps develop policy and funding initiatives to respond to a wide range of transit issues, including transit infrastructure. AoA is the only federal agency that has the authority to cross over agency boundaries to provide overall leadership on singularly aging issues and programs. When AoA was first established, Congress adamantly voiced its expectation that AoA have high visibility in the executive branch for developing and sponsoring a nationwide program to achieve the objectives set forth in the Act (Ficke, 1985).

The OAA amendments of 2000 required the Assistant Secretary of AoA to improve the delivery of services to rural areas by developing a best practices resource guide showing how rural needs can best be met and to provide training and technical assistance to help states in implementing best practices. Another significant new mandate was the requirement that AoA, in coordination with SUAs, AAAs, tribal organizations, and service providers, develop and publish before January 1, 2002, performance outcome measures for planning, managing, and evaluating activities performed under the Act. The 2000 amendments also, under Title II, established the Eldercare Locator and pension counseling as permanent programs and commissioned a White House Conference on Aging to take place before the end of 2005. One of the amendments made to the OAA in 2006 (see Exhibit 2.3) authorized the Assistant Secretary to promote three additional areas of focus. One is an effort named "Principles of Choices for Independence," which is a demonstration project to advance consumer-directed and community-based long-term care options. This included the creation of Aging and Disability Resources Centers in all 50 states designed to be "one-stop shops" for older adults and their families to receive information about long-term care options. Another change in the Act in 2006 was the authorization of the National Center on Senior Benefits Outreach and Enrollment program. The purpose of the program is to provide web-based support and other tools to inform older adults about the full range of federal and state benefits for which they may be eligible. The third area was civic engagement and charged the Assistant Secretary to work with the Corporation for National and Community Service to encourage civic engagement activities for persons of all ages. More recently, aging network support programs identified in the FY 13 budget under Title II have included the Senior Medicare Patrol Program, the National Alzheimer's Call Center, the Pension Counseling and Information program, the National Technical Assistance Resource Center for Lesbian, Gay, Bisexual and Transgender (LGBT) Elders, the National Education and Resource Center on Women and Retirement Planning, National Resource Centers on Native American Elders, National Minority Aging Organizations Technical Assistance Centers, and elder rights support activities (USDHHS, 2012c).

The AoA is often charged with implementing programs targeted for older adults that have been authorized under non-OAA legislation. For example, the Lifespan Respite Care Program was enacted in 2006 as an amendment to the Public Health Service Act of 2006 and authorized the Administration with implementing the program. Lifespan Respite Care programs bring together federal, state, and local resources and funding to help support, expand, and streamline the delivery of planned and emergency respite services while also providing for the recruitment and training of respite workers and caregiver training and empowerment (AoA, 2011f). The Lifespan Respite Care Act is intended to expand and enhance respite services in the states, improve coordination and dissemination of service delivery between the various programs available, improve access to programs, and improve the overall quality of the respite services currently available. Another example is the Chronic Disease Self-Management Programs funded under the ACA and designed to use state-of-the-art techniques to help older adults manage and treat chronic conditions (USDHHS, 2012c).

Title III, the largest program under the Act, authorizes the development of local services to help older persons. It has been described as the heart and soul of the OAA. Title III gives authority for the development of programs to assist older persons through grants to states. States, in turn, award funds to local planning and service areas (PSAs) whose boundaries have been designated by the state. SUAs administer the AoA grants at the state level, and the AAAs administer the AoA grants for the PSAs. An allocation formula based on the number of persons aged 60 and older residing in the state as of the most recent census determines the amount of funding each state receives. It follows, then, that Florida and California, which have large numbers of older adults 60 years of age and older, will receive larger federal allocations than states with fewer older adults, such as Colorado or Vermont. States must provide a minimum 15% match to the federal AoA grant. These matching funds vary greatly by state and help to increase the overall resources available under the OAA. SUAs keep 10% of their federal allocation for administration of the SUA. The balance is allocated to the PSAs by a more complex formula devised by the SUA using federal guidelines. The allocation formulas typically are based on census data numbers for persons aged 60 years or older—and for low-income, minority, rural, and frail individuals within this category—who reside in each PSA. AAAs must also provide local matching, which may be either cash or in-kind support, such as the value of volunteer hours or value of donated space and equipment to carry out a particular program.

The local AAA is responsible for:

- developing the area plan for a comprehensive and coordinated system of services to meet the needs of older persons;

- funding service provider agencies to fill gaps in priority service areas; and

- serving as the advocate and focal point for older people within its PSA.

Throughout the country, AAAs exhibit many organizational designs and structures based on local needs and preferences. The AAA office within a PSA may be a unit of general-purpose local government, such as a county, city, or regional council of government, or a public or nonprofit private agency. In any given location, an AAA can be a part of a council of governments or regional planning commission, part of a county unit of government or city government, part of an educational institution, or a freestanding private nonprofit organization.

Under Part A of Title III, both SUAs and AAAs must develop multiyear plans describing in detail how a coordinated, comprehensive service delivery system will be provided. AAAs must also designate, where feasible, a focal point for service delivery in each community, giving strong consideration to multipurpose senior centers. The Act requires that the AAA establish a council to advise the agency on the development of multiyear plans, funding, and administration, as well as programs and services. The local councils may conduct public hearings and review and comment on all community policies, programs, and actions that affect older persons in their regions. Advisory council membership must be made up of older adults (including individuals of color and older individuals residing in rural areas) who are participants or who are eligible to participate in programs assisted under this Act, family caregivers of such individuals, representatives of older individuals, service providers, representatives of the business community, local elected officials, providers of veterans' health care (if appropriate), and the general public. Other members may represent older individuals, local elected officials, and the general public. This mandate for grassroots participation in the planning and administration of local AoA programs has given a voice to thousands of older adults on services that affect their daily lives.

Title III, Part B of the Act is the supportive services component (see Exhibit 2.4). The mission of Part B is to develop a continuum of community-based services to assist older persons in remaining independent in the community for as long as is reasonably possible. To that end, AoA regulations state that AAAs must provide assurances that an adequate proportion of funds is allotted to service providers in their PSAs that provide

- *access services*, such as information and referral, outreach, case management, escort, and transportation;

- *in-home services*, which include chores, homemaking, personal care, home-delivered meals, and home repair and rehabilitation;

- *community services*, including senior centers, congregate meals, day care, a nursing home ombudsman program, elder abuse prevention, legal aid, employment counseling and referral, health promotion, and fitness programs; and

- *caregiver services*, such as respite, counseling, and education programs.

In most cases, AAAs do not provide these services directly. Instead, they subcontract with other organizations to deliver the services.

Title III, Part C allows for a separate federal allocation from Title III to the states and then downward to AAAs for the operation of congregate and home-delivered nutrition programs. The national nutrition program for older adults (described in more detail in Chapter 10), a result of 1972 amendments to the OAA, is a major service component under Part C. It allows AAAs to fund both congregate (group) and home-delivered meals for older adults 60 years of age and older and their spouses. The 2000 amendments gave more flexibility to transfer funds between the Supportive Services Part B budget and the Nutrition Services Part C budget. AAAs following state guidelines may now transfer up to 30% of funds between Parts B and C. This is up from the previous 20%. Also, in response to the dramatic increase in numbers of frail older adults, the OAA 2000 amendments allow AAAs following state guidelines to transfer up to 40% of funds (up from 30%) between a congregate meals budget and a home-delivered meals budget. The outline of the Title III service categories listed in Exhibit 2.4 speaks to the wide range of flexible options AAAs have locally to develop a comprehensive offering of services to meet the particular needs of their PSA. In 2010, 236 million congregate or home-delivered meals were provided to older adults (AoA, n.d.-g).

Title III, Part D was added to the Act in the 1992 amendments. Originally, Part D was a relatively small program that was intended to address home care needs but was never adequately funded. With the 2000 amendments, this aspect of Part D was consolidated into Part B, where home care has traditionally been an allowable service. Title III, Part D has been renamed "Disease Prevention and Health Promotion Services," which was originally Part F and was incorporated into the OAA with the 1987 amendments. First funded with the 1992 amendments to the Act, it has been minimally funded and has remained a small program. AAAs may provide disease prevention and health promotion services and information at

---

Exhibit 2.4 Community-Based Supportive Services Funded Through Area Agencies on Aging

Services to facilitate access

- Transportation
- Outreach
- Information and referral
- Client assessment and case management

Services provided in the community

- Congregate meals
- Multipurpose senior centers
- Casework, counseling, emergency services
- Legal assistance and financial counseling
- Adult day care, protective services, health screening
- Housing, residential repairs and renovation
- Physical fitness and recreation
- Preretirement and second-career counseling
- Employment
- Crime prevention and victim assistance
- Volunteer services
- Health and nutrition education

- Transportation
- Elder abuse education and training
- Mental health education and services

Services provided in the home

- Home health, homemaker, home repairs
- Home delivered meals and nutrition education
- Chore maintenance, visiting, shopping, letter writing, escort, and reader services
- Telephone reassurance
- Supportive services for families of elderly victims of Alzheimer's disease and similar disorders

Services to residents of care-providing facilities

- Casework, counseling, placement, and relocation assistance
- Group services, complaint and grievance resolution
- Visiting, escort services
- Long-term care ombudsman program

Source: Ficke (1985) and the OAA of 1965, as amended.

multipurpose senior centers, at congregate meal sites, through home-delivered meals programs, or at other appropriate sites. As with all AAA programs, disease prevention and health promotion should be targeted to the most needy. According to the Act, disease prevention and health promotion services include:

- health risk assessments,
- routine health screening,
- nutritional counseling,
- health promotion programs,
- physical fitness,
- home injury control services,
- mental health promotion,
- education concerning Medicare benefits,
- medication management screening and education,
- information on age-related diseases and chronic disabling conditions, and
- gerontological counseling and counseling regarding other social services.

One of the most significant developments with the 2000 amendments was the addition of a National Family Caregiver Support Program, or Title III, Part E of the OAA. This new program built on existing services at the local level that already provided relief to families helping to care for frail loved ones. Family caregivers and relative caregivers such as grandparents of children not more than 18 years of age are now able to receive services such as information and assistance, counseling, support groups, caregiver training, respite care, and other supplemental services. Congress's addition of Family Caregiver Support as a funded service under the OAA is attributable to immense lobbying on the part of family caregivers and the aging network. An initial $125 million was allocated to this effort. The 2006 amendments allow mental health screening, outreach, and services to be funded under Title III. In FY 2010, this program served 700,000 caregivers, and a survey of caregivers using the program found that 77% reported that services definitely enabled them to provide care longer than otherwise would have been possible, and 89% reported that services helped them to be a better caregiver (AoA, 2012g). Overall, in 2010, 90 million units of service were provided to older adults and their caregivers under Title III-B, D, and C programs (AoA, n.d.-e)

In addition to service programs, AoA, under *Title IV*, awards funds to support research, demonstration, and training programs (a list of resource centers is presented in Exhibit 2.5). Research projects collect information about the status and needs of various subgroups of older adults in the population that is used to plan services and opportunities that will assist them. Demonstration projects test new program initiatives that better serve older adults, especially those who are vulnerable, to identify and disseminate best practices to be used by agencies in the aging network (USDHHS, 2011a). AoA also provides funds to educational institutions to develop curricula and training programs for professionals and paraprofessionals in the field of aging (AoA, 1995a). This title makes the OAA unique among federal programs in its ability to be a catalyst for new approaches to meeting the local needs of older persons and their families (Region VIII Office, n.d.).

Exhibit 2.5   Resource Centers Supported by the Administration on Aging

Aging Network Business Practice, Planning and Program Development, National Association of Area Agencies on Aging, http://www.n4a.org/programs/capacity-building-program

The Aging Network's Volunteer Collaborative, National Association of Area Agencies, http://www.agingnetworksvolunteercollaborative.org

Aging and Disability Resource Center Technical Assistance Exchange, The Lewin Group, Inc., http://www.adrc-tae.org/

Alzheimer's Technical Assistance Resource Center, Research Triangle Institute, http://www.adrc-tae.org/tiki-index.php?page=AboutADSSP

Community Innovations for Aging in Place (CIAIP) Technical Assistance Center, Visiting Nurse Service of New York, http://www.ciaip.org/

Evidenced-Based Disease and Disability Prevention National Resource Center, National Council on Aging, Inc., http://www.healthyagingprograms.org/

National Aging Information and Referral Support Center, National Association of States United for Aging and Disabilities, http://www.nasuad.org/I_R/ir_index.html

National Center for Benefits Outreach and Enrollment, National Council on Aging, Inc., http://www.centerforbenefits.org

National Center on Elder Abuse, Administration on Aging, UC Irvine's Center of Excellence on Elder Abuse & Neglect and University of North Dakota, National Indigenous Elder Justice Initiative, http://www.ncea.aoa.gov/ncearoot/Main_Site/index.aspx

The National Center for Long-Term Care Business and Strategy, National Association of Area Agencies on Aging (n4a) 1730 Rhode Island Ave. NW, Suite 1200, Washington, DC 20036, 202-872-0888

National Consumer Protection Technical Resource Center, Hawkeye Valley Area Agency on Aging, http://www.smpresource.org

National Education and Resource Center on Women and Retirement Planning, Women's Institute for a Secure Retirement, http://www.wiserwomen.org

National Legal Resource Center, Center for Social Gerontology; National Senior Citizens Law Center; American Bar Association Commission on Law and Aging; National Consumer Law Center and Center for Elder Rights Advocacy; http://nlrc.aoa.gov/

National Long-Term Care Ombudsman Resource Center, National Consumer Voice for Quality Long-Term Care, http://www.ltcombudsman.org

National Minority Aging Technical Assistance Centers

National Caucus and Center on the Black Aged - Elderly African Americans, http://www.ncba-aged.org

Asociacion Pro Personas Mayores – Hispanic Elderly, http://www.anppm.org

National Asian Pacific Center on Aging – Asian American and Pacific Islander Elders, http://www.napca.org/

National Resource Center for Participant Directed Services, Trustees of Boston College, http://www.participantdirection.org

National Resource Center on Lesbian, Gay, Bisexual and Transgender (LGBT) Aging, Services & Advocacy for GLBT Elders (SAGE), http://www.lgbtagingcenter.org

National Resource Centers for Native American Elders

University of Hawaii - Native Hawaiian Elders and family caregivers, http://manoa.hawaii.edu/about/contact.html

University of Alaska Anchorage - Alaska Native Elders, http://elders.uaa.alaska.edu/contact.htm

University of North Dakota - American Indians, Alaska Natives and Native Hawaiians, http://ruralhealth.und.edu/projects/nrcnaa

National Pension Assistance Resource Center, The Pension Rights Center, http://www.pensionrights.org

Technical Assistance Centers for Family Caregiver Support Programs, Family Caregiver Alliance, http://www.caregiver.org

Source: AoA (2012a).

For Your Files: Nevada's Senior Medicare Patrol Demonstration Project Funded Under Title IV

The Nevada Senior Medicare Patrol (SMP), started with Title IV funding, was designed to educate Medicare beneficiaries and their caregivers to become critical health care consumers enabling them to identify suspicious situations or billings. Under this project, Nevada SMP effectively reached beneficiaries throughout the state by initiating presentations and information about Medicare fraud issues, how to avoid being a victim of fraud, and information about the SMP's volunteer program. Over the project period (2006–2010), virtually all areas of the state were visited, and 111 outreach/education events, 87 group educational sessions, and approximately 140 one-on-one counseling sessions/SMP presentations were conducted in senior centers, recreation centers, community centers, and tribal centers.

The SMP messages were enhanced by collaborations in events, organizational meetings, SMP presentations, newsletter articles, and website linkages with more than 50 organizations and task forces including Nevada Elder Abuse Task Force; Nevada Health Care Fraud Task Force; Attorney General's Bureau of Consumer Protection and Chief of Investigations; Governor's Office of Consumer Health Assistance; Aging Services Directors Association; Nevada Senior Coalition; Nevada Beneficiary Coalition; National Committee to Protect Social Security and Medicare; Community Coalition on Victim Rights; Clark County Senior Advisory Council and Senior Advocate Office; University of Nevada, Reno Sanford Center for Aging; Provider Hospital Groups and Medicare Contract Groups; Clark County Public Guardian Office; Nevada Senior Resource Network; and a number of senior, community, and community health centers and civic organizations.

Several different radio campaigns were held during this grant period in collaboration with the Nevada Broadcasters Association. In 2008 and 2009, radio campaigns aired over 12 weeks featured statewide public service announcements in both Spanish and English.

Since the SMP inception in September 2006, Nevada SMP logged approximately 297 complaints, of which close to 88% have been resolved. The program has been transferred from the Attorney General's office to the Nevada Aging and Disability Services Division and continues to operate in Nevada (AoA, 2010a, pp. 110–111).

For more information, contact the Nevada Aging and Disability Services Division, SMP, at 702-486-3403 or on their website: http://www.nvaging.net/ship/ship_main.htm#SMP.

As of 2010, literally hundreds of projects had been funded through Title IV.

These projects were first directed to programs of practical action. For example, in 1968, 29 grants for more than $2 million were made by AoA to fund projects designed to gain new knowledge on the nutritional needs of older persons. This demonstration project laid the groundwork for the national nutrition program for older adults (mentioned earlier) funded under Title III, Part C since 1977. Between 1973 and 1977, approximately 25 new research and demonstration grants were funded to research ways to maintain vulnerable older persons (e.g., those in poorer health) in their own homes or in appropriate community settings. Later, beginning in 1984, discretionary funds under Title IV were directed to social integration of older persons, strengthening of family supports, systems improvement, outreach to minorities, and improvement of capacity through the application of knowledge (Ficke, 1985).

During those early years, multidisciplinary research centers of gerontology also benefited significantly from Title IV grants. Among the first and more prominent centers that were funded by Title IV funds were the Institute of Gerontology at the University of Michigan, Wayne State University Institute of Gerontology, the Andrus Gerontology Center at the University of Southern California, and the Center for Aging and Human Development at Duke University. These centers were specifically mandated to recruit and train personnel in the field of aging, conduct basic and applied research, provide consultation to SUAs and AAAs, serve as repositories of information on aging, and help develop training programs on aging (Ficke, 1985).

Between 1978 and 1984, AoA expanded the recipients of Title IV grants to include "special emphasis" resource centers. Six centers were funded to concentrate on the concerns of income maintenance, health, employment, housing, older women, and education and leisure. The purpose of these centers was to help AoA fulfill its role as advocate for the nation's older adults and to bridge the gap between theory and practice through education and research. During the past 15 years, Title IV funds have made numerous contributions in the areas of long-term care, home and community-based services, elder abuse, legal services hotlines, and disaster assistance. For long-term care and home and community-based services, one of the most visible examples of Title IV support is the Eldercare Locator, an effort to help local and long-distance caregivers find the information they need by calling a toll-free number (more details on the Eldercare Locator can be found in Chapter 4). Title IV was virtually the only source of funding for states that were in the initial planning stages of developing home and community-based programs for older adults needing long-term care.

Title IV demonstration projects in elder abuse prevention have brought together individuals who provide social services to the aging and to those affected by domestic violence to more effectively address domestic violence that affects older women. With Title IV assistance, statewide legal hotlines have been established in 11 states, and most recently Title IV funding has supported disaster relief programs to victims of hurricanes, earthquakes, floods, and the Oklahoma City bombing. The 2000 OAA reauthorization included the following new projects: Career Preparation for the Field of Aging; Older Individual's Protection From Violence Projects; Health Care Demonstration Projects for Rural Areas; and Computer Training for Older Adults and Technical Assistance and Innovation to improve transportation. Whatever disagreement may exist about the viability of the OAA, most agree that Title IV has represented an atypical but largely successful effort by the federal government to advance knowledge on aging through applied research, training, and demonstration projects. New areas identified for funding in the 2006 OAA reauthorization included the Community Innovations for Aging in Place planning activities to help prepare communities for population aging, including assessing the needs of the older adult population; training and technical assistance to the SUA and AAAs; development, implementation, and assessment of technology-based service models; and activities that promote quality and improvement in support provided to caregivers. A 2010 compendium of AoA grants funded under Title IV identify funding for wide-ranging projects such as the community living program, pension counseling, health disparities among minority elders, Alzheimer's Disease support services, and model legal assistance hotlines (AoA, 2010a). In FY 2011, Aging Network Support Activities funded 24 grants with an average award of $279,465 (USDHHS, 2012c). Funding for support centers changes each budget year and more recently dropped from $43 million in 2005 to $24 million in 2006 to $0 in FY 2012 (AoA, 2007; National Association for Area Agencies on Aging [n4a], 2012). As a result of these budgetary ups and downs, many resource centers may be eliminated, their activities seriously limited, or the funding moved under Title II.

Title V establishes authority for the Senior Community Service Employment Program (SCSEP) for unemployed, low-income persons 55 years of age and older. Administered initially by the Office of Economic Opportunity and later by the U.S. Department of Labor (DoL), the program was added to the OAA in 1973 but continues to be administered by the DoL, although the most recent DoL budget proposes transferring SCSEP to the HHS and the AoA (USDoL, 2012a). During the past three decades, SCSEP has helped millions of low-income older workers, and in 2010 alone served 105,851 older adults (Green Thumb, Inc., 2001; USDoL, 2011a). Participants work part time, typically in service areas such as education, health and hospitals, recreation and parks, and senior centers. The program's goal is to place 30% of its positions in unsubsidized positions each year (USDoL, 2011a). A majority of the funds are administered through national organization grantees such as Easter Seals, Experience Works (formally known as Green Thumb), AARP, the National Council on the Aging, the National Urban League, and governors of every state who in turn support local employee assistance programs (USDoL, 2011a). Participants can also take advantage of One Stop Career Centers that provide services and support including job training referrals and career counseling (USDoL, n.d.). Title V projects contribute to the general welfare of communities through public service to local entities such as hospitals, senior centers, libraries, and historical sites while increasing employment opportunities for low-income older adults. Detailed information about Title V programs is provided in Chapter 8.

Title VI establishes authority for grants to Indian tribes to promote the delivery of supportive and nutrition services to American Indians and Alaska Natives that are comparable to services offered to other older persons under the Title III program. The rationale for making grants directly available to Indian tribes is to respect the needs of older Indians. Findings show that unemployment and poverty rates are much higher among Indians, housing is often substandard, and there are shortages of transportation, nursing homes, and home health care options for older Indians. Grants under Title VI to Indian tribes were first made in 1980, when AoA reported that $6 million funded 85 grants that ultimately assisted 20,000 elders. By comparison, in 2010 $38 million funded grants providing more than 9 million units of meals, nutrition education, outreach, transportation, legal, home health, ombudsman, homemaker, information and referral, caregiver, health and wellness, and other social services under the OAA, helping 255,770 elders (AoA, n.d.k, n.d.i).

Title VII, protection for vulnerable elders, was enacted as part of the OAA in 1992. The purpose of Title VII is to promote advocacy designed to protect the basic rights and benefits of vulnerable elders, especially those with great economic needs. According to the OAA, Title VII has a dual focus. The first is to bring together long-term ombudsman programs; programs for the prevention of abuse, neglect, and exploitation; and state elder rights and legal assistance development programs. The second is to facilitate the coordination of and linkages between the three programs in each state.

The purpose of the long-term care ombudsman program is to identify, investigate, and resolve complaints concerning the residents of nursing homes and board-and-care homes. The ombudsman program is discussed in greater detail in Chapter 19. Programs for the prevention of elder abuse, neglect, and exploitation are designed to provide public education about elder abuse and conduct outreach to help identify cases of abuse, neglect, or exploitation. These programs are also responsible for offering training and technical assistance about elder abuse to professionals working with older adults. The state elder rights and legal assistance development program requires that SUAs establish programs to provide leadership in improving the quality and quantity of legal assistance programs. Elder abuse and legal assistance programs are discussed in Chapter 13. First-time funding for the Adult Protective Services (APS) program was authorized by the Elder Justice Act of

2010 (included in Subtitle H of the Affordable Care Act). APS funding will provide demonstration grants to test innovative approaches to reducing and addressing elder abuse in states and in tribal settings. This funding will generate knowledge that can then be used to inform state and local efforts across the country to design and implement better approaches to protect our Nation's older adults from abuse (USDHHS, 2012c).

FUNDING FOR THE OLDER AMERICANS ACT

Exhibit 2.6 lists funding levels for OAA programs and other non-OAA programs that the AoA is responsible for implementing for selected years between 2009 and 2012. As shown in the table, overall funding has declined from FY 2010 level of $2.4 billion to $2.0 billion in FY 2012. In addition, programmatic funding has declined over the last two years with the exception of the Health Care Fraud and Abuse program, the State Health Insurance Assistance program, and the Chronic Disease and Self-Management program, which had increases in funding.

Exhibit 2.6   Older Americans Act Budget Authority for Fiscal Years 2009–2012 (dollars in thousands)

Title	Activity	FY 2009	FY 2010	FY 2011	FY 2012
II	Program Administration	18,696	19,976	19,939	23,063
II (Sec. 201, 202)	**Network Support & Demonstrations**				
	Health and Long-Term Care Programs	28,000	–		
	Aging Network Support Activities	13,694	8,198	8,184	7,873
III (Sec. 311) (B, Sec. 321) (C1, Sec. 331) (C2, Sec. 336)	**Health and Independence**				
	Home and Community-Based Supportive Services	361,348	368,290	367,611	366,916
	Congregate Nutrition[1]	434,269	440,718	439,901	439,070
	Home-Delivered Nutrition	214,459	217,644	217,241	216,831
VI (Sec. 613, 623, 631)	Nutrition Services Incentive Program	161,015	160,991	160,693	160,389
	Preventive Health Services	21,026	21,026	20,984	20,945
	Native American Nutrition and Support Services	27,208	27,708	27,653	27,601
III-E (Sec. 371) VI (Sec. 613, 623, 631)	**Caregivers Services**				
	National Family Caregiver Support Program	154,220	154,197	153,912	153,621
	Native American Caregivers Support Services	6,389	6,388	6,376	6,364
IV (Sec. 411)	**Program Innovations**	18,172	27,873	19,068	–

(Continued)

Exhibit 2.6 (Continued)

Title	Activity	FY 2009	FY 2010	FY 2011	FY 2012
V (Dept of Labor)	**Senior Community Services Employment Program**	571,925	825,425	449,100	448,251
VII (Sec. 712, 721)	**Protection of Vulnerable Older Americans**				
II (Sec. 201, 202)	Long-Term Care Ombudsman Program	16,327	16,825	16,793	16,761
	Prevention of Elder Abuse & Neglect	5,056	5,055	5,046	5,036
	Senior Medicare Patrol Program	–	9,438	9,420	9,402
	Elder Rights Support Activities	–	4,103	4,096	4,088
	Health Care Fraud & Abuse	–	3,779	3,312	10,710
II (Sec. 201, 202)	**Consumer Information, Access, & Outreach**				
	Aging and Disability Resource Centers	[2]	23,684	16,469	16,457
OBRA 1990	State Health Insurance Assistance Program		46,960	52,000	52,115
	Medicare Enrollment Assistance Program		30,000	–	–
	National Clearinghouse for Long-Term Care Information			3,000	3,000
Public Health Service Act (PHSA Sec. 398)	**Alzheimer's Disease Supportive Services Program**	11,464	11,462	11,441	4,011
PHSA (Title XXIX)	**Lifespan Respite Care**	2,500	2,500	2,495	2,490
PHSA (Sec. 243, 247b(k)(2)) and Patient Protection & Affordable Care Act	**Chronic Disease & Self-Management Programs**	–	–	–	10,000
	Total	2,086,504	2,432,236	2,014,734	2,004,994

Source: USDHHS (2010b, 2011a, 2012c).

[1] The American Recovery and Reinvestment Act of 2009 provided nutrition services programs an additional $100 million to supplement these programs. This amount is not included in the 2009 funding noted in the table.

[2] In 2009 this program was funded under Title II Health and Long-Term Care Programs.

OUTCOMES OF THE OLDER AMERICANS ACT

The OAA has been law for almost five decades. Its grand objectives, spelled out in Title I of the Act, have remained intact. The governmental structures at the federal, state, and local levels have reached mature and stable plateaus, and a wide variety of programs have been put into place nationwide. To what extent has the OAA, then, accomplished its original goals? Little comprehensive research exists to support either a positive or a negative claim—in part because of the difficulty in measuring such broad goals. Some say that the OAA has failed because it has not adequately served older adults of color. For example, although there has been an increase in the number and percentage of older adults of color receiving services, they continue to represent only a small percentage of the total number of participants (AoA, n.d.-e). While OAA programs target those with the greatest social and economic need, reaching those who are poor, isolated, and living in rural communities continues to be challenging.

In her landmark book *The Aging Enterprise*, Estes (1979) identifies a number of shortcomings associated with the passage of the OAA. Although her comments were made years ago, they are still being considered today. First, Estes states that the OAA does nothing to alleviate the economic and social conditions that determine the quality of life of older Americans. Indeed, securing a "brown bag" of groceries for older adults who have limited food does nothing to help them escape the poverty that causes daily worry about obtaining food. Moreover, the social structures that have led some older adults into marginal economic status, such as providing mechanisms for ensuring adequate retirement income for lifelong homemakers, are not addressed. Estes contends that existing social policy for aged persons simply preserves the existing social class distinctions. Second, Estes argues that the insistence on age-segregated programs creates tension between social groups and makes older adults targets of blame for the country's economic hardships. The rise in the discourse about rising health care costs associated with Medicare and Social Security seem to offer support for this concern. Finally, Estes notes that funding the OAA reassures the public that aged persons are adequately being cared for while nothing is being done to change the functioning of social class. She recommends that structural changes be made in income, retirement, and employment policies that accentuate class differences; that universalist policies be adopted which, among other things, would facilitate intergenerational bonding; and that universal health care be enacted.

Those who support the OAA point to millions of older adults who receive services through OAA programs in spite of the limited amount of funding provided to the aging network providers. These services are important for maintaining current levels of well-being as well as for assisting those who have low levels of functioning. Thus the programs and services supported by the OAA help elders with better levels of well-being maintain their physical and social vitality as well as assist those at risk of physical decline and social isolation. Services available under the OAA help people such as the Wrights, described at the beginning of the chapter; to whom would they turn if the aging network ceased to exist? Moreover, locally based AAAs must be responsive to the unique needs of the people they are directed to serve. For example, as the population has aged and there are increasing numbers of frail elders, local AAA funding has shifted to concentrate more on programs that help meet the needs of these individuals. An example of a program that has improved the lives of frail elders is the nutrition program. A study of the national nutrition program for older adults showed that the nutritional well-being of participants has measurably improved (Ponza, Ohls, & Millen, 1996). Others point to the success of many AAAs in leveraging other resources, both public and private, to support needed services.

Should the success of the OAA be measured against the degree to which it accomplishes its goals stated in Title I? Such lofty aspirations are laudable, but they are impossible to reach given the Act's limited resources and the variations in the organizational capacity of many AAAs across the country (Hudson, 2010). We will revisit the OAA in Chapter 20 and consider the future of the Act. In Chapter 3, we examine some of the factors associated with service use by older adults and some theoretical models that can be used to explain why some older adults choose not to seek services.

Patterns of Service Use and Theories of Help-Seeking Behavior

Katherine Hahn is an 80-year-old retired physician who lives alone with her two dogs in a condominium in Phoenix. She never married, and her only living relative is her brother, who lives in Germany. Recently, she has not been well, and dirty laundry, trash, and old newspapers have begun to accumulate in the entryway into her apartment, where there is a terrible stench. She has become increasingly frail and unable to descend her stairway safely to get outside. As a result, she is unable to take her dogs outside, so the dogs wear diapers. The neighbors are starting to complain to the building's management. She refuses all attempts to help her.

Most older adults enjoy good health, are active well into later life, and are content with retirement; the role changes that accompany later life, however, have the potential to be quite disruptive unless adequate support is available. For example, widowhood is often associated with a decrease in income, a loss of emotional support, and a decline in physical health that can complicate simple daily tasks such as shopping and preparing meals. Most communities offer a number of community and social support services to help older adults cope with their changing social, personal, and financial circumstances.

Community and support services can improve the well-being of recipients, but how many older adults use the services available to them? A review of the literature about the use of community service programs reveals a common theme: only a small percentage of older adults report using services (Casado, van Vulpen, & Davis, 2011; Cohen-Mansfield & Frank, 2008; Krout, 1983; J. Mitchell, 1995; Sun, 2011). Consider Katherine Hahn's situation. She could use the assistance of a home health aide or homemaker. Certainly, she could use a volunteer to walk her dogs. But she refuses any assistance. How can we explain this paradox? Moreover, many older adults in our communities need assistance. But on whom do they rely most often to meet those needs? In this chapter, we present information about the social care older adults receive from informal and formal networks, and look at how the informal and formal networks interact to assist older adults. Next, we examine possible reasons why older adults might not be inclined to use community services and present some social psychological theories that help explain help-seeking behavior. We end this chapter with a discussion about how social theory can be used to help understand patterns of service use among older adults.

SOCIAL CARE FOR OLDER ADULTS

When we encounter a problem, need help getting something done, or just need someone to talk to, what do we do? Most of us probably first seek help or advice from someone we know in our *informal network*—a friend or family member—rather than from a resource in the *formal network*. Older adults also show a preference for turning to the people with whom they are familiar and who are involved in their daily lives. Researchers have discovered that older adults turn to their informal network of family and friends for help before they turn to the formal network (Cantor, 1983, 1991; Horowitz, 1985; Litwak, 1985; Suitor & Pillemer, 1990). When seeking help from members of the informal network, older adults exhibit a hierarchical preference for assistance from spouses and children first, and then friends and neighbors (Cantor, 1979; Horowitz, 1985; Palley & Oktay, 1983; Spillman & Pezzin, 2000). The care given by kin and non-kin in the informal network is generally long term, is motivated by a desire to reciprocate for past assistance, is offered free of charge, generally requires a low level of knowledge or training, and plays an important role in contributing to the well-being of older adults (Barker, 2002; Doty, 1986; McPherson & Wister, 2008; Travis, 1995). Spouses, children, siblings, and other family members provide older adults with personal care, rehabilitation after surgery or an acute illness, emotional support, and social support services such as meal preparation, transportation, and mediation with bureaucracies (Brody, 1981; S. H. Matthews & Rosner, 1988; McPherson & Wister, 2008; Sangl, 1985; Shanas, 1979; R. Stone, Cafferata, & Sangl, 1987). A voluminous amount of research exists documenting that family caregivers of older adults assume this significant role at great expense to their financial, psychological, and physical well-being (e.g., Biegel, Sales, & Schultz, 1991; Montgomery & Kamo, 1989; Scharlach & Boyd, 1989; Strawbridge & Wallhagen, 1991; Vitaliano, Zhang, & Scanlan, 2003) although there are often concomitant positive feeling of providing support (Tarlow et al., 2004). Siblings and friends also provide support to one another in later life, and their help is more likely to comprise emotional support, companionship, and small acts of kindness such as bringing in the mail or watering plants rather than assistance with the tasks of daily living (Barker, 2002; Bedford, 1989; D.C. Jones & Vaughan, 1990; B. Wellman & Wortley, 1989). There is, however, some evidence beginning to emerge suggesting that non-kin maybe providing some level of caregiving assistance to older adults who lack children or other kin that they would otherwise seek support from (Barker, 2002).

In contrast to the informal network, the formal network consists of agencies that operate within a bureaucratic structure, generally have no prior emotional relationship with their clients, and provide care for a limited or specified amount of time (A. Lipman & Longino, 1982; Litwak & Misseri, 1989). The community resources that we discuss later in this book represent the formal network that exists to enhance the well-being of older adults. As Travis (1995) points out, the formal network also consists of agencies that are nonservice in nature and includes religious, ethnic, and social groups. When families become caregivers to frail older adults, they in essence become gatekeepers to the use of formal services. There has been considerable interest regarding when and how the informal network interacts with the formal network.

INFORMAL AND FORMAL INTERACTION

Although families offer a tremendous amount of care to older family members, there are occasions when older adults and their families turn to the formal network for assistance. Because the informal network plays such an important role in delivering and securing assistance for older adults, researchers have been interested in creating conceptual approaches to aid in understanding the interaction between the informal and formal network.

Litwak (1985) proposed the dual specialization model, suggesting that informal and formal networks carry out responsibilities that are best suited to each. For example, the informal network can respond to unscheduled or unplanned needs, and the formal network can offer scheduled, structured care provided by trained professionals. Being available to assist a frail older adult in living in the community with frequent trips to the bathroom at various times in the middle of the night is best provided by a caregiving spouse or child; checking on vital signs once a day is a task better suited to a trained individual in the formal network. According to Litwak's model, both the informal and formal networks work best when they perform the tasks to which they are most suited.

The supplemental model (Stoller, 1989; Stoller & Pugliesi, 1988) acknowledges that the informal network is the primary source of social care but that formal services are used to supplement assistance provided by the informal network when its resources are not able to meet the caregiving needs. The informal network relies on formal services to augment, rather than replace, its caregiving activities.

The research on the interplay between the formal and informal networks has been sparse primarily due to the complicated way in which families and older adults move in and out of tapping into formal and informal support. As Bonsang (2009) points out, this interface is complex and depends on informal support availability, level of an older adult's disability and need, level of burden, and availability of formal support. Clearly, more longitudinal research is needed to determine the patterns of formal network use during later life and during the course of the caregiving career. The conceptual models discussed here can alert the practitioner to be cognizant of the different ways in which the informal network reaches out to the formal network and to realize that the formal network frequently assists both the older adults and their informal network. We turn next to a review of the factors associated with service use.

Service Use by Older Adults

Researchers have identified a number of factors related to service use, but studies often report conflicting results regarding which factors predict service use. These differences are in part due to the use of dissimilar independent variables when predicting service use and the different community resources studied. Despite these methodological limitations, we can make some generalizations about the variables associated with service use. Characteristics such as age, transportation, gender, marital status, living arrangement, geographical location, race and ethnicity, health status, and awareness of services have all been found to be associated with the use of community services. Specifically, as age increases, so does service use (Chappell & Blandford, 1987; Krout, 1985b; McCaslin, 1989; Webber, Fox, & Burnette, 1994). Older women are more likely to use services than are older men (Coulton & Frost, 1982; McCaslin, 1989). Those with access to transportation are more likely to use services (Krout, 1983; McCaslin, 1989; J. Mitchell, 1995). Older adults living in rural communities are generally less likely to use community resources than are their urban counterparts (Krout, 1983; Spense, 1992; Sun, 2011). Older adults who are married are less likely to use services than are older adults who live alone (Krout, 1983; Spense, 1992), and older husbands who are caring for their elderly wives have been found to use services more than wives who are caring for their husbands (Coe & Neufeld, 1999). Whites are significantly more likely to use community services than are their non-White counterparts (Carlton-LaNey, 1991; Fellin & Powell, 1988; Guttman, 1980; Li, 2006; Spense, 1992), and those whose health needs are greater are more likely to use services (Calsyn &

Winter, 2001; Coulton & Frost, 1982; Strain & Blandford, 2002). Finally, not surprisingly, higher levels of awareness are linked to greater service use (Burnette, 1999; Casado et al., 2011; Strain & Blandford, 2002).

Currently, much of the research investigating service use by older adults has focused on the relationship between demographic and social characteristics and service use. More research is needed to indicate the psychosocial reasons *why* older adults do or do not use community services.

Psychosocial Barriers to Service Use

Studies of help-seeking behavior have identified several social-psychological barriers that might explain why older people do not use programs that could help them. Some years ago, A. Lipman and Sterne (1962) suggested that older adults are reluctant to use services because they wish to maintain an image of self-reliance and competency. A person's image of self-reliance may be compromised when experiencing a decline in physical health and no longer able to continue some activities. When the perception of self-reliance and competency is compromised, asking for formal assistance only verifies this personal shortcoming. Moen (1978) found that respondents in her study were reluctant to admit needs and did not want to use services that they associated with "welfare" programs. Furthermore, American culture puts a high value on independence and self-reliance, and, as a result, people feel uncomfortable when they "impose" on others for assistance. In addition, older adults from different cultural backgrounds and experiences may have varying views of the appropriateness of seeking assistance from formal service providers.

Along with the cultural norms and values people hold about self-reliance, their self-perceptions and social comparisons with others can influence the act of seeking assistance. For example, many older adults do not see themselves as old. At age 93, the grandfather of one of the authors stated that he did not want to go to the senior center to socialize with those "old" people. Perhaps, like many other older adults, his view of himself did not fit his image of who uses services or attends programs designed for older adults. Similarly, Powers and Bultena (1974) suggest that older respondents in their study might have been reluctant to use services because they perceived that programs were meant for older adults who were worse off than themselves.

Another barrier to seeking help is the desire to avoid embarrassment (Shapiro, 1983). The act of asking someone for assistance implies having problems that one cannot resolve on one's own. For the current cohort of the oldest-old, who survived such hardships as the Depression, this admission might be difficult. Moreover, when recipients seek formal services, they are forced to make their personal problems public (Williamson, 1974), which for some may cause embarrassment.

These psychosocial variables (i.e., independence, self-reliance, and embarrassment), although illuminating, are somewhat limited because they do not explore the help-seeking context in greater detail. Below we discuss theoretical models that can help explain service use among older adults.

PSYCHOSOCIAL THEORIES OF SERVICE USE

Within the fields of gerontology, sociology, and psychology, several theories or models can be used to help explain who is likely to use services and why some older adults might not be willing to seek assistance. Although researchers have not specifically applied some of these models and theories to older adult populations, they offer a way to think about the factors that might be associated with service use. These theories are psychosocial in that they draw on social as well as psychological dimensions.

Continuity Theory

Continuity theory (Atchley, 1971, 1989, 1997) is a theory of adult development based on the premise that, as adults develop, they become invested in mental pictures that organize their ideas about themselves and their external environment. Moreover, these ideas are actively constructed as people age. As adults reach middle age, they have a good idea of their strengths and weaknesses, and use these ideas to make choices that take advantage of their strengths. Thus, Atchley (1997) states that, when making choices in life,

> people will be attracted to past views of self . . . the coping strategies that have been successful, ways of thinking that have been effective, people that have been supportive and helpful, and environments that have met the need for security and predictability. (p. 272)

Application of continuity theory to help-seeking behaviors suggests that the coping strategies used by older adults throughout their lives are likely to predict the circumstances under which they will seek or accept help. Remember the story of Katherine at the beginning of the chapter? She refused all attempts to help improve her health and living arrangements. No doubt, spending her life as a doctor—especially at a time when there were few women physicians—fashioned her self-perception and ways of contending with difficulties. She was probably an independent, self-sufficient woman and found that she could successfully cope with most of life's challenges by herself. On the basis of this assumption about her past ways of handling difficult situations, the application of continuity theory to her situation evokes no surprise at her reluctance to accept assistance. Longitudinal research on help-seeking behavior and the use of formal services employing the continuity theory would help to better clarify how past views of self and coping strategies developed throughout the life course can influence help-seeking behavior in later life.

Social Behavior Model

Andersen and Newman (1973) developed the social behavior model in an attempt to explain why individuals use health services. More recently, researchers have relied heavily on this model for guidance when investigating the use of social services. The model (shown in Exhibit 3.1) suggests that using services is a function of older adults' predisposition to use the service, enabling factors that either facilitate or impede use of a service, and the need for the service (Andersen, 1995; Andersen & Newman, 1973).

According to the social behavior model, certain individuals are more inclined than others to use services because of personal characteristics that are present before the need for a service arises. These predisposing characteristics include the demographic factors of age and gender. They also include social structure characteristics of marital status, education, occupation, ethnicity, and social networks that are thought to determine the status of a

Exhibit 3.1 Social Behavior Model

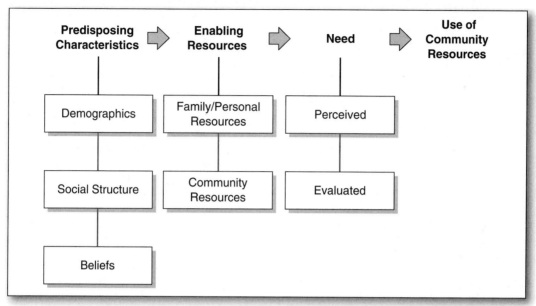

Source: Adapted from Andersen (1995). Copyright American Sociological Association. Used with permission.

person in the community, the ability to cope with the problem at hand, and the resources available to deal with the problem. General beliefs or attitudes about support services might also predict service use.

Even those who are predisposed to using services will not do so unless they can access those services. Enabling characteristics that facilitate the use of services include personal and family characteristics of income level, insurance coverage, access to transportation, and awareness of service. At the community level, enabling characteristics include the availability of the service and the distance to the service. Finally, service need can be either an individual's subjective assessment of need or an evaluated need provided by a professional. Researchers have found that predicting service use cannot be influenced by need alone unless the person is predisposed to use the service and then has the necessary enabling resources.

Let us illustrate how we can use this model to predict whether an older adult will attend a congregate meal site. Walter is 78 years old and has lived alone since his spouse of 45 years died two years ago. His monthly income is $1,050 a month, and he lives in a small one-bedroom apartment. Although he is in good health and able to drive, he does not go out much and easily becomes despondent when thinking of his spouse. Walter has found that he is uncomfortable with shopping and cooking because his wife was responsible for most of those duties. As a result, he often skips breakfast and lunch. After learning about his plight, a friend tells him about the congregate meal program offered three times per week at the senior center and invites Walter to go with him. Walter steadfastly refuses and states, "I do not need to eat like I used to, and I am getting along just fine." How can we explain Walter's reluctance to attend the congregate meal program? At first glance, he has many characteristics presented in the social behavior model that should be related to attending the program. He has the resources that would enable him to pay the suggested donation for the meal, he has transportation to the site, and he is aware of the service. Walter does not, however, perceive that he has an unmet nutritional need. In his mind, he can do without going to the congregate meal program, and he does not see how he could benefit from attending. Unless there is a change in Walter's perceived need for the program, he probably will not attend.

The social behavior model has had varying success in predicting actual community service use. Researchers using this model have found that the predisposing characteristics of being older, female, unmarried, and more highly educated, and the enabling characteristic of income, are associated with increased likelihood of service use (Krout, 1983; S. A. Peterson, 1989). But these characteristics do not explain use as well as awareness and need. Although awareness of services is strongly related to service use, it is often not sufficient to predict use. Researchers have reported that even when respondents were aware of community programs, their use of programs continued to be low (Krout, 1984; J. Mitchell, 1995; Powers & Bultena, 1974). Cohen-Mansfield and Frank (2008) posit that those not accessing services, for which they have an assessed need, may not be aware of their need or are unaware of the potential a service can have on alleviating their need. Overall, however, perceived need is most often the best predictor of service use. Researchers using the social behavior model should also investigate the role cultural barriers play in facilitating or inhibiting service use (Scharlach et al., 2006). In this next section, we describe some theories designed to predict help-seeking behavior developed primarily from the field of psychology.

THE PSYCHOLOGY OF HELP-SEEKING BEHAVIOR

People probably can remember a time when they were sick enough to see a doctor but did not do so until a friend or family member cajoled them into going. Or perhaps they can recall a time when they drove around hopelessly lost but refused to stop and ask for directions. Why do individuals refuse to ask for help when clearly they would be better off if they did? According to the psychology of help-seeking behavior, seeking assistance is more complicated than might be expected.

Decisions about whether to seek help involve weighing the psychological costs of asking for assistance against the benefits that might occur. In contrast to the social behavioral model, the help-seeking theories we discuss here take into account the psychological processes of a person who is considering seeking assistance. In this next section, we present a summary of the reactance theory, the attribution theory, the equity theory, and the threat-to-self-esteem model. We base this summary on the work of Fisher, Nadler, and Whitcher-Alagna (1983), who provide an in-depth review of how each of these theories can be used to predict help-seeking behavior.

Reactance Theory

The reactance theory (J. W. Brehm, 1966) suggests that people value freedom, which is the belief that one has the choice to engage in a particular behavior. When one's freedom is threatened (either perceived or actual), a negative psychological state (reactance) occurs, and people respond in ways that attempt to restore this valued state. The degree of reactance experienced by an individual depends on how important the freedom is to the indiv the number of freedoms lost or threatened, and the strength of the threat (J. W. Brehm, 1966; S. S. Brehm & Brehm, 1981; Chadee, 2011). The threat can be personal, where one feels threatened through interaction with known individuals, but the threat can also be impersonal in that it arises through interactions with institutions and its employees (Chadee, 2011). Thus, reactance can occur when the threat emerges from an impersonal source and when there is no direct personal threat to freedom. For example, when recipients perceive that the aid or assistance will threaten their freedom or autonomy, they are likely to react negatively and may refuse aid if they think there are "strings attached" that could compromise freedom (Fisher et al., 1983). Furthermore, as recipients seek to reestablish their freedom or autonomy, they may also form a negative impression of the person who is trying to provide the assistance (Gergen, Morse, & Kristeller, 1973).

How can we use reactance theory to explain why an older adult might choose not to seek assistance? Consider the case of Lydia, an 82-year-old widow living alone in a mobile home that she and her husband bought some years ago. Her monthly income consists of a Social Security check of $625 that she receives as a surviving spouse. An outreach worker informs Lydia that she is probably eligible for SSI, which would provide her with additional income as well as Medicaid coverage for her health care needs. She refuses, stating that she does not want to give any information about her personal affairs to a government worker. She fears that once she gives them any personal information and begins to receive SSI, the government could invade other aspects of her personal life or restrict what she does with her money. According to the reactance theory, even though a personal threat to Lydia's autonomy does not exist, she does not want to go through a process that she perceives will indirectly cause harm to her autonomy. As a result, she chooses not to accept any financial assistance.

Attribution Theory

Think about the last time someone helped you out of a difficult situation. Do you recall asking yourself why that person decided to help you? When contemplating whether to ask for help, did you wonder why you needed help with that problem? Attribution theory states that individuals formulate attributions to understand, predict, and control their environment and help explain why certain events occur (Kelley, 1967). Individuals assign attributions to both internal (self) and external (environment) factors to help them understand the occurrence of events or behaviors.

Let us examine the first question: Why did that person help you? If you have been on the receiving end of some assistance recently, you might have pondered for a moment *why* the person helping you chose to do so. What was the person's real motivation for helping you fix your flat tire or assisting you to solve a computer or smartphone problem? How we formulate an answer to this question plays an important role in whether we will allow someone to help us.

According to the attribution theory, a recipient of assistance will want to know what motivated the helper's behavior (Fisher et al., 1983). In deciding what the helper's motive is, the recipient can attribute the helping person's behavior to three possible motives. Fisher et al. suggested that the recipient might think that the person providing the assistance (a) acted from genuine concern, (b) acted for ulterior motives, or (c) performed the action because the person's role demanded it. These possible inferences readily apply to seeking assistance from helpers in the older person's formal network. If the older adult believes that the person providing assistance does so because that person's role requires it or that the helper acts from genuine concern, chances are that the older adult will be less hesitant about seeking assistance from a formal source.

Another application of the attribution theory is its use in answering another important question linked to seeking help when people need it—why do we need help? Remember, the basic premise of the attribution theory is that individuals scan their environment to explain some of their behaviors or actions. According to the theory, if individuals cannot explain their behaviors by external (environmental) factors, then they will look inward for internal factors (personal disposition). In the process of trying to determine why they need help, they will look for three types of information: the distinctiveness of the behavior (does the behavior always occur?), consensus (are others responding similarly?), and consistency (how often does the behavior occur?).

The recipient assesses each of these dimensions in any help-seeking situation. An internal or external attribution depends on the combination of different levels of distinctiveness, consensus, and consistency (Fiske & Taylor, 1991). For example, if you decide that you *always* have trouble with computers (low distinctiveness), that you have had difficulty using computers ever since you first started using them (high consistency), and that other people do not seem to have the same trouble you do with computers (low consensus), then you are likely to attribute your computer trouble to an internal attribute (you cannot learn new things). In contrast, if you have experienced difficulty with only one particular computer in the computer lab (high distinctiveness), you infrequently have trouble using computers (low consistency), and you notice others in the computer lab having the same difficulty (high consensus), then you will probably attribute your troubles to an external factor (the computer is a lemon).

This reasoning process is an important determinant in the decision to seek assistance. For example, if recipients feel that they need assistance because of a personal inadequacy (internal attribution), then their self-perceptions will be low, and help seeking may not occur (Fisher et al., 1983). On the other hand, if individuals perceive that many people need help for a similar condition (high consensus), they will make an external attribution and will be more likely to accept assistance (Gerber, 1969; Tessler & Schwartz, 1972).

How can the attribution theory be used to understand why a caregiver might not use the services of an adult day program? Consider the situation of Jacque, an adult daughter. Her mother, Olivia, is 82 and has lived alone since her spouse died 11 years ago. In the past six months, Jacque has seen her mother's physical condition steadily worsen—she is becoming more forgetful, and her unsteady gait causes her to fall frequently. Jacque has helped with shopping, meals, and other errands along with working and caring for her own two children. Her work and family obligations make it impossible to constantly supervise her mother during the day, and she is becoming increasingly worried about Olivia's well-being. A friend tells Jacque about the local adult day program and suggests she take Olivia. What are the chances that Jacque will use the services of the adult day program?

If we apply the attribution theory to this situation, we can expect that when Jacque is deciding whether to take her mother to the program, she will think about why she would need to use the services of an adult day program. She may come to the conclusion that taking her mother to the program demonstrates that she does not have the personal fortitude to take care of her (an internal attribution). She may, on the other hand, attribute the need for assistance to her mother's condition (external attribution). If her reasoning follows this latter line of thinking, she will probably be more likely to use the adult day program. If she formulates an internal attribution, she will be less inclined to use the service.

Equity Theory

Social exchange theories suggest that individuals interact with one another through the exchange of valued objects or sentiments. Several similar versions of exchange theories exist, including Walster, Berscheid, and Walster's (1973) equity theory. This theory is based on the premise that individuals strive to maintain equity within their relationships (Adams, 1965). Individuals who feel they are getting more than they should and who feel indebted to others react negatively to these situations in which equity is compromised (Fyrand, 2010; Rook, 1987). When inequities occur, individuals experience a certain degree of distress and attempt to rectify the imbalance either by altering the tangible elements of the interaction process or by psychologically reformulating the interaction context. Furthermore, equity theory states that the greater the degree of inequity, the greater the degree of stress experienced because of the inequity (Hatfield & Sprecher, 1983). In a help-seeking situation, recipients will feel inequality when they have a higher ratio of outcomes to inputs (Walster et al., 1973).

A number of researchers reported that individuals on the receiving end of assistance who were unable to reciprocate were less likely to seek or ask for assistance (DePaulo, 1978; Greenberg & Shapiro, 1971; Manton, 1987). When researchers introduced reciprocity into an inequitable situation, recipients reported feeling better about the assistance they were receiving (Wilke & Lazette, 1970). In situations in which introducing reciprocity is not possible, changing a recipient's perception of the helping context can be just as useful in restoring a sense of equity (Fyrand, 2010; Greenberg & Westcott, 1983; Roberto & Scott, 1986). If we apply this idea to receiving assistance from the formal network, older adults may avoid feeling indebted by differentiating between programs in which they are entitled (e.g., Social Security) and those that are needs based (e.g., food stamps; A. Lipman & Sterne, 1962). There is a sense of equity in programs such as Social Security because older adults have *paid* into the program—and they perceive that they are receiving financial benefits to which they are entitled. In contrast, the number of older adults who participate in programs in which recipients are always on the receiving end and provide nothing in return for those benefits may be low.

Equity theory also can be used to explain help-seeking behavior. Consider the situation of Hanna, 72, who suffers from rheumatoid arthritis that severely limits her ability to attend activities outside her home. Before her arthritis limited her activities, she worked part time and was a volunteer at the local hospital. Although she enjoyed working, she always remarked on how much satisfaction she experienced when helping patients. She describes herself as an independent person, having always provided for her own needs. Because her arthritis keeps her from volunteering and getting out as much as she would like, she finds herself becoming more and more isolated. She reads in the newspaper about a friendly visiting program, a service in which a volunteer provides social companionship and assistance with errands. She wonders how she could ever compensate someone for coming and spending time with her—she feels that she has nothing to give the volunteer in return. If Hanna feels she will be unable to reciprocate the help she receives, it may be difficult for her to accept the assistance of the volunteer.

Threat-to-Self-Esteem Model

The threat-to-self-esteem model (Fisher et al., 1983) is based on the assumption that most help-seeking situations contain a mixture of both positive and negative elements (see Exhibit 3.2). Whether the helping situation is perceived as positive or negative

Exhibit 3.2   Formalized Threat-to-Self-Esteem Model

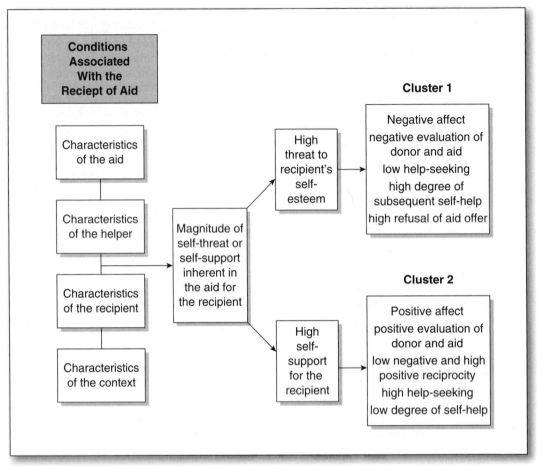

Source: Adapted from Fisher et al. (1983).

depends on the characteristics of the (a) aid, (b) helper, (c) recipient, and (d) context. If recipients perceive the aid as highlighting their inferiority or dependency, they will view the aid as *self-threatening.* In contrast, if they see the aid as positive, they will perceive the assistance as *self-supportive.* If the helper is similar in age or status to the recipient, or has a higher status than that of the recipient, the recipient is likely to see the aid as highlighting their inferiority, and the helping situation becomes self-threatening (Fisher & Nadler, 1976; Nadler, Fisher, & Streufest, 1976). Recipient characteristics also can influence how the help-seeking episode can influence the perception of the help-seeking behavior. Researchers have found that recipients who were ego-involved in the task and who valued autonomy were more threatened by receiving the assistance (DePaulo & Fisher, 1980; Nadler, Sheinberg, & Jaffe, 1981). Evidence suggests that those with high self-esteem are more reluctant to receive help than those with low self-esteem (Nadler & Mayseless, 1983).

Best Practice: Equity Theory in Action

Partners in Care is a service credit exchange program in Severna Park, Maryland, designed to create community by linking frail elderly and disabled adults with neighbors who volunteer their time to help with occasional tasks and errands. Participants may provide services, receive services, or both. For each hour of service donated by volunteers, an hour of service credit is earned. That credit may be used at a later time or donated back to the program for frail elderly who cannot volunteer themselves.

Volunteer services are matched to individual needs and may include providing grocery shopping, transportation, handyman help, yard work, or friendly visits. Volunteers are encouraged to use their individual talents, interests, and creativity as Partners in Care. The goal of these services is to help seniors and adults remain in their own homes. Each hour of volunteer work earns an hour of credit for the volunteer. Groups of volunteers are encouraged to collaborate efforts for larger projects.

For more information about Partners in Care Partnerships or services, call 410-544-4800, or toll-free 1-800-227-5500, or visit www.partnersincare.org.

Accordingly, the recipient will perceive the characteristics associated with the receipt of aid as either self-threatening or self-supporting. This, in turn, will influence the recipient's decision to seek assistance. If the recipient perceives the help as predominantly self-threatening, the recipient's reaction will be negative (Cluster 1 in the model shown in Exhibit 3.2). On the other hand, if the recipient views the assistance as primarily self-supportive, the recipient's reaction will be positive (Cluster 2 in the model).

Let us look at how the threat-to-self-esteem model can help predict help-seeking behavior. Consider Mabel and John, who have lived in a small rural community for 25 years. Mabel is 75 and still works at the local school district as a secretary. She is quite proud of the many years she has worked and is well known in the community. John, 84, retired 15 years ago and has remained healthy until recently. John has begun to experience back problems, high blood pressure, and arthritis that limit his mobility. He has successfully recovered from angioplasty for clogged arteries in his heart and neck. Because of John's health problems, Mabel thinks it is time to look into additional insurance that will supplement their Medicare coverage. Mabel has collected information from various insurance companies but is having trouble determining which policy is best. The local Area Agency on Aging has trained a number of older adults who live in the community to be insurance counselors and assist other older adults in comparing Medigap policies. Mabel refuses to use the service because she does not want to "look stupid" in front of the people she knows. In this situation, Mabel perceives that both the situation and the characteristics of the donor are self-threatening and most likely will not seek the assistance of an insurance counselor.

APPLICATION OF THEORY IN PRACTICE

Theories can be powerful tools in understanding and predicting the patterns and behaviors of others. The theories and models described in this chapter, summarized in Exhibit 3.3,

Exhibit 3.3   Summary Table of Psychosocial Theories

Theory	Author(s)	Summary
Continuity Theory	Atchley, 1971, 1989, 1997, 1999	Continuity theory holds that, in making adaptive choices, middle-aged and older adults attempt to preserve and maintain existing internal and external structures, and they prefer to accomplish this objective by using strategies tied to their past experiences of themselves and their social world. Change is linked to the person's perceived past, producing continuity in inner psychological characteristics as well as in social behavior and in social circumstances. Continuity is thus a grand adaptive strategy that is promoted by both individual preference and social approval (Atchley, 1989, p. 183).
Social Behavioral Model	Andersen, 1995; Andersen & Newman, 1973	Using services is a function of predisposing (e.g., age, race/ethnicity, marital status, gender), enabling (e.g., income, access to transportation, awareness of services), and need (e.g., subjective assessment or professional evaluation) variables.
Reactance Theory	J. W. Brehm, 1966; S. S. Brehm & Brehm, 1981	Individuals value states such as freedom and autonomy, and when these valued states are threatened, a negative state occurs (reactance).
Attribution Theory	Kelley, 1967	To understand, predict, and control one's environment, individuals assign attributions to themselves and the external environment.
Equity Theory	Walster et al., 1973	Individuals strive to maintain equity within their relationships, and when perceived inequities occur, individuals react negatively and attempt to rectify the imbalance.
Threat to Self-Esteem	Fisher et al., 1983	Help-seeking situations are a combination of positive and negative perceived characteristics of the type of aid being provided, the person helping, the recipient, and the context.

can give practitioners and students a better understanding of why older adults may or may not use the services and programs that would enhance their well-being. If service providers are aware of the different models and theories of help-seeking behavior, they can work to deliver their services in a way that addresses issues of equity or self-esteem. Using attribution theory, adult day program directors can convey a message to overworked caregivers that can help them reformulate the attributions they construct about using the services of an adult day program. Changing caregivers' internal attribution that using adult day care services is an indication that they are personal failures to an external attribution will increase the likelihood of program use. Simply informing older adults of the services that exist in communities will not guarantee that they will use the services. Understanding and acknowledging the psychosocial and cultural barriers to accepting help will increase the use of community-based services by older adults in times of need.

SUGGESTIONS FOR FURTHER READING

In this chapter, we have provided only a brief overview of different psychosocial theories that can help in understanding service use among older adults. Some suggested readings about each of the theories are listed below if you would like to learn more about each of these theories.

Continuity Theory

Atchley, R. C. (1989). A continuity theory of normal aging. *The Gerontologist, 29*(2), 183–190.
Atchley, R. C. (1999). *Continuity and adaptation in aging: Creating positive experiences.* Baltimore, MD: Johns Hopkins University Press.
Pushkar, D., Chaikelson, J., Conway, M., Etezadi, M., Giannopoulus, J., Li, K., & Wrosch, C. (2010). Testing continuity and activity variables as predictors of positive and negative affect in retirement. *Journal of Gerontology, 65B*(1), 42–49.

Social Behavioral Model

Andersen, R., & Newman, J. F. (2005). Societal and individual determinants of medical care utilization in the United States. *Milbank Quarterly, 83*(4), 1–28.
Phillips, K. A., Morrison, K. R., Andersen, R., & Aday, L. A. (1998). Understanding the context of healthcare utilization: Assessing environmental and provider-related variables in the behavioral model of utilization. *Health Services Research, 33*(3), 571–596.
Wolinsky, F. D., Coe, R. M., Miller, D. K., Prendergast, J. M., Creel, M. J., & Chavez, M. N. (1983). Health services utilization among the noninstitutionalized elderly. *Journal of Health and Social Behavior, 24,* 325–337.

Reactance Theory

Brehm, S. S., & Brehm, J. W. (1981). *Psychological reactance: A theory of freedom and control.* New York, NY: Academic Press.
Chadee, D. (2011). Toward freedom: Reactance theory revisited. In D. Chadee (Ed.), *Theories in social psychology* (pp. 13–43). London, UK: Blackwell.
Dillard, J. P., & Shen, L. (2005). On the nature of reactance and its role in persuasive health. *Communication Monographs, 72*(2), 144–168.
Woller, K., Buboltz, M. P., Walter, C., & Loveland, J. M. (2007). Psychological reactance: Examination across age, ethnicity, and gender. *American Journal of Psychology, 120*(1), 15–24.

Attribution Theory

Martinko, M. J., & Thomson, N. F. (1998). A synthesis and extension of the Weiner and Kelley attribution models. *Basic & Applied Social Psychology, 20*(4), 271–284.
Stajkovic, A. D., & Sommer, S. M. (2000). Self-efficacy and causal attributions: Direct and reciprocal links. *Journal of Applied Social Psychology, 30*(4), 707–737.
Weiner, B. (2000). Intrapersonal and interpersonal theories of motivation from an attributional perspective. *Educational Psychology Review, 12*(1), 1–14.
Weiner, B. (2011). An attribution theory of motivation. In P. A. M. Van Lange, A. W. Bruglanski, & E. T. Higgins (Eds.), *Handbook of theories of social psychology* (Vol. 1, pp. 135–155). Thousand Oaks, CA: Sage.

Equity Theory

Argyle, M. (1992). Receiving and giving support: Effects on relationships and well-being. *Counseling Psychology Quarterly, 5*(2), 123–133.

Fyrand, L. (2010). Reciprocity: A predictor of mental health and continuity in elderly people's relationships. A review. *Current Gerontology and Geriatrics Research, 2010.* doi:10.1155/2010/340161.

Jung, J. (1990). The role of reciprocity in social support. *Basic & Applied Social Psychology, 11*(3), 243–253.

Lu, L. (1997). Social support, reciprocity, and well-being. *Journal of Social Psychology, 137*(5), 618–628.

Messick, D. M., & Cook, K. S. (Eds.) (1983). *Equity theory: Psychological and sociological perspectives.* New York, NY: Praeger.

Threats to Self-Esteem

Goodwin, R., Costa, P., & Adonu, J. (2004). Social support and its consequences: "Positive" and "deficiency" values and their implications for support and self-esteem. *British Journal of Social Psychology, 4*(3), 465–474.

Nadler, A. (1987). Determinants of help-seeking behaviour: The effects of helpers' similarity, task centrality and recipient's self esteem. *European Journal of Social Psychology, 17*(1), 57–67.

Newsom, J. T. (1999). Another side to caregiving: Negative reactions to being helped. *Current Directions in Psychological Science, 8*(6), 183–187.

Schütz, A. (1998). Coping with threats to self-esteem: The differing patterns of subjects with high versus low trait self-esteem in first-person accounts. *European Journal of Personality, 12*(3), 169–186.

PART II

The Continuum of Services

Information and Assistance

Gary was panicked. His mother, Ruth, was coming home from the hospital in two days. Ruth, 81, had suffered her third stroke. She was confused and weakened on her right side but not paralyzed. Gary knew that his mother could not return to her apartment at this time, but he could not imagine Ruth living with him. Because he was currently employed at two jobs, he simply could not provide the care and attention she needed. His girlfriend suggested that he look in the community services section of the phone book for help. There he found Carelink listed under senior services. He didn't know what to expect, but he knew he had to start somewhere. Pete, the Carelink information and referral specialist, spent 20 minutes suggesting several options for Gary. When Gary talked with his girlfriend that evening, he told her that he still felt overwhelmed but that he had had no idea there were so many services for seniors with problems such as his mother's.

It is easy to see why Gary was overwhelmed with the idea of caring for his mother. Who would supervise her during the day? Who would cook her meals and administer her medications when he was at work? What about rehabilitation therapy? Although people such as Gary know that there must be services and programs in their community that can help, they often do not know where to begin to look. Not knowing who to call for assistance can result in leaving a personal or familial crisis unresolved; finding help, however, can be extremely difficult. As Levinson (1988) points out, the volume of services is so great that the result is a complex and fragmented network that makes finding information problematic for the average person. Information and referral/assistance (I&R/A) services are designed to help older adults and their families to access the services they need. Chelimsky (1991) defines I&R/A as "the active process of linking someone who has a need or problem with an agency that provides services meeting that need or solving that problem" (p. 2). In this chapter, we review the policies that helped create I&R/A services, describe the different types of programs and the people they serve, and look at the challenges that lie ahead for I&R/A services.

POLICY BACKGROUND

Information and referral services trace their origins to a social support agency created in the 1870s called the Social Service Exchange. The Social Service Exchange was created to prevent duplication of relief giving and increase the efficiency of screening "worthy" from "unworthy" applicants (McCaslin, 1981). By 1946, there were 320 agencies participating in the SSE, but the number had dropped to 97 by 1963 (Long, Anderson, Burd, Mathis, & Todd, 1971).

During this period, the Social Service Exchange was being replaced by different I&R/A systems. In the 1940s, Britain and the United States set up information centers to assist World War II veterans in finding appropriate resources. By 1949, however, the majority of these centers had shut down as well (Long et al., 1971). Also during this time, the United Community Funds and Councils of America, the predecessor to the United Way, began to provide information about social welfare resources and, with the creation of the Public Health Service, began to expand I&R/A efforts into health and aging resources (Levinson, 1988; Long et al., 1971).

A boost to the concept of I&R/A services came in the 1960s with the increase in public and private sector programs, which included legislation promoting the creation of I&R/A services to persons who were chronically ill, mentally ill, and aged (Levinson, 1988). In addition, the Older Americans Act (OAA) of 1965 instructed the Administration on Aging (AoA) to create a network of I&R/A services. Amendments to the OAA in 1978 provided that the AoA would act as a clearinghouse for all information related to the needs and interests of older persons and would provide access to services that included transportation, outreach, and I&R/A (Lowy, 1980). I&R/A services are currently funded along with other programs under Title III-B (Support Services and Senior Centers) of the OAA. The most current data available from the AoA indicated that in 2009, OAA funded I&R/A programs across the United States and served 12.4 million individuals (AoA, n.d.-c). Overall I&R/A funding in 2009 was $56.1 million, representing 37% of the Title III funding total.

The OAA defines I&R/A as a service for older adults that (a) provides individuals with current information on opportunities and services available to the individuals within their communities, including information relating to assistive technology; (b) assesses the problems and capacities of the individuals; (c) links the individuals to the opportunities and services that are available; (d) ensures, to the maximum extent practicable, that the individuals receive the services they need and that they are aware of the opportunities available through the establishment of adequate follow-up procedures; and (e) serves the entire community of older individuals, particularly older individuals with the greatest social and economic need and those at risk for institutional placement.

In part because the OAA requires the AoA to establish I&R/A as a priority service, the AoA has actively been involved in promoting and enhancing I&R/A services. For example, the National Association of State Units on Aging (NASUA) received a grant from the AoA in 1990 to establish the National Information and Referral Support Center (NIRSC) to strengthen the capacity of I&R/A activities under the OAA. The support center has served as the focal point for education and training of I&R/A providers across the country. During the first three years of the project, the support center developed a series of guides designed to promote consistency and improve the quality of I&R/A services. More recently, the NIRSC offers technical assistance documents that educate I&R/A specialists in areas of diversity, Medicare, communication skills, best practices for I&R/A, disaster preparedness information, and information technology support. In addition, the support center is encouraging the exchange of information about I&R/A services through an online "Strategy Exchange," which compiles successful approaches and ideas to enhance aging I&R/A. In collaboration with the Alliance of Information and Referral Systems

(AIRS), NIRSC has developed a certification for I&R/A Specialists in Aging. The certification, specifically related to working in the aging field, is a documentation of one's ability in the field of I&R/A, reflecting specific competencies and related performance criteria that describe the knowledge, skills, attitudes, and work-related behaviors needed by practitioners to successfully execute their duties.

Another national initiative to enhance I&R/A services is the AoA's creation of the Eldercare Locator. This nationwide I&R/A service, created in 1991, is administered by the National Association of Area Agencies on Aging (n4a) and NASUA. The service links callers or online users with I&R/A networks of state and local organizations that assist older adults and their families. These policy initiatives have been instrumental in providing technical support to I&R/A services. Under the 2006 amendments to the OAA, the AoA is also charged with building awareness of programs that provide benefits to older adults and to work with states and local Area Agencies on Aging (AAAs) to carry out outreach and benefit enrollment assistance. The AoA established the National Center on Senior Benefits Outreach and Enrollment in partnership with the National Council on Aging (NCOA), which, among other activities, maintains web decision support and enrollment tools and a clearinghouse on best practices in enrolling older adults with the greatest economic need, and collaborates with federal partners administering federal programs to provide training on the effective outreach strategies. Ten outreach centers were established in 2009 to implement person-centered outreach strategies in a coordinated approach to effectively locate and enroll economically vulnerable older adults and adults with disabilities into public benefit programs. A "person-centered" approach to benefits outreach and enrollment relies on personalized, one-on-one strategies to help individuals and families in need via seamless benefits screening and application processes (National Center for Benefits Outreach and Enrollment Programs, 2010). Targeted programs for enrollment outreach include Medicare Part D Extra Help, Medicare Savings Programs, Medicaid, Supplemental Nutrition Assistance Program, Low Income Home Energy Assistance, and State Pharmacy Assistance Programs (where available) In 2011, 10 additional national center grantees were selected from across the country (NCOA, 2011b).

The National 211 Initiative, another I&R/A program, has been underway since 1997. It was developed by a national partnership between AIRS and United Way and is modeled after the 911 phone number for emergencies. The 211 number is a way for individuals and families to search for health and human services information and referral services in their communities. In 1997, the I&R/A United Way of Metropolitan Atlanta created the nation's first 211 initiative that provides a free 24-hour telephone information and referral service, using a database of over 2,000 agencies to match callers to social services, and volunteer and donation opportunities (United Way of Connecticut, 2001). In 2000, the Federal Communications Commission authorized the 211 number to be used across the country for information and referral for human service information and referral. As of October 2011, 211 served over 260 million Americans—over 86% of the entire population—covering all or part of 50 states (including 16 states with 100% coverage) plus Washington, DC and Puerto Rico. As of July 2011, the 2-1-1 website had recorded over 5.5 million visitors. Canada also uses the 211 system, which currently covers over 56% of the population or 19 million people (Alliance of Information and Referral Systems [AIRS], 2012). In this next section, we examine the I&R/A program structure and services and provide a profile of users of I&R/A services.

Across the Globe: I&R/A in Scotland:
The Scottish Helpline for Older People (SHOP)

SHOP is national helpline in Scotland that assists older adults and those who care for or work with older adults find programs and services or information. Staff will also make referrals to other appropriate experts as needed. In addition to telephone access to information, SHOP offers a website and other online resources to assist in locating information and organizations that can help with a range of inquires, from health and housing to benefits, finances, leisure, work, and advocacy. SHOP was established in 2004 and is managed by Age Concern and Help the Aged in Scotland. The service is provided free of charge and receives the majority of its funding from the Scottish Government. SHOP receives around 15,000 calls annually.

For more information, visit http://www.ageconcernandhelptheagedscotland.org.uk

USERS AND PROGRAMS

Although I&R/A services play an important role in linking older adults with needed services, few scholarly evaluations of I&R/A services have been conducted during the past 30 years. Moreover, local studies that have evaluated I&R/A services are unpublished and not readily accessible (McCaslin, 1981). As a result, who uses I&R/A services and the outcomes of such use remain unclear. The few studies that have been conducted on I&R/A programs are reported below.

In 1975, the AoA embarked on a six-year research and demonstration project to develop a more useful and comprehensive system of I&R/A centers (Long, 1975). An evaluation of services provided by a demonstration project—the Wisconsin Information Service (WIS)—was conducted. Thirteen I&R/A sites were created and evaluated throughout Wisconsin from 1972 to 1974. Researchers found that 90% of inquiries were made by telephone and that slightly less than half (40%) of the respondents said that they had found out about the service through word of mouth. More than 75% of respondents who were informed about WIS through outreach efforts followed through with a contact to a recommended agency. A similar percentage of callers followed through with a call to a recommended agency; when referral appointments were made, however, 82% followed through with the recommended contact. All the WIS centers in the study served a high proportion of older adults. In addition, a higher percentage of older adults (55.6%) than younger adults (18.8%) received escort and/or transportation services.

For Your Files: Eldercare Locator

The Eldercare Locator is sponsored by the AoA, the n4a, and the NASUA. Fully operational since November 1992, the Eldercare Locator is a nationwide directory assistance service designed to help older persons and caregivers locate local support resources for aging Americans. This service links

(Continued)

(Continued)

callers with the I&R/A networks of state and local AAAs. The Locator receives 207,000 calls annually, and the website, which also has an online chat option, receives, on average, 300,000 unique
visits annually and can handle 150 different languages.

When contacting the Eldercare Locator, callers speak to a friendly, trained professional who has
access to an extensive list of I&R/A services. The Eldercare Locator will provide the names and phone
numbers of organizations within a desired location, anywhere in the country. Anyone may call the
toll-free number, 800-677-1116, Monday through Friday, 9:00 a.m. to 8:00 p.m. Eastern Time.

Source: NASUA (n.d.).

Two years later, Mark Battle Associates (1977) provided additional information about
I&R/A services for the AoA by conducting a national study of 62 I&R/A programs across the
country. The researchers collected data from I&R/A directors and staff, State Units on Aging
(SUAs), or AAAs, and users about the organizational structure, type of services offered, and
client satisfaction. They reported that I&R/A services that were age segregated were more
likely to provide a more comprehensive array of services than I&R/A services that were age
integrated. The average number of calls about or from older adults was 179 per month, and
the range of callers was from 2 to 11,000. Of the users, 75% indicated that the I&R/A staff
had fully or partially resolved their problems, and almost all users (97%) indicated that they
were pleased with the way in which their interviews were conducted. A similarly high percentage (92%) indicated that the I&R/A service did a good job in assisting them. The most
common problems of older callers were related to financial matters and Social Security,
transportation, health problems and care, and home health care. Housing maintenance and
repair, food and nutrition, and homemaker services were also frequently mentioned.

The different nuances of I&R/A programs with regard to data collection make it difficult
to identify consistencies across programs. In addition, simply collecting the data can be
problematic. For example, to protect the caller's identity, some I&R/A agencies often do
not collect information about the caller's race, income, or other demographic information
(U.S. General Accounting Office [GAO], 1991b). This makes it hard to generalize about the
type of older adults who use I&R/A systems and the problems for which they are seeking
assistance. The studies that have been conducted, however, can inform us about the types
of older adults seeking services and can serve as a starting point for more rigorous empirical investigations.

Coyne (1991) examined the demographic characteristics and use patterns of 257 callers
to a statewide I&R/A service specializing in Alzheimer's disease and related dementia. Results
indicated that the average age of respondents was 50 years and that the majority were
women (78%). In addition, the majority were married and working full time (71% and 58%,
respectively). Slightly fewer than half the callers were direct caregivers (44%), and 31% were
family members of caregivers. The majority of callers also indicated that they were pleased
with the services they received. For example, 96% reported that they had received the information they requested and thought the information was helpful. Of callers who received
referrals to specific community agencies, 65% reported that they had contacted or used the
referral. More recently, A. Barrett and Schimmel (2010) examined OAA program participant's
combinations of services they reported using. Their research, which was a nationwide study,

revealed that depending on which program participants were using, the use of I&R/A ranged between 17% and 26%. For example, 26% and 21% of participants in the congregate meal and transportation programs, respectively, also reported using I&R/A. Participants in these programs also reported having fewer functional limitations indicating that users of I&R/A services were healthier than those who did not use I&R/A services.

Researchers have also investigated the effectiveness of various outreach efforts by I&R/As, such as direct mailings of resource directories and door-to-door canvassing in targeted neighborhoods. For example, Cherry, Prebis, and Pick (1995) examined the effects of a mass-mailed *Senior Access Directory* to 35,000 older adults over the age of 60 living in northwest Indiana. To evaluate the effectiveness of the mailing in increasing service awareness and use, staff asked all callers 9 days before the mailing and 10 days after the mailing how they had found out about the agency and whether they had used the directory. More than 80% of the respondents indicated that the directory had increased awareness of services. Moreover, 44% reported that receiving the directory had prompted some action, such as talking to family members or calling an agency listed in the directory. Finally, calls to United Way more than doubled, increasing from 52 before to 122 after the distribution.

Best Practice: Information and Referral/Assistance Services— National Center for Benefits Outreach and Enrollment

In 2008, AoA awarded a $1.9 million grant to the NCOA to establish the National Center for Benefits Outreach and Enrollment. The establishment of the National Center was one component of an initiative to integrate services and benefits and to implement new outreach provisions incorporated into the OAA in the 2006 reauthorization.

One of the key tasks of the National Center has been to establish and support Benefits Enrollment Centers (BECs) to help low-income seniors and younger adults with disabilities find and apply for all the benefits programs for which they are eligible. In late 2008, the Center issued a request for proposals from local and state organizations to receive grants up to $100,000 to become BECs. The purpose of these grants was to develop and implement *coordinated, community-wide, person-centered systems* for benefits outreach and enrollment—with the primary focus being on undersubscribed public benefits programs, including the following:

Medicare Part D Extra Help (or Low-Income Subsidy)

The Medicare Savings Programs (MSP)

Medicaid

The Supplemental Nutrition Assistance Program (SNAP, formerly the federal Food Stamp program)

State Pharmacy Assistance Programs (where applicable)

The Low Income Home Energy Assistance Program

During the period from March 2009 to June 2010, the BECs reached out to more than 280,000 individuals and screened 223,547 for benefits eligibility. Sixty-six percent of these individuals were found

(Continued)

(Continued)

eligible for at least one benefit program, 60% of the eligible individuals filed applications for public benefits, and 70% of the individuals reached by BECs were provided with one-on-one benefits counseling.

Here are two examples of outreach activities funded by these grant dollars:

AgeOptions, Chicago, Illinois

Target area: suburban Cook County, Illinois (130 communities)

AgeOptions, in partnership with eleven agencies, created BECs throughout suburban Cook County. Six of the 11 BEC sites served ethnic populations of older adults and persons with disabilities who spoke limited English. These partners broke down barriers to accessing public benefits programs by creating and distributing materials that were culturally and linguistically appropriate. AgeOptions BEC sites tackled benefits coordination at the grassroots level by linking core programs, such as Medicaid and SNAP (which share an application in Illinois), with MSPs. Initially, the BEC sites conducted outreach to individuals, but as a second tier of their efforts, the sites provided outreach to professionals, significantly expanding the scope of the message.

Total individuals screened/total eligible for at least one benefit: 4,513/3,839

Total applications submitted: 5,095

Total value of benefits: $5,505,371

South Alabama Regional Planning Commission (SARPC)
Area Agency on Aging, Mobile, Alabama

Target areas: Mobile, Baldwin, and Escambia Counties in southwestern/coastal Alabama

SARPC incorporated BenefitsCheckUp as part of its service delivery system and developing Aging and Disability Resource Center. The BEC created a series of road show benefits enrollment events that included partners and allowed the public to receive both screening and on-site application assistance with core benefits from partner agencies. In addition to these events, SARPC offered its target audiences several ways to access screenings and enrollment: (a) phone screening, (b) completion of a paper BenefitsCheckUp form and mailing it into the office for follow-up, (c) daily offering of on-site appointments for application assistance, or (d) online access to its own private label version of BenefitsCheckUp.

The SARPC road show was put to use when the Deepwater Horizon oil spill occurred in the Gulf of Mexico in April 2010. SARPC and its partners went to affected communities along the Gulf Coast to help those in need access key social and economic benefits.

Total individuals screened/total eligible for at least one benefit: 7,013/6,567

Total applications submitted: 5,782

Total value of benefits: $6,025,826

Ten more outreach centers were funded in April 2011. For more information, visit http://www.centerforbenefits.org/centers.html.

CHARACTERISTICS OF PROGRAMS

Where and how do older adults and their families access I&R/A services? The location of the agency responsible for providing I&R/A services, the target population served, and the scope of information and services provided all vary by community. For example, I&R/A programs can be located in government offices, public or private agencies, voluntary associations, public libraries, or community centers (McCaslin, 1981). Local AAAs may directly deliver I&R/A services or may contract with other agencies to deliver I&R/A services to older adults. Moreover, I&R/As may target services to the general population or to a specific population, such as older adults, families with children, or persons with disabilities or chronic conditions. They may provide information about all types of community resources and services, or may specialize in one information area, such as services for persons with Alzheimer's disease. I&R/A services may have information about national, state, or local services (Levinson, 1988). Despite these myriad differences, all I&R/A programs have the same goal: to help individuals identify, understand, and effectively use programs they could benefit from accessing. A well-designed I&R/A will provide the following elements:

- *Information Provision.* Information is given to an older person, caregiver, or another provider in response to an expressed need concerning opportunities and services available to him or her.

- *Referral Provision.* Referral is made via a process of determining the individual's needs through an assessment, identifying appropriate resources and organizations capable of meeting those needs, assisting inquirers in making an informed choice, and actively linking the person to a particular resource or choice of resources.

- *Advocacy/Intervention.* Advocacy can involve helping an individual explain his or her situation in the "agency's language" in an effort to obtain a needed service to which he or she is entitled. Or advocacy can involve articulating the needs of a specific group of older persons to community policy makers, planners, and service providers to ensure the service delivery system meet the collective needs of the community.

- *Follow-Up.* Follow-up is conducted with an older person, his or her caregiver, or the service provider or agency to which the individual was referred, to determine whether the inquirer has received the appropriate service. Follow-up is mandated for inquirers in endangerment situations and in situations where the inquirer does not have the necessary capacity to follow through and resolve his or her problems. I&R/A agencies must also specify a percentage of inquiries for which follow-up is required to assess overall service performance. (National Aging I&R/A Support Center, 2002, p. 1)

DEVELOPING AND MAINTAINING A RESOURCE FILE

The foundation of a good I&R/A service is its resource database. It must be accurate and up to date and must include detailed information about community agencies. The following standards guide the development of a resource database: (a) inclusion/exclusion criteria are developed to determine which agencies and programs are in the resource database; (b) data elements that provide a standard profile used for each organization are developed; (c) there is a process developed for indexing the resource database/search methods along with a classification or taxonomy system; and (d) regular maintenance of the database is established (National Aging I&R/A Support Center, 2002, p. 9).

A critical component of a useful I&R/A service is the completeness and accuracy of its database. According to the guidelines established by the National Aging I&R/A Support Center, the database should include the following information about community agencies:

- Unique record identification number;
- Code to identify the organization responsible for maintaining the record (to facilitate combination, in a single database, of records maintained by different organizations);
- Organization name (legal name), and aliases including former name(s), popular names, and popular acronyms;
- Program name, if applicable;
- Street and mailing addresses (main location and branches);
- Telephone number(s) including TDD/TTY, fax, website address, and electronic mail addresses for the agency, its sites, and specific services, if applicable;
- Hours and days of operation;
- Services provided and target populations served;
- Eligibility requirements and exclusions (e.g., age, gender);
- Documents that may be required by the organization for application (e.g., birth certificates);
- Geographic area served;
- Application process;
- Languages other than English in which the service is offered (bilingual staff or interpreter services);
- Legal status (e.g., nonprofit, government, for-profit, unincorporated group);
- Fee structure for service, if any (the phrase *sliding scale* may be sufficient; use "none" or the equivalent when applicable);
- Method of payment accepted (e.g., Medicaid, Medicare, private insurance);
- Name and title of the organization's administrator/director; and
- Date the information was last verified. (AIRS, 2005, p. 16)

AIRS (2005) recommends that I&R/A services also collect information about the characteristics of the inquirer. Collecting information about the inquirer's socioeconomic status and demographic characteristics, including language requirements, the nature and extent of the problem, and the level of assistance needed can assist in problem-solving activities as well as provide valuable information about gaps in community resources.

PROMOTION OF INFORMATION AND REFERRAL SERVICES

The functions of an I&R/A program are useless unless older adults and their families know how to access I&R/A services. Unfortunately, studies of awareness of community resources consistently identify I&R/A services as the least known by older adults (Denton et al., 2010; Krout, 1983). Clearly, if I&R/A programs want to empower older adults and their families who are "information poor," they must be made aware of I&R/A services and benefits (Levinson, 1988).

The *National Standards* document (Whaley & Hutchinson, 1993b) recommends that I&R/A services promote their agencies through personal contact, public service announcements, news stories, printed materials, telephone directories, and displays. Indeed, research shows that baby boomers and older adults would prefer using formal (e.g., doctor's offices, service providers) and informal (e.g., friends and family) networks, and media and print material (e.g., newspaper/magazine articles, brochures and pamphlets, television) to obtain information about community resources (Brossoie, Roberto, Willis-Walton, & Reynolds, 2010; Denton et al., 2010). Research is also beginning to understand how preferred ways of accessing I&R/A information differ by age group, which can help I&R/A agencies target outreach programs. For example, in Brossoie et al.'s (2010) research, baby boomers were more likely than older respondents to report their willingness to contact community-based entities such as an AAA and the Eldercare Locator, and to prefer the radio, health and wellness fairs, and telephone hotlines. However, the advent of the digital age has now introduced a new avenue to promote I&R/A services as the Internet is becoming a more important means of disseminating I&R/A services (Brossoie et al., 2010; Denton et al., 2010). In Brossoie et al.'s sample, baby boomers were more likely than older respondents to prefer the Internet as a way to learn about services and programs, as 43% of respondents indicated websites would be an important way to access information. Moreover, a third of those respondents indicated they would also seek information from Facebook, Twitter, and YouTube.

In addition, I&R/A systems should network with other community agencies to encourage interagency linkages and target subpopulations of older adults such as foreign-language groups, low-income persons, persons of color, persons who are socially isolated, and persons with hearing or vision impairments. Canvassing targeted neighborhoods is another strategy often used to inform older adults about I&R/A services. When canvassing neighborhoods, outreach workers can make contact with older adults who may be unaware of the help that community services can provide (Cushing & Long, 1974).

FUNCTIONS OF INFORMATION AND REFERRALS

As shown in Exhibit 4.1, I&R/A programs can provide a range of services within each I&R/A function. The functions of an I&R/A include basic I&R/A activities, support services that facilitate use of needed services, and advocacy (Levinson, 1988; Whaley & Hutchinson, 1993a). Within each function, a range of services is provided to older adults. Ideally, all I&R/As should offer services along the I&R/A continuum to inquirers, and the I&R/A specialists should conduct interviews to determine the extent of I&R/A assistance that inquirers need.

Exhibit 4.1   Extent of Provider Intervention in Information and Referral/Assistance Services

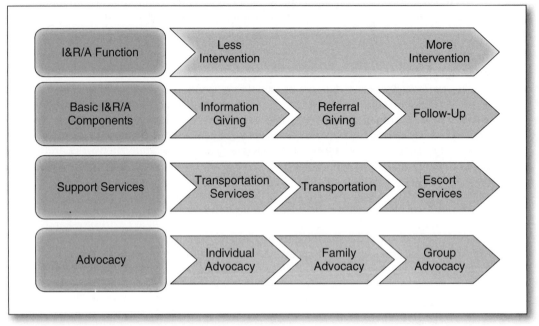

Source: Adapted from Levinson (1988, p. 44). Used by permission.

INFORMATION AND REFERRAL PROCESS

Exhibit 4.2 illustrates the I&R/A process. When inquirers contact the I&R/A service, an I&R/A specialist determines the needs of the caller, the appropriate resources needed to address the identified needs, and whether referral giving or simply information giving is necessary. The specialist also provides follow-up and assesses the need for advocacy. Each of these steps is discussed below.

Information Giving

At the least, an I&R/A service responds to the request of an inquirer about a particular agency or service by providing basic information about the appropriate agency. The I&R/A staff member gives the inquirer the agency's name, address, and phone number or an explanation of the agency's application process (Whaley & Hutchinson, 1993a). For example, if a caregiver calls and requests information about local adult day programs, the I&R/A service will give the caller the name, address, and phone number of all local adult day programs. Other information that could be helpful to the caller, such as hours of operation or type of service provided. At this stage, detailed information about how the intake system works for a particular agency, or the agency's policies and procedures, could also be given.

Exhibit 4.2   Delivery Process of Information and Referral/Assistance Services

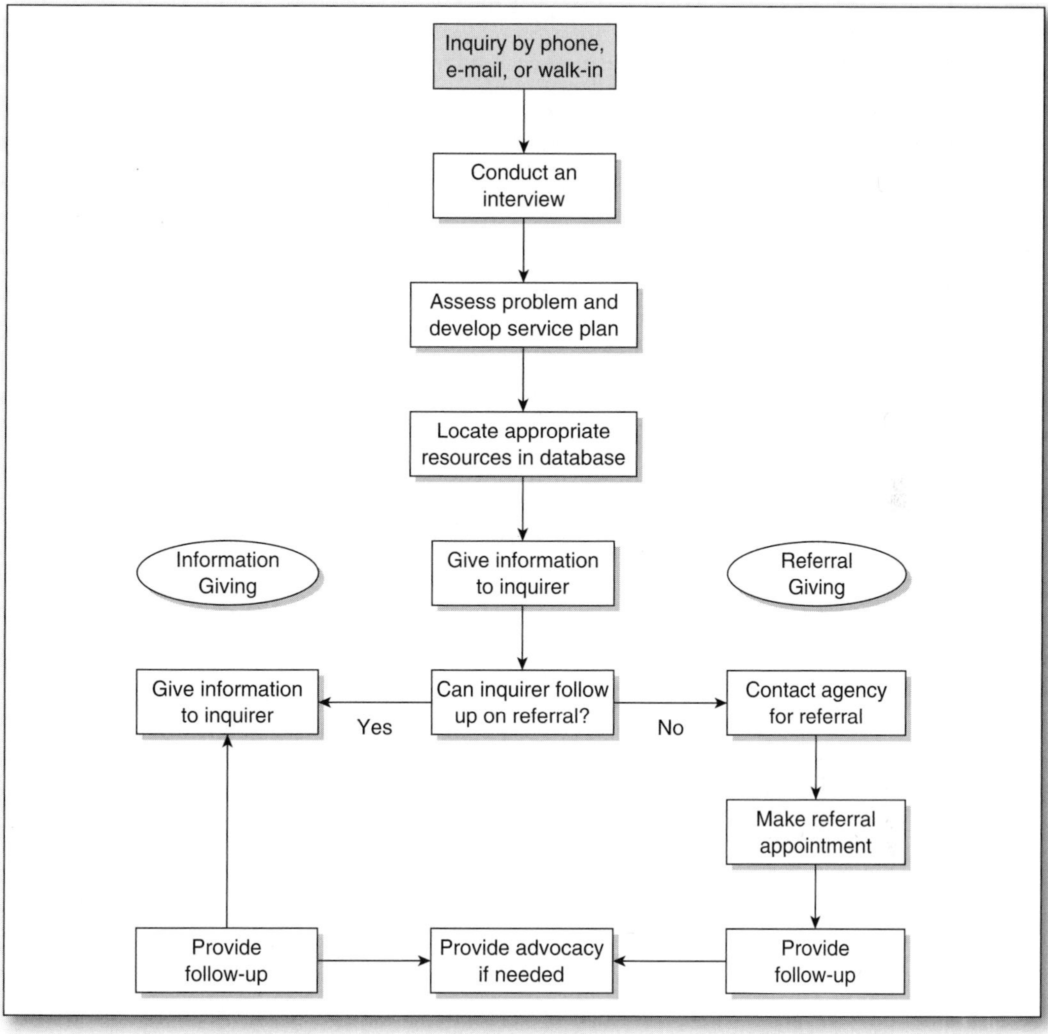

```
                    ┌────────────────────┐
                    │  Inquiry by phone, │
                    │ e-mail, or walk-in │
                    └────────────────────┘
                              │
                    ┌────────────────────┐
                    │    Conduct an      │
                    │    interview       │
                    └────────────────────┘
                              │
                    ┌────────────────────┐
                    │ Assess problem and │
                    │ develop service plan│
                    └────────────────────┘
                              │
                    ┌────────────────────┐
                    │ Locate appropriate │
                    │ resources in database│
                    └────────────────────┘
                              │
    ( Information      ┌────────────────────┐    ( Referral
      Giving )         │  Give information  │      Giving )
                       │    to inquirer     │
                       └────────────────────┘
                              │
┌──────────────┐   ┌────────────────────┐   ┌──────────────┐
│ Give information│←─│ Can inquirer follow│─→│ Contact agency│
│ to inquirer   │Yes│ up on referral?    │No │ for referral  │
└──────────────┘   └────────────────────┘   └──────────────┘
        ↑                                           │
        │                                    ┌──────────────┐
        │                                    │ Make referral│
        │                                    │ appointment  │
        │                                    └──────────────┘
        │                                           │
┌──────────────┐   ┌────────────────────┐   ┌──────────────┐
│   Provide    │←──│  Provide advocacy   │←──│   Provide    │
│  follow-up   │   │   if needed         │   │  follow-up   │
└──────────────┘   └────────────────────┘   └──────────────┘
```

Source: Adapted from Levinson (1988, pp. 147–149). Used by permission.

Referral Giving

Referral giving is a more involved process than information giving. In referral giving, the I&R/A staff are actively involved in assessing the needs of the caller, matching those needs with the appropriate agency, and linking the caller to the appropriate agency either by providing the caller with agency information or by calling the agency and arranging for services (Whaley & Hutchinson, 1993a).

Let's use Gary and his mother as an example of how referral giving works. When Gary calls the I&R/A service, he explains that his mother, who has suffered a series of strokes, will be coming to live with him. Because Gary has no idea what services could help him, the I&R/A specialist must assess the needs of Gary and his mother. After assessing the nature and extent of their problem, the I&R/A specialist can give Gary options for keeping his mother at home. He may be able to care for his mother with help from in-home health services, Meals on Wheels, and the use of an adult day program. The I&R/A specialist may also determine whether Gary's mother qualifies for help in paying for community-based long-term care services. Finally, the I&R/A specialist determines whether it would be appropriate to contact these agencies directly to notify them of Gary's forthcoming contact or to make an appointment on his behalf.

Contacting the agency on behalf of the caller is especially critical in situations in which the caller does not speak English, is hesitant or uncertain about dealing with bureaucracies, or does not have the personal resources or cognitive abilities needed to negotiate through the process. The complexity of the problems that the inquirer has might require that the I&R/A specialist make multiple referrals, repeated contacts with the inquirer, and numerous contacts with appropriate agencies (Levinson, 1988). I&R/A programs that help inquirers access the services they recommend are commonly referred to as *information and assistance (I&A)* or *enhanced I&R/A* programs, rather than I&R/A programs.

Follow-Up

All I&R/A programs should follow up on referral cases, including those who received only information, to determine whether inquirers contacted the recommended community service and, if not, why they did not; what assistance was given; and any additional needs that may have arisen (Whaley & Hutchinson, 1993a). Follow-up allows the I&R/A specialist an opportunity to provide additional assistance securing other services if needed. Moreover, follow-up can provide the I&R/A with valuable information about waiting lists or other problems (e.g., eligibility requirements) that inquirers encountered in trying to access recommended services (Huttman, 1985).

Advocacy and Intervention

In some instances, the I&R/A specialist will need to act as an advocate on behalf of an individual or groups of clients. The I&R/A specialist may need to act as an advocate when clients have difficulty receiving services for which they are eligible, when they have been mistreated, or when they are unable to effectively represent themselves (Whaley & Hutchinson, 1993a). The I&R/A specialist also can act as an advocate on behalf of a group of older adults by articulating service gaps and needed policy changes to community and government leaders.

Best Practice: Information and Referral/Assistance Services

There are a number of state and local AAAs that use unique strategies to promote the use of I&R/A services. Here are two examples of best practice in I&R/A activities.

Southern Maine Area Agency on Aging, Scarborough, Maine

In 2006, the Southern Maine Area Agency on Aging's (SMAA) Community Links program reached out to area physicians who specialize in the treatment of older adults to discuss the types of information assistance physicians are able to provide their older patients. It became clear that they could not effectively help their patients resolve needs outside the scope of their practice. SMAA provided information about the services it offers to the medical staffs and developed a list of protocols for appropriate referral to the agency. With the agreement of patients, the primary care physician completes a form to identify unmet needs and faxes it to SMAA. Elder advocates, all of whom are licensed social workers, then contact the patient/caregiver, and using the extensive database of community resources, makes the referral to address the specific needs of the older adult. The contact form, with a description of what the elder advocate has done, is returned to the primary care physician. Positive outcomes include 100% of respondents who reported that the direct referrals where helpful, SMAA understood their questions and helped them identify resources, and they felt confident turning to the agency for help.

For more information, contact the SMAA at 800-427-7411 or visit http://www.smaaa.org/index.php.

The Area Agency on Aging and Aging Resource Center for Northeast Florida, Jacksonville, Florida

When the ElderSource staff were brainstorming about the challenges they had in helping older adults understand the types of programs and services that are available to them, it occurred to them that verbally describing programs using language such as "respite" and "congregate meals" was confusing to clients. To address this challenge, ElderSource created a virtual Tour of Services DVD to visually show various services in action. Instead of describing a congregate meal program, the DVD shows elders participating in a congregate meal program. The DVD has been used in various ways, including outreach to community groups, and it also continuously runs in the ElderSource lobby. The DVD is also used to train new employees or student interns.

For more information about the Virtual Tour DVD, contact Linda Levin, MA, Director of Eldersource, at levinl@myeldersource.org. Their website is http://www.myeldersource.org.

INFORMATION AND REFERRAL SERVICES WITH A NATIONAL SCOPE

As previously mentioned, the Eldercare Locator is an I&R/A service funded by the AoA and sponsored by the NASUA and n4a. It is a nationwide directory service designed to help older persons and caregivers locate services. Inquirers can call a toll-free number to receive assistance. Callers are asked to provide the information specialist with the county and city name or zip code, and the type of problem or service desired. The Eldercare Locator also can be accessed from the Eldercare Locator site, www.eldercare.gov. The Alzheimer's Disease Education and Referral (ADEAR) Center is an example of a national specialized information and referral/assistance site, created by the U.S. Congress in 1990 (National Institute on Aging, 2011). ADEAR has a staff of Information Specialists available to answer questions about Alzheimer's disease (AD) and assist inquirers by making referrals to local supportive services. The site also has a live chat function and a toll-free number for callers. ADEAR also provides free publications about AD symptoms, diagnosis, related disorders, risk factors, treatment, caregiving tips, home safety tips, and research. Another specialized national I&R/A site is operated by the Alzheimer's Association, which offers information and support to people with memory loss, caregivers, healthcare professionals, and the public. Their website provided information, services, and support to more than 5.6 million visitors, and the 24/7 Helpline received nearly 250,000 calls in 2010 (Alzheimer's Association, n.d.).

CHALLENGES FOR INFORMATION AND REFERRAL SERVICES

As the number of private and public programs and services for older adults continues to grow, it will become more and more difficult to locate the appropriate service in a time of need. I&R/A services will need to respond to a variety of challenges.

For Your Files: The Alliance of Information and Referral Systems

AIRS is an agency that was formed in 1973 to improve the access to services through the use of I&R/A systems. It currently has a professional membership association of over 1,200 organizations, supporting over 28 state and regional affiliates. AIRS provides training and support of I&R/A activities and offers a certification process for I&R/A practitioners. AIRS also provides publications about I&R/A, conducts national training conferences, and acts as a clearinghouse for I&R/A. AIRS publications include a newsletter, the *Journal of the Alliance of Information and Referral Systems*, and the *National Directory of I&R/A Services in the United States and Canada*. The AIRS website also has other resources including a white papers series on key I&R/A issues and guidelines for practices that cover special topics such as disaster I&R/A resources. Inquirers can reach AIRS by calling 703-218-AIRS (2477) (or e-mail info@airs.org). The AIRS website is a great place to start when you are looking for more information about I&R/A: www.airs.org.

Enhancing Information and Referral Services

At the request of the Special Committee on Aging, the GAO (1991a) examined 12 I&R/A programs that experts believed were illustrative of the promising ways in which I&R/A systems served older adults. The GAO's research revealed effective methods of delivering I&R/A services used by the programs. On the basis of these findings, the GAO made four recommendations for I&R/A programming that continue to be relevant many years later. The first was locating I&R/A services where older populations live or frequently visit, such as grocery stores, drugstores, and shopping centers. For example, the Waxter Center for Senior Citizens in Baltimore, Maryland, has located 14 I&R/A offices in neighborhood senior centers; of those, 6 are located in minority neighborhoods. The second recommendation was to hire professional staff, including persons of color, to serve diverse cultural populations. The AAA in Billings, Montana, uses Native American I&R/A workers to make home visits to isolated older adults at six Indian reservations. The effectiveness of using minority I&R/A staff to work with racial and ethnic communities was documented by the Office of Senior Information, Referral, and Health Promotion in San Francisco. They found that in the year after hiring a Black outreach worker, the program served 405 more Black clients.

Employing a Chinese American outreach worker also increased the number of Chinese clients served by the program.

The third recommendation was the use of automated information resources and telephone technology to effectively provide information. Strategies included the use of automated information booths at sites throughout the community, multilingual telephone message lines, and computer bulletin boards. As we mentioned earlier, Internet access to I&R/A services is becoming a common form of outreach. For example, Exhibit 4.3 shows the Iowa Association of AAAs' I&R/A home page designed for caregiver's (www.i4a.org). Posting interactive information on the Internet provides an additional avenue for older adults and their caregivers to access information and inquirers can access information anytime and anywhere they have access to the Internet. It is important to note, however, that access to the Internet continues to vary by age group. Only 20% of adults aged 74 older have Internet access in their homes, and only 30% indicate that they go online. This compares to 68% of younger boomers aged 46 to 55 years who have Internet access in their homes and 81% who indicate that they regularly go online (Zickuhr, 2010). Although Internet access is in the process of becoming the norm for most age groups and households, the current cohort of older adults is not likely to use these online resources. Thus, offering face-to-face or phone contact will continue to be an important element in increasing the access to I&R/A services.

Publicizing I&R/A services to older adults and their caregivers through active outreach methods was the fourth recommendation. Suggestions for active outreach included publicizing services in locations such as convenience and grocery stores. Printed materials continue to be an important way to market and publicize I&R/A services. As the use of "smart" cell phones (with camera and Internet access) becomes more ubiquitous, the use of Quick Response codes (QR) will be another way to use technology to connect users to information. The QR, which is a specific matrix barcode, is beginning to appear on printed materials such as brochures, posters and postcards. When scanned by a smartphone, it takes users directly to a website with more information. As discussed earlier, the use of social media sites such Facebook and other sites such as YouTube to inform older adults and their families about I&R/A services will become more mainstream in very near future.

Future efforts of increasing access to information must include locating I&R/A services in multiple locations or providing options for multiple entry points to information. One model of expanding access is for a single I&R/A agency to establish smaller satellite locations perhaps in more nontraditional locations such as schools or shopping areas. Another approach would be to provide multiple entry points through non-I&R/A agencies that would assist clients because service providers not associated with I&R/A programs are often the first point of contact for older adults. In this model, I&R/A agencies work in collaboration with other agencies to train their staff to engage in basic I&R/A assessment to assist and refer people. Hence, staff must be familiar with I&R/A programs as well as services available in communities. It should not matter where older adults start their inquiry for assistance—the "no wrong door" approach—and persons working with older adults must know where to send their clients for further assistance.

Enhancing Information and Referral Databases

Additional empirical evaluations are needed to provide a profile of I&R/A programs and services as well as the effectiveness of I&R/A and outreach services. I&R/A studies could examine the problems that inquirers have, the short- and long-term outcomes of I&R/A intervention, and training needs of staff. In addition, if most people receive information outside a formal I&R/A service, such pathways to service access need to be identified.

Exhibit 4.3   Home Page of the Iowa Association of AAAs' Iowa Family Caregiver I&R/A Website

Source: www.i4a.org.

Supporting the Future of Information and Referral

Although none of the 45 resolutions put forth by the delegates of the 2005 White House Conference on Aging specifically identified I&R/A, it was included as a means of achieving proposed actions. For example, the delegates proposed to support working caregivers by encouraging and offering incentives for employers to provide information and referral services and to educate Employee Assistance Programs about Eldercare Locator and other information resources. NASUA (2000) published a position paper about information and referral titled *Vision 2010: Toward a Comprehensive Aging Information Resource System for the 21st Century*. NASUA believes that for the OAA information and resource system to be easily and universally accessible, and the best and most comprehensive source of information for older Americans, their families, and the public, the following are needed:

- *Leadership.* With the OAA network at the national, state, and local levels taking a proactive role in responding to increases in demand for information and related services;

- *Comprehensiveness*. So that the aging information resource system becomes, in essence, a one-stop-shopping source for consumers;

- *Responsiveness*. To better serve the diverse population of older consumers and their families by attending to the wide range of special needs and interests they represent;

- *Integration*. Establishing linkages with programs in aging, health and educational institutions, state and community service agencies, the federal government, and business to promote seamless information delivery;

- *Adequate Funding*. With increases commensurate to increasing needs and demands for services by a growing number of older persons and their families;

- *Skilled Personnel*. Sufficient in number to meet the anticipated number of requests for information and to provide counseling, decision-support, and advocacy assistance appropriate for empowering consumers;

- *Technology*. To maximize communication and reach greater numbers of user audiences cost-effectively; and

- *Marketing*. To ensure that older persons and their families across America have an understanding of and access to the information resource system. (NASUA, 2000, p. 7)

Indeed, knowing how best to use all the various ways now available to inform older adults and their families about the existing programs and services will continue to challenge providers of I&R/A services.

Best Practice: Using New Technologies to Provide I&R/A

New technologies, including YouTube and social media websites such as Facebook, are increasingly being used as ways to provide information about programs and services.

ElderSource, the AAA in northeast Florida, won a national award from the National Association of Area Agencies on Aging in the category of Caregiving, Technology, and You Name It! ElderSource created, with the help of a volunteer caregiver, a caregiver's podcast. The podcast provides valuable information to persons giving care to an older adult how to access and receive services. The information can also be accessed at www.myeldersource.org and downloaded to MP3 players for easy reference.

Source: ElderSource (n.d.).

Facebook is also being used as a means to get information about to older adults, their families, and professionals working with older adults. Here are a few examples:

- Seniors' Resource Center, Denver, Colorado, provides information about services and events as well as a monthly blog.

- SPOTLIGHT Senior Services Las Vegas's Facebook page provides a valuable resource program and support system for health care professionals who assist senior adults in Southern Nevada.

CASE STUDY

Finding and Asking for Help

Frank is an 83-year-old Hispanic man who has had several small strokes during the past three years. The strokes have weakened him, and on occasions, he is mildly confused. He and his wife, Maria, have been married for 35 years. Maria is Frank's second wife and is 26 years younger than him.

When Frank retired, they moved to a large urban community in which both have relatives. Although Frank and Maria do not have children, Frank has three daughters from his first marriage, whom he rarely sees. Maria attends her neighborhood church regularly and does some volunteer work for the parish. Otherwise, they lead a quiet life.

Since Frank's retirement, Maria has worked at a nursing home as a laundry assistant. Eventually, the many years of hard field work and an injury from lifting laundry culminated in a serious lower back condition. She had two back surgeries; neither surgery was successful. The arrangements for the second surgery were bungled because the surgery was not approved by her health maintenance organization (HMO). The HMO refused to pay for the surgery, and Frank and Maria are now responsible for a $20,000 medical bill that they are unable to pay.

Maria is no longer able to work. She would like to take over the payments of the HMO insurance that the nursing home gave her as a benefit. These payments are $326 per month. The local hospital charity fund has made the payments for a couple of months but cannot continue the assistance much longer. Fortunately, Frank is covered by Medicaid. A detailed examination of their financial condition shows that they are barely able to make ends meet. They have expenses of $825 per month and income of $823 per month, derived from the $594 per month Social Security received by Frank and $229 per month received by Maria. Now that Frank is no longer able to drive, transportation is a serious problem for the couple. At Frank's insistence, Maria never learned to drive. With her own health in jeopardy, no health insurance coverage, and little income of her own, Maria worries constantly about how she will take care of Frank and what she will do if something happens to him. Maria's good friend from church decides to take matters into her own hands and call a senior I&R/A number that she heard about on the radio.

Case Study Questions

1. Would you agree that Maria's friend is calling an appropriate resource with regard to Frank and Maria's situation? Why or why not?

2. List and describe each factor that has a role in justifying Maria's concern about Frank's future and her own.

3. If you were the I&R/A specialist assigned to this case, what additional information about Frank and Maria's situation would you want to know?

4. What do you think is Maria's greatest concern? What do you believe is her greatest problem? If not the same, which problem should be addressed first? Defend your answer.

5. What community resources would you recommend for Frank and Maria? List at least five.

6. How comfortable would you be as an I&R/A specialist that Maria and her friend could follow through on their own with the information that you have provided them? If concerned, what might you do to ensure that some of the suggested resource agencies were contacted?

LEARNING ACTIVITIES

1. Watch your daily local newspaper (either their online or print version) for a week. How many aging network agencies advertise their programs or services during that time? What are the pros and cons of using newspapers as a source of information about aging services and programs? Call the newspaper to determine how much it would cost programs to advertise.

2. Using the case study in this chapter about Frank and Maria, identify the resources you think they need. Because the majority of older adults continue to rely on print material, go to the library and select two phone books—one of an urban city and one of a rural community in your state. If possible, select unfamiliar cities and try to identify the community resources you would call that could assist them. What problems did you encounter in locating those services in the phone book? Were there noticeable differences between the rural and urban locations?

3. See if you can locate a hard copy of a senior resource book in your community. How many calls did you have to make before you located a copy? Examine the resource book closely. How is it organized? How much detailed information does the resource book provide about each service or program? What changes would you recommend?

4. What type of community resources does your community have online—including agency websites, Facebook, and YouTube? What was your approach to finding information online (e.g., if you used search engines, what keywords did you use?), and how easy or hard was it to find information and services for older adults? How difficult would it be for an older adult to search through the results? Compare the information you found online with the information you were able to identify in the phone book in Activity 2 above—does one method yield more information than another?

FOR MORE INFORMATION

International Resources

1. 211 British Columbia Services Society (BC211): www.bc211.ca/index.html

   BC211 was the first Canadian I&R agency to be accredited through the Alliance of Information and Referral Systems (AIRS) and operates in the Metro Vancouver, Fraser Valley and Squamish-Lillooet Regional Districts. Their Red Book, a directory of community, government and social services, is online.

2. Stockholm, Sweden- Support and Care for the Elderly Information: www.stockholm.se/FamiljOmsorg/Aldreomsorg/

   This web site provides Swedes in Stockholm information about the many services available to older adults.

National Resources

1. National Resource Center on Native American Aging, Center for Rural Health, the University of North Dakota, School of Medicine and Health Sciences, 501 North Columbia Road, Mail Stop 9037, Grand Forks, ND 58202-9037, http://ruralhealth.und.edu/projects/nrcnaa

   The National Resource Center on Native American Aging's mission is to identify and increase awareness of evolving Native elder health and social issues. In addition to providing training and resources to aid in working with Native American elders and communities, they support a nationwide interactive map that shows the location of Native elderly services.

2. B'nai B'rith, 1640 Rhode Island Avenue NW, Washington, DC 20036; phone: 202-857-1099; www.bnaibrith.org

   B'nai B'rith is the world's oldest and largest Jewish service organization. The Center for Senior Services page on Facebook, regular column in *B'nai B'rith Magazine*, and community seminars also provide useful education and valuable resources for seniors and their families.

3. National Asian Pacific Center on Aging, Melbourne Tower, 1511 3rd Avenue, Suite 914, Seattle, WA 98101; phone: 206-624-1221; www.napca.org

   This private organization works to improve the delivery of health and social services to Asian Pacific older adults and maintains a national network of service agencies.

4. National Information and Referral Support Center, 1225 I Street NW, Suite 725, Washington, DC 20005-3914; phone: 202-898-2578; www.nasuad.org/I_R/ir_index.html

   The support center provides technical assistance to those who deliver I&R/A and I&A under the OAA. It publishes the *Information and Referral Reporter* quarterly.

Web Resources

1. Florida Department of Elder Affairs: http://elderaffairs.state.fl.us/index.php

   Visitors to Florida Department of Elder Affairs (FDOEA) website can find information regarding elder services through the Elder Helpline Information and Assistance service for every county in Florida. The FDOEA also has an extensive consumer resource guide available online at http://elderaffairs.state.fl.us/english/CRG/TC.html.

2. Minnesota Board on Aging's Senior LinkAge: www.mnaging.org/advisor/SLL.htm

   The Senior LinkAge line offers free statewide information and assistance service provided by six AAAs that cover all 87 counties of Minnesota and helps connect elders and their families to local services.

3. U.S. government's official web portal: www.usa.gov

   This is the official information and services website of the U.S. government. The Senior Citizens' Resources page has a number of different links for more information on education, housing, consumer protection, health, taxes, and travel: www.usa.gov/Topics/Seniors.shtml.

4. Administration on Aging, Washington, DC: www.aoa.gov

   The AoA's home page has an extensive number of links to other national organizations and programs of interest to older adults and their families.

CHAPTER 5

Volunteer and Intergenerational Programs

Twice a week, 78-year-old Hazel volunteers at a local adult day care center. She helps with the hands-on care of participants. Her volunteer duties include helping people to eat, walking with them to the bathroom, and just sitting and talking with them. She also does what the director calls tender loving pushing. Hazel enjoys volunteer work. When interviewed by a local newspaper, Hazel said, "I hope if something happens to me, there will always be someone to care."

With the growth of the older adult population and the decline in resources, community agencies often seek assistance from seniors in delivering their programs and services. In many communities, senior volunteerism has developed into a highly organized and often large-scale activity. It is not uncommon to find older volunteers, such as Hazel, working within their local churches, civic or religious groups, hospitals, nursing homes, schools, and human service agencies. In fact, almost one fourth (23.6%) of volunteers in the United States are aged 65 and older, contributing 1.7 billion hours of service to communities across the country (U.S. Department of Labor [USDoL], 2011d). Older volunteers devote a median of 96 hours annually—nearly 2 hours weekly—to volunteer activities, with about 9% volunteering 10 or more hours a week (Population Reference Bureau, 2011).

However, participation in formal volunteer opportunities represents only part of the picture. Older adults also volunteer informally, without support or direction from formal organizations (Corporation for National and Community Service [CNCS], 2006; Zedlewski & Schaner, 2006). Informal volunteering includes self-initiated activities such as providing transportation, helping around the house, and providing companionship to individuals outside of the household (Zedlewski & Schaner, 2006). Findings from the 2002 National Health and Retirement Study indicate that 60% of all adults aged 55 and older engage in some form of volunteer activity (R. W. Johnson & Schaner, 2005). Approximately 10% engage in formal volunteer activities only, 23% are involved in both formal and informal activities, and slightly more than 38% engage in informal volunteer activities only. Estimates of the dollar value of volunteerism suggest that in 2002, $44.3 billion was donated through formal volunteer activities and another $17.8 billion by volunteering time through informal channels (R. W. Johnson & Schaner, 2005).

Despite the need for volunteers and the willingness of many seniors to volunteer, many are never asked; thus, older adults are often an untapped resource for volunteer positions. Just 43.8% of adults aged 65 and older volunteer on their own (USDoL, 2011d); most others were asked by someone in the organization (35.4%) or a relative, friend, or co-worker (13.4%). When asked to volunteer, more than three fourths of older adults accept the invitation (Civic Ventures, 2006).

Most individuals give multiple reasons when asked why they volunteer. A 2003 AARP survey of community service and charitable giving practices of 2,069 persons aged 45 and older found that 40% or more of volunteers were motivated to do so because (a) they believed it was a personal responsibility to help others; (b) it made life more satisfying; (c) the organization had an established track record; (d) it helped their own community and made a difference on issues; (e) it helped keep them active; (f) someone they knew was affected by the issue; (g) it was an expression of their religious beliefs; (h) it provided an opportunity to use their skills; and (i) it was something family and friends can do together. Differences in motivations do not appear significant across racial and ethnic groups. Blacks, Hispanics, Asian Americans, and non-Hispanic Whites identified the main motivation behind volunteering as a personal responsibility to help others.

The manner in which people volunteer, however, does appear to vary across racial and ethnic groups. According to the findings of the AARP (2003) study, Black elders volunteered an average of 17 hours per month and were more likely to engage in informal volunteering than other groups. They tended to volunteer through religious organizations focusing on meeting the needs of the homeless, problems in their neighborhood, advancing the rights of minorities, and tutoring or mentoring others. Eighty-five percent of Asian American older adults volunteered an average of 15 hours a month with a primary focus on advancing minority rights and supporting the arts. Hispanic elders reported giving the most time of all minority groups: 22 hours a month. Helping other Hispanics—considered very important in their culture—was the focus of their volunteer activities. Non-Hispanic White older adults, the largest volunteer group, were more likely to engage in volunteer activities to help animals, protect the environment, assist public servants, and support the arts.

Other study variables that distinguished among older adults' motives for volunteering were gender and age (AARP, 2003). Women identified a greater number of motivations as being very important to them than did men. Volunteers aged 70 and older were much more likely than volunteers aged 45 to 69 to view keeping active as a very important motivation for volunteering.

Organizations need to consider a variety of factors when recruiting older volunteers, including the individuals' experience, their perceptions of need, and personal interests (L. R. Fischer & Schaffer, 1993). Older adults who have volunteered before are easier to recruit than inexperienced volunteers. Thus, it is important for organizations to recruit baby boomers as volunteers prior to their retirement. The good news is that boomers are willing to participate in volunteer activities as long as they can balance their work, leisure, community responsibilities, and other pursuits (CNCS, 2006). A comparison of volunteering among the first cohort of baby boomers (born 1946 to 1955) with earlier cohorts showed an increased rate of volunteerism among boomers, which suggests that volunteer-based organizations in the coming decades will have a larger pool of senior volunteers than ever before (Einolf, 2009).

In this chapter, we begin by examining federal support for volunteer programs. Next, we profile senior volunteers and describe the various volunteer programs designed specifically for older adults, including those with an intergenerational focus. We conclude with a discussion of the current and future issues facing senior volunteer programs.

POLICY BACKGROUND

The idea of structured programs to promote senior volunteerism first emerged in 1963 when President Kennedy pushed for the establishment of a National Service Corps.[1] This organization was to "provide opportunities for service for those aged persons who can assume active roles in community volunteer efforts" (Special Committee on Aging, 1963, p. 14). Although Congress defeated the proposal for the Corps, there was strong pressure from the Senate to include senior participation in programs (e.g., VISTA) sponsored by the newly created Office of Economic Opportunity.

President Johnson supported his predecessor's idea of using the experiences and talents of older adults within their local community but with a new focus on engaging poor people in service endeavors. His vision was to create new roles and functions for older people while providing them with income support via employment and providing services to local communities. In 1965, the first service program targeting low-income seniors, the Foster Grandparent Program, emerged. Seniors who enroll in this program provide one-on-one assistance to children with special and exceptional needs (ACTION, 1992). Initially, the Office of Economic Opportunity administered the program. In 1968, the Foster Grandparent Program moved to the Department of Health, Education, and Welfare, where it stayed for three years until it was incorporated into the then newly created agency ACTION (the federal domestic volunteer agency).

In 1971, ACTION became the new administrative home of the Foster Grandparent Program and several other service-oriented programs, including the largest and most versatile program for older adults, the Retired and Senior Volunteer Program (RSVP). This program differs from the Foster Grandparent Program in that older adults have the opportunity to volunteer in a variety of community projects. They are not limited in their participation by income guidelines, they do not receive a stipend, and participation does not require a minimum time commitment. A third senior-specific service program, the Senior Companion Program, began in 1974. Modeled structurally on the Foster Grandparent Program, this program recruits low-income seniors to serve frail and homebound elders. We will discuss each of these programs in greater detail later in the chapter.

Through the early 1990s, ACTION funded, monitored, and supported local public and private nonprofit organizations that sponsored these service projects. In 1993, President Clinton worked with Congress to pass the National and Community Service Trust Act. This Act created the AmeriCorps initiative and established its administrative entity, the CNCS. ACTION programs became part of this umbrella organization. It is estimated that every federal dollar invested in national service yields $2.01 worth of essential services; thus, the market value of service initiatives supported by the CNCS grantees top $2 billion annually (Save Service in America, 2011)

In 2009, President Obama signed the Edward M. Kennedy Serve America Act, which reauthorized and expanded national service programs administered by the CNCS (2011b). This Act improved opportunities for older Americans by expanding age and income eligibility for Foster Grandparents and Senior Companions, authorizing a Silver Scholars program under which adults aged 55 and older who perform 350 hours of service receive a $1,000 education award (an award that can also be transferred to a child or grandchild), and

---

[1]Unless otherwise noted, the information in this section comes from a discussion of the origins of senior service by Freedman (1994).

establishing Serve America Fellowships and Encore Fellowships, which allow individuals to choose their service site from among registered sponsors.

USERS AND PROGRAMS

Characteristics of Older Volunteers

Several background characteristics distinguish among older volunteers. For example, the likelihood of volunteering declines with advancing old age and increasing health concerns (Zedlewski & Schaner, 2006). Approximately 20.0% of persons aged 70 to 74 years, compared with 17.3% of persons aged 75 to 79, 12.7% of persons aged 80 to 84, and 7.2% of persons over age 85, participate in volunteer activities (Federal Interagency Forum on Aging-Related Statistics, 2000). On average, older persons under the age of 75 volunteer 3.6 hours per week, whereas individuals 75 years of age and older average 3.1 volunteer hours per week (Saxon-Harrold & Weitzman, 2000).

Although it is commonly believed that women are more likely to volunteer than men, the existing research does not substantiate this perception, particularly in late life. About 23% of older men and 25% of older women volunteer (USDoL, 2011d). We do know, however, that gender plays an important role in understanding the experiences of volunteers in later life. Older men have been found to volunteer informally more often than women once differences in work status, education, and health between the sexes are taken into account (Zedlewski & Schaner, 2006). An investigation of volunteerism among 1,113 middle-aged and older women living in Washington found that the majority of women (73%) volunteered for a group or organization at some time in their lives; 39% were currently volunteering at the time of the survey (Bowen, Andersen, & Urban, 2000). Current volunteers were more likely to be White, married, better educated, and in better health than nonvolunteers or past volunteers. Four motivations—values, social expectations, increased knowledge, and enhanced esteem—were endorsed more highly by current volunteers than by past volunteers.

Race and ethnicity affect the likelihood of volunteering. Both White and Black older adults volunteer formally and informally more often than Hispanic elders (Zedlewski & Schaner, 2006). Although the helping tradition is strong in Hispanic and other minority communities, volunteers often provide help informally rather than as members of formal volunteer programs (AARP, 2003). Individuals also are inclined to volunteer for groups that bring people of their own race and ethnic background together and provide service to individuals who are similar to themselves. For example, Black adults aged 45 and older focus the majority of community service efforts on advancing the rights of minorities and those in their neighborhood. Hispanic adults, many of whom are immigrants themselves, are most likely to be providing volunteer help to other immigrants (AARP, 2003).

Social class is strongly associated with volunteerism in later life. Individuals with higher incomes and more education are more likely to seek out volunteer opportunities (F. Tang & Morrow-Howell, 2008). Perhaps, because they are more likely to have been connected to volunteer activities through employment, they are more likely to volunteer in their retirement years than those with less education, they lower incomes (Harvard School of Public Health, 2004; Zedlewski & Schaner, 2006). These individuals are also more likely to stay with their volunteer assignments and to report more satisfaction with the volunteer experience than individuals who have less volunteer experience (AARP, 2003).

Other personal characteristics associated with volunteerism in later life include geographic residence, health, marital status, employment status, and religious involvement. A greater percentage of older adults living in rural areas volunteer (26.8%) compared to those living in suburban (23.6%) and urban (19.1%) areas (CNCS, 2011a). Older individuals who perceive themselves to be in good health are more likely to volunteer than those in poorer health, and married older people are more likely to volunteer than elders who are not married. Nearly 72% of adults between the ages of 65 and 74 who continue to work for pay volunteer compared to 60% of individuals not working. Of adults aged 75 years and older who continue to work for pay, more than 66% volunteer compared with approximately 45% of their nonworking peers. This supports the adage, "If you want to get something done, ask someone who is busy" (CNCS, 2006). Older people who actively practice their religion are much more likely to volunteer than people who do not. Indeed, helping with church activities is one of the most common ways older people volunteer (Butrica, Johnson, & Zedlewski 2009; Krause, 2009).

In addition to religious organizations, other common organizations for which older volunteers work are social and community services, health-related organizations, and educational or youth services (USDoL, 2011d; see Exhibit 5.1). While most older adults (67.1%) volunteer for one organization, 20.8% volunteer for two organizations, and 11.8% volunteer for three or more organizations. The most common types of responsibilities they assume within these organizations include collecting, preparing, distributing, or serving food (13.1%); providing professional or management assistance (9.3%); engaging in general labor or supplying transportation to others (7.9%); providing general office services (7.8%); raising funds (7.7%); and being an usher, greeter, or minister (7.6%). About 44% of older volunteers began with their main organization after being asked to volunteer, most often by someone in the organization.

Exhibit 5.1   Types of Organizations for Which Volunteer Work Was Performed by Persons Aged 65 and Older in 2010 (percentage)

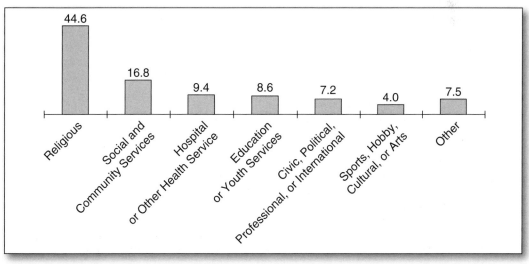

Source: USDoL (2011d).

Federal Senior and Volunteer Programs

As previously discussed, several volunteer programs receiving federal support can be found throughout cities and towns nationwide. In this section, we describe the activities of four well-known programs—RSVP, Senior Companions, the Foster Grandparent Program, and Counselors to America's Small Business (SCORE)—and present information about new initiatives by the Administration on Aging (AoA) to support senior volunteerism.

Retired and Senior Volunteer Program (RSVP)

RSVP offers men and women aged 55 and older the opportunity to put their talents and experience to work in community-defined, community-supported projects. Although RSVP is one of the largest federally funded volunteer organizations in the country, the program represents a true partnership between federal, state, and local government and the private sector in each community. In 2011, RSVP received $50.2 million in federal funds and $42.9 million in nonfederal funds in support of its programs (CNCS, 2012). The federal government awards grants to community sponsors of RSVP for program operation. This support may amount up to 70% of a program's total budget. Individual RSVP project sponsors are public agencies, private nonprofit organizations, and institutions that promote vital local interests and offer financial support to the project. The sponsor has full responsibility for the development and management of the project.

RSVP projects respond to community needs by matching the interests and abilities of seniors with rewarding part-time opportunities. The volunteers choose their assignments from a broad list of possibilities provided by the local RSVP office. They serve without compensation, but may receive reimbursement for program-related out-of-pocket expenses including meals and transportation. RSVP provides all volunteers with appropriate accident and liability insurance when on assignment at their host stations (Electronic Code of Federal Regulations, 2011c). Examples of organizations that serve as host agencies for the volunteers include health centers, hospitals, schools, libraries, crisis centers, correctional facilities, senior centers, nursing homes, government agencies, universities, and community service programs. Among the many services provided by RSVP volunteers are home renovation, independent living services for older adults, mentoring and tutoring programs for immigrants and children, disaster relief, respite care, and volunteer recruitment/management (CNCS, 2011a, 2011b).

In 2011, there were 685 RSVP grantees across the nation (CNCS, 2012). They managed 296,100 volunteers who contributed 60 million hours of service. Twenty percent of RSVP volunteer stations are in rural areas (Senior Corps—RSVP, 2005). Approximately 73% of RSVP volunteers are women; 19% are between the ages of 55 and 65, 68% are aged 66 to 84, and 12% are aged 85 or older. The majority of RSVP volunteers are White (90%), 7% are Black, and 1% are Asian, American Indian/Alaskan Native, or Native Hawaiian/Pacific Islander; 4% of volunteers are Hispanic (Senior Corps, 2009). Using Independent Sector's (2012) valuation of volunteer labor of $21.79 per hour, the estimated value of services provided in 2011 was approximately $1.31 billion, representing a 26.1-fold return on the federal dollar.

RSVP volunteers help their volunteer stations to meet a wide variety of needs and serve millions of people across eight primary service areas: health and nutrition (30% of volunteer hours); community and economic development (18% of volunteer hours); education (8% of volunteer hours); housing (2% of volunteer hours); the environment (2% of volunteer hours); public safety (4% of volunteer hours); homeland security and disaster recovery/relief (1% of volunteer hours); and other human needs services (35% of volunteer hours; Senior Corps, 2009). In 2011, 65,000 organizations were supported through RSVP—volunteers mentored 80,000 children, worked with 16,000 children of prisoners, and served 676, 000 frail older adults (CNCS, 2012).

According to a majority of volunteer station supervisors, RSVP volunteers help the volunteer stations better serve the community "to a great extent" by improving the quality of services and helping free up paid staff time (Senior Corps—RSVP, 2005). In addition, a majority of station supervisors credited the RSVP volunteers with helping to expand the types of services available to clients, increasing the number of clients served, increasing public support for the program, recruiting non-RSVP volunteers, and reducing the time and effort needed to recruit volunteers.

In 1984, RSVP went international (RSVPI), receiving sponsorship from organizations such as Rotary and the Red Cross (Garson, 1994). In 2000, the University of Maryland's Center on Aging assumed administration of the RSVPI program (RSVPI, 2010b). Since its inception, RSVPI has carried out projects in more than 30 countries spanning six continents, including South Africa, China, Colombia, Italy, Japan, Australia, and the United Kingdom. Objectives of RSVPI include (a) increasing the number of volunteers age 50 and older, (b) creating sustainability in current volunteer forces, (c) developing networks of collaborative partnerships to improve community awareness and establish mechanisms for problem solving, (d) providing technical assistance in the development and implementation of training programs, and (e) implementing recruitment and retention strategies that encompass diverse volunteer service models that reflect local cultural values, norms, and community issues (RSVPI, 2010c). RSVPI volunteers serve as mentors in schools; provide support to hospitals, businesses, and environmental and government agencies; act as translators and tourism guides; help with food distribution and nutrition education programs; and support service activities for older adults to remain living in their homes (RSVPI, 2010a).

Best Practice: The Nevada Rural Counties Retired and Senior Volunteer Program

The Nevada Rural Counties RSVP serves 15 of the state's 17 counties. In 2008, over 1,200 RSVP volunteers in rural Nevada provided more than 160,000 hours of volunteer service to over 184 public and nonprofit community agencies and individual older adults. RSVP plays a vital social services leadership role for the communities it serves. It continues to expand its role of not only assisting the low-income and homebound seniors in the service areas, but also serving all persons in need and enhancing the quality of life of all citizens.

One of the volunteer opportunities in which older adults are engaged is the Senior Farmer's Market Nutrition Program. The goal of the Farmer's Market program is to increase the consumption, production, and distribution of locally grown fruits, vegetables, and fresh unprocessed herbs, while supplementing nutritional needs for seniors. For example free coupons for fresh fruit and vegetables are provided to older adults living in Carson City, Nevada, who have individual incomes of less than $20,036 per year and $26,955 for a couple. The program is a cooperative effort by the U.S. Department of Agriculture, RSVP, the Nevada Department of Administration—Commodity Food Distribution Program, the Nevada Department of Agriculture, the Nevada Certified Farmers' Market Association, and the Nevada Division for Aging Services.

For more information, contact Nevada RSVP, P.O. Box 1708, Carson City, NV 89702. Phone: 775-687-4680, ext.10, http://nevadaruralrsvp.org.

Senior Companion Program

The guiding premise of the Senior Companion Program is that the best way to help people is to help them help each other (ACTION, 1990b). Senior Companions provide emotional support and assistance to primarily older adults who are frail, homebound, and living alone. They usually serve two to four clients on a weekly basis. They serve 15 to 40 hours a week, often as members of a comprehensive care team, helping homebound older adults live independently. For example, Senior Companions may provide physical and emotional assistance to individuals with physical disabilities or cognitive limitations, those recovering from substance abuse problems or major medical interventions, and older adults who are frail. Senior Companions are a "safety net" for their clients, providing an extra set of eyes and ears and being ever alert to their changing needs (Senior Corps—Senior Companions, 2005).

Senior Companions are low-income individuals, 55 years of age and older. They receive a stipend of $2.65 an hour, accident and liability insurance, meals while on duty, reimbursement for transportation, monthly training, and a physical examination annually (Electronic Code of Federal Regulations, 2011a). To be eligible for a stipend, the Senior Companion may not have an annual income from all sources in excess of 200% of the poverty line. Prior to their assignment, Senior Companions are provided a physical examination to ensure that they will be able to provide supportive service without injury to themselves or the clients served, and receive 40 hours of preservice training. Volunteer stations provide 4 hours of in-service training per month for the Senior Companions. Senior Companions are recognized for their work at award luncheons and other special recognition events.

In 2011, Senior Companion Programs received $46.8 million in federal funds and $22.9 million in nonfederal funds (CNCS, 2012). Local communities sponsor the Senior Companion Programs; project directors must raise at least 10% of their project funds from nonfederal sources. Most of the nonfederal funding comes from state and local governments, private social service agencies, United Way, private businesses, and fundraising campaigns. Each project has an advisory council whose members act as liaisons between projects and their communities.

In 2011, there were 220 Senior Companion projects across the nation (CNCS, 2012). The projects employed 13,600 volunteers. The majority of the Senior Companions (85%) are women; approximately 40% of the volunteers are from minority groups, with Black elders constituting the largest percentage (33%; Senior Corps—Senior Companion, 2005). The volunteers contributed 12.2 million hours of service, serving 60,940 frail older adults and providing respite for 7,900 caregivers (CNCS, 2012). Of its 5,000 public, nonprofit, and faith-based community volunteer stations, social service organizations and human needs agencies compose 25% of all volunteer stations, followed by multipurpose centers (23%) and community development nonprofit organizations (21%). About 14% of these volunteer stations were in rural areas (Senior Corps—Senior Companion, 2005). The estimated the value of Senior Companions' service at about $265.8 million, representing a 5.7-fold return on federal dollars invested in the program.

Senior Companions are an integral part of the support network of frail older adults, the majority of whom are over 75 years old, live in very low-income circumstances, or live alone (Senior Corps, 2008). Senior Companion activities impact the quality of lives of older adults across multiple venues. These include health and nutrition (37% of volunteer hours; 275,000 people served), community and economic development (4% of volunteer hours; 77,000 people served), education (1% of volunteer hours; 22,000 people served), housing

(<1% of volunteer hours; 5,400 people served), public safety (<1% of volunteer hours; 1,100 people served), disaster preparedness/relief (<1% of volunteer hours; 1,800 people served), and other human needs services (58% of volunteer hours; 111,000 people served; Senior Corps—Senior Companion, 2005).

According to the majority of volunteer station supervisors, Senior Companions help the volunteer stations better serve the community "to a great extent" by expanding the types of services available to clients and improving the quality of services (Senior Corps—Senior Companion, 2005). More than half of clients report that if their Senior Companion did not visit them, they would not be able to afford a replacement that would help them continue to live independently (Senior Corps, 2008). Senior Companions improve the quality of their clients' lives by providing social and emotional support to their clients. In addition, they serve as additional pairs of "eyes and ears" to watch over clients. As noted by one station supervisor, Senior Companions serve as "a safety net through their observational and reporting skills to catch residents early in a decline so treatment intervention comes prior to a significant decline" (Senior Corps—Senior Companion, 2005, p. 6). In addition, a majority of station supervisors credited the Senior Companions with helping to increase the number of clients served, helping free up the time of paid staff, increasing public support for the program, recruiting non–Senior Companion Program volunteers, and reducing the time and effort needed to recruit volunteers.

Foster Grandparent Program

The Foster Grandparent Program initiated its first 21 demonstration projects in 1965 (ACTION, 1990a). The first Foster Grandparent Program served very young children in institutions such as pediatric hospital wards and public homes for children with developmental disabilities, orphans, and other children without families. Today, Foster Grandparents help a broader array of children and youth who experience academic or personal problems. Depending on the needs of the community and the skills and interests of the Foster Grandparents, these volunteers may be found in a variety of settings, including schools, hospitals, child care centers, correctional centers, and drug treatment centers. In 2011, there were 325 projects established throughout the United States staffed by 27,900 volunteers (CNCS, 2012). The volunteers contributed 24 million hours and served 232,300 young people and 7,000 children of prisoners. Approximately 90% of Foster Grandparent volunteers are female; 56% are White elders, and 38% are Black elders (Senior Corps—Foster Grandparents, 2005). The volunteers carried out the program at 10,000 volunteer stations. Public and private primary schools composed 45% of all volunteer stations followed by Head Start centers (19%) and non–Head Start educational preschools (16%). About 16% of these volunteer stations were in rural areas, and 10% were associated with faith-based organizations (Senior Corps—Foster Grandparents, 2005). In 2011, the program received $110.7 million in federal funding and $33 million in nonfederal support (CNCS, 2012). The estimated value of this service is $523 million, representing more than a 4.7-fold return on federal dollars invested in the program.

As with Senior Companion Programs, sponsors of Foster Grandparent Programs must provide at least 10% of the project's funding themselves or through other nonfederal sources. An independent advisory council, consisting of professional and lay members of the immediate community, assists each project. Project directors assign volunteers to a volunteer station. Each volunteer station formally agrees to supervise and assist the Foster Grandparents serving under its direction.

To be eligible for the Foster Grandparent Program, volunteers must be at least 55 years old, low income (less than 200% of the poverty line), no longer in the regular workforce, and capable of serving children with exceptional or special needs without detriment to themselves or the children served. Individuals must commit to serving the program 15 to 40 hours per week (Electronic Code of Federal Regulations, 2011b). In return for their service, Foster Grandparents receive a stipend of $2.65 an hour, accident and liability insurance, meals while on duty, reimbursement for transportation, monthly training, and annual physical examination (CNCS, 2012). Before beginning their volunteer work, all Foster Grandparents receive a physical examination and a minimum of 20 hours of preservice training. They also receive an additional 20 hours of orientation training and 4 hours of in-service training per month that builds on and enhances their skills and knowledge relative to their volunteer assignments. In addition, each Foster Grandparent annually receives recognition of his or her services to the community at a formal public recognition event—this acknowledgment is perhaps as important as the monetary rewards.

Foster Grandparent activities focus primarily on four areas: education (80% of volunteer hours; 935,000 children and youth served), health and nutrition (12% of volunteer hours; 234,000 children and youth served), human needs services (6% of volunteer hours; 214,000 children and youth served), and public safety (2% of volunteer hours; 95,000 children and youth served; Senior Corps—Foster Grandparent, 2005). Most of relationships between young people and their Foster Grandparent last for seven months or longer, reflecting the practice of pairing Foster Grandparents with students over the course of a school year. Participating in the program leads to positive outcomes for the children and youth, including improving relationships with others, enhancing self-esteem, improving school attendance, increasing participation in school activities, and enhancing study habits and overall academic performance (Senior Corps, 2008). According to volunteer station supervisors, Foster Grandparents help the agencies better serve the community "to a great extent" by improving the quality of services, helping expand the types of services to the children and youth, increasing support for the organization, or improving community relations (Senior Corps—Foster Grandparent, 2005).

Senior Corps of Retired Executives (SCORE)

SCORE, "Counselors to America's Small Business," is a nonprofit association dedicated to entrepreneur education and formation of small businesses. Formed in 1964, SCORE is a resource partner with the Small Business Administration. More than 13,000 SCORE volunteers are members of 364 chapters offering assistance in more than 800 locations throughout the United States and its territories (SCORE, 2010). SCORE volunteers, who include retired CEOs of large corporations, former small business owners, computer consultants, doctors, lawyers, government officials, and university professors, provide real-world knowledge to entrepreneurs through face-to-face counseling, educational training workshops and seminars, and online assistance. In 2010, SCORE counselors volunteered 1.25 million hours, mentoring and training 590,550 small business owners (SCORE, 2011; SCORE Foundation, 2011). In addition, entrepreneurs can find dozens of online guides, in both English and Spanish, and templates for business plans, loan requests, and more. SCORE also provides programs and materials for specific groups of individuals including 50-plus entrepreneurs, women, minorities, and rural entrepreneurs (SCORE, 2010). SCORE clients started 58,637 new businesses in 2010 that created 71,449 jobs; they also helped 11,045 small businesses save an estimated 17,629 jobs (SCORE Foundation, 2011). These businesses generated $19.4 billion in gross revenue, with an average of $185,737 per business. Of SCORE 2010 clients, 30% were aged 45 to 54, 23% were aged 55 to 64 and 7% were 65 years of age or older.

Other Federally Sponsored Volunteer Initiatives

Since 2008, the AoA has provided support to the National Council on Aging (NCOA) to develop the Multi-Generational Civic Engagement Initiative (AoA, 2009a). This initiative provides technical assistance and other support to local programs that can become national multigenerational and civic engagement models for using older volunteers in meaningful direct services, as well as administrative, technical, or developmental activities. Projects focus on three target populations: older relatives caring for grandchildren, families caring for children with special needs, and caregivers of frail older adults. To learn more about the programs funded, go to http://www.epa.gov/aging/press/othernews/2009/2009_0605_ons_1.htm.

In 2010, the AoA funded the creation of the Aging Network's Volunteer Cooperative to engage senior volunteers nationwide in the aging network (AoA, 2011c). The goal of the Center is to help organizations use volunteers more effectively, especially the baby boomers; develop AoA's and the Aging Network's leadership in civic engagement; and expand the aging network's use of volunteers. The Center will conduct research on civic engagement, convene thought-leaders to help develop a plan of action on volunteerism for the Aging Network, develop communication and outreach tools to reach aging services leaders and volunteers across the country, create training programs and technical assistance resources for volunteers and volunteer coordinators, and identify and promote best practices.

Public and Private Volunteer Programs

Although the federal government provides primary funding sources for large-scale senior volunteer programs, public agencies and private foundations often partner to offer financial support for volunteer programs specifically designed to engage older adults in volunteer activities in their communities (see Exhibit 5.2). For example, with initial support from the Environmental Protection Agency (EPA), the University of Maine developed and implemented a statewide environmental leadership training program for adults aged 50 and older to increase civic participation in local, county, and state planning decisions that affect the built environment (Maine Senior Environmental Leadership Corps, 2011). The ENCorps leadership program is designed to focus on smart growth and environmental volunteerism. Volunteers participate in a leadership training summit and work with local organizations and personalized action plans developed at the summit. The first cohort of 140 volunteers volunteered in a variety of settings including land trusts, historical societies, downtown revitalization projects, town planning boards, and several revitalization projects in rural Maine. The project has strong sustainability prospects due to its partnership with the Maine Community Foundation and the Atlantic Philanthropies. The Helen Andrus Benedict Foundation (2011) is dedicated to helping older adults in Westchester County, New York, remain actively engaged in their communities. It funds multiple late life volunteer ventures including the Carter Burden Center for the Aging where seniors create art, craft, and practical items for local libraries, family emergency shelters, and food programs and the WorkSearch Online Employment Center at Westchester Community College, which is managed by older volunteers and supported in partnership with the AARP Foundation.

In addition to involving older adults in service to their communities, many public and private organizations provide seniors with the opportunity to give back to their professions (Wilson & Simson, 1993). For example, the American Bar Association developed the Second Season of Service Network, which links lawyers transitioning from full-time practice with organizations that can use their volunteer services (see http://www.abanow.org/2007/08/

Exhibit 5.2 The Civic Enterprise: A Network for Civic Engagement in Late Life

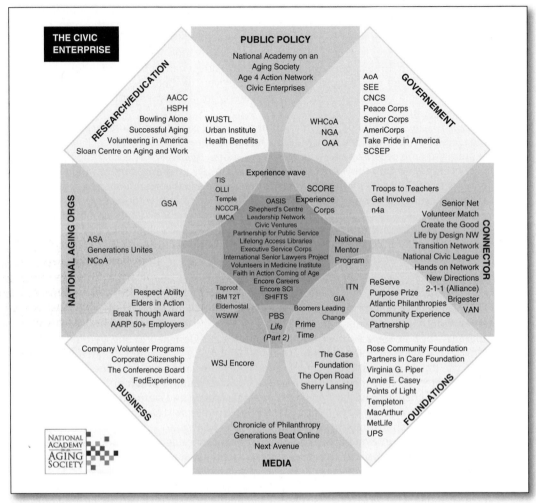

Source: O'Neill, Wilson, and Morrow-Howell (2010). Used by permission.

aba%E2%80%99s-second-season-of-service-initiative-focuses-on-the-new-senior-lawyer).
In Idaho, at the Kootenai Medical Center, retired nurses volunteer in the general medical unit
where they discuss diagnoses with patients, listen to their worries, help them prepare questions for their doctors, and smooth their departures from the hospital (Taggart, 2005). The
Volunteer Homeland Reserve Unit, comprised of retired law enforcement officers from local,
state, and federal agencies across the country who now reside in southern Nevada (see www
.vhru.com/index.htm), is yet another example of retired professionals volunteering to help
meet the needs of their communities. Unfortunately, little information is available about the
participants and outcomes of these local volunteer programs.

Intergenerational Programs

Many senior volunteer programs are intergenerational.[2] These programs bring together two or more independent agencies or organizations that serve different client populations. Persons served by intergenerational programs come from diverse economic, ethnic, and cultural backgrounds. They represent mainstream, special needs, or at-risk individuals from infancy through centenarians. Most intergenerational programs focus on bringing the generations together to promote the development of relationships and to provide support and services. Although intergenerational programs are structured so that all age groups benefit from the interactions, quite frequently, one age group is the provider of services or support, and another age group is the recipient of services.

The establishment of the Foster Grandparent Program formally introduced intergenerational programming to the American public. Since its origination, the number of intergenerational programs has continued to grow exponentially throughout the United States. In this section, we will highlight intergenerational programs and opportunities in the areas of education, recreational activities, and support programs.

Best Practice: Aetna Life and Casualty Senior Volunteer Program

Through public–private partnerships, alliances have been created between business and the aging network to solve problems jointly in more efficient and effective ways. Aetna Life and Casualty, based in Hartford, Connecticut, is an excellent example of how a large corporation can connect with a community to serve the needs of older adults. Beginning in 1980, Aetna started using corporate attorneys, paralegals, and support staff to assist older adults in a wide range of cases. The program was initiated in response to publicity about the legal needs of older adults regarding public benefits, wills, probate, age discrimination, landlord–tenant rights, consumer credit, divorce, and victim assistance.

Aetna is recognized as one of the first to use corporate lawyers to provide pro bono services to individuals. This program serves a definite need for clients who do not meet the guidelines of other legal programs funded through federal and state governments. Aetna reports that lawyers who donate time for this program experience a high level of satisfaction because they are greatly appreciated by their clients.

For more information, contact Connecticut Lawyers Legal Aid to the Elderly phone: 860-273-8164, or visit http://ctlawhelp.org/self-help-guides/elder-law/legal-assistance-elders-connecticut.

Educational Programs

From preschool through college, students and older adults are working together to enhance their learning opportunities. Developed at Cornell University, Garden Mosaics is a science education and community action program in which youth of ages 10 to 18 learn about plants and planting practices from older gardeners (Garden Mosaics, n.d.; Kennedy & Krasny, 2005), whereas teenagers in rural Virginia provide one-on-one computer instruction

---

[2]For more in-depth information about the history, development, and outcomes of intergenerational programs, see Brabazon and Disch (1997), Kuehne (2000), and Newman, Ward, Smith, Wilson, and McCrea (1997).

to caregivers of persons with Alzheimer's disease (Duesing & Pace Maxwell, 2007). In Florida, the Eckerd College Academy of Senior Professionals provides intergenerational learning opportunities for faculty and college students alike through numerous avenues such as tutoring, the use of seniors as discussant and resource colleagues, the use of seniors as coaches for educational teams, joint participation in service learning projects, and auditing of classes by older adults (Eckerd College, n.d.). In a broader, statewide educational initiative for college students who are aspiring teachers, student-teachers are matched with retired teachers who serve as mentors through the Kentucky Education Association's Intergenerational Mentoring Program (Saitz, 2009). By sharing insights and providing an attentive ear, mentors provide crucial support to education students as they face the multiple challenges of early teaching experiences. The situation is reversed in Philadelphia, where Project SHINE (Students Helping in the Naturalization of Elders) mobilizes college students to address the language, naturalization, and everyday needs of elderly refugees and immigrants (Skilton-Sylvester & Garcia, 1998–1999; http://www.projectshine.org).

With funding from the CNCS, Generations Together and the Association for Gerontology in Higher Education established a partnership to promote and support the development of intergenerational service learning models at colleges and universities throughout the United States. This innovative method of teaching and learning integrates community service activities into academic curricula; intergenerational service learning focuses specifically on the issues affecting the community's older adults. As a result of this project, a variety of intergenerational courses and service projects are being implemented nationwide (McCrea, Nichols, & Newman, 1998–2000). The National Service-Learning Clearinghouse was established in 1994 as a program of Learn and Serve America to support the service-learning community in higher education, as well as in primary and secondary schools, community-based organizations, and tribal programs (CNCS, 2010; National Service-Learning Clearinghouse, 2012). Its website provides information about service-learning programs and resources for practitioners, and researchers (go to http://www.servicelearning.org/about-nslc). The site also hosts e-mail discussion lists, and center staff members are also available to provide information and technical assistance.

Recreational Activities

Parks and recreation centers, senior centers, and fitness clubs are but a few organizations offering joint recreational activities and programs for younger and older adults. For example, as a result of society's focus on exercise, intergenerational fitness programs link children and youth with older adults (Duquin, McCrea, Fetterman, & Nash, 2004; Flora & Faulkner, 2006; Friedman & Godfrey, 2007). These programs allow older adults to participate in leisure and fitness programs while providing the opportunity for students to learn about the aging process. Gardening is another recreational activity easily shared between older adults of all functional levels (e.g., nursing home residents, homebound elders with physical disabilities, healthy elders) and children or young individuals (Gigliotti, Jarrott, & Yorgason, 2004; Predny, 2004). Roots & Branches Intergenerational Theater grew out of New York's Jewish Association for Services for the Aged Theater Ensemble (Roots & Branches Theatre, 2001; Vorenberg, 2004). While training young actors to work with older adults, it builds understanding and respect between generations by challenging stereotypes about age and aging through original theater, workshops, and other projects. The work of Roots & Branches springs from interactions that transcend age, culture, religion, and class.

Across the Globe: Magic Me Intergenerational Arts Programs

Magic Me is the United Kingdom's leading provider of intergenerational arts projects. Based in East London, the program works with seniors recruited through over 50's clubs and resource centers, nursing homes, adult day care centers, and community or cultural organizations. Local school students and other young volunteers are partnered with the older adults, and the mixed groups come together regularly, usually on a weekly basis. Participants are encouraged and supported to work together, so that real relationships can develop as they engage in art activities designed to stimulate both age groups. Projects have used story-telling, creative writing, photography, weaving, drama, dancing, puppetry, carnival, mosaic, ceramics, painting and poetry to bring together young and old participants.
   For more information go to www.magicme.co.uk/

Support Programs

Probably the most popular model of intergenerational support programs is having older adults providing formal care for young children (Newman & Riess, 1992; Smith & Newman, 1992, 1993). FACES-SF (formerly the Whitney Young Child Development Center) in San Francisco operates three full-time child care sites to meet the needs of the working poor in an industrial area of the city. Older volunteers serve more than 400 children from infants to sixth graders, providing a broad spectrum of multicultural and developmentally appropriate activities (E. Larkin, 1998–1999; http://www.facessf.org). The Friendly Listener Intergenerational Program in Madison, Wisconsin, pairs third, fourth, and fifth graders with older active and homebound volunteers who call children who are home alone after school at preappointed times to check in and to talk (National Eldercare Institute on Health Promotion, 1995). At Hawthorne Elementary School, for example, RSVP provides the program (see https://www.madison.k12.wi.us/012). Older adults involved with Mount Sinai School of Medicine's Family Friends Program support families living in East and Central Harlem that have a child with special needs by visiting with the child at home or working with children who are waiting to see the doctor in the pediatric practice (Mount Sinai Medical Center, 2011). Seniors, however, are not the only ones providing care and support. College students across the United States often provide support to local elders. At the University of North Carolina at Chapel Hill, for example, the Youth for Elderly Service program offers students the opportunity to provide companionship and social support to elders in five different community retirement homes (Campus Y UNC Chapel Hill, n.d.). A unique initiative in Salt Lake City, Utah—the Adopt-a-Native-Elder program—was created to build a "Bridge of Hope" between Native American elders and younger adults from other cultures. The program supports the elders who live in the cultural and spiritual traditions of the Diné People who predominantly live in remote portions of the Diné (Navajo) reservation. Volunteers support older adults choosing to adhere to Navajo traditions by financing food runs for elders, providing specific items for important traditional ceremonies, funding deliveries of firewood, donating medical supply boxes for home care needs, giving yarn for traditional rug weaving, and sustaining the memorial blanket program (Adopt-a-Native Elder Program, n.d.).

Shared Site Programs

Intergenerational shared sites are settings where children, youth, and older adults participate in services and/or programs concurrently at the same site or on the same campus (Generations United, 2011b). Participants interact during regularly planned intergenerational activities, as well as through informal encounters. Common models of shared sites include adult day care and child care programs, child care in senior housing and long-term care facilities, and after-school programs held at senior centers. For example, the Seagull Schools at Kapolei on Oahu is a joint preschool and adult day care facility (Medelson, Larson, & Greenwood, 2011). Incidental and planned interactions are accomplished through purposeful activities and aided by the architectural design of the facility, which includes having playgrounds that encircle the senior care facility and a large covered lanai that acts as a shared outdoor space for a variety of events that include exercise, entertainment, and relaxation. Hope Meadows in Central Illinois is a small-town residential neighborhood that supports up to 12 families adopting vulnerable children from the foster care system and 40 households of older adults (E. T. Mitchell, 2011). Seniors volunteer to work with the children in the Hope Meadows community a minimum of six hours per week in exchange for reduced rent on their apartments. Constructed in 2008, the Harry and Jeanette Weinberg Intergenerational Center is the first intentionally built shared site facility in the Baltimore–Washington region (Ricker, 2011). It serves persons with and without disabilities from birth through age 100 and older as well as their family caregivers. Interactive, intergenerational activities take place daily and include planned, individual interaction (e.g., arts and crafts, reading, storytelling) as well as small and large combined group activities (e.g., musical performances and singing exercises). While there are many benefits of shared sites programs for both older adults and the children and youth involved, public policies often create barriers that delay or prevent the creation of shared sites because of issues regarding funding streams, zoning, or regulatory requirements (Generations United, 2011b).

For Your Files: The Illinois Intergenerational Initiative

The Illinois Intergenerational Initiative is a coalition of individuals and organizations committed to enhancing education through intergenerational efforts, involving young and old in solving public problems and promoting vital communities through service and learning. The initiative is a Higher Education Cooperation Act partnership composed of statewide education and aging organizations such as the AARP, the Illinois Retired Teachers Association, the University of Illinois and Southern Illinois University systems, and the Illinois Association of School Boards. Accessing the initiative's website allows individuals to download publications on starting intergenerational programs, aging across the curriculum, and ideas for intergenerational projects. Individuals can also access the quarterly intergenerational newsletter, *Continuance,* online.

For more information, visit the organization's website at www.iii.siuc.edu/.

CHALLENGES FOR VOLUNTEER AND INTERGENERATIONAL PROGRAMS

Many successful volunteer programs provide thousands of hours of volunteer services; without these volunteers, many nonprofit community organizations would not be able to maintain their current level of services. Because senior volunteers are critical to the delivery of services, programs need effective strategies to recruit and retain volunteers. Volunteer coordinators face many challenges as they attempt to staff and carry out their programs, including finding volunteers to work during the day, coordinating volunteer efforts efficiently, and identifying new sources for recruiting volunteers (Substance Abuse and Mental Health Services Administration [SAMHSA], 2005; Urban Institute, 2004).

Tapping Untapped Potential

Many older people currently do not participate in any formal volunteer program. Barriers to volunteering include employment and family obligations, health, lack of knowledge of volunteer programs, perceived lack of skills, lack of transportation, and a belief that programs should pay people for their work. Thus, agencies must implement aggressive and systematic recruitment efforts to recruit older individuals (F. Tang & Morrow-Howell, 2008; Wilson & Simson, 2006). Programs must also make a greater effort to recruit older adults from diverse ethnic and cultural backgrounds. Initiatives targeting nonreligious adults, Hispanics, and the more disadvantaged (those with low education levels and low incomes) might yield big payoffs because these individuals report the lowest levels of volunteer activity (Zedlewski & Schaner, 2006). Lesbian, gay, bisexual, and transgender elders represent another untapped source of volunteers. Organizations can best engage older individuals by ensuring that volunteer opportunities are open to all, regardless of sexual orientation and gender identity and expression (J. M. Grant, 2010).

In addition, the current corps of senior volunteers is aging. Greater efforts need to focus on the recruitment of the baby boomers and young-old individuals to supplement, and at some point replace, older volunteers. More than half of adults aged 55 and older who do not currently volunteer have an interest in volunteering either now or in the future (MetLife Foundation, 2007). Although older nonvolunteers report that the most important factors in their decision to volunteer is to be working on a cause that they care about and securing a position that is interesting, is challenging, and will allow them to learn new skills and explore new interests, they also want positions that are nearby or convenient and fit their schedules. Programs also must develop new positions and opportunities for those elders who may be growing older but who still wish to give their time to support community programs and initiatives. The older generations' growing use of Internet technology (Zickuhr, 2010) may provide opportunities for older people to volunteer without having to leave their homes.

Training Volunteers

Training volunteers to complete their assignments efficiently and effectively remains a challenge for charities and nonprofit organizations. Providing skills training, ongoing support, and sufficient supervision is necessary to attract and retain volunteers, particularly those with less education or experience (F. Tang & Morrow-Howell, 2008). Recognition of the importance of providing ongoing training and feedback to volunteers is a capacity-building option not yet embraced by most organizational cultures. Only three out of five charities and one out of three congregations report employing a staff person to coordinate services and train volunteers. In that group, only 66% report possessing the skills they feel they need to train and manage their volunteer corps. Yet most would agree that making an ongoing investment in maintaining volunteers benefits program recipients, which in turn justifies greater volunteer investment (Eisner, Grimm, Maynard, & Washburn, 2009; Urban Institute, 2004).

Retaining Volunteers

The first three to six months are crucial in the life cycle of a volunteer. During this time, agencies are most likely to lose senior volunteers. To enhance retention of volunteers, agencies must be selective in their recruitment efforts. Once volunteers are recruited, retention is higher when programs match their interests and skills with appropriate assignments. According to a study by the CNCS (2007), to increase volunteer retention, it is important to keep volunteers engaged. Baby boomers and older adults with a high attachment to their volunteer work have high volunteer retention rates. The more time a volunteer spends volunteering with an organization and the more volunteer activities a volunteer is involved with, the more likely she or he is to keep volunteering. Thus, volunteer managers should focus on finding ways to cultivate greater interest and involvement among volunteers.

Reasons older volunteers give for leaving their positions include a higher priority of another productive activity or commitment, declining health, and problems with the program administration (F. Tang, Morrow-Howell, & Choi, 2010). To address these issues, volunteer managers need to consider greater role flexibility. Having the opportunity to set their own work schedules and ability to leave their positions temporarily may help with the retention of volunteers. Ensuring volunteers have a clear understanding of their roles and program expectations can help alleviate conflicts with staff and program participants and enhance the volunteer experience. Long-term volunteers who experience feelings of burnout also may leave their volunteer positions. These feelings result from grief (especially for individuals working with persons who are seriously ill or who are dying), frustration, intrusion on their private lives, and the time demands of their assignments. Volunteer leaders need to protect their volunteers by setting limits on both the type and amount of service asked of them.

Funding Volunteer Programs

One of the national strategies put forth by delegates of the 2005 White House Conference on Aging (2006) for promoting new and meaningful volunteer activities and civic engagement for seniors included increasing funding to support the RSVP, Senior Companion Program, and Foster Grandparent Program. Unfortunately, these federally sponsored programs have experienced cutbacks and flat funding levels in the past several years. Volunteers are not free. They require investments in training and supervision. Thus, the effective use of volunteers is a necessity for operating a cost-effective volunteer program (SAMHSA, 2005). A lack of adequate resources also limits the scope and effectiveness of many volunteer programs for older adults. Financial and technical support that enhances the recruitment and retention of volunteers would greatly expand the scope of services offered by many programs.

Evaluating Volunteer Programs

Most volunteer and intergenerational programs put only minimal effort into evaluating their programs (L. R. Fischer & Schaffer, 1993; Jarrott, 2005, 2011). Regular system-wide evaluations are necessary to identify both the strengths and weaknesses of existing programs and the effectiveness of the services that the volunteers provide. Often, when evaluations are conducted, they are published as final reports submitted to the administration of the national program or to the sponsor of the individual project. Evaluation information needs to be made more available and accessible to increase public knowledge about volunteer and intergenerational programs, garner community support for volunteer and intergenerational programs, and secure funding for expansion and/or maintenance of these programs (Butler, 2006; Jarrott, 2005, 2011).

Supporting the Future of Senior Volunteer Programs

Among the top 50 resolutions put forth by delegates of the 2005 White House Conference on Aging, two gave specific attention to volunteer programs. Specifically, delegates called for

- the development of a national strategy for promoting new and meaningful volunteer activities and civic engagement for current and future seniors; and

- reauthorization of the National and Community Service Act to expand opportunities for volunteer and civic engagement activities.

CASE STUDY

Reconnecting With the Community

Maggie is a 75-year-old woman whose husband, Warren, died of cancer three years ago. Maggie and Warren were a close couple. They had many interests in common and were known in their neighborhood for their activities with the local Audubon chapter. A county wetland area was preserved largely because of their efforts. Warren was the advocate, and Maggie quietly helped with the organizing and details. This was the way they approached everything in which they were involved. When Warren died, Maggie was completely devastated. It was as if she had lost her right arm. Warren had been the outgoing person in their relationship, and she felt lost.

Maggie is a bright woman and would have gone to college if finances had permitted. Her daughters, Kathy and Michelle, did further their education and currently teach in nearby communities. For the past year, the daughters have watched their mother become ever more detached and isolated from the community. She stopped attending the Audubon chapter meetings, which she had always enjoyed. She dropped out of her bridge club and even stopped going to church. Maggie was literally pining away. Nothing seemed to get through to Maggie, no matter how many conversations her daughters had with her about the importance of getting on with her life. It seemed that the normal grieving process had continued for too long and was having a dramatic impact on their mother. Kathy and Michelle regarded their mother as a healthy, vital woman whose quality of life was deteriorating needlessly.

Case Study Questions

1. Maggie's daughters are urging her "to get on with her life." On the basis of your reading of the chapter, what benefit would volunteering bring to Maggie's situation?

2. What personal characteristics of Maggie's would be important for someone to consider when proposing volunteer opportunities to her? Why?

(Continued)

(Continued)

3. Think about the volunteer programs discussed in this chapter and any others of which you are aware. What volunteer situations might appeal most to Maggie?

4. Ultimately, it will be Maggie's decision whether she will become reinvolved in her community as a volunteer. What role could her daughters play in helping to direct their mother toward an interest in a volunteer program or activity?

5. Drawing on your own personal experiences and observations, discuss with the class examples of older adults as volunteers who impressed you. Why did they impress you?

6. The chapter pointed out that recruiting and retaining older volunteers is a great challenge. What suggestions do you have that could increase recruitment and retention of older volunteers?

LEARNING ACTIVITIES

1. Interview the director of a senior volunteer program. Find out who volunteers, in what type of programs, and in what type of activities.

2. Meet with a group of older adult volunteers. Find out what they do, why they do it, and how volunteering has affected their lives. What are the benefits of volunteering? What did you learn about their programs, experiences, and the impact of senior volunteers? After this experience, do you see yourself volunteering when you are older? What types of volunteer activities interest you?

3. Interview staff members at a program that has older adult volunteers. What type of benefits do they see in having the volunteers? What types of activities or duties are assigned to volunteers? What would be the effect on their program if they did not have the volunteers?

4. Attend an in-service training that is designed for older volunteers or those working with them. What was the emphasis of the training?

5. Identify online campaigns that nonprofit organizations use to recruit senior volunteers. In what ways has the online forum enhanced volunteer recruitment possibilities? What might be some added challenges of volunteer recruitment and management introduced by online volunteer recruitments strategies?

6. Observe or volunteer for an intergenerational program. Was one age group the focus of service more than the other? What types of activities or services were there? Did the participants seem to enjoy themselves? Were there problems or issues that arose? What was your overall impression?

7. Search YouTube for examples of senior volunteer and intergenerational programs. What are the similarities and differences among the programs?

FOR MORE INFORMATION

International Resources

1. International Consortium for Intergenerational Programmes (ICIP); http://www.icip.info/

   ICIP is the only international membership organization focused solely on promoting intergenerational programs, research, practice, and public policy from a global perspective.

2. European Approaches to Inter-Generational Lifelong Learning (EAGLE) Toolkit for Intergenerational Activities; http://www.eagle-project.eu/welcome-to-eagle/the-eagle-toolkit-for-intergenerational-activities

   This toolkit provides a framework for practitioners, policy makers, and educators interested in developing intergenerational programming grounded in research on best practices. Case studies of intergenerational programs across Europe are featured.

3. Global Volunteers—Boomers Reach Out Abroad; http://www.globalvolunteers.org/serve/boomers.asp

   Global Volunteers is a private, nonprofit, nonsectarian, nongovernmental organization engaging short-term volunteers on micro-economic and human development programs in close partnership with local people worldwide. Baby boomers compose about 30% of the volunteers who participate in Global Volunteers "Adventures in Service."

4. Centre for Intergenerational Practice (CIP)—Toolkits and Guides page; http://www.centreforip.org.uk/resources/toolkits-and-guides

   The CIP, an initiative of the Beth Johnson Foundation, was founded in 2001 to support the development of intergenerational practice throughout the United Kingdom and to promote understanding of the potential for intergenerational programming to address social issues. Their web portal provides links to a multitude of toolkits, guides, and resources for intergenerational programming that have evolved out of CIP efforts.

5. United Nations Economic Commission for Europe (UNECE) Policy Brief on Ageing No. 10: *Tapping the Potential of Volunteering;* http://live.unece.org/fileadmin/DAM/pau/_docs/age/2011/Policy-briefs/10-Policy-Brief-Volunteering.pdf

   Published in January 2011, this brief addresses the UNECE strategy "to ensure full integration and participation of older persons in society." Topics covered include examples of best practices, volunteering by and for older persons, and broad policy/programming recommendations for optimizing late life volunteer engagement.

National Resources

1. Corporation for National and Community Service, 1201 New York Avenue NW, Washington, DC 20525; phone: 202-606-5000; www.nationalservice.gov

   The corporation oversees AmeriCorps, the National Senior Service Corps, the Foster Grandparent Program, RSVP, and the Senior Companion Program. Information about each of the programs is available on request.

2. Generations United, 1331 H Street NW, Suite 900, Washington, DC 20005, phone: 202-289-3979; www2.gu.org/HOME.aspx

   Generations United is a national membership organization focused solely on improving the lives of children, youth, and older people through intergenerational strategies, programs, and public policies. They represent more than 100 national, state, and local organizations, serving as a resource for policy makers and the public on the economic, social, and personal imperatives of intergenerational cooperation.

3. National Caucus and Center on Black Aged, 1220 L Street NW, Suite 800, Washington, DC 20005; phone: 202-637-8400; www.ncba-aged.org

   The National Caucus and Center on Black Aged is a nonprofit organization that works to improve the quality of life for older Black Americans. One of its programs, the Living Legacy Program, promotes intergenerational dialogue between older and younger individuals.

4. Volunteers of America, 1660 Duke Street, Alexandria, VA 22314; phone: 800-899-0089; www.voa.org

   Volunteers of America is a national nonprofit organization that offers programs and services to meet the needs of local communities. The organization offers services that assist the young and old, persons with disabilities, and persons with alcoholism. It sponsors foster grandparent and senior volunteer programs and publishes a quarterly newsletter, *Volunteers Gazette*.

5. *Journal of Intergenerational Relationships: Programs, Policy, and Research*, Taylor & Francis, Inc., 325 Chestnut Street, Suite 800, Philadelphia, PA 19106, phone: 800-354-1420; www.routledgementalhealth.com/journals/details/1535-0770/

   This is the only international journal focusing exclusively on the intergenerational field from a practical, theoretical, and social policy perspective. It provides readers with information about the latest intergenerational research, policy, programming strategies, and evaluation.

Web Resources

1. Generations Together: An Intergenerational Studies Program: www.gt.pitt.edu

   Generations Together is an intergenerational program in the University of Pittsburgh's Center for Social and Urban Research. The home page offers information about the development and evaluation of intergenerational programs, as well as information about the development of intergenerational studies as an academic discipline.

2. The Intergenerational Center: www. http://templeigc.org/

   The home page of Temple University's Intergenerational Center offers information about cross-age programs, training and technical assistance, and other resources for intergenerational programming. The site also has links to other resources for intergenerational programmers.

3. Strom Thurmond Retirement and Intergenerational Studies: http://sti.clemson.edu

   This home page explains the Intergenerational Entrepreneurship Demonstration Project, a pilot program that uses new retirees as volunteer mentors to at-risk youth. The retirees help the young people operate their own country market in a renovated dairy barn. Website visitors can access the newsletter and barn catalog online.

4. The Virtual Volunteering Project: www.serviceleader.org/

   This website offers information to agencies that wish to expand their volunteer efforts to the Internet and provides resources to volunteers who wish to volunteer online. Examples of helpful information provided by this website include how to involve volunteers through the Internet, how to set up a virtual volunteering program, and how to include people with disabilities in online volunteering.

5. AARP's Volunteer website: www.aarp.org/giving-back/

   AARP's volunteer website provides information about volunteer activities and programs in AARP chapters throughout the country and provides resources for those interested in volunteering nationally or locally.

6. VolunteerMatch: www.volunteermatch.org

   VolunteerMatch is a national nonprofit, award-winning online service dedicated to "strengthening communities by helping good people and good causes connect." This organization provides volunteer recruiting services for over 80,000 nonprofit organizations nationwide.

Education Programs

Jim and Donna Wagner retired to a small rural community of 3,000. They chose the community for its geographical location, climate, and proximity to relatives. Although they enjoy small-town living, they miss the many educational and cultural opportunities that larger communities offer. Six months after they settled into their new home, Donna decided to visit the tiny Senior Center on Main Street. After lunch, she remained with a group of seniors for a class on famous women of the World War II era. The other seniors told Donna that the local community college had brought many classes to their center through the years. They liked that the classes were noncredit and affordable. They also mentioned that the county Cooperative Extension agent frequently came to town and offered classes on health, self-care, and financial management for retirees.

Educators recognize now, more than ever before, that learning does not stop when adults enter the later stages of life. Although the process of learning changes during the life course (e.g., older adults take longer to assimilate information and are less likely to use memory schemas), study after study confirms that humans maintain the capacity for learning throughout their lives (Craik & Salthouse, 2008). Like Donna and her new friends at the Senior Center, many seniors find participating in educational programs to be an enriching experience. Most older adults, however, prefer attending classes outside traditional academia. They want the opportunity to actively participate in classes that are of interest to them and relevant to their lives now and in the future.

The idea of lifelong education first appeared in the research literature in the 1930s. By definition, lifelong education implies a cradle-to-grave approach to learning and recognizes that people can be learners at 18 or 80 (Manheimer, Snodgrass, & Moskow-McKenzie, 1995). It differs from the traditional lockstep model of education that assumes one's life path extends in a straight line. A lifelong education model provides a more fluid perspective that considers individuals as learners and, often simultaneously, as teachers who have a broad range of needs throughout their life course (Feldman, 1991).

EDUCATIONAL LEVEL OF OLDER ADULTS

Contributing to the lifelong learning phenomenon is the current education level of older adults and the future increase in the overall level of formal education achieved by Americans. Exhibit 6.1 shows the educational attainment of men and women aged 65 years and older in 2010. Approximately 80% of older men and women had completed high

Exhibit 6.1   Educational Attainment of Persons 65 and Older by Sex in 2010 (percentage)

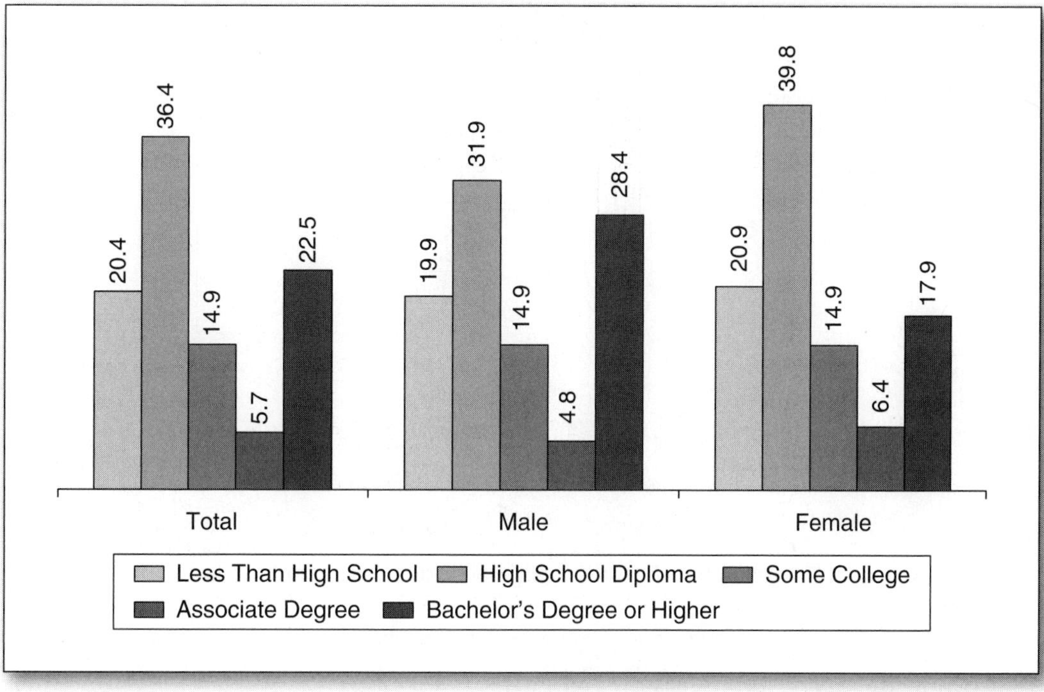

| Less Than High School | High School Diploma | Some College |
| Associate Degree | Bachelor's Degree or Higher |

Source: NCES (2011).

school; about 28% of older men and 18% of older women reported having a bachelor's degree or higher (National Center for Education Statistics [NCES], 2011).

Education levels among older adults, however, vary considerably by race and ethnicity. In 2010, approximately 84% of non-Hispanic White elders, compared with 74% of Asian elders, 65% of Black elders, and 47% of Hispanic elders had completed high school (NCES, 2011; see Exhibit 6.2). Approximately 35% of Asian elders and 24% of non-Hispanic White elders, compared with 15% of Black elders and 9% of Hispanic elders, had completed a bachelor's degree or higher.

The educational status of future cohorts of older adults will be dramatically different. It is anticipated that there will be more older adults with college degrees than older adults with less than a high school education. By the year 2030, more than 85% of older adults will have at least a high school education. As shown in Exhibit 6.3, approximately 87% of older men and 88% of older women will have completed high school, and approximately 31% of older men and 28% of older women will have attained a bachelor's degree (He, Sengupta, Velkoff, & DeBarros, 2005). In addition, the difference between the percentages of Asian, non-Hispanic White, Black, and Hispanic older adults with a high school education will grow smaller. Approximately 93% of Asians, 95% of non-Hispanic Whites, and 89% of Blacks aged 25 to 29 have graduated from high school; however, only 69% of Hispanics aged 25 to 29 have graduated from high school (U.S. Census Bureau, 2011b). Of persons aged 25 to 29, 36% of Asians, 31% of non-Hispanic Whites, 15% of Blacks, and 11% of Hispanics have a bachelor's

Exhibit 6.2   Persons 65 and Older With High School Diplomas or College
Degrees by Race in 2010 (percentage)

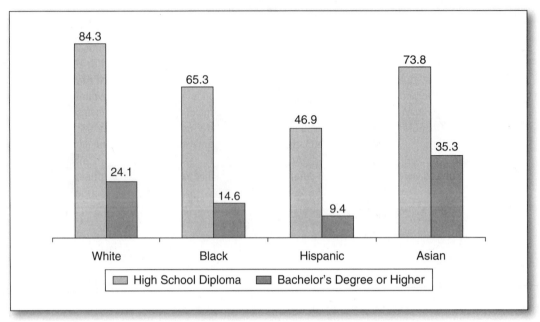

Source: NCES (2011).

degree. These differences in educational levels will no doubt influence the types of educational programs offered to older adults. In addition to basic education programs, there will be a renewed interest in the concept of lifelong education.

Literacy in the Older Adult Population

Although literacy proficiencies tend to increase as level of education increases, a significant percentage of older adults continue to have limited literacy skills. Findings from the 2003 National Assessment of Adult Literacy, which measures the English literacy (EL) of America's adults aged 16 years and older living in households and prisons, suggest that, although the average literacy of adults aged 65 and older increased between 1992 and 2003 (Kutner et al., 2007), adults in this age group had the lowest average literacy of any age group and accounted for the largest percentage of adults with below basic prose (i.e., no more than the most simple and concrete literacy skills; Kutner, Greenberg, & Baer, 2005). Among adults aged 65 and older, 23% had levels of literacy below basic prose literacy, 27% had levels below basic document literacy, and 34% had levels below basic quantitative literacy. Yet the number of older participants in EL programs is lower than for other adult age groups; less than 62,000 older adults were enrolled in EL programs in 2008–2009 (American Institutes for Research, 2010). Older adults' literacy skills and abilities influence every aspect of their lives and are of major concern to government agencies, health care entities, and social institutions.

Exhibit 6.3   Educational Attainment of the Elderly by Sex in 2030 (percentage)

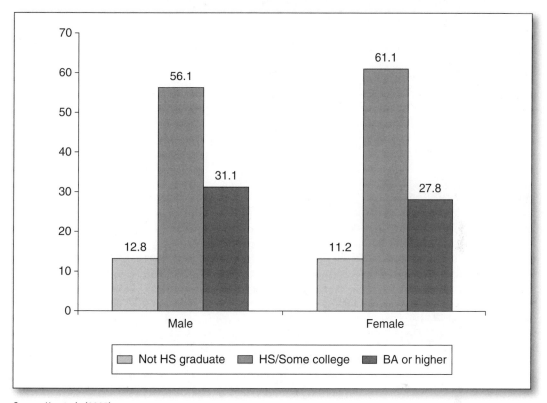

Source: He et al. (2005).

LIFELONG EDUCATION

Moody (1976, 1988) contends that society's focus on lifelong education has emerged through five chronological stages indicative of changes in attitudes toward later life. In the late nineteenth and early twentieth centuries, education for older adults was in the *rejection stage*, with the prevailing belief being that older adults neither needed nor deserved more learning opportunities. Society viewed education as the preparation of children and youth for the future, an investment not justifiable for older adults. From the late 1950s through the mid-1970s, beliefs about education moved through the *social services stage*. During this time, society viewed education for older adults as worthwhile if it had a special therapeutic value. Education programs focused primarily on the problem areas of growing older and the responsibility of social institutions to meet elders' needs through service programs (D. Peterson, 1985). By the mid-1970s, a shift began from the segregationist "social problem" perspective to an assumption that older adults should remain active and involved in their communities and in society. In this *normalization stage*, educators and practitioners minimized the differences between older and younger adults. Older adults seeking educational opportunities were placed in existing educational pathways. A decade later, the *self-actualization stage* emerged, in which learning in later life held special transformative possibilities for personal growth. Practitioners emphasized psychological and spiritual concerns as part of the educational milieu for older adults. Most recent is the *emancipation stage*, in which personal growth is intertwined with current community events. The focus is on the empowerment of older adults to actively participate in all realms of life.

In this chapter, we explore the opportunities for lifelong learning for individuals living throughout the United States. We begin by examining the federal government's support for education programs for older adults. Next, we present a description of the types of educational programs available for seniors and a profile of older adults who attend these programs. In the final section of this chapter, we discuss the challenges facing education programs currently and in the future.

For Your Files: Seniors and Literacy

The Centre for Literacy of Quebec (www.centreforliteracy.qc.ca) is home to one of Canada's largest and most comprehensive special collections on literacy and related topics. In 2004, staff developed the *Seniors and Literacy* annotated bibliography, which provides references and annotations of research articles, project reports, resource guides, and other documents that address the issue of seniors' literacy levels and practices. It includes websites from a range of governmental and nonprofit agencies in Canada and around the world. The annotations are descriptive and do not analyze or evaluate the material. To download a copy, go to www.centreforliteracy.qc.ca/sites/default/files/seniors.pdf.

POLICY BACKGROUND

Historically, support specifically for the education of older adults represents only a small fraction of the total federal expenditures for education. Provisions made under Title I of the Higher Education Act of 1965 provided colleges and universities the opportunity to direct some of their resources and staff to program development for older people. Most of the support for educational programs for older adults during the late 1960s through the mid-1970s, however, came from demonstration projects funded by federal agencies such as the National Endowment for the Arts and the National Endowment for the Humanities (Manheimer, 1992). Despite enthusiastic claims of success, these projects usually terminated at the end of their grants. Without outside money, most institutions closed older adult education programs because attending to the education needs of older adults was not high on the priority lists of traditional colleges and universities.

Following the gradual recovery from the post–Vietnam War recession, an increasing number of nontraditional-aged adults began to go back to school. Continuing education and lifelong learning became popular concepts. In 1976, Congress passed the Lifelong Learning Act. Hailed as "a landmark of social legislation," it had the goal of providing lifelong learning opportunities for all citizens "without regard to restrictions of previous education or training, sex, age, handicapping condition, social or ethnic background, or economic circumstances" (Weinstock, 1978, p. 16). The Act was the first legislation to specially mention older adults and retired persons as potential recipients of educational resources. Unfortunately, Congress did not provide funding for the Act.

Although state and local governments have the responsibility for developing public and continuing education, the federal government, through the office of Vocational and Adult Education, has been instrumental in setting national priorities for education opportunities for persons of all ages. For example, under the Adult Education and Family Literacy Act, Title II of the Workforce Investment Act of 1998, federally funded, state-administered adult education programs address the needs of older adults by emphasizing functional competency and grade-level progression from the lowest literacy level, with provision of EL instruction, through attainment of the General Education Development (GED) Certificate. States operate special projects for older persons through individual instruction, use of print and educational technology, home-based instruction, and curricula focused on coping with daily situations. In 1998, adult education programs served 246,067 adults 60 years of age or older (U.S. Department of Education, 1998). In addition to adult literacy programs, a variety of federal programs have supported informal educational activities of interest to older adults, including consumer education, older reader services, community schools, continuing education, and health education.

The Administration on Aging (AoA), under the provisions of the Older Americans Act (OAA), also plays an important role in encouraging older adults to seek educational opportunities and in developing educational programs for older adults. The 1987 amendments to the OAA instructed local Area Agencies on Aging (AAAs) to identify the postsecondary schools in their area that offered tuition-free education to older adults and to distribute the findings to senior centers and other locations (U.S. Senate Special Committee on Aging, 1991b). State and local AAAs also are involved in a number of grassroots education programs aimed at providing older adults with the knowledge they need to enable them to lead more productive lives by broadening their occupational, cultural, and social awareness. For example, AAAs sponsors educational programs in health and nutrition, injury prevention, preretirement and legal concerns, employment, and consumer education.

USERS AND PROGRAMS

There is great diversity among learners within the older adult population. Like any age group, older adults are heterogeneous and multidimensional in learning needs and abilities. They come from all educational levels and have interests in a variety of subjects from the liberal arts to programs more focused on issues of aging (e.g., health care, finances). Variation also exists in the educational programs designed to meet the needs of the aging population. In this section, we examine three primary settings for formal education programs for older adults: (a) institutions of higher education, (b) community-based organizations, and (c) at-home programs. For each setting, we describe the types of programs available and the older adults who participate in them.

Institutions of Higher Education

In 2009, 16,818 Americans 65 years of age and older were enrolled in undergraduate credit programs at four-year institutions of higher education throughout the United States

(NCES, 2010a), representing 4% of the total undergraduate population. Women constituted 59% of the "older" undergraduate population. The institutions classified 93% of the older students as part-time students. In addition, 8,194 older adults were enrolled in graduate programs, composing about 3% of all postbaccalaureate students. Women made up 54% of this population of graduate students. Of older students, 72% were pursuing their graduate degrees on a part-time basis.

For Your Files: Leadership Training for Older Persons

Leadership Training for Older Persons is a program for underserved adults aged 50 years and older from low-income or minority communities. The program enables participants to gain the skills, knowledge, and confidence necessary to become effective leaders and to advocate for their peers in the community. Through classroom sessions and time spent on community projects, participants learn practical skills such as how to organize and lead meetings, public speaking, using community resources, teamwork, and advocacy strategies. Since its inception, over 50 new community leaders have "graduated" from the program.

For more information, contact North Carolina Center for Creative Retirement, Reuter Center, CPO # 5000, The University of North Carolina at Asheville, One University Heights, Asheville, NC 28804-8516; phone: 828-251-6140; www2.unca.edu/ncccr/.

Most states have established guidelines within their statutes for tuition waiver programs for older adults. State requirements, as well as individual university requirements, vary with respect to minimum age, number of credits for which a person may enroll, the type of course (i.e., credit or noncredit), and the availability of space. Although 60% of accredited degree-granting educational institutions offer tuition waivers for older adults, very few older adults take advantage of the tuition waiver policy (Lakin, Mullane, & Robinson, 2008). Many older adults are unaware of the waiver programs, and others do not take advantage because of the requirements. Waivers often depend on space availability, are restricted to specific types of courses (credit bearing or noncredit), have an income cap for eligible participants, and require proof of state residency, documentation of retirement, and a high school diploma (Brandon, 2009). For example, in Ohio, residents 60 and older can audit classes free at 13 public universities and 23 community colleges, space permitting, with the professor's approval (G. Brown, 2011). Once enrolled, older students can take full advantage of the classroom experience, completing as much or as little of the course assignments as they choose. They are usually not required to buy books, but they may be required to pay registration, parking, and other fees.

University-based retirement communities located on or near campus often allow residents to attended classes free. The Kendal at Oberlin retirement community in Ohio, for example, has enjoyed a close and mutually beneficial relationship with Oberlin College from its very beginning (Kendal at Oberlin, 2005). Residents attend concerts and recitals at the Oberlin Conservatory, as well as lectures of all sorts, and can audit classes at no cost with permission from Oberlin professors. Similarly, Oak Hammock, on the campus of the University of Florida, offer residents a "focus on lifelong learning" and has developed the Institute for Learning in Retirement, which offers free classes through a joint venture with both the University and Road Scholar (Oak Hammock at the University of Florida, n.d.).

Community Colleges

Community colleges are major providers of educational programs for older adults. In 1970, community colleges became the focus of the expanding instructional network on aging. The AoA awarded a grant to the American Association of Community and Junior Colleges to encourage the organization "to develop an awareness of the needs of older Americans and to explore ways in which these community-oriented institutions might contribute to an improvement in the quality of life in the nation's elderly population" (Korim, 1974, p. 5). Because of this project, community colleges begin developing new programs for older people in the mid-1970s. Expansion of programs has been slow. By the early 1990s, only about one quarter of colleges reporting having programs and services for older adults (L. Weiner, 2007). Since that time, programs for older adults, particularly those focusing on workforce training, have grown significantly. In 2009, 48,736 older adults enrolled in courses or programs taught through two-year institutions (NCES, 2010b). The majority (95%) of the older adults were part-time students.

At several community colleges around the country, the Next Chapter (formerly Life Options) programming is being developed to respond to the educational and social needs of aging baby boomers (Goggin & Ronan, 2004). Such programs are designed to help adults approaching the traditional age of retirement make a successful transition to the next phase of their lives. A theme common to these programs is that they are not modeled on traditional seniors programs; their focus is derived from market research and opinion surveys that clearly indicate baby boomers are not attracted to the retirement options that traditionally have been available for aging adults. To adapt to and capitalize on the changing demographics and emerging social trends, Goggin and Ronan (2004) propose a number of things that community colleges need to do to address the educational needs of the aging boomers:

- Develop a clear understanding that this new student cohort has explicit desires and expectations

- Prepare new programs and services based on the expressed desires of adults at this life stage

- Adapt existing service learning, leadership training, and workforce development models to the needs and interests of post-midlife adults

- Create a simple and specific access point for existing and new programs that will appropriately serve this group

- Partner with other community organizations such as libraries, community centers, other community-based organizations, and government agencies to build a collaborative network for life planning, meaningful engagement, continued learning, and community connections

- Educate the workplace and the nonprofit sector about the ways they will need to change in order to take best advantage of the contributions these experienced adults can make

The American Association of Community Colleges' Plus 50 Initiative (2008–2011) was created to build the capacity of community colleges nationwide to develop programming that engages the Plus 50 learner (Learning for Action Group, 2010). The Initiative, funded by the Atlantic Philanthropies, supported a pilot group of 13 two-year institutions to develop or expand college offerings in three areas: workforce training and career development, learning and enrichment, and volunteering. Grantee colleges developed new courses and redesigned existing ones, as well as developed and expanded support services that enabled access to community college programming. Approximately 15,000 individuals aged 50 and older enrolled in courses associated with the program during the Initiative. While colleges maintained their inventory of learning and enrichment course offerings for older adults (13,000+ unique courses), in response to the economic recession the number of workforce training courses offered specifically for Plus 50 learners rose sharply, from 54 in 2007 (baseline) to 1,147 by 2010. The majority of Plus 50 students reported that they were "somewhat" or "very" satisfied with the program, including the colleges' learner-centered support services. There is strong evidence of program sustainability: strategic plans at seven of the pilot grantees include Plus 50 programming; 11 colleges have written Plus 50 programming into the annual budget; and 12 colleges have allocated continued staff time to Plus 50 programs.

Best Practice: Joliet Junior College Plus 50 Workforce Center

The Plus 50 Workforce Center in Joliet, Illinois, promotes mentoring, volunteering, ageless learning, and re-careering programs for individuals aged 50 and older. Programs and services of this Center focus specifically on the adult learner who is facing the opportunities and challenges of leaving a current job and choosing a retirement job or second career. The Center offers a comprehensive system of quality employment, education, and training services that support local and regional economic development initiatives. Programs and workshops, as well as access to a comprehensive resource area, are customized to meet the needs of the mature job seeker.

For more information, contact The Plus 50 Workforce Center, Joliet Junior College City Center Campus, 214 N. Ottawa Street, Joliet, IL 60432; phone: 815-280-1500; http://www.jjc.edu/continuing-education/workforce-development/Pages/mature-workforce.aspx.

Lifelong Learning Institutes

Lifelong Learning Institutes (LLIs), formerly known as Learning in Retirement (LIR) programs, are community-based organizations of retirement age people dedicated to meeting the educational interests of its members. The first LLI was established in 1962 at the New School in New York City. Throughout the 1960s and 1970s, other colleges and universities replicated or adapted the educational model. During the 1980s, several national conferences introduced the concept to a wider audience and spurred the development of many more groups. In 1988, 30 LLIs collaborated with Elderhostel, Inc. to form the Elderhostel Institute Network (EIN), with the goal of helping establish new institutes, providing resources and services to established Institutes, and developing an all-inclusive organization of institutes for learning in retirement (EIN, 2012b). Between 1988 and 1999, more than 200 new ILRs were started in North America under the auspice of the EIN. Each independent institute who became an affiliate of EIN paid annual dues to help support the services of the national office. Located at educational institutions large and small, private and public, and in communities both urban and rural, LLIs provide unique, noncredit academic programs developed and attended by the members themselves—an educational community of older learners.

By 2002, the LIR movement had matured, and established institutes did not need the same level of services from EIN as in the past. Dues were eliminated and services were streamlined. EIN has now become a "virtual" organization of more than 300 institutions of higher learning across North America, with services provided via the Elderhostel website (EIN, 2012a). In addition, EIN expanded its network by inviting programs for older adults that demonstrate high academic standards, but do not necessarily have a college/university connection, to join. There are between 300 and 500 of these programs as well, bringing the North American total for learning programs for older adults to around 1,000 (EIN, 2012b).

Another network of LLIs, the Osher Lifelong Learning Institutes (OLLIs), formed with support from the Bernard Osher Foundation (OLLI, 2010). In 2004, the Foundation designated the Osher Institute at the University of Southern Maine as the National Resource Center for the current network of 117 Osher Lifelong Learning Institutes (see http://usm.maine.edu/olli/national/). The Center disseminates information on effective educational programming for older learners. In addition to providing information and connections via its website, the Center publishes a national research journal, plans an annual national conference, and provides a number of other ways for OLLIs to connect with one another.

Regardless of type or network affiliation, the most successful LLI programs share several characteristics. These programs are designed to serve the learning needs and interests of the local older adults involved in the program; offer a broad-ranging educational program; are nonprofit, charging a modest tuition or membership fee; often have a need-based scholarship program; publicly commit themselves to affirmative action goals; use volunteer teachers or course leaders who are members of LIR; offer social, cultural, and physical experiences that complement the curriculum and are appropriate for the program participants; and provide for participant involvement in planning, evaluating, teaching, and, where appropriate, administering the program (Young, 1992).

Across the Globe: University of the Third Age (U3A)

University of the Third Age (U3A) is a "learning for leisure" educational enrichment forum for adults in their postretirement years. A global phenomenon, U3A are in more than 30 countries around the world. U3A began in France in 1972 at the University of Toulouse. In the French model, faculty members and working academics act as course facilitators and lecturers for classes in a wide range of subjects offered to older adults. The U3A movement in the UK began in 1981. It comprises learning cooperatives, which draw upon the knowledge, experience, skills, and interests of their own members to organize and provide programs (http://www.u3a.org.uk). The nine U3A programs in Finland are all associated with universities and have been providing a myriad of courses to retirees since 1985. South Africa's U3A system, launched as a single Cape Town cooperative in 2000, now boasts 24 independent local programs across the country, engaging participants in a wide variety of classes led by experienced volunteers and amateur enthusiasts (http://kesayo.jyu.fi/ikaantyvienyliopisto/en). The Malaysian U3A system, established in 2007, is a hybrid of the British and French models (http://u3amalaysia.wordpress.com). Programs in their infancy, such as the U3A in Singapore, are still defining the parameters of their programming (http://www.sace.org.sg/page3.php).

For more information go to http://www.u3a.org.za/History.html.

Elderhostel: Road Scholar Program

Conceived as a means of getting older adults directly involved with stimulating activities and with each other, Elderhostel combines the excitement and challenge of travel with the enrichment of academic courses on substantive subjects.[1] The founders offered the first program during the summer of 1975. Throughout that summer, 220 older individuals came to one of five New Hampshire colleges to participate. By 1980, all 50 states and several Canadian provinces offered Elderhostel programs. In 1981, Elderhostel offered its first international programs in Great Britain and Scandinavia. In 2004, Elderhostel launched Road Scholar, an adventurous, experiential travel-study opportunity structured to meet the interests and capabilities of baby boomers. To reach out to groups of older adults who were less likely to participate in Elderhostel programs, Elderhostel created its diversity outreach program in 2006 to attract African Americans to its lifelong learning experiences and, in 2007, began to offer Day of Discovery programs at retirement communities. In 2010, Elderhostel began to operate its programs under the name Road Scholar to capture the essences of the program experience—"learning from expert instructors, enhanced by direct discovery of an idea, issue, subject or place" (Road Scholar, 2012b).

Road Scholar is a nonprofit educational organization; its national office is in Boston. There are five U.S. area offices, a UK office, and headquarters program staff that support and guide 340 institutions worldwide in developing and maintaining individual Road Scholar programs. The travel organizations and program leaders, who for the participants are the most visible part of the organization, develop and host the individual Road Scholar programs under the guidelines of the administrative offices. They are responsible for all aspects of running a program, from lodging and meals to courses, learning activities, and instructors.

Road Scholar is a network of educational and cultural sites, including colleges and universities, state and national parks, museums, and environmental/outdoor educational centers. Coordinators at each site design and operate individual Road Scholar programs. Although most program sites offer varied programs from year to year, they typically include at least one course about the cultural or historical significance of their geographic location. In recent years, "full-immersion" programs have developed in which participants spend their whole time studying one topic such as "The Cajun Experience in Music, Food, and Dance" (for more information, visit http://www.roadscholar.org).

In 2011, Road Scholar offered nearly 6,500 programs in every American state, Canada, and 150 other countries to approximately 100,000 participants (Road Scholar, 2011). The typical Road Scholar program in the United States brings together a group of 15 to 35 persons over the age of 55. Programs from the easiest level, in which participants must be able to handle their own luggage, climb a few stairs, and get from sleeping accommodations to classrooms and dining rooms, to the most challenge programs that require participants to have a high level of physical fitness and appropriate expertise in the program activities (e.g., backpacking in the Grand Canyon; hiking the Appalachian Trail in four states; trekking in Nepal) to be able to engage in full days of fast paced, strenuous physical challenges. The average duration of the U.S.-based programs is five to six days, while the average duration for an international-based program is two to three weeks, with participants spending time

---

[1]Unless otherwise noted, the background information about Road Scholar comes from Elderhostel Institute Network (2012a) and Road Scholar (2012b). Current statistical data about the program came from Road Scholar's website (www.roadscholar.org) and national office.

at several different study sites (Road Scholar, 2012a). During their learning adventure, participants delve into the subject matter through lectures, field trips, and extracurricular events for the sheer joy of learning—there are no tests!

The original "hostel" lodging in dormitories on college campuses has given way to comfortable hotels, inns, conference centers, and other more luxurious, yet affordable, accommodations. Not only do programs cover a wide range of topics and activities; they are offered in variety of formats including adventures afloat, independent city discoveries, national parks, and outdoor adventures. In 2011, the average cost for programs in the continental United States was $150 per day; international programs cost about $275 per day. The cost includes accommodations, meals, lectures, activities, transportation within the program, taxes, gratuities, and a travel assistance and insurance plan.

Older adults attend Road Scholar programs because they want to expand their knowledge. They are a self-selecting group of highly motivated individuals. Most Road Scholars report an annual income of $62,000 or more, and more than 80% have attended college. To help increase the social, educational, and economic diversity of Road Scholar's participant group, Elderhostel offers approximately 600 Road Scholar Scholarships annually. The scholarship award is up to an $800 credit, which recipients may apply to any program in the United States and Canada (Road Scholar, 2012a).

Many participants wish to spend time with their grandchildren and share the wonders and experiences Road Scholar programs provide. In response, intergenerational programs have been developed (see www.roadscholar.org/programs/grandparenttravel.asp). In 2011, almost 300 intergenerational programs were offered across the United States. Trip options included visiting national parks, camping, participating in outdoor activities, and expanding cultural experiences. Although most intergenerational programs are designed for one adult to be paired with one child in attendance, Road Scholar Family Programs are open to any combination of older and younger learners within a family, and are geared to multiple generations but are suitable for two generations (read more about family programs at www.roadscholar.org/programs/familyprograms.asp).

Community-Based Organizations

Many community-based agencies and organizations also provide educational programs for older adults. Several favorable characteristics account for the popularity of community-based education programs with older students, including their location, the schedule of program offerings, and the format of the offerings (Courtenay, 1990). Because the primary mission of the sponsoring organization is to be responsive to all the residents, these educational programs generally are dispersed throughout the community. Senior centers, hospitals, community centers, churches, and libraries often provide educational programs and/or the physical space for such programs. Almost without exception, older adults prefer educational programs offered from late morning to mid-afternoon during the week. The availability of alternative scheduling makes community-based organizations especially accommodating to the needs of the older learner. They also have an advantage over colleges and universities in that they are not under educational accreditation/standards requirements, do not need extensive registration procedures, and have nearby parking or free transportation. Although they typically do not have the resources to offer every type of educational experience, community-based organizations do have the flexibility to provide a wide range of subject matter.

Libraries have established a variety of onsite education programs specifically for older adults (Manheimer et al., 1995; M. A. Wolfe & Brady, 2010). Participants take part in learning activities such as minicourses, book and film discussions, forums on consumer and health issues, and life enrichment programs. For example, the Queens Borough Public Library in Queens, New York (www.queenslibrary.org) offers programs on topics related to disabilities and aging, including information about community resources for older adults and health and wellness programs.

The Older Adult Service and Information System (OASIS) is a public–private partnership offering programs through a national network of community-based sites designed to enrich the lives of older adults through lifelong learning and service opportunities. The OASIS Institute in St. Louis is the national headquarters, which oversees educational, cultural, health, and volunteer outreach programs at OASIS sites for adults aged 50 and older. Sponsored by multiple corporate and nonprofit agencies, the OASIS program has centers operating in 40 U.S. cities and 24 states with more than 370,000 members. Organizations that host OASIS centers include Macy's stores, fitness centers, the Junior League, healthcare providers, senior centers, and shopping malls. Membership is free, with older members from all socioeconomic, cultural, and educational backgrounds in the program (OASIS, 2011a). In 2010, 6,339 older adults participated in 1,003 classes offered through OASIS Connections Program, designed to teach computer skills for use in the workplace, volunteer roles, and in their personal lives (OASIS, 2011b). Other members participated in OASIS' evidence-based health education programs to increase their physical activity, improve nutrition, and manage chronic conditions. Almost 6,000 OASIS members served as volunteers in the Intergenerational Tutoring Program, helping 21,293 students strengthen their reading and language skills, while more than 700 OASIS volunteers led peer-education classes in the arts, humanities, health, and technology.

Shepherd's Centers of America is a national network of 60 local Shepherd's Centers that encourage older adults to lead meaningful, purposeful lives (Greater Kansas City Community Foundation, 2012). The local nonprofit interfaith community organizations provide seniors health enhancement, cultural enrichment, and lifelong learning opportunities. One program, Adventures in Learning, provides college-type classes in an environment in which older adults share their knowledge, talents, skills, and interests with peers (Shepherd's Center of America, 2012). They are the teachers, students, planners, and participants in the program. Other educational programs include computer classes, defensive driving

For Your Files: Women Work!

Women Work! educates displaced homemakers—women who have lost their principal means of self-support through events such as widowhood or divorce—to assist them in achieving economic self-sufficiency. Local programs based in community organizations (e.g., community colleges, employment centers) offer vocational testing, employment training, tuition assistance, and job referral services. The program also produces *Network News*, a quarterly newsletter for displaced homemaker advocates; *Women Work!*, a biannual newsletter for displaced homemakers; and *Women Work! Program Directory*, a listing of job training and education programs nationwide.

For more information, contact WomenWork! at the National Network for Women's Employment, 1625 K Street, Suite 300, Washington, DC 20006, phone 202-467-6346; www.womenwork.org.

classes, and intergenerational programs. The centers charge a nominal fee for participation. Classes are held through affiliate locations nationwide and cover a wide range of topics, including workplace etiquette, leadership, business practices, personal well-being, health, and travel.

The Cooperative Extension System also provides community-based education programs for older adults focusing on family, health, aging, and caregiving issues as well as leisure and home-based activities. This nationwide educational network established through legislation is a partnership of the U.S. Department of Agriculture, and over 100 state land-grant universities and colleges (U.S. Department of Agriculture, 2006a). For a listing of aging programs and resources offered through Cooperative Extension in each state, see www.csrees.usda.gov/nea/family/pdfs/aging_resources.pdf.

Although people may think of community-based education as occurring primarily in a classroom setting, outdoor programs also present older adults with learning opportunities. For example, Camp Cheerio, nestled in the Blue Ridge Mountains of North Carolina, offers adults aged 50 and older the opportunity to enjoy camping experiences similar to those traditionally offered to youth and teens. During the five-day camp sessions, participants stay in cabins and have the option to participate in activities such as fishing, guided morning walks, arts and crafts, ping-pong, archery, riflery, skeet shooting, table/card games, bingo, and tennis. During these programs, older adults learn the importance of good physical and mental health and develop new skills such as camping, canoeing, and working in a group situation. To learn more about Senior Adult Camp, visit the Camp Cheerio website at www.campcheerio.org/sac/index.php.

At-Home Educational Experiences

With the advance of technology, both well and frail older adults can take part in new educational ventures from the convenience of their own homes. These programs reduce structural barriers (e.g., inconvenient timing, hard-to-reach locations) that often discourage older adults from attending university or community-based courses and programs.

For many years, special programs from public and state libraries have provided educational services to older adults via bookmobiles, cable television, and books by mail (Manheimer et al., 1995). In addition, librarians and volunteers provide reading programs and materials to persons who are homebound and residents of nursing homes and other institutional settings. The Alameda County Library branches in California, for example, offer a full range of programming specifically targeting seniors. Their services include Active Living educational programs; a Homeward Bound program through which volunteers deliver and share library resources with home- and institution-bound adults of any age; computer classes and assistive technology; BiFolkal Senior Activity Kits, which are multisensory kits that can be use to help older adults trigger memories, communicate, and belong; and provision of "talking" and large print books for individuals with sensory impairments (Alameda County Library, 2009).

SeniorNet, a nonprofit membership organization based in San Francisco that began in 1986, offers computer training and networking capabilities to adults 50 years of age and older. Community organizations (e.g., banks, senior health organizations, financial service companies, private foundations) sponsor local SeniorNets by furnishing computer equipment, scanners, and digital cameras, and contributing to the cost of establishing and maintaining the sites. Using a "seniors teaching seniors" model, over 3,000 seniors serve as mentors, instructors, and learning center administrators to teach members how to use computers at the sites. In 2011, 65 learning centers and affiliates were located throughout the United States, housed in a variety of settings, including senior centers, community centers, public libraries, schools and colleges, clinics and hospitals, and Indian reservations and other underserved areas (M. M. Williams, 2011). A typical center contains 6 to 10 computers. In addition to providing basic and advanced computer instruction, most centers offer open lab time where students can use computers to practice their skills or to work on individual projects. A 12-month membership in SeniorNet, which provides access to any local classroom learning center, is $40 for the first year and $30 each year thereafter (SeniorNet, 2011).

SeniorNet also offers online classes through their Online Learning Center Campus. For $199, members receive access 24/7 to over 300 senior-friendly lesson plans covering computer operating systems, numerous software programs (e.g., Microsoft Word, Excel, PowerPoint, Adobe Photoshop), and other technology-related topics, as well as a complimentary membership in SeniorNet. A nationwide online "electronic community" also fosters long-distance information sharing among the program's approximately 8,000 members through a variety of online discussion boards called SeniorNet Round Tables (M. M. Williams, 2011). Members, particularly those not living near a site, have the opportunity to interact with one another, participate in network forums, and seek and give information through databases and special-interest groups. Members also receive newsletters and discounts on computer-related and other products and services.

The goal of Seniors Surf the Net is to provide older adults living in central Pennsylvania access to reliable information about local services, medical care, and community events from a single web portal. Multiple local human service agencies joined with the Dauphin County Area on Aging and Comcast Cable to create the website. To help seniors become more comfortable and proficient in accessing Internet sites, hands-on training sessions are provided throughout the year by a Comcast representative at a local computer lab. In 2006, over 40 older adults received instruction on how to surf the net. More information can be obtained at www.dauphininfo.com.

Some older adults find self-directed learning opportunities such as Internet courses and webinars appealing. These programs often are offered through the continuing education division of many colleges and universities and public or private organizations. Their independent structure may be attractive to some older adults. In particular, older individuals who are self-disciplined and internally motivated to learn, who live in rural or more remote areas, or who have limited mobility or transportation can participate in courses of personal interest without leaving their homes. With the aging of the baby boomers, the number of older adults accessing educational opportunities online is expected to increasing dramatically (Guess, 2007). However, distance education is not a viable solution for all older adults, in part because it does not sufficiently provide the sense of community that drives many older adults to pursue higher education (Lakin, Mullane, & Robinson, 2007). In addition, both older students and educators face challenges in a virtual classroom (Willis, 2006). While learning features that foster interactivity, older adults also need to be mastering course content. This requirement for divided attention may be particularly challenging for older learners. Conversely, instructors may have a harder time identifying their older students' particular strengths and learning styles in a virtual rather than a traditional classroom.

> ### For Your Files: Computer Learning Through SeniorNet
>
> SeniorNet provides adults aged 50 and older with information and instruction on computer technologies so they can use their new skills for their own benefit and to benefit society. More than 80,000 older adults have been introduced to computers at SeniorNet learning centers. All centers share common goals and objectives, but each has its own activities. Here are some examples:
>
> - The center in Bakersfield, California, has joined with the Senior Aid Program at the Mexican American Opportunity Foundation to prepare Spanish speakers to go back into the workforce.
> - In Honolulu, a group of members produced a 10-minute video about Hawaii, the college (Honolulu Community College), and SeniorNet, using both video and computer technology.
> - The Chicago Department of Aging established a learning center on the South Side to serve its predominantly African American population. It is open seven days a week and has about 20 seniors stopping by daily.
> - The instructors of the Peoria, Illinois, center helped set up computers in nursing homes and retirement homes and now go online with the residents.
>
> For more information, visit the SeniorNet website at www.seniornet.org.

CHALLENGES FOR EDUCATIONAL PROGRAMS

Not all older adults participate in educational programs equally. People of lower socioeconomic status, racial minorities, residents of rural areas, and those with less formal education historically have participated in adult education programs at lower rates than their counterparts (M. A. Wolfe & Brady, 2010). But, as we previously noted, future cohorts of older adults from all walks of life will have higher levels of formal education, so participation by older adults in formal and informal learning situations is likely to increase. The demand for increased opportunities for lifelong learning will no doubt challenge people to rethink the role of education as well as where and how such educational experiences are delivered. We end this chapter by addressing several current and future challenges facing education programs for older adults.

Increasing Participation of Older Adults

The growth in the number of older learners is not necessarily reflected in increasing enrollments within most traditional postsecondary institutions. The main focus of higher education has always been on collegiate and postcollegiate students. The pedagogical norm at most colleges and universities does not suit the unique needs of older adults (Manheimer, 2002; Yankelovich, 2005). Most older adults are not attracted to lengthy course commitments or to lecture halls in which traditional college-age students listen passively. Thus, to attract more older adults, institutions of higher education may need to rethink their curricula, course content, and didactic delivery style (Duay & Bryan, 2008).

For older adults who do choose to enroll in educational programs and courses at colleges and universities, the cost of attending usually is not a primary concern. The problems concern access. The campus environment can be far more challenging and frustrating for older adults than younger students who more readily adapt to the college life. Inconvenient parking facilities, lack of concern for physical safety of those walking to and from the classroom (e.g., poor lighting), and lack of physical comfort (e.g., uncomfortable chairs, lack of climate control, unpleasant and unattractive classrooms) discourage older adults from enrolling in classes (M. Moore & Piland, 1994). Moore and Piland (1994) suggest that colleges conduct a "physical environment audit" (p. 316), with active involvement from older adults, to illustrate appropriate areas of the campus for older adult learner activities and to suggest realistic alterations in others that could house senior educational services. In addition, colleges and universities may need to make several significant administrative changes to meet the needs of older students. For example, they must consider the schedule time and place of course offerings, transportation from parking lots to classrooms, the support services available to the older students, and the relevance of the learning to real-world issues facing older adults (Lakin et al., 2008).

In addition to physical barriers, older adults face demographic, psychological, social, and financial barriers when contemplating entering the higher education arena (Lakin et al., 2007). A pervasive obstacle to participation in lifelong education by today's older adults is that they have a lower level of educational experiences than younger adults. Older adults often hold negative self-images about their ability to learn that make them apprehensive about mixing with younger students. Although society expects adults to fulfill many roles in their later years (e.g., retiree, grandparent), the role of student is not commonly encouraged. Older adults consistently cite costs as a barrier in their pursuit of higher education (Lakin et al., 2008). Adults actively enrolled in lifelong learning programs report that finding money from one semester to the next was a continuous struggle. Although many older adults are aware that grant sources exist, they perceive the amount of work necessary to find and apply for awards prohibitive, particularly when available funding sources rarely cover part-time enrollments or courses for personal enrichment.

Institutions of higher education sponsoring senior educational courses and programs must address the inclusion of participants from all races, cultures, and socioeconomic groups. Today, the majority of the older learners attending traditional classroom courses or participating in nontraditional programs (e.g., LLI, Road Scholar programs) are those with the highest levels of education, income, and employment. Although LLI and Road Scholar programs provide scholarships to encourage attendance by individuals from all economic strata, their attempts to recruit a more diverse group of older individuals have not been very successful.

Expanding the Content and Delivery of Education Programs

In addition to efforts to make formal educational opportunities more accessible to older adults, attention must be directed toward the content of educational experiences. According to R. Fischer (1992), colleges and universities have at least four major responsibilities to older adult learners. First, they need to help them understand the values, culture, and technology of today. Second, higher education must act as a catalyst for mobilizing young-old adults for productive roles in society for the 20 to 30 years of life after retirement. Third, colleges and universities have a responsibility to foster diversity in intellectual, cultural, and social life by educating students of all ages about aging and ageism. Finally, higher education has the responsibility of enhancing the effective use of society's limited resources by reducing older adults' needs for health and social services.

Higher education must rethink program delivery formats to attract older adults to its classrooms. Instead of delivering linear certificate and degree programs, colleges and universities need to find ways to deliver education in chunks, or "skill-ettes," so that older adults can easily acquire education for new careers or existing jobs (Lakin et al., 2008). A potential benefit of this paradigm is that older adults might be more inclined to enter a more formal program after successfully completing condensed courses. In addition, having knowledgeable and effective instructors who respect their views and ability to learn is a key influence on older adults' satisfaction with a learning experience (Duay & Bryan, 2008). Yet most college professors have limited knowledge about teaching older adults. Pincas (2007) described several issues that teachers of older people need to understanding to be most effective, including conditions for learning, competence and capability of older learners, relationships between learners and teachers, learners' prior knowledge and competencies, need for continuing participation, and the importance of self-fulfillment.

Ensuring the Quality of Educational Programs

Quality control is an issue of concern for all educational programs. Community-based educational offerings for older people have diverse sponsors, program types, audiences, and content. There is no central system of support for monitoring of these activities, so their patterns depend on the preferences of administrators and the needs of local communities. This often makes them responsive to the wishes of the older learner but does not facilitate development of easily described categories of programs, nor does it provide much assistance in predicting a program's success with other sites and sponsors (D. Peterson, 1990).

Financing Education Programs

A concern for institutions of higher education is the method of financing educational activities for older people. Federal and foundation funds are not nearly sufficient for the number of programs currently operating or planned. D. Peterson (1990) suggests that long-range funding must come from the states or from the sponsoring institutions themselves. Public institutions will need state support in revising program priorities to meet the needs of the aging population. Typically, state support is primarily for credit students, with non-credit enrollees paying most of their program costs. One proposed strategy for seeking state funds for older adult education programs is tying requests to other policy issues that serve the state (Lakin et al., 2008). For this to work, legislators need to be convinced that any funds spent educating older adults will yield real payoffs, for example, by older adults filling positions in high-need service areas in their states.

Yet another concern is the limited funding that directly supports the availability of community educational opportunities. With decreases in federal dollars for educational programs, community-based programs will need to further develop private sponsorships. Although many foundations have given local awards, only a few have devoted large amounts of money to this area and have continued support of educational programs through several years (D. Peterson, 1990).

Addressing the Future of Senior Education Programs

The role and purpose of education for future cohorts of older adults will no doubt be as varied as the older population itself. As noted in several resolutions made by delegates to the 2005 White House Conference on Aging (2006), educational opportunities for older adults will need to address their different needs and make use of innovative and lifelong learning models that are culturally and linguistically appropriate. According to McClusky (1974), older adults have five needs that educational programs can address. Education programs can help older adults address *coping needs*—those that help individuals deal with the social, psychological, and physiological changes brought about by aging. Courses on health, physical exercise, adjustment to retirement, and learning how to live with losses are examples of education that addresses coping needs. *Expressive needs* are activities in which older adults derive satisfaction, pleasure, or meaning. Given that much of learning during the life course is related to skill acquisition, there may be a greater demand for these types of educational opportunities by future cohorts of older adults. *Contribution needs* of feeling wanted and needed, and fulfilling a useful role, can be addressed through educational opportunities that allow older adults to act as mentors or peer counselors. Educational programs that empower older adults so they can have influence and control over their quality of life deal with *influence needs*. Courses that address these needs teach older adults about their legal rights or how they can assume leadership roles within their communities. Finally, individuals' needs to feel better off in later life compared with an earlier time in life are *transcendence needs*. Any educational experience that allows older adults to advance artistically, occupationally, educationally, or physically has the potential of addressing transcendence needs (Tomstam, 2005).

CASE STUDY

Can Further Education Help a Downsized Worker?

Martin, 50, entered the workforce shortly after graduation from high school. His first job was with a state highway department, in which he worked as a construction supervisor for seven years. He was caught up in a reorganization and was laid off from that job. For the past 25 years, he has been employed with a major private sector highway-construction firm for which he has performed many duties, including work as a materials tester, safety officer, office manager, and highway-construction supervisor. Martin and his wife, Nancy, who is an administrative assistant with the U.S. Forest Service, have been earning excellent wages and benefits for more than 20 years. They have two children: a daughter in her second year of college and a son employed in a successful position with a major insurance company.

Two months ago, Martin was officially informed by his company that his job would be eliminated by the new owners. Once again, Martin found himself in a downsizing situation in which the higher salaried positions were being eliminated to cut the operating expenses of the company. As a dislocated worker, Martin thought that this time around he would have considerably more difficulty finding a job, especially without the benefit of more education.

Martin had always wanted to pursue educational opportunities beyond high school, so he and Nancy had stressed the benefits of higher education with their children. Fortunately, Martin and Nancy have been careful with their finances. Even with a daughter in college, they were not panicked about Martin losing his job. Their finances were such that Martin was thinking that this might be a good time for him to reevaluate his educational opportunities.

Case Study Questions

1. This chapter discusses three philosophical perspectives about lifelong learning. Which of those perspectives most closely pertains to Martin's situation? Why?

2. What statistics and studies described in the chapter could you cite to Martin that would reassure him that a decision to return to a higher education learning environment need not be threatening because of his age?

3. What differences in attitudes might Martin encounter as a middle-aged learner in the 1950s and the 2000s?

4. If you were counseling Martin on his options, which options described in the chapter might best meet Martin's educational goals? Which generic educational programs and services might not meet Martin's needs at this time in his life?

5. If Martin decides to enroll at a local college, what problems, barriers, and frustrations might he have to overcome as an older learner? Cite chapter discussion to support your answer.

LEARNING ACTIVITIES

1. Investigate what educational opportunities are available to older adults in your community, at your college, or at other institutions. Find out about the older adults who are involved in these classes. What are their reasons for being interested in taking these classes?

2. Interview older participants in a Road Scholar program or other educational programs about the experience. What did the participants gain from it, what did they like and dislike, and why are they involved?

3. Sit in on a class that is geared toward older adults. How is it similar to or different from classes you attend? Interview students or the teacher of the course. What type of experiences have they had? What do they like, and what would they change? Is this something they do or plan to do on a continuing basis?

4. Interview someone involved in arranging Road Scholars or other types of educational opportunities for older adults. How did she or he decide what to offer? To whom are the classes marketed? How successful has the program been?

5. Introduced in Congress on May 12, 2011, the goal of the Lifelong Learning Accounts Act of 2011 is to establish lifelong learning accounts as an incentive for employees ages 18 through 70 to save for career-related skills development and to promote a competitive workforce through lifelong learning (Council for Adult Experiential Learning, 2011). Unfortunately, the bill was not enacted. Go to www.govtrack.us to search for other proposed bills supporting education for older adults.

FOR MORE INFORMATION

International Resources

1. Association for Education and Ageing (AEA), 132 Dawes Road, LONDON SW6 7E; phone: (00 44) (0) 207 385 4641; http://associationforeducationandageing.org

   Formed in 1985, AEA is an international membership organization that involves older learners in dialogue with professionals and volunteers who provide and support learning. It focuses on combining the interests of research, practice, and policy concerning later life learning in all its forms.

2. United Nations Educational, Scientific, and Cultural Organization (UNESCO) Institute for Lifelong Learning; http://www.uil.unesco.org

   The UNESCO Institute for Lifelong Learning (UIL) is a nonprofit, policy-driven, international research, training, information, documentation, and publishing center. It promotes lifelong learning policy and practice with a focus on adult learning and education, especially literacy and nonformal education and alternative learning opportunities for marginalized and disadvantaged groups. The UIL provides technical support to member states through consulting services, program monitoring, and evaluation, advocacy, networking, and capacity building.

3. United Nations Economic Commission for Europe (UNECE) Policy Brief on Ageing No.5: Lifelong Learning; http://live.unece.org/fileadmin/DAM/pau/ggp/iwg/Prague/ECE.WG.1.5.e-corr.pdf

   This policy brief, published in March 2010, summarizes the best practices developed by and challenges facing European countries who have committed to the UNECE's goal of promoting lifelong learning and adapting the educational system to address changing economic, social, and demographic conditions.

4. Projection of Populations by Level of Educational Attainment, Age, and Sex for 120 Countries for 2005–2050; http://www.demographic-research.org/Volumes/Vol22/15/22-15.pdf

   The authors of this report provide projections for 120 countries by five-year age groups, sex, and four levels of educational attainment for the years 2005–2050. Taking into account differentials in fertility and mortality by education level, they present systematic global educational attainment projections according to four widely differing education scenarios, showing a possible range of future educational attainment trends around the world.

5. *International Journal of Education and Ageing.* 78 Northampton Road, Market Harborough, Leicester, LE16 9HF United Kingdom; www.associationforeducationandageing.org/international-journal-of-education-and-ageing.html

   This journal brings together international research, scholarship and practice on education, learning, and aging in a critical and accessible manner. Authors explore the interface of learning with social, economic, health, and other aging policy and practice, across Europe and worldwide.

National Resources

1. American Library Association (ALA), Adult Services Division, 50 Huron Street, Chicago, IL 60611; phone: 800-545-2433; www.ala.org

   The ALA's activities are focused in many areas, including developing innovative programs that support libraries in acquiring new information technology and training people in its use and supporting libraries as centers for culture, literacy, and lifetime learning.

2. National Center for Creative Aging (NCCA), 4125 Albemarle Street NW, Washington, DC 20016-2105; phone: 202-895-9456; www.creativeaging.org

   Founded in 2001, the Center promotes three initiatives: civic engagement, health and wellness, and lifelong learning, integral to its mission of bringing arts programs to older adults. The NCCA has established individual and organizational memberships into 20 statewide networks organized by regions: Midwest, Northeast, Southeast, Northwest, and Southwest.

3. *Gerontology and Geriatrics Education.* Taylor & Francis, Inc., 325 Chestnut Street, Suite 800, Philadelphia, PA 19106, phone: 800-354-1420; www.routledgementalhealth.com/journals/details/0270-1960/

   Articles published in this journal focus on the exchange of information related to research, curriculum development, course and program evaluation, classroom and practice innovation, and other topics with educational implications for gerontology and geriatrics. It is designed to appeal to a broad range of students, teachers, practitioners, administrators, and policy makers.

4. *Educational Gerontology.* Taylor & Francis, Inc., 325 Chestnut Street, Suite 800, Philadelphia, PA 19106, phone: 800-354-1420; www.routledgementalhealth.com/journals/details/0360-1277/

   This journal publishes original research in the fields of gerontology, adult education, and the social and behavioral sciences. Researchers from around the world will benefit from the exchange of ideas for both the study and practice of educational gerontology.

Web Resources

1. National Institute for Literacy: http://lincs.ed.gov

   The home page of the National Institute for Literacy offers information about literacy forums and, Listservs (e-mail discussion groups), regional and state literacy resources, and links to other Internet resources.

2. SeniorNet, 1 Kearny Street, Third Floor, San Francisco, CA 94108; phone: 415-352-1210; www.seniornet.org/php/default.php

   Don't forget to drop by the SeniorNet site. Find out more about the program, the members, and the activities at various sites.

3. The American Society on Aging Lifetime Education and Renewal Network (LEARN): www.asaging.org/learn

   The goal of LEARN is to increase providers' knowledge of the nature and promise of lifelong learning to enhance both the quality and quantity of educational programs available to older adults. It provides updates on program models, adult learning, public policy issues, new research, funding sources, and training opportunities. The network also helps educators connect with peers to exchange ideas and information related to this specialized field.

4. Generations on Line: www.generationsonline.com

   This organization provides both a service for access and a product for learning aimed at older adults who cannot afford or choose not to enroll in computer training or Internet training. The specially programmed self-training software introduces older adults to the Internet and provides four basic functions: e-mail, discussion, research, and a gateway to popular sites. The software is provided at a minimal cost to senior centers, libraries, retirement homes, and other locations where older adults might congregate.

Senior Centers and Recreation

Last fall, a distraught daughter called the San Francisco Senior Center (SFSC) and asked the Social Services Director for advice to help her 85-year-old Italian American mother, Jane, who had suddenly stopped talking. After an extensive discussion with the daughter, the Social Services Director suspected that Jane had been suffering from isolation and depression, which are documented as common and sometimes deadly in the elder population. The Social Services Director suggested that both Jane and her daughter visit SFSC to observe the activities and meet senior participants. Coming from a large city back East where she walked frequently, Jane was naturally attracted to the Aquatic Park location's Gardening and Walking Group, whose members walk from the center to the Fort Mason Community Garden each Wednesday. As Jane continued to come to SFSC, she found many walking companions who enjoyed walking and visiting this San Francisco garden while sharing their concerns about the challenges of aging. Jane has since become known as "fast Jane" for her ability to out-walk even the youngest participants in the group. In addition, Jane participates in the healing class each Monday, and almost every day she visits the center where her new friends look forward to her company (San Francisco Senior Center, 2010).

Stop for a moment and think about the activities in which you participate during your free time away from work or school. Do you read a good book? Garden or fix things around the house? Exercise? Jump in the car and take a short day trip? Play golf or tennis? Attend a concert or a movie? Gather with friends for a coffee? Now think about the benefits you derive from participating in your favorite leisure activity. Does it help you unwind? Make you feel connected with others? Gain a sense of accomplishment? Feel productive? Improve your mood? Researchers have been interested in identifying the functions and types of leisure activities people participate in, and the social, psychological, and physical benefits of leisure participation in later life, as well as the patterns of leisure participation over the life course.

According to Dumazadier (1967), leisure has three main functions—relaxation, entertainment, and personal development—and thus acts as a buffer against major life stresses. Stebbins (1992) introduced a model of leisure that further refined leisure activities as either serious or casual leisure. *Casual leisure* comprises those activities that are immediate, are intrinsically rewarding, and are a relatively short-lived pleasurable activities requiring little or no training to enjoy it, such as a walk in the park. *Serious leisure* is defined as the "systemic pursuit of an amateur, hobbyist or volunteer activity that is sufficiently substantial and interesting for a participant to find a career there in acquisition and expression of its special skills and knowledge"

(p. 3). Stebbins and others purport that qualities of serious leisure activities can play an important role in contributing to the elements of successful aging, including lifelong learning and personal growth, keeping active, engaging in creative and meaningful activities, involvement in a social network, and development of close personal relationships. Indeed, researchers have found that leisure activities can replace a work role, expand on preretirement skills and interests, and assist in maintaining a positive self-concept and contribute to a "successful aging" experience (C. A. Brown, McGuire, & Voelkl, 2008; J. R. Kelly, Steinkamp, & Kelly, 1987; Paillard-Borg, Wang, Winblad, & Fratiglioni, 2009; Riddick & Stewart, 1994).

In addition, participating in leisure activities can help older adults such as Jane deal more effectively with stressful life events through shared companionship and friendship, can reduce feelings of loneliness, and can increase the ability to cope with significant life changes such as widowhood and retirement (Aday, Kehoe, & Farney, 2006; D. Coleman & Iso-Ahola, 1993; Kleiber, Hutchinson, & Williams, 2002). There is evidence that involvement in formal leisure activities has been positively associated with increased happiness, decreased depressive symptoms, and improvements in psychological well-being (Menec, 2003; Musick & Wilson, 2003). Engagement in physical leisure activity has also been associated with maintenance or prevention of negative physical health declines (DiPietro, 2001).

According to researchers, most of our leisure patterns are highly individualized and relatively stable across our life course until very late in life, when an intervening variable, such as health status or functional ability, forces a change (J. R. Kelly, Steinkamp, & Kelly, 1986; R. E. Lee & King, 2003; Paillard-Borg et al., 2009; Singleton, Forbes, & Agwani, 1993; Stanley & Freysinger, 1995). One of the few longitudinal studies conducted on changing patterns of leisure activities among people over the age of 50 was conducted by Janke, Davey, and Kleiber (2006). They examined leisure participation patterns over an eight-year period in three subdomains of leisure activities: informal leisure activities, which include socializing with friends and family, visits with others, and telephone conversations; formal leisure activities, which include participation in clubs and organizations; and physical leisure activities, which include participation in sports or exercise of both low and high intensity. Results indicated that participation in informal leisure activities remained consistent until late in life (mid-80s and older) when participation declined markedly. Over time, two factors influenced informal leisure participation rates: retirement was associated with an increase in informal leisure activities, and an increase in the number of functional limitations was associated with a decline in informal leisure participation rates. Older adults' participation in formal leisure activities declined at a faster rate later in life (early to mid-80s), and, as the severity of functional limitations increased over time, participation rates declined. Participation in physical leisure activities remained fairly consistent until the eighth decade of life when rates of participation declined significantly. However, physical and mental health was found to be related to rates of participation in physical leisure activities. As physical health declined and the severity of depressive symptoms increased, rates of participation in physical activities decreased. Janke and colleagues concluded that, overall, leisure activities remain fairly stable over time, and the changes that do occur in patterns of leisure activity are influenced more by health status, not age per se.

One source of leisure activities for older adults is the senior center. According to Krout (1989), a *senior center* is a designated place with a broad array of services and activities targeted to older people. It offers opportunities for social interaction, development of strong friendships, and promotion of feelings of self-worth and community belonging. In this chapter, we begin by reviewing the federal policies that have contributed to the growth of senior centers. This is followed by a discussion of who attends senior centers, the various models of senior centers, and the types of programs offered. In the final section, we present the challenges that lie ahead for senior centers.

POLICY BACKGROUND

The first senior center was established in 1943 in New York City (Leanse, Tiven, & Robb, 1977). The founders established the William Hodson Community Center to help alleviate loneliness among older adults observed by social workers in the city's Welfare Department. According to the center's first director, the center needed to offer older adults a meeting place but, more importantly, needed to offer services that would help participants remain in the community (Perspective on Aging, 1993). California was the location of the next two senior centers, which offered a variety of recreational and educational services (Kent, 1978; Maxwell, 1962). By 1966, there were 340 centers; today, approximately 11,000 senior centers are located across the country, serving one million older adults everyday (National Council on Aging [NCOA], 2011d; D. L. Wagner, 1995a).

According to the National Institute of Senior Centers (NISC, 1978), senior centers are based on the philosophy that aging is a normal developmental process, that human beings need peers with whom they can interact and who are available as a source of encouragement and support, and that adults have the right to have a voice in determining matters in which they have a vital interest. As such, the center is a major community institution that is geared to maintain good mental health and to prevent breakdown and deterioration of mental, emotional, and social functioning of the older person (p. 5). Similarly, the NCOA (2005, para. 3) defines a senior center as a place where older adults come together for services and activities that reflect their experience and skills, respond to their diverse needs and interests, enhance their dignity, support their independence, and encourage their involvement in and with the center and community.

As senior centers emerged as a significant community resource for older adults, the Older Americans Act (OAA) played an important role in the creation and support of more facilities. In the original Act (1965), funds were available for senior center operations under Title IV, and dollars under Title III supported many of the programs offered at these sites.[1] The 1973 amendments of the OAA created a new Title V under which senior centers became the focal point of providing services to older adults. These amendments introduced the term *multipurpose senior center* and provided funding for renovation or acquisition of facilities to be used as multipurpose centers—community organizations designed to be the center for developing and delivering a range of services. Amendments in 1978 eliminated Title V and placed support for senior centers under Title III. In addition, the amendments required that, when feasible, Area Agencies on Aging (AAAs) designate a central point for the delivery of services and give special consideration to senior centers. In part because of this increased support for senior centers under the OAA, the number of senior centers increased dramatically. By the end of the 1970s, there were an estimated 6,000 to 7,000 centers. As funding for OAA programs in the 1980s flattened and declined, few additional legislative changes affected senior centers. In Title III under the OAA 2000 amendments, a *multipurpose center* was defined as

> a community facility for the organization and provision of a broad spectrum of services, which shall include, but are not limited to provision of health (including mental health), social, nutritional and educational services and the provision of facilities for recreational activities for older persons. (§ 102 [33])

---

[1]Unless noted otherwise, the history of senior centers comes from Krout (1989).

In 2005, the delegates of the White House Conference on Aging (2006) put forth the following resolutions and strategies to encourage the redesign of senior centers for broad appeal and community participation:

- Support an expanded role for senior centers as focal points for community-based services and civic engagement for senior centers as independent service through (a) combined service for all economic levels, cultural competence, and diversified populations and generations (volunteer opportunities, transportation, nutrition, etc.) and mental health services; and (b) NISC accreditation. (p. 115)

- Support efforts to modernize and upgrade facilities and programming that will attract and serve existing and new generations through (a) healthy aging—physical, emotional, and mental health services; (b) civic engagement to provide community support; and (c) design for all economic levels and capabilities. (p. 115)

- Impose a federal requirement that all 50 states, territories, and tribes establish statutes defining "multipurpose senior centers" as the community-based focal point for planning and coordination for the organization and provision for a broad spectrum of services suited to the diverse needs and interests of self-determining older persons. (p. 116)

- Create a separate and distinct title in OAA for multipurpose senior centers which are a system serving older adults, caregivers, and their families. (p. 116)

- Support policies and encourage efforts to create and expand opportunities and partnerships that integrate senior centers, health care systems, service providers, communities, business, and public and private organizations to serve culturally diverse populations across all social and economic lines. (p. 116)

The OAA reauthorization in 2006, however, did not contain language that would affect senior center operations. Although Title III monies fund senior centers, those dollars must also support the other programs designated under Title III. Krout (1990) notes that the average percentage of federal contributions to senior centers fell from 29% in 1982 to 19% in 1989. Currently, slightly more than half of all senior centers ($n = 5,900$) receive some funding from OAA monies; senior centers in 21 states receive less than 50% of their funding from OAA allocations (Administration on Aging [AoA], 2011d). Thus, many centers are funded entirely or in part by local nonprofit organizations; local, state, and federal governments; and charitable organizations such as the YMCA, United Way, and Catholic Charities.

USERS AND PROGRAMS

It is estimated that 15% of older adults participate in senior center activities annually (NCOA, 2005). Most of the research on senior centers during the past four decades has focused on identifying organizational characteristics of senior centers, characteristics of participants, and types of programs and services offered. As you will see in the review below, much of the research on demographic characteristics of senior center participants and the role these characteristics play in predicting senior center participation paints a somewhat contradictory picture. This is no doubt reflective of the fact that most of the research on senior centers uses local or state samples which reflect the diverse communities in which centers are located and the differences in the type of programs and activities provided by centers.

Characteristics of Senior Center Participants

Early studies of senior center participants reported equal percentages of female and male participants (Krout, 1983; Silvey, 1962; Storey, 1962), whereas more recent studies reveal that the majority of participants are women (Jellinek, Pardasani, & Sackman, 2010a; Krout, Cutler, & Coward, 1990; Strain, 2001; Turner, 2004). Early studies of senior center participants found that participants were primarily in their 60s (Harris & Associates, 1975; Storey, 1962). More recently, researchers have found that senior center participants are older than nonparticipants (Calsyn, Burger, & Roades, 1996; Jellinek et al., 2010a), and others have found a curvilinear relationship between age and senior center attendance, as those least likely to participate are the young-old and the old-old (Aday, 2003; Krout et al., 1990; Turner, 2004). When examining frequency of attendance and age, the results have been inconsistent. Strain (2001) found that, over a four-year period, there was no relationship between frequency of attendance and age. However, Miner, Logan, and Spitz (1993) found that frequency of attendance was related to age. Older participants were more likely to report that they attended the senior center frequently than were their younger counterparts, who were more likely to report rarely attending. There was no discernible pattern between age and attending senior centers "sometimes." Miner and colleagues concluded that observations by senior center directors that younger participants were interested only in occasional trips and special events appear to be supported by these findings. More recent research suggests that age of participants may be related to the model or programming of senior centers. Pardasani and Thompson (2010) found that senior centers that could be characterized as operating as a community center model offering more intergenerational programming reported that they are attracting younger participants, whereas centers with a focus on providing programs that support a continuum of care have seen an increase of older clientele over the age of 75. In summary, the research supports the notion that senior center participants are aging in place and that younger cohorts are not currently frequent users of senior center activities. This may change in the near future as senior centers have begun to actively recruit baby boomers. We will return to this issue later in the chapter when we discuss the future of senior centers.

Are older adults of color less likely to be senior center participants? Calsyn and Winter (1999) found that race was not a predictor of senior center participation. Other studies have found race to predict participation. Some researchers have found that older adults of color were less likely than their White counterparts to attend senior centers (Aday, 2003; Krout, 1987b, 1988; Leanse & Wagner, 1975). More recently, a citywide study of senior center participants in New York City found 47% of participants were African American, Hispanic, or Asian American, and 46% were White (with 7% not reporting; Jellinek et al., 2010a); interestingly, in the sample of nonparticipants among non-Caucasians, a larger percent of African Americans and Hispanics indicated they were nonparticipants. There may be some evidence that racial and ethnic group participation varies by geographic location of the center. A national sample of recreation and senior center directors were asked to estimate the percentage of their participants by ethnic group (Wacker & Blanding, 1994). Overall, older Blacks constituted an average of 8% of the participants, older Hispanics 5%, and Asian and Native Americans 2% each. The percentage of minority participants, however, varied across programs. For example, the percentages of older Black and Hispanic participants ranged from 0% to 95% and from 0% to 98%, respectively. Similar percentages were noted for older Asian Americans and Native Americans. These variations in participant characteristics may reflect the location of the center; senior centers located in neighborhoods having high numbers of older adults of color probably report higher percentages of minority users. Overall, older adults of color are underrepresented at most senior centers, except for those centers primarily serving them.

For Your Files: The Los Angeles Gay and Lesbian Center

The Los Angeles Gay and Lesbian Center serves lesbian, gay, bisexual, and transgender elders aged 50 and over. The Center's mission is successful aging in place. In this effort, the Center provides a broad array of social, educational, and support services to lesbian, gay, bisexual, and transgender (LGBT) seniors and baby boomers, all of which are free or low-cost. The program provides one-on-one case management to those in need of support and resources, including case management services and referrals related to affordable housing, benefits, home health assistance, bereavement, isolation and loneliness, as well as mental health and legal issues. The Center also provides more than 70 health and wellness activities, enrichment classes, monthly dinners, cultural excursions, educational seminars, and intergenerational programming to over a 1,000 seniors and boomers each year.

For more information, contact the Los Angeles Gay and Lesbian Center, 1125 N. McCadden Place, Los Angeles, CA 90038, 323-860-7322, or seniors@lagaycenter.org. http://www.laglc.org/

Health and functional status appear to differentiate users of senior centers from nonusers. Early studies (Hanssen et al., 1978, Harris & Associates, 1975) found that those with poor functional ability and poor health were less likely to attend. Cox and Monk (1990) found in their study of 282 senior centers in New York that only 10% of participants were classified by directors as frail. Similarly, in another study, only a small percentage of participants had a disability that required special programming accommodations (Wacker & Blanding, 1994). For example, an average of less than 9% of participants had physical disabilities or hearing impairments, 6% had visual impairments, and only 3% had cognitive impairments. Krout et al. (1990) also reported that older adults with fewer problems with activities of daily living were more likely to attend a senior center than were their less well counterparts, and Aday (2003) found that only 2.6% and 20.9% of senior center participants in seven states had self-rated health as poor or fair, respectively. Strain (2001) also found that those who had attended a senior center in the past six months had fewer Instrumental Activity of Daily Living (IADL) limitations than did nonparticipants. Most recently, Jellinek et al. (2010a) found that individuals with disabilities or needing assistance with walking were less likely to participate in senior center activities. One exception to these findings was a study by Miner et al. (1993). The authors found that frequency of attendance did not differ by functional ability; seniors with disabilities who had ever attended a senior center participated as frequently as did their healthier counterparts.

They concluded that, although functional disability may make a difference in whether older adults ever attend a senior center, it does not influence how often they attend. Strain (2001) also found that changes in participation patterns of senior center participants over time were not related to the changes in IADL limitations. The overall the majority of studies, however, conclude that participants are less likely to have physical limitations than nonparticipants.

Socioeconomic status measures of education and income have been found in some studies to be predictors of senior center attendance. Attendees are more likely than nonattenders to have lower incomes (Calsyn et al., 1996; Krout, 1990; Strain, 2001), and it is has been suggested that those with higher incomes have other, more expensive, alternatives for leisure activities and supportive services (Miner et al., 1993) and are less likely to participate in senior center activities. Demographic data of participants suggest that senior centers serve neither the very rich nor very poor but are attracting older adults whose incomes are lower than those of the older adult population in general (D. A. Wagner, 1995a). When examining the relationship between education and senior center participation, Krout et al. (1990) found participation was highest among those with mid-levels of education, and Jellinek et al. (2010a) found 37% of participants reported their education level as high school or less, whereas nonparticipants with postgraduate education were less likely to participate. In contrast, two other studies found no relationship between education and attendance (Krout, 1991; Strain, 2001). Other participant characteristics associated with senior center attendance have been higher levels of social interaction (Krout et al., 1990), having a desire to have more contact with friends and family, size of family networks (Di & Berman 2000), living alone (Aday, 2003; Jellinek et al., 2010a; Strain, 2001), and being unmarried (Calsyn et al., 1996; Di & Berman, 2000; Jellinek et al., 2010a; Turner, 2004). Finally, lack of attendance may also reflect lifelong patterns of participation in voluntary or community associations (Krout, 1989).

In summary, although findings from national, state, and local data are somewhat contradictory, we can make some generalizations about the typical senior center participant, who is generally a woman in her middle 70s, of lower to middle economic status, living alone, White, in good physical health, and with slightly less than a high school education.

BARRIERS TO SENIOR CENTER PARTICIPATION

What factors prevent older adults from attending senior centers? Some evidence suggests that many older adults living in the community are simply unaware of the different activities and services offered at senior centers (J. Walker, Bisbee, Porter, & Flanders, 2004). Indeed, Krout (1981, 1982, 1984) found that, although a high percentage of respondents were aware of the existence of senior centers, nonparticipants knew little about senior center programming. Transportation can also be a factor in participation. Transportation problems and lack of transportation services to and from senior centers has been found to be a hindrance to senior center attendance (Jellinek et al., 2010a; Jirovec, Erich, & Sanders, 1989; Ralston, 1982; J. Walker et al., 2004).

Researchers have identified other personal perceptions that inhibit senior center participation. Nonusers often report that they believe senior centers are for those who are "old and frail," or say they are reluctant to attend because they do not want to be labeled as a "senior citizen" or, generally speaking, senior centers were not meant for them (Jellinek et al., 2010a; Leanse & Wagner, 1975; J. Walker et al., 2004). Other nonusers perceive that participants are cliquish and unwelcoming, that they are uncomfortable because the groups attending the center are either too small or too large, or that there was a lack of interest in attending (Jellinek et al., 2010a; J. Walker et al., 2004).

For Your Files: Manzano Mesa Multigenerational Center

The Center for all Ages Manzano Mesa Multigenerational Center in Albuquerque, first opened in 2002, is for seniors, youth, and the entire community. Activities are especially designed for seniors and youth, and include everything you can find at a senior center as well as activities for youth aged six and up. Programs for older adults include health screening and promotion, senior fitness programs, legal services, estate planning, and many other classes and activities. The Manzano Multigenerational Center provides both breakfast and lunch for seniors. Services for youth include both before- and after-school care for children, as well as many recreational and cultural programs.

For more information, contact the center at 505-275-8731; http://www.cabq.gov/seniors/centers/manzano-mesa-multigenerational-center.

MODELS OF SENIOR CENTERS

As senior centers sprang up across the nation in different social contexts and locations, they developed different organizational structures. Taietz (1976) was the first to identify the different models of senior centers. On the basis of his study of senior centers across the country, he suggested that centers could be categorized as based on either a social agency model or a voluntary organizational model. Senior centers based on a social agency model have programs designed to meet the needs of older adults, with those who are poor and disengaged being the likely participants. In contrast, the voluntary organization model assumes that older adults who are more active in voluntary organizations and who have strong attachments to the community are the ones who will participate in senior centers. Krout (1989), however, argued that such a dichotomous distinction might not accurately reflect the wide variation of senior centers and their participants. For example, although some participants attend senior centers for recreational and educational opportunities, they may have other unmet nutritional and health needs.

Moreover, the model that a senior center adopts may be linked to its geographical location. For example, rural senior centers differ from urban centers in several organizational characteristics: They are likely to have smaller budgets, fewer paid staff, and fewer resources (Krout, 1987a). Thus community size makes a significant difference in program planning activities, interagency networking, and the types of services and activities that senior centers offer. Centers located in smaller communities are less likely to create new programs, work with other aging and nonaging organizations in joint projects, and make referrals to other agencies (Wacker & Blanding, 1994). Not surprisingly, programs in larger communities are able to offer a wider range of services, including support groups, outreach, and job and employment counseling. The same pattern holds true with activities: Rural centers are less likely than centers located in urban areas to offer many cultural, educational, social, recreational, and outdoor activities.

More recently, Pardasani and Thompson (2010) analyzed data from a national study (Pardasani, Sporre, & Thompson, 2009) of senior center directors ($n = 147$) for the NISC to identify emerging models of senior centers. Using the directors' responses, they identified the following six models based on the most significant center programmatic characteristics: (a) community center, (b) wellness center, (c) lifelong learning/arts, (d) continuum of care/transitions, (e) entrepreneurial model, and (f) café model. The models, defining characteristics, impact, and examples are presented in Exhibit 7.1. Although the centers in this study often exhibit programmatic characteristics of more than one model, the identified models provide an organizing framework for senior centers as they consider how to adjust their operations in the future. Moreover, because the focus of each model is different (e.g., wellness, lifelong learning), the impact on participants' social psychological and physical well-being and on the larger community will likely vary. As we will discuss future challenges facing senior centers in more detail at the end of the chapter, Pardasani and Thompson's research confirms that directors of senior centers are reexamining how to adapt to the changing landscape of our aging society. Although more research is needed to verify these new senior center models, it is an important first step in understanding how centers are embracing and advancing innovative programming.

Exhibit 7.1   Innovative and Emerging Models of Senior Centers

Model Type/ *Impact*	Defining Characteristics	Example(s)
Community Center *Increase participation by young-old; far-reaching community impact*	• Target population: children, youth, adults and active older adults • Mission/programming focus: multigenerational; recreational, educational, cultural, fitness, nutritional, and intergenerational programming; grandparent caregiver support programs; has state-of-the-art recreational facilities • Location: one main site • Funding: primarily from public funds and membership fees	• Fort Collins Senior Center, Fort Collins, CO • Manzano Mesa Multi-generational Center, Albuquerque, NM
Wellness Center *Increase participation by young-old; impact on other providers via focus on collaboration and coordinated programming*	• Target population: active older adults age 50+ • Mission/programming focus: improve health and well-being through evidence-based health promotion models; recreational and exercise/fitness programming; health education and screenings; has state-of-the-art health and fitness center and use of innovative technology • Location: one main site • Funding: membership dues and service fees	• Baltimore County Senior Centers, Baltimore, MD • OPC Center, Rochester, MI

Model Type/ *Impact*	Defining Characteristics	Example(s)
Lifelong Learning/ Arts *Increase participation by young-old; impact on other providers via increased coordinated programming*	• Target population: active older adults age 50+ • Mission/programming focus: intellectual stimulation, personal growth, and enhanced quality of life; continuing education and knowledge acquisition through workshops, courses, and travel programs; recreational and health education; culturally and linguistically diverse programming • Location: may have multiple sites in partnership with other community organizations • Funding: public and consumer fees	• The New Center for Learning, Five Towns Senior Center, Woodmere, NY
Continuum of Care/ Transitions *Increase participation by adults aged 75+; impact on other providers via structured system of linkages to continuum of community care services*	• Target population: older adults age 50+; specific programs for frail and homebound elders • Mission/programming focus: comprehensive services and programs that meet the gradual and changing needs of older adults as they "age-in community"; act as focal points of coordination of information, access, and service delivery; recreational and health education programming; meals, adult day care, and respite; homebound support services and medical transportation • Location: main site and often multiple sites in partnership with other community organizations; home-based services • Funding: service fees, private insurance, and limited public funding	• Avenidas Village, Avenidas, Palo Alto, CA • The Senior Center, Senior Center Plus Program, Ann Arundel County, MD
Entrepreneurial Center *Tends to attract more men, newly retired, those interested in civic engagement; impact on other providers via focus on collaboration and coordinated programming*	• Target population: active older adults age 50+ • Mission/programming focus: civic engagement, volunteerism; create programs that generate income; recreational and health education programming; structured programming that provides participants training, placement, and coordination services for community volunteering • Location: one main site, new or remodeled, that is contemporary, "hip" • Funding: philanthropic funding rather than public funding; generating earned income	• Lou Walker Senior Center, Lithonia, GA

(Continued)

Exhibit 7.1 (Continued)

Model Type/ *Impact*	Defining Characteristics	Example(s)
Café Program *Attracts broad range of older adults*	• Target population: active older adults age 50+ • Mission/programming focus: a community gathering place open to community members; non-age-segregated; limited range of recreational and health education programming, performing arts, information and referral; café-style meals • Location: one main site • Funding: service and meal fees; private fund-raising	• Mather LifeWays, Chicago, IL • Borchardt Cyber Café, St. Barnabas Senior Center, Los Angeles, CA

Source: Pardasani et al. (2009) and Pardasani and Thompson (2010).

Best Practice: Serving Rural Seniors

Weld County covers 4,004 square miles in north-central Colorado—an area larger than Rhode Island, Delaware, and the District of Columbia combined. The challenge was how to set up and support senior programs in the county's 31 smaller communities, which range from 99 to 19,009 in population. The solution began in March 1975 after a VISTA volunteer had spent three months assessing both the needs of the rural Weld seniors and the barriers to providing services to them. Without exception, the response from the agencies was the same: "Weld County is so large we simply do not have the staff to do outreach work in the rural communities. Everything is concentrated in Greeley; we have nothing in the small towns."

With this information in hand, a plan was developed and approved by the county commissioners to bring the services and the seniors in the rural areas together. Small-town governments were encouraged to hire a senior aide for 20 hours per week with the promise that the county would pay the aide's salary through an employment and training program for the first year. At the end of the first year, 11 senior aide sites were in place. Today, 21 sites are active, most fully supported by their towns.

Through the years, the senior aide program has grown not only in terms of numbers of sites in place but also in its program offerings. Originally, most senior aides worked out of their homes, offering simple information and referral activities. Today, nearly all the aides work in viable senior centers; some aides have become full-time town employees; and all use volunteers in their centers. Many have new, modern centers and offer a respectable range of recreational outings, educational classes, regular senior meals, and intergenerational programs.

A unique and successful aspect of this program is the monthly half-day training meetings that provide a forum for training and information exchange. The meetings continue to this day and rotate among the participating towns, giving each aide a better understanding of the similarities and differences among the communities. A technical advisor, provided by the AAA, helps the senior aides develop their monthly agendas. These meetings include a wide range of informative programs designed to help the aides provide up-to-date information and quality senior services to their communities. The senior aging network uses the monthly meetings to get the word out about their services and how to access them. The advisor also travels to each town to provide one-on-one technical assistance when needed. In 1980, the senior aides incorporated under the name WELDCO'S, Inc. They applied for general fund dollars from the county commissioners and have received a yearly allocation that they divide among themselves. Aides use the funds to help pay utilities, buy craft materials, pay for a fundraising event, purchase equipment, and take seniors on outings. Records show that the program generates more than 750 volunteer hours annually for the senior centers and their communities. Community volunteers, coordinated by the aides, also assist with the overwhelming transportation needs generated in this large, rural county. The program continues to grow and thrive, providing valuable assistance and opportunities for seniors in small towns.

For more information, contact Weld County Area Agency on Aging, P.O. Box 1805, Greeley, CO 80632; phone: 970-346-6950, ext. 6132; www.weldaaa.org.

PROGRAMS OFFERED AT SENIOR CENTERS

The variety of services and activities offered by senior centers can be classified in several ways. NISC classified senior center activities on the basis of participant characteristics. For example, senior centers can provide services to community institutions, group services such as education and group social work, and individual services such as health maintenance and counseling (Lowy & Doolin, 1985). In contrast, Krout (1985a) distinguished between activities and services offered through senior centers. *Activities* are programs offered by the center for personal enrichment and enjoyment, whereas *services* are designed to relieve or prevent problems for at-risk older adults. Although the type and number of services and activities offered by senior centers have expanded through the years, centers have always offered creative activities such as arts and crafts; recreational activities such as cards, bingo, parties, and dances; and services such as information, referral, and meals (Krout, 1985a; Leanse & Wagner, 1975; Wacker & Blanding, 1994). Although the availability of services and activities offered at senior centers will vary by the location and size of the center, the services and activities likely to be available at most local centers are listed in Exhibit 7.2.

Krout's (1985a) national survey of senior centers reported that more than 75% of centers offered information and referral, outreach and transportation services, meals, health education, and screening. More than half of the centers offered home-delivered meals, friendly visiting, telephone reassurance, consumer information, crime prevention, financial/tax services, housing information, legal assistance, and assistance with Social Security and Medicare. Less than one quarter offered adult day care services, job training and placement, protective services, and peer counseling.

A comparison of Krout's (1985a) data with an early study conducted in 1975 by Leanse and Wagner revealed that the types of services offered by senior centers have diversified and grown, especially services such as home-delivered meals, classes and lectures, and active recreational activities (Krout, 1989a). Findings from a national sample of both senior centers and recreation programs serving older adults were similar to Krout's (1985a) findings in that the majority of senior centers offered health services such as fitness classes,

Exhibit 7.2   Types of Services/Programs and Activities Offered at Senior Centers

Recreational opportunities	Intergenerational programming
Health and wellness	Information and referral
Educational opportunities	Support groups and counseling
Meals and nutritional education	Social and community action opportunities
Transportation	Employment assistance
Arts and humanities	Volunteer activities
Employment assistance	

Source: Adapted from Wagner (D. L. 1995a).

blood pressure checks, vision and hearing tests, and health education, and provided meals, transportation, and outreach (Wacker & Blanding, 1994). Fewer than half offered housing support/assistance, employment counseling, crisis counseling, or adult day care. Although senior centers were providing the usual craft and social activities, few were providing outdoor recreation activities or more physical activities such as swimming, golf, and tennis. This study also revealed a trend in the inclusion of intergenerational programs: 70% of senior centers offered some type of intergenerational activity. Examples of intergenerational programming included lunch buddies, whereby older adults are paired with schoolchildren to eat lunch together twice a month, pen pal programs, and a gift shop for kids at the senior center. Jellinek et al. (2010b) asked New York City's senior center participants ($n = 3,200$) and directors ($n = 150$) to identify from a list of 79 programs and services the ones offered at their respective centers. Listed in Exhibit 7.3 are the programs and services grouped by the percentage of centers offering the programs—50% or more of the centers, 25% to 49%, and less than 25%. The results indicate that recreational and health and fitness programs continue to be offered by greater percent of centers; however, a noticeable percentage are also offering social service programs such as care assistance (75%), telephone reassurance (43%), transportation (43%), and housing assistance (43%).

Exhibit 7.3   New York City Senior Centers Offering Various Programs and Services (percentage)

PROGRAM TYPE	Percentage Offered		
	50% or more	**25%–49%**	**<25%**
Recreational	Trips	Painting or sculpture	Creative writing
	Parties	Dominoes	Book club
	Bingo	Drama	Gardening
	Movies	Choral group	Poetry club

PROGRAM TYPE	Percentage Offered		
	50% or more	**25%–49%**	**<25%**
	Dancing Cards Cultural events Discussion groups Knitting, crocheting, sewing Arts	Billiards Intergenerational programs Mahjong Foreign language classes	Beauty parlor Storytelling Bowling Therapeutic arts Fashion show Chinese chess Box office Piano lessons Radio station Spa Go
Health and Fitness	Meals and nutrition Education Walking club Health screening Blood pressure screening Yoga TaiChi Programs with local medical providers	Aerobics Health fairs Evidence-based health programs Vision testing Alzheimer's programs Hearing testing	Annual mammography Cancer screening Massage therapy Weightwatchers Weight training AA meetings Tennis Programs for blind seniors Programs for deaf seniors
Social Services	Case assistance	Transportation Telephone reassurance Housing assistance Friendly visiting Counseling Tax assistance Support groups Assistance to immigrants	Legal services Food pantry Caregiver services Escort for chores
Education and Other	Volunteer opportunities Computer classes	Advocacy/social action Educational classes HIV/sexuality education ESL/citizenship classes	HIV testing College-level courses

Source: Jellinek et al. (2010a).

Wacker and Blanding (1994) examined the relationship between programmatic charac-teristics and the age of center participants. Centers with a higher percentage of adults over 70 years of age compared with the percentage of participants under age 70 offered significantly different types of programs. For example, programs with older participants were likely to offer more health-related services (e.g., health education, blood pressure checks, vision and hearing tests) and support services (e.g., nutrition, outreach, transportation, legal aid) than were programs with a younger clientele. More research is needed to determine whether the participant profile influenced programmatic differences or whether the programs offered drew a particular type of participant.

Not surprisingly, differences in programming exist among centers with varying budgets and locations. Centers with larger budgets and more staff are likely to offer a higher number of services and activities (Krout, 1987a; Wacker & Blanding, 1994), and there appears to be a relationship between budget size and location. Two studies by Krout (1984, 1987a) found that budgets of senior centers in rural communities were smaller than budgets of centers located in more urban areas.

Senior centers also serve as a focal point for services and, in many cases, as a source of information and referral for participants. A handful of studies reported that those attending senior centers believed that their center was a source of information about other community services and played an important intermediary role between themselves and other service providers (see West, Delisle, Simard, & Drouin, 1996). Programs with predominantly older participants referred their participants to support services and long-term care services more often than did programs with predominantly younger participants. For example, more referrals were made to legal aid and nutrition programs, as well as to case management services, nursing homes, home health agencies, and adult day care programs. Thus, as a source of information and referral, senior centers must be aware of a wide range of community services and must respond to changing needs as participants age in place in their programs.

Best Practice: Innovative Programming at Senior Centers

NISC, in collaboration with the NCOA, identified a number of examples of innovative programming at senior centers across the country. Here are examples from two senior centers:

Town N Country Senior Center, Tampa, FL—Health Education

The Town N Country Senior Center serves 3,500 older adults annually and has worked to develop programs that offer their members reliable information and activities to help them manage and improve their own health. Here are some examples of health education programs offered at Town N Country:

- *Pack Your Bag* focuses on the importance of medication management and allows seniors to meet one-on-one with pharmacists to review their daily medications and supplements for potential interactions. (Sponsored by CVS/pharmacy.)

- *Patchwork of Hope Network* points patients with shingles and postherpetic neuralgia, or after-shingles pain, to resources that help. (Sponsored by Endo Pharmaceuticals.)

- *A Look Within: What to Know, What to Do, What to Ask* highlights the importance of MRI safety for people with pacemakers. (Sponsored by Medtronic.)

For more information, contact the Town N Country Senior Center, 7606 Paula Drive, Tampa, FL 33615, 813-873-6336.

Madison Senior Center, Madison, WI—Keeping Older Adults Engaged

The Madison Senior Center has worked to engage older adults by providing volunteer opportunities that are challenging, collaborative, and designed specifically for each individual. Over the last 15 years, the Center has developed and refined processes for volunteer recruitment, candidate application and selection, assessment of senior skills and experience, and focused training materials. Using team leaders to train, place, and support volunteers, the Center now has over 300 volunteers of all ages and provides 8,000 hours of service annually.

For more information, contact the Madison Senior Center, 330 West Mifflin Street, Madison, WI 53703, 608-266-6581; http://www.cityofmadison.com/seniorCenter/volunteer/index.cfm.

Source: NCOA (2010a).

In an attempt to promote formal, national quality-control standards for senior centers, NISC instituted an accreditation process in 1998. The accreditation process is based on a peer review process, an onsite visit, adherence to standards issued by NISC, and a recommendation to accredit by the National Senior Center Accreditation Board (NCOA, 1998). As of 2011, over 200 senior centers met the accreditation self-assessment requirements and peer review process (NCOA, 2011c). In addition, some states have also instituted a certification process. For example, North Carolina has developed a certification process that designates senior centers as Centers of Merit or Centers of Excellence based on the scope and quality of outreach and access to services, programs and activities, planning, evaluation, input from older adults, staffing, operations, and the physical plant (North Carolina Division of Aging and Adult Services, 2011). Currently, 48% of the state's senior centers are certified as either centers of "Merit" or "Excellence."

Across the Globe: Hikarigaoka Senior Center, Nerima, Tokyo, Japan

The Hikarigaoka Senior Center serves residents 60 years of age or older living in Nerima City, which is a ward (or neighborhood) in Tokyo, Japan. Similar to many senior centers in the United States, the Hikarigaoka Senior Center offers a number of educational and recreational programs and services such as

- table tennis, Mahjong competition, chess, Go board game, and dance;
- oral health education, introductory course on using mobile phones, first aid and emergency care, classical Japanese literature, cooking classes (for men), dementia education, pottery classes, and karaoke competition; and
- films, mandolin concerts, and senior circle arts festival.

For more information, visit the Hikarigaoka Senior Center's website at http://www.nerima-swf.jp/service/tsusyo/hikarigaokakourei/index.html.

ADDRESSING DIVERSITY

As discussed in Chapter 1, the percentage of older adults of color has been rising steadily and is expected to increase from 19.6% of the older adult population over age 65 to 41.5% in 2050 (Federal Interagency Forum on Aging-Related Statistics, 2010). In addition, gay/lesbian elderly are becoming more "visible," and it is estimated that between 3% and 8% of elders are LGBT (Cahill, South, & Spade, 2000).

As discussed previously, the general pattern of senior center attendance by nonmajority older adults remains low. Barriers to participation can be attributed to system or community barriers such as lack of transportation or geographical segregation. In many communities, both large and small, neighborhoods are often segregated by socioeconomic class and race, thus making attending senior centers in other neighborhoods difficult. Indeed, senior centers located in urban neighborhoods tend to have elders from specific ethnic or racial backgrounds, whereas participant diversity among suburban centers is more difficult to achieve.

Organizational characteristics such as lack of culturally aware programming or culturally competent staff (E. Kim, Kleiber, & Kropf, 2001; Pardasani, 2004a, 2004b) or individual barriers such as a perceived lack of a welcoming environment by a majority of participants can act as barriers to participation. A history of discrimination no doubt makes it difficult for many older persons to feel comfortable attending senior centers when they are in the minority. To address the issue of increasing diversity among senior center participants and to provide programs that appeal to and support the unique needs of these subpopulations, two approaches or models of centers have emerged. As shown in the model in Exhibit 7.4, one approach to addressing diversity has been the Open + Targeted Model where the older adults targeted for participation represent the entire senior community. Increasing diversity among members is addressed via outreach efforts to specific subpopulations within the senior community or to incorporate the unique elements of ethnic diversity within the center's programming. An example of this approach is the San Francisco Senior Center, which has a mission to serve seniors who are economically and ethnically diverse, who are well or frail, and who live alone, with family, or with caregivers. Although the senior center targets the entire senior population in San Francisco, there are programs targeting specific groups such as the Chinese Outreach Program and the Senior Literacy Project. Another example of the Open + Targeted Model is the Pimmitt Hills Senior Center in Falls Church, Virginia, that identifies itself as a multicultural center whose participants include elders from China, Taiwan, Iran, and South America. In addition to offering exercise, leisure, educational, and arts activities, Pimmitt Hills incorporates other programming such as English as a second language classes, Persian calligraphy, Iranian cultural music and dance, Chinese calligraphy, and an American cultural seminar.

The second model or approach to addressing the diversity among elders in a community is the Targeted Model, where senior centers serve a specific subpopulation of elders and provide programming and services that address the unique needs of that group. Examples of the Targeted Model are the Yu-Ai Kai Japanese American Community Senior Service in San Jose, California; the Hispanic Senior Center in Cleveland, Ohio; and the Korean American Senior Center in Chicago. The programming offered to participants is more specific to the needs of the subgroup the center is targeting. For example, the Korean American Senior Center in Chicago provides culturally and linguistically isolated Korean American seniors with support and assistance, culturally familiar meals, adult literacy and translation assistance, cultural arts, and citizenship classes, and delivers home care and counseling services through culturally sensitive staff. Over 100 Korean elders partake in the noontime meal

Exhibit 7.4   Two Models of Serving Diverse Older Adults in Senior Centers

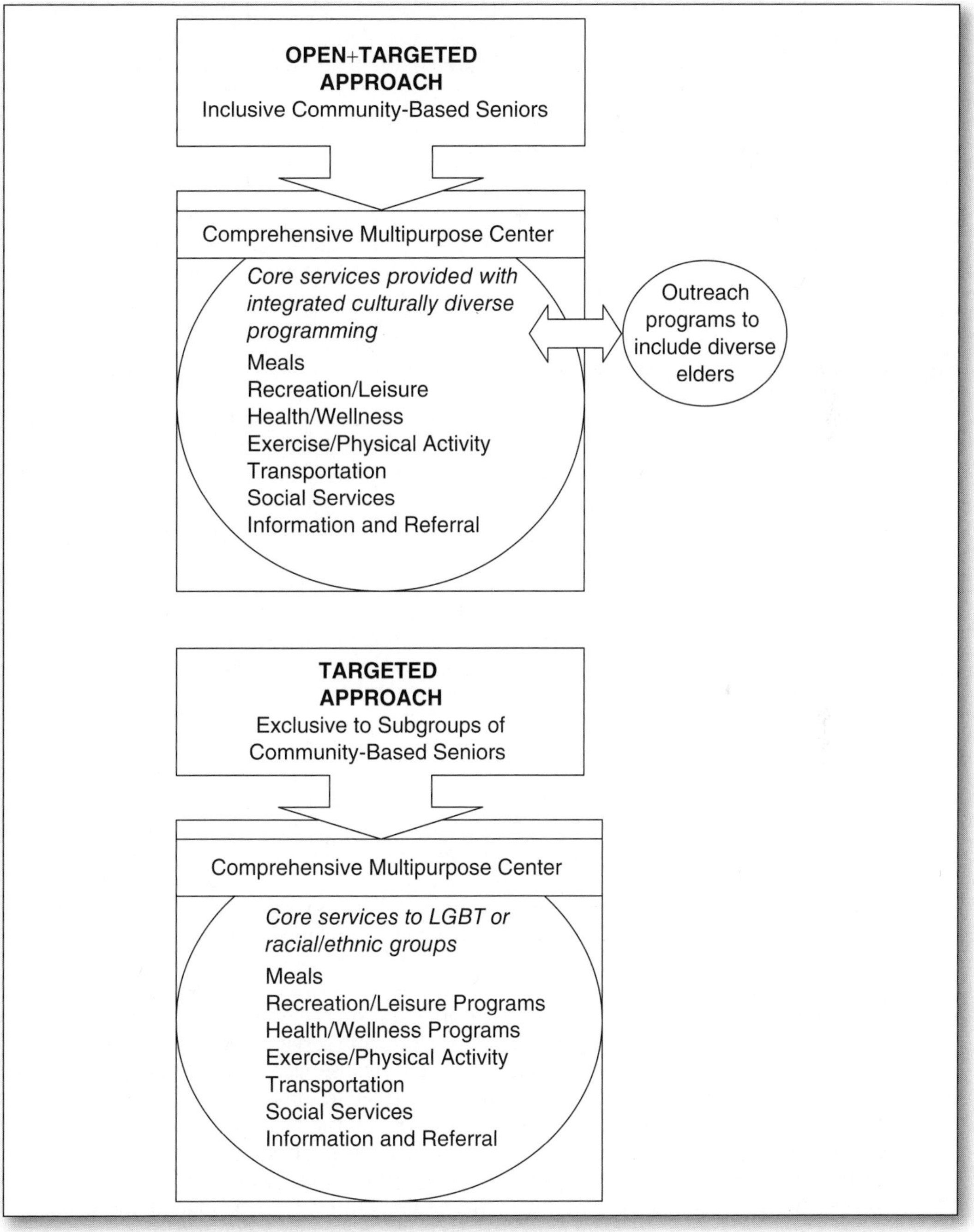

OPEN+TARGETED APPROACH
Inclusive Community-Based Seniors

Comprehensive Multipurpose Center

Core services provided with integrated culturally diverse programming
Meals
Recreation/Leisure
Health/Wellness
Exercise/Physical Activity
Transportation
Social Services
Information and Referral

Outreach programs to include diverse elders

TARGETED APPROACH
Exclusive to Subgroups of Community-Based Seniors

Comprehensive Multipurpose Center

Core services to LGBT or racial/ethnic groups
Meals
Recreation/Leisure Programs
Health/Wellness Programs
Exercise/Physical Activity
Transportation
Social Services
Information and Referral

every day. Another example is the LGBT Senior Center in Cleveland that convenes twice a week at the Lesbian and Gay Community Center in Cleveland and offers social events, fitness programs, and lunch; or the Gay & Lesbian Center Village at Ed Gould Plaza in Hollywood, California, which offers support and counseling as well as social and educational events. As our older adult population becomes increasingly diverse, senior centers will have to determine the approach or model that best serves all the elders in their communities.

CHALLENGES FOR SENIOR CENTERS

Senior centers provide older adults with a place to pursue leisure activities, to socialize with others, and to receive important health, social, and educational services and information. As the United States experiences social and demographic changes, senior centers will face a number of challenges adapting to this changing environment.

Who Will Senior Centers Serve in the Future?

Senior centers, with their important historic mission of being the focal point of community programs and services for older adults, are now faced with trying to serve a diverse generational mix of older adults of young-old and recently retired to the oldest old, all of whom differ from one another in a number of ways. Current senior center participants, who are in their mid to late 70s and older, have a history of joining community groups, may have limited leisure and recreation choices, and have different leisure and recreation preferences from their younger counterparts. The "greatest generation" born in the 1920s and 1930s currently composes the majority of senior center participants and as a cohort have a history of joining clubs and organizations. Recent work by Putnam (2000) has brought to our attention the fact that membership and participation in a variety of local and civic organizations has been declining at an accelerated rate during the past 25 years. Between 1970 and 1990, average attendance by Americans at some type of monthly club meeting has fallen off by almost 60%. The fact that many senior participants are "aging in place" at senior centers established in the mid-1970s is reflective of a generation with a long history of civic involvement, whereas their children and grandchildren are much less engaged in most forms of community life. The difference can be summed up this way: Fewer baby boomers belong to a bowling league compared with their parents; however, there is an increase in number of boomers bowling in a nonleague setting. Thus, senior centers will have to look to ways to re-engage and connect with baby boomers that have grown up with a different concept of group association and membership and do not have the same pattern of joining community organizations as did their parents.

In addition, senior centers will need to determine how best to serve the different programmatic needs of both the current older participants and the younger baby boomers. Senior centers have historically offered an array of program and services that may be seen as more traditional in nature (e.g., bingo, pool and billiards, meal services). To be more responsive to baby boomer interests, senior centers are adjusting programmatic offerings to match baby boomers recreation and leisure interests. Younger cohorts who will be recruited to attend senior center activities will carry with them leisure and recreation interests that will no doubt differ from those of the current cohort of older participants. Some possible programmatic changes might include incorporating the latest technology for information and entertainment; acting as brokers for arranging individual leisure pursuits, including adventure leisure activities and eco-tourism; changing food programs to accommodate a wider variety of discerning tastes; and extending hours of operation to include evenings and weekends. To attract a more active, more health-conscious cohort of older adults, many senior centers are reconstituting themselves into "vital aging" centers that foster self-development and intellectually challenging opportunities (e.g., language courses, cooking, financial management, lectures, exhibits) and health education and wellness (including personal trainers and public health and nutrition consultants; MacNeil, 2001; Marken, 2005). Others suggest that providing opportunities to engage in altruistic activities, civic engagement, and intergenerational activities will also be attractive to a new generation of older adults (Eaton & Salari, 2005; Marken, 2005; A. L. Williams, Haber, Weaver, & Freeman, 1998; D. L. Wagner, 1995b).

Hostetler (2011) characterizes baby boomers as wanting a more individualize approach that would allow them to choose among a number of individual lifestyle opportunities including travel, leisure, creative pursuits, continuing education, and volunteering. Addressing the different desires of baby boomers will create some challenges for senior centers. One concern is that by catering solely to the needs of baby boomers, senior centers will become more like health or country clubs with a fragmented array of choices that promote autonomous, individual lifestyles and do not promote a sense of community or generational exchange among participants. In addition, altering programming to cater to the interests of baby boomers means that senior centers will also have to determine how to serve their oldest-old participants who are more frail. Unfortunately, there is a dearth of information about how senior centers currently serve at-risk older adults, the impact of involving at-risk older persons with well participants, and how at-risk older adults can successfully be recruited in senior center activities (Krout, 1993b). Cox and Monk (1990) also point out that if senior centers are going to include frail elders in their programs, they must receive assistance from other agencies in obtaining diagnostic, program, and service resources. They found that senior center directors perceived that the well participants would be resistant to including impaired older persons into their programs. Several directors in their study reported being concerned about becoming "babysitters" for nursing home residents.

The last issue that senior centers are addressing as they work to attract baby boomers is the retooling of the image associated with senior centers. Research has clearly established that baby boomers are reluctant to join senior centers because "senior" centers overtly identify participants as being an older adult in a youth-oriented society (J. Walker et al., 2004) and because of the negative social stigma of aging often linked to senior centers as places where knitting and bingo serve an aged membership. Thus, many senior centers have changed their names and have eliminated the word *senior* from their titles. In a survey of 244 senior center directors, 63% were in favor of changing the name *senior center* (Kelley, 2005, cited in NCOA, 2006). Some communities have already made the name change. Senior centers in Lincoln, Nebraska, are now called ActivAge Centers (Lincoln Area Agency on Aging, 2006). It is likely that this trend will increase in the coming years as senior centers move to "reinvent" their images. Of course, not everyone is in favor of moving away from using the term senior center. Using senior center in the name clearly identifies it as a place for older adults, and thus increases the likelihood that community members will recognize the purpose of the organization.

Hostetler (2011) sums up the dilemma faced by senior centers this way:

> [Senior centers] are called upon to serve at least two distinct groups of clientele, separated by age and cohort (and often by socioeconomic status), while also combating ageist stereotypes. Although many of the programs and services likely to attract aging baby boomers are expensive (to centers and/or senior "customers"), ignoring this demographic is not a viable option. But when senior centers target

younger seniors by counteracting stereotypes, they ironically risk reinforcing the same ageist beliefs about at least certain groups or cohorts of older adults (e.g., by marginalizing or even denigrating traditional senior center activities like bingo). (p. 174)

How Will Senior Centers Respond to Diversity Among Seniors?

How will senior centers respond to the increasingly diverse elderly population in their communities? Which model should communities embrace to accommodate this growing diversity—the Open + Targeted Model or the Targeted Model? Clearly, research is needed that measures the individual and organizational benefits of each type of model. However, one way we can begin to think about how senior centers are organized to address diversity is to employ the social capital framework (Putnam, 2000), which refers to understanding the social connections that are created within our communities and organizations. Two concepts of social capital that are germane to our discussion are the dimensions of bonding and bridging. *Bonding* refers to networks that are, by choice or necessity, inward looking and reinforces exclusive social identities among homogenous groups. Senior centers that can be characterized as Targeted Models, such as those which serve exclusive subgroups of older adults of color or LGBT elders, have a high degree of bonding among their members and provide those within this social network with an environment in which they feel welcome and where they receive both practical and emotional support. *Bridging* characterizes social networks that are outward looking and encompass people across diverse social divides such as race and social class, yet who share broadly similar demographic characteristics (Woolcock, 2001). Senior centers that fit the Open + Targeted Model could be considered to have a high degree of social bridging. Bridging outcomes include increased levels of trust and reciprocity, and serve to build connections between diverse heterogeneous groups. As Halpern (2005) notes, both bridging and bonding have different types of benefits, but a social network based too much on one or the other is likely to be a disadvantage to individuals and to communities. According to Halpern, a healthy and effective community needs a blend of both forms of social capital. Interestingly, there is some evidence to suggest that if particular social and ethnic groups have protected enclaves where bonding can occur, they will be more likely to form bridges with people who are very different from themselves. If senior centers can organize themselves around the concepts of bonding and bridging, they may be able to more effectively address the cultural diversity that exists within their communities. Senior centers must consider offering culturally diverse meals and activities, increasing staff sensitivity, and dealing with issues of inclusion by the majority group (Ralston, 1991). Just as U.S. society continues to struggle with racial segregation and racism within many of its cities, senior centers will no doubt be confronted with these same issues as they strive to be more inclusive of minority elders.

The Senior Center of the Future

So what will senior centers look like in the future? Although Schoeffler (1995) argues that, at a minimum, every senior center must provide information and referral services and be used as an intake location for delivering other community services, it is hard to know for certain what form or function senior centers will embrace in the coming years. But what is certain is that if senior centers wish to continue to be effective places, they must be flexible and adapt to the changing natures of our communities and elderly population by developing new models and approaches that serve both current and future older adults without unintentionally marginalizing older participants. Conducting frequent needs assessments and hiring staff trained in gerontology will be critical to maintaining the viability and relevancy of senior centers in the coming years and to meeting the challenges that lie ahead. In the near future, senior centers will be challenged to respond to the needs and demands of a new generation of older adults. Perhaps, as a result, senior centers of the future will bear little resemblance to the senior centers that currently exist.

CASE STUDY

Loneliness of a Caregiver

Alex, 70, laid down the natural science journal he was reading and thought for a moment about the turn of events in his life since his wife, Susan, had been diagnosed with Alzheimer's disease five years earlier. When he retired from the university and she from public school teaching, they had literally catapulted into a new life of worldwide travel and volunteer work with the local Friends of the Library and several conservation groups. Their life contained all the excitement and stimulation they had hoped it would when they began planning for their retirement. Hardly a day passed when they were not socializing with friends and other volunteers. Even Alex's lifelong lapses into depression had virtually disappeared.

At first, after Susan's diagnosis, they kept up a good front. Few of their social contacts realized what was happening to Susan. Now, he thought, everything has changed. Susan needed constant supervision. Other than their two daughters, who visited once a month, a couple of neighbors who dropped in to say hello, and the home health aide, Alex had few contacts with the outside world. It embarrassed him to think that twice in the last year, he had checked into emergency care at the hospital on orders from his doctor to have a psychiatric evaluation. Once, he was released; the other time, he was admitted for three days of psychiatric tests and counseling.

(Continued)

(Continued)

On his worst days, Alex wonders why he is alive. On better days, he's gratified that he is still able to take care of his wife. At the same time, he also wonders how much longer he can tolerate the isolation and loneliness. His psychiatrist and the home health aide are advising him to hire a respite worker to come in and sit with Susan a couple of afternoons a week so that he can visit the downtown senior center.

Case Study Questions

1. Why do you believe Alex's psychiatrist and his wife's home health aide are recommending that he connect with the local senior center? Cite research in this chapter that supports your response.

2. On the basis of what you know about Alex, what the literature says about the typical senior center participant, and theories of service use, what are the chances that Alex will follow the advice of his psychiatrist?

3. Describe a typical senior center offering of activities and services. Which of these offerings might be most beneficial to Alex? Why?

4. What barriers to becoming involved in the senior center do caregivers like Alex face? What other community support services could be helpful at this time?

5. Why do you think Alex and his wife did not join the senior center at the time of their retirement? What research supports your answer?

6. Describe a senior center program that would be most appealing to Alex.

7. What are the benefits to Alex, Susan, and society in helping Alex reconnect with his community?

LEARNING ACTIVITIES

1. Interview two or more people who are in their 50s about their leisure and recreational activities. Do they participate in casual or serious leisure activities? How do they think the pattern of their leisure activity will change as they become older or retire? Would they be interested in joining a senior center when they get older? Why or why not? What type of activities do they think senior centers should provide to people in their generation? If possible, interview a group with diversity based on gender, sexual orientation, income, and race.

2. Visit the local senior center. What activities are available there? What percentage of program offerings are for recreation? What percentage are social support services? On the basis of your

review, do you think this center acts as a focal point for older adults in your community? Using Pardasani and Thompson's (2010) models of senior centers, which model does your local senior center emulate?

3. Interview the director of a local senior center. What percentage of the participants are aging in place? What strategies has the center used to attract younger participants? What, in the director's opinion, is the most innovative program the center offers? If money were no object, what program or service would the center provide?

FOR MORE INFORMATION

International Resources

1. Age UK Lambeth: www.ageuk.org.lambeth/

   The Age UK Lambeth runs the Vida Walsh activity centre in the Brixton area in London and offers a range of activities for people over 55. The Centre offers a handyman service, befriending service, lesbian and gay groups, information and advice as well as classes, and recreation and leisure activities.

2. Seniors Activity Centres (SACs), Silver ACE,

   Singapore: www.ntueldercare.org.sg/

   SACs are neighborhood drop-in centers for seniors and offer social and recreational programs and activities, lunches, outings, and support services such as monitoring of frail elderly, guidance, advice and information, and a place to turn to for help in times of emergency.

3. Federation of Senior Citizens' Club in Kyoto, Japan: www.k-furouren.or.jp/

   There are over 110,000 Federation of Senior Citizens' Clubs in Japan with more than 7 million members. The Club in Kyoto offers a wide variety of activities including physical fitness and health education programs, friendly visits to home bound, painting and calligraphy, community service days as well as intergenerational activities.

National Resources

1. National Institute on Senior Centers, 1901 L Street NW, 4th Floor, Washington, DC 20036, phone: 202-479-1200; http://www.ncoa.org/national-institute-of-senior-centers/

   NISC is funded under a cooperative agreement between the AoA and the NCOA. The institute is a resource for multipurpose senior centers and community focal points. The institute offers training, technical assistance, and materials, and sponsors research initiatives.

2. National Senior Games Association (NSGA), PO Box 82059, Baton Rouge, LA, 70884-2059 phone: 225-766-6800; www.nsga.com/

   The mission of the NSGA is to motivate senior men and women to lead a healthy lifestyle through the senior games movement. The NSCA governs the Summer National Senior Games, better known as the Senior Olympics, which is the largest multisport event in the world for seniors. It supports and sanctions member state organizations that promote the year-round participation of older adults in events such as archery, badminton, basketball, shuffleboard, table tennis, horseshoes, volleyball, cycling, swimming, softball, tennis, triathlon, and golf.

3. National Recreation and Park Association (NRPA), 22377 Belmont Ridge Road, Ashburn, VA 20148-4501; phone: 800-626-6772); www.nrpa.org

   The Leisure and Aging Section of the NRPA represents and assists professionals who are involved with helping older adults remain healthy and active through participation in recreational pursuits.

Web Resources

1. Here are a few good examples of senior center websites

   A. Pasadena Senior Center: http://www.pasadenaseniorcenter.org

   The mission of the Pasadena Senior Center is "improving the lives of seniors through caring service with opportunities for social interaction, recreation, basic support and needs services, education, volunteerism and community activism." Their website lists activities, events, and services for and about seniors, and can be viewed in six different languages. Visitors can access information about recreation and leisure programs and activities, volunteer opportunities, community news, and other community services for older adults.

   B. Iowa City/Johnson County Senior Center: http://www.icgov.org/default/?id = 1215

   The mission of the Senior Center is to "promote optimal aging among older adults by offering programs and services that promote wellness, social interaction, community engagement, and intellectual growth. The Center serves the public through intergenerational programming and community outreach." You can access their 68-page catalog of programs and services— everything from yoga to tango dancing to bingo.

   C. Northshore Senior Center, Bothell, WA: http://northshoreseniorcenter.org

   The home page of the Northshore Senior Center provides information about how to join the center, volunteer opportunities, and the computer learning center. Visitors can access the Center's newsletter and catalog.

2. Shepherd's Centers of America: www.shepherdcenters.org

   Shepherd's Centers of America is an interfaith, nonprofit organization whose primary purpose is to enrich the lives of older adults. The home page explains the philosophy behind the centers and provides a list of centers across the country.

Employment Programs

At 57 years of age, John suddenly found himself unemployed when his company downsized in the midst of the latest economic recession. He had worked in almost every area of the lumber business and had expected to work for the same company until he retired. The new owners offered him a position at half the salary he had been earning. With at least eight years until retirement and his youngest child still in college, John simply could not accept the offer. He was frightened about his financial future. Through a friend, he heard that the local employment service operated a federally funded program for adults aged 55 and older. John qualified for the program as a displaced worker and because of his age. His employment specialist helped him regain his self-confidence and set new employment goals. The program enrolled him in a correspondence course and an on-the-job training program with a local appraisal company. After successfully completing his training, the employment counselor helped John establish himself as a self-employed appraiser.

In 1986, the first of the baby boomers turned 40 and became "older workers." By 2006, many of these individuals were seriously contemplating the date of their retirement. The onset of the Great Recession in 2007 significantly changed the retirement plans of older workers, with many needing to extend the time they had anticipated working to regain some financial stability. But some individuals, like John, found that their age worked against them in maintaining their current positions, seeking new jobs, or requesting training—although most employers rate older workers highly on such traits as loyalty, dependability, and attitude toward work.

We begin this chapter by examining work-related policies that protect older workers. We then profile older workers and their employers, with particular focus on federally supported employment-training programs designed specifically for older adults. We conclude the chapter with a discussion of the challenges facing older worker and employment programs.

POLICY BACKGROUND

Protecting Older Workers

The Age Discrimination in Employment Act (ADEA), first passed in 1967, is the single most important law protecting the rights of older workers. It provides that workers over the age of 40 cannot be arbitrarily discriminated against because of age in any employment decision, including hiring, discharges, layoffs, promotion, wages, and health care coverage

(R. Brown, 1989). The 1986 amendments to the ADEA prohibit most employers from setting a mandatory retirement age. There are, however, a few exceptions to the ADEA. For example, the ADEA does not protect workers who are employed by companies that have fewer than 20 employees, and the ADEA permits the mandatory retirement of "executives or persons in high policy-making positions" (p.186) at age 65 if their annual retirement pension benefits equal or exceed $44,000. With the shift in aging of the population, the ADEA's role in maintaining or encouraging the employment of older workers and its impact on those beyond what has been considered the "normal" retirement age of 65 will become relatively more important than it has been in the past (Neumark, 2009). In addition to the ADEA, more than 40 states have their own laws against age discrimination in employment that often provide greater protection than the federal law.

Congress also enacted the Older Workers Benefit Protection Act in 1990 to make clear that discrimination based on age in virtually all forms of employee benefits is unlawful. Specifically, it applies to employee benefits and benefit plans established or modified on or after its enactment (October 16, 1990; April 14, 1991, for private employers). The major goal of the Act is to establish regulations prohibiting age discrimination for most employee fringe benefits (Wiencek, 1991). It provides statutory recognition of early retirement programs and enacts into law the "equal benefit" or "equal cost" principle, requiring employers to provide older workers with benefits at least equal to those provided for younger workers, unless the employers can prove that the cost of providing an equal benefit is greater for an older worker than for a younger worker.

The Americans With Disabilities Act (ADA) of 1990 also provides additional protection for older workers. Although disabilities are not a result of normal aging, the ADA classifies many ailments associated with older adults as disabilities. Older adults who have been unemployed because of disability will have substantially improved opportunities to re-enter the workforce. Under the law, individuals must be considered for employment if they can perform the essential functions of the position with reasonable accommodations.

In 2000, then-President Bill Clinton signed into law the Senior Citizens' Freedom to Work Act, eliminating the earnings limitation for Social Security for those adults older than normal retirement age. The passing of this law was heralded by some members of Congress as the "dawn of a new age for older Americans." The goals of the act are twofold: to allow those older adults already working to receive more wages and to encourage more older adults to get into the labor force. Critics point out that the overwhelming majority of older adult retirees had little to gain by the Freedom to Work Act because only about one in five taxpayers older than age 65 report wages or earned income from employment. A review of labor statistics in 2002 indicated that little has changed for older adults, yet evidence suggests that, over time, benefits will be seen (Song, 2003–2004). Recent analyses have suggested that eliminating the earnings test for older workers, while not affecting employment decisions of most retired adults, has encouraged a larger number of men with marginal wage rates (those just around the test threshold and beyond) to continue working full time after age 65 (Michaud & Van Soest, 2008). As of yet, however, there is no evidence that the Freedom to Work Act has influenced older adults to delay applying for their Social Security benefits (Y. Lee, 2010).

Training for Older Workers

The federal government has been instrumental in creating employment programs for older workers. These include Experience Works, the Senior Community Service Employment Program (formally known as the Green Thumb Program), Community Service Employment for Older Americans under Title V of the Older Americans Act (OAA), the Senior Environmental Employment (SEE) Program, and the Agriculture Conservation Experienced Services (ACES) Program. Each of these will be explained in greater detail later in this chapter.

The Job Training Partnership Act (JTPA) of 1982 implemented a comprehensive workforce development initiative with several programs that provide employment and training activities. In general, under Tittle II-A of the JTPA, programs provided basic educational and occupational skills training to persons who were economically disadvantaged and other persons with multiple barriers to employment (e.g., age discrimination) to prepare them for employment and economic self-sufficiency (Hale, 1990). Although all adults, regardless of age, could use JTPA services, participation by older adults was low. In 1995, 176,000 adults participated in JTPA II-A programs beyond initial assessment; of these, only 3,513 (2%) were 55 years of age or older (Gross, 1998). The Title II-A 5% Set-Aside program was designed to provide funding specifically for older adults (age 55+) with low income (i.e., no more than 100% of the poverty guidelines or 70% of the lower living standard income level). These programs provided training for placement of older individuals in employment with private business. Approximately 66% of the states administered Title II-A 5% Set-Aside programs through the state JTPA office. In 20% of the states, the State Unit on Aging (SUA) administered the program. Older adults also were eligible for training through Title III of JTPA, which provided monies for training, placement, and other assistance for dislocated workers as well as for long-term unemployed persons with limited opportunities for employment or reemployment in the area in which they resided. The Workforce Investment Act of 1998, which became fully effective on July 1, 2000, superseded JTPA, and the programs were discontinued.

The Workforce Investment Act of 1998 (WIA) authorized national, state, and local workforce development activities through legislative reform that created a comprehensive workforce investment system (U.S. Department of Labor [USDoL], 2011b). The reformed system is intended to help Americans of *all ages* access the tools they need to manage their careers through information and high-quality services, and to help U.S. companies find skilled workers. The law has seven key principles: (a) streamlining services through better integration at the street level in the One-Stop delivery system; (b) empowering individuals through access to Individual Training Accounts (ITAs) at qualified institutions, information and guidance from a system of consumer reports, and the support available through the One-Stop system partners; (c) universal access; (d) increased accountability from state and local entities managing the workforce investment system; (e) enhanced role for local workforce investment boards and the private sector, with local, business-led boards acting as the "boards of directors" of the local workforce investment system; (f) state and local flexibility; and (g) improved youth programs linked more closely to local labor market needs and community youth programs and services, with strong connections between academic and occupational learning.

President Obama's proposed Jumpstart Our Business Startups Act (2011) also contained several provisions that would have assisted older workers who are trying to re-enter the job market (Rafter, 2011; White House, 2011). Specifically, the proposed legislation called for a $4,000 tax credit for employers hiring long-term unemployed workers and even higher tax breaks for businesses hiring unemployed veterans. The Act also proposed a Pathways Back to Work program that would have (a) extended unemployment benefits to workers choosing work sharing over layoffs, (b) allowed the unemployed to receive new skills training while on unemployment benefits, and (c) empowered states to implement wage insurance to help with rehiring of older workers. Unfortunately, this Act was not passed by Congress. Watch for it in future sessions of Congress.

For Your Files: Sloan Center on Aging and Work at Boston College

The Sloan Center on Aging and Work integrates evidence from research with insights from workplace experiences to inform organizational decision making through publications and multidisciplinary dialogue with business leaders and scholars. It focuses on a broad range of issues such as workplace flexibility, innovative workplace practices, working in retirement, diversity among older workers, and family caregivers of the elderly. Examples of publication titles include *The New Unemployables— Older Job Seekers Struggle to Find Work During the Great Recession, Talent Management and the Prism of Age*, and *Working in Retirement: A 21st Century Phenomenon*.

For more information, contact Sloan Center on Aging and Work at Boston College, 140 Commonwealth Avenue, Chestnut Hill, MA 02467; phone: 617-552-9195; www.bc.edu/research/agingandwork.

USERS AND PROGRAMS

Characteristics of Older Workers

Labor force participation by older men and women has increased over the past couple of decades. In 2011, about 40.2% of people aged 55 and over were in the labor force (Rix, 2011). Of these older workers, 17.7% were aged 65. Many factors contributed to this change including: (a) changes to Social Security, (b) a shift in pension type from defined benefit to defined contribution plans; (c) increased education levels (people with more education work longer), (d) improved health and longevity; (e) less physically demanding jobs, (f) decline of employer-provided retiree health insurance; and (g) more women working (wives typically are younger than their husbands and husbands and wives like to coordinate their retirement; Munnell, 2011). Interactions among these various factor has resulted in the age retirement age of 64 for men and 62 for women.

Although labor force participation by older adults has increased, the overall proportion of older people working decreases with age. In 2008, 76% of men between the ages of 55 and 61 and 53% of men aged 62 to 64 were in the civilian labor force (Federal Interagency Forum on Aging-Related Statistics, 2010; see Exhibit 8.1). About 36% of men between the ages of 65 and 69, and 17% of men aged 70 and older were in the labor force. While older men are more likely to be employed than older women, older women show a similar pattern of decline in labor force participation as older men. Approximately 65% of all women aged 55 to 61 and 42% of women aged 62 to 64 were working, yet only 26% of women between the ages of 65 and 69, and 8% of women aged 70 and older were employed.

Rates of labor force participation also vary between members of various ethnic groups. As shown in Exhibit 8.2, in 2008 non-Hispanic White and Hispanic men had higher rates of participation than did older Black men. Among men aged 62 to 64, 55% of non-Hispanic White men, 56% of Hispanic men, and 45% of Black men were employed. For men aged 70 to 74, a higher percentage of non-Hispanic White men were employed (22%) than either Blacks (19%) or Hispanics (19%). A lower percentage of women than men were employed

Exhibit 8.1 Labor Force Participation by Age and Gender in 2008 (percentage)

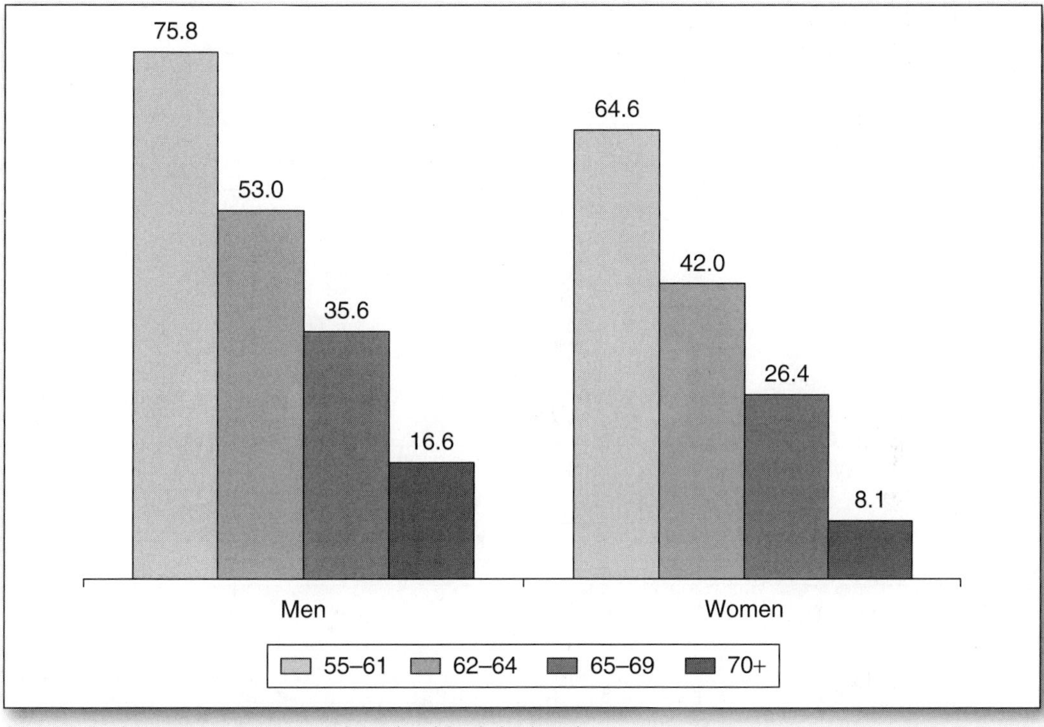

Source: Federal Interagency Forum on Aging Related Statistics (2010).

at every age and in each ethnic group. Among older women, a higher percentage of non-Hispanic White women and Black women were employed than Hispanic women. At age 62 to 64, 44% of non-Hispanic White women, 44% of Black women, and 38% of Hispanic women were employed (R. W. Johnson, Haaga, & Simms, 2011).

According to the Bureau of Labor Statistics (BLS, 2010a), the majority of workers aged 55 or older are employed in nonagricultural industries in education and health services, wholesale and retail services, and professional and business services (see Exhibit 8.3). They compose approximately 20% of all workers in each of the industries shown. Education and health services account for the largest share of older women workers, whereas similar percentages of older men work across a variety of areas.

Of persons aged 55 and older in the labor force, about 70% work full time (BLS, 2010c). Older women are more likely to be among the part-time workers than older men (35.9% vs. 23.6%, respectively). Workers aged 50 and older are more likely than younger workers to be self-employed (17% vs. 12%) or small business owners (9% vs. 5%; Sloan Work and Family Research Network, 2009). Of adults over age 65 employed in nonagricultural industries in 2010, 16.7% were self-employed (BLS, 2010b). A greater percentage of older men were self-employed than older women (19.7% vs. 13.4%).

The availability of unearned income, particularly the availability of pension income, is a key factor in determining whether older individuals continue working after receipt of

Exhibit 8.2   Labor Force Participation in 2008 by Age, Sex, and Race (percentage)

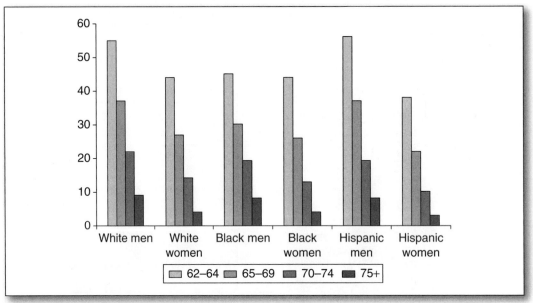

Source: R. W. Johnson et al. (2011).

Exhibit 8.3   Employed Persons Aged 55+ in Nonagricultural Industries in 2010 by Sex and Race (percentage)

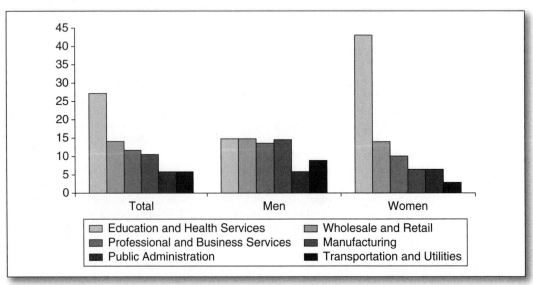

Source: BLS (2010a).

Social Security benefits. Only about 10% to 12% of older men and 6% to 8% of older women who receive income from a private pension or retirement savings plan remain in the workforce (Purcell, 2000). According to the 2006 Metlife National Survey of Aging Workers, 72% of retirees say they continue working because they need the income to live, 54% want to stay active and engaged, 43% want to engage in meaningful work, 43% desire to maintain their lifestyle, and 41% want to build up retirement savings. Seventy-five percent of older adults aged 66 to 70 work because they want to stay actively engaged (DeLong & Associates, 2006).

Despite rising unemployment rates that began with the start of the recession in December 2007, millions of older Americans have succeeded in remaining employed. Workers aged 55 and older have a lower unemployment rate (6.9%) than persons aged 25 to 54 (8.0%). However, between December 2007 and July 2011, the unemployment rate increased by a greater percentage for older workers (115.6% change) than younger workers (95.1% change). Once older workers become unemployed, they experience a longer period of unemployment than do other workers. For example, individuals aged 55 and older report being unemployed an average of 52.7 weeks, and those younger than aged 55 report being unemployed an average of 36.5 weeks. As of July 2011, more than half of older unemployed workers (53.9%) were among the long-term unemployed, that is, they had been out of work for 27 or more weeks (Rix, 2011). Approximately 3% of older persons not in the labor force in 2011 indicated that they would like to be working (BLS, 2011b). The most common reasons for not looking for work were discouragement over job prospects, illness or disability, and family responsibilities.

Employers of Older Workers

Federal Employment and Training Programs

The federal government provide the majority of employment and training programs for older persons. Experience Works (formerly known as Green Thumb) is the oldest and largest operator of employment and training programs for older Americans. It was founded in 1965 by the National Farmers Union, as part of President Johnson's War on Poverty. Originally designed to put older, rural Americans to work to beautify the nation's parks and highways, the program began with 280 participants in four states. Today, the program provides employment, training, and service opportunities for more than 50,000 older Americans each year (Experience Works, 2011). The program is funded by grants, contracts, and foundations, as well as contributions from organizations and individuals. Experience Works operates the largest Senior Community Service Employment Program (SCSEP) in the country (described below), in partnership with the DoL and state funders, serving over 20,000 older Americans in 30 states and Puerto Rico (Experience Works, 2009).

In 1969, Congress funded a demonstration project to promote useful part-time opportunities in community-service activities for unemployed low-income older adults. The success of this project resulted in statutory financing in 1973 for SCSEP (Walter, 2011[1]). In 1978, this program became Title V of the Older Americans Act (OAA). The federal allocation for SCSEP for FY11 was $450 million. The OAA requires that 75% of all federal SCSEP

---

[1]Unless otherwise noted, the background information about the Senior Community Service Employment Program comes from Walter (2011).

funds be spent on participant wages and benefits. Although the DoL manages the SCSEP, it allocates the funds to 18 national organizations (e.g., AARP Foundation; the Asociacion Nacional Pro Personas Mayores; Easter Seals, Inc.; Experience Works; the National Caucus and Center on Black Aged; the National Council on the Aging; the National Indian Council on Aging; the National Asian Pacific Center on Aging) and 56 states and territories to administer SCSEP. The governors of each state decide which state agency in government has the authority for program management and oversight. In most states, the SUA has this responsibility.

SCSEP programs provide subsidized minimum-wage jobs in community service positions in public and nonprofit organizational settings for persons aged 55 and older whose incomes are no more than 125% of the poverty level (Walter, 2011). Priority enrollment is granted first to veterans and their qualified spouses, then to persons aged 65 and older, or individuals who have a disability, have limited English proficiency, have low literacy proficiency, live in a rural area, have low employment prospects, or are homeless or at risk of homelessness. Senior participants work an average of 20 hours a week for the minimum wage and minimal benefits. Participants may remain in the SCSEP program for a maximum of 48 months, although SCSEP participants may receive a program waiver to extend their time beyond the durational limit. Each state and national SCSEP grantee determines which waiver factors (e.g., severe disability; frail; aged 75 or older), if any, they will accept. Ultimately, the goal is to place these individuals in unsubsidized employment. Nationally, the unsubsidized placement rate is about 47%; this figure, however, varies widely by sponsor (USDoL, 2011a).

Although regulations allow contractors to provide training to participants, they devote few financial resources to this activity. Most of the efforts go into creating community jobs for participants and matching participants with existing jobs. SCSEP workers provide whatever services are needed locally. Programs deliver two thirds of their services to the general community; the remaining services assist the older population in the community. The largest service categories are social services and education. In 2008, SCSEP participants engaged in 48,883,907 hours of community service work, providing a total economic value of $989,899,116 worth of work to their host agencies and communities (Washko, Schack, Goff, & Pudlin, 2011). Most SCSEP participants are female (64%); about 51% are minorities, 48% live in a rural area, 55% are aged 65 and older, and 20% have a disability (USDoL, 2011a; Washko et al., 2011).

For Your Files: Job-Seeking Online

Older workers wanting to re-enter the workforce can find job openings as well as online support for their search and interview process through online employment services such as the Employment Assistance section of Retired Brains (www.retiredbrains.com) and Senior Job Bank (www.senior jobbank.com). The employment sites are supported by employer ads and do not charge the prospective worker a fee. Sites often have web links to resume writing tips, career evaluation tools, and other practical resources for job search success.

A smaller workforce program first authorized in the OAA of 1978 under Title V is the Section 502(e) experimental projects. The purpose of these projects is to ensure second-career training and the placement of eligible Title V participants in jobs in the private business sector. In contrast to the SCSEP program, 502(e) programs can pay participants more than federal minimum wage, can subsidize a greater number of hours per week, and can offer greater flexibility in the income eligibility requirements for program participants. Enrollees may have incomes of up to 150% to 165% of the poverty level, compared with 125% for SCSEP. Unfortunately, there is no separate appropriation for 502(e) programs. Sponsors must divert part of their Title V funding to run these training-oriented programs. The first year of implementation for the experimental projects was Program Year 1983. An examination of the early 502(e) projects estimated that the number of experimental project participants was about 3% of the total SCSEP enrollment (Centaur Associates, 1986). Women constituted about 70% of program enrollees. Most of these 502(e) placements were in health, clerical, and services occupations. With the 2006 amendments to the OAA, no more than 1.5% of Title V funds were allowed to be allocated to carry out demonstration projects, pilot projects, and evaluation projects addressing the employment and training needs of eligible individuals under section 502(e).

In 1984, the Environmental Programs Assistance Act authorized the Environmental Protection Agency (EPA, 2008) to establish a program of grants/cooperative agreements to federal, state, and local environmental agencies for projects of pollution prevention, abatement, and control. To implement this program, the EPA and other federal and state environmental offices fund cooperative agreements with six national aging organizations authorized by the Secretary of Labor. Known as SEE (Senior Environmental Employment Program), the National Older Worker Career Center (NOWCC) operates this public–private partnership program. Participating in SEE provides opportunities for retired and unemployed older adults aged 55 and older to use their skills to support a wide variety of government agencies with environmental programs. Located at sites across the United States, SEE employees may obtain full- or part-time positions that involve responsibilities ranging from clerical duties to technical and scientific tasks. SEE enrollees are not employees of EPA but receive wages and benefits including paid federal holidays, health insurance, and vacation and sick leave. In 2010, starting pay rates for SEE employees ranged from $7.27 to $12.72 per hour, depending on the level of skill required and responsibilities involved (Senior Service America, 2010). Since its inception, the program has expanded to over 1,500 participants supporting the EPA; the Departments of Interior, Army, Commerce, Defense, and Energy; and the White House (NOWCC, 2012a).

The Agriculture Conservation Experienced Services (ACES) Program offers individuals aged 55 and older temporary paid assignments to provide technical services in support of the conservation-related programs of the U.S. Department of Agriculture (USDA; Senior Service America, 2010). Authorized by the Food, Conservation, and Energy Act of 2008, the program is patterned after the SEE program. To be eligible for the ACES Program, individuals must be at least 55 years old and legally eligible to work in the United States. ACES enrollees are not employees of either the USDA or a state agriculture department but receive wages and benefits including paid federal holidays, vacation, and sick leave. Positions range from technical, no degree required with prior experience (e.g., soil conservation technicians, engineering technicians) to professional or expert with advanced or doctoral degree required with a minimum of 20 years of related on-the-job experience. Entry-level wages range from $11.33 to $30.80 per hour. Enrollees work from 16 to 40 hours a week. The ACES program fills over 155 positions in 24 states and the District of Columbia (NOWCC, 2012b).

Across the Globe: Silver Human Resource Center (SHRC)—Japan

Established in Tokyo in 1974, Japan's Silver Human Resource Center (SHRC) provides retired persons aged 60 and older part-time employment opportunities. There are SHRCs in 1,600 municipalities throughout Japan with more than 790,000 members. Each Center contracts work through corporations, households, public organizations, and other entities, which it then allots to registered members based on work content, frequency, and volume. Opportunities include indoor and outdoor general work (e.g., park cleanup, janitorial work), facility administration (e.g., administration of parking lots, schools, community centers), specialized knowledge (e.g., accounting, translating, editing), technical skills (e.g., carpentry, plumbing, painting), office work (e.g., reception work, filing, addressing of envelopes), customer interface/door-to-door work (e.g., pamphlet distribution, payment collection, meter reading), and human services (e.g., traffic control, housekeeping). Older members receive a financial compensation from the Center based on the content of the work they performed and the number of hours they worked.

Source: Weiss, Bass, Heimovitz, & Oka (2005).

Private Sector Employers

Most employers view older workers as mature and stable contributors to their organizations. Older workers are perceived as having lower absenteeism rates than younger workers and as possessing good work ethics (Tourigny & Pulich, 2006). However, the same employers tend to believe that older workers cannot learn new things, take on new responsibilities, and be productive beyond the scope of work they have traditionally completed. Employers also do not view older workers as needing to build their careers. Thus, they are reluctant to invest too much time, energy, and money in older workers because they do not see it as a good return on their investment.

Many employers hold the belief that older workers cannot learn new things and are unable to use computer technology in the workplace. However, research indicates that older workers are not afraid of using computers; they just have not had as much opportunity to use them as younger workers (Rizzuto & Mohammed, 2005). Most older adults agree that they would be happy to learn if offered the opportunity. Their success is based on their willingness to learn and employers' commitment to their achievement.

Some companies view workers over the age of 50 as an asset rather than a liability. One such company, USB Financial Services in Winston-Salem, North Carolina, purposefully employs more financial advisors who are aged 50 or older than not. USB management recognized that clientele were more receptive to the advice of older advisors than younger advisors. In a business move that runs counter to current management thinking that younger workers are more cost-effective, USB management sought and trained older workers who were successful in their previous careers as financial advisors (Craver, 2007).

With the aging of the work force, the federal government is considering ways of changing its current recruitment and hiring practices to reach new sources of talent, including the millions of highly skilled and experienced older workers who are approaching retirement age, or are already retired, from all sectors of the economy (Partnership for Public Service, 2008). To help address these critical needs, in 2008 the Partnership for Public Service launched the FedExperience pilot program with federal agencies, corporate partners, and other stakeholders to match government's critical hiring needs with the talents of experienced, older workers (Partnership for Public Service, 2011). The program matches IBM retirees and employees nearing retirement with mission-critical staffing needs at the Department of Treasury, the Federal Aviation Administration, and the Department of Energy, Environmental Management. The Partnership for Public Service helps promote job opportunities at these agencies to IBM employees with matching skill sets and experience; identifies opportunities to streamline hiring processes; provides career transition resources; encourages flexible work arrangements; and establishes mentoring programs and other employee-friendly practices.

Best Practice: Mature Services

Mature Services, Inc. in northeastern Ohio offers a number of employment services to middle-aged and older adults who want to enter or re-enter the workforce. Their Mature Staffing Systems network provides job search support, job fairs, meetings with employers, and a computer resource room. It also includes a full-service staffing agency that works to match mature job seekers with employers.

For more information about this employment program, contact Mature Services, 415 S. Portage Path, Akron, OH 44320; phone: 330-762-8666; www.matureservices.org.

CHALLENGES FOR OLDER WORKERS AND EMPLOYMENT PROGRAMS

Society is redefining the meaning of work and retirement. It is not uncommon for today's workers to pursue multiple careers throughout their lifetimes. Workers who pursued one lifelong career may retire from it only to continue working in another field or in their primary field while receiving some retirement income. In addition, given the changing demographics of society, there will be increasing numbers of older workers, as well as a greater need for them. We end this chapter by examining several challenges facing older workers and employment programs as they address the changing needs and values of an aging workforce.

Promoting and Increasing Enrollments in Job Training Programs

One of the top 50 resolutions put forth by delegates to the 2005 White House Conference on Aging (2006) was to promote incentives for older workers to continue working and improve employment training and retraining programs to better serve older workers. Strategies for implementing this resolution include providing greater access to education and training for older workers via education grants, providing tuition waivers, developing new financing mechanisms like a training education 401K, and requiring local workforce investment boards to set aside a minimum amount of funds to support the training of older workers. Eligibility requirements also need to be reconsidered as they currently limit the number of middle-aged and older persons who take part in SCSEP programs. Program administrators at the state and local levels need to start a more aggressive awareness campaign to increase the number of older adults enrolled in SCSP and other job training program.

Providing Opportunities for Older Workers

In both the public and private sectors, training is a key element in the successful integration of older workers in the labor force. The rapid introduction of new technologies and productive innovations requires a reorientation by employers and workers of all ages toward the concept of lifelong learning and skills upgrading (DeLong & Associates, 2006). In addition, business must look beyond the "McJobs" opportunities for older workers (Hushbeck, 1990) and support the use of older workers to their full potential (Adler & Hilber, 2008; Ghilarducci & Turner, 2007; Hedge, Borman, & Lammlein, 2006).

In rural areas, the agricultural economic base, low population density, and relative isolation from larger urban areas often limit the employment opportunities for older workers. The aging network needs to become more involved in offering and facilitating training programs that prepare older workers for the more limited employment opportunities in rural areas as well as helping them prepare for their retirement years.

Older women, particularly those from nonmetropolitan areas, experience higher rates of underemployment than either their male peers or younger women (Sloan Center on Aging and Work, 2009). Entry or re-entry into the labor force may be difficult for some older women without recent job experience. Upon finding a job, older women typically receive less pay and fewer benefits than older men. Older women earn 55 cents for every dollar that older men earn, and only 80% have access to health insurance through their employer (Sloan Work and Family Research Network, 2009). These women may benefit from special programs designed to better integrate them into the labor force to gain better positioning. One such program, formed in 1981 to empower displaced homemakers and help them in achieving economic self-sufficiency, is the National Displaced Homemakers Network. In 1993, it reorganized and changed its name to Women Work! The National Network for Women's Employment, in recognition of the range of economic transitions women face throughout their lives. Today, Women Work! (www.womenwork.org) is one of the leading organizations advocating for women to train and qualify for jobs in the information technology field and nontraditional occupations. Recognized as experts on employment and training issues, Women Work! and its nationwide network affect policy by working with lawmakers, business leaders, nonprofit organizations, and labor unions to create and strengthen programs and policies for women.

Increasing Self-Employment

Many baby boomers reaching retirement age want to continue working. For those not willing or able to remain in their current position, the most flexible way to remain in the workforce is through self-employment. However, there is relatively little research on self-employment among middle-aged and older workers. In a 2003 MetLife study of retirees, 36% of 60- to 65-year-olds and 42% of 66- to 70-year-olds identified themselves as being self-employed. Some workers reported feeling forced into self-employment due to age discrimination at their workplace and limited employment options elsewhere (DeLong & Associates, 2006). Others reported that both push and pull factors drive the decision to become self-employed (Zissimopoulos & Karoly, 2007). For example, poor health appeared to be a push factor, suggesting that older workers with a work-limiting health condition are better able to accommodate their condition and continue working if they are self-employed compared with employment in the wage sector. Higher wealth was considered a pull factor, acknowledging that access to capital was a significant determinant of becoming self-employed in late life.

Supporting Encore Careers

As many as 9.5% of individuals aged 44 to 70 years old are pursuing encore careers, combining income, meaning, and social purpose (Civic Ventures, 2008; Freedman, 2007). Most older adults currently in encore careers are leading-edge boomers who came from professional and white-collar jobs, have at least some college education, are women, and live in cities or suburbs. Workers interested in encore careers are more likely than those not interested to describe retirement as a time to begin a new chapter in their life rather than a time to take it easy (71% vs. 43%, respectively; Civic Ventures, 2008). They are working in many different areas including education, health care, government agencies, and nonprofit organizations. To encourage more older adults to pursue encore careers and ease the transition into the social sector will require support and action from policy makers, including improving access to affordable health care, ending financial penalties for continuing to work while receiving a pension, developing programs that help match people who want to work for nonprofits and government agencies with interested employers, and supporting accelerated education and retraining programs for experienced people interested in learning new ways to use their skills in work that helps their community (Civic Ventures, 2008).

Educating Employers

Stereotypes of aging still hold fast in the workplace (Dennis & Thomas, 2007). Older workers confront more restricted job opportunities than do otherwise identical younger workers. With the changes in demographics, employers may face a shortage of skilled, knowledgeable workers and a loss of institutional knowledge. Thus, employers large and small need to develop a greater awareness and understanding of older workers as resources and assets (Cappelli & Novelli, 2010; Rothwell, Sterns, Spokus, & Reaser, 2008). Furthermore, employers need accurate information about the myths and realities of older workers. Many employers would probably be surprised to know that older workers have lower rates of absenteeism, experience less stress on the job, and remain productive workers.

Preparing for Retirement

Regardless of how, at what age, or why older adults leave the workforce, they are often ill prepared for life as a retirees. Teaching men and women about finances and other retirement issues should begin early in their work careers. This introduction to retirement issues serves two purposes: consciousness raising and information dissemination (Burtless, 2006; Shagrin, 2000). Personnel offices, training offices, and employee counseling services within organizations should provide workers with adequate information concerning financial options for retirement because many individuals are unaware of, or do not fully understand, their retirement benefits. This may be a particular concern for women and low-income individuals who, because of financial concerns, may not even consider retirement as an option or have exacerbated fears about retirement (T. H. Brown & Warner, 2008; Wong & Hardy, 2009).

Several private organizations are testing models of flexible retirement options. These programs help upcoming retirees make an easier transition from work to retirement. Companies view such programs as a cost-effective means for solving their labor shortages. For example, the National Rural Electric Cooperative Association, which won an AARP Best Employers for Workers over 50 Award in 2008, has a "phased retirement" option for its older workers. When employees reach retirement age under their pension plan, the pension may start even if they continue working on a full- or part-time basis. Other benefits, like health insurance, also continue to be available during the phased retirement period (USDoL, 2000; AARP, 2008b). Other companies offer cafeteria-like options for older workers on a preretirement basis, such as part-time work, flextime, and vacation-work combinations. Another approach used by some companies is internal job redesign that allows for work-schedule adjustments based on demographic and lifestyle changes as employees age (Bond, Thompson, Galinsky, & Prottas, 2002; Clark & Quinn, 2002). Preretirement planning and flexible retirement plans stand to benefit both employers by allowing them to implement knowledge transfer and mentoring programs, and employees by providing adequate time to prepare for the transition from work to retirement.

CASE STUDY

Beginning the Journey to Financial Independence at Midlife

Sally, a 58-year-old widow, has had no income for the last six months. She is unable to pay her rent and has had to move in with her sister. Before medical problems forced her to quit her job, Sally had been employed for three years at the local university, clerking in the student bookstore. Her supervisor was complimentary about her organizational skills and how well she worked with the students and faculty. It was a pleasant job, although far from her original career goals. As a young woman, she had aspirations of becoming a chaplain or working in some aspect of the ministry, or at least in some type of helping profession. Marriage and family interrupted this dream. She left school one semester and a thesis shy of a Master of Divinity degree. During the past 30 years, a series of unfortunate events has left Sally with few resources. Other than her three uninterrupted years working in the student bookstore, her work history is patchy. Mostly, Sally fulfilled a traditional role as homemaker until her husband died four years ago. To keep in touch with her love of helping people, she volunteers at least five hours per week in the social ministries of her large church.

Sally and her husband had no children, and her sister is her only living relative. Although Sally appreciates her sister's kindness, she desperately wants to be independent. When she finally rebounded from her recent medical problems, she began looking for work. She has been searching for a job for four months with no promise of employment—at least employment that can support her. Sally is angry and frustrated. She is sure she is being discriminated against. She suspects that her age and being overweight are contributing to her lack of success. Overall, Sally's self-esteem at this point in her life is low, and she is running desperately short on financial resources.

Case Study Questions

1. What protection does Sally have against discrimination? How realistic is it that these protections will alleviate her present situation?

2. On the basis of statistics on older workers, in what fields is Sally most likely to find employment? How do these jobs relate to her employment goals?

3. Sally could continue her job search on her own. Eventually, she might be successful. What other employment assistance might she explore? Do you believe she would qualify for these employment programs? Why?

4. Although Sally is classified as an older worker, how does her situation differ from that of a worker 65 or 70 years of age? What impact does being female have on her situation, if any?

5. Which of the special employment programs for older workers described in the chapter would be most appropriate for Sally? Why? If you were the older worker employment specialist working with Sally, what would be your goals for her?

LEARNING ACTIVITIES

1. At what age would you like to retire? From what job do you see yourself retiring? How far up the career ladder will you have climbed? What will be your ending salary? What steps do you need to take throughout your adult life to achieve these goals?

2. Interview an employee counselor who deals with retirement planning. What information and training does the counselor provide? What types of employees (e.g., women, men, age, position) seek or attend retirement planning? When does the counselor recommend that employees start to plan for retirement? How much savings/pension should the average employee try to secure for retirement?

3. Plan your retirement. Will you pursue an encore career, travel, take classes—or do it all? If planning an encore career, describe what it would be, and peruse a senior job line to check on availability, pay, and requirements (experience and skills).

4. Interview someone who has retired from one career and has now embarked on another. How did the individual decide on the second career? How did the person find the position, learn skills, and so on? How is the second career different from the previous one?

5. Interview an advocate, attorney, or someone who deals with age discrimination in employment. What type of cases has the person handled? How successful are people in fighting age discrimination? What types of positions or older adults seem more prone to age discrimination?

6. Search for an active SCSEP in your area. Ask the program manager about the successes and challenges of the program. How does the manager anticipate the program will change with the aging of the baby boomers?

FOR MORE INFORMATION

International Resources

1. AARP International: www.aarpinternational.org/

   AARP International provides resources on a number of topics related to aging including economic and retirement security. Subtopics include research and news on age discrimination, the mature workforce, and pensions and can be searched by world region.

2. AARP International Forum on the Future Workforce: New Strategies for New Demographics: http://aarpintorg.stage.bridgelinedigital.net:8020/conference/conference_show.htm?doc_id = 669747

   To explore innovative strategies implemented across the globe to address the effects of population aging on the future workforce, AARP and the European Commission convened an international forum that brought together experts and innovators representing government, industry, and social partners. This report, the product of this international forum, covers new approaches to reengineer the workplace, re-career older workers, recast public perceptions about aging, and restructure the regulatory environment to create incentives for continued employment.

3. Centre for Senior Policy: http://www.seniorpolitikk.no/informasjon/english

   The Centre for Senior Policy is a Norwegian advocacy group that publishes reports and news briefs (with English translations) related to older workers. Their mission is to reduce rates of early retirement and raise awareness of the benefits of an older workforce.

4. United Nations Economic Commission for Europe (UNCE) Policy Brief on Ageing No. 9—Age-Friendly Employment: Policy and Practices: http://live.unece.org/fileadmin/DAM/pau/_docs/age/2011/Policy-briefs/9-Policy-Brief-Age-Friendly-Employment.pdf

   This policy brief covers the challenging context facing the UNCE, goals, strategies, and best practices related to Commitment 5 of the UNCE Strategy on Aging: "to enable labor markets to respond to the economic and social consequences of population aging."

National Resources

1. Experience Works, 2200 Clarendon Boulevard, Suite 1000, Arlington, VA 22201; phone (toll free): 1-866-EXP-WEKS; www.experienceworks.org

   Experience Works empowers low-income older Americans aged 55 and older to remain productive and independent by providing them with training opportunities to help them find jobs in their local communities.

2. U.S. Department of Labor, Office of Public Affairs, 200 Constitution Avenue NW, Room S1032, Washington, DC 20210; phone: 202-639-4650; www.doleta.gov/seniors

   The DoL produces numerous reports and statistical analyses that include information about the aging workforce. In addition, the DoL is responsible for the Senior Community Service Employment Program for low-income older adults over age 55.

3. AARP, 601 E Street NW, Washington, DC 20049; phone: 1-888-OUR-AARP; www.aarp.org

   AARP is a nonprofit organization helping older adults maintain independence, dignity, and purpose. AARP has a number of publications about older workers and preretirement planning.

4. Equal Employment Opportunity Commission, 1801 L Street NW, Washington, DC 20507; phone: 1-800-669-4000; www.eeoc.gov

   The Equal Employment Opportunity Commission enforces the Age Discrimination in Employment Act and investigates age discrimination complaints.

Web Resources

1. America's Job Bank, U.S. Department of Labor: www.ajb.dni.us

   This online listing links visitors to a computerized network of 1,800 state employment offices and their active job listings. There are approximately 250,000 positions listed in America's Job Bank files. There is no cost to employers for posting their vacancies or to job seekers.

2. National Council on the Aging's MaturityWorks Alliance: http://www.ncoa.org/enhance-economic-security/mature-workers/

   MaturityWorks is devoted to employment and training issues affecting middle-aged and older workers. Website visitors can link to the National Council on the Aging's workforce resources, other workforce-related sites, and the Senior Community Service Employment Program sites.

3. Urban Institute: www.urban.org

   The Urban Institute, a nonprofit policy research organization located in Washington, DC, investigates the social and economic problems confronting the nation, including those facing older workers.

4. National Older Worker Career Center (NOWCC): www.nowcc.org

   NOWCC is a nonprofit organization that expands employment and training opportunities for America's fast-growing population of workers aged 40 and over. This website also provides information on the Senior Environmental Employment Program (SEE), which offers nation-wide opportunities for individuals aged 55 and over to apply skills and experience ranging from clerical to scientific and assists the U.S. Environmental Protection Agency in pollution prevention and control projects.

5. The SPRY (Setting Priorities for Retirement Years) Foundation: www.spry.org

   SPRY is an independent, nonprofit 501(c)(3) research and education organization that helps people prepare for successful aging. SPRY emphasizes planning and prevention-oriented strategies in four key areas: health and wellness, mental health, financial security, and life engagement. The SPRY Foundation's report, titled *Redefining Retirement: Research Directions for Successful Aging Among America's Diverse Seniors*, suggests that minority seniors do not share the traditional idea of age-related retirement and retirement planning. Visit the Foundation's website to read this and other SPRY reports.

CHAPTER 9

Income Programs

Scott and Stacy are somewhat anxious as they wait for their appointment with a retirement planner. Like many couples in their mid-40s, they have not given serious thought to retirement. Most of their financial planning has centered on preparation for sending their two children to college. After hearing so much in the media lately about whether Social Security will be there for them when they retire, they are wondering whether they are making the best plans for their own future. Unanswered questions for them at this time include the following: Will Social Security be a retirement resource for them? Are they saving enough money and in the right way to supplement their Social Security? How do their work pensions fit into all this? What level of income will they need in retirement for quality of life they desire? What sources of help could they turn to if something terrible and unforeseen happened to their income security?

The economic circumstances of older Americans have improved substantially during the past three decades, with average incomes and assets for persons over 65 rising dramatically. Median incomes for older adults have risen, whereas the share of older adults in poverty has dropped, even during the recession that began in December 2007. As shown in Exhibit 9.1, the percentage of older adults living in poverty declined from 15.3% in 1975 to 8.9% in 2009 (Federal Interagency Forum on Aging-Related Statistics, 2010; Issa & Zedlewski, 2011). The decrease in the percentage of older adults living in poverty coincides with the passage of public programs for income security (Moon & Ruggles, 1994). About 8.9% of older Americans lived in poverty in 2009 ($10,289 for single individual living alone at or over the age of 65, and $12,968 for a couple with at least one older member; Issa & Zedlewski, 2011). The percentage of older adults living in poverty, however, varies significantly by age, gender, race, and ethnicity. In 2009, the poverty rate for persons age 65 to 74 was 8.1% compared with 9.2% for persons between the ages of 75 and 84, and 11.6% for persons 85 years of age and older. Almost 11.0% of older women live in poverty compared with 6.6% of older men. In contrast to the 6.6% of non-Hispanic White older adults living in poverty, 18.9% of Black older adults, 15.8% of Asian older adults, and 18.3% of Hispanic older adults live in poverty (Issa & Zedlewski, 2011). The percentage of older adults living in poverty also was higher for those who never married and lived alone (20.0%) than for married couples (4.6%), for older adults with no high school diploma (18.6%) compared to those who completed high school (7.2%) or had at least a bachelor's degree (4.3%), and for older adults in poor health (16.7%) compared to those in good, very good, or excellent health (6.8%). Poverty rates were also higher among older gay (4.9%) and lesbian (9.1%) couples when compared with older heterosexual couples (4.6%; Goldberg, 2009).

Exhibit 9.1   Poverty Rates for Older Adults, 1975 to 2009 (percentage)

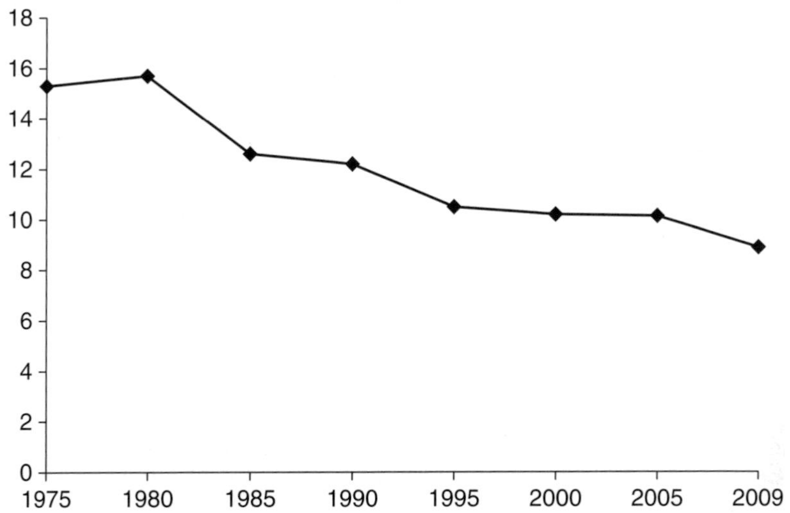

Source: Federal Interagency Forum on Aging-Related Statistics (2010); Issa and Zedlewski (2011).

Older adults whose income is below the poverty rate represent only a portion of older persons living in low-income households. In 2009, an additional 24.9% of older adults lived near poverty, defined as having an income at or above the federal poverty level but below two times it (Issa & Zedlewski, 2011). There is variation among older adults living near poverty. About 20.9% of persons aged 65 to 74 were living near poverty compared to 28.5% of persons aged 75 to 84, and 32.6% of persons aged 85 and older. Almost 28.3% of older women lived near poverty compared to 20.4% of older men. A lower percentage of non-Hispanic White older adults and Asian older adults lived near poverty (23.7% and 19.9%, respectively) than Black older adults (31.3%) and Hispanic older adults (32.5%). The percentage of older adults living near poverty also was higher for those who never married and lived alone (25.1%) than for married couples (18.3%), for older adults with no high school diploma (37.7%) compared to those who completed high school (25.4%) or had at least a bachelor's degree (11.8%), and for older adults in poor health (34.3%) compared to those in good, very good, or excellent health (21.2%).

In 2010, the median income for older married-couple households was $48,858 for male-headed households and $43,831 for female-headed households, which was approximately twice as high as the median income for nonmarried persons aged 65 or older of either sex (Wu, 2011a). Marital status is only one of many factors that contribute to marked income diversity among subgroups of elders. For example, median income of families declines steadily as age of the head of household increases, and advanced age is associated with an increased risk of becoming impoverished (K. Johnson & Wilson, 2010; Wu, 2011a). The median income of families headed by people aged 65–69 was $42,314, while median family income for families headed by individuals aged 85+ was $21,305 (Wu, 2011a). Approximately 39% of people over age 75 lived under 200% of poverty, compared to 29% of individuals aged 65–74 (Employee Benefit Research Institute [EBRI], 2011b). Older women living alone, regardless of age, had a lower median income than their male counterparts (Wu, 2011a). Relative to gender and marital status, however, education level appears to be an even more powerful predictor of income after age 65. The mean income for older adults in 2010 without a high school diploma was just $16,089, as compared to $64,459 for individuals with a graduate degree (EBRI, 2011b).

Racial and ethnic minority status is also an important correlate of income disparity after age 65 (see Exhibit 9.2). Older Hispanic adults of any race continue to report the lowest incomes among older adults in the United States. The median household income for older Hispanic men is $15,707—two thirds the median household income of older non-Hispanic White men ($26,564). Older Asian men have the second highest median household income of $20,834, although older Asian women have a median household income far below that of White and Black women ($11,977 vs. $15,443 and $13,145; U.S. Census Bureau, 2011d). Moreover, older men in all minority groups have higher median incomes than their female counterparts (AARP Public Policy Institute, 2010; U.S. Census Bureau, 2011d).

Thus, the differential income distributions between older women and older men, and between older Whites and minority elders result in a greater reliance on income support programs by older women and by older non-Whites (AARP Public Policy Institute, 2010). In this chapter, we provide the policy background for three primary income programs: Social Security, pensions, and Supplemental Security Income (SSI). We then describe the users of these programs and conclude with challenges facing income programs as the next century approaches.

Exhibit 9.2   Median Income of Persons 65 Years and Older by Race, Ethnicity, and Sex in 2010

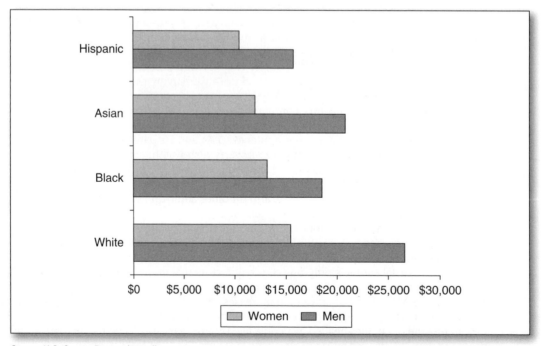

Source: U.S. Census Bureau (2011d).

POLICY BACKGROUND

Social Security

The Social Security Act of 1935 established the basic Old Age Benefits program and a federal–state system of unemployment insurance. In 1939, Congress added survivors' and dependents' benefits, and in 1956, it expanded Social Security to include disability insurance to protect workers with severe disabilities. Although numerous adjustments have been made to the Social Security system since its inception, there have been few major programmatic changes (see Chapter 2 for details).

Exhibit 9.3 summarizes the various programs available under Social Security. Workers and employers each pay 6.2% of earnings up to a cap, which was $106,800 in 2011, to the Social Security Trust Fund (Reno, Lamme, & Walker, 2011). To be eligible for retirement benefits under the Old Age, Survivor, and Disability Insurance (OASDI) program, a worker must have worked in covered employment for 40 calendar quarters. Coverage is nearly universal for work done in the United States; it covers about 95% of all jobs. In 2010, about 157 million persons worked in employment or self-employment covered under the OASDI program. Persons aged 62 and older comprise 80% of the more than 54 million people receiving Social Security benefits: 10% aged 62 to 64, 37% aged 65 to 74, 23% aged 75 to 84, and 10% aged 85 + (Social Security Administration, 2011b).

The three basic categories of benefits under Social Security are (a) retirement benefits, (b) disability benefits, and (c) dependents' and survivors' benefits. Once a worker qualifies for retirement benefits, she or he (together with the survivors) first becomes eligible to claim early retirement benefits at age 62. To receive disability benefits, a worker must have a physical or mental impairment that prevents any substantial gainful work, and the disability must be expected to last, or to have lasted, 12 months, or to be expected to result in

Exhibit 9.3   Benefits Provided Under Social Security in January 2011

Type of Benefit	Who Qualifies	Average Monthly Benefits Paid to Recipient[1]	Number of Beneficiaries
Retirement	Full retirement benefits are payable at age 65 for persons born in 1937 or earlier, with reduced benefits available as early as age 62. The age to receive full benefits is gradually rising by two months per birth year for persons born between 1938 and 1960. Beginning in 2027, full retirement benefits will be payable at age 67. Reduced benefits continue to be available at age 62.	Workers retiring at full retirement age: $1,166 Workers retiring at full retirement age and aged spouse: $1,911	Social Security pays monthly retirement benefits to more than 37 million retired workers and their families. More than 9 out of 10 Americans who are age 65 or older receive Social Security benefits.

(Continued)

Exhibit 9.3 (Continued)

Type of Benefit	Who Qualifies	Average Monthly Benefits Paid to Recipient[1]	Number of Beneficiaries
Disability	Workers are considered disabled if they have a severe physical or mental condition that prevents them from working. The condition must be expected to last for at least 12 months or to result in death. Once benefits begin, they continue for as long as the worker is disabled. A worker who receives disability payments for two years becomes eligible for Medicare.	Disabled worker: $1,050 Disabled worker with a young spouse and one or more children: $1,807	More than 8 million disabled workers under 65 and 1.980 million dependents receive Social Security.
Dependent's and survivor's benefits	Children under 18 A child who is under 19 but still in high school A child who is 18 or older but who becomes disabled before age 22 A widow(er) who is caring for children under age 16 or disabled A widow(er) age 60 or older, or a widow(er) age 50 or older who is disabled	Surviving children: $752 Surviving spouse and two dependent children: $2,390 Widow(er) alone, nondisabled: $1,134 Widow(er) alone, disabled: $681	Social Security pays monthly survivor benefits to 6.36 million Americans.

Source: Reno et al. (2011) and Social Security Administration (2011b).

[1]Social Security benefits generally increase each year by a cost-of-living adjustment (COLA) that is based on the consumer price index for urban wage earners (CPI-W). Because of the recession, the CPI-W declined and inflation remained low; thus, no COLA was paid in 2010 or 2011.

death (National Academy of Social Insurance, 2011). To be eligible for dependents' and survivors' benefits, the worker has to have had enough credits to qualify for her or his own retirement or disability benefits.

Pension Benefits

The Civil Service Retirement Act was enacted in 1920, providing pension coverage for the first time to federal civilian employees (Schultz, 2001). A year later, the implementation of private, employer-sponsored pension plans was encouraged by the passage of the

Revenue Act of 1921. This legislation exempted both the income of pension and profit-sharing trusts, and the employer contributions to these plans from income taxation.

Through the years, serious problems (e.g., inadequate funds, misuse of funds) have undermined the worker protection provided under employer-sponsored programs. In response to abuse and mismanagement in the private pension system, Congress enacted the Employee Retirement Income Security Act of 1974. It was the first comprehensive effort to regulate private pensions. The major objectives of this Act are to (a) ensure that workers and beneficiaries receive adequate information about their employee benefit plans, (b) set standards of conduct for those managing employment benefit plans and plan funds, (c) determine that adequate funds are being set aside to pay promised pension benefits, (d) ensure that workers receive pension benefits after they have satisfied certain minimum requirements, and (e) safeguard pension benefits for workers whose employers end their pension plans (B. Coleman, 1989).

A major shift in the type of pension programs provided by employers began in the 1980s. In the mid to late 1980s, plans established by single employers dominated the labor market. By 2005, many plans were insolvent or were absorbed by multi-employer plans (Pension Benefit Guaranty Corporation, 2006). Regardless of the origin of the plan, types available include defined benefit and defined contribution plans.

Defined benefit pension plans promise to pay a yearly pension benefit to workers who qualify on the basis of age and service. These plans provide retirees with a steady income stream that commences with retirement and continues until that person's, or in some cases the spouse's, death. In almost every defined benefit plan, the employer assumes the risk of making sure that adequate money is available to pay the promised benefit (Barocas, 1994). When an employer offers a defined benefit plan, participation is generally automatic, as it does not require the employee to make any contributions (Costo, 2006). As a result of the recent recession, some state pension plans are requiring increased contributions from employers, which often results in the costs being passed to employees (National Conference of State Legislatures, 2011). The economic downturn and pending demographic changes also have strained private pension plans. Many workplaces will likely raise contributions from employees, and company's whose plans are in the worst condition may find increasing employer contributions or reducing benefits insufficient to address their underfunding and demographic challenges (U.S. Government Accountability Office, 2010).

Defined contribution plans specify employer and employee contributions but do not guarantee future benefits. Funds accumulate in an account, and the returns to the accumulated funds determine the retirement benefits. The employee is responsible for investing the contributions. The most common and frequently employed defined contribution arrangements are 401(k) plans (Gale, Orszag, Burman, & Hall, 2004).

In 2010, 54.5% of all full-time, year-round wage and salary workers participated in a retirement plan (Copeland, 2011). Surveys of *private sector* employees found that 49% of these workers participated in employment-based retirement plans, with 19% participating in defined benefit plans, and 41% participating in defined contribution plans (Bureau of Labor Statistics [BLS], 2010d, 2011a). Among all wage and salary workers, men participate at a higher level in retirement plans than women, largely due to lower salaries and higher rates of part-time employment among women. However, when comparing BLS (2011a) full-time, year-round workers, a slightly greater percentage of women participate in retirement plans than men (55.5% vs. 53.8%, respectively; Copeland, 2011). In addition, fewer Hispanic and Black Americans participate in retirement benefits plans than White Americans, although the gap in participation narrows when comparing employees across earnings levels.

Across the Globe: Canada's Guaranteed Income Supplement

Canada provides a wide range of income assistance programs to older adults based on varying needs and circumstances, including the Guaranteed Income Supplement. This program, aimed at reducing poverty among Canadian seniors, offers extra financial assistance to low-income older adults who are receiving a pension but meet income eligibility requirements. Eligible seniors receive additional annual benefits of up to $600 for single seniors and $840 for couples. Single recipients with an annual income of $2,000 or less, excluding pension benefits, and couples with an annual income of $4,000 or less receive the full increase. This program is expected to improve the financial security and well-being of more than 680,000 of Canada's most vulnerable seniors.

Source: Service Canada (2012).

Supplemental Security Income

Administered by the Social Security Administration, the SSI program provides income support to persons aged 65 and older and to children and adults who are blind or have a disability. Established in 1972, SSI replaced the federally aided state programs that had prevailed for several decades. Distribution of the first SSI payments occurred in January 1974. The program has not experienced any significant changes since its original legislation.

SSI acts as an important safety net for older adults receiving few or no Social Security benefits. Under this program, each eligible person living in his or her own household, having limited or no other income and few assets, receives a monthly cash payment. Eligibility and federal payment standards are nationally uniform and strict. To receive SSI, a person must be aged 65 or older, blind, or have a disability, and must have assets (excluding a home, car, and personal belongings) of no more than $2,000 for an individual and $3,000 for a couple (Social Security Administration, 2011b). In addition, the recipient's monthly income (e.g., Social Security, pensions, bank account interest, stock dividends) must not exceed the guidelines established by each state. Many recipients receive only partial SSI benefits because benefit levels are reduced by one dollar for each dollar of countable income. In 2011, the maximum federal SSI benefit was $674 a month for individuals and $1,011 for couples, which amounts to approximately 91% of the official poverty guideline for single adults and 115% for couples (Legislative Analyst's Office, 2011; Social Security Administration, 2011b).

For Your Files: Office of Financial Protection for Older Americans

The Office of Financial Protection for Older Americans, established in 2011 within the Consumer Financial Protection Bureau, is tasked with improving the financial decision making of seniors and preventing unfair, deceptive, and abusive practices targeted at seniors. The purpose of the Office is to help seniors navigate financial challenges that can arise in late life by educating and engaging them about their financial choices in the area of long-term savings, retirement planning, and long-term care; reaching out to and coordinating with senior groups, law enforcement, financial institutions, and other federal and state agencies to identify and prevent scams targeting seniors; using information from the field along with direct input from seniors to identify trends and bad practices in a timely and effective way; and protecting seniors from fraud and deception in financial counseling services (National Council on Aging, 2011d).

To find out more, visit http://www.consumerfinance.gov/older-americans.

Source: National Council on Aging (2011a; 2011d).

USERS AND PROGRAMS

Social Security is an important source of income for many families and is the primary source of money income for older adults. As shown in Exhibit 9.4, retired workers (64%), survivors of deceased workers (12%), disabled workers (15%), and spouses and children of retired and disabled workers (9%) receive Social Security benefits under one of its programs (Social Security Administration, 2011b). Nine of every 10 older adults receive income from Social Security. Moreover, 22% of married older adults and 43% of nonmarried older adults depend on Social Security for 90% or more of their income. Of all adult beneficiaries, 44% are men and 56% are women. Although the percentage of men among retired worker beneficiaries (80%) is much higher than that of women (61%), the percentage of women receiving retired worker benefits has increased significantly since the inception of the program when only 12% received these benefits. Among older adults, White (90.8%) and Black (84.1%) elders are somewhat more likely than Hispanic elders (79.4%) to receive Social Security (Wu, 2011b).

The monthly Social Security benefit amount a retired worker will receive depends on the worker's age and earning record. Nearly one half of all new retired worker benefits are awarded at age 62, and more than two thirds are awarded before age 65. According to the Social Security Administration (Reno et al., 2011), the average monthly benefit for retired workers in 2011 was $1,166; the maximum monthly benefit for workers retiring at full retirement age was $2,366. Older male retirees received an average monthly benefit of $1,323 compared with $1,023 received by older female retirees (Social Security Administration, 2011b).

About 40% of persons aged 65 and older receive pension income, including both private and government employee pensions (Wu, 2011b). The proportion of retirees receiving pension income is greater in the middle and higher income brackets than in the low to moderate income brackets. Gender is a influencing factor in rates and amounts of retirement annuity and pension income, with 43.2% of men and only 29.4% of women over age 65 receiving annuity and/or pension income in 2008 (McDonnell, 2010). There were also discrepancies in amounts of income from these sources, with men receiving a mean amount of $19,557 per year and women having a mean annuity and/or pension income of $12,137 per year. A greater percentage of White older adults (43.4%), compared with Black (32.4%) or Hispanic (20.3%) older adults, received pension benefits (Wu, 2011b).

Approximately 1.7 million older adults received military benefits (Wu, 2011b). The median benefit paid to Veterans aged 65 and older was $8,400. The military retirement program, touted as the best pension in the United States, provides full benefits that begin immediately on retirement, requires no financial contribution from military personnel, pays at least 50% of basic pay to those with 20 years' service and 75% after 30 years of service, and does not subject benefits to an earnings test.

In 2010, approximately 2 million older adults received SSI benefits. The average monthly amount for an older beneficiary was $405; the maximum federal monthly SSI check was $674 for an individual and $1,011 for a couple (Social Security Administration, 2011b). Older women were more likely than older men to receive SSI benefits (68% vs. 32%, respectively). African American (10.3%) and Hispanic (11.4%) older adults were more likely to receive SSI than were their White (2.5%) counterparts (Wu, 2011b).

Exhibit 9.4   Number (in Thousands) of Social Security Beneficiaries by Type of Benefit (2010)

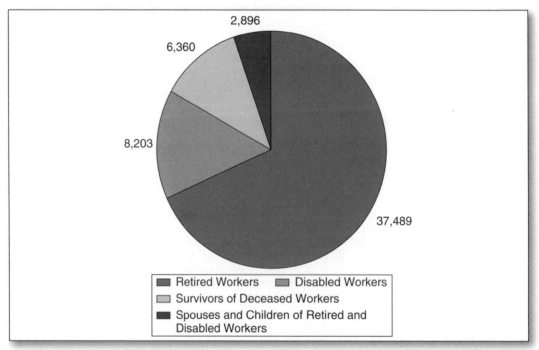

Source: Social Security Administration (2011b).

Best Practices: Tax Counseling for the Elderly (TCE) Program

The Tax Counseling for the Elderly (TCE) Program offers free tax help to individuals who are aged 60 or older. Trained volunteers from nonprofit organizations provide free tax counseling and basic income tax return preparation for senior citizens. Volunteers who provide tax counseling are often retired individuals associated with nonprofit organizations that receive grants from the IRS. As part of this IRS-sponsored TCE Program, AARP offers the Tax-Aide counseling program. In 2011, this program had 6,100 Tax-Aide sites nationwide (e.g., senior centers, libraries) and 35,000 active volunteers who served 2.6 million taxpayers during the filing season. For more information on TCE or to find an AARP Tax Aide site near you, call 1-888-227-7669 or see www.aarp.org/money/taxes/aarp_taxaide.

CHALLENGES FOR INCOME PROGRAMS

There is growing consensus among business, government, and academic experts that most Americans have limited financial literacy and do not realize how much it costs to retire (Behrman, Mitchell, Soo, & Bravo, 2010; Eschtruth, 2006; Lusardi & Mitchell, 2011). Younger workers think they have plenty of time to prepare for their retirement years and often do not take advantage of company-sponsored retirement plans or savings initiatives. Midlife employees recognize the need to plan proactively for retirement but often view themselves as unable to save more. As a group, they appear conservative and do not understand much about such topics as budgeting, types of investments, risk, and the time value of money. Older employees tend to fall into one of two groups: those who have planned well and those who have not. Environmental, personal, and social circumstances prevent many older adults from having a financially secure retirement (Perlman, Kenneally, & Boivie, 2011). We end this chapter by discussing some challenges facing income programs as the number and proportion of persons entering the retirement years grow.

Bouncing Back From the Recession

The economic turndown that began in 2008 has had serious repercussions for most individuals, including adults approaching retirement. Older employees have experienced a greater decline in their 401(k) account balances than younger employees because their account balances were not very large to begin with, and because the incremental contributions of younger employees could make up for a substantial portion of the decline (Madrian, cited in Majmundar, 2010).

While the recession also has influenced the retirement lives older adults, minority elders are particularly vulnerable to the economic crisis. They often entered their later years with very limited assets and resources. More than half of African American (52%) and Hispanic (56%) older adults (compared to 32% White elders) are economically insecure, meaning they have inadequate resources to maintain a basic standard of living for the remainder of their lives (Meschede, Sullivan, & Shapiro, 2011). A 2010 AARP survey found that about one third (34%) of African Americans aged 45 and older indicated that they had stopped contributing to their 401(k), IRA, or other investment accounts during the year prior to the survey. In addition, 26% of African Americans compared to 18% of the general population had withdrawn funds from their retirement saving accounts (Perron, 2010). Policy reforms focused on retirement security are needed to improve the economic well-being of the aging population. Initiatives designed to help low-skilled employees would be of particular benefit to African American workers and other groups with limited education as would initiatives to boost private savings and provide wage subsidies (R. W. Johnson et al., 2011).

Maintaining a Person's Standard of Living

Many workers are unaware of how much they need to save for their retirement. Findings from the 2011 Retirement Confidence Survey (RCS) found that although 74% of the workers surveyed stated that they have saved money for retirement, less than one half (42%) reported that they have tried to calculate how much money they will need to save for a comfortable retirement (Employee Benefit Research Institute, 2011a). Experts often promote a "three-legged stool" model for financial preparation for retirement. Personal savings, Social Security, and pension income represent the three components or "legs" of the retirement income stool (Barocas, 1994). As previously mentioned, Social Security benefits are a significant source of retirement income for many older adults, yet there is a large gap for most workers between their Social Security benefits and the income needed to maintain their current living standards in retirement. The challenge is to encourage broader pension coverage, particularly for low-wage workers, and to encourage financial planning for retirement.

One of the main ways workers can be encouraged to save for retirement is through an employer-sponsored retirement savings plan, such as a 401(k). Seventy-nine percent of all workers in the RCS indicated that they participate in such a plan with their current employer (Employee Benefit Research Institute, 2011a). Workers who participate in this type of plan are more than twice as likely as those who do not participate to have savings and investments of $50,000 or more (52% vs. 23%, respectively). Yet the majority of workers contributing to employer-sponsored saving plans are uncertain about how much they should be saving so that they can maintain their current lifestyle when they retire, and how much money they can expect to receive in retirement from their current saving plan.

Financial planning for retirement is a difficult and complex task. Preparation must occur on more than just the individual level. Companies must invest more in preretirement planning as a means of helping employees take greater responsibility for their retirement income. The challenge for both the public and private sector is to (a) increase the availability of preretirement education for all individuals; (b) improve the quality of available programs by ensuring that programs assist employees in evaluating their current financial state, defining their personal goals, and identifying a financial game plan to make certain that the resources are available to achieve their personal goals; and (c) encourage people to begin preparing for retirement at an early age (McKinsey & Company, 2009; Volunteers of America, 2011).

Enhancing the Income of Older Women

Studies have shown that women make substantially less than men in the labor market. This discriminatory pattern influences women's pensions, Social Security benefits, annuities, and bank savings. In addition, women who divorce or separate from their husbands may lose any resources developed during a marriage (e.g., rights to an ex-husband's pension and other financial assets). These women also may have discontinuous work careers that decrease their ability to achieve pension-vesting rights and lower the wages on which retirement income is calculated (Rappaport, 2007). To improve the income adequacy for women, policy makers must address the inequities of Social Security, particularly for working women, as well as inequities in private pension systems and methods of providing protection to the surviving spouse.

Increasing Participation in Income Programs

The federal government estimates that about 37% of older adults eligible for SSI do not participate in the program (Rupp, Strand, Davies, & Sears, 2007). Two key reasons appear to be lack of knowledge about it and the stigma associated with being involved with a means-tested program (Schultz, 2001). In recent years, the Social Security Administration has undertaken activities to increase awareness and participation in the program (e.g., public service announcements) but with little success. Another factor that may prohibit individuals from seeking SSI payments is the income and resource test. SSI limits the amount of assets, earned income, and unearned income the individual may have and still qualify for benefits. The asset limit ($2,000) has not been increased since 1984, and the disregards for earned and unearned income ($65 and $20 per month, respectively) have not been changed since the program began (Corporation for Enterprise Development, 2010; Social Security Administration, 2012c).

Ensuring the Long-Term Financing of Social Security

As people are living longer and receiving Social Security benefits for longer periods of time, the total benefits paid annually by Social Security are increasing. Some economists predict that the cost of benefits will exceed the amount of payroll taxes collected within the next decade. In the past, efforts to deal with Social Security's financial difficulties have generally featured cutting benefits and raising tax rates on a pay-as-you-go basis. The pay-as-you-go approach means that taxes collected by workers in a given year are spent to pay benefits in the same year. The Social Security Trust Fund, which holds the money, is more of a money-transfer system, not a savings program. Therefore, the collection of Social Security tax is sensitive to the ratio of the number of current workers and those receiving benefits (J. Brown, Hassett, & Smetters, 2005). In 1950, the ratio was 16:1; by 2010, it had dropped to 2.9:1. It is projected that there will be 2.1 workers for each beneficiary in 2029. In 2010, for the first time, payroll taxes were not enough to pay scheduled benefits and administrative expenses (Social Security Administration, 2011b). Some economic forecasters estimate depletion of the trust funds by 2036, at which time payroll taxes and other income flow into the fund will cover only about 77% of the program costs.

Government officials and Congress agree that the Social Security System needs to change but are unable to agree on a single plan for dealing with the predicted financial difficulties. The general debate surrounds two fundamentally different views: (a) Social Security is an antiquated system unsustainable in an aging society that should be replaced by a system of privatized accounts, and (b) Social Security is not "broken" or in "crisis" but is a valuable system of social insurance, particularly for poor and disabled retirees, that is simply in need of moderate changes to ensure long-term stability (Nuschler, 2010). President Obama—who views Social Security as a crucial source of income for many vulnerable seniors, individuals with disabilities, and survivors of deceased workers—is strongly opposed to privatization and favors protecting and strengthening the existing Social Security system (White House, 2012a, 2012b). Although the President has established some "guiding principles" of reform (e.g., restoring strength of Social Security for future generations and establishing long-term solvency; not slashing basic benefits for current or future generations), it is not yet clear what specific reforms will be put forward. The National Academy of Social Insurance put forth a series of alternatives for improving benefits while reducing or eliminating the anticipated shortfall. Strategies proposed include lifting the taxable wage cap (over 10 years) to cover 90% of wages, raising the FICA rate by 1/20 of 1% a year over 20 years, to 7.2% in 2035, and dedicating a 0.25% financial speculation tax to Social Security (Reno et al., 2011).

Maintaining and Enhancing Income Programs in the Future

Obtaining financial security in later life will require that employment opportunities exist for older workers who wish to remain or re-enter the workforce, that public and private pensions expand the number of workers covered, and that Social Security benefits continue to act as the third leg of the financial retirement stool. The delegates to the 2005 White House Conference on Aging (2006) proposed numerous strategies for strengthening the Social Security Program, including (a) maintaining the entire Social Security (SS) system without privatization, including survivor benefits, the disability program, and the current cost-of-living adjustment (COLA) formula; (b) investing a portion of SS Trust Fund in equity and bond markets and dedicating the inheritance tax for estates to the SS Trust Fund; and (c) retaining the progressive defined benefit structure by removing caps on earnings for SS contributions. Perhaps the increase in the number of older adults facing retirement decisions in the next decade will facilitate a change in policy about work, retirement, and income security in retirement.

CASE STUDY

When the System Fails

Sonny, who is 66 years old, and his wife, Magdalena, who just had her 63rd birthday, never expected to find themselves in such a financially precarious position and so frustrated with their own government at this point in their lives. When they were married 45 years ago, they had made so many plans. They were proud that their hard work had realized a modest retirement savings and that their three children were responsible, hardworking young adults. Sonny was especially proud of his service to his country during World War II.

Sonny retired at age 65 with a Social Security benefit of $1,000 per month and a union retirement benefit of $400 per month. Magdalena had never worked outside the home. She had no credits toward Social Security, and at age 63 was not eligible to draw an early Social Security retirement benefit on Sonny's credits of work or apply for Medicare. Nevertheless, their income had been adequate because their home and vehicles were paid for and they had no other outstanding debts.

Their retirement dreams began to fade as Magdalena's health deteriorated. Side effects from diabetes, diagnosed when Magdalena was 15 years old, have caused kidney failure. Magdalena is now receiving dialysis twice a month and spends part of her time in a wheelchair. She is also considered legally blind. The predicament for Sonny and Magdalena now is that the health plan that covered Magdalena's medical expenses expired because it had limited time coverage from Sonny's former employer, that Magdalena is not eligible for SSI because their income of $1,400 per month is too much to qualify, and that she cannot qualify for private insurance because of her pre-existing condition. Although a Social Security regulation permits persons with dialysis to qualify for benefits including Medicare before age 65, Magdalena has twice been denied this benefit on the grounds that she is not disabled. Their savings have been completely depleted to pay for Magdalena's dialysis and other medical expenses. To their anger, shame, and frustration, Magdalena is receiving a six-month limited health benefit from their state's medically indigent uninsurable program. At the end of the six months, they will still have another year of uncovered medical expenses before Magdalena can qualify for Social Security unless they can find some help to turn this situation around.

One day at the dialysis center, Magdalena was talking with the receptionist about not understanding why Social Security would refuse her application for early disability under the special dialysis rule. Why would Social Security not consider Magdalena disabled?

Case Study Questions

1. Are Sonny and Magdalena justified in their frustration? Do they have the right to expect a source of income maintenance and health insurance coverage, given their situation?

2. Name as many help source agencies or programs that you can think of that Sonny and Magdalena might have contacted regarding this situation.

3. It is obvious that money is tight for this couple at this time. One human services professional might see the best course of help as being to put Sonny and Magdalena in touch with a variety of charity programs that could help them with food, clothing, utilities, and free medical service. Another professional might see the best course as being to appeal their case to Social Security. Which professional would you be and why?

4. Describe the characteristics of a community service environment in which a dialysis center receptionist cares and knows where to refer a patient for help in a matter such as Magdalena's?

5. Often, in working with older adults, professionals speak of clients who "fall through the cracks." What do you think this expression means? Do you think Sonny and Magdalena fit this description? Why or why not?

6. What could have been a worst-case scenario for this couple? How typical do you think their situation is? What does it show about the importance of income-maintenance programs for many older adults?

LEARNING ACTIVITIES

1. Visit the "One Away" website (http://www.oneaway.org/), a campaign sponsored by the National Council on Aging to call greater attention to the fact that 13 million seniors are one event away from economic disaster. Review several of the personal stories posted by more than 4,500 seniors and identify common themes in their challenges of surviving on fixed incomes while expenses like healthcare and food increase.

2. Put together a monthly budget that includes expenses such as rent or mortgage, food, utilities, medical expenses, entertainment, insurance, and other items that you believe are necessary for a comfortable and satisfying lifestyle. What would you need currently to support yourself? Project your income needs to maintain that lifestyle at age 70. What changes may occur in your income needs? What is your plan to ensure that your income is sufficient?

3   Interview someone from your local Social Security office. What issues does the office primarily deal with in relation to income and benefits? Whom do the office staff see more—women or men? What is the clients' typical level of income? Do many of the recipients have alternative income sources? Does the office offer information on income planning for retirement? What counseling and information services does the office provide, and for what are beneficiaries most likely to ask?

4.   Investigate retirement-income plans. How accessible is the information (both to obtain and to understand)? What places carry the information, and to whom is it targeted? Are there specific brochures for women, men, minorities, and different income levels, and in languages other than English?

5.   Estimate how much of your earnings you may be able to replace through pension plans if you live in the United States or elsewhere by using the pension calculator provided by the Organization for Economic Co-operation and Development (www.oecd.org/els/pensionsystems/ pensionsataglancepensioncalculator.htm). Identify which countries have the highest and lowest rate of return and how pension benefits may differ for men and women.

6.   Talk to two family members to find out what plans they have made for their income needs in their old age. Do they feel that their income will be adequate? If you could, what suggestions would you make to help them plan for an adequate income in retirement?

FOR MORE INFORMATION

International Resources

1.   Social Security Programs Throughout the World: www.ssa.gov/policy/docs/progdesc/ssptw

This publication highlights the principal features of social security programs in more than 170 countries. A set of tables in provides information for each country on the types of social security programs, types of mandatory systems for retirement income, contribution rates, and demographic and other statistics related to social security.

2.   Global Action on Aging Social Pensions: http://www.globalaging.org/pension/world/social/social pensions.htm

Based in New York at the United Nations headquarters, the mission of this organization is to report on older people's needs and potential within the global economy. Its website provides links to articles, reports, and sources of information about social pension programs, many of which focus on developing countries worldwide.

3.   Elderly Poverty and an Ageing World: Conditions of Social Vulnerability and Low Income for Women in Rich and Middle-Income Nations: http://www.lisproject.org/publications/liswps/ 497.pdf

This Luxemburg Income Study Working Paper (No. 497; Smeeding, Gao, Saunders, & Wing, 2008) examines the problems of population aging, low incomes, and social spending on elderly adults in a comparative perspective, with a focus specifically on older women in several rich and middle-income nations.

4. Social Security Programs Throughout the World: The Americas 2011: http://www.ssa.gov/ policy/docs/progdesc/ssptw/2010-2011/americas/index.html

   This fourth issue of a four-volume series of *Social Security Programs Throughout the World* reports on the countries of the Americas. The combined findings of this series, which also includes volumes on Europe, Asia and the Pacific, and Africa, are published at six-month intervals over a two-year period. Each volume highlights features of social security programs in the particular region.

National Resources

1. Social Security Administration, 6401 Security Boulevard, Baltimore, MD 21235; phone: 800-772-1213; www.ssa.gov

   The Social Security Administration is responsible for the administration of Social Security and SSI programs. Free publications are available.

2. Pension Rights Center, 1350 Connecticut Avenue NW, Suite 206, Washington, DC 20036-1739; phone: 202-296-3776; www.pensionrights.org

   The Pension Rights Center works to protect the pension rights of workers, retirees, and their families. The center publishes handbooks and packets on pension law and retirement systems.

Web Resources

1. Social Security Online: www.ssa.gov

   The Social Security website is one of the most comprehensive sites in the aging network. Visitors can request a copy of their earnings record, browse information about the history and legislation of Social Security, access publications online, and review statistical information about benefits and beneficiaries.

2. Benefits Link: www.benefitslink.com/index.html

   Benefits Link is a free nationwide link to information and services for employers sponsoring employee benefit plans, companies providing products and services for plans, and participating employees. There are links to new benefits information, public discussions of benefits design, Internet resources, and online benefits newsletters.

3. U.S. Department of Labor: www.dol.gov

   The U.S. Department of Labor's site has a number of resources, including a link that provides pension information.

4. The Center for Retirement research at Boston College: http://crr.bc.edu

   The Center for Retirement Research at Boston College provides decision makers in the public and private sectors with critical information to better understand the issues facing an aging population. The Center's research program spans the four main areas that affect a household's retirement income: (a) Social Security, (b) employer-sponsored pension plans, (c) household saving, and (d) labor market trends among older workers.

5. Social Security Administration (SSA) "For Women": www.ssa.gov/pressoffice/forwomen.htm

   The Social Security Administration has launched this website to provide basic Social Security information on retirement, survivors, disability, and SSI benefits that pertain to women.

6. BenefitsCheckUp: www.benefitscheckup.org

   The National Council on the Aging created BenefitsCheckUp to help older adults quickly identify federal and state assistance programs that may improve the quality of their lives. Family and friends can also obtain facts about benefits for which their loved ones may qualify.

7. The National Council of La Raza (NCLR): www.nclr.org

   NCLR is a private, nonprofit, nonpartisan organization established to reduce poverty and discrimination and to improve life opportunities for Hispanic Americans. Policy reports on the website include, for example, "The Great Debate: Social Security Reform, What's at Stake for Latinos" and "We Need the Work: Latino Worker Voices in the New Economy."

8. Improving the Lives of LGBT Older Adults: 11 Issue Briefs: www.lgbtmap.org/policy-and-issue-analysis/improving-the-lives-of-lgbt-older-adults-issue-briefs

   Services and Advocacy for Gay, Lesbian, Bisexual, & Transgender Elders partnered with the Movement Advancement Project (MAP) and the Center for American Progress (CAP) to develop 11 policy briefs to expand on key issues that were raised in the original "Improving the Lives of LGBT Older Adults" report. Issue briefs address financial concerns such as "Social Security" and "Pension Plans."

Nutrition and Meal Programs

The door opens, and Alice beams with pride as she ushers you into her apartment. She prepares lunch, but you notice that there's nothing in the fridge. It's empty. That's the first sign. She offers you coffee, and you get Nescafé. That's the second sign. You know that she's giving you the last food she has until she visits a food pantry later in the week, a wonderful, welcoming agency that receives its food from the Greater Boston Food Bank. You have no choice but to eat Alice's food. Refusing to do so would hurt her more than the hunger that hurts her most every day. Alice relies on emergency food assistance to survive. She lives on her small Social Security income to pay her rent and utility bills and to buy clothes and food. "I have lived through the Depression, and know how to stretch a dollar," she explains. "But it's just not enough."[1]

The consumption of food is not only a biological necessity for health and vitality but also a social activity that is rich with symbolism. It is often an integral part of holiday gatherings and celebrations of all types. Although most of us are aware of the social nature of food consumption, we are only vaguely aware of the necessity of good nutritional habits. Good nutritional habits are important in all stages of life, but in later life, as individuals grow older, age-related changes in various body systems as well as in social relationships can place them at risk of inadequate nutritional intake. In this chapter, we review the extent of malnutrition and hunger among older adults, the physical and psychosocial factors that influence nutritional status in later life, the policies that support nutrition programs of older adults, the types of nutrition programs available, and the characteristics of those who use such programs.

NUTRITIONAL STATUS AMONG OLDER ADULTS

When reviewing the literature concerning the nutritional status among older adults, one can easily be confused by the different terminology used. For example, *malnutrition*, although usually linked to a lack of sufficient food intake, literally means "bad nutrition" and includes nutritional states of undernutrition and overnutrition (Keller, 1993). With regard to *undernutrition*, evidence supports the notion that many older adults are at risk of

---

[1]This story is based on true events and provided by the Greater Boston Food Bank and the Food Bank for New York City website in 2007.

poor nutritional intake, food insecurity, or hunger (see Exhibit 10.1 for definitions and questions used to measure these terms). A study conducted by the U.S. Department of Agriculture's (USDA) Economic Research Service found that 7.9% (2.33 million) of adults aged 65 and older experienced food insecurity and 2.6% (773,000) of elderly households experienced very low food security with hunger (Coleman-Jensen, Nord, Andrews, & Carlson, 2011). Ziliak and Gundersen (2011) examined data from the Current Population Survey, which is a nationally representative survey conducted by the U.S. Census Bureau, to examine the extent of food insecurity among people aged 40 and older. The survey includes 18 questions that compose the Core Food Security Module, which measures the food insecurity status of households in the United States. They found that in 2009, among adults age 50 and older, 15.6 million persons faced the threat of hunger (i.e., marginally food insecure), 8.8 million faced the risk of hunger (i.e., were food insecure), and 3.5 million faced hunger (i.e., were low food secure). This is an increase of 66%, 79%, and 132%, respectively, from the levels of food insecurity in 2001 among this population. For those in their preretirement years, aged 50 to 59 years, 8.1 million were marginally food insecure, 4.9 million were food insecure, and 2.1 million were very low food secure. Among older adults aged 60 and older, the comparable numbers were 7.5 million, 3.9 million, and 1.4 million, respectively. Data also showed that food insecurity of any type increased among older adults during the two years between 2007 and 2009. The percentage increase in marginal food insecurity among those aged 50 to 59 from 2007 to 2009 was 38% and 20% among those over aged 60 and over. Food insecurity increased by 38% among those aged 50 to 59, and 25% among those aged 60 and over. The percentage increase for those aged 50 to 59 with very low food security rates was 69% and 17% for those over age 60.

In another attempt to measure the extent of food insecurity in the United States, Feeding America (formally America's Second Harvest) conducted a study of more than 37,000 agencies operating food programs across the country and more than 62,000 clients of emergency food programs (Mabli, Cohen, Potter, & Zhao, 2010). Results indicated that 18.6% of the clients served by Feeding America's food program sites have elderly adults (age 65 and over) as members of the household. Of the adult clients (excluding food program clients under age 18), 29.6% were between the ages of 50 to 64 and 14.2% were over age 65, and the majority accessed food at a food pantry rather than at a food kitchen or shelter. Thirty-nine percent of households with older adults reported being food insecure without hunger, with 18.8% reporting being food insecure with hunger, up from 2005 percentages of 35.8% and 16.2%, respectively. In addition, many of the elderly clients who received food from pantries, kitchens, or shelters reported that they were making choices between purchasing food and paying for household expenses. For example, 34.9%, 23.3%, and 29.6% reported having to choose between food purchases and utilities or heating fuel, rent or mortgage, and medical care, respectively.

Older adults who do not have adequate nutritional intake are at risk of negative physical outcomes. Researchers have found a link between food insecurity and increased risk of additional health problems, reduced muscle mass, a compromised immune system, and mortality (Chandra, 1992; N. G. Choi, 1999; DiMaria-Ghalili & Amella, 2005; Kamp, Wellman, & Russell, 2010; Roberts, Hajduk, Howarth, Russell, & McCrory, 2005; W. S. Wolfe, Olson, Kendall, & Frongillo, 1998). Furthermore, inappropriate diets may induce diseases such as coronary heart disease and a reduction in general well-being (Kannel, 1986; J. S. Lee & Frongillo, 2001; Saxon, Etten, & Perkins, 2010).

With regard to overnutrition, the growing number of adults in the United States who have been classified as overweight or obese is a growing public health concern (Flegal, Carroll, Ogden, & Curtin, 2010). In 2007–2008, the prevalence of obesity among men and women aged 60 and over was 37% and 33%, respectively. Given the prevalence of obesity

Exhibit 10.1   USDA's Revised Labels and Definitions of Food Security

General Categories (old and new labels are the same)	Detailed Categories			Indicators Used to Measure Food Security (in adult-only households)
	Old Label	New Label	Description of Conditions in the Household	
Food Security	Food security	High food security	No reported indications of food-access problems or limitations	1. Worried whether our food would run out before we got money to buy more 2. Food that we bought didn't last, and we didn't have money to get more 3. Couldn't afford to eat balanced meals 4. Cut the size of meals or skipped meals 5. Cut or skipped meal in 3+ months 6. Ate less than we felt we should because there wasn't enough money for food 7. Hungry, but didn't eat, because there wasn't enough money for food 8. Lost weight because there wasn't enough money for food 9. Did not eat for a whole day because there wasn't enough money for food 10. Did not eat whole day, 3+ months
		Marginal food security	One or two reported indications, typically of anxiety over food sufficiency or shortage of food in the house Little or no indication of changes in diets or food intake	
Food Insecurity	Food insecurity without hunger	Low food security	Reports of reduced quality, variety, or desirability of diet Little or no indication of reduced food intake	
	Food insecurity with hunger	Very low food security	Reports of multiple indications of disrupted eating patterns and reduced food intake	

Source: USDA (n.d.) and Coleman-Jensen et al. (2011).

among younger adults, this percentage is expected to increase (Flegal et al., 2010; Salihu, Bonnema, & Alio, 2009). Similar to undernutrition, overnutrition has negative health consequences, including overall poor health outcomes, mobility disability, and increased risk of diabetes, arthritis, stroke, and mortality (Salihu et al., 2009; H. K. Vincent, Vincent, & Lamb, 2010). We discuss the issue of obesity in more detail in Chapter 11.

PHYSICAL AND PSYCHOSOCIAL FACTORS THAT INFLUENCE NUTRITIONAL STATUS

A number of physical and psychosocial factors are thought to influence nutritional status (see Exhibit 10.2). For example, changes that older adults experience in taste, smell, and vision may inhibit their ability to enjoy food (Morley, 2001; Saxon et al., 2010). In addition, changes in the digestive system and the ability to chew may impair the digestion of food and make eating less enjoyable. Chronic conditions such as arthritis, orthopedic impairments, cataracts, and hypertension have been found to be negatively associated with poor nutritional intake (Dwyer, 1991; Payette & Shatenstein, 2005). For example, impairments that affect mobility, such as arthritis, can make shopping, preparing, and eating difficult. Individuals with cognitive impairments are at obvious risk of poor nutrition. Loss of memory, disorientation, and impaired judgment can reduce food intake (J. V. White, Ham, & Lipschitz, 1991). Because the use of medications—either over-the-counter or prescribed—is high among older adults, they are at risk of experiencing adverse drug–nutrient interactions as well as adverse effects on appetite and cause the depletion of certain minerals (Omran & Morley, 2000; J. V. White et al., 1991).

Not only do physical changes make the task of eating more difficult, but changes in the social environment can also have a detrimental effect on dietary patterns. Throughout our lives, eating is an activity that we rarely do in isolation. It is a social activity associated with various rituals in our culture. Think about the food rituals in your family. Do you have a special place you like to go to eat when celebrating a birthday? Do you look forward to eating or cooking certain meals during the holidays? Are there special restaurants you enjoy? Chances are that these rituals are enjoyed with friends and family. And on those occasions when you are alone, you are probably less likely to cook and more likely to eat something of questionable nutritional value from a fast-food restaurant. Because eating is such a social activity, social isolation can result in negative changes in eating patterns. Indeed, researchers have found that living alone is associated with a lack of interest in preparing and consuming food and a less favorable dietary pattern (Davis, Randall, Forthofer, Lee, & Margen, 1985; Locher et al., 2005; V. C. Ryan & Bower, 1989; U.S. Census Bureau, 2004a). For example, in a national study of 6,525 adults aged 50 or older, Davis, Murphy, Neuhaus, Gee, and Quiroga (2000) found favorable dietary patterns among those adults living with a spouse compared to those in other living arrangements. Men living alone had a higher mean number of low nutrient diets compared with men who were living with a spouse. Among women, those living alone compared to those living with a spouse had a higher mean number of low nutrients.

Included among those living alone are widowed older adults. Older adults who are widowed may be at risk of poor nutritional habits because of changes in income and social interaction patterns. Moreover, being responsible for new roles associated with meal preparation (e.g., shopping, cooking) for which they were not previously responsible can have negative dietary consequences. Although some evidence supports the relationship between living arrangement and dietary intake, other studies have found no relationship (Green et al., 1993; Schafer & Keith, 1982). Such variations may suggest that simply measuring whether one lives alone does not adequately capture other life circumstances that may be confounding nutritional intake, such as the

---

Exhibit 10.2 Factors Affecting Nutritional Status in Older Adults

Physical

Cognitive status and dementia-related behaviors

Chronic and acute illness

Oral/dental health status

Chronic medication use

Dependence and disability

Psychosocial

Social support

Economic status

Emotional problems

Ethnic status

Accessibility and availability of food programs

Advanced age

Source: Adapted from J. S. Goodwin (1989), Omran and Morley (2000), and J. V. White et al. (1991).

length of time one has lived alone, degree of loneliness, number of social contacts, and living with others in a non-spouse household (Davis et al., 2000).

Income has an obvious effect on the quality and amount of nutritional intake, and older adults with low incomes have less money to spend on food, thus increasing chances of an inadequate diet. The U.S. Government Accountability Office (2011) reported that among elderly households with incomes below 130% of poverty, the proportion classified as food insecure rose from 17.6% in 2006 to 24.0% in 2010. Various researchers have found that poor elderly persons compared to nonpoor elders consumed less of essential nutrients and have a greater level of nutritional risk (Bowman, 2007; J. S. Lee & Frongillo, 2001; Locher et al., 2005). In addition, those living in poverty may not have accessibility to health care services needed to diagnose and treat diseases linked to poor nutritional status.

Rural older adults are also at risk of inadequate nutritional intake (Sharkey & Haines, 2002). This may partly be because rural older adults have more risk factors associated with increased food insecurity. Rural elders are more likely than their urban counterparts to have incomes below the poverty level, to have more health problems, to have fewer social and health services, and to be socially isolated (Administration on Aging [AoA], 2010d; Gamm, Hutchison, Bellamy, & Dabney, 2002; Quandt & Rao, 1999; Schwenk, 1992; U.S. Department of Health and Human Services [USDHHS], 2011c). Rural elders who are older, male, and non-White and have low incomes are more likely to have inadequate nutritional intake (Ralston & Cohen, 1994; Vitolins et al., 2007).

Older adults of different racial and ethnic groups are also at risk of experiencing nutritional problems. A national study found that the level of food insecurity among African American and Hispanic elders was more than double that of White elders (Ziliak & Gundersen, 2011). Although tremendous variations exist among and between ethnic groups in their history and cultural characteristics, they often share some sociodemographic characteristics that make them susceptible to poor nutritional intake. In general, Black, Hispanic, and Native American older adults are more likely than their White counterparts to have incomes below the poverty line, to have lower levels of education and poorer health status, and to need assistance with everyday activities than do older Whites (Federal Interagency Forum on Aging-Related Statistics, 2010). These increased levels of functional impairment, low income, and education put older adults of color at an increased risk of malnutrition and unbalanced diets (Saxon et al., 2010). Moreover, language difficulties that exist among some older adults such as first-generation Asian Americans and Hispanics can act to isolate them from nutrition education and programs. The promotion of optimal nutritional status among older adults of different race and ethnicities requires staff to be culturally competent to be sensitive to the cultural variations in diets (Kamp et al., 2010).

In response to the nutritional needs of older adults, a network of nutrition services and programs has been created. We describe these efforts in the following section.

POLICY BACKGROUND

Congress initiated nutrition programs for older adults with the passage of research and demonstration projects in 1968 under Title IV of the Older Americans Act (OAA). Four years later, Congress authorized the Nutrition Program for Older Americans as Title VII; however, the program was not implemented until 1973 (U.S. Senate Special Committee on Aging, 1993). Congress reorganized the nutrition program in 1978 by placing it under Title III in the OAA.

The purpose of the nutrition program for older adults under the OAA is to provide nutritionally balanced meals and nutrition education, opportunities for social interaction, and other support services (U.S. Senate Special Committee on Aging, 1993). In the 2006 amendments of the OAA, specific goals for the program identified were

- to reduce hunger and food insecurity;
- to promote socialization of older individuals; and
- to promote the health and well-being of older individuals by assisting such individuals to gain access to nutrition and other disease prevention and health promotion services to delay the onset of adverse health conditions resulting from poor nutritional health or sedentary behavior.

Under the 2006 OAA legislation, congregate meal programs were required to provide at least one hot meal five or more days a week in a congregate setting, adult day program, or multigenerational site (except in rural areas and where it is deemed unfeasible); such programs may include nutrition education services. The act also authorizes home-delivered meal programs that deliver at least one hot, cold, frozen, dried, or supplement meal at least five days a week (except in rural areas and where it is not feasible). Each meal must provide a minimum of one third of the recommended daily allowances and be prepared with the advice of dietitians. The 2006 amendments also provided for nutrition screening, nutrition education, nutrition assessment, and counseling. Finally, the OAA legislation authorized an evaluation of the effect of the nutrition projects on improvement of the health status, including nutritional status, of participants; prevention of hunger and food insecurity of the participants; and continuation of the ability of the participants to live independently. Research will also examine the cost-benefit analysis of nutrition projects, including the potential to affect costs of the Medicaid program, and an analysis of how nutrition projects may be modified to improve the nutritional outcomes of the participants.

Funding for nutrition services is allotted to the states and U.S. territories based on a formula that is reflective of their relative share of people age 60; to receive the allotment, states are required to provide a matching share of 15% (Colello, 2011). Exhibit 10.3 shows the level of OAA funding for nutrition services both in actual dollars and 2010 constant dollars, which adjusts the amounts for inflation. Although the amount of funding has increased slightly from 1990, when the amounts are adjusted for inflation, the amount has dropped steadily from 1990 funding levels, which was $958.5 million, to $817.8 million in 2011, which reduces the purchasing power and therefore number of meals served (Colello, 2011). The congregate meal and home-delivered meals programs use funds from other sources to supplement the costs of providing meals. Based on the most recent data available, only 37% of the cost of a congregate meal and 23% of the cost of home-delivered meals comes from Title III funds. The remainder comes from participant contributions; state, local, and private funds; and the Nutrition Services Incentive Program, which provides cash or commodities to support the meal program (Millen, Ohls, Ponza, & McCool, 2002). The Nutrition Services Incentive Program, formally administered by the USDA until it was transferred to the AoA in 2000, provides nutrition programs with high-protein foods, meat, and meat alternative commodities. Programs can opt to receive a cash payment in place of donated food (AoA, 2003). As shown in Exhibit 10.3, funding for the Nutrition Services Incentive Program in 2011 was $160.9 million (AoA, 2012e). Funding for nutrition services is also provided under Title VI, which is a grant program for tribal organizations to help them deliver social and nutrition services to older American Indians, Alaskan Natives, and Native Hawaiians. In 2011, Title VI grantees received $27.6 million in Title VI funds for nutrition and supportive services.

Exhibit 10.3 Funding for Nutrition Services Programs Under the Older Americans Act for Selected Years Between 1990 and 2011

	Actual and *amounts converted to 2010 constant dollars*, in millions				
Fiscal Year	**Congregate Meals**	**Home-Delivered Meals**	**Total**	**NSIP**	**Total**
1990	$351.9 *($587.2)*	$78.9 *($131.8)*	$430.8 *($719.0)*	$143.4 *($239.5)*	$574.3 *($958.5)*
2000	$374.3 *($474.1)*	$146.9 *($186.2)*	$521.2 *($660.3)*	140.0 *($159.8)*	$661.4 *($837.6)*
2005	$387.2 *($432.5)*	$182.8 *($204.1)*	$570.0 *($636.6)*	$148.5 *($165.9)*	$718.6 *($802.6)*
2007	$398.9 *($419.7)*	$188.3 *($198.1)*	$587.2 *($617.8)*	$147.8 *($155.5)*	$735.0 *($773.4)*
2009[1]	$434.2 *($441.6)*	$214.4 *($218.1)*	$648.6 *($$659.7)*	$161.0 *($163.7)*	$809.7 *($823.3)*
2010	$440.7 *($440.7)*	$217.6 *($217.6)*	$658.3 *($658.3)*	$161.0 *($161.0)*	$819.4 *($819.4)*
2011	$439.9 *($439.9)*	$217.2 *($217.2)*	$657.1 *($657.1)*	$160.9 *($160.7)*	$818.0 *($817.8)*

Source: AoA (2012e), Colello (2011), Napili and Colello (2010), and O'Shaughnessy (2004).

[1] In 2009, American Recovery and Reinvestment Act funds added $100 million to the initial FY 2009 appropriations of for nutrition services programs; this amount is not included in the total for 2009.

Supplemental Nutrition Assistance Program (Food Stamp Program)

The first U.S. food assistance programs were developed in the 1930s during the Depression, when the government purchased surplus agricultural commodities and distributed them to the poor (Kuhn et al., 1996). In 1964, Congress established the Food Stamp Program using coupons, and in 1971, it enacted national eligibility standards, although the states still had a choice of food assistance programs. By 1974, however, the Food Stamp Program became a nationwide mandatory program (Lipsky & Thibodeau, 1990). In 2008, Congress enacted significant changes to the Food Stamp Program, including changing the name of the legislation from the Food Stamp Act to the Food and Nutrition Act, and encouraged states to change the name of the program to Supplemental Nutrition Assistance Program (SNAP.)[2] The goal of SNAP is

---

[2] Although states continue to use various names for their food stamp program, we will use the new name Supplemental Nutrition Assistance Program (SNAP) for clarity.

to promote the general welfare, to safeguard the health and well-being of the Nation's population by raising levels of nutrition among low-income households . . . to alleviate . . . hunger and malnutrition . . . [by] permit low-income households to obtain a more nutritious diet . . . by increasing food purchasing power for all eligible households. (P.L. 110–246 [Sec. 2])

To be eligible for benefits, participants must meet a somewhat complicated mix of gross, net income, and asset guidelines, and those over age 60 have slightly different eligibility guidelines. In addition, states have the option to slightly vary the eligibility and assets requirements. Older adults who receive Supplemental Security Income (SSI) automatically meet the eligibility requirements for SNAP; however, SSI recipients in California are not eligible for SNAP because the state includes extra money in the amount it adds to the federal SSI payment instead of adding SNAP benefits (USDA, 2012b). In 2010, SNAP served approximately 2.9 million older adults aged 60 and over, representing almost 16% of all SNAP participants, up from 15% in 1992 (A. Barrett, 2006; Eslami, Filion, & Strayer, 2011); 18%, 10%, and 6% of elderly SNAP participants are African American, Hispanic, and Native American elders, respectively. The participation rate for SNAP-eligible elderly adults has been and continues to be significantly lower than for any other age group (Cunnyngham, 2004; Leftin, 2010; Rosso, 2001), although the percentage of participants increased slightly between 2008 and 2009 (Leftin, 2010). In 2008, Fuller-Thomson and Redmond conducted a national study to identify the characteristics of eligible older adults who were not receiving SNAP benefits. Their research found that two thirds of older adults living in poverty were not receiving benefits, and that those aged 85 and over were three times less likely than those aged 65 to 74 to be participating in SNAP. Reasons for nonparticipation include perceived lack of need, lack of information about the program, low expected benefits, and stigma associated with applying for assistance (McConnell & Ponza, 1999; Sing, Cody, Sinclair, Cohen, & Ohls, 2005). In 2010 the average monthly SNAP benefit for elderly individuals varied by household type. For all elderly individuals, the average SNAP benefit was $144, compared to $119 for elderly beneficiaries living alone, $198 for elderly-only households, and $285 for elders living with nonelderly individuals (Eslami et al., 2011).

Nutrition Screening

As we discussed previously, older adults are at risk of malnutrition, and a nutritional assessment is a critical first step in early intervention. Of the many nutrition assessment tools that have been used over the last 20 years, the Mini Nutritional Assessment (MNA) has become one of the most highly regarded assessment tools among researchers and geriatricians (Bauer, Kaiser, Anthony, Guigoz, & Sieber, 2008; Charney, 2008). The development of the MNA began in 1990 in an effort to identify a valid and reliable nutrition assessment tool that could be used with elders regardless of their level of dependence, cognitive functioning, and residential setting. The MNA, both the full version (18 questions) and short form (6 questions; see Exhibit 10.4), is thought to be the most established tool for nutrition screening in older adults as it has been well validated in international studies in a variety of settings (Bauer et al., 2008; Guigoz, 2006). The MNA is now available in 24 different languages as well as an iPhone application (Nestlé Nutrition Institute, n.d.).

In the next section, we discuss the various nutrition programs that have emerged from both the public and private sectors, and provide a profile of nutrition program participants. We end this chapter with a discussion of the challenges facing nutrition programs.

Exhibit 10.4   Mini Nutritional Assessment (MNA)® Short Form Nutritional Screening Tool

Nestlé Nutrition Institute

Mini Nutritional Assessment
MNA®

Last name: _____   First name: _____

Sex: _____   Age: _____   Weight, kg: _____   Height, cm: _____   Date: _____

Complete the screen by filling in the boxes with the appropriate numbers. Total the numbers for the final screening score.

Screening

A Has food intake declined over the past 3 months due to loss of appetite, digestive problems, chewing or swallowing difficulties?
0 = severe decrease in food intake
1 = moderate decrease in food intake
2 = no decrease in food intake   ☐

B Weight loss during the last 3 months
0 = weight loss greater than 3 kg (6.6 lbs)
1 = does not know
2 = weight loss between 1 and 3 kg (2.2 and 6.6 lbs)
3 = no weight loss   ☐

C Mobility
0 = bed or chair bound
1 = able to get out of bed / chair but does not go out
2 = goes out   ☐

D Has suffered psychological stress or acute disease in the past 3 months?
0 = yes   2 = no   ☐

E Neuropsychological problems
0 = severe dementia or depression
1 = mild dementia
2 = no psychological problems   ☐

F1 Body Mass Index (BMI) (weight in kg) / (height in m^2)   ☐
0 = BMI less than 19
1 = BMI 19 to less than 21
2 = BMI 21 to less than 23
3 = BMI 23 or greater   ☐

IF BMI IS NOT AVAILABLE, REPLACE QUESTION F1 WITH QUESTION F2.
DO NOT ANSWER QUESTION F2 IF QUESTION F1 IS ALREADY COMPLETED.

F2 Calf circumference (CC) in cm
0 = CC less than 31
3 = CC 31 or greater   ☐

Screening score   ☐☐
(max. 14 points)

Save

12-14 points: ☐   Normal nutritional status
8-11 points: ☐   At risk of malnutrition   Print
0-7 points: ☐   Malnourished   Reset

Ref.   Vellas B, Villars H, Abellan G, et al. *Overview of the MNA® - Its History and Challenges.* J Nutr Health Aging 2006;10:456-465.
Rubenstein LZ, Harker JO, Salva A, Guigoz Y, Vellas B. *Screening for Undernutrition in Geriatric Practice: Developing the Short-Form Mini Nutritional Assessment (MNA-SF).* J. Geront 2001;56A: M366-377.
Guigoz Y. *The Mini-Nutritional Assessment (MNA®) Review of the Literature - What does it tell us?* J Nutr Health Aging 2006; 10:466-487.
Kaiser MJ, Bauer JM, Ramsch C, et al. *Validation of the Mini Nutritional Assessment Short-Form (MNA®-SF): A practical tool for identification of nutritional status.* J Nutr Health Aging 2009; 13:782-788.
® Société des Produits Nestlé, S.A., Vevey, Switzerland, Trademark Owners
© Nestlé, 1994, Revision 2009. N67200 12/99 10M
For more information: www.mna-elderly.com

Source: Reprinted with permission from the Société des Produits Nestlé S.A.

USERS AND PROGRAMS

Nutrition programs for older adults, much like the continuum-of-care model discussed in Chapter 1, exist on a continuum based on functional status and socioeconomic need. Balsam and Osteraas (1987) developed the continuum of community nutrition services. As shown in Exhibit 10.5, older adult nutrition programs exist within a continuum of community nutrition programs and serve both independent and frail older adults. We explain the different nutrition programs that serve older adults in more detail below.

Congregate Meal Sites

As previously mentioned, the OAA nutrition program under Title III-C provides funds to support congregate meal programs. The program, funded by OAA dollars, reaches millions of older adults. In 2009–2010, congregate meal sites funded under the OAA provided almost 96.4 million meals to 1.7 million older persons (AoA, 2012h). The goals of congregate meal programs are to (a) provide low-cost meals to older adults; (b) encourage well-being through social interaction and maintenance of good health; and (c) provide nutrition education, screening, counseling, and outreach (AoA, 1995c; Mullins, Cook, Mushel, Machin, & Georgas, 1993). For both the congregate and home-delivered programs (discussed below), services must be targeted at persons with the greatest social and economic need, with particular attention to low-income older persons, including low-income minority older persons, older persons with limited English proficiency, older persons residing in rural areas, and those at risk for institutionalization. Individuals 60 years of age and older and their spouses can eat a nutritionally balanced hot meal for a suggested donation, and programs are not allowed to base participation on income level. Other groups eligible for congregate meals include persons under age 60 with disabilities who live in housing occupied primarily by elderly

Exhibit 10.5   Continuum of Community Nutrition Services

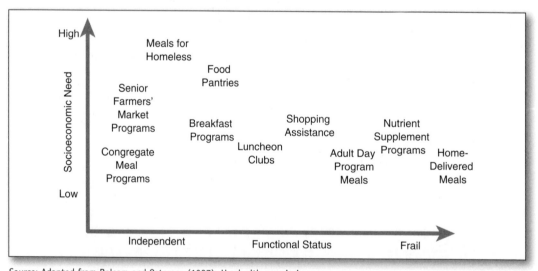

Source: Adapted from Balsam and Osteraas (1987). Used with permission.

adults where congregate meals are served; persons with disabilities who reside at home with, and accompany, older persons to meal sites (Colello, 2011). Suggested donations range from $2 to $4; 94% of congregate meal participants and 73% of home-delivered meal participants make a contribution for their meal (Ponza, Ohls, & Millen, 1996). Congregate meal sites are located in a variety of places, including senior centers, schools, churches, and restaurants. Meals, which must be offed at least one per day, five or more days per week, may be prepared on site or prepared at a central kitchen and delivered to sites. All congregate meal programs serve lunch. Approximately 13% have a supper option during the week, and 11% serve weekend congregate meals. Almost 75% of the programs offer modified meals (e.g., low fat, low cholesterol, low salt) to accommodate special diets.

Congregate meal programs also offer nutrition education programs, screening, and information about other community programs. Approximately 85% of congregate meal programs offer information and referral services to participants (Ponza, Ohls, Millen, et al., 1996). Providing participants with information and referral services makes congregate meal programs an important link in coordinating and delivering non-nutrition programs to older adults. Other congregate meal programs sponsored by nonprofit organizations such as the Salvation Army provide meals to low-income individuals and families of all ages. Unfortunately, the number of older adults who receive meals through these community congregate meal sites has not been documented.

Home-Delivered Meals

Home-delivered meals in most communities are provided by private nonprofit agencies or programs funded under the OAA. More than one home-delivered meal program may exist in any community and serve different target populations; Meals on Wheels is perhaps the most recognized home-delivered meal program in the country. Individuals aged 60 and older, who are homebound and their spouses of any age, as well as those under age 60 with disabilities if they reside at home with the homebound elder, may participate in home-delivered meal programs (Colello, 2011). Most programs have a suggested donation amount or a sliding fee scale based on income. Programs deliver one or more hot, chilled, or frozen meals directly to the recipient's home each day during the week. Many programs offer frozen meals for recipients to use during the weekend.

More recently, nutrition programs have begun offering medical nutrition therapy for older adults who are nutritionally at risk or malnourished. According to the National Policy and Resource Center on Nutrition and Aging (1996), the medical nutrition therapy process is designed to help older adults who are at risk of malnutrition to obtain appropriate nutrition. On the basis of an assessment of the nutritional status of an at-risk older adult by a dietitian, a nutritional care plan is developed. The plan might recommend a change in daily diet or the incorporation of high-nutrient food into the diet. In addition, the food itself may need to be altered—for example, chopped or pureed to help those who have difficulty chewing or swallowing. Nutritional supplements or liquid meals might also be needed to meet an individual's nutritional needs. Because of the increased cost of providing medical nutrition therapy, the funding for such programs comes from client fees, contributions, and private payers.

In addition to the nutritional value that home-delivered meal programs offer their participants, volunteers play an important role in meeting clients' social needs. Volunteers who deliver the meals are often the only source of social contact for meal recipients, and in some cases, they help clients with grocery shopping or other errands. Because of the increase in the number of frail older persons, many home-delivered meals have waiting lists. The most recent national survey found that 41% of home-delivered meal programs have waiting lists of persons needing home-delivered meals, and the mean length of time on a waiting list is between two and three months (Ponza, Ohls, Millen, et al., 1996). The total number of home-delivered meals has increased dramatically over the past 20 years. From 1980 to 1996, it increased by 227%, due in part to an increase in funding for home-delivered meals over the years (U.S. Senate Special Committee on Aging, 2000). In 1998, home-delivered meals funded under Title III-C of the OAA provided some 129.7 million meals to 896,153 older adults; in 2004, the number of home-delivered meals totaled 143 million to 968,062 older adults (AoA, n.d.-b; AoA, 2001a). The most recent data available show that in 2009–2010, 145.4 million home-delivered meals were provided to 868,076 older adults (AoA, n.d.-e, n.d.-g).

Best Practice: Two Coasts, Two Meals on Wheels Programs

San Francisco

In 1970, a group of civic-minded individuals living in San Francisco noticed a need among their elderly community. The people in need required nutritious meals delivered to their homes and friendly assistance with small tasks that they were unable to take care of themselves. To fill the need, this small group of dedicated volunteers started Meals on Wheels of San Francisco (MOWSF). They fixed the meals in their own neighborhood kitchens and then delivered them to their homebound neighbors. As the need for this service grew beyond anyone's expectations, Meals on Wheels volunteers, in their own cars, were supplemented with professional drivers and refrigerated delivery vehicles. Eventually, full-time social workers, nutritionists, and administrative staff were hired. In 1995, MOWSF opened its own state-of-the-art kitchen.

In 1988, Meals on Wheels served 500 seniors per day. In 2010, the program served an average of 1,700 homebound participants daily and delivered 922,530 meals to older adults over a 12-month period. The MOWSF launched home-delivered grocery pilot program to assist homebound elders. There is also a large volunteer force that provides additional services such as shopping, reading, and helping with pet care. Dieticians provide nutrition education services and case managers, and other professional staff assist clients with referrals to help meet social or health needs.

For more information, contact Meals on Wheels of San Francisco, Inc., 1375 Fairfax Avenue, San Francisco, CA 94124, phone: 415-920-1111; www.mowsf.org.

New York City

In 1981, Gael Greene and James Beard founded Citymeals-on-Wheels by raising private funds to supplement the government-funded weekday meal delivery program. Citymeals now funds weekday and weekend, holiday, or emergency meals to homebound elderly New Yorkers who can no longer shop or cook for themselves. The program also provides Vitamin D supplements and a mobile food pantry that contains canned goods and rice. The program served 6,000 older adults in its first year. During 2010–2011, Citymeals funded the preparation and delivery of 1.7 million meals to more than 16,918 homebound elderly New Yorkers.

For more information contact Citymeals-on-Wheels, 355 Lexington Avenue, New York, NY 10017, phone: 212-687-1234; www.citymeals.org; e-mail: info@citymeals.org.

Sources: MOWSF (2010) and Citymeals-on-Wheels (2012).

Senior Farmers' Market Nutrition Program

The Senior Farmers' Market Nutrition Program (SFMNP), was established through the 2008 Farm Bill and provided $20.6 million annually through FY 2012. The purpose of the SFMNP is to (a) provide fresh, nutritious, locally grown fruits, vegetables, herbs, and honey from farmers' markets, roadside stands, and community-supported agriculture (CSA) programs; and (b) increase the consumption of agricultural commodities by expanding or aiding in the development and expansion of domestic farmers' markets, roadside stands, and CSA programs (USDA, 2011b). The SFMNP awards grants to states, territories, and Indian tribal governments who in turn provide coupons to low-income elders, aged 60 and older, with incomes not greater than 185% of the federal poverty rate. Eligible elders receive coupons that can be exchanged for the locally grown items listed above. The SFNMP benefit level may not be less than $20 per year or more than $50 per year, and in FY 2010, 844,999 older adults participated in the program. The program currently operates in 42 states and six tribal nations, and over 25,000 farmers, farmers' markets, and roadside stands, as well as 163 CSAs, participate in the program.

Food Banks

Many communities have created food banks that serve families and individuals with low incomes. Food banks distribute to qualified individuals government commodities or food that has been donated by private citizens, farmers, food manufacturers, grocery stores, and restaurants. The Food and Nutrition Service, under the USDA, supports two community food security programs: the Commodity Supplemental Food Program (CSFP) and the Emergency Food Assistance Program (TEFAP). The CSFP assists low-income older adults over 60 years of age in addition to low-income pregnant and breastfeeding women, new mothers up to one year postpartum, infants, and children up to age 6. The program is available in 38 states and the District of Columbia. To qualify for assistance, older adults must be residents and have incomes at or below 130% of the poverty income guidelines. Food packages include items such as cereal, rice, pasta, canned meat, fruits, and vegetables (USDA, 2011a). The number of older adults participating in the CSFP has increased over the past 15 years from 219,000 persons in 1996 to 568,854 in 2011 (USDA, 2011a; U.S. Senate Special Committee on Aging, 2000). The TEFAP, administered by the USDA, distributes to low-income individuals foods such as butter, flour, cornmeal, green beans, tomatoes, beef, and pork at no cost. In 2005, the program donated $154 million worth of surplus food. In 2010, that amount totaled $565.6 million to purchase food under the TEFAP (USDA, 2006b, 2012a).

Food recovery and gleaning are programs that collect excess food for delivery to community food banks. Food recovery programs work with wholesale food markets or retail grocers to salvage edible but not sellable ripe fruits and vegetables. In Portland, Oregon, a program called "Fork It Over" coordinates a food rescue program where food banks and pantries pick up surplus restaurant food. Many fresh and prepared foods are donated, including unserved menu items, unserved buffet foods, produce, dairy items, deli items, catered foods, baked goods, meats, and seafood. This program recovered approximately 10,614 tons of food, much of which would have otherwise been landfilled had it not been donated (McGuire, 2002). Another way communities have gathered surplus food to distribute to low-income individuals is to harvest unusable produce left after a commercial harvest. These "gleaning projects" have played an important role in preventing hunger in their communities. One gleaning program, through the faith-based organization called the Society of St. Andrew, had more than 30,000 volunteers who helped salvage and distribute more than 18 million pounds of produce through their Gleaning Network in 15 states in 2010 (Society of St. Andrew, n.d.).

Brown Bag Programs

Brown bag programs are also supplemental food programs for low-income seniors. Typically, low-income older adults can receive a grocery bag containing fresh or frozen produce, breads, and canned foods. Food for these programs comes from local grocery stores and private donations from food drives. Distribution sites, home-delivery availability, frequency of distribution, and eligibility guidelines vary by community and by program. One example of a brown bag program is the Greater Boston Food Bank's "Let's Bag Hunger" program. The program has seven Elderly and Family Brown Bag programs in the Boston area, which serve more 7,400 participants each month. This initiative provides a free 15-pound grocery bag filled with milk, cheese, pasta, rice, ground beef, tuna, peanut butter, green beans, and oatmeal once a month (Greater Boston Food Bank, 2012).

Shopping Assistance Programs

As noted above, many older adults have difficulty grocery shopping. Chronic conditions make traveling to grocery stores and selecting and carrying groceries home problematic. Lack of private transportation makes shopping burdensome as well. No doubt many of the participants who receive home-delivered meals are in need of assistance with grocery shopping. Communities have responded by offering shopping assistance services that escort older adults to food markets or deliver groceries to their homes. Volunteers, in conjunction with public transportation, often help with shopping assistance. Volunteers travel to the homes of older adults, escort older adults to the grocery store, assist them in shopping, and return home. Grocery delivery programs allow older adults to call in their grocery order to be filled and delivered by volunteers. A study that surveyed a random sample of nutrition programs across the country found that approximately 43% of meal programs for older adults provided escort shopping services and that 15% offered grocery delivery services (Balsam & Rogers, 1988).

For Your Files: Campus Kitchens Project

The Campus Kitchens Project (CKP) is a community service for high school and college students and resourceful anti-hunger program for communities around the country. As they note on their website, "What we do is kind of a no-brainer. We know there are people in every community who need nourishing meals. And, we know that every college campus has unserved food in its dining halls and brilliant students in its classrooms. So we put them all together."

The CKP is a student-run program that works with thousands of students each year to recycle food from their high school or college cafeterias, the leftover food is turned into nourishing meals, and then delivered to those who need it most. An example of CKP outreach to older adults is from the University of Nebraska at Kearny. The program helps Arlene Jones, 92, a retired school teacher, with her noontime meal. Arlene suffers from macular degeneration, a disease that results in loss of vision in the center of the visual field, and has limited her ability to cook. She lives alone, moves with a walker, and can no longer peel potatoes, chop vegetables, or read recipes like she used to. In an interview about the program, Arlene said she receives more than just hot meals when the students visit. "I love to chat with them and find out where they are from and what they are majoring in. Being a school teacher, that is what I am interested in."

For more information and a list of local CKP visit their website: http://www.campuskitchens.org/national.

Users of Congregate and Home-Delivered Meal Programs

Who attends congregate meal programs? Who participates in the home-delivered meal program? Do these programs serve the neediest among the older population? To answer these questions, researchers have conducted studies to identify participant characteristics and benefits of attending meal programs on both the national and local levels.

There have only been two national studies investigating Title III nutrition program participants and outcomes. One of those studies was the longitudinal study of the OAA nutrition program outcomes initiated in 1978 (U.S. Department of Health, Education, and Welfare, 1979). The purpose of the evaluation was to assess program impacts on participants and to identify program characteristics and other factors that influence participant outcomes. Researchers collected information from a random sample of 91 meal sites and conducted interviews with program staff and representatives from related organizations. In addition, a sample of nutrition program participants was compared with a sample of nonparticipants. The evaluation gathered specific information about dietary and health status, isolation, life satisfaction, longevity, and independent living. Results revealed that the majority of participants had incomes below the poverty level and that one quarter of the participants were minority group older adults. Participants had higher rates of social activity compared with the sample of nonparticipants. The majority attended once a week or more, and the more frequent attendees were long-term participants who were poor, more than 75 years of age, in poor health, living alone, and ethnic minorities. In the final report, Kirschner Associates (1983) concluded that the attendance did increase the nutrient intake of participants; participants also ranked the benefits of social interaction higher than the benefits of the meals.

Almost 15 years later, another comprehensive two-year evaluation of the Title III nutrition program was undertaken. The purposes of the study were to evaluate the program's effect on participants' nutrition and socialization compared with those of similar nonparticipants; to evaluate who used the program and how effectively the program served targeted groups in most need of its services; to assess how efficiently and effectively the program was administered and delivered services; and to clarify funding sources and allocation of funds among program components (Ponza, Ohls, Millen, et al., 1996). Data were collected from 55 State Units on Aging, 350 Area Agencies on Aging, 100 Indian tribal organizations, a representative sample of 200 nutrition projects, a nationally representative sample of 1,200 congregate meal participants and 800 home-delivered meal participants, and personal interviews with a nationally representative sample of 600 nonparticipants eligible for the congregate meal program and 400 nonparticipants eligible for the home-delivered meal program. The majority of congregate meal participants were women (69%); 45% had been participating in the congregate meal program for more than five years (Ponza, Ohls, Millen, et al., 1996). The average age of the participants was 76 years, and 26% needed special transportation to get to the meal site.

Ponza, Ohls, Millen, and colleagues (1996) found that participants were more disadvantaged regarding income, living arrangements, and physical health than the older adult population in general. For example, between 80% and 90% of participants had incomes that were 200% below the poverty level—a rate that was two times higher than that of the overall U.S. older adult population. Moreover, more participants were living alone (60%) than the overall older population (25%). With regard to physical health, participants typically had two chronic health conditions, and almost a quarter reported difficulty in doing one or more everyday tasks. Racial and ethnic minorities accounted for 27% of congregate meal participants. The congregate meal participants were also found to be nutritionally at risk. Following the protocols under the Nutritional Screening Initiative, 64% of participants had characteristics associated with moderate to high nutritional risk, and over 55% received half or more of their daily food intake from their congregate meal. Approximately two thirds of participants were either over- or underweight, placing them at increased risk for nutritional and health problems. This same research also evaluated specific outcomes of improved nutritional status and increased social contacts. They found that the nutrition program significantly influenced participants' overall nutritional intake. On a daily basis, participants had higher percentages of recommended daily allowances than did nonparticipants, and overall dietary intakes were better than those of nonparticipants as well. Results indicated that when compared with nonparticipants, participants had, on average, more social contacts per month. Overall, the results indicate that nutrition programs are accomplishing the mission of improving the dietary and social well-being of an at-risk population.

More recently, a national survey of OAA congregate meal program participants shows that slightly more than half were aged 75 and older, 48% lived alone, 13% had annual incomes of less than $10,000, and 57% indicated that the congregate meals provided one half or more of their daily food intake (Colello, 2011). The results also confirmed that socialization provided by congregate meal programs plays an important role among participants. Eighty-seven percent of participants indicated that they see friends more often due to their participation in the congregate meal program.

Over the years since the inception of congregate meal sites, researchers conducting studies of local older adult nutrition programs report similar outcomes, with some variation of the ethnic makeup of participants. A study in the late 1970s of the Boston area congregate meal program participants ($N = 174$), found that the majority of participants were White (93%), female (69%), and widowed (44%; Posner, 1979). The average age of participants was 73 years, and most participants were living alone. One fifth had incomes below the poverty level, and 44% had incomes that were at or below 125% of the poverty level. Respondents were asked to identify what they thought was the program's value for them. The opportunity for a nutritious meal and the opportunity for socialization were the two top reasons given by respondents for attending the meal program. Participants indicated that they realized financial as well as food-purchasing benefits (31% and 50%, respectively). That is, their participation in the nutrition program helped reduce the amount of food they bought. Significantly more older adults who lived alone realized these benefits. More than half the respondents indicated that attending the program had a positive impact on the social aspects of their lives. This included meeting more people and socializing more with peers (26%), reduced loneliness and improved morale (22%), and increased social activities outside their homes (22%). Finally, 47% of participants indicated that they engaged in social activities outside the meal program with peers whom they had first met at the site.

Similarly, in their study of 888 local congregate meal participants, Mullins et al. (1993) found that the majority of participants were female (70%), White (65%), widowed (47%), and living alone (51%). A surprising number had relatively few associations with children, grandchildren, and siblings, and had fewer close relationships than did respondents who received home-delivered meals. Moreover, more than one quarter (26%) reported levels of loneliness greater than the median. Half the congregate meal participants rated their health as either fair or poor, and 66% indicated that they had a health problem that affected their daily activities. Many of the participants also indicated that their economic condition was problematic; more than half (54%) reported that not having enough money to live on was a somewhat or very serious problem. Respondents were also asked if they felt healthier because of their participation in the nutrition program. More than three quarters of congregate meal participants indicated that attending the program was related to feeling healthier and making more friends.

Another study investigated the social and nutritional outcomes of a random sample of participants ($N = 140$) at 13 rural areas and eight urban congregate meal sites in Colorado (Wacker, 1992). The majority of respondents were female (83%), and 43% were widowed. Slightly more than half the respondents reported their health status was good (52%), and 31% indicated their health was fair. Most had a high school education (47%), whereas 29% reported having less than a high school education. Reflecting data from national studies showing that meal programs primarily serve those with low incomes, many of the study participants reported a similar financial picture. When asked about their financial well-being, 32% said they had just enough income to make ends meet; 47% indicated that they had enough to make ends meet, with a little extra left over sometimes. A significant majority of respondents had been attending the program for three or more years, and attended at least once per week. When participants were asked why they attended the program, the most popular reasons given were socializing with others (84%), getting an affordable meal (75%), and liking the food being served (72%). In addition, 75% indicated that the meal program was an important part of their diet. Of those who indicated that they had changed their health habits (e.g., reduced amount of fat and sodium in their diets), 17% said that the nutrition education presented at the meal program influenced them to change.

Finally, a study of OAA nutrition program participants in Georgia showed that congregate meal participants were predominately female (75.3%) and White (67.8%), had at least a high school education (67.3%), and rated their health as good or excellent (54.7%; J. S. Lee, Sinnett, Bengle, Johnson, & Brown, 2011). Results also showed that 29.8% of participants were food insecure, and 51.4% were deemed to be at high nutritional risk. The study also identified that 47.2% of those on a wait list for congregate meal programs were food insecure.

Examinations of users of home-delivered meal programs have shown that recipients have more physical limitations, are more socially isolated, and have lower incomes than those who attend congregate meal programs (AoA, 1983; Colello, 2011; Joung, Kim, Yuan, & Huffman, 2011; Mullins et al., 1993; Ponza, Ohls, Millen, et al., 1996). Home-delivered meal participants are a more frail and at-risk population than those who attend congregate meal programs. According to the national study of the OAA Title III meal program mentioned above, the average age of a home-delivered meal participant is 78 years; 70% are female, 60% live alone, and 95% receive five or more meals per week. One quarter were minority and ethnic elders, and almost half (48%) of participants had incomes below 100% of the DHHS poverty guidelines. When meal participants were asked how many times per month they saw relatives, friends, or neighbors, 38% reported never or less than once. Home-delivered meal participants have more than twice as many physical impairments as the overall elderly population. Over 75% report experiencing difficulty doing one or more everyday tasks, and 43% reported a recent stay in a hospital or nursing home. Approximately one third also receive personal care and homemaker services from other agencies. These meal participants are also nutritionally at risk. Eighty-eight percent were determined to be at moderate or high nutritional risk, and more than one third saved part of the program meal to eat as a second meal or as part of a second meal or snack. Other research has confirmed that the majority of homebound older adults have poor diets compared with persons who attend congregate meal programs (Ponza, Ohls, Millen, et al., 1996; Steele & Bryan, 1986; Stevens, Grivetti, & McDonald, 1992). J. S. Lee and colleagues (2011) found that among their Georgia sample of home-delivered meal participants, 74.3% had high nutritional risk and 48.7% were food insecure.

These demographic and health characteristics of home-delivered meal participants were also found in the 2009 national survey of OAA participants—70% were aged 75 or older, 56% lived alone, and 25% had annual incomes below $10,000 (Colello, 2011). Recipients of home-delivered meals were frailer than congregate meal participants, as 40% and 15% needed assistance with one or more activities of daily living (ADLs), and three or more ADLs, respectively; 85% reported needing assistance with one or more instrumental ADLs. In summary, both congregate meal and home-delivered meal participants are among the most vulnerable elderly adults with regard to their levels of social interaction, nutritional status, and physical health.

CHALLENGES FOR NUTRITION PROGRAMS

On the basis of empirical research during the past two decades evaluating the outcomes of nutrition programs, one can conclude that these programs are indeed successful and that programs funded under the OAA are serving older adults who are at risk of poor nutritional intake with meals that are critical to their daily food consumption. These programs also provide older individuals with social contacts that are beneficial for their psychological well-being. Despite these successes, meal programs for older adults face a number of critical issues.

Enhancing Awareness and Use of Nutrition Programs

Older adults who participate in nutrition programs derive nutritional and psychological benefits, yet many other older adults who also could benefit from attending do not participate. S. A. Peterson and Maiden (1991) explored the variables associated with awareness and use of congregate meal programs in a sample of 358 community-dwelling older adults. Those who were aware of the programs had more personal and social resources and less nutritional need. Those using nutrition programs, however, had fewer personal and social resources and greater nutritional need. Such research illustrates the need for more studies about the factors associated with awareness and use of programs to assist with outreach efforts. On the basis of their two-year evaluation of the senior nutrition program, Ponza, Ohls, Millen, and colleagues (1996) made the following recommendations for future directions of nutrition programs:

- As the percentage of persons in the oldest-old category increases, the need for home-delivered meals may increase.

- Programs must endeavor to better meet the specialized nutrition needs of their participants, including more choices in types of meals, and more options for meals available during the day and on weekends.

- Changes in the delivery of health care will also have an impact on nutrition programs. As individuals continue to be discharged more quickly from hospitals and nursing homes, nutrition programs will be serving an even more frail and functionally impaired population than in the past.

- There continue to be waiting lists at some nutrition sites for home-delivered and congregate meals, and high percentages of home-delivered and congregate meal participants continue to be nutritionally at risk. Programs will be challenged to serve the underserved population in an era of shrinking public and private dollars.

The demand for OAA Nutrition Program (OAANP) services over the past few years during the Great Recession has increased dramatically, whereas the funding, when adjusted for inflation, has declined substantially over the last 20 years (Colello, 2011). In 2009, local AAA meal programs reported a 79% increase in demand for home-delivered meals, and a 42% increase for congregate meals (K. E. Brown, 2010). Within one state, Georgia, approximately 5,000 older adults requested OAANP services and 57.4% were placed on a waiting list (J. S. Lee et al., 2011). Supplementing OAA funding with alternative funding from businesses, civic organizations, and foundations will be sources of financial support that programs must tap to maintain and expand services (Balsam & Rogers, 1991).

Serving a Diverse Older Population

Meal programs for older adults must be ever mindful of meeting the nutritional needs of an ethnically diverse population. Programs must ensure that the social atmosphere, as well as the meals, is welcoming to racial and ethnic elders by having culturally sensitive staff, preparing ethnic meals, offering culturally appropriate nutrition education materials, and obtaining input from minority participants (Briggs, 1992; Mower, 2008). Others have commented on the need to reach out to the most needy older persons. For example, Balsam and Rogers (1991) argue that outreach for nutrition programs must include older adults who are "socially impaired"—those who are socially isolated, homeless, live in single-room occupancy dwellings, suffer from substance abuse, or are deinstitutionalized. Because such persons might not be readily welcomed at congregate meal sites, programs targeted to older adults at the margins of society might be created (Doolin, 1985). Adding to and customizing meals will also mean that more dieticians knowledgeable in working with older adults will be needed to help guide and advise expanding nutrition programs (N. S. Wellman, Rosenzweig, & Lloyd, 2002).

Implementing Meal Programs for a New Generation of Older Adults

Finally, nutrition programs will have to change as the population ages and as cohorts with different needs and preferences replace the current participants. Because evidence indicates that nutrition and eating habits vary across age groups (Wurtman, Lieberman, Tsay, Nader, & Chew, 1988), the menus and meals offered through nutrition programs will no doubt need to accommodate those differences as well.

Supporting the Future of Senior Nutrition Programs

The delegates at the White House Conference on Aging (2006) passed a resolution and strategies that address a number of the challenges previously discussed. The delegates recommended the following to promote the importance of nutrition in health promotion and disease prevention and management:

- Form a public–private nutrition and fitness alliance that would become the authoritative source for seniors and caregiver, and promote through a national media campaign.

- Respond to the special nutritional needs of individual seniors to enhance independent living by reauthorizing the OAA to include the flexibility to use nontraditional food sources and by strengthening the congregate and home-delivered meal programs to increase services up to seven days and expanding Senior Farmers' Market Nutrition Program nationwide.

- Through the reauthorization of the OAA (Title III), expand funding to ensure adequate nutrition (eliminate undernutrition) and provide reliable nutrition education/information delivered by registered dieticians or technology that can then empower individuals.

- Use existing nutrition sciences to concurrently deliver physical activity and exercise information and programs to older adults.

CASE STUDY

Good Nutrition—Making Independence Possible

Manuel, 75, is a shy bachelor who has lived with his mother all his adult life except during two years when he was stationed overseas with the army. After his discharge, he returned home and worked as a cook for the local National Guard for 12 years. Everyone in town talked about the good old-fashioned food that Manuel prepared. When the local National Guard facility closed, Manuel became a self-employed janitor. He continued to work without giving retirement a second thought. His work, his flower garden, and taking care of his mother were his main activities in life. Manuel's income, barely $617 per month, supported his modest lifestyle.

One day, when Manuel was driving to the hardware store to buy garden supplies, a semitrailer broadsided him. The accident was serious and was Manuel's fault. He was rushed to the hospital with internal injuries and a broken leg and collarbone. During the hospitalization, medical tests revealed that Manuel was diabetic. His diabetes had gone untreated because he had simply ignored symptoms that had plagued him for many years. The untreated diabetes, it now seemed, was the cause of his eyesight deteriorating so rapidly in the year before the accident.

After four weeks, the hospital discharged him to a nursing home, where he spent three months in a skilled care unit. This was a difficult time for Manuel. He was making progress overcoming his injuries, but not the chronic pain in his neck. In addition, his mother died, and he felt terrible that he was unable to be with her before her death. His only remaining family was his estranged sister.

Manuel's greatest desire was to return home. He reminded the nursing home staff and his doctor of that at every opportunity. He desperately missed his garden and the few neighbors with whom he used to chat over the fence. Finally, after weeks of listening to Manuel complain about neck pain and not being able to go home, his doctor ordered more x-rays, which showed that Manuel's neck was broken. He was fitted for a halo cast and told by his doctor that he could return home only if he followed a strict diabetic diet and did not drive.

Case Study Questions

1. Why is nutrition such a central factor in Manuel's plan of care?

2. What community-based food programs would you recommend for Manuel? Which program would you choose as the best option for Manuel? Why?

3. Is Manuel a good candidate for living at home alone if he follows the doctor's instructions? Why or why not?

4. What reasons would you give to defend Manuel's chances for successfully returning home?

5. What reasons would you give to defend Manuel's chances for having to move back to the nursing home?

LEARNING ACTIVITIES

1. Have an older adult relative keep a nutrition diary for one week to track what was eaten and when. Keep track of your own nutritional intake for that same week. Examine both diaries. How are they different? Similar? Are there any deficiencies in either diet? What improvements could be made in both diets?

2. Visit or volunteer at the local food bank. How many of the clients are older adults? How often is food distributed? What are the eligibility criteria for participation? How does the food bank obtain food to distribute?

3. Sign up for a congregate meal at a nearby site. How many people attend? How many times during the week are meals served? What is the suggested donation? What was the ethnic makeup of participants? Would the type of meals served attract older adults of different ethnic backgrounds?

FOR MORE INFORMATION

International Resources

1. The British Dietetic Association: www.bda.uk.com/about/index.html

   The British Dietetic Association is the professional association and trade union for dietitians. Their website has nutrition resources and publications on a wide variety of topics for both professionals and laypersons.

2. AgeUK - Healthy Eating: http://www.ageuk.org.uk/health-wellbeing/healthy-eating-landing/

   The AgeUK's website has a number of healthy eating resources for older adults including the "Healthy eating guide: Your guide to eating well" and "Healthy eating: fact vs fiction".

3. International Life Sciences Institute- Project PAN (Physical Activity and Nutrition): www .ilsijapan.org/English/ILSIJapan/COM/CHP_PAN.php

   The Physical Activity and Nutrition (Project PAN) works to promote healthier lifestyles among people in their advanced years. One of their initiatives is called the "TAKE10!" for the elderly. The major features of the TAKE10! program include: 1) targeting behavioral changes such as increasing physical exercise and improving dietary practices, 2) ability to adapt the program at a reasonable cost to either the elderly and 3) ability to use the instruction package to easily incorporate the program into existing nursing care prevention programs or municipal peer-leader training programs.

National Resources

1. National Resource Center on Nutrition, Physical Activity & Aging, Florida International University, University Park, OE200, Miami, FL 33199; phone: 305-348-1517; http://nutrition andaging.fiu.edu; e-mail: nutritionandaging@fiu.edu

   The Resource Center on Nutrition, Physical Activity & Aging works with the AoA to improve the nutritional status of older adults by disseminating nutrition information, providing technical assistance and training, and examining nutrition policies.

2. American Dietetic Association, 216 West Jackson Boulevard, Chicago, IL 60606; phone: 800-877-1600, ext. 5000 (publications); www.eatright.com

   The American Dietetic Association is the professional society for dietitians. In addition to other services for its members and a consumer nutrition hotline, the association has numerous publications helpful to consumers, such as *Staying Healthy: A Guide for Elder Americans*, *Older Adults Food Guide Pyramid*, and *Recommendations of Food Choices for Women*.

3. Food and Nutrition Information Center, U.S. Department of Agriculture, National Agriculture Library Building, Room 105, 10301 Baltimore Avenue, Beltsville, MD 20705-2351; phone: 301-504-5719; http://fnic.nal.usda.gov

   The Center provides information to professionals and the general public on nutrition and acquires and lends printed and audiovisual materials dealing with nutrition.

4. Meals on Wheels Association of America (formerly the National Association of Meal Programs), 203 S. Union Street, Alexandria, VA 22314; phone: 703-548-5558; www.mowaa.org

   The Meals on Wheels Association of America provides education and training to those who plan and conduct congregate and home-delivered meals programs.

5. *The Journal of Nutrition in Gerontology and Geriatrics,* Taylor & Francis, www.tandfonline.com/loi/wjne20

   The Journal of Nutrition in Gerontology and Geriatrics publishes research on nutritional care for older adults. The journal includes client education suggestions and covers essential aspects of nutrition, from the clinical correlation between the pathophysiology of diseases and the role of nutrition to the psychosocial aspects of eating. In addition to scholarly studies, it also highlights evidence-based interventions for use in community settings.

6. The National Association of Nutrition and Aging Services Programs, 1612 K Street, NW, Suite 400, Washington, DC 20006; phone: 202-682-6899; www.nanasp.org

   The National Association of Nutrition and Aging Services Programs (NANASP) is a professional membership organization with members drawn primarily from persons working in or interested in the field of aging, community-based services, and nutrition and the elderly. NANASP is recognized as a primary leadership organization in the field of aging in shaping national policy, training service providers, and advocating on behalf of seniors.

Web Resources

1. Food in Later Life Research Project, University of Surrey, Guildford, Surrey, GU2 7XH, UK; www.foodinlaterlife.org/senior410.html; e-mail: m.raats@surrey.ac.uk

   The Food in Later Life Research Project is a longitudinal research project funded by the European Union to examine the relationship between food intake, nutritional well-being, health, and quality of life among older people and to disseminate and consult with professionals who are in a position to enhance older people's nutritional well-being, health, and quality of life through food and service provision. Twelve countries will be involved in the study, including the United Kingdom, Italy, Germany, Sweden, Demark, Portugal, and Spain. The project website contains many resources on the topic of the nutritional well-being of older adults.

2. Jean Mayer USDA Human Nutrition Research Center on Aging at Tufts University, 711 Washington Street, Boston, MA 02111; 617- 556-3000; http://hnrca.tufts.edu/

   The mission of the Jean Mayer USDA Human Nutrition Research Center on Aging at Tufts University (HNRCA) is to explore the relationship between nutrition, aging, and health by determining the nutrient requirements that are necessary to promote health and well-being for older adults and examining the degenerative conditions associated with aging. In addition to providing nutrition resources and information, the HNRCA introduced the MyPlate for Older Adults, which corresponds with MyPlate, the federal government's new food group symbol. MyPlate for Older Adults calls attention to the unique nutritional and physical activity needs associated with advancing years. MyPlate for Older Adults is available to print out on the USDA HNRCA website.

CHAPTER 11

Health Care and Wellness

Marge had intended for years to get serious about losing weight. She could not believe it when her physician told her she was diabetic. She had just celebrated her 65th birthday, she felt great, and she was as active as she had ever been. Marge discussed her options for treatment with her doctor and decided to try diet and exercise because her sugar levels were only a little above normal. However, she knew her personality and lifestyle well enough to be aware that she could not do this on her own. Her doctor suggested that she contact the Lifetime Wellness Center through the local hospital. The center encouraged her to enroll in a "Slim for Life" class sponsored by the American Heart Association and attend a "Managing Diabetes" class sponsored by the hospital. After eight weeks of classes, Marge believes she is on her way to getting control of her weight problem. She also knows the consequences of her actions and that if she needs more help, the Wellness Center is there to support her.

Although changes in physical health are inevitable as individuals age, it is possible to live a healthy life well into the ninth decade. Early detection of conditions such as Marge's diabetes and the assistance of wellness programs will make it possible for her to manage her illness for many years. Indeed, older adults are living longer partly because of the advances in preventive and traditional medical care and improved access to health care services through Medicare. In this chapter, we provide a summary of the health status of older adults, the newly enacted Affordable Care Act, and the Medicare and Medicaid programs. We conclude this chapter by describing health promotion and wellness programs available to older adults and looking at future challenges for health care policy and health promotion programs.

HEALTH STATUS OF OLDER ADULTS

Overall, the majority of older adults consider their health to be *good*, *very good*, or *excellent* (Mirel, Wheatcroft, Parker, & Makuc, 2012). Although self-assessment is certainly one way to measure health status, the presence or absence of chronic or acute disease and the degree of inability in level of functioning are other measures of health status (R. A. Kane & Kane, 1981). Although older adults suffer more frequently from chronic than acute conditions, the consequences of acute illness are more severe for older adults than for younger adults. For example, an equal number of older adults and younger adults get respiratory infections, but death rates are 30% higher for older adults who get these infections (Hooyman & Kiyak, 2002; Hoyert, Heron, Murphy, & Kung, 2006). In contrast, older adults are more likely than younger adults to have chronic illnesses—those that are long term, often permanent, and result in a disability that requires management rather than a cure. Marge's diabetes is a good example of a chronic condition that will require health management for the rest of her life. According to the National Center for Health Statistics (He, Sengupta, Velkoff, & DeBarros, 2005), more than 80% of older adults over 65 have at least one chronic condition.

The presence of chronic conditions varies across subpopulations of older adults. For example, as shown in Exhibit 11.1, older women are more likely than older men to suffer

Exhibit 11.1   Prevalence of Selected Chronic Conditions of Persons Aged 65+ by Gender, 2009–2010 (percentage)

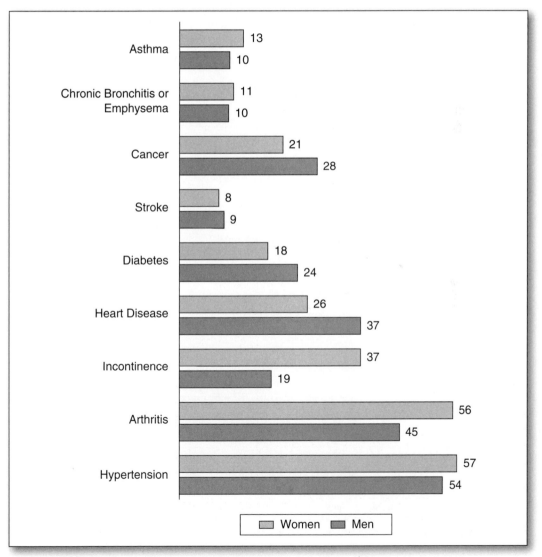

Source: Federal Interagency Forum on Aging-Related Statistics (2010) and Centers for Disease Control and Prevention, 2012a).

from chronic conditions such as arthritis, hypertension, incontinence, and asthma; men more likely to suffer from heart disease and diabetes. Similarly, older adults of color suffer from chronic conditions at rates that are often significantly higher those of White older adults. Exhibit 11.2 show the prevalence of chronic conditions experienced by Hispanic, Black, and White older persons. Black and Hispanic older adults are more likely to suffer

Exhibit 11.2   Prevalence of Selected Chronic Conditions of Persons Aged 65+ by Race and Ethnicity, 2010 (percentage)

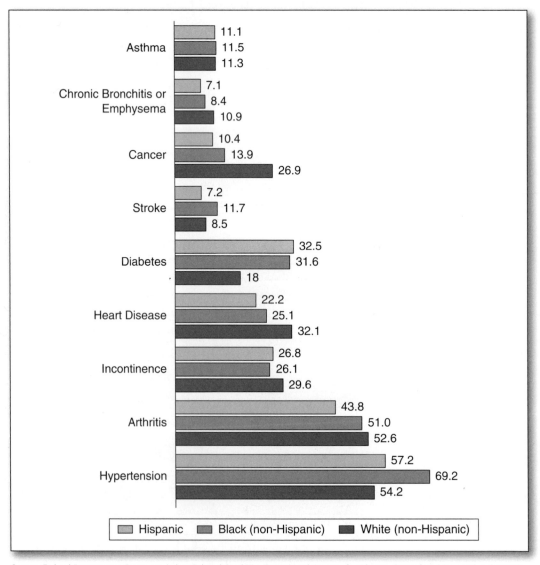

Source: Federal Interagency Forum on Aging-Related Statistics (2010) and Centers for Disease Control and Prevention (2012a).

from diabetes than White elders. Elderly Blacks are also more likely to suffer from hypertension, arthritis, diabetes, and stroke than are Hispanic and White elders. Elderly Hispanics are more likely to suffer from heart disease than their counterparts. In addition, 85% of older Hispanic adults suffer from at least one chronic condition; by the age of 45, many experience chronic health impairments, such as arthritis, heart disease, and diabetes, similar to those of a typical White 65-year-old (Cuellar, 1990). Older Native Americans have even greater rates of chronic conditions. Older Native Americans are more likely to have arthritis, congestive heart failure, stroke, asthma, prostate cancer, high blood pressure, and diabetes than the general population aged 55 and older (Moulton et al., 2005).

A more recent health concern among the aging population is the increasing number of overweight and obese individuals. Currently, 73.2% of older adults aged 75 and older are considered overweight, and of those, 26.6% are considered obese (Centers for Disease Control and Prevention, 2012d)—percentages that have increased by 17% and 13%, respectively, since 1988 (see Exhibit 11.3). In addition, the prevalence of being overweight

Exhibit 11.3   Trends in Weight Among Older Adults Aged 65 to 74 and 75 and Over, Selected Years 1988–2010 (percentage)

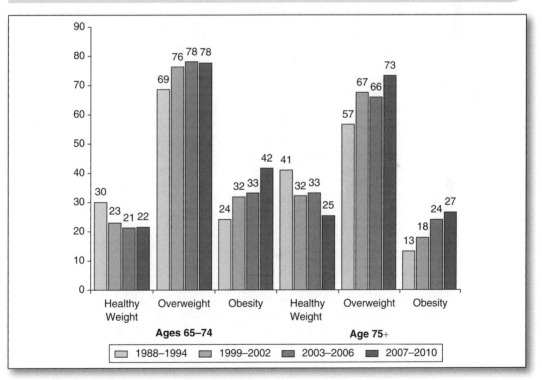

Source: Centers for Disease Control and Prevention (2012d).

Normal weight: body mass index (BMI) greater than 18.5, less than 25; overweight: BMI greater than 25, less than 30; obese: BMI greater than 30, less than 35.

Notes: Percentages do not sum to 100 because the percentage of persons with BMI less than healthy weight is not shown and the percentage of persons with obesity is a subset of the percentage with overweight.

and obese in the 65 to 74 population is higher than those aged 75 and over, as 77% of persons aged 65 to 74 are overweight and 41.5% of those are considered obese, percentages that are also up significantly from 1988. Individuals who are overweight and obese have increased likelihood of being in poorer health, suffering from more chronic health conditions, and being limited in their ability to carry out activities of daily living (Strum, Ringel, & Andreyeva, 2004).

Older adults are also living with HIV and dying from AIDS. According to the National Center for Health Statistics (Kochanek, Xu, Murphy, Miniño, & Kung, 2011), more people over age 65 died of AIDS than did children and youth under the age of 25. The number of persons aged 65 and older who died from AIDS increased significantly from 1999 to 2009 (1,631 to 2,556, respectively) compared to persons aged 24 and younger (302 to 155, respectively; Centers for Disease Control and Prevention, 2012e). As of December 2009, there were an estimated 77,401 persons aged 55 and older diagnosed with AIDS (Centers for Disease Control and Prevention, 2011).

Persons living with chronic conditions, including HIV/AIDS, experience functional limitations for which they need assistance. Functional limitation, one measure of an individual's health status, is the inability to perform personal care tasks and home-management activities. Personal care tasks, commonly referred to as *activities of daily living* (ADLs), include tasks such as bathing and grooming, toileting, dressing, and eating. Home-management activities, or *instrumental activities of daily living* (IADLs), include tasks such as shopping and preparing meals, doing housework, and handling personal finances. National data reveal that 37.5% of older adults living in the community have difficulty in performing ADLs or IADLs, and more older women are likely to have a functional limitation than older men (41.4% vs. 32.6%; Federal Interagency Forum on Aging-Related Statistics, 2010). As shown in Exhibit 11.4, older women are more likely than older men to have trouble doing a number of activities, including walking, light and heavy housework, transferring (e.g., in/out of bed), shopping, and bathing. Just as older women and older adults of different ethnic and racial groups suffer from multiple chronic impairments, they are also likely to have multiple limitations in their everyday activities. In a sample of community-dwelling older adults, 15.3% of women compared with 7.8% of men could not do IADLs without assistance (Centers for Disease Control and Prevention, 2012a). A similar disparity existed between older Whites and other racial and ethnic groups in functional abilities: 45% of Blacks, 58% of American Indians or Alaska Natives, and 46% of Hispanics had one or more functional limitations in IADLs and ADLs, compared with 38% of non-Hispanic Whites over 65 years of age (Centers for Disease Control and Prevention, 2012a, 2012c; Waldrop & Stern, 2003).

A related indicator of functional limitation is the need for assistance in carrying out ADLs and IADLs. Not surprisingly, the need for assistance with daily activities increases with age. As shown in Exhibit 11.5, 7.9% and 13.7% of older adults aged 75 to 84 need assistance with ADLs and IADLs, respectively. The need for assistance increases to 19% and 32% for those over age 85 who need assistance with ADLs and IADLs.

Older women are more likely than older men to need assistance with major ADL and IADL tasks, such as assistance with bathing, dressing, eating, transferring between bed and chair, toileting (ADLs) and preparing meals, doing housework, shopping (IADLs). Although the percentages of women and men aged 65 to 74 who need assistance with everyday activities are similar (25% and 17%, respectively), by age 85 and older, 58% of women need assistance with everyday activities compared to 38% of men (see Exhibit 11.6).

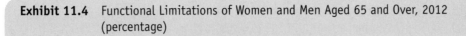

Exhibit 11.4 Functional Limitations of Women and Men Aged 65 and Over, 2012 (percentage)

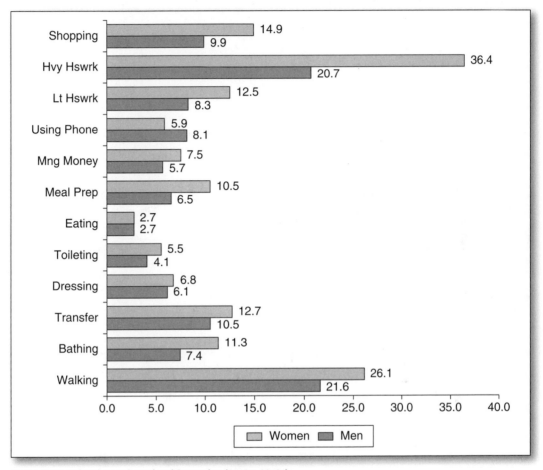

Source: Centers for Disease Control and Prevention (2012a, 2012c).

Similar to older women, older adults of different ethnic and racial groups experience a higher number of chronic conditions and functional limitations than do older Whites and therefore are more likely to need assistance with everyday activities. As shown in Exhibit 11.6, a higher percentage of older Blacks and Hispanics report needing assistance in everyday activities than do older non-Hispanic Whites ages 65 to 74, and a higher percentage of Hispanics report needing assistance in everyday activities than do non-Hispanic Whites and Blacks at age 85 and older (Centers for Disease Control and Prevention, 2012a, 2012c).

In summary, most older adults do enjoy relatively good health; however, as people grow older and move into later life, they acquire more chronic conditions and experience fewer acute conditions, although the latter can result in life-threatening illnesses for some.

Exhibit 11.5   Persons Needing Assistance With ADL and IADL Needs by Age, 2010 (percentage)

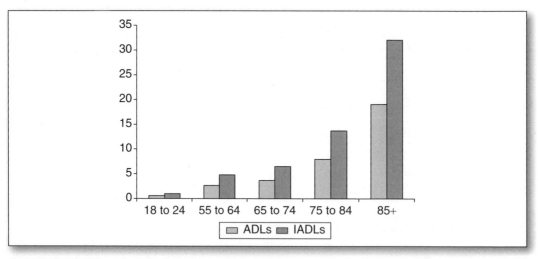

Source: Centers for Disease Control and Prevention (2012a, 2012c).

Exhibit 11.6   Persons Needing Assistance With ADL and IADL Needs by Age, Gender, and Race, 2010 (percentage)

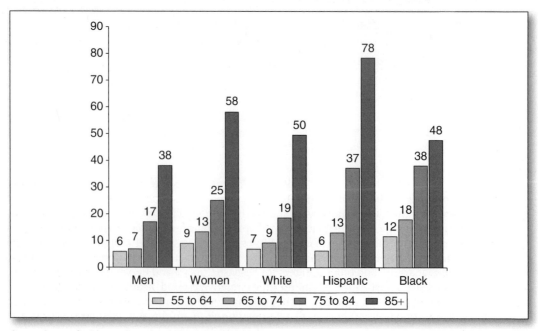

Source: Centers for Disease Control and Prevention (2012a, 2012c).

Note: Data do not total 100% as data for IADL and ADL needs were summed.

Furthermore, health status varies between older women and men, between Whites and older adults of different racial and ethnic backgrounds, and between persons of different ages. In general, women, racial and ethnic elders, and those over age 85 have more chronic illnesses and more functional limitations, and are more likely to need assistance with major activities.

These health characteristics have significant implications for the delivery of health care and health promotion programs. For example, in later life, adults need health care programs and services that address chronic, rather than acute, conditions. They also need access to and coverage of rehabilitation services, including assistance with assistive technology devices that are designed to maintain functional independence. Furthermore, health promotion and prevention programs can assist in preventing illness as well as in maintaining functioning. Later in this chapter, we will discuss the health promotion and wellness programs designed to improve the health status of older adults. In this next section, we provide an overview of the federal health insurance programs—Medicare and Medicaid.

For Your Files: AbleData

Assistive technology devices help people maintain independent living by helping them perform ADLs. Assistive technology devices have been used by persons with disabilities for years; with the growing number of older adults with chronic conditions, however, such devices can effectively assist more older adults with their functional limitations. AbleData, sponsored by the National Institute on Disability and Rehabilitation Research, is a national database of information on assistive technology and rehabilitation equipment from domestic and international sources. AbleData contains information on more than 40,000 assistive technology products that consumers can search on the web or by phone. AbleData also offers fact sheets about devices and topics related to assistive technology, consumer guides to assist with product selection, and other publications for consumers of assistive technology devices. AbleData can refer callers to resources that can help them make their companies accessible. Visit AbleData's fully accessible facilities at 8630 Fenton Street, Suite 930, Silver Spring, MD 20910; phone AbleData for more information at 800-227-0216; or access the website, www.abledata.com.

FEDERAL HEALTH CARE POLICY

Patient Protection and Affordable Care Act

The most significant change to health care policy to be enacted in the last 40 years was the passage of the Patient Protection and Affordable Care Act (ACA) P.L. 111-152, signed into law by President Obama on March 23, 2010.[1] The ACA expands health care coverage through a number of different public and private approaches. The ACA will provide health access to approximately 32 million currently uninsured adults and attain almost universal coverage through a combination of public programs and private insurance options, incentives for employers and small businesses to cover employees, expansion of Medicare and Medicaid programs, and changes to provisions allowable under private insurance policies (Kaiser Family Foundation [KFF], 2011b). In addition, the ACA has provisions designed to

---

[1]Unless otherwise noted, the summary of the ACA is from the Kaiser Family Foundation (2011b).

control health care costs and improve the health care delivery system. The provisions of the Act are phased in from 2010 to 2014.

With regard to the expansion of health care coverage under the ACA, the changes in effect as of 2012 are

- a temporary program operated by the federal and state government to provide health coverage to individuals with pre-existing medical conditions who have been uninsured for at least six months;

- dependent coverage for adult children up to age 26 for all individual and group policies;

- a prohibition against individual and group health plans placing lifetime limits on the dollar value of coverage, rescinding coverage except in cases of fraud, and denying children coverage based on pre-existing medical conditions or from including pre-existing condition exclusions for children; and

- requiring that new health plans provide at a minimum coverage without cost-sharing for certain preventive services, recommended immunizations, preventive care for infants, children, and adolescents, and additional preventive care and screenings for women including contraception. (KFF, n.d.)

By 2014, the Act requires most U.S. citizens and legal residents to have health insurance and those low-income adults not covered under Medicaid or who have private insurance through their work and employers will be able to purchase plans through American Health Benefits Exchanges (HBE) and Small Business Health Options Program (SHOP) Exchanges. These Exchanges will be administered by a government agency or nonprofit where employers and individuals can purchase coverage with cost sharing assistance for low income individuals (KFF, n.d.). The health plans must offer guarantee issue and renewability of health insurance regardless of health status, and the ACA prohibits annual limits on the dollar value of coverage. Small businesses will be encouraged to offer qualified coverage through SHOP Exchanges and tax breaks. The Exchanges will offer buyers a choice between four categories of coverage plus a separate catastrophic plan that provides a comprehensive set of services and limits annual cost sharing. The Act makes significant changes to the Medicare and Medicaid programs and we will discuss those changes in the sections that follow.

Medicare

Medicare is a national health insurance program authorized in 1965 under Title XVII of the Social Security Act as a complement to those receiving Social Security benefits. Originally, Medicare covered older adults age 65 and over, but since its passage, coverage has been extended to persons who are entitled to Social Security disability for 24 months or more, persons with end-stage kidney disease requiring dialysis or transplant, and noncovered persons who elect to buy into Medicare. Beginning in 2001, persons with Lou Gehrig's disease are allowed to waive the 24-month waiting period and can be covered under the Medicare program (Klees, Wolfe, & Curtis, 2011). The Centers for Medicaid and Medicare Services (CMS) administer the program under the direction of the U.S. Department of Health and Human Services (HHS).

There are two original parts to Medicare: *Part A, Hospital Insurance*, which covers costs associated with inpatient hospitalization and some post-hospitalization care, and *Part B, Supplemental Medical Insurance*, which covers physician, outpatient care, and other medical services. A new third part of Medicare, sometimes called *Part C*, was established in

1997, and later renamed the *Medicare Advantage Program* in 2003; it expanded beneficiaries' option for participation in private sector health care plans. The 2003 changes in Medicare also introduced *Part D*, which established a new prescription drug program (Hoffman et al., 2006; see Exhibit 11.7). Part A is funded by taxes on earnings; employers and employees each pay 1.45% of payroll, and self-employed persons pay 2.9%. Starting in 2013, a payroll tax of 0.9% will be collected on earned income over $200,000 for single filers and $250,000 for joint filers (Klees et al., 2011). Older households and Social Security beneficiaries with incomes above a certain amount also contribute to the Part A funding through payroll taxes. Part B is funded primarily through income-related premiums paid by beneficiaries and general federal revenues. Individuals exceeding a threshold income level (starting at $85,000 for individuals and $170,000 for couples) will pay slightly higher

Exhibit 11.7   Overview of Medicare Coverage

Original Medicare Plan		OR	**Medicare Advantage Plans**
Part A Hospital	Part B Medical		Part C this option combines Part A (Hospital) and Part B (Medical) coverage
Medicare provides this coverage. Part B is optional. Beneficiaries have a choice of doctors.			*Private insurance companies approved by Medicare provide this coverage.* Generally, beneficiaries must see doctors in the plan.

+	+
(optional)	

Prescription Drug Coverage Part D	**Prescription Drug Coverage**
Beneficiaries can choose this coverage. Private companies approved by Medicare run these plans. Plans cover different drugs. Medically necessary drugs must be covered.	Most Part C plans cover prescription drugs; if not, beneficiaries may be able to choose this coverage. Plans cover different drugs. Medically necessary drugs must be covered.

+	

Medigap (Medicare Supplement Insurance) Policy	**Medigap (Medicare Supplement Insurance) Policy**
Beneficiaries can choose to buy this private coverage (or an employer/union may offer similar coverage) to fill in gaps in Part A and Part B coverage. Costs vary by policy and company.	Persons joining a Medicare Advantage Plan do not need and can't be sold a Medicare Supplemental Insurance (Medigap) policy.

Source: Centers for Medicare and Medicaid Services (CMS, 2011).

premiums that will cover 35%, 50%, 65%, or 80% of the average program cost for aged beneficiaries compared to the standard base premium that covers 25% (Boards of Trustees of the Federal Hospital Insurance Trust Fund and the Federal Supplementary Medical Insurance Trust Fund, 2012). The ACA freezes these income threshold levels through 2019. Thus premiums for Part B cover approximately 25% to 80% of program costs, and general federal revenues cover the remainder (Boards of Trustees, 2012). Reviewing and paying claims under both Part A and Part B are done by intermediaries called Medicare Administrative Contractors, organized by geographical area, creating a single point of contact for all claims. In 2010, over 47 million people were enrolled in Part A, 44 million in Part B, approximately 12 million have chosen to participate in Part C, and Part D covered over 34 million enrollees (Boards of Trustees, 2012; Klees et al., 2011).

Who Is Eligible for Medicare?

All persons who are eligible for Social Security or Railroad Retirement benefits are also eligible for Medicare benefits. In addition, individuals who are entitled to Social Security Disability or Railroad Retirement Disability Benefits for at least 24 months and government employees with Medicare-only coverage who have been disabled for 29 or more months are also entitled to receive Part A benefits. Therefore, individuals qualify for Medicare if they or their spouses worked for 10 years (or 40 quarters) in employment that paid into Social Security. Those who lack a sufficient number of quarters can purchase Part A benefits if they also buy Part B coverage. In 2012, individuals who wished to buy Part A coverage could do so for $451 (CMS, n.d.-c). For individuals who have earned enough quarters, there is no premium cost associated with Part A; older adults choosing to participate in Part B, however, pay a monthly premium. Beginning in January 2012, the amount of the Part B monthly premium is based on the beneficiary's gross income. Individuals with incomes less than $85,000 pay $99.90, those with incomes between $85,000 and $107,000 pay $139.90, those between $107,000 to $160,000 pay $199.80, and those above $160,000 pay monthly premiums of $259.70. All beneficiaries must meet the $140 per year deductible for physician services (CMS, n.d.-d).

Coverage

Exhibits 11.8, 11.9, 11.10, and 11.11 present detailed explanations of the coverage provided by Part A, Part B, and Part D. Medicare Part A provides coverage of inpatient hospital services up to 90 days per benefit period[2] plus 60 days of lifetime reserve days, skilled nursing facilities for 100 days following a 3-day hospital stay, intermittent home health services if skilled care is needed, and hospice care (Health Care Financing Administration [HCFA], 2001c). Medicare Part B helps pay for the cost of physician services, outpatient hospital services, medical equipment and supplies, and other health services and supplies. The ACA expands coverage of preventive services (see Exhibit 11.10) to 19 different services, reduces or eliminates deductibles and copayments, and covers annual wellness visits and a personalized prevention/wellness plan (CMS, n.d-a). Payments made by Medicare under Part A for inpatient hospital costs are based on the patient's diagnosis (referred to as *diagnostic related group*, or *DRG*). The patient's DRG dictates the payment the hospital will receive as well as the length

---

[2]A benefit period begins on the first day a beneficiary receives in-patient hospital benefits and ends after being discharged from the hospital or skilled facility for 60 consecutive days

Exhibit 11.8 Medicare Coverage, Part A

Services	Benefit Period[a]	Medicare Pays	Beneficiary Pays
Hospitalization Semi-private room, meals, regular nursing services, intensive care, operating and recovering room, drugs, laboratory tests, x-rays, and all other medically necessary supplies	*First 60 days*	All approved charges but $1,156	$1,156
	Days 61–90	All but $289 per day co-insurance	$289 per day for each benefit period
	Days 91–150	All but $578 per day co-insurance	$578 per day each benefit period
	150+ days	Nothing	All
	Lifetime reserve days		"Lifetime reserve days" are 60 extra days of coverage that can use during the lifetime of the beneficiary.
Inpatient mental health care in a psychiatric hospital	*Same as above*	Same as above Inpatient mental health care in a psychiatric hospital is limited to 190 days in a lifetime	Pay $578 per day during the 60 days of coverage All after 190 lifetime days
Skilled Nursing Facility Semi-private room and board, skilled nursing and rehabilitative services, and other services and supplies	*Days 1–20*	100% of covered services	Nothing
	Days 21–100	All but $144.50 per day	$144.50 per day
	100 +	Nothing	All costs
Home Health Part-time or intermittent skilled care, home health aide services, durable medical equipment and supplies, physical therapy, occupational therapy, and speech-language pathology	Unlimited as long as Medicare conditions are met	100% of the cost of covered home health care; 80% of approved amount for durable medical equipment	Nothing for services; 20% for durable medical equipment
Hospice Pain relief, symptom management, and support services for the terminally ill	For as long as doctor certifies and patient has six months or less to live	100% of charges; no deductible	A co-payment of up to $5 for outpatient prescription drugs and 5% of the Medicare-approved amount for inpatient respite care

(Continued)

Exhibit 11.8 (Continued)

Services	Benefit Period[a]	Medicare Pays	Beneficiary Pays
Blood When furnished by a hospital or skilled nursing facility during a covered stay	Unlimited if medically necessary	All but first three pints per calendar year	For first three pints then 20% of the Medicare-approved amount for additional pints of blood

Source: CMS (2011).

[a]A benefit period begins on the first day a beneficiary receives in-patient hospital benefits and ends after being discharged from the hospital or skilled facility for 60 consecutive days.

Exhibit 11.9 Medicare Coverage, Part B

Services	Benefit Period[a]	Medicare Pays	Beneficiary Pays
Preventive Services See Exhibit 11.10			
Medical Expenses Doctors' services, inpatient and outpatient medical and surgical services and supplies, physical and speech therapy, diagnostic tests, durable medical equipment, and other services	*Unlimited if medically necessary*	80% of approved amount after deductible	Deductible, plus 20% of approved amount and limited charges above the approved amount
Clinical Laboratory Services Blood tests, urinalyses, and more	*Unlimited if medically necessary*	Generally 100% of approved amount	Nothing for services
Home Health Care Part-time or intermittent skilled care, home health aide services, durable medical equipment and supplies, and other services	*Unlimited as long as Medicare conditions are met*	100% of the cost of covered home health care; 80% of approved amount for durable medical equipment	Nothing for services; 20% for durable medical equipment
Outpatient Hospital Services Services for the diagnosis or treatment of illness or injury	*Unlimited if medically necessary*	Approved amount minus co-pay or co-insurance amount	Co-pay or co-insurance amount
Blood When furnished by a hospital or skilled nursing facility during a covered stay	*Unlimited if medically necessary*	80% of approved amount after $100 deductible and starting with the 4th pint	For first three pints plus 20% of approved amount for additional pints
Mental Health Services	*Unlimited if medically necessary*	50% of approved amount	50% of approved amount

Services	Benefit Period[a]	Medicare Pays	Beneficiary Pays
Ambulance Services	*Unlimited if medically necessary*	80% of approved amount	20% of approved amount
Eyeglasses (limited)	*One pair of eyeglasses or contact lenses after cataract surgery*	80% of approved amount	20% of approved amount

Source: CMS (2011).

[a]A benefit period begins on the first day a beneficiary receives in-patient hospital benefits and ends after being discharged from the hospital or skilled facility for 60 consecutive days.

Exhibit 11.10   Medicare-Covered Preventive Services

Service	Who Is Eligible	How Frequently	Beneficiary's Costs
Initial Preventive Physical Examination (IPPE) or "Welcome to Medicare Exam"	Enrollees in Part B within first 12 months of enrollment	Once-in-a-lifetime benefit per beneficiary	Prior to 01/01/2011—No deductible; but copayment/coinsurance apply As of 01/01/2011—None
Annual Wellness Visit (AWV)—New Benefit in 2011	Enrollees in Part B after first 12 months of enrollment who have not received an IPPE or AWV within the past 12 months	Annually	None
Ultrasound Screening for Abdominal Aortic Aneurysm (AAA)	Part B enrollees with certain risk factors for abdominal aortic aneurysm	Once in a lifetime based on referral resulting from a "Welcome to Medicare Exam"	Prior to 01/01/2011—No deductible; but copayment/coinsurance apply As of 01/01/2011—None
Cardiovascular Disease Screenings	All Part B enrollees	Every five years	None
Diabetes Screening Tests	Part B enrollees with certain risk factors for diabetes or diagnosed with pre-diabetes	Two per year for beneficiaries diagnosed with pre-diabetes; one per year if previously tested, but not diagnosed with pre-diabetes, or if never tested	None
Diabetes Self-Management Training (DSMT)	Part B enrollees diagnosed with diabetes	First year: up to 10 hours of initial training Subsequent years: up to 2 hours of follow-up training annually	Deductible and coinsurance/copayment

(Continued)

Exhibit 11.10 (Continued)

Service	Who Is Eligible	How Frequently	Beneficiary's Costs
Medical Nutrition Therapy (MNT)	Certain Part B enrollees diagnosed with diabetes, renal disease, or who have had a kidney transplant within the last three years	First year: three hours of one-on-one counseling Subsequent years: two hours	Prior to 01/01/2011—Both deductible and copayment/coinsurance As of 01/01/2011—None
Screening Pap Test	Female Part B enrollees	Annually if at high risk for developing cervical or vaginal cancer, or childbearing age with abnormal Pap test within past three years Every 24 months for all other women	Prior to 01/01/2011—None for tests not requiring physician interpretation; for tests requiring physician interpretation, no deductible but copayment/coinsurance apply As of 01/01/2011—None
Screening Pelvic Exam	Female Part B enrollees	Annually if at high risk for developing cervical or vaginal cancer, or childbearing age with abnormal Pap test within past three years Every 24 months for all other women	Prior to 01/01/2011—No deductible; but copayment/coinsurance apply As of 01/01/2011—None
Screening Mammography	Female Part B enrollees aged 35 and older	Aged 35 through 39: one baseline Aged 40 and older: annually	Prior to 01/01/2011—No deductible; but copayment/coinsurance apply As of 01/01/2011—None
Bone Mass Measurements	Female Part B enrollees who are estrogen deficient and at clinical risk for osteoporosis All Part B enrollees: with vertebral abnormalities receiving (or expecting to receive) glucocorticoid therapy for more than three months with primary hyperparathyroidism; or being monitored to assess response to osteoporosis drug therapy	Every 24 months More frequently if medically necessary	Prior to 01/01/2011—Deductible and coinsurance copayment As of 01/01/2011—None
Colorectal Cancer Screening	Part B enrollees age 50 and older	**Normal risk:** Fecal Occult Blood Test (FOBT) every year, Flexible Sigmoidoscopy every four	Prior to 01/01/2011—FOBT, none; all others, no deductible but copayment/coinsurance apply

Service	Who Is Eligible	How Frequently	Beneficiary's Costs
		years (or at least 119 months after a screening colonoscopy); Screening Colonoscopy every 10 years (or at least 47 months after a screening flexible sigmoidoscopy); Barium Enema **High risk:** FOBT every year, Flexible Sigmoidoscopy once every four years; Screening Colonoscopy every two years (or at least 47 months after a screening flexible sigmoidoscopy); Barium Enema	As of 01/01/2011—None except deductible and copayment/coinsurance apply to Barium Enema, and co-payment/coinsurance apply to screening colonoscopy where polyps or other abnormalities are found and treated
Prostate Cancer Screening	Male Part B enrollees aged 50 and older	Annually	Digital rectal examination—Deductible and copayment/coinsurance Prostate-specific antigen (PSA) test—None
Glaucoma Screening	Part B enrollees: with diabetes mellitus, family history of glaucoma, African Americans aged 50 and older, or Hispanic Americans aged 65 and older	Annually	Deductible and copayment/coinsurance
Seasonal Influenza Virus Vaccine	Part B enrollees	Once per influenza season in the fall or winter; but Medicare may provide additional flu shots if medically necessary	None
Pneumococcal Vaccine	Part B enrollees	Once in a lifetime; but Medicare may provide additional vaccinations based on risk if at least 5 years have passed since receipt of a previous dose	None
Hepatitis B (HBV) Vaccine	Certain Part B enrollees at intermediate or high risk who are not at the time of the vaccine positive for antibodies for hepatitis B	Scheduled dosages required	Prior to 01/01/2011—Both deductible and copayment/coinsurance apply As of 01/01/2011—None

(Continued)

Exhibit 11.10 (Continued)

Service	Who Is Eligible	How Frequently	Beneficiary's Costs
Tobacco Cessation Counseling	All Part B enrollees who use tobacco when counseled by a Medicare-recognized counselor	Two cessation attempts of up to four intermediate or intensive sessions per year	Prior to 01/01/2011—Both deductible and copayment/coinsurance apply As of 01/01/2011—None
Human Immunodeficiency Virus (HIV) Screening	Beneficiaries who are at increased risk for HIV infection or pregnant	Annually for beneficiaries at increased risk Three times per pregnancy for beneficiaries who are pregnant	None

Source: CMS (n.d-a).

of stay on which the payment is based. Under the DRG system, payments to the hospital for a given Medicare patient may be more or less than the hospital's cost—thus, the hospital either absorbs the loss or enjoys a profit. Payments for other services under Part A (home health, skilled nursing facility, and hospice) are paid on a "reasonable cost" billed by the provider. Under Part B, Medicare pays physicians on the basis of a "reasonable charge," which is the lowest of either the submitted charges or a fee schedule based on a relative value scale (HCFA, 2001c). If a provider agrees to accept the approved rate as full payment for services, the provider "accepts assignment." If the provider does not accept assignment for the services provided, the beneficiary is responsible for the remaining balance of the cost of the service and what Medicare will pay. Other services covered under Part B, such as durable medical equipment and clinical laboratory services, are also paid on a fee schedule. Outpatient and home health coverage under Part B is paid on a reasonable cost basis.

According to Klees et al. (2011), in 2010, Part A provided benefits of $244.5 billion to 39 million aged adults and 8 million disabled enrollees. Part B provided coverage to approximately 37 million elderly enrollees and 7 million disabled enrollees totaling $209.7 billion.

Medicare beneficiaries can select to receive benefits under the Part C or Medicare Advantage program. This program offers beneficiaries the option to enroll in plans offered by health maintenance organizations (HMOs), preferred provider organizations (PPOs), and private fee-for-service plans (PFFS). To enroll, beneficiaries must live in a locale in which these private sector plans are available. Under Medicare-managed care plans, Medicare pays a set amount of money every month to a private insurance company participating in the Medicare Advantage (Part C) program, and beneficiaries must use doctors and hospitals that are members of the plan and must obtain a referral from their primary care provider to see a specialist. Private fee-for-service plans are offered by private insurance companies, and, as with the managed care plans, Medicare pays a set amount of money every month to the private insurance company. Beneficiaries must go to selected health care providers and hospitals, receive prior authorization for certain medical treatments, and pay Medicare's Part B premium and possibly an additional monthly premium. The insurance company decides how much it will pay and how much the beneficiaries pay for the health services provided.

Under the ACA, the Medicare program will gradually phase down payments to the providers of these plans (which is currently 9% to 13% higher on average than local fee-for-service costs) to be more closely aligned to the average cost of the traditional Medicare program (KFF, 2010a). In turn, providers will receive monetary incentives for offering high quality plans and for increased cost effectiveness. In addition cost-sharing requirements must not be higher than traditional Medicare for chemotherapy, renal dialysis, and skilled nursing care and enrollees will be able to improve prescription drug coverage (KKF, 2010a). Beneficiaries pay the monthly Part B premium, and most plans require a co-payment ($5 to $10) for each doctor visit and possibly an additional monthly premium. Some plans offer additional benefits such as prescription drug coverage.

In 2011, 12 million Medicare beneficiaries chose to be in the Medicare Advantage (Part C): 65% were in HMOs, 18% in local PPOs, 9% in regional PPOs, and 8% in in private fee-for-service or other plans (Gold, Jacobson, Damico, & Neuman, 2011; Klees et al., 2011). Since the creation of Part C, the number of organizations providing plans under Medicare Advantage contracts has fluctuated. In the early years of the program, the number of available plans declined from 346 in 1998 to 212 in 2005 (Gold, Hudson, & Davis, 2006; HCFA, 2001b). The decline in the number of private companies offering Medicare Advantage plans to beneficiaries forced over 1.7 million enrollees back to the original Medicare program or another Medicare Advantage provider. Since 2005, the number of Medicare Advantage plans has increased markedly, but continues to fluctuate. There were 2,098 plans in 2007, 2,623 in 2008, 2,830 in 2009, 2,314 in 2010, and 2,011 in 2011 (Gold, Jacobson, Damico, & Neuman, 2010). In addition, benefits under many of the Medicare Advantage plans have become less generous in some aspects and more generous in others. In 1998, 78% of enrollees were in Medicare Advantage plans that had no additional premium cost and that included coverage of outpatient prescription drug coverage. By 2011, the percentage of enrollees in plans that did not have additional premiums dropped to 52%; however, the average enrollee's monthly premium dropped from $44 in 2010 to $39 in 2011 (Gold et al., 2011; HCFA, 2001b).

Cain (1996) has identified a number of advantages that Medicare beneficiaries enjoy when they join HMOs. They usually do not have to pay deductibles or co-insurance payments required under Part A or Part B, and HMOs agree not to charge more than Medicare's approved amount. Therefore, for many older adults, HMOs are an alternative to buying supplemental Medigap policies. In addition, HMOs often provide a wider range of services, including preventive health care, outpatient mental health services, prescription drugs, and eyeglasses. Disadvantages include restrictions on choice of doctor and hospitals not associated with the HMO; there is also a fear that older adults will not get the health services they need (R. L. Kane et al., 1996). Other problems include misunderstandings among enrollees about the terms associated with HMO enrollment, restrictions, and denial of services, and simply a lack of awareness of the availability of plans (Wilson, cited in National Association of Area Agencies on Aging, 1996; Mittler, Landon, Zaslavsky, & Cleary, 2011). Gold et al. (2006) examined the characteristics of benefits and premiums offered by Medicare Advantage plans in 2006 and found that the structure of the benefits and premiums was complex, "presenting beneficiaries with even more Medicare Advantage plan types that vary in how they function and in how benefits and cost sharing are structured" (p. 17). They concluded that, because of the complexities of plans, beneficiaries will need a great deal of support and assistance as they try to choose between the original Medicare Part A and B, and Medicare Advantage.

As mentioned earlier, Medicare now provides prescription drug coverage. Drug coverage can be obtained either under Part D through the additional purchase of a private plan authorized under the Medicare program or as a part of a Medicare Advantage plan. Medicare beneficiaries enrolling under Part D are encouraged to join when they are first eligible to do so, or they pay a penalty as long as they have Medicare. Individuals who have drug coverage from another source, such as a previous employer, can choose not to enroll in Part D. Beneficiaries may switch prescription drug plans during the enrollment period each year (November 15–December 31) and under other situations as approved by Medicare (e.g., moving out of the service area of the plan). As of 2011, 29.5 million older adults received prescription coverage under Part D, and of this total, 10.7 million were enrolled in Medicare Advantage drug plans (KFF, 2011a).

Each calendar year, those enrolled in Part D pay a base monthly premium (the average is expected to be $39 but varies by plan) and a yearly deductible (not greater than $320 in 2012; KFF, 2011a). Starting in 2012, enrollees will pay an additional premium surcharge above the plan's base amount based on their Modified Adjusted Gross Income. The additional surcharge ranges on a sliding scale from $11.60 for beneficiaries with incomes greater than $85,000, to $66.40 for those with incomes greater than $214,000 (Klees et al., 2011). No plan may have a deductible higher than the amount set each year. After the deductible has been reached, the plan covers 75% of the next $2,930 of the prescription drug costs, and the beneficiaries pay the remaining 25%. After this initial coverage amount has been met, a coverage gap—often referred to as the *donut hole*—is in effect. The donut hole is the gap in coverage after the plan and the beneficiary reach a predetermined amount that has been spent on coverage ($2,930 in 2012). Once this amount has been spent, the beneficiary gets a 50% discount on the cost of brand-name drugs and therefore pays 50% of brand-name drugs and 86% of generic drugs until they reach an out-of-pocket amount ($4,700 in 2012), and then catastrophic coverage begins. During the catastrophic coverage, the plan covers up to 95% of prescription costs or $2.60/$6.50 for each drug until the end of the calendar year (CMS, 2011; Klees et al., 2011; see Exhibit 11.11). Under the ACA, changes designed to address the donut hole problem include providing a $250 rebate to beneficiaries, introducing the discounted payment rates of 50% and 86% on brand-name and generic drugs mentioned above (both now in effect), and the gradual phased out of the donut hole in 2020 (Klees et al., 2011).

For older adults to benefit from Part D, they must be able to sort through a myriad of plans available in their area and identify which plan has better coverage for the prescription drugs they use. The Medicare website has an interactive Medicare Plan Finder (www.medicare.gov/find-a-plan) to help consumers sort through their options. Prescription drug coverage in a select plan can also change, thus enrollees may have to reevaluate their plans on a regular basis. Enrollment patterns and benefits will need to be studied in the future. One early study found that over half of respondents reported being confused about the changes and viewed the task of choosing a plan as stressful (Hibbard, Greene, & Tusler, 2006).

Exhibit 11.11   Medicare Prescription Drug Coverage, Part D

Medicare Part D Coverage—2012		
Prescription Drug Spending	**Medicare-Approved Plan Pays**	**Beneficiary Pays**
Up to $320	Nothing	Up to $320 deductible amount
$320 to $2,930	75% of drug costs	Co-pay of 25% of drug costs
$2,931 to $4,700 (donut hole)	Generic drugs—14% of drug costs	86% of generic drug costs or 50% of brand-name drug costs up to out of pocket costs totaling $4,700
Over $4,700	95%	5% or between $2.60 (generic) and $6.50 (brand-name)

Source: CMS (2011) and KFF (2011a).

Medigap Policies

Many older adults purchase Medicare supplemental insurance policies, commonly referred to as *Medigap policies*. Medigap policies are designed to assist with the costs of health care services not covered by Medicare. Medigap policies usually pay deductibles, co-payments, and the remaining 20% of the approved charges for physician and hospital services. Limited coverage is sometimes provided for prescription drugs, home care, and preventive care.

Medicaid

In the same year in which Congress enacted Medicare (1965), Medicaid became law as Title XIX of the Social Security Act. Medicaid provides three types of medical assistance for some categories of low-income adults, children, and elderly individuals: (a) health insurance for acute care, (b) long-term care and home care, and (c) supplemental coverage for low-income Medicare beneficiaries (called *dual-eligibles*) for services not covered by Medicare and Medicare premiums, deductibles, and cost sharing. Unlike Medicare, Medicaid is funded through the joint effort of federal and state governments to help states pay for the health care of those who are needy. The federal government provides broad national Medicaid program guidelines and funding to the states. Until 2014, when the ACA expands Medicaid coverage, every state that participates develops its own eligibility standards; determines the type, amount, and scope of benefits and the rate of payment for services; and administers its own program (Klees et al., 2011). In addition, states can apply to the federal government for a Medicaid waiver that allows states to test new benefits or financing or to implement a major restructuring of the Medicaid program. As a result of these variations, Medicaid programs vary by state, and not all low-income individuals are eligible for Medicaid, and a person deemed eligible for Medicaid in one state may not qualify for Medicaid in a different state.

The passage of the ACA will significantly expand the Medicaid program by making changes to eligibility criteria and coverage. The elements of the ACA that effect older adults are described in more detail below.

Who Is Eligible for Medicaid?

As mentioned above, states have some flexibility in setting Medicaid eligibility guidelines. They determine who will be covered and the income guidelines necessary to be eligible. Eligibility falls into two categories: the categorically eligible and the medically needy. Those who are *categorically eligible* (e.g., limited income families with children, children, pregnant women, people with severe disabilities, elderly adults) must meet certain income and asset guidelines established by the state. Some groups of categorically needy persons, however, are required by federal law to receive Medicaid coverage. For example, persons who receive federal income maintenance assistance, such as current and some former Supplemental Security Income (SSI) recipients, low-income Medicare beneficiaries, and individuals who were eligible for Aid to Families With Dependent Children (AFDC)[3] as of July 16, 1996, must receive benefits (HCFA, 2001a). States also have the option of covering other categories of individuals. These groups include (a) certain aged, blind, or disabled adults who have income above those requiring mandatory coverage but below the federal

---

[3]Under the Welfare Reform Act called the Personal Responsibility and Work Opportunity Reconciliation Act of 1996, AFDC is replaced by Temporary Assistance to Needy Families (TANF). Under this legislation, states have been given more leeway to determine Medicaid eligibility for families with children.

poverty level; (b) institutionalized individuals with income and resources below specified limits; (c) persons who would be eligible if institutionalized but who are receiving care through home and community-based services; and (d) recipients of state supplementary payments, such as old age pensions (Klees et al., 2011).

Some states opt to include individuals who are considered *medically needy* but who have too much income to qualify as categorically needy. Under this option, states allow members of selected groups (e.g., aged, blind, or disabled persons) to spend down to Medicaid income eligibility guidelines by using their medical expenses to offset their excess income, thus reducing their income level to meet the Medicaid guidelines. Two groups recently added to the list of medically needy individuals that states may cover are women who have breast or cervical cancer and persons with tuberculosis (TB) who are uninsured (Klees et al., 2011).

Coverage

States participating in Medicaid must provide basic medical services to Medicaid beneficiaries. The following medical services are provided to those who qualify:

- Inpatient hospital services,
- Outpatient hospital services,
- Physician services and medical and surgical services of a dentist,
- Nursing facility services,
- Rural health clinic services,
- Home health care for persons eligible for skilled nursing services,
- Laboratory and x-ray services,
- Nurse practitioner services, and
- Services from a federally qualified health center.

States also may receive federal assistance if they choose to provide other optional approved medical services. Some optional medical services covered by Medicaid include the following:

- Clinic services,
- Intermediate care facility services,
- Optometrist services and eyeglasses,
- Prescribed drugs,
- Prosthetic devices,
- Transportation services,
- Rehabilitation and physical therapy services,
- Dental services,
- Hospice,
- Home and community-based care,
- Case management services,
- Psychologists, and
- Diagnostic, screening, preventive, and rehabilitation services.

States may also limit the amount and duration of these services. Payment for services may be made directly to the provider on a fee-for-service basis or be paid to providers such as HMOs through prepayment agreements. The provider must accept the Medicaid payment as payment in full, and the amount must be enough to enlist providers so that the covered services are available. States may also require beneficiaries to pay nominal co-payments or a deductible for certain services; persons in long-term care facilities must contribute most of their income as a copayment for long-term care coverage (Klees et al., 2011).

After obtaining permission from CMS, states can require beneficiaries to enroll in managed care plans and can offer home and community-based services to those individuals with chronic impairments who are eligible for Medicaid. In 2010, 71.5% of the Medicaid population was enrolled in a managed care plan, compared to 63% in 2000 (CMS, 2010c). Currently, all states but New Hampshire, Alaska, and Wyoming have enrolled some percentage of Medicaid beneficiaries in a managed health care plan. Twenty-eight states—Arizona, Arkansas, Colorado, Connecticut, Delaware, Georgia, Hawaii, Idaho, Illinois, Iowa, Kansas, Kentucky, Louisiana, Maryland, Michigan, Mississippi, Nebraska, Nevada, New Jersey, North Carolina, Oklahoma, Oregon, Pennsylvania, South Carolina, South Dakota, Tennessee, Utah, and Washington—have over 75% of their Medicaid recipients enrolled in Medicaid managed care plans (CMS, 2010d). States also can request a waiver called a Program of All-Inclusive Care for the Elderly (PACE) that allows them to offer a package of services to persons who, without community support services, might otherwise be institutionalized. Such services include case management, adult day program services, respite care, and homemaker/home health care.

As mentioned above, Medicaid also provides benefits to persons who qualify for Medicare. For persons who are eligible for both Medicare and Medicaid (i.e., dual-eligibles), Medicaid pays all the premiums, deductibles, and co-insurance costs associated with Part A and Part B. Medicaid may also pay for services beyond what is covered under Medicare (e.g., hearing aids, skilled nursing after 100 days). The Medicare program must pay for services before any payments are made by Medicaid.

Other Medicare beneficiaries who can receive assistance from Medicaid are those who have incomes at or below 100% of the federal poverty line (FPL) and whose resources are at or below 200% of the SSI guidelines (HCFA, 2001a). There are three categories of these beneficiaries, and all receive some assistance in paying the cost-sharing provisions in Medicare. *Qualified Medicare beneficiaries* (QMBs) whose income is at or below 100% of the FPL receive some assistance from Medicaid for payment of the cost sharing provisions in Medicare in Parts A and B. *Specified low-income Medicare beneficiaries* (SLMBs) who have incomes above 100% of the PL but below 120% of the PL and *Qualified individuals* (QIs) whose incomes are above 120% but below 135% of the FPL also receive assistance from Medicaid in paying Part B premiums. Finally, dual-eligible persons receive assistance with the cost of copayments and premiums required under Part D prescription drug coverage. In 2010, Medicaid provided some level of assistance to 9.1 million dual-eligible persons (Klees et al., 2011).

Persons who are over the age of 65 represent 10% of persons enrolled in Medicaid (4.6 million) and account for 23% of Medicaid spending (Klees et al., 2011). Data indicate that much of the Medicaid spending for this group is for long-term care—an amount totaling almost $48 billion, or 25% of total Medicaid spending, and paying an average of $29,533 per nursing home beneficiary (Klees et al., 2011; KFF, 2012a). In an attempt to moderate the growth in health care costs for low-income and dual-eligible persons (which represents 38% of Medicaid costs; KFF, 2012a), managed care has emerged as a way to control health care costs. Another way legislators have acted to control Medicaid spending on long-term care costs has been the recent enactment of legislation allowing all states to enact legislation that links the purchase of long-term care insurance with Medicaid. In

February 2006, Congress passed legislation that permits Medicaid to cover long-term care needs beyond the terms of the policy, with policy holders not required to "spend down" their assets to meet the Medicaid eligibility guidelines (Capretta, 2007).

The passage of the ACA will significantly expand Medicaid's eligibility criteria described above. Currently, the majority of states do not include low-income nondisabled, nonpregnant adults without dependent children or others who are not currently eligible in one of the categories listed above—a nationwide total of about 15 to 27 million uninsured people between the ages of 19 and 64 (Kenney et al., 2012; Urban Institute, 2012). Beginning in 2014, the categorically eligible criteria for nonelderly will be eliminated, and the program will determine eligibility based on a person's Modified Adjusted Gross Income. Thus, all non-Medicare-eligible adults, children, parents, and pregnant women with incomes below 138% of poverty ($\sim$ $15,000 for an individual or about $30,656 for a family of four in 2012, with no asset test) will be eligible for Medicaid (CMS, 2012a; Kenney et al., 2012; KFF, 2010b). In addition, all newly eligible beneficiaries will be guaranteed a benchmark of health care benefits. Those who receive SSI or qualify as "medically needy" will remain Medicaid eligible as well.

New to Medicaid will include an option to provide Health Homes for beneficiaries with at least two chronic conditions (or one chronic condition and are at risk for another), which will offer a more holistic approach designed to reduce fragmentation of care. The Health Home program will offer integrated care management and coordination, health promotion, transition care from inpatient to other settings, and referrals to social services (KFF, 2012c). Other long-term care services under the ACA include the following:

- Expands the scope of services and increases eligibility to individuals with incomes up to 150% of the FPL, covered under the Home and Community Based Services (HCBS) program;

- Extends the Money Follows the Person (MFP) demonstration program until 2016 that supports options for individuals with disabilities and older adults who live in an institution to transition back to the community; and

- Establishes the Community First Choice Option that allows states to provide support to qualified individuals who need institutional care but wish to live in non-institutional settings to receive support that covers the cost of attendants and other services. (KFF, 2010b)

In 2012, the Supreme Court deliberated over the legality of the ACA and the federal government's (a) requirement that U.S. citizens have health insurance (called the *individual mandate*), (b) expansion of Medicaid, and (c) withholding of all existing Medicaid funds from states that were not in compliance in the new Medicaid program. The Court found that the individual mandate is constitutionally permissible, and the Medicaid expansion described above was allowed along with the other provision of the ACA, but it restricted the federal government's enforcement authority of withholding all Medicaid funding as a penalty only the ACA Medicaid funding. Thus states can choose not to participate in the revised Medicaid program; however, there are strong incentives for states to participate. The federal government will pay 100% of those newly eligible individuals from 2014 to 2016 and 90% after 2016 (KFF, 2011b). Keep up with the most recent implementation of the ACA by visiting http://healthreform.kff.org.

Medical Benefits for Retired Veterans

The federal government provides health care coverage for retired members of the uniformed services, as well as their spouses and children, through the TRICARE program. TRICARE provides coverage for civilian hospital services, doctors, and other health care services and supplies. With a few exceptions, retirees who become eligible for Medicare lose their previous TRICARE coverage, and they become dual enrolled in Medicare and the TRICARE for Life program. Under this program, beneficiaries are required to enroll and pay for Medicare Part B premiums, and Medicare becomes their primary payer. TRICARE for Life is similar to other Medigap policies that act as a second payer to Medicare, paying for out-of-pocket costs for services provided under Medicare. In addition, TRICARE for Life will pay for some health care services not covered by Medicare, including pharmacy benefits, extended hospital and skilled nursing home care, and mental health counselors (U.S. Department of Defense, 2001).

HEALTH PROMOTION AND WELLNESS

The focus on health promotion and wellness has been driven, in part, by the desire to enjoy a high level of functioning in later life. Growing evidence shows that individuals who engage in healthy lifestyle behaviors have positive health outcomes. For example, 7 of the 10 leading causes of death (e.g., heart disease, stroke) can be reduced by changes in lifestyle, including proper nutrition, exercise, reduced alcohol consumption, and not smoking (Belloc & Breslow, 1972; Saxon et al., 2010). For older adults in particular, health promotion activities can prevent illness in those who are healthy, prevent those who are ill from becoming disabled, and help older adults who are disabled to preserve function and prevent further disability (Institute of Medicine, 1991). Therefore, numerous health promotion programs targeting older adults have emerged. The Older Americans Act (OAA) has supported the funding of evidence-based health promotion programs, and the Administration on Aging (AoA) has been instrumental in supporting initiatives designed to enhance the well-being of older adults. These efforts will be discussed below.

Policy Background

The 1992 amendment to the OAA authorized the creation of *Part F, Disease Prevention and Health Promotion Services*, under Title III. Under the 2000 amendments, the health promotion programs under Part F were moved to Part D and included funding of the following health promotion programs:

- Health risk assessments;
- Routine health screenings;
- Nutrition counseling and education;
- Health promotion programs relating to chronic conditions;
- Alcohol and substance abuse, smoking cessation, weight loss, and stress management;
- Physical fitness programs, group exercise, music therapy, art therapy, and dance movement;
- Home injury control services;

- Mental health;

- Education about the availability of preventive services covered under Medicare;

- Medication management;

- Information about age-related diseases;

- Gerontological counseling; and

- Counseling regarding social services and follow-up health services.

Funding for preventive health services under Part F for fiscal years 2010 through 2012 was $21.0 million, $20.9 million, and $20.9 million, respectively (USDHHS, 2010b, 2012c).

Health Promotion Programs Funded Under the OAA

During the past three decades, the AoA has been instrumental in sponsoring a number of nationwide initiatives designed to promote health and wellness of older adults. The National Health Promotion Initiative sponsored by the AoA and the U.S. Public Health Service in 1986 was designed to facilitate collaboration between state and local health departments, state and local Area Agencies on Aging (AAAs), and volunteer organizations in developing and implementing health promotion programs (FallCreek, Allen, & Halls, 1986). The initiative targeted four areas of health promotion—injury control, proper drug use, better nutrition, and improved physical fitness. The initiative was responsible for the development of resource materials, including *Health Promotion and Aging: A National Directory of Selected Programs* (FallCreek et al., 1986), *A Healthy Old Age: A Sourcebook for Health Promotion With Older Adults* (FallCreek & Mettler, 1982), and *Health Promotion and Aging: Strategies for Action* (FallCreek & Franks, 1984).

In 1989, the AoA launched the Historically Black Colleges and Universities Initiatives to address the health promotion needs of older adults of color. Ten schools were awarded grants under this initiative to develop strategies and demonstration projects to promote better self-care habits among minority older persons. Health promotion strategies included church-based health promotion programs, programs for low-income older Blacks living in inner cities and rural areas in Georgia using peer counselors, and the creation of videotapes and instructional guides targeted to older African American audiences through public access television (USDHHS, 1993).

In the 1990s, a major initiative sponsored by the AoA was the Action for Health: Older Women's Project. The goal of the Action for Health: Older Women's Project was to demonstrate the feasibility of developing and implementing an innovative community-based, peer educator–facilitated health and wellness promotion program for older minority and low-income women (Herman & Wadsworth, 1992). In 1994, the AoA became a participant in the National Coalition on Disability and Aging to focus attention on the common concerns of aged persons and persons with disabilities. The delivery of care under managed care was just one of the topics coalition members examined.

In the 2000s, the AoA collaborated with the Centers for Disease Control and Prevention's Healthy People 2010 initiative to focus on diabetes, cardiovascular disease, and rates of immunization in older ethnic minority groups. The AoA earmarked $1 million to support the initiative called Racial and Ethnic Approaches to Community Health 2010 (REACH 2010) (AoA, 2000). Agencies in four communities were awarded demonstration grants designed to educate older ethnic minorities about diabetes, cardiovascular disease, and immunizations. The four agencies were (a) the Boston Public Health Commission, which targeted its efforts to older African Americans; (b) the Latino Education Project of Corpus Christi, Texas, which targeted older Latinos; (c) the National Indian Council on Aging, which targeted Indian and Alaskan Native populations; and (d) Special Services for Groups of Los Angeles, California, which targeted individuals of Southeast Asian descent.

A new effort to direct funding toward "evidence-based" health promotion and prevention programs began in 2003. Evidence-based prevention programs use interventions based on results from scientific studies published in peer-reviewed journals. During 2003, the AoA funded 12 grants totaling over $2 million per year for three years to implement evidence-based prevention programs in the community. The areas of focus were

- falls prevention,
- physical activity,
- sound nutrition,
- medication management,
- disease self-management, and
- depression. (AoA, 2003)

Examples of programs funded in 2003 included the Chronic Disease Self-Management for African-American Urban Elders program in Philadelphia, Pennsylvania; the Neighborhood Centers, Inc., Activity Centers for Seniors, in Houston, Texas; and the A Matter of Balance fall-prevention program in Portland, Maine. In 2004, the AoA partnered with the President's Council on Physical Fitness and Sports, the National Institute on Aging, the Centers for Disease Control, and other federal agencies to launch the *You Can! Steps to Healthier Aging* campaign, a social marketing campaign designed to increase the number of older adults who are active and healthy by using a partnership approach to mobilize communities. More than 2,700 community organizations joined the campaign (AoA, n.d.-d). In 2006, the AoA continued to support health promotion and prevention activities in the five areas mentioned above, and awarded $13 million to 16 states to implement evidence-based programs in senior centers, nutrition programs, senior housing, and faith-based organizations (AoA, 2006b).

In the current decade, the focus on health and wellness continues to be on providing programs to elders living in medically underserved geographical areas that have the greatest economic need and that are evidence-based (Klees et al., 2011). Funding under OAA Preventive Health Services in 2012 include (a) health promotion information and outreach through a variety of entities including the Aging and Disability Resources Centers, AAAs, parks and recreation centers, faith-based organizations, and congregate meal sites; (b) health screenings and risk assessments for a variety of conditions, including diabetes, hypertension, high cholesterol, and hearing and vision loss; and (c) health promotion intervention programs that are evidence based.

In 2012, the AoA expanded the 2003 definition and criteria of *evidence-based programs* (EBPs) under Title III-D. The new definition states that EBPs are those that have been empirically demonstrated to be effective in helping to promote the adoption of healthy behaviors, improve health status, or reduce the use of medical services, and created three new tiers or levels of EBP. The three new criteria are (a) minimum criteria—demonstrated through evaluation and ready for implementation; (b) intermediate criteria—outcomes published in a peer-review journal or effective with an older adult population, and evidence that the outcomes are ready to be implemented; and (c) highest level criteria—outcomes based on an experimental or quasi-experimental research design, full translation of findings in the community, and dissemination of products to the public (AoA, 2012c). Exhibit 11.12 provides a partial listing of health, prevention, and wellness programs currently supported by the AoA.

Area of Focus	Program Description	Current Projects—Examples
Alzheimer's Disease Supportive Services Program (ADSSP) Funded under Public Health Services Act and administered by the AoA http://www.aoa.gov/AoARoot/AoA_Programs/HPW/Alz_Grants/index.aspx	ADSSP supports state efforts to expand the availability of community-level supportive services for persons with Alzheimer's Disease and Related Disorders (ADRD) and their caregivers.	*COMPASS II: Early Stage Directions Program—Oklahoma Department of Human Services* The purpose of this collaborative partnership is to reach persons with dementia (PWD) in the early stages (ES) of ADRD, and their families, to equip and support them, mitigating later crises. *Managing Difficult Behaviors: A Standardized Intervention to Help Family Caregivers (STAR-C)* This is a standardized intervention to help family caregivers identify, reduce, and manage difficult behavioral symptoms of their relative with Alzheimer's disease. The STAR-C manual provides detailed instructions for the consultants, family caregiver assignments, and handouts.
Behavioral Health Behavioral health is a state of mental and emotional well-being and/or choices and actions that affect wellness http://www.aoa.gov/AoARoot/AoA_Programs/HPW/Behavioral/index.aspx	States are enhancing the ability of their systems to educate, identify, refer, and provide appropriate services/interventions for older adults, persons with disabilities, and caregivers with or at risk for behavioral health disorders.	ElderVention This program provides prevention education for older adults who are at risk for depression and suicide. Region I AAA, Phoenix, AZ *The Older Americans Behavioral Health Technical Assistance Center* This is a partnership between the Substance Abuse and Mental Health Services Administration and the AoA to provide states and communities with learning opportunities and support for behavioral health services for older adults. Webinars and issue briefs are available.
Chronic Disease Self-Management Program (CDSMP) Funded by the American Recovery and Reinvestment Act of 2009 http://www.aoa.gov/AoARoot/AoA_Programs/HPW/ARRA/Index.aspx	The CDSMP enables older Americans with chronic diseases to learn how to manage their conditions and take control of their health. In 2010, AoA awarded grants to 45 states, Puerto Rico, and the District of Columbia to deliver evidence-based self-management programs to older adults with chronic diseases.	*The Stanford Chronic Disease Self-Management Program* The Chronic Disease Self-Management Program is a workshop given for two and a half hours, once a week, for six weeks, in community settings such as senior centers, churches, libraries, and hospitals.

Area of Focus	Program Description	Current Projects—Examples
Disease Prevention and Health Promotion Services (DPHPS) OAA Title IIID http://www.aoa.gov/AoARoot/AoA_Programs/HPW/Title_IIID/index.aspx	Programs under the DPHPS and EBDDP provide education and implementation activities that support healthy lifestyles and promote healthy behaviors.	*Tai Chi for Arthritis Program (Tier 1 program)* Medical studies have shown that practicing this program reduces pain significantly, prevents falls for the elderly, and improves many aspects of health.
Evidence-Based Disease and Disability Prevention Program (EBDDP) http://www.aoa.gov/AoARoot/AoA_Programs/HPW/Evidence_Based/index.aspx		*Steps to Healthy Aging: Eat Better & Move More (Tier 2 program)* A community-based nutrition and physical activity program for older adults that delivers a 12-week program consisting of mini-talks on nutrition and walking. *A Matter of Balance (Tier 3 program)* This program emphasizes practical strategies to reduce fear of falling and increase activity levels. Elders learn to view falls and fear of falling as controllable, set realistic goals to increase activity, change their environment to reduce fall risk factors, and exercise to increase strength and balance.
Older Adults and HIV/AIDS http://www.aoa.gov/AoARoot/AoA_Programs/HPW/HIV_AIDS/index.aspx	The Older Adults and HIV/AIDS website provides resources for aging professionals and others interested in designing programs for older adults about the prevention and treatment of HIV/AIDS.	*The Graying of HIV/AIDS: Community Resources for the Aging Services Network Webinar* *National Resource Center on LGBT Aging HIV and Aging Resources*
Older Adults and Oral Health http://www.aoa.gov/AoARoot/AoA_Programs/HPW/Oral_Health/index.aspx	Supports programs to help address the oral health needs of older adults.	*Area Agency on Aging (AAA) District 7, Inc.'s Ohio State University Geriatric Dentistry Program Appalachian Outreach Project* The program provides mobile dental services to older adults in Pike County, Ohio.

Source: AoA (2012f).

Health Promotion Programs and Users

For many years, older adults were not targets of health promotion programs (McGinnis, 1988). As S. N. Walker (1989) pointed out, health promotion programs excluded older adults because it was thought that they could not benefit from activities in which the benefits would emerge in the future. In addition, many believed that health promotion programs would not be successful in changing the lifelong behaviors of older adults. Fortunately, both of these notions have been proven to be incorrect and health promotion programs that target older adults have become more frequent in recent years.

Health promotion programs for older adults have shifted from focusing on the management of specific disease conditions to including prevention of illness and injury and the enhancement of health (S. N. Walker, 1989). Thus health promotion programs can address a multitude of concerns and be defined in a variety of ways. For example, Teague (1987) defines *health promotion* as any combination of health education and related organizational, political, and economic interventions designed to facilitate behavioral and environmental changes that prevent, delay the occurrence of, or minimize the impact of disease or disability while promoting the independence and wellbeing of older adults (p. 23).

Health promotion programs can be illness specific, such as programs designed to reduce high blood pressure, or can be broad based and include physical fitness, stress management, nutrition, and environmental awareness. In addition, there are different levels of health program intervention strategies (O'Donnell & Ainsworth, cited in Teague, 1987). *Educational health promotion* programs provide participants with information designed to increase awareness, education, and behavior change. Health education can be delivered through lectures, flyers and posters, health fairs, and resource libraries. *Evaluation screening* programs test past, current, and potential health problems. Fitness assessments are perhaps the most popular evaluation screening programs. *Prescription* programs are used in conjunction with evaluation screening and give participants the information they need to correct or prevent a current health problem. Finally, *behavior change support* programs provide participants with evaluation screening, a prescription for change, and the support system needed for participants to be successful in changing health habits.

Across the Globe: Health Promotion Program—Well for Life, State Government of Victoria, Australia

The Well for Life program is designed to improve nutrition and physical activity for older people living at home in the community. The Well for Life Resource Kit is an initiative of the Department of Health, Public Health and Aged Care Branches in Australia. The Resource Kit has been developed for staff of primary health and community service organizations that provide care and services for older people living at home.

According to their website, the Resource Kit addresses nutritional, physical activity, and emotional well-being issues for older people and their care givers, using primary health and community services and includes:

Guide to action: a facilitator's guide that includes case studies, a good practice checklist for physical activity and nutrition, and an action plan template to record agreed actions.

Nineteen help sheets: providing information and tips to increase awareness and knowledge of physical activity and nutritional needs to inform discussion, strategies and action on physical activity, and nutrition.

Education supplements: training modules and case studies on physical activity and nutrition to support quality improvement in organizational practice.

Resources: information on resources and programs that may improve physical activity and nutrition for older people living at home. (paras. 1–4)

For more information go to www.health.vic.gov.au/agedcare/publications/wellforlife_nutrition.htm.

Health promotion programs may be sponsored by hospitals, universities, churches, departments of public health, local AAAs or aging network members, insurance companies, and community organizations such as the Red Cross. Programs may be delivered in a variety of settings, including shopping malls, senior centers, hospitals, senior housing, and local schools.

Although information about health promotion activities is widely available, little empirical published research documents who participates in formal health promotion programs. Admittedly, the generalizability of such research is limited because of the wide variation in program content, format, and participant characteristics. A handful of studies, however, can provide a tentative understanding of participation rates and benefits.

Best Practice: REACH Program, Corpus Christi, Texas

A major effort to help address these health disparities is the Centers for Disease Control and Prevention's Racial and Ethnic Approaches to Community Health (REACH 2010) Program, which supports community-based coalitions in the design, implementation, and evaluation of innovative strategies to reduce or eliminate health disparities among racial and ethnic minorities. One example of a successful REACH 2010 Program is the Latino Education Project (LEP), in the Corpus Christi, Texas, area, which targets midlife and older Latinos—a population that suffers disproportionately from diabetes and its complications. The need for assistance in these small, rural, and isolated communities is great. Approximately 80% to 95% of the residents are Hispanic, and almost 50% are aged 60 or older. This area has been classified as medically underserved for decades, and the high cost of health care, lack of access to health insurance, and limited community resources contribute significantly to health disparities. LEP activities focus on enabling and mobilizing key community institutions and organizations to respond to the diabetes crisis among midlife and older Hispanics. Communitywide health forums bring together health care providers, advocates, elected officials, radio, television and newspaper representatives, and local leaders to identify the best strategies for the prevention, early diagnosis, and management of diabetes. Small study circles allow for personalized attention, focusing on individual behavioral change through the selection of healthier foods, promoting and facilitating physical

(Continued)

(Continued)

activity, and mobilizing informal support networks. Lay health educators (Promotores de Salud) use their leadership skills to assist communities and individual participants to access resources on their own. The educators provide case management that leads to healthier behaviors, better health, and improved management of diabetes. As a result of these activities, LEP participants have increased their levels of physical activity and consumption of water, fruits, and vegetables, as well as improved communication with their health care providers. For more information, go to www.cdc.gov/reach.

Source: Centers for Disease Control and Prevention & Merck Company Foundation (2007, p. 3).

Some evidence suggests that participants in health promotion programs have higher incomes and education, have higher levels of community involvement, and are more often women (Given & Given, 2001; Lefebvre, Harden, Rawkowski, Lasater, & Careton, 1987; Martinson, Crain, et al., 2010; Pirie et al., 1986). For example, Buchner and Pearson (1989) examined the characteristics of participants in an HMO senior health promotion program. Demographic factors associated with participation included being older and female, having higher levels of income and education, and being a nonsmoker. Ratings of general health status were not related to participation, and participants were more likely to have lower mental and social health ratings than nonparticipants. E. H. Wagner, Grothaus, Hecht, and LaCroix (1991) evaluated a senior health program involving a sample of people who were 65 years and older and who were enrolled in an HMO. The health promotion program consisted of a nurse educator visit to assess health risks, follow-up classes, written materials, and a review of prescription medications. Researchers interviewed the enrollees who chose not to participate. Nonparticipants had lower levels of education and family income, were less likely to be members of community organizations, were more likely to smoke, and had more negative self-evaluations of chronic conditions and health status than participants. Other studies comparing participants and nonparticipants in health promotion programs generally conclude that participants are individuals who already have preventive attitudes toward health care and engage in a variety of preventive health behaviors (Carter, Elward, Malmgren, Martin, & Larson, 1991; van Heuvelen et al., 2005).

For Your Files: National Institute on Aging Physical Activity Resources

The National Institute of Aging (NIA) has two health and fitness resources that you might find useful when encouraging older adults to engage in fitness activities. One guide is *Exercise & Physical Activity: Your Everyday Guide.* This illustrated booklet describes ways for older people to exercise safely and stay motivated. Drawings and, in the online version, animations show the correct positions for specific exercises. Also included are worksheets to help older adults track their progress as well as a chapter on healthy eating.

This guide is the centerpiece of *Go4Life*, NIA's national campaign to help older adults fit exercise and physical activity into their daily life. To find out more about how *Go4Life*, visit their website at http://go4life.nia.nih.gov.

NIA also has developed *Go4Life DVD—Everyday Exercises From the National Institute on Aging*. This DVD features strength, balance, and flexibility exercises that can be done at home, at work, at the gym—almost anywhere.

For more information, visit www.nia.nih.gov/health/publication/exercise-physical-activity-your-everyday-guide-national-institute-aging-0.

Finally, there is some concern that health promotion programs do not have lasting results (Hickey & Stilwell, 1991; Warshaw, 1988). Lalonde, Hooyman, and Blumhagen (1988) investigated the long-term effectiveness of the Wallingford Wellness Project. This project was a three-year community-based health promotion demonstration project that offered 21 weeks of education and behavior change training to persons 55 and older in physical fitness, stress management, nutrition, and environmental awareness and action. An experimental group ($n = 90$) was recruited from the community, and a comparison group ($n = 44$) was recruited through social groups. Follow-up studies revealed that the project was most effective in the short term—up to six months following graduation from the program. Participants reported sustaining behavior changes initiated in physical fitness, stress management, and nutrition; these behavioral changes declined, however, when measured six months later. With regard to retaining health information, participants sustained their increase in health information over pretest levels, except for nutrition information. The project was ineffective in reducing health service use among participants. In contrast, Buchner and colleagues (1997) examined the impact of a community-based exercise program where participants engaged in aerobic exercise and strength training. Researchers found that there were positive outcomes in strength, aerobic capacity, and fall reduction at the end of the program. Moreover, 58% of the participants were engaging in unsupervised exercise three or more times per week nine months after they started the program. In a review of 29 physical activity health promotion programs, A. C. King, Rejeski, and Buchner (1998) found that the majority of studies reported that the respondents had physical activity levels or fitness levels that were greater than their baseline levels and better than control groups. More recently, researchers have been examining the factors associated with interest in and adherence to health promotion activities. Effective strategies for promoting participation include the use of behavioral or cognitive-behavioral strategies, such as goal setting, along with health education and instruction (Ettinger et al., 1997), locations that are easily accessible (Grove & Spier, 1999), providing individualized assessments and counseling (Fox, Breuer, & Wright, 1997), using a combination of group and home-based program delivery format (A. C. King, Haskell, Taylor, Kraemer, & DeBusk, 1991; Rejecki & Brawley, 1997), and taking into account cultural differences (Zhan, Cloutterbuck, Keshian, & Lombardi, 1998). Martinson, Sherwood, and colleagues (2010) found that encouraging older adults to maintain their activity levels after they have completed a health promotion program can be successful. They found that telephone and mail-based physical activity maintenance reminders of older adults who completed the Keep Active Minnesota program was effective at helping participants maintain their physical activity levels up to 24 months after the program ended. Clearly, more rigorous studies are needed to evaluate and compare the effectiveness of different types of health promotion and wellness programs offered to older adults.

Best Practice: EnhanceFitness

EnhanceFitness is a health promotion program managed by Senior Services of Seattle/King County in collaboration with Group Health Cooperative and the University of Washington Health Promotion Research Center. The program is a low-cost, evidence-based exercise program that can help active and near-frail older adults become more active, energized, and empowered to sustain independent lives. EnhanceFitness focuses on stretching, flexibility, balance, low-impact aerobics, and strength-training exercises. The EnhanceFitness program does not require expensive equipment or a large space and is led by certified fitness instructors who receive training and a detailed manual, which will give them the expertise they need to lead three one-hour classes each week. Empirical research from over 80 sites around the country showed that the program significantly improved overall fitness and health. Results found that 13% of participants reported improvement in social function, 52% reported improvement in depression, and 35% reported improvement in physical functioning. Another study of participants in ethnic community sites with nutrition programs showed that these participants, although less physically fit to start with when compared to White communities, showed greater improvement than those in White sites. EnhanceFitness has won awards from the National Council on Aging, the AoA, and the HHS. For the results of the research on program effectiveness, see Belza et al. (2006).

For more information about EnhanceFitness, contact Project Enhance, Senior Services of Seattle/King County, 2208 Second Avenue, Suite 100, Seattle, WA 98121; phone: 206-448-5725; http://www.projectenhance.org/EnhanceFitness.aspx.

CHALLENGES FOR HEALTH CARE AND HEALTH PROMOTION PROGRAMS

Serving Diverse Groups of Older Adults

Extending health promotion and prevention programs to all elderly individuals, especially those hard-to-reach populations, will be critical as the aging population increases in number. Outreach efforts and programs must endeavor to serve elders with lower education and incomes, who are ethnically and racially diverse, as well as those who are physically frail and have multiple chronic conditions. Effective health promotion intervention programs must take into consideration the social and environmental barriers to participation that are unique to those with lower socioeconomic characteristics (Prohaska et al., 2006). Health promotion programs must also be sensitive to the cultural characteristics of their participants and be cognizant of differences in language, perceptions, and life experiences (Zhan et al., 1998). For example, Ralston (1993) identified programmatic strategies for health promotion programs targeting older Blacks, including using an educational framework with scheduled classes to deliver information, using Black churches to sponsor programs and using peer leaders to act as liaisons between older adults and the health care delivery system. In addition, health promotion programs must be sensitive to participants' social and environmental context. Something as simple as instructing older inner-city participants to take daily walks may be unsuccessful because they fear walking in their neighborhood or simply lack sidewalks that are safe to walk on (Brawley, Rejeski, & King, 2003; Minkler & Pasick, 1985). Although providing education about preventive health behaviors is an important factor in changing personal behavior, scholars have criticized health promotion programs for focusing too much on individual behaviors while ignoring social factors that negatively impact poor health, including poverty, racism, sexism, ageism, and environmental hazards (Hickey & Stilwell, 1991; Minkler & Pasick, 1985).

Health promotion programs will be meaningless if issues such as access and affordability to health care services continue to be problematic for many low-income older adults. Moreover, older adults should not be overlooked when developing health promotion programs because of an erroneous perception that older adults are unwilling or unable to make healthy lifestyle changes (Chernoff, 2001).

Increasing Research and Program Evaluation

Empirical research must continue to examine the factors associated with participation in and benefits of health promotion programs. Researchers should continue to investigate models that can assist in identifying the motivational forces that are associated with participation in a wide variety of formal health promotion programs (Pascucci, 1992). Professionals designing health promotion programs must also develop evidence-based programs that are based on what research findings show "works," and it is equally important that these programs be evaluated for their effectiveness and sustainability (Bryant, Altpeter, & Whitelaw, 2006). White House Conference on Aging (2006) delegates recommended that state health departments and local aging network agencies promote, implement, and evaluate evidence-based health promotion and disease prevention programs at the local level for all citizens.

Supporting Health Programs and Policies in the Future

Traditional health care, with its focus on acute care, does not adequately address the health care needs of older adults who must live with and manage chronic conditions. Older adults need regular primary care to help them prevent illness and maintain their health. Preventive services for the control of high blood pressure, cancer screenings, immunizations, and therapies to help manage chronic conditions are key to extending a healthy life in later life. The changes made to Medicare, via the ACA, that extend access to preventive and wellness services by eliminating copayments for those service have already seen positive results. Almost 800,000 Medicare beneficiaries received an Annual Wellness Visit, and 5.5 million used preventive benefits including, most prominently, mammograms, bone density screenings, and screenings for prostate cancer over a six-month period when these provisions were enacted via the ACA (CMS, n.d.-a).

Delegates to the White House Conference on Aging (2006) recommended a number of strategies and resolutions designed to enhance the health status of older adults. These included

- expanding Medicare to include oral health services, vision services and eyeglasses, hearing services, and other emerging preventive services; and

- increasing federal funding to the National Institutes of Health, the Centers for Disease Control, and Title III of the OAA to reduce health disparities and promote health promotion programming for all minority populations, including gays, lesbians, bisexuals, transgender, and seniors with disabilities.

Finally, the delegates adopted four resolutions related to health and health promotion:

- Reduce health care disparities among minorities by developing strategies to prevent disease, promote health, and deliver appropriate care and wellness.

- Improve the health and quality of life of older Americans through disease management and chronic care coordination.

- Prevent disease and promote healthier lifestyles through educating providers and consumers on consumer health care.

- Improve health decision making through the promotion of health education, health literacy, and cultural competency.

Indeed, the challenge facing U.S. society in the next century is creating a health care system that provides all its members, of every age, with accessibility to health care, including regular preventive care, primary care, and health promotion programs.

CASE STUDY

Health Concerns After Retirement

David, 65, retired a year ago from a high-level executive position with a major auto company. His retirement meant the end to 25 years of long hours in fast-paced, high-stress management work. It also meant the end to grueling overseas travel and weeks of separation from his family. During this past year, David has been helping his wife, Evelyn, move into a smaller, but new, home. He has had a lot of time to think about what he would like to do next. David has decided to use his experience by developing a part-time international consulting business that would allow him to work in his home office part time.

Lately, David has been feeling tired and sleeping poorly. He decided that he should take advantage of Medicare's new "Welcome to Medicare" preventive visit with his doctor and have a complete checkup before launching into his new endeavor. He was both anxious and excited about meeting his new doctor, recommended by another retired executive. He told David not to expect to leave this doctor's office with a prescription in hand after a 30-minute visit. The friend was right. The checkup ended up taking two weeks and consisted of a thorough recounting of David's medical history, family medical history, and lifestyle choices. It also included an examination and a series of laboratory tests.

When David returned for the results of his evaluation, he was presented with some startling facts. His doctor told him frankly that he was headed into a lifetime of chronic health problems unless he drastically changed his lifestyle. Specifically, his blood pressure and blood sugar levels were too high, and his insomnia problems were probably due to too much alcohol consumption on a daily basis. The doctor complimented David for quitting smoking 10 years earlier. However, because of the other factors, and because David's father died of heart disease, David was still at risk of heart disease and other complications. The doctor strongly recommended some major lifestyle interventions.

Case Study Questions

1. Would you say that David's doctor is being responsible by strongly recommending lifestyle changes for David? What research supports your answer? Why might David not have encountered such medical recommendations 10 or 15 years ago?

2. In what ways does David fit or not fit the profile of someone who would participate in a health promotion program? Would you say that David has a preventive attitude about his situation?

3. The chapter describes four possible models of health promotion programs. Describe each model and explain how each might apply to David's situation.

4. Without knowing the specific community in which David and his doctor live, where generally might David look for health promotion support for his lifestyle-change work? Find out what health promotion programs are available in your city. Based on what you find, what would you recommend for David?

5. First and foremost, David's doctor is concerned with David's health and well-being. In light of current health care trends, how is this case an economic concern for the doctor and for society?

LEARNING ACTIVITIES

1. Interview an older adult about his or her physical health. What chronic conditions does the individual have? How do these interfere with activities of daily living? What has the person done to adjust to any impairments? Does the person use any assistive technology devices (low or high tech) to help with activities?

2. Ask an older family member or friend to share with you a recent hospital or doctor's bill and the Medicare invoice that corresponds to that health care episode. After gaining the person's permission (and ensuring confidentiality), report to the class the type of health care episode, the amount the health care provider charged, the amount Medicare paid, the amount paid by a Medigap policy (if there is one), and the amount paid by the patient. How easy or difficult was it to gather this information from the invoices sent by each provider?

3. Go to the Medicare.gov site and investigate whether PPOs or HMOs are in your area. Check the website and find out what model of PPO or HMO they adhere to and compare the plans with Medicare and a standard Medigap policy. What are the differences in coverage?

4. What health promotion programs are available in your community for older adults? Who sponsors these programs? What services and information are offered in these programs?

FOR MORE INFORMATION

International Resources

1. The World Health Organization: Ageing and Life Course: www.who.int/ageing/en/index.html

   WHO is the directing and coordinating authority for health within the United Nations and is responsible for providing leadership on global health matters, setting norms and standards, providing technical support to countries and monitoring and assessing health trends. The WHO website has health and wellness information about older adults from across the globe.

2. EuroHealthNet - Healthy Ageing: www.healthyageing.eu

   This EuroHealthNet website captures a expansive range of practical examples of health promotion interventions, of initiatives that promote healthy ageing in the European Union, and makes available key resources you can use to promote healthy ageing. A great website to visit.

3. Healthy Seniors: Portal for Aging and Health in the Americas: www.healthyolderpersons.org/

   The Aging and Health in the Americas Portal has a number of resources including a directory of international policies designed to promote health, links to individuals and institutions committed to the health and well-being of older adults in the Americas and aging and health resources.

4. AGE Platform Europe: www.age-platform.eu/en

   AGE Platform Europe is a European network of around 167 organizations of and for people aged 50 + which aims to promote the interests of senior citizens in the European Union. Check out their publication *How to Promote Ageing Well in Europe: Instruments and Tools Available to Local and Regional Actors.* The site has a number of publications and other resources addressing healthy aging.

5. Canadian Fitness and Lifestyle Research Institute: www.cflri.ca/eng

   The mission of the Canadian Fitness and Lifestyle Research Institute is to enhance the wellbeing of Canadians through research and communication of information about physically active lifestyles to the public and private sectors. The site has links to numerous publications on staying active and fit, many directed toward older adults.

National Resources

1. American Heart Association, 7272 Greenville Avenue, Dallas, TX 75231; phone: 800-242-8721; www.heart.org

   The American Heart Association funds research and conducts public education programs on the prevention and control of heart, stroke, and cardiovascular disease. It distributes a number of pamphlets in English and Spanish for older adults, including *Benefits of Physical Activity for Older Adults* and *Exercise Tips for Older Americans.*

2. The Center for Healthy Aging, c/o National Council on Aging, 1901 L Street NW, 4th Floor, Washington, DC 20036; phone: 202-479-1200; http://www.ncoa.org/improve-health/center-for-healthy-aging/

   The Center for Healthy Aging encourages and assists community-based organizations serving older adults to develop and implement evidence-based health promotion/disease prevention programs. Evidence-based programming translates tested program models or interventions into practical, effective community programs that can provide proven health benefits to participants. The website contains information and support for evidence-based health promotion programs in the areas of chronic disease, disabilities, fall prevention, health promotion, medication management, mental health/substance abuse, nutrition, and physical activity. Examples of evidence-based programs are also available on the website. You can also find NCOA on Facebook and Twitter.

3. The Centers for Medicare and Medicaid Services—Medicare.gov, P.O. Box 340, Columbia, MD 21045; phone: 410-786-3000 or 800-638-6833; www.cms.gov

   The CMS coordinates the Medicare program and has publications for consumers, including *Medicare and You* and *Guide to Health Insurance for People on Medicare.*

4. National Caucus and Center on Black Aged, Inc., 1220 L Street NW, Suite 800, Washington, DC, 20005; phone: 202-637-8400; www.ncba-aged.org

   The National Caucus and Center on Black Aged has publications on its website including *The Healing Zone Health Update Newsletter* and *Health Status of Older African Americans.*

   The Arthritis Foundation offers health education programs, brochures, and a bimonthly magazine about resources and programs to help persons with arthritis. Local chapters sponsor exercise programs, support groups, and resource materials.

Web Resources

1. National Institute on Aging

   National Institute on Aging offers a wealth of health-promotion-related information. It recently launched the Go4Life program. Go4Life is an exercise and physical activity campaign from the National Institute on Aging at NIH designed to help older adults fit exercise and physical activity into their daily life. Motivating older adults to become physically active for the first time, return to exercise after a break in their routines, or build more exercise and physical activity into weekly routines are the essential elements of Go4Life. Go4Life offers exercises, motivational tips, and free resources to older adults get ready, start exercising, and keep going. The Go4Life campaign includes an evidence-based exercise guide in both English and Spanish, an exercise video, an interactive website, and a national outreach campaign. You can stay connected through Facebook or following the helpful exercise tips via Twitter.

2. National Center for Chronic Disease Prevention and Health Promotion: www.cdc.gov/nccdphp

   The center has a site with links to statistical and educational information about chronic disease, disease prevention and control, and community health promotion.

3. The Henry J. Kaiser Family Foundation Health Reform Source: http://healthreform.kff.org

   There's no doubt about it . . . the new ACA is bringing some significant changes to the health care landscape in the United States, and there is a great deal of misinformation about what the law does and does not require. The Henry J. Kaiser Family Foundation, which is a nonpartisan source of facts, information, and analysis for health care policy, has created a website—Health Reform Source—that is devoted to explaining the ACA to laypersons. Check out *Illustrating Health Reform: How Health Insurance Coverage Will Work*, a short, animated movie—featuring the "YouToons"—on YouTube that explains the problems with the current health care system, the changes that are happening now, and the changes coming in 2014: http://www.youtube.com/watch?v=vmdbllWOOzs.

CHAPTER 12

Mental Health Services

Phil, a 78-year-old widower, lived independently until about six months ago. At that time, he realized he no longer could get around without the help of a walker. Just as he was accepting this restriction, his eye doctor told him that nothing more could be done to treat his macular degeneration. Now Phil is legally blind. Because of his independent nature, the eye specialist referred him to a rehabilitation counselor for persons with visual impairments. Although Phil made progress on learning new skills, the counselor became increasingly concerned about his extreme mood swings from anger to despondency and referred him to the mental health center's peer counseling program. After a few weeks of talking one-on-one with the peer counselor, Phil agreed to participate twice per week in a group of other older adults with similar experiences. Phil likes the idea of talking through his problems with someone his own age. He says, "I am getting the help I need without people thinking I am crazy."

Approximately 21% of people aged 65 and older in the United States report having a lifelong psychiatric illness (Gum, King-Kallimanis, & Kohn, 2009). Older women are about 1.5 times more likely than older men to have a psychiatric disorder (24.0% vs. 16.7%). Lifetime prevalence rates are even higher among the baby boomers (43.7%); thus, the number of older adults with psychiatric problems is likely to increase significantly over the next few decades. As these statistics suggest, some older adults have had serious mental illnesses (e.g., anxiety disorders, bipolar disorders, substance-use disorders) most of their adult lives; others have had periodic episodes of mental illness throughout their lives. Approximately 8.5% of older adults report psychiatric problems within any given year. For older adults like Phil, factors such as a decline in physical health, loss of independence, lower socioeconomic status, multiple stressful life events, and limited social support seriously influence their mental health status for the first time in their lives.

This chapter focuses on mental health services for older adults and their families. We begin by examining federal support for mental health programs and services. Next, we profile older adults with mental health problems and describe the various types of programs designed specifically to address their needs. We conclude this part of the chapter with a discussion of the current and future issues in delivering mental health programs. The second part of the chapter examines mental health services targeted to caregivers of elders with physical and/or cognitive impairments.

POLICY BACKGROUND

The Community Mental Health Act of 1963 created a major shift in the provision of mental health services in the United States. It changed the focus of care from long-term, custodial, institutional care in state hospitals to active, outpatient, community-based care. A major goal of outpatient care for all individuals, including older adults, is to encourage maximum independence. This translates into the need for mental health programs and services aimed at keeping older persons within their own homes and communities.

Mental health services for older adults constitute only about 7.0% of Medicare expenditure (Garfield, 2011). Medicare coverage for mental health services was expanded in 1990 (via the Omnibus Budget Reconciliation Act [OBRA] of 1989), but coverage of specialized services is still limited. Although there are few limitations on the total number of hospitalization or inpatient days for psychiatric care in general hospitals, older persons treated for psychiatric conditions in specialty facilities are covered for 90 days of care per illness with a 60-day lifetime reserve (Medical Learning Networks, 2011). Coverage for inpatient care in freestanding psychiatric hospitals is limited to 190 days during an individual's lifetime. Prior to 2010, Medicare beneficiaries were required to pay a 50% copayment for outpatient psychiatric services, including psychotherapy and psychological and neuropsychological testing services. With the enactment of the Medicare Improvements for Patients and Providers Act of 2008 (Democratic Policy Committee, 2008), the amount of the beneficiary's copayment for services was reduced to 45% in 2010, and it will be incrementally reduced to 20% by 2014 (Medical Learning Networks, 2011). There is a 20% co-payment requirement for outpatient psychotherapy, medical management, diagnostic services, and professional services for evaluation. A 20% co-payment also is required for partial hospitalization programs that provide structured intensive services for those in acute psychiatric distress who would be hospitalized without these services.

OBRA (1989) also expanded the coverage for services provided by nonphysician providers. Psychologists and clinical social workers rendering mental health services are now eligible for direct reimbursement. Previously, reimbursement was made only when the services provided by these professionals were under the direct supervision of a physician.

In response to the changes put forward by OBRA, the National Association of Insurance Commissioners revised the model Medicare Supplemental (Medigap) insurance regulations. All Medigap policies are now required to cover the 40% co-insurance for outpatient mental health care under Medicare Part B, which will decrease to 20% co-insurance by 2014 (Centers for Medicare and Medicaid Services [CMS], 2011). Unfortunately, this change is prospective, so it does not apply to older adults holding Medigap policies in effect prior to their state's adoption of the new model regulation.

As part of Medicaid reform, Congress passed the Omnibus Budget Reconciliation Act of 1987. This legislation requires require states to have a Preadmission Screening and Resident Review (PASRR) program (Linkins et al., 2001). This means that all prospective nursing home applicants who have a primary or secondary diagnosis of a major mental disorder (i.e., schizophrenia, paranoid disorders, major affective disorders, schizo-affective disorders, atypical psychoses) must undergo a preadmission screening to determine whether they are appropriate candidates for nursing home admission and whether they need active treatment for mental illness. If the older adult requires specialized mental health services, the state Medicaid agency must provide or arrange for provision of such services. In 1996, Congress revisited the PASRR program and removed the requirement for annual resident review, replacing it with a requirement to conduct reviews when there are changes in a resident's physical or mental status (Linkins et al., 2001). Researchers report low rates of compliance with the implementation of recommended mental health services (Borson, Loebel, Kitchell, Domoto, & Hyde, 1997; Snowden & Roy-Byrne, 1998). In one study of nursing home residents with a psychiatric diagnosis, only 36% received a mental health visit during a 12-month period (Shea, Russo, & Smyer, 2000). Thus, it is not too surprising that about one fifth of all nursing homes receive a deficiency citation each year for mental health care as part of the federal survey and certification process (Castle & Myers, 2006).

In the 1990s, the number of Medicare participants increased, and the cost of maintaining the program rose exponentially. In response to accusations of alleged fraud and abuse of services, the federal government passed the Balanced Budget Act of 1997 to curtail spending and place tighter controls on Medicare providers. As a result, in 2001, the CMS implemented 15 demonstration sites to test the effectiveness of coordinating care for chronically ill, fee-for-service Medicare beneficiaries. The programs enrolled a diverse population of generally high-cost beneficiaries with chronic illnesses, with depression (18%) and dementia (9%) being the most commonly occurring mental health conditions. Participating beneficiaries received intervention to improve self-care, identify complications early, avoid hospitalization, and better coordinate treatments and medications for multiple conditions.

Although the participants reported satisfaction with the program and liked the support and monitoring they received, evaluation data over four years of operations revealed that most of the care coordination programs had limited or no improvements in quality of care, few achieved cost neutrality, and none reduced total Medicare expenditures when care coordination fees were included (Peikes, Brown, Chen, & Schore, 2008). Reasons suggested by the evaluators for so few program successes were that (a) most programs lacked extensive care coordination experience; (b) it is difficult to improve the self-care behavior of elderly beneficiaries as it is exceedingly difficult to change people's behavior; (c) some of the participating programs were part of medical care systems that already had well-coordinated care, thus programs may have had little opportunity to improve on the existing system; and (d) improvements in the quality of care do not necessarily result in reductions in hospitalizations or costs.

In 1999, the U.S. Supreme Court ruled in *Olmstead v. L.C.* that anyone receiving mental health services was to be served in the least restrictive environment possible. Implications for this ruling required states to develop a system of services to handle the needs of persons with mental illness for whom institutional placement is inappropriate. To meet recipient needs effectively, states were given the latitude to develop programs independently from other states. As a result, Medicaid services vary substantially among states. Coverage includes mandatory and optional services. General hospital inpatient care, physician services, outpatient services in general hospitals, emergency room services, and nursing home care are mandatory. These services focus on the needs of patients with acute illness episodes and persons who need to be in a nursing home. The optional services help persons with chronic mental impairments living in community settings. These services include care by nonphysicians, freestanding outpatient clinics, case management, rehabilitation, and home health care. Many states have not adopted Medicaid's optional elements. In those states that have, providers are often reluctant to participate because of the low rates of reimbursement. In addition, 10 states (Alaska, Connecticut, Hawaii, Indiana, Maryland, Mississippi, Montana, New Hampshire, New Mexico, Wyoming) have home- and community-based services waivers to serve adults of all ages with mental health and substance use needs (U.S. Department of Health and Human Services [USDHHS], 2010a).

In response to the Deficit Reduction Act of 2005, which called for further reduction of long-term care spending, CMS began exploring different approaches for delivering long-term support programs. Money Follows the Person (MFP) is a system of flexible financing for long-term services and supports, which enables available funds to move with the individual to the most appropriate and preferred setting as the individual's needs and preferences change. This approach supports the concept of least restrictive environment and allows the consumer to remain in the community, thus reducing unnecessary institutionalization. With the passage of the Affordable Care Act March in 2010, the government provided an additional $2.25 billion (paid out through 2016) to encourage new states to participate in MFP and allow existing demonstration programs to continue strengthening and expanding (CMS, 2011). By February 2011, 43 states and the District of Columbia had MFP programs. Although original number targets for transitioning people into community care through this program proved unobtainable due to lack of affordable housing and inadequate community workforce supply, states have accelerated transitions over recent years, with 13,000 transitions already completed or in progress by July 2010 (Kaiser Commission on Medicaid and the Uninsured, 2011b). It is important to note, however, that older people with mental illness and developmental disabilities have been the least likely candidates for transition due to their extensive health and long-term service needs.

The Social Security Administration administers several programs that provide cash payments or other benefits to persons with mental disabilities. Persons with adequate work histories usually receive monthly cash payments as Social Security benefits, and persons with minimal resources and insufficient work history usually receive a monthly payment under the Supplemental Security Income (SSI) program. Based on the number of SSI recipients aged 65 and older, approximately 20%, or 400,000 people, receive government disability payments because of their mental disorders (Karlin & Norris, 2006; Social Security Administration, 2006).

Older Americans Act (OAA) funds also may be used to support mental health services for older adults under Title III-B and III-F. Title III-B, which allocates spending for a wide range of supportive services, includes funding for mental health programs. Local Area Agency on Aging (AAA) funds can be used to support mental health programs and services designed to enable older adults to attain and maintain mental well-being. Funding also may be authorized under Title III-F, which funds disease prevention and health promotion services. Health promotion services can include screening for the prevention of depression, coordination of community mental health services, provision of educational activities, and referral to psychiatric and psychological services. Thus, local AAAs have the opportunity to fund a wide variety of mental health programs and services under the OAA.

USERS AND PROGRAMS

Characteristics of Mental Health Clients

In 2009, approximately 11% of noninstitutionalized persons aged 65 or older had a diagnosable mental, behavioral, or emotional disorder that interfered with their ability to carry out one or more major life activities (Substance Abuse and Mental Health Services Administration [SAMHSA], 2012a). Of these individuals, 1.4% had a serious mental illness, and 2.4% experienced major depressive episode (e.g., a period of at least two weeks when a person experienced a depressed mood or loss of interest or pleasure in daily activities and had a majority of specified depression symptoms). A greater percentage of older women than older men reported having a mental illness (14.0% vs. 6.5%, respectively). Approximately 11.0% of White and Hispanic older adults experienced mental illness as compared to about 9.0% of Black/African American older adults. Of older adults residing in nursing homes in 2004, 6.0% had a primary diagnosis of mental illness.

Depressive symptoms and disorders are the most common reasons for referring older persons for mental health services (see Exhibit 12.1). As many as 11% of community-dwelling older adults and 49% of elders living in long-term care facilities suffer from depressive symptoms (Institute of Medicine [IOM], 2012). Older women report a higher prevalence of depressive symptoms than their male counterparts (Federal Interagency Forum on Aging-Related Statistics, 2010). In the majority of cases, when older adults experience depressive symptoms, it is viewed as a reactive depression (i.e., the person is reacting to a major life loss or transition) rather than as stemming from other etiologies. However, 3.0% to 4.5% of community-living older adults (about 1.2 million to 1.7 million people) have a major depressive disorder (IOM, 2012). Prevalence rates for depressive disorders are generally higher for the age group 65 to 74 than for individuals aged 75 and older.

Other reasons why older adults are referred for mental health services include Alzheimer's disease and other dementias, affecting approximately 13% of individuals 65 years of age and older (Alzheimer's Association, 2012b); suicide behaviors—16% of all suicides deaths are committed by adults 65 years of age and older (Centers for Disease Control and Prevention, 2007); and alcohol dependence and abuse, which affects up to 15% of older adults (Bartels, Blow, Brockmann, & Van Citters, 2005). The prevalence of mental health disorders also differs among older minority elders (Jimenez, Alegria, Chen, Chan, & Laderman, 2010).

Exhibit 12.1   12-Month Prevalence Rates and Estimated Number of Community-Living Older Adults With Mental Health and Substance Abuse Conditions

	Prevalence Rate (%)	Estimated Number (in millions)
Mental Health Conditions		
Depressive disorder	3.0–4.5	1.2–1.8
Major depressive episode	3.0–4.3	1.2–1.7
Depressive symptoms	1.1–11.1	0.4–4.3
Generalized anxiety disorder	1.1–2.1	0.4–0.8
Panic disorder	0.8–1.1	0.3–0.4
Obsessive-compulsive disorder	0.8	0.3
Bipolar disorder	0.2–0.8	<0.05–0.1
Schizophrenia	0.2–0.8	<0.05–0.3
Suicide plans and attempts	<.02	<0.05
Substance Use Conditions		
Alcohol dependence or abuse	<0.2–1.9	<0.05–0.7
Drug dependence or abuse	<0.2–0.2	<0.05–0.1
At-risk drinking	5.2	2.0
At-risk drug use	0.9	0.4

Source: Institute of Medicine (2012).

Asians older adults have the lowest prevalence rates of mental health conditions across all ethnic/racial group groups. As shown in Exhibit 12.2, Hispanic older adults have higher 12-month prevalence rates of depressive disorders, major depressive episodes, and panic disorders as compared to White and Black older adults.

Exhibit 12.2   12-Month Prevalence Rates of Mental Health and Substance Abuse Conditions Community-Living Older Adults by Race and Ethnicity (percentage)

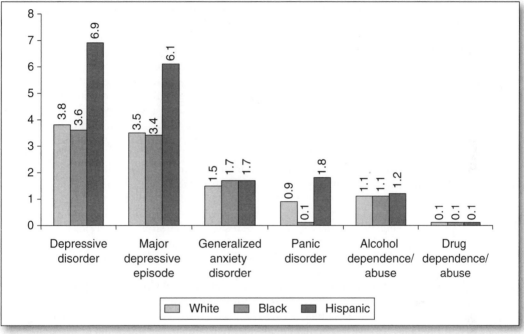

Source: IOM (2012).

Best Practice: Lifespan's Geriatric Addiction Program

Lifespan, founded in 1971, has provided services to Rochester, New York, area older adults and caregivers for over 40 years. In 2001, it began implementing the Geriatric Addiction Program (GAP) after discovering that many older adults did not fit well within traditional treatment programs, which are usually geared toward a younger population. GAP provides intervention, assessment, linkage, and counseling within older adult substance abusers' homes. As of 2010, GAP had served 981 adults 55+ with addiction problems. Program evaluation data show a reduction in substance use or abstinence with an increase in health, safety, and functioning for 88% of clients. Since its inception, GAP has also trained 1,731 professionals and 1,415 nonprofessionals and caregivers in the recognition and dynamics of geriatric addictions.

For more information, contact the GAP staff at 1900 S. Clinton Avenue, Rochester, NY 14618; phone: 585-244-8400; http://www.lifespan-roch.org/substance-abuse.htm.

Older adults are less likely than younger adults to seek specialty mental health services (Karlin, Duffy, & Gleaves, 2008). Only 10% of community-living adults aged 65 and older with mental health conditions receive treatment, compared with 25% of younger adults with similar conditions. Several demographic variables are associated with the lack of use of mental health services among older adults, including age, gender, race, and ethnicity, as well as the stigma they associated with mental health problems, lack of knowledge about specialty mental health settings, lack of culturally and linguistically appropriate services, and lack of transportation to services (Black, Rabins, German, McGuire, & Roca, 1997; IOM, 2012). Family members and professional providers who share the misperception that mental disorders are a "normal" part of aging further compound the problem of under-identification and treatment.

Although rural elders are one of the greatest at-risk groups for experiencing mental health problems (SAMHSA, 2004), only about 5% of rural community mental health centers' patients and 2% to 4% of rural private patients with psychiatric problems are older adults (Karlin & Norris, 2006). Several factors adversely influence the appropriate use of mental health services by rural elders, including sociodemographic, economic, and cultural issues; the lack of mental health professionals to work with aged individuals; funding cutbacks; lack of transportation; and the stigma surrounding mental illness and its treatment (Karlin & Norris, 2006; Sanders, Fitzgerald, & Bratteli, 2008; Solway, Estes, Goldberg, & Berry, 2010).

Residents of long-term care facilities also benefit from mental health services. The three major nursing home resident groups needing such services are persons who are physically ill but cognitively capable; persons who are mentally ill but cognitively capable; and persons with dementia. Although different therapeutic issues arise and different interventions are needed for each group, all long-term care residents face similar situations in which they may require emotional support, including making the transition into the facility, establishing relationships with staff, adapting to the institution's schedule, adjusting to new roles with family caregivers or to a lack of family caregivers, and accommodating to a new activities schedule (Lichtenberg, 1994). Unfortunately, results of a national survey revealed that less than one fifth of older residents in nursing homes who need mental health services receive them (Smyer, Shea, & Streit, 1994). Those receiving mental health services were more likely to have a specific mental health diagnosis, exhibit mood disturbances, and enter the nursing home from a psychiatric hospital. This suggests that services were more likely directed toward individuals with more severe impairments. In addition, residents in small nursing homes and residents of nursing homes in rural areas have the greatest unmet need for mental health services (Reichman et al., 1998).

Across the Globe: Specialist Mental Health Services for Older People

Throughout Australia, there is a range of regional government-supported programs tailored to meet the unique needs of older adults with mental health issues. For example, in New South Wales, teams are available to offer psychiatric and medical diagnosis and assessment, triage, case management, and treatment of mental health disorders (long term, recently emerging, or dementia-related) for older adults 65 in community, long-term care, or acute-care hospital settings. These specialized teams are multidisciplinary, including consultant psychiatry, neurology, nursing, occupational therapy, rehabilitation, clinical psychology, social work, physiotherapy, speech pathology, podiatry, and dietetic services. Whenever possible, consumers and caregivers are involved in treatment planning. In addition, caregivers are encouraged to participate in available support services and programs.

Sources: NSW Ministry of Health (n.d.).

Mental Health Programs

For most older adults, mental health intervention does not mean going into a counselor's office or receiving help from a specialized mental health care center. As few as 2% to 4% (Karlin & Norris, 2006) of persons seen in private psychiatric offices and only 5% of patients who receive community mental health services are 65 years of age and older (Center for Mental Health Services, 2007). This can be attributed to several factors:

- Most centers are not widely accessible and tend to be isolated from the mainstream of community health and social services for older adults (Chumbler, Cody, Booth, & Beck, 2001).

- Mental health service programs have not aggressively engaged in outreach and case finding; rather, they tend to rely on referrals and self-identification of potential clients (Chumbler et al., 2001).

- Reimbursement for treatment of mental disorders under Medicare varies from year to year and is substantially lower and less comprehensive than for physical disorders (Hinrichsen, 2010).

The aging service network provides a wide range of mental health services for older adults. The results of a national mail survey of AAAs (Bane, Rathbone-McCuan, & Galliher, 1994) indicated that the most common services available in rural planning and service areas (PSAs) were telephone reassurance, mental health screening, individual counseling, and Alzheimer's support groups. In mixed PSAs (i.e., areas with rural, urban, and suburban counties), the most common mental health services were Alzheimer's support groups, counseling, and mental health referral and materials. Great variability in the community resources that facilitate these services to older adults was found in both the rural and mixed PSAs. For example, more than 80% of respondents in both areas reported the availability of adult protective service intervention for older persons with mental health problems, whereas only 12% of the rural PSAs and 31% of the mixed PSAs reported having a mobile mental health team that traveled to the person's home.

Mental health services and counseling may take place in a health care setting (i.e., physician's office or clinic), the client's residence (i.e., own home or nursing home), a senior center, or an adult day center. For example, in Tallahassee, Florida, a professional counselor is available two days a week at the local senior center to help seniors work through their problems (go to http://www.talgov.com/seniors/seniors-services.aspx). The Geriatric Services Team in Baltimore County, Maryland, provides oversight and consultation for services for older adults with serious and persistent mental illness. Services include the PEERS program, which matches volunteers to elderly people, and the county's Consumer Drop-In

Centers (see http://www.baltimorecountymd.gov/Agencies/health/healthservices/mental/mhsvc.html#geriatric). The Halton Geriatric Mental Health Outreach Program in Ontario is designed to provide specialized services to older adults with complex mental health needs (e.g., mental health problems accompanied by significant medical illness or functional needs; late-onset severe mental illness). Services are brought to where the person resides (e.g., their own home, long-term care facility) because the person cannot or will not access the help they need through traditional services (visit http://www.rgpc.ca/about/regions/sgs_details.cfm?SGSID = 51). Mental health specialists in Alabama report that brief, home-delivered psychosocial intervention can be an effective approach for treating rural older adults with emotional complaints such as depression, anxiety, and loneliness (Kaufman, Scogin, MaloneBeach, Baumhover, & McKendree-Smith, 2000). The KateMills Snider Geriatric Psychiatry Outreach Program (GO program) serves older adults with mental illness who live at home but are unable to get to an outpatient treatment facility (Johnston et al., 2010). Although there is no minimum or maximum number of visits, older adults are seen an average of four times in person with about 30 additional contacts per GO participant with their family caregivers members, community agencies, and other physicians.

Relatively few community-based services are available to older adults with serious or chronic mental illness who are at risk for, or have a history of, psychiatric hospitalization (Center for Mental Health Services, 2004). Many successful programs that serve older adults with serious mental health problems feature outreach as a key service. Older adults receiving outreach services have shown increased likelihood of receiving case management services, decreased mental health symptoms, and decreased incidence and length of psychiatric hospitalization. Services modeled after the Gatekeepers program, which uses community members as frontline assessors, have been successfully implemented with older adults in both urban and rural areas. Evaluation of the Gatekeeper program showed that it saves healthcare costs while decreasing ED visits and hospitalizations for older adults (D. L. Barrett, Secic, & Borowske, 2010).

Although community-based treatment of older adults with mental health problems is preferred by both older adults and mental health professionals, a small proportion of older individuals need more intensive care provided by institutions. In 2005, persons older than age 65 represented 4 % of all individuals receiving inpatient psychiatric services (Center for Mental Health Services, 2007). Symptoms of depression, anxiety, dementia, paranoia, delusional ideation, and alcohol and drug abuse are the most likely reasons for admission of older persons to psychiatric hospitals. The need for hospitalization is dependent on the severity of symptoms and the older person's ability to carry out activities of daily living. In addition, patients frequently have concomitant physical illnesses that also must be addressed.

The geriatric mental health and substance use workforce is a loosely defined set of providers who assess, diagnose, treat, manage, and care for older adults who have or are at risk for mental health and substance use conditions (IOM, 2012, p. 138). This workforce includes primary care physicians, psychiatrists, nurses, psychologists, social workers, marriage and family therapist, counselors, peer support specialists, community health workers, and direct care staff. They work in settings such as community mental health centers, inpatient settings, HMOs, public and private agencies, hospitals, nursing homes, and private practice. The number of specifically trained individuals to provide mental health services targeted for geriatric patients is small. The IOM (2012) estimates the current number of geriatric mental health and substance specialists in the United States to be less than 500,000.

Trained paraprofessionals, known as *qualified mental health professionals* (QMHPs), also provide psychological and psychosocial interventions with older adults under the supervision of experienced professionals. Criteria for QMHPs are determined by the states. In some cases, they offer formal mental health services, whereas in others they provide informal support. Paraprofessionals work alone, in conjunction with, or under the supervision of trained professionals. One type of paraprofessional program that has grown rapidly during the past two decades is peer-counseling programs for older adults. These programs train and supervise older adults to provide counseling and support to other older individuals. Peer counselors typically address a broad range of issues including depression, loneliness, problems that result from physical impairments, and other concerns related to aging, gender, and ethnicity. They receive supervision from a professional counselor employed by the agency sponsoring the program. Programs often begin because they are a cost-effective means of providing mental health services for older adults. The benefits of peer-counseling programs for older adults include the following:

- Many older people talk more readily to older people than to professional therapists.
- Peer counselors serve as positive models for their clients.
- Peer counseling enriches the lives of both the client and the counselor.
- Peer counselors may be more effective than professionals because they are often more aware of the problems of older people. (Bratter & Freeman, 1990)

A growing number of mental health and aging coalitions are engaged in efforts to improve the availability and quality of mental health prevention and treatment services to older adults and their families through education, research, and increased public awareness. For example, the National Coalition on Mental Health and Aging (NCMHA) provides guidelines for building state and community mental health and aging coalitions. Older mental health consumers voice their concerns and promote awareness of the need for home and community-based mental health services through participation in the Older Adult Consumers of Mental Health Alliance (OACMHA; www.oacmha.com). The main purpose of OACMHA is to improve the quality of and access to mental health services for older adults (Bazelon Center, 2000). The SAMHSA, in collaboration with the National Council on Aging, developed a toolkit for health and social services providers in the aging services field with health promotion and health education activities to prevent substance abuse and mental health problems in older adults (SAMHSA, 2012b).

Best Practice: Gatekeeper Program

This program, originally developed in 1978 in Spokane County, Washington, is designed to seek out and offer assistance to at-risk older adults who have little or no support system to act in their behalf as they experience serious difficulties that compromise their ability to live independently. This is accomplished through "gatekeepers," nontraditional referral sources such as postal workers, meter readers, phone operators, and others who come into contact with older adults on a regular basis. Gatekeepers receive training to identify and refer at-risk older adults to appropriate support agencies that can intervene and solve a problem before it becomes a major crisis. The Gatekeeper model has been applied nationally and internationally to train employees to identify and refer isolated, at-risk older adults residing in their own homes.

For more information about the Gatekeeper Program, visit its website at www.smhca.org/gatekeeper.aspx.

CHALLENGES FOR MENTAL HEALTH PROGRAMS

The graying of America and the deinstitutionalization of persons with mental illness has resulted in increased attention to the mental health needs of older adults. Although significant improvements in the delivery of mental health services have been made since the passage of the Community Mental Health Act in 1963 and the funding of mental health programs under the OAA, many challenges remain to improve the delivery of mental health services to older adults (National Association of Mental Health Planning and Advisory Councils, 2007).

Connecting the Delivery Systems

The two primary systems involved in providing community services to older adults with mental health concerns are the public mental health system (primarily community mental health centers) and the aging service network. A formal relationship between community mental health centers and the aging network, however, is often the exception rather than the rule. This is unfortunate for older adults because those centers with formal relationships with local AAAs tend to provide a larger range of services to older adults, provide services to older adults in more settings, and provide mental health services to higher proportions of older adults than do those without formal affiliations (Kuiken, 2004). Thus, joining forces appears to be the most effective and efficient means of reaching and serving older adults with mental health concerns.

Reaching Diverse Groups

Older adults from minority groups use mental health services to a lesser extent than their White counterparts, yet they appear to have the same, if not greater, need for such services. Use is affected by language barriers, limited access to information regarding available services, transportation, cultural dissimilarity, and reduced social and economic resources (Abramson, Trejo, & Lai, 2002; Barrio et al., 2008; Solway et al., 2010). Because individuals from ethnic minority groups represent a rapidly increasing segment of the total older adult population, mental health services must recognize the importance of cultural sensitivity and cross-cultural training of mental health professionals as one means of eliminating the barriers to, and promoting the use of, mental health services by ethnic minority elders.

The rural older adult population also is vastly underserved by the mental health system (Karlin & Norris, 2006; Neese, Abraham, & Buckwalter, 1999). As in most other service sectors, rural providers are faced with the issues of availability, accessibility, and acceptability of mental health services. Strategies put forth for improving the development and delivery of geriatric mental health services to rural areas include increasing the number and quality of rural mental health providers; adapting or developing diagnostic techniques to improve case identification among rural elderly; providing culturally sensitive mental health services; strengthening informal and formal care linkages in rural communities; developing innovative service delivery models building on the strengths of rural settings; and emphasizing fluidity as well as continuity in treatment models (Chalifoux, Neese, Buckwalter, Litwak, & Abraham, 1996).

Lesbian, gay, and bisexual (LGB) populations have higher rates of mental health distress than the general population due to chronic social stigma and stressors (Fredriksen-Goldsen & Muraco, 2010). For example, a California study found that approximately one fourth of aging LGB adults (27.9%) report that they needed help for emotional or mental health problems; this compares to about compared to 14% of aging heterosexual adults (Wallace,

Cochran, Durazo, & Ford, 2011). Among LGB older adults who reported needing help, approximately 78% sought mental health services and had a higher number of visits than heterosexual older adults. The authors of the study speculated that higher use of mental health services by the aging LGB adults may be due to a greater intensity of need to cope with day-to-day experiences of discrimination or less mental health support available from biological families. Several organizations provide materials and technical support for communities striving to improve the quality of mental health and support services available to the aging LGBT population, including the National Resource Center on LGBT Aging (www.lgbtagingcenter.org); Services and Advocacy for GLBT Elders (www.sageusa.org); and the American Society on Aging (www.asaging.org/lain).

Training Providers

The demand for mental health services is likely to increase as baby boomers tend to use mental health services more frequently than the current cohort of older adults and are less stigmatized by seeking mental health care. The number of health care professionals available to treat the growing number of older adults with mental health problems is inadequate. Unfortunately, mental health specialists have little required training in geriatrics, geriatric specialists have little required training in mental health, and most general providers do not have extensive requirements in either area (IOM, 2012). The United States needs a workforce that is able to address the complex health care needs of older adults, with basic knowledge of geriatric mental health and substance use; expertise in team-based, collaborative care; cultural competence; and multilingual skills (p. 245). The development of both primary training and continuing education programs are needed to help psychologists and other mental health professional develop attitude, knowledge, and skill competencies for professional practice with older adults (IOM, 2012; Karel, Gatz, & Smyers, 2012).

Providing Mental Health Programs in the Future

During the 2005 White House Conference on Aging (2006), delegates passed a resolution to improve recognition, assessment, and treatment of mental illness and depression among older Americans. One specific strategy for implementing this resolution was to assure access to affordable, comprehensive, quality mental health and substance abuse services in a variety of settings. With the baby boomers having had higher average rates of mental health service use throughout their lives and their willingness to use such services expected to continue as they age, there is clearly a need for developing more mental health services and preparing a substantially larger workforce capable of providing the services (IOM, 2012).

Because the vast majority of older adults exist in and interact with a family network, professionals must also address the mental health needs of those within the family network. We now turn our attention to the mental health needs of family caregivers.

MENTAL HEALTH SERVICES FOR FAMILY CAREGIVERS

In 2010, 14.9 million family members and other unpaid caregivers (e.g., friends, neighbors) provided 17 billion hours of care to persons with dementia, Alzheimer's disease, mental confusion, or forgetfulness (Alzheimer's Association, 2011). One potential consequence of providing care for older adults with physical and cognitive impairments is an increased risk of mental health problems among family caregivers. Caregivers are highly vulnerable to stress-related physical and emotional complaints. Between 40% and 70% of family caregivers suffer from symptoms of depression, with about one fourth to one half of these caregivers meeting the diagnostic criteria for major depression (Taylor, Ezell, Kuhibhatla, Ostbye, & Clipp, 2008; Zarit, 2006). Caregivers whose family member has emotional or mental health problems are more likely than other caregivers to report a decline in their own health (28% vs. 12%, respectively; Zarit, 2006).

Although caring for one's spouse or parent is fairly common practice, particularly for midlife and older women, a family care situation receiving greater attention is that of grandparents assuming full-time parenting responsibilities for their grandchildren. Approximately 2.6 million children live in homes where grandparents are the householder and have primary responsibility for them (AARP, 2012b). Of these families, approximately 1 million children have no parent present in a home (AARP, 2012a; Kreider & Ellis, 2011). The majority of grandparents rearing grandchildren are under the age of 60 (67%), married (73%), and female (62%). More than half of them are in the labor force. Almost 20% live below the poverty threshold (AARP, 2012a), and nearly half have incomes between 1 and 3 times the poverty line (Livingston & Parker, 2010). Older adults of all race and ethnic groups are raising grandchildren: 51.1% are White not Hispanic; 24.2% are African American; 18.7% are Hispanic/Latino; 2.9% are Asian, 2.0% are American Indian or Alaskan Native; and 0.3% are Native Hawaiian and Other Pacific Islander (AARP, 2012a). Some grandparents report increased physical and mental health problems that they associate with assuming parenting responsibilities for their grandchildren (Grinstead, Leder, Jensen, & Bond, 2003; Roberto, Dolbin-MacNab, & Finney, 2008). For example, grandparents parenting their grandchildren often report feeling isolated, particularly if their new roles and responsibilities deprive them of emotional and instrumental support from others as they experiences changes in their social support networks.

Community services for caregivers include psychoeducational programs, support groups, respite care, and individual or family counseling to help manage their emotional reactions to the changes in their loved ones. With advances in technology, caregivers also engage in education and interventions programs via telephone calls, the Internet, video or audiotapes, computers, and interactive television (National Alliance for Caregiving, 2011; R. Schulz, Lustig, Handler, & Martire, 2002). These services and programs may be partially funded or supported by state, local, and nonprofit voluntary agencies. In the following sections, we describe policies supporting family caregivers, the characteristics of caregivers who use mental health services, and the types of services available to them. We end with a discussion of the challenges facing programs trying to reach and serve these caregivers.

POLICIES AFFECTING FAMILY CAREGIVERS

Congress has introduced a number of bills to support family caregivers (e.g., Family Medical Leave Act of 1993—see Chapter 11; Lifespan Respite Care Act of 2006—see Chapter 18). As previously noted, in 2010, Congress passed the Patient Protection and Affordable Care Act (ACA), implementation of which will occur over the course of the next several years. The ACA recognizes families in their caregiving role, addresses their experience of care, and provides them with opportunities for education and training (Feinberg & Reamy, 2011). A number of provisions in the law call for demonstrations and pilot programs that will assist caregivers with the care of their family members (Family Caregiver Alliance, 2011).

For example, the *Independence at Home* demonstration will allow persons with multiple chronic conditions to have medical professionals come to their homes. This will alleviate the burden on family caregivers to provide (or secure) transportation to various medical appointments. The *Community-Based Care Transitions Program* will assist in creating and funding collaborative partnerships between hospitals and community-based organizations to implement evidence-based care transitions services for Medicare beneficiaries who are at high risk for hospital readmission. Hospital discharges often thrust family members into a new caregiver role, many times with little to no training for high-level care responsibilities.

The Caregivers and Veterans Omnibus Health Services Act of 2010 created a new system of comprehensive support for caregivers of veterans of wars since September 11, 2001, and a program of general caregiver support services for family caregivers of all veterans (Feinberg, Reinhard, Houser, & Choula, 2011). This initiative provides stipends for family caregivers of veterans, information and training, respite, counseling, and ongoing supportive services (Family Caregiver Alliance, 2011). In conjunction with this initiative, the VA also created a website with additional information for caregivers of veterans (www.caregiver .va.gov) as well as a toll-free National Caregiver Support Line (1-855-260-3274).

The National Plan to Address Alzheimer's Disease (USDHHS, 2012d) was authorized in legislation passed in 2011 called the National Alzheimer's Project Act (NAPA; http:// www.gpo.gov/fdsys/pkg/PLAW-111publ375/pdf/PLAW-111publ375.pdf). In addition to creating and maintaining an integrated National Plan, NAPA requires that the Secretary of USDHHS

- coordinate Alzheimer's disease research and services across all federal agencies;
- accelerate the development of treatments that would prevent, halt, or reverse the course of Alzheimer's disease;
- improve early diagnosis and coordination of care and treatment of Alzheimer's disease;
- improve outcomes for ethnic and racial minority populations that are at higher risk for Alzheimer's disease; and
- coordinate with international bodies to fight Alzheimer's globally.

The ultimate goal of the National Plan is to prevent and effectively treat Alzheimer's disease by 2023. To jump-start the plan, on February 7, 2012, the Obama administration announced a historic $156 million investment in Alzheimer's disease research and practice. This investment includes (a) immediately increasing the National Institutes of Health's Alzheimer's disease research funding by $50 million in FY 2012; (b) sustaining and growing the Alzheimer's disease research investment; and (c) supporting people with Alzheimer's disease and their families and educating the public and providers.

USERS AND PROGRAMS

Characteristics of Caregivers Using Mental Health Programs

Family caregivers who seek support from mental health professionals present a wide array of problems and concerns. A study of 51 family caregivers who participated in weekly individual counseling sessions revealed nine pressing issues and problems: improving coping skills (time management, dealing with stress, and other coping mechanisms); family issues regarding spouse, siblings, and children; responding to the older person's emotional and behavior needs; physical well-being and safety; legal and financial affairs; quality of relationship with the care receiver; eliciting formal and informal support; feelings of guilt and inadequacy; and long-term planning (G. Smith, Smith, & Toseland, 1991). These problems and issues are consistent with reviews of research of caregiving demands (cf. Dilworth-Anderson, Williams, & Gibson, 2002; Roberto & Jarrott, 2008; R. Schulz & Martire, 2004; Torti, Gwyther, Reed, Friedman, & Schulman, 2004; Yee & Schulz, 2000) and suggest areas in which practitioners need to be prepared to help caregivers with a broad range of problems and concerns.

Mental Health Programs for Family Caregivers

Programs designed to meet the mental health needs of family caregivers include individual counseling, support groups, and educational programs (Bourgeois, Schulz, & Burgio, 1996; Cooke, McNally, Mulligan, Harrison, & Newman, 2001; Qualls, & Noecker, 2009; Zarit, 2008). Evaluations of these intervention strategies suggest positive outcomes for the caregivers who participate (Elliott, Burgio, & DeCoster, 2010; Lewis, et al., 2009; Yin, Zhou, & Bashford, 2002). However, most caregiver interventions are implemented primarily with urban caregivers. Whereas the types of support need are consistent across geographic areas (Chwalisz, Clancy Dollinger, O'Neill Zerth, & Tamkin, 2011), rural caregivers typically have access to fewer services and must rely more heavily on informal sources to support them in their caregiving journey (Wilken & Stanback, 2011).

With respect to individual counseling, spouses of persons with Alzheimer's disease reported less depression after their participation in brief psychodynamic psychotherapy. This approach offered caregivers the opportunity to understand how past conflicts influenced their reactions and responses to their current situation (Trotman & Brody, 2002). After completion of brief cognitive-behavioral therapy (CBT), whereby participants were taught to identify and modify the negative thoughts that contributed to the development and maintenance of depression, caregivers reported a significant reduction in symptoms associated with depression (D. A. Walker & Clarke, 2001). Similarly, caregivers enrolled in a CBT intervention demonstrated a significant reduction in anxiety over time (Akkerman & Ostwald, 2004). Reductions in anxiety were maintained over a six-week follow-up period, suggesting that CBT may offer caregivers skills that will help in modulating anxiety throughout their caregiving career. A review of studies conducted with primary care partners for physically frail elders also revealed positive outcomes for those who received treatment, compared with a no-treatment group (Cooke et al., 2001). Caregivers participating in counseling demonstrated more effective coping skills, improved psychological well-being, and improved relationships with care receivers as compared to caregivers who did not receive counseling.

Support groups—a popular form of caregiver intervention—are widely available. Most groups are limited to six to eight sessions. Almost all include both education and support, focusing on seven major themes: information about the care receiver's situation; the group and its members as a mutual support system; the emotional impact of caregiving; self-care; problematic interpersonal relationships; the development and use of support systems outside the group; and home care skills (Brubaker & Roberto, 1993). The typical support group comprises predominantly middle-class women, mostly the wives and daughters of individuals with some form of cognitive impairment (Bourgeois et al., 1996). Support groups are generally not well attended by minority individuals caring for older relatives. In some minority families, lack of participation may be due in part to the caregivers' reliance on other family members or informal helpers for caregiving assistance and strong cultural norms of family responsibility (Qualls & Roberto, 2006). The use of telephone (Toseland, Naccarato, & Wray, 2007; Winter & Gitlin, 2007) and Internet-based (Family Caregiver Alliance, 2006) support interventions offers an alternative option for those caregivers who find it difficult to leave their loved one or live in areas where a support group is not available. Reviews of the efficacy of support groups in improving caregiver outcomes have been mixed, perhaps due to differences in their purposes and approaches as well as research designs (Hornillos & Crespo, 2012).

Numerous educational programs have been developed to meet the needs of individuals faced with the challenges of providing care for frail, aging relatives (Toseland, Haigler, & Monahan, 2011). Most of these programs are for spouses and adult children who have assumed the primary responsibility for a family member experiencing physical or cognitive decline. Programs cover a variety of topics, including community resources, sensory changes, communication skills, normal aging, behavioral changes, living arrangements, coping with stress, and chronic illness. Among the few program descriptions and evaluations published in family and gerontology journals, several commonalities exist. First, the presentation formats are similar. A two-hour session offered during several weeks is the most popular model. Second, almost all programs use a multiple-topic approach. Third, although the majority provides similar content, most programs are designed for a specific target population (Brubaker & Roberto, 1993). Because psychoeducational programs typically do not carry the stigma often associated with counseling or other invention programs, they often have greater appeal to ethnic and racially diverse caregivers. For example, Hispanic and Latino caregivers who participated in an eight-week class designed to teach specific cognitive and behavioral skills for coping with the frustrations of caregiving assessed the program favorably and reported increased knowledge, hope, and self-confidence, along with decreased guilt and despair (Gallagher-Thompson, Arean, Rivera, & Thompson, 2001).

A large multisite research project funded by the National Institute on Aging and National Institute for Nursing Research in the late 1990s investigated the efficacy of several interventions for reducing the burden on diverse groups of family caregivers to older adults while improving the quality of care (R. Schulz et al., 2003). Each site in the Resources for Enhancing Alzheimer's Caregiver Health (REACH) study tested distinctive interventions targeted at particular caregiving populations with individually designed interventions including home visits, psychoeducational support classes, family interventions, and telephone-linked computer tools to foster communication among professionals and family caregivers. Overall, the findings suggest that active interventions were superior to control conditions in reducing (a) caregiver burden, (b) caregiver depression, (c) burden for women and those with high school or lower education, and (d) depression for Hispanic caregivers, non-spouses, and those with less than a high school education. Further description of the study sites, conditions, and multisite outcomes are published in a special section of *Psychology and Aging* (2003, vol. 18, no. 3), and site-specific methodologies and findings are published in a special section of *The Gerontologist* (2003, vol. 43, no. 4).

Many Cooperative Extension programs and resources provide support in meeting the mental health needs of caregivers of frail elders. Through the facilitation of formal educational programs and support groups, as well as through online support tools, family members learn how to more effectively carry out their roles and responsibilities as primary caregivers while reducing feelings of stress and burnout. For example, North Carolina Cooperative Extension agents and specialists are part of a statewide network using the *Powerful Tools for Caregiving* curriculum to educate caregivers about taking care of their family members as well as themselves (North Carolina Cooperative Extension, 2011). The program focuses on coping with stress, communicating with family members and care receivers, decision making, and arranging for caregiver down time. *The Healthy Caregiver Decision Tool* (http://tools.extension.org/decisiontool/main.html/32), developed by the Kansas State University Cooperative Extension Service, is an online tool designed to help caregivers find resources to optimize their own physical and mental health (Kansas State Research and Extension, 2011).

For Your Files: Caregiver Support Groups in America

The Self-Help Support Group On-Line is a searchable database that includes information on over 800 national, international, and demonstrational model self-help support groups, ideas for starting groups, and opportunities to link with others to develop new national or international groups. This database uses information provided by the American Self-Help Clearinghouse, a department of the Behavioral Health Center of Saint Clare's Health Services in Denville, New Jersey, which publishes *The Self-Help Sourcebook.*

For more information, call the American Clearinghouse at 973-625-3037; or visit www.mentalhelp .net/selfhelp.

Almost three fourths (74%) of family caregivers are employed at some point in their caregiving experience, and 69% report making work accommodations (i.e., arriving late/ leaving early, cutting back on hours) because of caregiving (Feinberg et al., 2011). Family caregivers can face financial hardships if they must leave the labor force to meet caregiving demands. For example, lifetime income-related losses as a result of leaving the workforce in midlife to provide elder care ranges from $283,716 for men and $324,044 for women (MetLife Mature Market Institute, 2011b). Since the pioneering efforts of the Travelers Companies in the mid-1980s, workplace support for caregivers has increased (D. L. Wagner, 2003). Employers provide support for their employees with elder care needs through their policies (e.g., job-sharing options, flextime, medical, personal, or family leave time), benefits (e.g., insurance, tax credits, dependent care reimbursement plans, subsidized care), and services (e.g., education, information and referral, counseling, and case management). For example, a leader in "caregiver-friendly" policies, S. C. Johnson in Wisconsin, offers (a) in-home assessments/consultations, facility evaluations, family consultations, and ongoing care management and monitoring through their own Employee Assistance Program; (b) long-term care insurance that employees can purchase for eligible parents/grandparents; (c) partial monetary reimbursement for acute care costs (e.g., hospital charges) when a dependent elder is too sick to be cared for by his or her regular caregiver; (d) an overnight care program that provides dependent care reimbursement when employees travel for work and have to hire a caregiver for dependent care; and (e) pretax dependent daycare reimbursement accounts (Caregiver Connection, 2010).

CHALLENGES FOR FAMILY CAREGIVER MENTAL HEALTH PROGRAMS

As the number of physically, cognitively, and emotionally frail older persons increases and more family members occupy the role of caregiver, the emotional support provided by mental health services will be in greater demand. A number of challenges need to be addressed to meet the mental health needs of family caregivers.

Increasing Participation in Programs

A limited number of caregivers attend mental health–related programs or use services that may enhance their ability to provide care. This may be because many do not identify themselves as caregivers or because they may lack a caregiving alternative that would allow them to attend therapy or other types of programs. When caregivers do access these services, it usually is because they have reached a crisis stage. Health care and other service providers need to inform caregivers of the availability of supportive services and encourage their use before caregivers experience distress. Caregivers need to be continually reminded to "take care of themselves." They also need reassurance that using services does not mean that they are failing to meet their caregiving responsibilities but rather that through the use of such services, they are maintaining and enhancing their coping abilities. Employers also need to recognize the benefits of mental health programs for their employees who are family caregivers and to make those services available through employee assistance programs.

Reaching Diverse Groups

Despite research demonstrating that minority caregivers experience burden and depression, they are less likely to participate in caregiver support programs. Because cultural norms may make it difficult for caregivers to turn to the formal network for support, services must be sensitive to the differing personal and cultural expectations held by caregivers of diverse ethnic and racial groups, sexual orientation, and geographical regions. The American Psychological Association's (2002) guidelines for providing service to culturally diverse populations provide a foundation from which to design effective interventions for families providing care. Specific principles include awareness and acknowledgment that culture is a primary aspect of human existence, and that culture and ethnicity inevitably shape behavior. Sensitivity to, knowledge of, and understanding of the cultural backgrounds of both the intervener and the family member are required in persons and programs seeking to assist individuals. Of particular importance is sensitivity to the individual's cultural background and preferences, including language, family values, community, and religious systems.

Providing Mental Health Programs in the Future

The delegates of the 2005 White House Conference on Aging (2006) passed two resolutions specifically addressing the needs of family caregivers:

- To develop a national strategy for supporting informal caregivers of seniors to enable adequate quality and supply of services
- To support older adult caregivers raising their relatives' children

For caregivers of older adults, growing consensus suggests the need for more comprehensive and multicomponent interventions. Such interventions must be individually tailored to meet the specific goals, values, and preferences of both family caregivers and the person needing care (Feinberg et al., 2011). More programs that provide a combination of education, skills training, coping techniques, and counseling show positive results, but more research is needed.

CASE STUDY

Schizophrenia Complicates Care Needs

Katherine is a 77-year-old divorced woman who has a diagnosis of schizophrenia. Although Katherine has most likely been a schizophrenic since her early 20s, she was not formally diagnosed until her mid-50s. Since her diagnosis and subsequent treatment, Katherine has enjoyed long periods when she has felt good. Like many mental health patients, however, when Katherine is feeling good she stops taking her medicine. Gradually, mood changes occur that escalate to hostile and paranoid behavior. On many occasions, she has had to be hospitalized in the psychiatric care unit of the local hospital. The length of time under such care varies, depending on how long it takes to regulate her medication.

Despite her illness, Katherine raised four sons. Two of her sons are dead, one lives out of state and takes no interest in his mother, and the fourth and youngest son, Tom, lives nearby. Tom tries to help his mother, but it isn't easy. She keeps to herself and does not let people—even her son—get close to her. In her community, she is known as a character who doesn't mince words. Although she is fiercely independent, she is dedicated to her church. One of her favorite rituals is communion, which she always takes twice a year.

Now age has compounded her problems. Katherine is overweight, is unsteady on her feet, and has arthritis and poor vision. It is increasingly difficult for her to get around. At this stage, her isolated, simple life is also becoming problematic. She requires more services such as transportation, shopping assistance, and daily monitoring to make sure she is taking her medication. Although her disease has leveled out some, she continues to have relapses when she is noncompliant with her medicine. These events are more frequent than necessary. Both her son Tom and her mental health worker of three years are concerned about her future.

Case Study Questions

1. Which mental health research data discussed in this chapter best describe Katherine?

2. Do you think Katherine's mental health diagnosis, coupled with her physical problems, makes her more at risk of institutionalization? Why or why not?

3. Katherine probably would not qualify for nursing home care as a Medicaid recipient solely because of her physical health. Under what circumstances described in the chapter could Katherine receive nursing home care paid for by Medicaid?

4. Fortunately, Katherine has the services of a professional mental health worker. From which of the mental health programs described in the chapter has Katherine most likely been receiving services?

5. What types of support may be available for Tom to help him understand and care for his mother?

LEARNING ACTIVITIES

1. Interview a mental health professional who works with older adults. What are some of the primary issues with which many older adults need assistance? What are some of the difficulties in getting older adults to participate in mental health services? Why has this professional decided or been chosen to work with older adults? How might the skills needed be similar to or different from those needed to work with other populations?

2. Ask a mental health service provider to share with you copies of the assessment tools that are used for younger and older adults. Are they similar or different? Would you have difficulty in answering some of the questions?

3. Search the Internet for the availability of peer-counseling programs for older adults across the country. Compare their approach, focus, and type of support they provide to older adults with mental health concerns.

4. Find out if your college or university provides geriatric mental health training. If so, in what department is the program located? How many students are enrolled? What is the curriculum? Where are graduates of the program employed?

5. What are the benefits of offering mental health services for older adults and their family caregivers? What are some of the barriers, and what might agencies and communities do to break down the barriers? What might keep you from accessing mental health services currently and in the future?

FOR MORE INFORMATION

International Resources

1. World Health Organization Ageing and Mental Health Resources: http://www.who.int/mental_health/resources/ageing/en/index.html

   This webpage provides access to multiple publications presenting global perspectives on late life mental health issues.

2. *Integrating Mental Health into Primary Care: A Global Perspective*: http://www.who.int/mental_health/policy/services/integratingmhintoprimarycare/en/index.html

   This report provides the rationale and practical steps for successfully integrating mental health into primary health care—a process considered particularly important for optimizing mental health supports for older adults. The authors describe how integration improves health outcomes, provide lessons from countries that have successfully integrated their mental and primary health services, and discuss 10 common principles that guide successful mental health integration, regardless of country resource level.

National Resources

1. National Institute of Mental Health, Public Information & Communications Branch, 6001 Executive Boulevard, Room 8184, Bethesda, MD 20892-9663; phone: 1-866-615-6464; www.nimh.nih.gov

The National Institute of Mental Health conducts and supports research to learn more about causes and treatment of mental and emotional disorders. Available are free publications including *Facts on Stress* and *Older Adults: Depression and Suicide Facts*.

2. Mental Health America, 2000 N. Beauregard Street, 6th Floor, Alexandria, VA 22311; phone: 703-684-5968 or 800-969-6642; www.mentalhealthamerica.net

Mental Health America provides inquirers with information about mental health topics and has a wide variety of written information about mental health topics.

3. The Geriatric Mental Health Foundation, 7910 Woodmont Avenue, Suite 1050, Bethesda, MD 20814; phone: 301-654-7850; www.gmhfonline.org/gmhf

The Geriatric Mental Health Foundation was established by the American Association for Geriatric Psychiatry to raise awareness of psychiatric and mental health disorders affecting older adults, eliminate the stigma of mental illness and treatment, promote healthy aging strategies, and increase access to quality mental health care. Review the Foundation's website for mental health information for older adults and their families, to find a geriatric psychiatrist, and for information about programs and events.

4. Alzheimer's Association, 225 North Michigan Avenue, Floor 17, Chicago, IL 60601; phone: 800-272-3900; www.alz.org

The Alzheimer's Association sponsors education programs and support services to patients and families who are coping with Alzheimer's disease. The Association offers a 24-hour hotline with information about Alzheimer's disease and local chapters and resources. Educational materials are also available.

5. *Clinical Gerontologist*. Taylor & Francis Group, 325 Chestnut Street, Suite 800, Philadelphia, PA 19106; www.tandf.co.uk/journals/WCLI

This journal presents timely material relevant to the needs of mental health professionals and all practitioners who deal with older clients and their families. All articles in this practitioners' journal feature timely, practical material relevant and applicable to the assessment and management of mental disorders in later life.

6. *Aging & Mental Health,* Taylor & Francis Group, 325 Chestnut Street, Suite 800, Philadelphia, PA 19106; phone: 800-354 1420; www.tandf.co.uk/journals/titles/13607863.asp

This journal provides a leading forum for this rapidly expanding field, which investigates the relationship between the aging process and mental health. It encourages an integrated approach between the various biopsychosocial processes and etiological factors associated with psychological changes in the elderly, and emphasizes the various strategies, therapies, and services which may be directed at improving the mental health of older adults.

Web Resources

1. American Psychological Association (APA): www.apa.org

The APA has developed a variety of resources for professionals working with older adults and family caregivers including the *Caregiver Briefcase* (www.apa.org/pi/about/publications/caregivers/index.aspx). Included in the briefcase in information about common caregiving problems, how to identify and reach caregivers, roles psychologists have in working with family caregivers, assessment tools and effective interventions, conducting caregiver research, educating and teaching about caregiving, advocating for family caregivers, and resources for diverse populations and age groups.

2. Mental Help Net: www.mentalhelp.net/

   This is quite a site! It offers more than 4,200 individual resources on mental health issues. Links to a reading room, professional resources, self-help resources, and other mental health web resources are listed. Definitely worth the visit when you have some time to spend between classes!

3. Psych Central, Dr. John Grohol's Mental Health Page: http://psychcentral.com/resources

   This psychWeb pointer helps visitors locate information on the web and is organized by topic or alphabetically. There is an incredibly lengthy list of general support resource links to other sites on the web with a brief description. It is the most comprehensive mental health listing we have found.

4. Mental Health America: www.mentalhealthamerica.net/

   Mental Health America's website contains information on depression, coping with loss, and other topics of interest.

5. Substance Abuse and Mental Health Services Administration SAMHSA: www.samhsa.gov

   SAMHSA's mission is to reduce the impact of substance abuse and mental illness on America's communities. Their site provides access to general statistics, resources, research, publications, and so forth. As part of their treatment improvement protocols (TIP) series, SAMHSA offers publications on substance abuse among older adult specifically for older adult consumers, treatment providers, social service providers, and physicians.

6. National Family Caregiver Support Program Resources:

   www.aoa.gov/AoARoot/AoA_Programs/HCLTC/Caregiver/index.aspx#resources

   Sponsored by the U.S. Administration on Aging, this resource collection provides information for families, caregivers, and professionals providing support for older adults and grandparents, and relative caregivers of children not more than 18 years of age. Resources include caregiving tips, fact sheets, findings from national studies of caregiving, and contact information for state Family Caregiver Support Programs.

CHAPTER 13

Legal Services

Fernando telephones the local Area Agency on Aging requesting emergency food. The agency staff member arranges for food to be delivered and then asks Fernando why he has none. It seems that he has not received his Social Security check for two months. He did get a couple of letters from Social Security a few months ago, but he does not read well, so he set them aside and forgot about them. He did not pay his rent this month or last, and ran out of medicine two days ago. The agency staff member arranges for Fernando to receive daily meals and medication. She also calls the local senior legal assistance program and makes an appointment for Fernando. With the assistance of a senior legal aid attorney, his Social Security checks are reinstated, and his landlord has agreed not to evict him.

Fernando's situation illustrates how one problem—in this case, a lack of food—can in turn reveal a cascade of other additional problems, many of which are or become legal issues. Older adults may experience legal problems brought about by changes in work, family, and physical health. These problems can have devastating consequences on their quality of life. For example, a retired person may be unable to collect an expected pension. After the divorce of a child, the ex-son- or daughter-in-law might refuse to let grandparents visit grandchildren—or, because of other circumstances, grandparents may effectively find themselves parents once again, caring for grandchildren. On the death or divorce of a spouse, tangible property must be divided, and when physical or mental capacity wanes, substitute decision makers may need to be appointed to make decisions on behalf of an older adult. Legal problems may also occur because older adults do not have access to legal advice before signing legal documents (W. Moore, 1992).

In this chapter, we review the federal policies that facilitated the development of legal programs serving older adults. We then briefly discuss the legal problems that older adults often encounter and with which they consequently need assistance, and take a look at the different types of legal programs designed to serve older adults. We conclude the chapter by discussing the challenges that legal programs face in meeting the legal needs of older adults.

POLICY BACKGROUND

In 1974, Congress passed legislation that created the Legal Services Corporation (LSC). Its purpose is to provide low-income individuals with minimum access to legal assistance.

The LSC is a private, nonprofit organization directed by an 11-member board appointed by Congress and the president. The LSC receives federal funding to support local legal services programs in all 50 states. Since its inception, the LSC has not been without its critics, and there have been times over the course of LSC's history when the budget submitted by the White House proposed to eliminate the LSC and its programs. The low levels of funding for LSC programs through the years have resulted in a limited number of attorneys and paralegals available to handle cases and caused many offices to limit the type of cases accepted and the number of people served. For example, the LSC Act of 1974 defined minimum access to legal assistance as having two legal services attorneys for every 10,000 poor persons. Currently, however, there is only one LSC-funded attorney for every 6,415 poor persons. This compares with approximately one attorney for every 429 persons with incomes above the poverty line (LSC, 2009).

Individuals can receive legal assistance through a local legal services office, provided that their income does not exceed 125% of the poverty line and their legal problem is civil rather than criminal. The majority of cases handled by legal services staff on behalf of older adults include housing issues, such as landlord–tenant disputes and subsidized housing complaints; family issues, such as divorce; and public benefits issues, such as Social Security, Medicare and Medicaid, and Supplemental Security Income (SSI). The recent economic crisis has increased the number of individuals living in poverty and increased the number of economy related legal issues such as home foreclosures, bankruptcy, and landlord–tenant disputes, and the demand on LSC programs has also increased. Of the 931,965 cases closed by legal services advocates in 2010, 12.9% involved legal assistance to clients older than age 60 (LSC, 2010). As mentioned above, funding levels for LSC has been rather volatile over the last 20 years, and funding has decreased, gone up slightly, or remained flat. For FY 1995, Congress appropriated $415 million to fund the LSC programs; one year later, the appropriation was $278 million, and by 2005, funding was at the same level it was in 1981—approximately $330 million (LSC, 2006). In FY 2010, federal funding inched past the 1995 level to $420 million (LSC, 2010). As a result, the number of local legal services offices dropped from 269 in 1999 to 136 in 2010. In addition, a number of national and state support centers that provided technical legal assistance and expertise on a variety of poverty law issues were eliminated.

Older Americans Act Support of Legal Assistance

Legal programs became eligible for funding under the Older Americans Act (OAA) in 1973. Amendments to the OAA in 1981 required that Area Agencies on Aging (AAAs) spend an "adequate proportion" of Title III-B dollars on legal services. A subsequent amendment in 1987 required State Units on Aging (SUAs) to set minimum percentages that AAAs must spend on providing legal assistance. The amendments in 2000 simply require that AAAs provide an adequate proportion of their funds for legal assistance. AAAs are also required to give priority to older adults with income, health care, long-term care, nutrition, housing, utilities, protective services, defense of guardianship, abuse, neglect, and age discrimination assistance legal problems (§ 305[11][E]). AAAs must contract with legal providers who have experience in delivering legal assistance, and must involve the private bar in efforts to improve older adults' access to legal assistance. In 2009–2010, $26.1 million in Title III funds was spent on legal assistance, providing close to one million legal assistance hours to older adults (Administration on Aging [AoA], n.d.-j, 2011g).

In addition to Title III-B dollars allocated to fund legal assistance programs, the Vulnerable Elder Rights Protection Activities program (Title VII), authorized in 1992 and again in the 2006 amendments to the OAA, directs funding for legal assistance support. Title VII monies are also used for states to establish focal point programs at the state level for elder rights policy review and advocacy. These state programs, called Legal Services Developers, must create statewide standards for legal service delivery, provide technical assistance to AAAs and legal service providers, promote training to representative payees and guardians, and promote pro bono programs in cooperation with the private bar. Title VII monies are also used for programs that are designed to prevent elder abuse, neglect, and exploitation. The 2006 amendments introduced a new term—*elder justice*. When used in a collective sense, elder justice means efforts to prevent, detect, treat, intervene in, and respond to elder abuse, neglect, and exploitation, and to protect individuals with diminished capacity while maximizing their autonomy. Elder justice also means the recognition of the individual's rights, including the right to be free of abuse, neglect, and exploitation. Funding is made available for programs that

- conduct public education about elder abuse and outreach to help identify possible cases of abuse and exploitation;
- promote the development of information and data systems for elder abuse reporting systems and conduct analyses of state information concerning elder abuse;
- conduct training on the identification, prevention, and treatment of elder abuse and exploitation as well as conduct training that assists the victims of elder abuse;
- promote the development of an elder abuse, neglect, and exploitation system to identify, investigate, and resolve cases;
- examine various types of shelters serving older adults, called *safe havens*, and testing various safe haven models that recognize the rights of older adults; and
- address underserved elders in rural locations, in minority populations, and low-income elders.

In addition, the 2006 amendments to Title VII added grants to promote statewide development and implementation of comprehensive multidisciplinary elder justice systems. These systems are characterized by an integrated, multidisciplinary, and collaborative system for preventing, detecting, and addressing elder abuse, neglect, and exploitation. Funds are designed to specifically support programs that provide widespread, convenient public access to the range of available elder justice information, programs, and services; that reduce duplication and gaps in the elder justice system; and that provide a uniform method for the standardization, collection, analysis, and reporting of data. Funding for programs under Title VII in FY 2010 was $21.8 million (U.S. Department of Health and Human Services [USDHHS], 2011a).

Finally, the AoA supports the delivery of legal assistance under Title IV that provides discretionary funds to support research and demonstration projects. Since 1998, Title IV dollars have supported the creation of legal hotlines for older adults. As mentioned in Chapter 2, OAA funds are used to provide national support and consultation to those who deliver legal assistance to older adults. For example, the Center for Social Gerontology and its National Support Center in Law and Aging, the National Senior Citizens Law Center, the National Legal Resource Center, the National Pension Assistance Resource Center, National Center on Elder Abuse, National Consumer Protection Technical Resource Center, and the National Bar Association's Black Elderly Legal Assistance Support Project are some programs that have been supported by OAA dollars.

In addition to the provisions supporting legal assistance for older adults under the OAA, the Elder Justice Act (EJA), subtitle H of the Patient Protection and Affordable Care Act, passed into law in 2010, supports a number of initiatives designed to protect vulnerable elders. The initiatives include

- establishment of a federal Elder Justice Coordinating Council that will advise the Secretary of Health and Human Services on how best to coordinate the activities of federal, state, and local entities concerned with elder abuse and exploitation;

- establishment of a 27-member expert advisory board charged with creating short-term and long-term strategic plans for elder justice;

- creation of a federal funding stream for state Adult Protective Services (APS) and dedicated resources at the HHS for collection and dissemination of data and best practices and other research related to APS;

- increasing resources for the Long-Term Care Ombudsman Program;

- creation of Forensic Centers and a National Training Institute for Surveyors;

- investment in incentives to enhance and expand long-term care staffing, which includes the creation of a national nurse aide registry;

- requirement for immediate reporting to law enforcement of crimes in a long-term care facility and establishment of civil monetary penalties for failure to report;

- creation of penalties for long-term care facilities that retaliate against an employee for filing a complaint against or reporting a long-term care facility that violates reporting requirements; and

- establishment of a nationwide program for national and state background checks on direct patient access employees of long-term care facilities. (Elder Justice Coalition, n.d.; National Council on Aging, n.d.)

The implementation of the provisions of the EJA is a collaborative effort of the HHS AoA, the Department of Labor (DoL), and the Department of Justice, and although funding for these initiatives were authorized in the Act, funds were not appropriated in FY 2012 (Elder Justice Act of 2009; USDHHS, 2012c).

USERS: LEGAL PROBLEMS OF OLDER ADULTS

Obtaining a profile of who uses legal assistance programs is a difficult task because many programs do not compile detailed information about client characteristics (e.g., marital status, age, income, education) or are hesitant to publicly reveal client characteristics to protect client confidentiality, or such data are provided only to local AAAs or SUAs and not published in academic journals. Thus, statistical information on Title III-B legal assistance clients is inadequate. Some inferences about client characteristics can be made, however, by examining the type of legal problems for which clients seek assistance. In addition, the type of cases that legal programs accept will affect the type of clients served by those programs. Moreover, legal assistance programs funded under the OAA target socially and financially needy older adults. An older adult with a sizable estate will no doubt be served by the family attorney or be referred to an estate lawyer rather than to a Title III legal aid program. In the next sections, we will review the civil and criminal legal problems of older adults and, when available, the extent to which older adults report having those problems.

Legal problems emerge in various ways. Older adults who lack an understanding about what constitutes a legal problem or how laws originate may not be able to identify that a legal remedy exists when problems occur. Persons who work with older adults also must be aware of potential legal problems so that referrals can be made to appropriate legal services.

Legal problems can be categorized as either civil or criminal. Civil legal problems are disputes between individuals or organizations, whereas criminal legal problems are those acts that threaten the well-being of the state and include crimes against the person such as assault, homicide, rape, and robbery. Civil legal problems commonly experienced by older adults are presented next, followed by criminal problems.

Family Issues

Divorce

In the year 2010, 10.6% of individuals 65 and older were divorced, but more older women were divorced than older men (11.4% vs. 9.6%, respectively; U.S. Census Bureau, 2011f). Although divorce is uncommon in later life and less frequent than in other age groups, its consequences can be financially devastating to older women who divorce. Many women in the current cohort of older adults have been lifelong homemakers who often have no financial support apart from those benefits associated with being a spouse. When husbands file for divorce, lifelong homemakers may discover that the house, utilities, bank accounts, credit cards, and automobiles do not have both names on titles and accounts. Divorce might even exclude the wife's access to her husband's pension. Such arrangements leave them financially vulnerable and in need of legal assistance to protect their rights to marital property.

Grandparent Visitation and Grandparents Raising Grandchildren

It is estimated that 56 million older adults are grandparents (Fields, O'Connell, & Downs, 2001). Researchers have documented that grandparents occupy important roles within the family network. For example, grandparents provide emotional and instrumental support, offer stability in times of crisis, assume parental responsibilities for grandchildren when parents are unavailable, and serve as the keepers of family history (Matthews & Sprey, 1984; Minkler & Roe, 1996; Wood & Liossis, 2007). Strong emotional bonds are not uncommon between grandparents and grandchildren (Hodgson, 1995; Pecchioni & Croghan, 2002; Roberto & Stroes, 1992).

Various disruptions in the nuclear family can fracture the relationship between grandparents and grandchildren. For example, divorce, death of a parent, adoption of a grandchild by a friend or relative, or termination of parental rights may sever intergenerational bonds. Until recently, grandparents had no legal recourse to aid them in re-establishing contact with their grandchildren. Now, however, all 50 states have enacted laws that allow grandparents to petition the court for visitation rights. State statutes vary with regard to who can petition, the circumstances that must be present in the nuclear family before visitation rights are considered, and how the court determines whether grandparent visitation would be in the best interests of the grandchildren.

Other grandparents have a different set of problems concerning their grandchildren. Growing numbers of grandparents have found themselves parenting their grandchildren (Minkler & Roe, 1996). According to the U.S. Census Bureau (2011c), 2.7 million grandparents are responsible for the basic needs (e.g., food, shelter, clothing) of the grandchildren they live with; these grandparents represent 43% of all grandparents who live with their grandchildren. Grandparents take on the parental role when, for a variety of reasons, parents are unable to care for their children. Grandparents who become parents often need assistance in filing for additional health or income benefits or in filing for adoption or custody.

Estate Planning

A will provides a means to specifically identify and distribute tangible property after death. Dying without a will (intestate) results in the distribution of property among family members in accordance with state law. Thus, the distribution of the assets of a person who has died intestate can be complicated, time consuming, and subject to conflicts among family members regarding the value and ownership of the property. Therefore, many older adults—even those with small estates—can benefit from drafting a will. In a statewide surveys of the legal needs of older adults in Utah, Georgia, North Carolina, and Michigan, problems with wills and estates were one of the top three legal issues with which older adults wanted help (Gunther & Ormsby, 2004; Lamb & Morgan, 2010; Michigan Office of Services to the Aging & Elder Law of Michigan, 2008; Thomas, 2006).

Income

Many older adults live on fixed incomes and rely wholly or in part on public income programs such as Social Security, SSI, Railroad Retirement, or veterans' benefits. Some 22% of older adults rely on Social Security for their sole source of income; 2 million receive SSI benefits (Social Security Administration, 2010, 2012b). Given the complex and complicated regulations that govern the administration of these programs, it is not surprising that many legal problems can arise.

Legal problems occur when program intake workers refuse to process applications because older adults do not have the documents needed to prove their age, work history, marital status, or financial status. In addition, eligibility criteria are often excessively complicated, confusing, or easily misinterpreted. State and federal programs such as old age assistance programs and SSI base eligibility on financial need, and applicants must prove that their income and asset levels are below eligibility amounts. Definitions of income and assets can create confusion because in-kind assistance, such as gifts of food, can count as income. An otherwise qualified individual may be denied access to critical financial assistance. Finally, legal problems can surface even after individuals are receiving benefits. For example, because eligibility for Social Security is based on work history, an error in an earnings record can result in a smaller benefit amount. Mistakes occur in an estimated 4% of earnings records (J. L. Matthews & Berman, 2010).

A second type of legal problem related to income assistance programs occurs when participants receive a notice of overpayment or notice of termination of benefits. Overpayments occur when income amounts exceed eligibility criteria or when the benefit amount paid to the recipient is miscalculated. For example, the father of one of the authors of this book sought legal assistance after he received a $13,000 overpayment notice from Social Security (the notice suggested that he send Social Security a check for the entire amount within 30 days!). Further investigation revealed that an error made by a Social Security technician in recording his working income into his monthly Social Security benefit amount for a three-year period had caused the overpayment. A legal services paralegal was able to negotiate with Social Security a repayment plan that took a small amount of money from his monthly check until the overpayment was paid.

Overpayments also can result when older adults receive income benefits from more than one program. Consider the case of Mary Espinosa, who received a small Social Security check, based on her husband's earnings, together with an SSI check, for a total monthly income of $425. Following Mr. Espinosa's death, Mary went to the Social Security office to report his death so that her technician could adjust her benefit amount. Mary continued to receive both checks until one day she received a notice of overpayment demanding that she repay $3,000 in SSI benefits. Mary did not realize that, although her SSI intake worker sat next to her Social Security intake worker in the same office, she needed to notify both workers of her change in circumstances. A legal advocate can determine whether the overpayment actually occurred and, if the situation warrants, can appeal the overpayment decision or, if necessary, can negotiate a repayment schedule.

Although older adults can appeal these adverse decisions, they may not understand why they have been denied benefits or have had their benefits reduced and may assume that nothing can be done. A reduction or termination of benefits could place the older adult in a position of being unable to pay for rent, food, or necessary medical assistance. Therefore, it is critical that older adults consult legal advocates when there are changes in benefit eligibility or amount. In a number of statewide legal needs assessments, problem with government benefits was one of the top legal needs of older adults (AARP, 2008a; Godfrey & Weber, 2007; Gunther & Ormsby, 2004; Thomas, 2006).

Employment

Age Discrimination

In 2012, 16.9% of persons aged 65 and older were working and 6.5 million workers over 55 were employed part time as well (USDoL, 2012b, 2012c). Older adults who wish to remain working or to obtain work may encounter age-based discriminatory employment practices. Although the number of older adults who have experienced workplace discrimination is unknown, researchers report that many managers have negative stereotypes about older workers. These include the perception that older workers will not perform as well as younger workers, that older workers are not cost-effective, and that older workers are not suitable for training (Gordon & Arvey, 2004; Rix, 1994; Sterns & McDaniel, 1994). Such attitudes and beliefs, although not supported by empirical research (see Commonwealth Fund, 1993; Posthuma & Campion, 2009), can lead to discrimination against older workers.

To counter age discrimination against older workers, Congress enacted the Age Discrimination in Employment Act (ADEA) in 1967. Although some exceptions exist, the ADEA prohibits employment discrimination against persons aged 40 or older. Under the Act, employers must not refuse to hire individuals on the basis of their age; discriminate with respect to compensation, terms, conditions, or privileges; limit, segregate, or classify employees in a way that adversely affects their employment status or opportunities because of age; or retaliate against employees who exercise their rights under ADEA (P. J. Strauss, Wolf, & Schilling, 1990). The ADEA also prohibits employment agencies from engaging in discriminatory employment practices. Older workers who feel they have been discriminated against can file a claim with the Equal Employment Opportunity Commission and may also have claims under state law. In 2005, the commission received 16,585 age discrimination complaints; by 2011, that number had risen to 23,465 (U.S. Equal Employment Opportunity Commission, n.d.). The number of age discrimination complaints is likely to continue to increase with the aging of the baby boomer cohort.

Pensions

For some older adults, private pension plans provide additional income in retirement. According to the Employee Benefit Research Institute (EBRI), the number of private pensions over the years has vacillated from 311,094 in 1975, to 733,029 in 1987, and to 730,031 in 1998, but most recently (2009) has declined to 706,667 (USDoL, 2011c). In 2008, 43.6% of all full- and part-time workers participated in an employment-based retirement plan (Topoleski, 2009). As of 2010, 66% of private sector workers, 94% of state and local public sector workers, and almost all federal workers were covered by a pension plan (EBRI, 2011c; Lichtenstein & Verma, 2003). Unlike Social Security, whose regulations apply uniformly to all older adults, pension plans vary from employer to employer. We reviewed the types of pension plans in more detail in Chapter 9.

The Employee Retirement Income Security Act (ERISA) of 1974 regulates the administration of pensions. Retirees can file a federal suit if pension benefits have been unfairly denied, if future benefits are affected by changes in the pension plan, if the plan or funds have been improperly managed, if other rights outlined in the plan are breached, or if the plan does not disclose information required by ERISA (J. L. Matthews & Berman, 2012). Although retirees have various legal safeguards to their pension funds, it is probable that the majority of retirees are unaware of their rights under ERISA.

Health Care

Medical Insurance

As with income assistance programs, older adults can encounter legal problems with Medicare and Medicaid. (We discussed these in greater detail in Chapter 11.) Most legal difficulties with Medicare Part A can occur when coverage is denied for services rendered. A denial most often occurs when the Medicare insurance carrier determines that services were not medically necessary, that services could have been provided on an outpatient basis, or that services were custodial rather than medical (J. L. Matthews & Berman, 2012). Disputes of payments under Part B usually concern the scope of coverage or the amount approved for payment by Part B carriers. Appeals against adverse decisions are made to the Social Security Administration.

Because Medicare does not cover all medical expenses and older adults must pay for deductibles and uncovered services out of pocket, many purchase supplemental insurance (Medigap) policies to help pay medical expenses. Unfortunately, older adults are often victims of Medigap insurance fraud—pressured to switch companies or to purchase duplicate policies, denied coverage because of pre-existing clauses, or refused for renewal of a policy for reasons other than nonpayment. In recent years, the selling of Medigap policies has come under scrutiny and regulation. Federal law requires each state to adopt standardized Medigap benefit policies. When violations in these regulations occur, advocates can pursue legal remedies with the state insurance commissioner or through a civil court.

Medicaid eligibility is based on income and asset levels and on being age 65 or older, blind, or disabled, or having dependent children. Because Medicaid is a state and federal program, income and asset levels for eligibility vary among states. Under the Medicaid program, adverse decisions with regard to eligibility and coverage can be appealed. Legal difficulties with health care insurance were mentioned as a legal problem experienced by 24% and 20% of elders in Georgia and Ohio, respectively (AARP, 2008a; Thomas, 2006).

Advance Directives for Health Care

Readers may remember hearing about the case of Terri Schiavo. Terri, age 26, collapsed in her home in 1990 and never regained consciousness. After she had been in a vegetative state for eight years, Terri's husband petitioned the court to have her feeding tube removed, but her parents opposed this decision. In part because Terri had only made oral declarations of what her end-of-life decisions would be, and because her parents did not believe she was in a vegetative state, legal appeals—including involvement by the Florida Legislature and the U.S. Congress—continued until February 2005. A final legal decision to remove the feeding tube from Terri was made on March 18, 2005, and Terri died on March 31, 2005, at the age of 41 (University of Miami Ethics Program, n.d.). Due to this and two other similar end-of-life cases that have gained national attention—the Karen Ann Quinlan case in 1975 and the Nancy Cruzan (*Cruzan v. Harmon*) case in 1990—and the increase in the number of persons who wish to remain in control of health care decisions after they are unable to articulate their desires, states have enacted laws that allow for the creation of advance directives. *Advance directives* are legal documents that convey the wishes of an individual regarding personal health care decisions and that must be executed while the individual is still competent. Two types of advance directives are the durable power of attorney for health care and the living will.

Older adults who want to articulate their health care wishes can do so in many states by executing a durable power of attorney for health care decisions. A durable power of attorney appoints an agent to make health care decisions outlined in the document. A living will also provides a legal mechanism that enables individuals to express their wishes regarding life-sustaining treatment. Living wills are narrower in scope because they authorize the withdrawal of certain life-sustaining procedures only in situations in which the individual has a terminal illness or is comatose (Alexander, 1991). Only a small percentage of community-dwelling older adults report that they have executed a living will. Hopp (2000) found that 29% had executed either a living will or a durable power of attorney. In contrast, two national studies that examined the circumstances of older adults who had died in a nursing home, in a hospital, or at home found that 70.8% and 67.6% had an advanced directive (Silveira, Kim, & Langa, 2010; Teno, Gruneir, Schwartz, Nanda, & Wetle, 2007). Providing preventive legal assistance to older adults by drafting these documents before they are needed can reduce the occurrence of problems in the future.

Consumer Fraud

Older persons are prime targets of consumer fraud and deceptions. According to the Federal Bureau of Investigation, the amount of money being scammed primarily from older adults is approximately $500 million a year from telemarketers and $25 billion a year on bogus health products (Federal Bureau of Investigation, 2005; U.S. Senate Special Committee on Aging, 2000). Older adults tend to be more vulnerable to certain types of telemarketing fraud, including sweepstake fraud, lottery club scams, magazine sales scams, and reverse mortgage and other types of banking fraud. For a variety of reasons, older adults may be more likely than others to be victims of consumer fraud. First, physical frailty or mental impairments may leave older adults at a disadvantage in understanding and negotiating with persistent salespersons. Second, older homebound persons may welcome opportunities to shop at home and may enjoy the company of friendly visiting salespersons and be more likely to be at home when the telemarketer calls. Third, older adults with low incomes may be especially susceptible to apparent opportunities to increase their incomes, take advantage of promised low prices, or send away for prize money. Federal and state consumer protection laws provide legal remedies for consumer fraud cases. Older victims of consumer fraud need to consult legal advocates to help them recover the costs of their fraudulent purchases.

Nursing Homes and Long-Term Care

Of older adults, 3.3%, or approximately 1.25 million persons, reside in long-term care facilities at any one time; of adults aged 65 and older, however, it is estimated that 30.5% of older adults can expect to stay in a long-term care facility (American Health Care Association, 2011; Laditka, 1998; U.S. Census Bureau, 2012a). A variety of legal concerns may unfold during a resident's stay in a long-term care facility. One source of legal problems can be the admission agreement. Studies evaluating the legality of nursing home admission agreements found that many contained illegal, questionable provisions or confusing provisions (Amborgi & Leonard, 1988; Pearson, 2004; Wacker, 1985). Unfortunately, when problems do occur with the provisions set forth in the admissions agreement, older adults or their family members may not realize that they have a valid legal challenge to those contracts.

A second concern is the enforcement of residents' rights. Federal and state governments have enacted numerous laws to protect the rights of nursing home residents and to promote a high standard of care. Nursing homes must provide care and services to residents in a way that promotes and maintains the residents' physical, social, and mental well-being (Eldeman, 1990). Federal law protects residents' rights, including the right to privacy, the right to speak freely, the right to refuse treatment, and the right to freedom of association (see Chapter 19). Although nursing home residents and their family members can call on an ombudsman to advocate on behalf of the resident, there may be instances when a breach of residents' rights calls for a legal remedy.

Substitute Decision Making

Imagine for a moment that you have failed to open your mail or failed to go online to monitor your monthly payments for a couple of months. What would be the consequences of such a seemingly innocent mistake? No doubt your utilities would be on the verge of being turned off. Your car payment and insurance bills would be overdue, and letters threatening repossession would be in the stack of unopened letters. Bank accounts would be left unattended and important notices left unanswered. Such a scenario is not hard to imagine happening to older adults who are cognitively impaired and unable to manage their personal financial affairs.

Older adults who need assistance managing their personal affairs have legal ways to appoint a substitute decision maker. Legal documents such as a power of attorney or durable power of attorney are used to appoint someone to manage financial affairs. Individuals must be mentally competent before they can execute these documents. A durable power of attorney, unlike the power of attorney, continues to remain in effect on the incapacity of the executor.

Another type of substitute decision maker is a guardian or conservator. Courts can appoint guardians or conservators who have the authority to make personal or financial decisions on behalf of an incompetent adult. Before a guardian or conservator can be appointed, the individual must file a petition with the court and prove that the older adult, called a *ward*, is mentally incompetent. Once appointed, guardians have the power to make decisions about every aspect of the ward's life, including living arrangements, financial affairs, health care, and social relationships. Because of the extensive nature of the guardian powers, guardianships should be sought only when other less restrictive options are unavailable (Keith & Wacker, 1994).

Criminal Legal Problems

Criminal legal problems include assault, robbery, rape, burglary, larceny, and motor vehicle theft. Many researchers report that older adults are fearful of being a victim of crime, with older adults of color and older women expressing greater levels of fear of crime than do older Whites and older men (Acierno, Rheingold, Resnick, & Kilpatrick, 2002; G. R. Lee, 1983; Michigan Offices of Services to the Aging, cited in Kart, 1997). Although older adults are fearful of being victimized, they are far less likely to be victims of crimes (Catalano, 2006; Truman, 2011) compared to younger adults. As shown in Exhibit 13.1, the crime rate for selected crimes

Exhibit 13.1 Victimization by Type of Crime and Age (rate per 1,000 persons)

Age	All Crime	Sexual Assault	Robbery	Assault
15 to 17	23.0	1.7*	2.7*	18.6
18 to 20	33.9	1.1	5.9	26.9
21 to 24	26.9	1.5*	3.7	21.7
25 to 34	18.8	1.3*	2.5	15.0
35 to 49	12.6	0.6*	1.5	10.4
50 to 64	10.9	<.05*	1.3	9.7
65+	2.4	0.1*	0.6*	1.7

Source: Truman (2011).

*Based on 10 or fewer sample cases.

against older adults is markedly less than the rate for adults under age 65. Even though older adults are less likely to be victims of crime, the outcome is often more physically, emotionally, and financially devastating than for younger victims of crime (Covey & Menard, 1988; Crandall, 1991). One of the more significant crimes affecting older adults is elder abuse.

Best Practice: National Association of Triads, Inc.

Representatives from the AARP, the International Association of Chiefs of Police, and the National Sheriff's Association developed the concept of triads in 1988 to promote older adults' safety, reduce their criminal victimization, and enhance the delivery of law enforcement services to them. In 1989, the first triad partnership was created in St. Martin Parish, Louisiana. Local triads are guided by SALT (Seniors and Law Enforcement Together) Councils, which plan activities and programs that are designed to benefit both law enforcement and older adults. There are triads in 36 states, and the National Association of Triads, Inc. is the organization that provides advice, support, technical assistance, and training to local triads.

For more information, contact the National Association of Triads, Inc. (NATI), 1450 Duke Street, Alexandria, VA 22314; phone: 703-836-7827; www.nationaltriad.org. Check out Ontario, Canada's, version of Seniors and Law Enforcement Together program at www.hrps.on.ca/CommunityPolicing/Seniors/SALT/Pages/default.aspx.

Elder Abuse

Elder abuse most often occurs within the family context, and perpetrators are usually the elders' primary caregivers (Pillemer & Finkelhor, 1989). Elder abuse includes physical, psychological, and financial abuse as well as neglect. Victims of physical and psychological abuse are often in poor emotional health; the victims of neglect are usually older women, with multiple frailties, who are cognitively impaired and socially isolated (Teaster, Dugar, Mendiondo, Abner, & Cecil, 2006; Wolf, 1996). The prevalence of older adults who have been injured, exploited, or mistreated by someone on whom they rely on for care is estimated to be between 2% and 10% (Lachs & Pillemer, 2004). The first national study of elder abuse conducted by the National Center on Elder Abuse at the American Public Human Services Association (formerly the American Public Welfare Association) found that some 551,000 older adults living in domestic settings were abused or neglected, or experienced self-neglect (AoA, 1998). All 50 states have legislation that allows for intervention and protection of vulnerable, disabled, or incapacitated adults. The responsibility for investigating such cases rests with either the state Social Services Department or the SUA (Wolf, 1996). Because a family member is most often the abuser, and because the older adult is often frail and dependent on the caregiver for assistance, intervention can be difficult. It is estimated that for every one case of abuse, neglect, exploitation, or self-neglect reported to authorities, five cases go unreported (American Public Human Services Association, 1998). For competent older adults, legal assistance can help evict or restrain the abuser; for incompetent victims, protective services can be implemented. The designated state agency, usually the Department of Social Services, offers protective services to help the victim resolve the abuse or, as a last resort, may seek a guardianship to protect the victim from exploitation. Protective services are also called to intervene in cases of self-neglect.

For Your Files: The Clearinghouse on Abuse and Neglect of the Elderly (CANE)

The Clearinghouse on Abuse and Neglect of the Elderly (CANE) at the University of Delaware is the nation's largest digital library of published research, training resources, government documents, and other resources on elder abuse. You can obtain citations and brief summaries of peer-reviewed journal articles, books, agency reports, transcripts of hearings, news articles, videos, memoranda of understanding, and online resources addressing the abuse and neglect, self-neglect, and financial exploitation of elders. CANE is a partner of the National Center on Elder Abuse (NCEA). NCEA is funded by the AoA, HHS. You can access the database at http://www.cane.udel.edu.

LEGAL ASSISTANCE PROGRAMS

Despite the creation of legal programs through the OAA and the LSC, many older adults—particularly low-income and minority elders—do not receive legal assistance with civil problems. This is particularly true for those older adults who have incomes just above the LSC guidelines mentioned earlier yet cannot afford the costs of a private attorney. Furthermore, the limited numbers of attorneys and paralegals staffing legal assistance programs means that these programs are serving fewer clients and accepting fewer numbers and types of cases. To address the lack of available legal assistance for older adults, SUAs and local AAAs have developed unique methods of delivering legal assistance and have formed partnerships with state and local private bar associations to broaden their involvement in the delivery of legal services for older adults. These different methods of delivering legal assistance are discussed below.

Legal Hotlines

According to W. Moore (1992), improving access to legal assistance must begin with improving the entry point to legal assistance and increasing the provision of preventive legal assistance. Legal hotlines have emerged as one way to address both problems. There are currently legal hotlines operating in 31 states, the District of Columbia, and Puerto Rico, which are supported by funding from the AoA. Residents of the state who are aged 60 and older can call a toll-free number and speak directly to an attorney (AoA, 2010a). Attorneys offer legal information or advice, refer those who need representation and can afford to pay for it to attorneys who charge a fixed rate per hour, or refer those who cannot afford legal assistance to a local legal services program. Users of hotline services, who frequently have low income, report high levels of satisfaction, and the majority would recommend the services to a friend. In 2005, a nationwide study of 23 legal hotlines reported a total of 96,005 calls with each hotline program handling an average of 4,572 calls (AARP Foundation, 2006). Advantages of a telephone hotline service include being accessible to persons who are homebound or without transportation, being able to give prompt information and thereby reduce the anxiety level of older adults, and being able to resolve simple problems quickly.

For Your Files: The Samuel Sadin Institute on Law

The Samuel Sadin Institute on Law at the Brookdale Center on Aging at Hunter College acts as a legal support program for social workers, paralegals, attorneys, and other professionals engaged in advocacy assistance to older persons who are poor. An interdisciplinary staff of attorneys and social workers has expertise in Medicare, Medicaid, SSI, Social Security disability, home care, health care decision making, adult protective services, Medigap, and long-term care insurance. The staff is available to provide technical assistance on public benefit laws and regulations to elected public officials and staff of other not-for-profit agencies. More than 2,500 professionals are trained annually, and telephone case consultations average 1,000 calls per month. The institute publishes many publications, including the *Benefits Checklist for Older Adults* and training manuals.

For more information, contact the Samuel Sadin Institute on Law, Brookdale Center for Healthy Aging & Longevity of Hunter College, 2180 Third Avenue at 119th Street, 8th Floor, New York, NY 10035; phone: 212-396-7835; www.brookdale.org.

Examples of legal hotline programs are the Legal Services of Northern California Senior Legal Hotline (n.d.) and the Access to Justice Foundation Legal HelpLine for Older Kentuckians (Godfrey & Weber, 2007). The Access to Justice Foundation Legal HelpLine for Older Kentuckians provides a statewide toll-free hotline offering legal advice, information and referral services. This program has been in operation since 1999 and has assisted over 18,000 clients. In Idaho, the Idaho Legal Aid Services' Senior Legal Hotline targets low-income and limited-English-proficiency seniors in rural areas, migrant worker seniors, Hispanic seniors, and Native American seniors. And in Maryland, the Senior Legal Helpline is intentionally working to extend outreach to Korean, Chinese, and Spanish elders (AoA, 2010a).

Bar Association Services

Edelstein (1996) outlined bar association services that may be useful to older adults. These include lawyer referral services, referral and information services, reduced-fee panels, volunteer lawyer panels, and outreach programs.

Lawyer Referral Services

A lawyer referral service is typically composed of a panel of attorneys who will give advice or represent individuals with legal problems. Callers are referred to an attorney who has some expertise with the type of legal problem encountered and who is located nearby. The initial consultation is provided free of charge or for a small fee, with no obligation to continue with that particular attorney. No prescreening is done on the legal merits of the case.

Lawyer Referral and Information Services

A lawyer referral and information service is similar to the lawyer referral service except that calls are screened more carefully for legal merit, and simple problems are often resolved before the referral is made. The service is provided at no cost or for a nominal fee, and there is no further obligation by the client to continue with the attorney.

Reduced-Fee Panels

Reduced-fee panels are coordinated by local or state bar associations and comprise attorneys who will provide legal assistance in specialized areas of law. For example, the Maryland State Bar Association sponsors a Sixty-Plus Legal Program through which participating attorneys offer low-cost assistance with wills, living wills, powers of attorney, and small estate administration for older adults with moderate or low incomes.

Volunteer Lawyer Panels

Some communities have created pro bono legal programs staffed with volunteer attorneys who provide free legal assistance to older adults. These pro bono programs usually require clients to meet some financial guidelines and often limit the type of legal problems they accept. One pro bono program enlists volunteer paralegals who deliver free legal services at "Saturday clinics" at a different site each month in minority communities (W. Moore, 1992).

State and local bar associations also are involved in educating older adults about potential legal problems. Bar associations may sponsor continuing education sessions about legal problems germane to older adults, produce legal handbooks for senior citizens, and sponsor "law days" for older adults.

Outreach Programs

The American Bar Association's Commission on Law and Aging funds a number of legal outreach programs through its Partnerships in Law and Aging Program. Outreach programs are designed to deliver legal services to isolated older adults. One example of such a program is the Urban Justice Center in New York City, which partnered with Harlem Hospital and the Columbia Law School to expand their Mental Health Project to represent low-income seniors at risk because of mental illness. The project provides comprehensive services to help clients obtain income, health benefits, obtain or retain housing, and avoid incarceration or institutionalization. In Shreveport, Louisiana, the Grandparents Raising Grandchildren Legal Assistance Program provides grandparents raising grandchildren with pro bono legal advice and representation in guardianship, custody, adoption, and related matters (Philpotts, 2010; Edelstein, 2004).

Dispute Resolution Programs

Mediation services offer individuals an alternative to the costs associated with traditional court litigation. Mediation is done through a neutral third party who guides the parties to a mutual resolution. Mediation is usually less expensive, less time consuming, and less stressful than traditional legal methods, and mediation settlements tend to be more lasting than settlements imposed by the courts (Edelstein, 1996).

Dispute resolution programs are emerging across the country as a viable alternative to going to court. Many dispute resolutions programs are sponsored by local or state bar associations and university law school programs. For many older adults who have legal problems, a dispute resolution program may be a better option than the traditional court system, although the extent to which older adults use dispute resolution services is unknown.

Money Management Programs

For some older adults, paying bills and managing finances becomes an overwhelming task because of health limitations or inexperience. Although family members frequently assist with money management tasks (R. Stone et al., 1987), many older adults who do not have an informal support network to turn to are not able to easily secure this type of assistance. Daily money management (DMM) programs have been created to assist older adults with their financial activities. These programs are provided through local social service agencies, AAAs, and nonprofit organizations. More recently, private for-profit DMM agencies have emerged across the country, and the American Association of Daily Money Managers has DMM certification program as well as a national list of certified money managers. These programs help clients with bill paying and check depositing, sorting through medical bills and filing claims to insurance companies, budgeting, and preparing durable powers of attorney or burial trusts (Choi-Allum, 2007; Tokarek, 1996).

Best Practice: Dispute Resolution Center

The Dispute Resolution Center in Saint Paul, Minnesota, is a private nonprofit organization founded to provide mediation, facilitation, training, and referral services in the Twin Cities. As a community resource, the center assists individuals, families, community groups, government agencies, and businesses in resolving conflicts. A majority of the individuals served by the center are people in lower income ranges. Through constructive means such as mediation and facilitation, the center has helped in thousands of matters to prevent the need for costly litigation.

The Dispute Resolution Center is a Certified Community Dispute Resolution Program under the guidelines administered by the Supreme Court. The center works with social service and government agencies, and handles between 400 and 500 cases on average each year. Community problems handled include matters of public safety concerning traffic and parking; rental arrangements; consumer-merchant disputes; neighborhood conflicts about noise, pets, and property lines; and small claims concerning money, property damage, or breach of contract.

To accomplish its goals of fostering open communication and encouraging positive responses to conflict, the Dispute Resolution Center recruits and trains a diverse group of volunteer mediators. The center benefits from more than 50 volunteers who represent a broad cross-section of the community. In 1998, the volunteers contributed approximately 2,000 volunteer hours as mediators, office workers, and board members.

The Dispute Resolution Center also provides workshops and presentations on conflict resolution and communication for community groups and organizations such as schools, colleges, landlord or tenant unions, community councils, block clubs, youth centers, and other audiences.

For more information, contact Dispute Resolution Center, 974 West Seventh Street, Saint Paul, MN 55102; phone: 612-292-7791; www.disputeresolutioncenter.org.

CHALLENGES FOR LEGAL PROGRAMS AND SERVICES

Removing Barriers to Legal Services

One important challenge for legal assistance programs is to identify and remove the barriers that impede older adults in obtaining legal relief. Statewide surveys of the legal needs of older adults have begun to document some of the barriers that act to keep older adults from seeking legal services. Among them are personal factors, such as a lack of knowledge about legal rights and where to find legal assistance. Lamb and Morgan (2010) found that although many older North Carolinians responded stated they did not have a need for legal advice, 18% to 45% of respondents reported problems with government benefits, housing, credit, or credit cards. Godfrey and Weber (2007) found that over a third of older Kentuckians (36.7%) did not recognize any of the organizations that provided legal assistance that listed on a survey. Similarly, Gunther and Ormsby's (2004) survey of older Utahans found that 56% never heard of legal services programs.

Across the Globe: Legal Aid for Older Adults in the United Kingdom

Community Legal Advice is a free and confidential advice service in England and Wales. Individuals living on a low income or on benefits, including older adults, may be eligible for free advice from legal advisers on issues such as benefits and tax credits, debt, education, housing, employment, and family problems. Callers to the Community Legal Advice helpline will be provided advice regarding the legal help needed and if they qualify financially will be eligible for legal aid representation. If callers are not eligible for legal aid representation, Community Legal Advice will put callers in touch with organizations that can help. Community Legal Advice has a free translation service available in 170 languages.

For more information, go to www.gov.uk/community-legal-advice.

As mentioned earlier, if older adults are not aware that a problem they are experiencing has legal remedies, they will not be inclined to seek out legal advice or assistance. Even when it may seem obvious to most that the problem encountered needs the assistance of a legal professional, for many older adults, the legal system seems complicated, foreign, and intimidating. It is often difficult to find an appropriate attorney, and frail older adults might not have the physical or mental stamina to fight what they imagine will be lengthy litigation, with its complications and confusing legalese. Furthermore, having a legal problem can elicit feelings of embarrassment, especially when the legal problem has occurred because of poor judgment or lack of foresight (Lamb & Morgan, 2010) that act to limit access to services.

Making Legal Programs More Accessible

Another challenge is to make legal programs easily accessible. Although a great deal of information about legal issues and legal assistance programs are available online, statewide surveys show that older adults prefer phone helplines, face-to-face consultations, or free handbooks on common legal questions (AARP, 2008a; Godfrey & Weber, 2007; Lamb & Morgan, 2010; Michigan Office of Services to the Aged, 2008) and are not comfortable accessing this information via websites.

Programs that do provide legal assistance are often not readily accessible to those without transportation (Lamb & Morgan, 2010) or people who live in rural areas. Although legal services may be available in a given community, if they are located away from low-income neighborhoods or segregated neighborhoods, such programs will be less available to these at-risk populations. Language barriers and a lack of cultural sensitivity can keep many older adults from various ethnic backgrounds from seeking legal assistance. This is especially significant because racial and ethic minority elders have greater unmet legal needs than do their White counterparts (AARP, cited in W. Moore, 1989).

Supporting Legal Programs in the Future

Finally, in recent years, legal assistance programs have been chronically underfunded and understaffed. The underfunding of legal aid programs has become more acute since advent of the Great Recession in 2009. For example, data show that in 2009, for every client serviced by a LSC-funded legal aid program, one person is turned away because of the lack of program resources (LSC, 2009). If the legal needs of low-income and middle-class older adults are to be addressed, funds for legal programs that serve older adults should be increased. The 2005 White House Conference on Aging (2006) delegates recommended resolutions that supported a number of new policies that ensured authorization of and adequate access to legal assistance programs. In addition, delegates recommended the implementation of programs and policies that affect older adults in a number of legal concerns. Some of the strategies included the following:

Access to Legal Services

- Ensuring access of seniors to legal services through funding of legal service providers

- Providing access to legal counsel for elderly in fraud and abuse situations

- Providing more adequate federal funding for civil legal aid nationwide for low- and moderate-income older Americans of diverse cultural backgrounds

Advance Directives

- Educating the public and legal and health care providers on end of life, and the legal and ethical obligation to follow advance care directives

- Developing health care and community collaborations with faith-based communities, aging service, and other community providers to promote advance care planning and completion of advance directives for all individuals

- Providing, through public education, mandatory courses on aging and end-of-life issues targeting elementary, junior high, and high school students

Preventing Elder Abuse and Fraud

- Enacting and fully funding comprehensive justice legislation to address elder abuse, guaranteeing protection for older Americans and building the capacity of APS programs in every state
- Developing innovative prevention and intervention programs for elder mistreatment—such programs should be culturally sensitive
- Enacting laws that specifically protect Native American elders from financial exploitation and abuse
- Establishing public–private partnerships for detection of abuse, neglect, and exploitation—for example, banks, utility companies, post office, press, and aging network
- Strengthening laws for prosecuting mail fraud from other countries using P.O. box clearinghouses
- Increasing training about elder abuse to all relevant professionals, including law enforcement and prosecutors to ensure maximum prosecution of offenders

Guardianships

- Expanding guardianship and protective services to include a complete and integrated set of services such as financial management, legal assistance, and cognitive evaluation
- Developing adequate systems to regulate and oversee guardians/conservators of incapacitated adults

As the number of older adults increases in the coming decade, there will no doubt be a greater demand for legal assistance programs and services. This increase in demand for services will likely occur without an increase in funding levels, and legal service providers and AAAs will be challenged to develop creative methods of legal education and service delivery.

CASE STUDY

A Widow in Legal Trouble

Jean is a 66-year-old woman who was widowed at age 65. She and her husband, Fred, had been married for 42 years when he died suddenly of a heart attack. For most of their working years, they managed apartments. Jean assumed the office duties, and her husband maintained the physical building and grounds. This employment gave them an apartment, utilities, and an income of approximately $20,000 per year. It was a dependable existence, and they were well liked and respected by their renters.

Like many husbands of that generation, Fred paid the bills and balanced the checkbook. Jean always depended on Fred to handle the couple's finances. After Fred's death, Jean, of necessity, had to take over the finances. Within two months, Jean realized that she was in deep trouble. Unbeknown to her, Fred had been taking cash advances from eight credit cards to support a gambling habit. The credit card receipts were arriving, it seemed to Jean, almost daily. To her horror and distress, the cash advances totaled $40,000. Now unemployed and frail from her advancing emphysema, Jean was barely getting by on $812 Social Security per month. Quickly, Jean realized that, after rent, utilities, groceries, prescription drugs, and other necessities, she could not pay off this incredible debt.

Jean's daughter, Susan, was sympathetic and supportive but unable to provide financial assistance. A few years earlier, Jean and Fred had invested the little savings they had in a grocery business for their daughter. This was an unsuccessful venture that eventually went bankrupt. The first credit collection calls have begun, and Jean is completely distraught. She finally mustered up the courage to tell her best friend what had happened, but then it took her another two weeks to pick up the telephone and call the senior paralegal program at the local area AAA.

Case Study Questions

1. Jean, like Fernando in the introduction to this chapter, has multiple problems. List all possible problems that could be brought on by Jean's husband's actions.

2. Which of Jean's problems are legal issues? Which fall into other service categories?

3. Of all Jean's problems and worries, what is the single thing that could be addressed that would bring her the most peace of mind? Defend your choice.

4. Considering the chapter's discussion of why older adults might hesitate to seek legal assistance, what factors in Jean's case substantiate her reluctance to call an attorney?

5. Jean's health situation suggests that possible end-of-life legal issues could be addressed. Referencing the chapter, suggest one or two other legal areas that could be approached with Jean.

LEARNING ACTIVITIES

1. Make an inventory of the legal aid programs that serve older adults in your community. What type of cases do they accept? Where do these programs refer people when they cannot take their cases? What is the breakdown of the cases they accept in a given year?

2. Contact your local District Attorney's Office and arrange an interview to find out about cases of elder abuse and fraud involving older adults that the office prosecutes each year. Does the office sponsor any public education for older adults about consumer fraud or elder abuse?

3. Make a list of the legal problems discussed in this chapter. Obtain permission from 10 older adults to ascertain whether they have had any of these legal problems in the last year. If so, ask them if they sought legal advice for the problem and the outcome of the situation. Be sure to keep your interviewees' names confidential when reporting your findings.

FOR MORE INFORMATION

International Resources

1. World Elder Abuse Awareness Day: http://www.inpea.net/weaad.html

   In an effort to bring worldwide attention to the issue of elder abuse, June 15 has been designated as World Elder Abuse Awareness Day (WEAAD) and is formally recognized as such by the United Nations. For more information and resources visit the International Network for the Prevention of Elder Abuse's WEAAD page listed above.

2. South Africa Older Persons Forum: www.saoph.org.za

   The role of the South Africa Older Persons Forum is to promote the rights and dignity of older persons, consult and advise government, comment on legislation and policy, foster the growth of community organizations, disseminate information and raise public awareness.

3. International Guardianship Network: www.international-guardianship.com/index.htm

   The International Guardianship Network provides support, information and networking opportunities for guardians worldwide and is working to put the legal proceedings of the UN Convention on the Rights of Persons with Disabilities into practice.

National Resources

1. American Bar Association, Commission on Law and Aging, American Bar Association, 740 15th Street NW, Washington, DC 20005-1019; phone: 202-662-1000; www.americanbar.org/groups/law_aging.html

   The commission focuses on the legal concerns of older adults and provides technical assistance, models of legal assistance projects, telephone and written assistance, publications, and speakers.

2. American Association of Retired Persons Foundation Legal Advocacy, 601 E Street NW, Washington, DC 20049; phone: 888-687-2277; www.aarp.org/research/legal-advocacy

   AARP Foundation Legal Advocacy is one of the few national organizations that defends and supports the legal rights of older Americans across the United States—assuring that they have a voice in our judicial system. Their legal work encompasses areas of federal and state laws that affect older Americans' day-to-day lives, including age and disability discrimination in employment, pensions and financial fraud including predatory lending, health and long-term care, disability, and government and public benefits

3. National Senior Citizens Law Center, 1101 14th Street, NW, Suite 400, Washington, DC 20005; phone: 202-289-6976; www.nsclc.org

   The center offers advice, litigation assistance, and training and program development assistance to legal services providers and state and local area agencies on aging.

Web Resources

1. AoA's Legal Assistance: www.aoa.gov/AoARoot/AoA_Programs/Elder_Rights/Legal/index.aspx

   This is a great place to start when looking for legal resources for older adults. AoA has compiled links to legal resources and resources about elder abuse. Updates to the page are made regularly.

2. SeniorLAW Center: www.seniorlawcenter.org

   SeniorLAW Center, in Philadelphia, provides free legal representation and legal education to older adults. The site provides information about a variety of legal issues of concern to older adults and also describes a number of special projects the center has, including the Legal Services for Hispanic Elders, Community-Based Neighborhood Legal Services and Community Clinics, KinCAN—Kinship Caregiver Assistance Network, and the Homebound Elderly Legal Project.

3. National Senior Citizens Law Center: www.nsclc.org

   The center has information about its services, manuals, and publications, as well as information about Social Security and SSI, Medicare, Medicaid, nursing home residents' rights, home care, pension rights, age discrimination and mandatory retirement, and OAA services.

4. National Guardianship Association: www.guardianship.org

   The National Guardianship Association (NGA) is a national association that advocates for excellence in guardianship. The NGA, started in 2008, represents more than 1,000 guardians, conservators, and fiduciaries from across the United States. The NGA has established national practice standards and formed the Center for Guardianship Certification, which now lists 2,000 individuals who have earned the designation of National Certified Guardian or National Master Guardian.

5. ABA Commission on Law and Aging: www.americanbar.org/groups/law_aging.html

   The Commission examines a wide range of law-related issues, including legal services to older persons, health and long-term care, housing needs, Social Security, Medicare, Medicaid, and other public benefit programs, and offers a number of online legal resources.

6. Senior Citizens Handbooks

   A number of legal assistance programs develop senior citizen's handbooks that offer information about a variety of legal issues such as health care, family issues, consumer issues, and long-term care. Here are a few examples of the many consumer senior legal handbooks available to elders and their advocates in many states:

   - State Bar of New Mexico, Senior Legal Handbook
     www.nmbar.org/Public/seniorlegalhandbook.html

   - Virginia State Bar, Senior Citizens Handbook
     www.vsb.org/site/publications/senior-citizens-handbook

7. National Center on Elder Abuse: www.ncea.aoa.gov/ncearoot/Main_Site/index.aspx

   The National Center on Elder Abuse is funded by the AoA and is operated through a partnership with a number of national organizations. The center's comprehensive website provides information about elder abuse and resources. Visitors can also access the quarterly newsletter, *NCEA Exchange.*

CHAPTER 14

Transportation

An older man in a wheelchair was picked up by a paratransit system in El Paso, Texas, to go from the nursing home where he resided to K-Mart. The trip did not take more than 15 minutes. During the trip, the man expressed how pleased he was to be getting out. He said that he had been a resident of the nursing home for seven years and that this was his first outing during that time that was not medically related (J. Peterson, 1995, p. 12).

It is difficult to understand how most of us would feel if we could not do something as common as take a trip to K-Mart. We jump in our cars at a moment's notice to run this or that errand. For most Americans, taking several trips per day to a variety of locations is a common occurrence. This gentleman, however, was grateful that accessible transportation was available and thrilled to be enjoying a nonmedical outing. The actual purpose of his trip may have been less important to him than the opportunity for an outing.

Mobility attained through the private automobile is the American way of life. We all remember the anticipation of getting our first driver's license. Most teenagers are excited to obtain a driver's license, and having a car is a rite of passage. Aside from deriving enjoyment from car travel, without transportation, we could not meet our basic needs. Going to work, buying groceries, seeing the doctor, meeting with friends—all become difficult and often impossible without transportation. Thus, we enter later life being accustomed to having the ability to come and go as we please.

Transportation plays a critical role in promoting physical, social, and psychological well-being of older persons. Physical health depends on access to medical facilities and other social services. The ability to maintain an active social life in old age depends on accessibility to family and friends as well as recreational and cultural activities. Key ingredients of psychological health that are enhanced by mobility are the ability to choose one's range of activities and promoting the feeling of belonging to the community (Wachs, 1979).

In this chapter, we review the legislative history of transportation services, the transportation patterns of older adults, and the different models of transportation services available. We conclude by identifying some of the challenges in meeting the transportation needs of an aging society.

POLICY BACKGROUND

Twentieth-century growth patterns, coupled with America's emphasis on travel by personal automobile, have contributed greatly to decline in travel options. Private transportation has come to dominate travel in this country to such an extent that the United States is less connected via public transportation now than it was in the late 1920s. Previously, through a series of easy transfers, passengers could travel from Burlington, Iowa, in the southeast corner of the state, along the Mississippi River, to Waverly in central Iowa—a distance of more than 150 miles—and back in the same day. The same journey today via public transportation would be impossible ("Community Service Is Key," 1994). Indeed, 79% of older adults over the age of 65 live in car-dependent suburban and rural communities (Rosenbloom, 2003). In an attempt to reverse this trend, federal and state transportation legislation has been enacted during the past four decades to increase transportation options for persons who are transit dependent.

Responsiveness to mobility needs began in the 1970s when the United States made significant gains in providing transportation options for elders and persons with disabilities. Beginning in 1970, an amendment to the Urban Mass Transportation Act of 1964 advanced the cause of transportation for older adults and persons with disabilities by mandating that these individuals have the same right as other persons to use mass transportation facilities and services. Spurred on by demands made by older adults, persons with disabilities, and their advocates, approximately 4,000 or more special-purpose transportation systems were in operation by the end of the decade (Ashford, Bell, & Rich, 1982). These programs varied from a single vehicle to a fleet of buses serving urban and rural areas, resulting in a mosaic of transportation programs across the country. During this same period, transportation was the "sleeper" issue at the 1971 White House Conference on Aging, ranking third in importance, preceded by income and health.

Another important statute of the 1970s, the Rehabilitation Act of 1973 (§ 504), directed federally assisted transit providers to offer half-fare service to older persons in off-peak periods. These regulations also required that local transit planning processes make special efforts to plan public mass transportation facilities and services that could effectively be used by older and disabled persons. Transportation planners and operators responded to Section 504 mandates by implementing special transportation systems for the older adults and persons with disabilities. These systems used smaller buses and vans, and could provide door-to-door service. Such systems became known as *paratransit* operations.

During the 1980s, the United States entered a second generation of specialized transportation developments. Although the 1970s were a decade of growth and development of specialized transportation systems, the 1980s were a decade of retrenchment in response to a general tightening of the availability of financial resources at all levels of government (Ashford et al., 1982). The 1980s were also a time when transportation systems emphasized cost-effectiveness and efficiency in providing public transportation. Federal legislation required that programs applying for federal transit funds create a transit development plan. These plans identified present and future needs and how transportation would be coordinated with other providers. Only with an approved plan could local or regional transit groups compete for federal transit funding. Today, transit development plans are still a requirement to receive federal transit funding.

In the 1990s, two laws were passed that greatly influenced public transit. The first was the Americans with Disabilities Act (ADA), signed into law in July 1990. This far-reaching law prohibits discrimination against people with disabilities in almost all aspects of American life and extends comprehensive civil rights to people with disabilities similar to those conferred on racial minorities by the Civil Rights Act of 1964. ADA requirements cover transportation services, facilities, and equipment of all entities, public and private. A key requirement of the ADA is that all new transit vehicles must be accessible to persons with wheelchairs. Fixed-route systems must offer a paratransit or specialized service for persons with disabilities who cannot access the fixed-route system. Furthermore, this paratransit service must be comparable to the fixed-route service in fares, hours and days of operation, response times, and geographic areas covered. The ADA also provides specific eligibility criteria for the comparable paratransit service for what constitutes disability. A recent review of the accomplishments of the ADA include 98% accessibility in the national fixed-route bus fleet; functional access to 648 of the 681 stations identified as key stations in the nation's oldest rail systems; access to 76% of the nation's intercity rail (Amtrak) stations that serve 97% of all boardings; access at 84% of the nation's light rail stations and 100% station access in several new light rail systems built since 1990; and 66.9 million trips provided via ADA complementary paratransit in 2008 (Hershey, Clark, Day, & Thatcher, 2010). Issues of concern that the authors identified in this review include a lack of accessibility for individuals to get to and from stops and stations, design issues with low-floor bus ramps, the reliability and availability of elevators in transit stations, and issues concerning wheelchair-securement systems.

The second law, the Intermodal Surface Transportation Efficiency Act (ISTEA) of 1991, made several significant changes to the federal transit program. One obvious change was renaming the federal agency that oversees the transit industry. The agency that had been called the Urban Mass Transportation Administration since its birth in 1964 was renamed the Federal Transit Administration (FTA). This name change reflected an awareness by Congress and the federal government that public transportation is vital to all citizens, urban and rural (Rucker, 1995). ISTEA specifically addressed the mobility needs of older persons, persons with disabilities, and those who are economically disadvantaged. The legislation also placed great emphasis on local, regional, and state planning and coordination; it made funding of capital and operating costs dependent on assurances that local transit systems were coordinated with regional and state transit plans. The most current transportation legislation was signed into law in 2005: the Safe, Accountable, Flexible, Efficient Transportation Equity Act: A Legacy for Users (SAFETEA-LU). Since the law was enacted, the percentage of local governments providing or delivering transportation programs increased 23% from 2005 to 2010 (National Association of Area Agencies on Aging, 2011b). The Act officially expired in 2009, and funding extensions for SAFETEA-LU every year since 2009 have been authorized by Congress, including $8.4 billion in American Recovery and Reinvestment Act (ARRA) funds in 2009. Most recently, Congress authorized $10.5 billion for SAFETEA-LU transit programs in FY 2011 (American Public Transportation Association [APTA], 2011). In 2012, the members of the House and Senate introduced legislation (H.R. 4348 and S. 1813) that would reauthorize the SAFETEA-LU law. Differences between the Senate and House bills were hammered out in a Congressional Conference Committee, and on July 6, 2012, President Obama signed H.R.4348, the Moving Ahead for Progress in the 21st Century (MAP-21) law, which now replaces the SAFETEA-LU legislation (MAP-21, P.L. 112-141).

USERS AND PROGRAMS

Transportation Patterns of Older Adults

Older Americans largely rely on private vehicles for their transportation needs; almost 90% of trips taken by older adults over age 65 are in a personal vehicle (National Cooperative Highway Research Program [NCHRP], 2006). Exhibit 14.1 shows the percentages of older urban, suburban, and rural adults who rely on various modes of transportation. The majority

Exhibit 14.1   Travel Modes by Gender and Residence for Persons Aged 65 Years and Older (percentage)

Mode	Urban	Suburban	Rural
Private vehicle	77.3	93.7	94.8
As driver	54.9	71.7	68.1
As passenger	22.4	22.0	26.7
Public transit	8.5	0.9	0.3
Walking	13.3	4.6	4.6
All other modes	0.9	0.8	0.3

Source: Rosenbloom and Waldorf (1999, p. 107).

of older adults, regardless of location, rely on private vehicles. The most current federal transportation statistics show that 32.9 million licensed drivers in the United States are over age 65, and it is estimated that by 2025, one in five drivers will be over the age of 65 (Federal Highway Administration, 2009; Lynott & Figueiredo, 2011). Because the number of older adults is increasing, a greater number of older adults are driving and thus miles traveled by older adults now account for 10% of total miles traveled among all age groups. Although there are more older drivers on the road, the average daily miles traveled by persons aged 65 and over has declined by approximately five miles in the years 2001 to 2009, perhaps due, in part, to increase gasoline prices (Lynott & Figueiredo, 2011). Contrary to public perception, up to age 70, the majority of older adults have good driving records and appear to perform as well as middle-aged drivers. Although younger drivers have the highest rate of fatalities per miles driven, older adults age 85 and older have a fatality rate that is higher than drivers between the ages of 25 and 74 for each mile driven (Federal Highway Administration, 2007).

Although we are seeing an increased number of older drivers, compared with younger drivers, a higher percentage of older adults do not drive. Twenty percent of older adults over age 65—some 7 million people—do not drive, compared with 6.9% of people between the ages of 19 and 64. Isolation is greater among older non-drivers than older drivers, as over half of non-drivers, compared with 17% of older drivers over age 65, or 3.6 million people, stay home on any given day and make fewer trips for social, family, religious, and medical reasons (Bailey, 2004; National Household Transportation Survey, 2001). A recent study found that 36.6% of survey participants who were 65 and older had some level of transportation deficiency, and 8.5% of them reported they had the problem frequently (S. Kim, 2011). Moreover, isolation of older non-drivers is greater among racial and ethnic elders and those living in the southern and Midwestern states (Bailey, 2004).

Non-drivers who have transportation needs must rely on either friends or family or use public transportation. Access to all forms of public transportation is markedly less in sprawling suburbs, small towns, and rural areas compared to urban areas; 51% of all Americans report that they do not have access to public transportation services (Bailey, 2004). Within the older adult population, 34% reported they had no transit available to use, and less than half of the baby boomer population is located within three quarters of a mile of a fixed-route transportation system. Where transit options were available, only 11.5% of older adults reported using transit and 53.8% indicated they did not use it (NCHRP, 2006). Those most likely to use transit were non-White and those living in city centers, and those least likely to use public transit were the oldest old, rural persons, and those with two or more activity of daily living (ADL) limitations. However, when we examine transit use by people aged 65 and older as a portion of all trips they take, the public transit share of trips increased by 40% between 2001 and 2009 (Lynott & Figueiredo, 2011).

Finally, one mode of transportation, walking, accounts for a great share of trips among older adults than either public transportation or taxis (Lynott & Figueiredo, 2011). Older adults now take almost 9% of their trips on foot.

Gender

Among the current cohort of older adults over the age of 65, women are less likely to hold a driver's license than are men (73% vs. 89%), are less likely to drive than men, and take fewer and shorter trips than do men (NCHRP, 2006; TRIP, 2012). Twenty-seven percent of women over age 65 indicate that they do not drive (NCHRP, 2006). Overall, older women in both rural and urban settings are less likely to rely on a private vehicle, and more likely to use public transportation, than are older men.

Health

Another factor influencing the mobility of older persons, and consequently use or nonuse of public transportation, is their health status and presence of physical disabilities that interfere with mobility. A national study of community-dwelling Medicare beneficiaries estimated that 14.1 million older adults have some degree of difficulty walking or climbing stairs (Shumway-Cook, Ciol, Yorkston, Hoffman, & Chan, 2005). The incidence of health-related mobility problems is substantially higher for women and is higher among rural residents (21%) than among urban residents (12%; National Eldercare Institute on Transportation, 1994). Fifteen percent of those who do not ride public transportation, even though it is available, said it was because of a health limitation (NCHRP, 2006). Thus older adults with mobility limitations are among those who are transit dependent.

Geographic Location

Geographic location also affects older adults' transportation options. Nationally, 76 million people are considered transit dependent, and rural areas account for 29 million, or 38% of the total (U.S. Census Bureau, 1996). By contrast, only 30% of urban residents are so classified. Another factor resulting in rural transportation deficiency is the loss of long-haul bus services to 15% of rural communities.

One way to analyze transit ridership by older adults is to break ridership patterns into urban, small urban, and rural components. This is useful because there are differences among these areas. The latest national study available showed that in the 33 largest cities (those with populations of more than 1 million), transit resources were substantial, yet many of the mobility needs of older adults were still unmet (National Eldercare Institute on Transportation, 1994). In those urban areas, only 6% of the total ridership and 13% of the noncommuter ridership were composed of older persons. In small urban areas (areas of 50,000 to 200,000 persons), the total served was substantially less than in the large urban areas. Furthermore, the total amount of service per senior was substantially less: 12.5 trips annually in small urban areas, 20 trips annually in areas with a population between 200,000 and 1 million, and 37 trips annually for the largest urban areas. Transit ridership by older adults in rural areas was even more limited. Approximately 41% of the nation's rural residents live in areas with no public transit service, and another 25% live in areas determined to have inadequate public transportation (having fewer than 25 trips per year; National Eldercare Institute on Transportation, 1994; Seekins & Spas, 1998; Stommes, Brown, & Houston, 2002).

Income and Race

Economic problems also magnify transportation problems. In 2009, 9% of older adults, or 3.5 million, were living in poverty (U.S. Census Bureau, 2011e). Elders living in rural areas were poorer than their urban counterparts (10% of older adults living in rural areas were poor, compared with 11.5% living in urban areas). Racial and ethnic minority elders are more at risk of being poor than are their White peers. For example, in 2010, approximately 8% of White elders were living in poverty, whereas nearly 18% of African Americans and Latinos aged 65 or older were poor (U.S. Government Accountability Office, 2011). Thus, the expense of maintaining a private vehicle is beyond the means of many low-income older persons and low-income non-White elders. In addition, 28% of older African Americans, 19% of older Latinos, and 9% of Asian Americans live in households without a car, and approximately 40% of African American, Asian, and Latino elders do not drive compared to 16% of White elders (Bailey, 2004). Older minority females of color are more likely to have a lack of transportation, which limits their activities, and thus face a greater level of transportation deficiency than do their White counterparts (S. Kim, 2011).

As shown in Exhibit 14.2, non-driving among older adults is greatest among those over age 85, women, non-Whites, poor, those living alone and in center cities, and those with a greater number of ADL limitations (NCHRP, 2006).

Barriers to Public Transit Use

As mentioned previously, 53.8% of older adults who have access to public transportation do not use it. Why is the rate of public transit use by older adults so low in areas where public transportation is available? A variety of barriers exist to keep older adults from using public transportation when it is available. If you have some free time one afternoon, try getting from your house or apartment to the senior center, grocery store, or medical clinic *via public transportation*, and try to envision yourself as an older adult. While on your trip, think about the following:

- How difficult was it to access a transit map and to figure out the route you needed to take to get to your destination? What times did the bus service not run?

- How difficult was it and how long did it take you to get to the bus stop? What would it be like waiting there in bad weather?

- How high was the first step into the bus?

- Were the seats comfortable? Could you get in and out of them easily?

- How many transfers did you have to make during your trip?

- How close did the bus drop you to your final destination?

- How long did it take you to complete your trip?

If you are a veteran of using public transportation, you probably do not think twice about making your way across town and completing your journey without much trouble, but how would an older adult fare? Those of you who use your car to get around probably experienced some uncertainty—we hope you did not get lost! But from an older adult's perspective, using public transportation can be challenging.

Exhibit 14.2 Non-Driving Among the Older Adult Population (percentage)

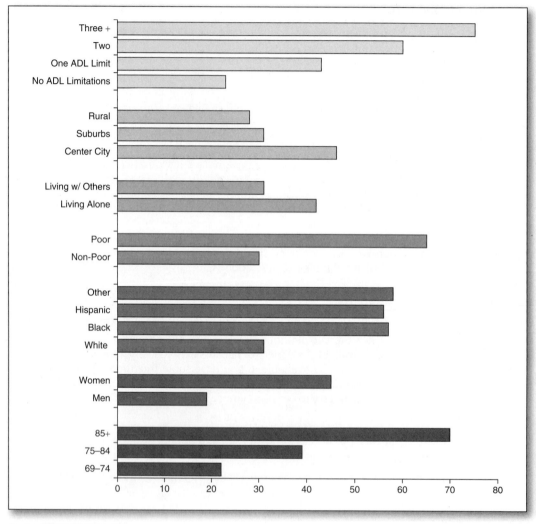

Source: NCHRP (2006, p. 19).

Note: ADL = activity of daily living.

Health and Physical Barriers

Health problems or other physical impairments can keep older adults from using fixed-route transit systems. Fifteen percent of older adults reported that they did not ride transit systems because of a health problem (NCHRP, 2006). Walking long distances to the nearest bus stop and bus stops that have inadequate shelters, no benches, and poor lighting are barriers to public transit by older adults. The buses themselves may pose problems because steps into the bus are often high and narrow, the seats are difficult to get into and out of, and buses are often overcrowded (Peck, 2010).

Fear of Crime

Fear of crime on public transit or near transit stops can be a significant barrier to public transit use by older adults. For example, one in five respondents in a national study cited a fear of crime associated with using public transit (Stowell-Ritter, Straight, & Evans, 2002). Other research has shown that most perceived crime-related experiences on public transit are classified as "quality-of-life" offenses, such as obscene language, verbal abuse, public drunkenness, vandalism, and disorderly conduct (Hardin, Tucker, & Callejas, 2001).

Bus Schedules

Another barrier to riding transit systems relates to bus schedules. Most transit systems are designed for commuters going to work, rather than to hospitals, clinics, and senior centers (Huttman, 1985). Older transit riders report a lack of frequency of bus service during the daytime and weekends, and insufficient destinations was the most frequently cited reason why older adults over age 65 in Southern California did not use the transit system (Ong & Haselhoff, 2005; Peck, 2010).

Best Practice: Lane Transit District, Eugene, Oregon

Lane Transit District (LTD) operates a one-on-one training initiative called the Bus Buddy Program. The program teaches seniors how to ride the bus in a relaxed way by breaking down barriers and building confidence. LTD recruits regular bus riders to serve as volunteers, known as Bus Buddies, and partners with local senior centers to match individual seniors with these volunteers. Bus Buddies teach seniors about the LTD transit system, as well as how to plan trips and navigate routes. Each Bus Buddy and senior pair then rides the bus together. Afterward, the pair discusses the trip, and the Bus Buddy answers any remaining questions about using public transportation in Eugene. In addition, seniors aged 65 and older can apply to be in the Honored Rider program. The program provides older adults a complimentary photo ID bus pass that entitles them to ride on the regularly scheduled LTD fixed-route bus service for free.

For more information, contact LTD, 1080 Willamette, Eugene, OR 97401-0470; phone: LTD Guest Services at 800-248-3861; http://www.ltd.org/ridingltd/accessibleservices.html.

Source: APTA (2005).

The National Eldercare Institute on Transportation (1992) conducted focus groups of older adults around the country to ascertain anecdotal information about transportation barriers. Older adults reported that the ideal transportation system would (a) have drivers who were courteous and patient, (b) require traveling shorter distances to destinations located within their neighborhoods, (c) have smaller buses that were for seniors and persons with disabilities only, (d) not require transferring, (e) have bilingual staff, and (f) have more flexible bus schedules to meet the needs of community people, not just workers.

Social Barriers

Racial and ethnic elders may face additional barriers that result from cultural perceptions and a lack of sensitivity by the transportation service system. For example, elders of color may shy away from all services, including transportation, because they have experienced hurtful discriminatory practices in the past. Other barriers include language and literacy barriers, discomfort if the rider is the only person of color using the transportation system, fixed-route services that do not adequately serve racial and ethnic neighborhoods, and service providers who assume that elders of color rely on their families for transportation (Heath, 1993; National Center on Senior Transportation, 2009). In addition, transit providers must be able to convey to a wide demographic of individuals the knowledge and information that the service exists, where the service travels, where and how to catch the bus or light rail, the arrival and departure times, and where to disembark (Hardin et al., 2001).

Across the Globe: Programs to Encourage Mobility Among Older Adults

In Europe, an older adult's mobility choices include many non-automobile options. For example, in the Netherlands, the combined percentage of older adults who walk, use public transportation, and ride a bicycle is greater than the percentage of those who drive cars.[1] In addition, in both the United States and Europe, as people age they take fewer trips by car, so alternative means of transportation becomes an important aspect of older adults' overall travel options. Two programs—one in Belgium and one in France—are examples of efforts to assist older adults to successfully use public transit and bicycles.

Belgium: OV-ambassadeurs—Public Transport Ambassadors

How does one take a bus, find information online about travel destinations and travel times, find bus stops, and pay for trips? Although these seem like simple questions to most of us, for some older adults, not knowing how to navigate public transportation can be a barrier to its use. Public Transport Ambassadors is a mobility project in Belgium that was founded by Mobiel 21, an organization promoting sustainable mobility, and the Flemish public transport organization. The aim of this initiative is to raise awareness among older adults in Flanders and Brussels on the importance of sustainable mobility and encourage them to use public transport more often. The Public Transport Ambassadors program offers classes that help older adults understand how to use public transport and practice the skills that are useful when travelling by bus, train, tram, or metro. The project's strength is that the workshops are organized by and for older adults. For more information visit their website: http://www.mobiel21.be/nl/content/ov-ambassadeurs.

France: L'école-vélo—Bicycle School for Elderly People

The association Fées du Sport has launched a school offering basic bicycle training and safety instruction for women and older adults. Originally created to promote women bicyclers, the association observed that many elderly people often need encouragement before they start riding with confidence. Despite this hesitation, bicycling can be a good resource for seniors because it increases their activity and mobility; riding a bicycle in a town is an effortless means of transport (particularly in flat regions) and is safe in towns that have bicycle paths. For these reasons, Fées du Sport has developed an initiative, L'école-vélo [the Bicycle School], which explains safety rules, riding skills, and how to navigate the urban environment. The association anticipates a very productive, intergenerational exchange among the younger members of the organization and the elderly adults who take advantage of the bike school. For more information, visit their website: http://www.fees-du-sport .com/a-bicyclette-lecole-velo-pour-adultes.

[1]Wegman and Aarts (2006).

Transportation Programs

Community transportation programs vary greatly in funding and design. Transit resources available to older persons have been described as a mosaic rather than as an integrated network. This mosaic is made up of public systems supplemented by transportation programs provided by nonprofit organizations, human service agencies, caregivers, and communities of faith (National Eldercare Institute on Transportation, 1994). A transportation program could be as basic as a group of volunteers working on their own or under the auspices of an umbrella human service agency to transport older adults to medical appointments and other important destination points in their community. At the other end of the spectrum, the transportation program could be a sophisticated, multifaceted system including a fixed-route service with a complementary paratransit service that is scheduled through a fully computerized central dispatch component. In each community, it is the challenge of the human service professional to find out what programs exist, and who is eligible for service and under what circumstances.

To best understand any discussion about transportation programs, one must have a basic knowledge of a few transportation terms that describe general types of transportation delivery systems (see Exhibit 14.3). Public transportation and specialized transit have been referenced several times in this chapter. *Public transportation* is defined as service that is available for any trip purpose to any person of any age and is operated by public agencies or supported by public funds to some extent. *Specialized transit*, on the other hand, is service that is provided for a variety of trip purposes and is open to older, disabled, or low-income persons but usually not to the general public. Specialized operators range from urbanized operators with large fleets of more than 30 vehicles, to rural systems with only one van and volunteer drivers. Another term, *incidental transit* or *human service agency transportation*, describes those programs in which transit is "incidental" to the agency's main program purpose. For example, mental health centers, senior centers, hospitals, and nursing homes often provide some transportation for their clients. The transportation, however, most likely is an optional service that the organization is providing to enhance its main program. *Commercial service* is defined as service provided by for-profit entities on a for-hire basis. Taxi services, shuttles, limousines, and charter services fall into this category.

Exhibit 14.3 Selected Transportation Terms

ADA: the Americans With Disabilities Act, a federal law requiring that facilities and services be made accessible to persons with disabilities

APTA: the American Public Transit Association, representing the interests of public transit agencies, particularly those in large urbanized areas

Complementary paratransit: a service that must be offered by fixed-route public transportation operators to persons with disabilities who cannot access or use regular fixed-route service

CTAA: the Community Transportation Association of America, representing the interests of specialized transit operators and those who operate in rural and small urbanized areas

Curb-to-curb service: a demand-responsive service system in which the passenger must come out to the vehicle

Deadhead: the time or distance that a transit vehicle does not spend in revenue service or moving passengers (e.g., the travel from a garage to the beginning of a route)

Demand-responsive service: a personalized, direct transit service usually provided for persons who are older or disabled on either an immediate demand basis or an advanced reservation basis; often used interchangeably with *paratransit, dial-a-ride,* or *specialized service*

Deviated fixed-route service: a fixed-route service that will deviate from its regular route to pick up special riders such as older or disabled persons and then return to its regular route without significantly detracting from its schedule

Door-through-door service: a demand-responsive system in which the driver goes into the home or final destination to provide more assistance, especially for frail or disoriented individuals

Door-to-door service: a demand-responsive service system in which the driver goes to the door of the passenger's residence and provides assistance if needed

E&D: elderly and disabled; in the past, the more common term was E&H (elderly and handicapped)

Fixed-route service: a regularly scheduled transit service operated over a set route

FTA: Federal Transit Administration; a federal agency in the U.S. Department of Transportation that provides funding for various transit services; formerly known as the Urban Mass Transportation Administration

Human services transportation: transportation provided to persons served by human service programs such as Medicaid and Title III of the Older Americans Act; most transportation is provided to older, disabled, or low-income persons on a demand-responsive basis

Incidental provider: an organization that provides transit only to its own clients, mainly as a service incidental to its primary service

Paratransit: transportation that is more flexible and personalized than conventional fixed-route, fixed-schedule mass transportation service but does not include exclusionary services such as charter or sightseeing trips (see also *demand-responsive service*)

SAFETEA-LU: Safe, Accountable, Flexible, Efficient, Transportation Equity Act: A Legacy for Users, signed into law in 2005, is the federal legislation for transit and highway programs; the Act provides funds for capital investment and programs that address special transit needs as well as research on transit issues; the Act has been replaced by the Moving Ahead for Progress in the 21st Century Act (MAP-21)

MAP-21: Moving Ahead for Progress in the 21st Century Act, signed into law on July 6, 2012, replaces the SAFETEA-LU as the federal legislation for transit and highway programs

Source: Mauser (1994), APTA (2005), and Community Transportation Association of America (2012).

Best Practice: Partners in Care and the Ride Partners Program

Partners in Care is a service credit exchange program located in Pasadena, Maryland, designed to create community by linking frail elderly and disabled adults with neighbors who volunteer their time to help with occasional tasks and errands. The goal of these services is to help seniors and disabled adults remain independent in their own homes. Participants may provide services, receive services, or both. For each hour of service donated by a volunteer, an hour of service credit is earned. The credit may be used by the individual at a later time or donated back to the program for others in need. Groups of volunteers are encouraged to combine their efforts for larger projects. The majority of tasks members provide involve transportation for a variety of needs. In 2009, members of Partners in Care had approximately 13,338 rides matched and drivers logged over 150,000 miles to complete a variety of tasks for individuals, including transportation to medical appointments, laboratory testing, mammograms, and pharmacy pickup. Partners in Care provides niche transportation support for those seniors who need extra help getting from their homes into a car, for trips at the edge of the normal work day, and for trips that may not be accommodated by family members or the Department of Aging van system.

The Ride Partners Program is a result of a collaboration among the Annapolis Department of Transportation, AmeriCorps, and Partners in Care, and provides out-of-county transportation. Members are encouraged to participate in these much-needed trips through a mileage reimbursement incentive and a sliding fee scale for participants.

For more information, contact Partners in Care, Inc., 6 S. Ritchie Highway, Pasadena, MD 21122; phone: 410-544-4800, or 800-227-5500; www.partnersincare.org.

Within these general categories of transportation programs are several types of service in terms of organization. A *fixed-route* service is a regularly scheduled service operated on a set route. A *deviated fixed-route* service is a fixed-route service that will deviate from its regular route to pick up special riders such as persons who are older or disabled, depending on its passengers' requests. Let's suppose a county transportation program runs several routes a week on scheduled days and at particular times to the county's rural senior centers to transport groups of seniors to a major shopping center. Depending on the needs of the seniors, the driver will pick up or drop off seniors in neighboring towns that are off the route. The driver is also able to change the destinations according to the needs of the group being transported. This system can modify the usual route to meet the needs of the riders. Opposite to fixed-route and deviated, or modified, fixed-route services is the *demand-responsive* system, a personalized service usually provided for older and disabled persons. It is provided on an immediate-demand basis or on an advance-reservation basis. This term is often used interchangeably with *paratransit, dial-a-ride*, or *specialized service.* This service can be curb to curb (the passenger must come out to the vehicle), door to door (the driver goes to the door of the passenger's residence and provides assistance if needed), or door through door (the driver goes into the home or final destination to provide more assistance, especially to frail or disoriented individuals). An important feature of demand-responsive service is that transportation services are tailored to the needs of individual riders. Most demand-responsive systems operate minivans, vans, or minibuses to provide this service. Passengers call, usually a minimum of 24 hours in advance, to schedule a van for an appointment. The transit scheduler will match the request with the appropriate vehicle and routes. Whether a transportation system is fixed route, modified fixed route, demand responsive, or a combination of service modes depends on the needs of the community and the resources available to meet those needs (Mauser, 1994).

Federal Transit Administration

Of the types of transportation described above, most visible are the programs funded with federal funds, which provide over half of all public money for transportation for older persons. Most of that money comes from two sources: the FTA and the U.S. Department of Health and Human Services (HHS; J. Lee, 1993).

Four principal funding sources through the FTA previously provided under the SAFETEA-LU legislation and now under the MAP-21 legislation are critical to meeting the mobility needs of older and disabled persons. One FTA program, called Rural Transit Formula Grants or Section 5311, apportions funds to states for public transportation in rural and small urban public transportation areas with populations under 50,000. In most Section 5311 programs, however, the majority of riders are older persons or persons with disabilities. The most recent national statistics show that Section 5311 transit systems provides an estimated 154.2 million trips per year and that elderly riders account for 31%, while 23% of riders are persons with disabilities. Section 5311 programs are made up of a network of approximately 1,200 public, private for-profit, and private nonprofit agencies that cover a service area of 3.5 million square miles and 91 million people. Demand-responsive service is the most common mode of service among Section 5311 providers (85%). Fixed-route service is provided by 51% of providers, and route- and point-deviation services are offered by 50% of providers (Community Transportation Association of America [CTAA], 2001). The remaining service is fixed route or modified fixed route. Funding for Section 5311 in 2006 was $388 million; in 2012, it was $385 million (FTA, n.d.; U.S. Department of Transportation, 2005c). Under the new MAP-21 law, the total federal investment in Section 5311 programs will grow by 30% from FY 2012 to FY 2014 (CTAA, 2012).

Section 5310, Transportation for Elderly Persons and Persons With Disabilities, is another FTA program that offers funds to assist with the purchase of capital equipment to agencies serving older persons and persons with disabilities. Each state determines specific program eligibility criteria since the legislation does not define "elderly" or "disabled" (Koffman, Raphael, & Weiner, 2004). Funds can be awarded to private nonprofit organizations and to public organizations as well. The SAFETEA-LU legislation increases coordination requirements and projects must coordinate with human service transportation plans

(U.S. Department of Transportation, 2005a). Nearly 3,700 transportation providers in the United States received Section 5310 funds, and over a 10-year period (1992–2001), 18,000 vehicles were purchased with Section 5310 funds (Koffman et al., 2004). Funding for Section 5310 in 2006 was $112 million; in 2012, funding for 5310 programs was $100 million (FTA, n.d.; U.S. Department of Transportation, 2005a). Under the new MAP-21 legislation, 60%, 20%, and 20% of 5310 funding must go to recipients in urban areas great than 200,000 in population, to urban areas between 50,000 and 200,000 population, and rural areas, respectively (CTAA, 2012).

Under the previous SAFETEA-LU legislation, Section 5317, New Freedom Program, provided funds to encourage service and facility improvements to address the transportation needs of persons with disabilities that go beyond what is required by the Americans With Disability Act. Projects must coordinate with locally developed human service transportation programs. Funding for 2006 was $78 million. and in 2012, funding was $77.5 million (FTA, n.d.; U.S. Department of Transportation, 2005b). The MAP-21 law now combines Section 5317 with Section 5310 program mentioned above. Section 5310 funding is expected to increase by 90% by FY 2014 (CTAA, 2012).

Section 5307, Urbanized Transit Formula Assistance, makes federal monies available for public transportation in urbanized areas, and formula grants are available to communities of 50,000 or larger for transportation planning, equipment costs, and operation costs. In addition, two new formula funds are available for New Small Transit Intensive Cities for urbanized areas under 200,000 and New Growing States and High Density States. Recipients of these funds may not serve nonurbanized areas and are not required to serve the entire urbanized area they represent. Congress authorized funding for these programs in 2012 totaled $3.4 billion (FTA, n.d.). The MAP-21 legislation continues the Section 5307 but adds a tier of funding based on the areas' share of low-income population, and funding is expected to rise by 7% by FY 2014 (CTAA, 2012).

Department of Health and Human Services

Under the HHS, transportation programs are funded primarily through the Older Americans Act (OAA), the Community Services Block Grant, and Title XIX and XX of the Social Security Act (see Exhibit 14.4). Title III, Part B of the OAA authorizes transportation services to facilitate access to supportive services, nutrition services, or both. How these monies flow to the states and local Area Agencies on Aging (AAAs) is explained in Chapter 2.

The network of Title III–funded older adult transportation providers includes more than 3,993 agencies, most of which are not AAA agencies (AoA, n.d.-e). Program data for FY 2010 show that Title III programs provided 1,483,816 one-way assisted trips and 25,852,102 unassisted one-way trips (AoA, n.d.-f, n.d.-g). Expenditures under Title III of the OAA in 2010 for transportation for older adults totaled $216,922,086, representing 8.5% of Title III expenditures. Because the AoA has historically discouraged the use of Title III funds for the purchase of vans, the major portions of these monies are allocated for operational rather than capital expenses (National Eldercare Institute on Transportation, 1994). Transportation services are also funded under Title VI, which provides funds to Native American Indian Tribes. Often, OAA funds are part of a public–private partnership to increase transportation services. A private or corporate entity will work with a government entity—in this case, the local AAA—to deliver a service to needy older adults as a way to maximize resources.

An example of such a public–private venture is in Bentonville, Arkansas, where the AAA issues coupons to elderly adults with low incomes and persons with disabilities to offset a

Exhibit 14.4   Important Sources of Transportation Support Through the U.S. Department of Health and Human Services

Funding Source	Eligible Recipients	Program Description
OAA – Title III	State agencies on aging and local AAAs that subcontract with local providers	Funds are available through Title III, Part B of the OAA to provide community-based systems of transportation, and legal and in-home services for elders, as well as for multipurpose senior centers.
OAA – Title VI	Tribal organizations and public or private nonprofit organizations that service Native American elders	Funds are available through Title VI of the OAA to provide nutrition, information and referral, transportation, and other services to Native American elders.
Community Services Block Grant	Funds are available to local agencies, often county based, to serve low-income persons.	Funds may be used for employment, education, housing, nutrition, energy, emergency assistance, and related needs such as transportation for elders, low-income persons, and the disabled.
Social Security Act – Title XX, Social Services Block Grant	State and local social service agencies	Funds enable states to address goals of reduced dependency on social programs; services can include transportation.
Social Security Act – Title XIX, Medicaid	State and local medical assistance agencies	Funds available through Title XIX of the Social Security Act enable states to provide health care services to medically needy low-income persons. States are to assure transportation to medical services for Medicaid beneficiaries.
Developmental Disabilities Basic Support Grants	State and local developmental disabilities agencies, often called Community Center Boards	Funds provide medical services, support services—programs that enable persons with developmental disabilities to become independent and productive; transportation is a key service for independence.

portion of the cost of a taxi trip with the local taxi company. The city gains a valuable service for its older adults and residents with disabilities. Meanwhile, the taxi company increases its ridership (Area Agency on Aging of Northwest Arkansas, 2012).

Two other important sources of support for public transportation are the Community Service Block Grant and Title XIX Medicaid, both HHS programs. Under the block grant program, states and Native American tribes receive funding to provide a broad range of social services for low-income persons. These funds are awarded on a formula basis to states, which pass the majority of these funds on to local nonprofit community action programs. Transportation services commonly are provided by many of these local programs.

Title XIX of the Social Security Act, the Medicaid Program, establishes and supports essential health care for low-income people—primarily older persons, persons with disabilities, and single-parent households with dependent children. Nonemergency medical transportation (NEMT) has been part of the Medicaid program since 1969, when federal regulations mandated that states ensure access to medical services for all Medicaid recipients who have no other means of transportation available to them. However, the ways in which transportation services are delivered vary widely from state to state. Some states offer a comprehensive array of transportation services that include taxis, vans, and public transportation passes, whereas other states simply provide gasoline vouchers or mileage reimbursement (Koffman et al., 2004). A CTAA study in 2000 (Raphael, 2001) reported that state and federal funding for NEMT services totaled $1.75 billion. States spend about 1% of Medicaid expenditures on transportation services and provide more than 100 million trips. Rural transit agencies are particularly reliant on Medicaid NEMT, which provides between 8% and 70% of their transportation budgets.

Successful transportation programs can tap many other sources of funding to meet the needs of mobility-dependent persons. Examples include other federal sources, foundations, advertising, rider fees, and special fundraising events (see Exhibit 14.5).

Exhibit 14.5   Some Other Federal Sources of Transportation Funding

Funding Source	Eligible Recipients	Program Description
Congregate Housing Services Program	Public bodies and private nonprofit corporations managing housing for elders and persons with disabilities	Funds are available to provide meals and nonmedical support services, including transportation services, to allow frail elders or disabled persons to maintain maximum independence in a home environment.
Foster Grandparent Program	State and local government agencies, private nonprofit organizations	Funds may be used to provide stipends, transportation, and other support services for low-income elders working as volunteers in programs serving infants, children, or youth with special needs.
Retired Senior Volunteer Program	State and local government agencies, private nonprofit corporations	Funds may be used to provide transportation and other support services for elders to work as volunteers in community service activities.
Senior Companion Programs	State and local government agencies, private nonprofit corporations	Funds may be used to provide transportation and other support services for low-income elders to work in community service activities serving elders with physical, mental, or emotional impairments.
Other Sources	Other sources of funding may include United Ways, fares, local tax initiatives, service clubs, foundations, contracts with programs to provide services to a specific group of recipients, and in-kind donations, to name a few.	

Source: Adapted from "Community Service Is Key" (1994) and Diebert (1996). Used with permission.

Best Practice: Partnering With Taxi Services

Many local communities that have taxi service have been partnering with these companies to provide transportation services to elderly and disabled adults. However, many vary in terms of their eligibility and cost.

Ozaukee County in Wisconsin offers a shared taxi service. Trips can be arranged in advance or for travel the same-day services are needed. The county is divided into five zones, and the cost is based on how many zones you travel. Riders share a taxi with others, and the cost of round-trip travel for older adults and persons with disabilities within one zone costs $4.50, and between four zones costs $10.50, which is slightly less than the full fare. You can find out more by visiting http://www.co .ozaukee.wi.us/ADRC//IA/Directory.pdf.

The Fairfax County (Virginia) Department of Transportation offers the "Seniors-On-the-Go" taxi program. The taxicab service is available countywide, and older adults can call one of three taxi cab services to arrange a ride. The program is limited to individuals over age 65 who are considered to have low incomes. Eligible seniors purchase taxicab coupons booklets worth $30 at a cost of $20 per booklet. The difference is subsidized by the Fairfax County government. You can find out more by visiting http://www.fairfaxcounty.gov/ncs/seniors.htm.

CHALLENGES FOR TRANSPORTATION PROGRAMS

As baby boomers age, adequately addressing their transportation needs will require a multifaceted approach because of their diverse transportation needs. As we mentioned previously, we are a country that has an automobile-centric culture, and we built our local communities and our state and national infrastructure based on the automobile as the primary mode of transportation. So as the number of older adult drivers increase, what can be done to support their safe driving? We also discussed that there is a significant number of older adults that do not drive and are in need of other transit options. Furthermore, much of rural America remains without transportation services. Although urban areas have greater public transit resources than rural areas, using those transit services is difficult for many urban dwelling older adults. How can we best address the transit needs of our aging population in a way that considers a both a community-level perspective and an operational and programmatic perspective?

Meeting Transit Needs by Creating Livable Communities

The key to providing an effective community transportation network will mean that community leaders must endeavor to offer a variety of viable transportation options—from walking to public transit to providing safe roadways—that are responsive to the varying levels of independence and the social and medical needs of older adults as well as other community members. Considering appropriate transportation options in all its forms is an important component in community design or what social scientists, urban planners, transportation engineers, and elected officials are generally referring to as a component of *livable communities*. Livable communities are those that have "affordable and appropriate housing, supportive community features and services and adequate mobility options. Together these facilitate personal independence and the engagement of residents in civic and social life" (Kochera, Straight, & Guterbock, 2005, p. 6). Thus, transportation is a key component of an interdisciplinary approach to creating livable communities in which older adults can successfully age in place. Livable community transportation accommodates a wide range of optimal transportation modes for people of all ages that are balanced and reliable (Grant et al., 2012). It also includes increasing opportunities for safe, comfortable walking and bicycling, improving the transit experience, providing information to support choices, and supporting *placemaking*, which is the connection between land use, transportation, and urban design. A placemaking approach to transportation includes considering street designs that promote traffic calming and "road diets," which reduces the number of traffic lanes to accommodate other modes of transportation such as walking and bicycling (Grant et al., 2012; see Exhibit 14.6). Creating communities that promote walking by fixing and widening walking paths (with places to rest), and improving the safety of crosswalks, including providing more time to cross streets, would help many older adults achieve mobility independence. Incorporating other transit options such as low-speed golf carts or scooters would allow many older adults who no longer drive to access social and community services.

In addition, providing transportation services to people living in the suburbs will become a critical issue in the coming years. Boomers will likely be aging in place in the suburbs (U.S. Senate Special Committee on Aging, 1991a), where the distance to services is great and often the only way to access these services is one's automobile. This graying of the suburbs where there is little or no access to public transportation will bring unique transportation challenges for local and county governments.

Of course, supporting a livable community transportation approach will require local, state, and federal funding. Transportation advocates across the country have called for an increase in the amount of federal and state transit funding as well as increased coordination among public entities. The Partnership for Sustainable Communities is one example of a joint effort between the U.S. Department of Housing and Urban Development, the U.S. Department of Transportation, and the U.S. Environmental Protection Agency (Partnership for Sustainable Communities, n.d.) to coordinate efforts to promote livable community transportation efforts and partnerships.

Improving Coordination of Resources

As community leaders consider how to envision livable community transportation, one of the biggest challenges that face public transit systems in our communities is the lack of transportation coordination. Transportation coordination includes activities such as the formation of partnerships; sharing of planning resources; joint identification of consumer needs; identifying and sharing available services, costs, and revenues; and reporting (Burkhardt, 2005). Any one or a combination of these efforts can lead to an increased level of service that provides improved mobility and access to a range of activities and services. The U.S. General Accounting Office (1991a) conducted a study of special transportation services for older adults. The authors reported that, of the 19 special transportation programs studied, 18 showed that fragmentation of special transportation is a pervasive, long-standing problem, and that in many communities, agencies operate in isolation from one another. This fragmentation occurs despite federal legislative mandates to encourage coordination. Multiple funding sources for special transportation services result in differing

Exhibit 14.6 Examples of Transportation and Livable Community

This is a picture of a recently designed street in Bogotá, Columbia, that provides ample mobility space to pedistrians, cyclists, and bus traffic. Notice the absence of cars. This mix of pedestrians and access to public transit is elder-friendly.

Photo credit: Karl Fjellstrom, The Institute for Transportation and Development Policy (ITDP) (CC BY 3.0)

These are before and after pictures of the newly remodeled East Boulevard in Charlotte, North Carolina, which is an example of good traffic calming in a neighborhood. The Boulevard used to be a four-lane, undivided road (left picture) that carried over 20,000 cars per day. East Boulevard now has bike lanes, a center turn lane, curb ramps, and improved pedestrian safety and comfort (right picture).

Photo credit: Charlotte Department of Transportation (2012). Used by Permission.

Source: Gallagher (n.d.)

program guidelines for operational practices. For example, programs under SAFETEA-LU and now the MAP-21 legislation encourages the charging of fares, whereas the OAA explicitly prohibits charging for services but allows voluntary donations. Another problem affecting coordination and efficiency is that many social service community agencies such as adult day programs, nursing homes, and senior centers purchase vans to respond to the needs of their clients. Often, these vans sit idle for long periods or are not at full capacity when in use. Not only does lack of coordination result in a community not being served adequately within its own boundaries, but there is also an incredible imbalance in service levels from community to community and in traveling from one community to another when public transportation is required. One community can be served adequately by a transit program while a neighboring community has no transit service at all. Even large metropolitan areas, which overall have better coverage from public transportation, have unserved population pockets, including suburban areas surrounding central cities. Less likely to be found is public transit service between communities, particularly small to mid-size communities. Currently, the federal government, through the MAP-21 legislation, places a heavy emphasis on local transportation coordination and a balanced, flexible-funding approach to transportation.

Coordination will continue to be critical as funding for transit programs declines or stays flat. Without adequate transportation to and from social and health care services, most social delivery programs lose much of their impact, and any reforms made in health care will be pointless without health care access. Another future funding challenge is the uncertainty of Medicaid and the transportation services it provides, as the federal and state governments continuously debate how to make this program more cost-effective. The future of Medicaid transportation funds is uncertain at best. There is also a push for many other federal programs to be "block granted" to the states in the future, thus leaving the states with considerably more flexibility than they currently have to determine how federal monies are expended. Will transportation for older and disabled persons be a priority against a myriad of other pressing human needs and limited budgets that states are facing?

Programmatic Concerns: Barriers to Public Transportation Use

Transit options in rural communities continue to be underdeveloped and insufficient to meet the needs of rural elders. Increasing dedicated funding through the Section 5311 Rural Transit Formula Grant program for a variety of public transportation in rural areas have been called for by rural transit advocates (DeGood, 2011). In addition, community agencies must continue to explore various transportation options that can serve to expand access. These include agency-focused models that offer specialized services or may serve the general public, cooperative efforts among social service agencies to enhance transportation options and scope, using volunteers or vouchers, and public–private partnerships with local taxi services (Research and Training Center on Disability in Rural Communities, 2007). Delegates from the 2005 White House Conference on Aging (2006) recommended strategies that would supplement public transit programs with volunteer transportation services, including

- tax incentives for community-based volunteer transportation programs; and

- removal of legal barriers for volunteers, including protection of unreasonable increases in automobile insurance rates when volunteers use their own cars to drive older adults.

In communities where public transportation is available, barriers to service use discussed earlier in the chapter must be addressed to increase ridership of young and old alike. As noted earlier, one barrier to using existing public transit includes a perception that using public transportation is not a safe means of travel. Improving lighting and increasing monitoring of transit stops could help address these fears. Adding transit stops in neighborhoods and providing more comfortable stops (with covers and benches) and adding transit stops at locations frequented by older adults could help improve access and use of public transportation. Often overlooked is the need for personal assistance getting on and off buses or vans. Many transit services require riders to use services independently, and this simple detail can keep some older adults with minor mobility issues from using public transportation.

Although many transit vehicles can accommodate persons with disabilities, there are specific changes to transit vehicles that could promote the use of public transportation among older adults. Transit vehicles with lifts to ease boarding, buses that "kneel" at curbside, and buses or light rail with cars that have low floors and low platform boarding will be needed to attract and serve an increasing number of elderly riders (APTA, 2003).

Elderly Drivers

While communities begin to consider long-ranging planning and changes facilitated by the livable community approach, realistically, travel by car will continue to be the primary mode of transportation for many older adults in the foreseeable future. They will be more likely to retain their driver's licenses compared with the current cohort of older adults and to have high expectations about driving (Eberhard, cited in Committee for the Study on Improving Mobility and Safety for Older Persons, 1988). Because America has supported a national policy during the past 60 years that places high priority on private automobile transportation, some argue that roadway designs, automobile engineering, and licensing and retraining of drivers are all critical considerations in enabling older adults to use their automobiles as long and as safely as possible.

One way to improve the safety of older adult drivers is to improve roadway characteristics. This would include such things as improving roadway markings by using retroflective pavement paint or wider striping, using advance street name signs placed ahead of intersections, making highway signs more legible, improving vehicle safety, and establishing, among other things, better designs for left-hand turn lanes (older drivers in particular have difficulty with left-hand turns; see Exhibit 14.7; Amparano & Morena, 2006). These are just a few examples of how a better-designed roadway system that takes the needs of older adults into consideration would go a long way in maintaining the mobility of older adults.

Technological advances in automobiles in the future will also contribute to increasing the safety of older adult drivers. For example, it is likely that in the near future, cars will have On Board Units (OBU) that can warn of impending unsafe traffic situations, adjust speeds to avoid collisions, provide improved vision for night time driving, provide advanced GPS services, detect road obstacles, provide audible alerts for lane drifting, or even override control of the vehicle to prevent injury or accidents (McCormick, Underwood, & Wang, 2012). The key to the effectiveness of these technological advances will be the ease of use by a population of older adult drivers that may not be as experienced in interacting with advanced technologies as younger adults might be.

Many states have also responded to the increase in older adult drivers by enacting various provisions for licensing standards applicable to drivers over a certain age in hopes of improving safety. For example, some states now require vision testing for adults after a certain age (ranges from 40 to 80 and older) when renewing their driver licenses, accelerating driver's license renewal cycles for adults over a certain age (ranges from 54 to 81), and mandating in-person renewals or mandating road tests (U.S. Government Accountability Office, 2007).

At some point, however, when seniors are no longer able to drive, programs that assist in helping older drivers make the emotional transition from driving to being dependent on other means of transportation will be critical in reducing the isolation that comes with the inability to drive (Stephens et al., 2005). The success of this type of program depends, of course, on the availability of other community transportation alternatives.

Addressing Mobility Challenges of Ethnically Diverse Elders

While livable communities by definition seek to provide mobility options for elders with different socioeconomic and ethnic and racial backgrounds, ethnically diverse elders have some unique transportation needs. The National Coalition on Mobility Needs of Culturally and Ethnically Diverse Elders convened by the National Center on Senior Transportation

Exhibit 14.7 Improving Roadway Safety

The U.S. Department of Transportation's Federal Highway Administration has created new guidelines for highway and other road signs that are designed to be more visible to elderly drivers. These new signs use different layouts and fonts. An example of this change is this Detroit-area overpass, which offers a side-by-side comparison of the old-style font (left sign) and the new Clearview font (right sign). Notice the larger amount of space within the enclosed loops of the lowercase letters in the sign using the Clearview font.

Source: Trentacoste (2010).

The use of a positive offset left-turn lane improves an older driver's ability to see past the opposing left-turning vehicle to more easily identify the oncoming traffic.

Source: U.S. Government Accountability Office (2007).

(NCST, 2009) identified the following six challenges associated with access to transportation services for diverse elders:

- A lack of translated materials, as well as limited literacy, in the native languages spoken by immigrant and American Indian elders;

- A lack of targeted outreach by the transportation system to culturally and ethnically diverse elders;

- Isolation and segregation of many culturally and ethnically diverse communities;

- Vast distances to travel to get to needed services, particularly for American Indian elders living on reservations;

- Cultural mores that prohibit getting help outside the family, and

- Economic challenges facing many culturally and ethnically diverse elders, resulting in dependence on publicly funded transportation services. (p. 4)

The Coalition recommended that the NCST, organizations within the aging and transportation services network, and community-based organizations that serve diverse elders work to address these transportation challenges through advocacy/regulatory and policy changes, data collection and research activities, local coordination of transportation, funding and grants, and training and information dissemination.

In summary, meeting the future transportation challenges of an aging population requires both community-based and programmatic planning perspective. It must focus on how to reconfigure our communities and our transit options so older adults and other community members have a range of mobility options from which to select based on their particular capabilities and situation.

CASE STUDY

A Need for Transportation Planning and Coordination

Daylight, Inc., is a small, social-model adult day program. Daylight's mission is to help older adults remain independent in the community and to give caregivers time apart from the daily stresses of caregiving. At first, the Daylight staff and board of directors thought that they would have to close due to lack of interest. But 15 years later, with consistent marketing, great personal effort by the executive director, and excellent support from an active board of directors, Daylight has increased its average attendance from 6 to 17 persons per day. Family calls and agency referrals to the program are coming in weekly. Two years ago, Daylight opened a satellite program 35 miles away to serve seven rural communities in the southern half of the county. Now there is a need for a modern facility and expansion of services to include weekend and overnight respite. Daylight has embarked on a major capital development project in partnership with a home health care agency. The proposed facility will house both agencies and permit program expansion and flexibility that are not currently possible.

At a recent annual planning retreat, the staff receptionist commented about the many callers who ask about the program but who ultimately do not enroll their family members in Daylight. After much discussion, the board directed the executive director to conduct a follow-up survey with those callers to learn why they chose not to use Daylight. A telephone survey was prepared, and volunteers called 37 families.

The survey results showed that 42% of the families contacted did not choose Daylight as a respite option because of the lack of transportation. Nearly 55% of those surveyed in the southern part of the county listed transportation as the principal barrier to enrollment. Transportation barriers were due to age, disability, and conflicting work schedules. When the executive director brought this information to the next board meeting, the board decided to form a task force to develop a plan of action for board consideration that would address the transportation problem.

Case Study Questions

1. Assume that you are a member of the task force. What additional information would you want to know before you proceed with the development of a plan of action to address these transportation barriers?

2. Daylight is planning to build a new facility. What relationship does this transportation issue have with the success or failure of the new facility, if any?

3. On the basis of what you have learned from reading the chapter, what types of transportation programs might you need to contact? What questions would you need to explore with these entities to write your report and proposal for the Daylight board of directors?

4. What transportation options should the task force explore? Describe at least three transportation options for Daylight, and list the advantages and disadvantages of each option.

5. How is this situation relevant to the chapter's discussion of the relationship between mobility needs of frail elders and home- and community-based services?

6. List the transportation terminology that best describes the typical Daylight passenger and the type of service most suited to this passenger.

LEARNING ACTIVITIES

1. Contact your state transportation association. To find the name and phone number of the transit association in your state, go to the Community Transportation Association of America's website, www.ctaa.org. Find out the association's stance on transit issues, gaps in service for older adult riders, and future public transit plans.

2. Select a destination to which an older adult might travel, such as the bank, Social Security office, senior center, grocery store, or doctor's office. Use the local public transportation system to get there. Try to select a location that is not close to your home. If you are familiar with

riding public transportation, select a location you have not been to before. Record your observations and make note of the following:

 a. How long did it take for you to get to the bus stop?
 b. How long did you have to wait?
 c. How long did it take to get to your final destination?
 d. How many older adult riders were there?
 e. How many barriers to riding public transportation could you identify that you think would make it difficult for older adults to ride the bus? Look for things such as these:

   • Bus stop location and condition
   • Height of steps into the bus
   • Seating
   • Ability to see upcoming stops

3. Make a note of your general feelings. Did you feel any apprehension? How hard was it to figure out your route and bus stop location? On the basis of your observations, what suggestions do you have for making public transportation older adult friendly?

4. Interview an older adult who is currently driving and one who uses public transportation. Ask the current driver: Has your driving changed through the years? Whom would you rely on if you were no longer able to drive? Would you consider using public transportation, and if not, why not? Ask the public transportation user what he or she likes and dislikes about public transportation, and what suggestions he or she has for improving transportation services.

FOR MORE INFORMATION

International Resources

1. The Institute for Transportation and Development Policy (ITDP):www.itdp.org

   The Institute for Transportation and Development Policy (ITDP) was founded in 1985 to promote environmentally sustainable and socially equitable transportation worldwide. ITDP helps cities to: build bus rapid transit (BRT) systems, develop high quality cycling and walking facilities, manage traffic demand, and promote pedestrian and transit-oriented development.

2.. The International Transport Forum: www.internationaltransportforum.org/Home.html

   The International Transport Forum at the OECD is an intergovernmental organization with 54 member countries. It acts as a strategic think tank for transport policy and has a comprehensive library of publications about transportation needs of the elderly.

3. Wandsworth Community Transport: www.wandsworthcommunitytransport.org.uk

   Take a trip to the United Kingdom and check out the transportation services offered by the Wandsworth Community Transport System

National Resources

1. Community Transportation Association of America, 715 15th Street NW, Suite 900, Washington, DC 20005; phone: 202-628-1480; www.ctaa.org

The association's website has links to state and local transportation systems, federal transportation news and budget information, and transportation funding sources that describe more than 90 transportation grants available, along with links to other related transportation sites.

2. National Center on Senior Transportation (NCST), http://seniortransportation.easterseals.com

National Association of Area Agencies on Aging co-administers the NCST with Easter Seals. The Center provides technical assistance, training, and support for innovations in transportation for older adults at the community level. The NCST targets its activities to aging organizations and to public and private transportation providers.

3. Aging and diversity resources

Here are two resources that provide a wonderful overview of the unique transportation need of culturally and ethnically diverse older adults:

a. *Crossing Great Divides: A Guide to Elder Mobility Resources and Solutions in Indian Country* was developed by the NCST in partnership with the National Rural Transit Assistance Program to offer a spark for action within each tribe to address the mobility needs of elders.

http://www.n4a.org/pdf/Crossing_Great_Divides_final.pdf

b. *EVERYONE RIDES: Transportation Access for Culturally and Ethnically Diverse Elders* identifies the challenges involved in addressing the mobility needs of culturally and ethnically diverse elders. The NCST consulted with national organizations, research centers, and transit organizations that target their services to culturally and ethnically diverse elders.

http://www.n4a.org/pdf/FINAL_PROOF_Everyone_Rides_booklet.pdf

Web Resources

1. National Complete Streets Coalition: www.completestreets.org

The National Complete Streets Coalition seeks to fundamentally transform the look, feel, and function of the roads and streets in communities, by changing the way most roads are planned, designed, and constructed so pedestrians, bicyclists, motorists, and transit riders of all ages and abilities can safely move along and across a complete street. Complete Streets' policies direct transportation planners and engineers to consistently design with all users in mind. Their website is full of resources, information, and examples of street redesign across the country.

2. Independent Transportation Network (ITN) America: http://itnamerica.org/index.php

ITN America affiliates, currently in nine states, provides rides with door-to-door, arm-through-arm service to thousands of seniors nationwide by allowing older people to trade their own cars to pay for rides, and enable volunteer drivers to store transportation credits for their own future transportation needs. ITN's Road Scholarship Program converts volunteer credits into a fund for low-income riders, and the gift certificate program helps adult children support their parents' transportation needs from across the street or across the nation. One program, ITNPortland, provides nearly 16,000 rides per year to nearly 1,000 members. Check out the video of the San Diego program at http://www.youtube.com/watch?v = HTV-vJcJ05A.

CHAPTER 15

Housing

It has been a year since Lois sold her home and moved into a federally subsidized senior housing complex. The move was a difficult decision, and the two years she waited for an opening were challenging and frustrating. But once settled into her new apartment, she had no regrets. Her modest income of $623 per month had been totally inadequate to meet the expenses of keeping up her home and paying for her heart medication, groceries, and utilities. She rarely had as much as a dime left over at the end of the month. She could not even begin to consider a major roof repair that was sorely needed. She misses her old neighborhood, but she does not miss the worries of taking care of a house and yard. Now that her money goes a little further, she can enjoy some outings with her new friends.

The majority of older individuals perceive their home as one of their most prized possessions. A home is much more than physical shelter. It gives those who dwell in it a sense of security, privacy, comfort, and independence. It also plays a major role in facilitating social interaction with family and friends (Kochera, Straight, & Guterbock, 2005). A home holds for its residents a multitude of memories and a sense of continuity in life. Findings from a recent AARP study suggest that the 90% of people aged 65 and older want to stay in their homes for as long as possible (Farber, Shinkle, Lynott, Fox-Grage, & Harrell, 2011). The quality and type of dwellings in which older adults live depend on many things, such as their income, age, marital status, gender, and race, as well as their health and functional status.

We begin this chapter by describing the theoretical concept of *person–environment fit* as a framework for understanding the relationship between older individuals' place of residence and their physical, psychological, and social needs. We then discuss the various independent and supportive housing arrangements in which older adults reside and policies that support these arrangements. The chapter concludes with a discussion of several emerging issues that are likely to influence the housing options and needs of older adults in the future.

THE PERSON–ENVIRONMENT FIT MODEL

For older individuals to be satisfied with their environment, an appropriate "fit" needs to exist between their level of competence and the demands of their environment (Lawton, 1980; Lawton & Nahemow, 1973). *Competence* refers to the upper limits of an individual's abilities and extends across several areas of functioning, including health, sensory-cognitive abilities, capacity for self-care, ability to perform instrumental activities, mastery, and social skills (Lawton, 1982). If the environment is too demanding for an older adult's competence, or if the environment puts too few demands on the older adult's competence, there is a poor fit.

Elders enjoy a range of comfort and display adaptive behavior when their physical and social living environments are compatible with their personal abilities and resources. A moderately challenging environment is beneficial because it encourages growth and therefore stretches the person's abilities. Too wide a discrepancy between personal competence and the demands of the environment results in maladaptive behavior and personal stress, and can impede the person's abilities to carry out activities of daily living (ADLs). For example, we know that living in their own homes is the preferred housing choice of most older adults. If, however, the home becomes too costly to manage or the older person is physically unable to maintain it, the demands of the environment may be too stressful. Relocation decisions often occur when older adults, or others in their support network, decide that they are no longer competent to remain living in their current housing environment.

When selecting a new housing option, older persons should avoid moving to a residence that requires too little from them or lacks the stimulation necessary to challenge their existence. When older adults find that their skills and abilities are limited by their environment, they often become bored and give up doing many things for themselves. Overstimulation by the environment can cause distress, but understimulation can be just as stressful for the individual and can result in greater dependence and feelings of helplessness (Lawton, 1982).

In summary, when one is considering outcomes related to the person–environment fit model, the preferences of the individual and the nature of the environment must be taken into account. The older adult's decision to move often is prompted by a need for greater physical, psychological, or social security (Parmelee & Lawton, 1990). An older person's security needs, however, may be in direct conflict with that person's need for autonomy and independence. To adapt successfully to a new, more structured living environment, older adults need to pursue a level of autonomy appropriate to their personal resources and competencies. We now turn to a discussion of the different types of housing environments that older adults occupy.

USERS AND PROGRAMS: INDEPENDENT LIVING ENVIRONMENTS

Independent living environments are designed for older adults who are able to manage daily activities, such as housekeeping, cooking, and personal care, with little assistance from others. Widely varying living environments exist that allow older adults to live independently. Each of these will be discussed below along with the programs and services that help older adults remain in independent living environments.

Single-Family Dwellings[1]

Most noninstitutionalized, community-dwelling older adults own or rent their dwellings. The majority live in detached, single-family dwellings (69%), whereas the remainder lives in multi-unit buildings (19%), mobile homes (7%), and semidetached houses (5%; see Exhibit 15.1). More than two thirds (70%) of older adults who own their homes have no

---

[1]Unless otherwise noted, the statistical information is on single-family dwelling characteristics.

mortgage debt, while 30% are making mortgage payments. Approximately 20% of elders are renters.

In 2010, approximately 81% of individuals aged 65 and older owned their homes. Personal variables such as age, race, gender, marital status, and income influence home ownership in later life. About 82% of persons aged 65 to 74 are homeowners, compared to 78.9% of individuals aged 75 and older. Ownership levels are higher for married-couple families (91.8%) than for men (68.3%) or women (70.4) who live alone in later life (U.S. Census Bureau, 2010). Older persons with incomes greater than $25,000 and White elders are more likely to be homeowners than their less financially well off and minority counterparts (see Exhibit 15.2). Approximately 85% of non-Hispanic White elders are homeowners compared with 68% of Black older adults and 63% of Hispanic elders.

Almost three fourths (74%) of elderly homeowners reside in the suburbs; 23% live in central cities, and 26% live in nonmetropolitan areas (B. Lipman, Lubell, & Salomon, 2010). While older renters are almost twice as likely as homeowners to live in a central city (40% vs. 23%), overall, more older renters live in the suburbs (43%) than either a central city (39%) or nonmetropolitan area (17%). It is common for older adults, particularly homeowners, to have lived in their current place of residence for more than 30 years (AARP Public Policy Institute, 2011). Although only about 6% of dwellings of older persons are considered physically inadequate (e.g., missing siding, broken windows, holes/cracks/crumbling in the

Exhibit 15.1   Types of Dwellings of Older Adults in 2009

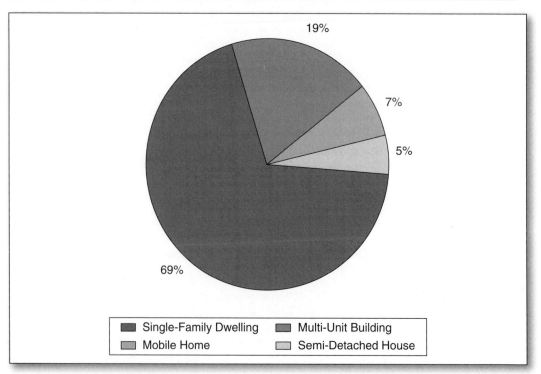

Source: U.S. Census Bureau (2011a).

Exhibit 15.2   Householders 65 Years of Age or Older Who Are Homeowners, by Race and Income

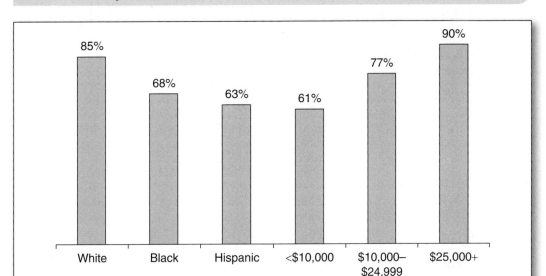

Source: U.S. Census Bureau (2005).

foundation, sagging roof, holes in the floor), many housing units may be neither safe nor suitable for older adults due to hazardous bathrooms, steep stair cases, and narrow door-ways (B. Lipman et al., 2010).

Although many older homeowners do not have a mortgage and consequently spend less on housing than do younger and middle-aged adults, approximately one third (34.8%) of aged homeowners spend 30% or more of their income on housing (U.S. Census Bureau, 2011a). Low-income elders are especially hard hit when it comes to the percentage of their income spent on housing costs. For example, older householders with an annual income of less than $10,000 are likely to spend $250 or more per month on housing costs, leaving them with $583 or less for living expenses. These older adults clearly represent the pre-dicament of being "house rich" but "cash poor."

Housing Programs

As mentioned at the beginning of the chapter, the majority of older adults, such as Lois, want to remain living in their own homes for as long as possible. This may be more difficult for older adults with low and middle incomes and those with houses in need of repair. Most communities offer programs that can provide economic and tangible assistance to make housing costs and repairs more affordable.

Home Equity Conversion Mortgage Programs

Older adults who own their homes can convert part of their home equity into cash while still living in their home through home equity conversion mortgage programs

(HECM). Since the program began in 1989, more than 660,000 loans have been made, with 74% put in place since the mortgage markets began to collapse in 2006 (Redfoot, 2011). To be eligible for an HECM, a homeowner must be 62 years of age or older, have a very low outstanding mortgage balance or own the home free and clear, occupy the property as the principle resident, not be delinquent on any federal debt, and have received U.S. Department of Housing and Urban Development (HUD)–approved reverse mortgage counseling to learn about the program (HUD, 2011a).

There are no restrictions on how the homeowner uses the income generated through an equity conversion program. Older adults may choose to use the income for home repairs, health care costs, or living expenses, or as a source of discretionary income. Borrowers may choose one of five payment options (HUD, 2011a):

- *tenure*, which gives the borrower equal monthly payments from the lender for as long as the borrower lives and continues to occupy the home as a principal residence;

- *term*, which gives the borrower equal monthly payments for a fixed period selected by the borrower;

- *line of credit*, which allows the borrower to make unscheduled withdrawals up to a maximum amount, at times and in amounts of the borrower's choosing until the entire line of credit is used;

- *modified tenure*, which combines the tenure option with a line of credit; or

- *modified term*, which combines the term option with a line of credit.

Once borrowers receive an HECM, they are obligated to occupy the home as a principle residence, make timely payments of the property taxes, maintain a homeowner's hazard insurance policy, and maintain the property in a condition equal to when they secured the loan (HUD, 2011a). Borrowers do not need to repay their HECM loan until they move, sell, or die.

Declining home values and the resulting collapse of the mortgage markets have had a major impact on reverse mortgage programs. While some of these changes have the potential to create more consumer choice in loan options, the costs of reverse mortgages have generally increased and the choices have become more complicated (Redfoot, 2011).

Although not a home equity program, a *property tax relief* program allows older homeowners to defer property tax payments until they sell their homes or die. There are three types of relief programs: homestead exemptions, property tax credit programs, and property tax deferral programs (Chervin, 2007). *Homestead exemptions* are reductions in the amount of assessed property value subject to taxation for owner-occupied housing. Most homestead exemptions provide the same reduction in the assessed property value for all eligible households. *Property tax credit programs* include homestead credit programs that provide the same reductions in property taxes to all eligible households or "circuitbreaker" programs in which tax credits decrease as income increases. *Property tax deferral programs* allow older and disabled homeowners to defer payment of all or a portion of their property taxes until the sale of their property or death. The deferred taxes become a lien against the value of the home. Eligibility requirements (e.g., age, income, homeowner status—owner or renter) for the property tax relief programs differ by state. A survey of 10,000 AARP member households found that households that meet the eligibility criteria of property tax relief programs often are unaware of their existence (Baer, 1998). In addition, seniors reported that they did not apply for these programs because they did not believe they needed property tax assistance or because they needed help with the applications.

Home Repair Programs

Home repairs and maintenance are a considerable expense for many older adults because the majority of older adults have lived in their homes for more than three decades. Although older homeowners are more likely than younger households to have paid off their mortgage, many of these homeowners nevertheless have high housing cost burdens. For example, 4.5% of older persons report housing inadequacies (Harrell & Houser, 2011). Specifically, 0.9% have an inadequate kitchen (i.e., lacking stove, refrigerator, or sink with faucet), 0.5%, have inadequate plumbing (i.e., without hot and cold running water, a flush toilet, or bathtub/shower), and 1.2% report overcrowding (i.e., more than two people per bedroom, or two or more people in a housing unit with no bedrooms). These inadequacies vary across states, with Alaska ranking first in percentage of 50+ households with inadequate kitchens (3.6%), followed by Oregon (1.9%) and Hawaii (1.6%). Alaska also has the most 50+ households with inadequate plumbing (4.5%), followed by New Mexico (1.6%) and Arizona (1.0%).

Physical housing problems are more frequent among older, frail, poor, and minority seniors. Besides needing specific repairs, many homes do not support frail older adults in conducting daily activities within the home. Older adults who are aging in place may need to modify their homes' structure to accommodate their physical limitations. Modifications in lighting, accessibility, mobility, and bathing facilities can improve functioning and enhance safety (AARP, 2005).

With the increasing demand for assistance with housing upkeep and repairs, a number of home repair programs have emerged across the country. Home repair programs provide assistance with home maintenance or minor repairs. The funding for many of these programs comes from community development block grants or Title III monies from the Older Americans Act (OAA). Programs vary with regard to the type of repairs they subsidize but typically include: emergency repairs for plumbing, electricity, heat, and leaking roofs; minor repairs; exterior painting; and the removal of debris.

Two programs that help low-income adults with the costs of heating and cooling their homes are the Department of Energy's Weatherization Assistance Program (WAP) and the Low Income Home Energy Assistance Program (LIHEAP). Under WAP, any household at or below 200% of poverty may be eligible for services (U.S. Department of Energy [DOE], 2011b). The DOE provides funds to all of the states, which contract with community action agencies, other nonprofits, and local governments to make repairs that improve the energy efficiency of low-income dwellings. The program provides energy-efficiency services to approximately 100,000 homes every year and has weatherized more than 6.4 million low-income homes since its inception in 1976 (DOE, 2011a). The average expenditure limit per home is $6,500 (DOE, 2011b). In addition to reducing the utility costs for homeowners, the program helps improve health and safety by reducing carbon monoxide emissions and eliminating fire hazards. Funding for the weatherization program in the FY 2009 was $250 million (DOE, 2011c).

Best Practice: Los Angeles Housing Department Handyworker Program

The Handyworker Program of the Los Angeles Housing Department provides free minor repairs to low- and moderate-income homeowners who are senior citizens 62 years of age and older or physically disabled. Emergency repairs that directly affect the occupants' health and safety also are provided to other low- and moderate-income homeowners. Eligible repairs are limited to work that does not require a city building permit or formal inspection. Typical services include the following:

- Emergency repairs, such as repair or replacement of broken doors and windows
- Accessibility improvements for the physically challenged, such as access ramps and hand railings
- Correction of safety hazards, such as repairs to porches, steps, and sidewalks
- Home security improvements, such as fences, security doors, and smoke detectors
- Habitability improvements, such as replacement of sinks, toilets, and floor tiles
- Exterior and interior painting

For more information, contact the Handyworker Program: phone: 213-808-8803 or 866-557-7368, or visit http://lahd.lacity.org/lahdinternet/HandyWorkerandHomeSecurePrograms/tabid/86/Default.aspx.

LIHEAP provides heating and cooling assistance to low-income families regardless of age either directly through vendors, or to property owners for home heating and cooling costs, energy crisis intervention, or low-cost weatherization. An eligible household's income must not exceed 150% of the poverty level or 75% of the state median income (Administration for Children and Families, 2011b). In 2009, about 39% of the households receiving energy assistance had at least one member 60 years of age or older (Berger & Yang, 2010). There is wide variation in states' average household benefit level for various types of fuel assistance. In 2007, the national average LIHEAP household benefit for heating costs was $265 and $321 for combined winter and year-round crisis benefits (U.S. Department of Health and Human Services [USDHHS], 2010c). Funding proposed for LIHEAP in FY 2012 was $2.5 billion, about one half the level of FY 2011 funding (Administration for Children and Families, 2011b; Jackson, 2011)

Home Sharing

When home expense becomes burdensome, home sharing can be a viable solution to managing those expenses. Shared housing is an arrangement in which two or more unrelated individuals share a home or apartment (AARP, 2005). "Tenants" often pay modest rent or provide services to the householder in exchange for room and board. For older adults with extra living space in their homes, this housing option can provide financial assistance, companionship in a familiar and comfortable setting, and help with household chores.

A study conducted by the AARP Foundation Women's Leadership Circle found that more than one third of the 1,200 women aged 45 and older surveyed said they would be interested in sharing a house with friends or other women—as long as it included private space (Mahoney, 2007). The biggest incentives for home sharing among the women were financial security and companionship. An earlier AARP study (2005) reported that of people aged 50 and older interviewed with a household income under $50,000 were more likely to find the idea very or somewhat appealing than those with a household income of $50,000 or more. Older home sharers who are economically secure and active but live alone typically are interested in having someone in their homes at night or someone who will do periodic home maintenance chores (e.g., shoveling snow) but do not expect routine daily assistance or companionship from their "boarder" (Jaffe & Howe, 1988).

Federal Housing Programs

Federal legislation has created a number of housing programs that assist older adults who have limited incomes through Section 8, Section 202, and public housing. In addition, programs under the auspices of the Rural Housing and Community Development Service offer housing assistance for older, low-income individuals living in rural areas.

Section 8

Project-Based Assistance. Under Section 8, rental subsidies are given to property owners who agree to rent to low-income individuals and families. The subsidy covers the difference between the tenants' contribution, an amount that totals 30% of their adjusted income, and fair market rents. From the inception of the Section 8 program, owners were able to develop properties dedicated for use by elderly households. Approximately 200,455 units, or about one half of of project-based Section 8 housing, is dedicated to elderly households (Perl, 2010).

Housing Choice Voucher Program. In contrast to the Section 8 project assistance component, the participants in the housing choice voucher program find their own housing, including single-family homes, townhouses, and apartments. They are free to choose any housing that meets the requirements of the program (e.g., rent that is not higher than the fair market value) and are not limited to units located in subsidized housing projects. Tenants are responsible for paying 30% of their income for rent. If the rent is higher than the fair market value, the renters are responsible for the difference (HUD, 2011b). In 2003, older adults (65+) were heads of households in 14.7% of tenant-based Section 8 housing (HUD, 2008b).

Section 202

Section 202 Supportive Housing for the Elderly Program is the only federally funded housing program designed specifically for older persons. It makes low-cost federal loans to nonprofit sponsors for new construction or rehabilitation of existing structures to provide subsidized rental housing for low- and moderate-income elders 62 years of age and older. Since its inception in 1959, the program has supported the creation of approximately 262,704 residential units designated for elderly households only (Perl, 2010). Beginning in 2002, appropriations have included funding to convert a small number of projects to licensed assisted living facilities. Tenants living in Section 202 units have incomes below 50% of their area's median income. The average Section 202 resident is female (71%), White (61%), 79 years old, with a mean annual income of $11,227, and has lived in her current residence for an average of 5.5 years (Haley & Gray, 2008). The majority of Section 202 units are located in central cities (51%) or suburban areas (34%) and usually offer supportive services, such as transportation, housekeeping, and home-delivered meals.

Although there is nothing in the HUD guidelines governing Section 202 (and certain project-based Section 8 housing) assistance programs specifically prohibiting the exclusion of children from these developments, the housing units are typically not equipped to serve families with both elderly residents and young children. To address the growing number of grandparents raising grandchildren, Congress enacted the Living Equitably: Grandparents Aiding Children and Youth (LEGACY) Act in 2003, which provided funding for housing units in the Section 202 program for elderly residents raising grandchildren or other relatives aged 19 or younger (Perl, 2010). In FY 2006, Congress appropriated $3.96 million for an Intergenerational Families Demonstration Project. In December 2008, HUD funded two projects: the Roseland Grandfamily Apartments in Chicago, consisting of 10 units, and Fiddler's Annex in Smithville, Tennessee, consisting of nine units (HUD, 2008c). Opened in 2011, residents of both projects receive a range of supportive services tailored to meet the needs of seniors, children, and the families as a whole (Generations United, 2011a). Roseland Place Grandfamily Apartments, for example, provides residents with access to recreational spaces, shared gardens, a central game/TV room, and an on-campus beauty salon (Mercy Housing, 2011; Trivedi, 2011).

Public Housing

Public housing is the oldest and largest federal housing program assisting individuals and families with low incomes, including older renters. In 1956, Congress for the first time gave preference to seniors in public housing (Milbank Memorial Fund, 2006). Throughout the 1960s and 1970s, a large number of developments were built specifically for low-income seniors. Today, approximately 76,000 public housing units are designated exclusively for older residents (Perl, 2010). With very few exceptions, these units are traditional apartments. Older adult renters occupy almost one half of public housing units, including over 50,000 seniors aged 83 and older (McNickle, 2007). Local public housing authorities usually operate these housing units, and renters pay rent no more than 30% of their adjusted monthly income. Older residents of public housing are older, poorer, and perhaps frailer than most elderly households. Almost one in five elderly public housing households is headed by someone aged 85 or older, compared with about one in nine nationwide. An estimated 20% of older adults living in public housing experience difficulty with at least one ADL, compared with about 12% of the general population (Brigl, 2001). Older women compose almost three fourths of public housing residents, and almost one half of all elderly public housing residents are minorities; approximately 25% of elderly residents are Black and 13% are Hispanic.

Many public housing communities employ on-site service coordinators who help elderly residents obtain supportive services that allow them continue to live in place, independently, without having to move to more expensive assisted care environments (HUD, 2010; McNickle, 2007). Service coordinators work with community service providers to tailor services to the needs of eligible residents, establish a system to monitor and evaluate service delivery and outcomes, and coordinate with other independent living programs to meet the needs of their elderly residents.

Rural Programs

Two housing programs are available to rural elders under the Rural Housing and Community Development Service program. Section 515 offers low-interest construction loans for rental and congregate housing for low-income individuals. Since it began operating in

1963, Section 515 has provided more than half a million affordable rental homes for the lowest income rural residents (L. R. Strauss, 2009). Section 515 financed over 38,000 units at its peak in 1979, but produced 2,800 units in 1995 and only 800 units in 2008. About 40% of Section 515 tenants are older adults (U.S. Department of Agriculture, Rural Development Program [USDA-RDP], 2011). Section 504 provides loans and grants to low-income rural residents 62 years of age and older to repair new or existing single-family housing. This program provides funds for removing electrical and fire hazards, replacing roofing, installing or improving water and waste-water disposal systems, and installing insulation and heating and cooling systems (USDA-RDP, 2004).

Naturally Occurring and Planned Retirement Communities

Although the majority of older adults live in age-integrated communities, almost one third of all older adults live in a naturally occurring retirement community (NORC) in which, by most definitions, at least half of the residents are 60 years of age or older (Ormond, Black, Tilly, & Thomas, 2004). NORCs emerge through long periods as people living in the same location age in place. NORCs evolve in three ways: "aged-left-behind," "aging in place," and "in-migration" (Hunt, 1998). The first two types of NORCs are populated primarily by long-term residents—the first by residents who stayed in a community characterized by out-migration; the second by older residents who gradually became the dominant population in a stable community. The third type is distinguished by the proportion of older residents who are new to the community. Residents aging in place in these communities may reside in an apartment type of building (i.e., vertical NORCs) or single-dwelling homes in a specific neighborhood (i.e., horizontal NORCs; Ivery & Akstein-Kahan, 2010).

Launched in 2002 with funds from Title IV of the OAA, the NORC Supportive Services Program (NORC-SSP) provides NORC building residents with a range of coordinated health and social services on-site or in proximity to it. This service delivery framework is designed to assist older adults to age in place with independence, dignity, security, and quality of life (Bedney, Goldberg, & Josephson, 2010; Ivery & Akstein-Kahan, 2010). In addition, NORC-SSPs provide older adults with the opportunity to participate in the development and operation of NORC programs. Between 2002 and 2010, Congress initiated 50 NORC-SSP demonstration projects in 26 states. Findings from a 2006 survey of NORC-SSP residents from 24 communities around the country suggested that the program is an effective way of increasing socialization and reducing social isolation of residents, linking older adults with services that can help them age in place, and promoting their health and well-being (Bedney et al., 2010).

For Your Files: B'nai B'rith

B'nai B'rith is the largest Jewish sponsor of nonsectarian, federally subsidized housing for older adults in the United States. B'nai B'rith, through its Senior Citizens Housing Committee, has been involved in a cooperative partnership with HUD to make available rental apartments for low-income older adults. It has a network of 42 apartment buildings in 26 communities across the United States, which encompasses more than 4,000 apartment units serving more than 8,000 persons. Each project has a volunteer board of directors that makes sure each apartment building is responsive to

(Continued)

(Continued)

its residents. Professional staff members offer support and assistance to individual apartment building boards of directors.

For more information, contact B'nai B'rith at 2020 K Street, NW, 7th Floor, Washington, DC 20006; phone: 202-857-6600 or 888-388-4224; http://www.bnaibrith.org.

About 7% of households aged 55 or older (approximately 2.5 million households) live in age-restricted communities, such as Leisure World in California and Sun City in Arizona, with owners and renters about evenly split (Metlife Mature Market Institute, 2011b). Such communities are more common in the South and West. Homeowners typically choose age-restricted communities to live in because such communities are easier living, quieter neighborhoods, and maintenance costs are included in fees (National Association of Home Builders Research Center, 2002). As for community attributes, the community clubhouse, proximity to shopping, and planned social activities are the most common reasons older adults gave for moving to a planned age-restricted community. It is easy to see that most of these residences support an active lifestyle. For example, the 18,000 residents (average age of 78) of Leisure World in Laguna Woods Village in Orange County, California, enjoy special-interest activities including fitness, swimming, golf, tennis, arts and crafts, and two computer-learning centers, plus the opportunity to participate in the Saddleback College Emeritus class program. Facilities include seven clubhouses, five swimming pools, a performing arts center seating 814, and the community's "living" amenity, the equestrian center. For more information, see www.lagunawoodsvillage.com.

Senior Cohousing and Other Intentional Communities

Cohousing, a form of residential development designed to promote the practice of caring for neighbors as they age while retaining individual privacy, is emerging as an appealing living arrangement for older adults (Wardrip, 2010a). Although the majority of the 115 cohousing communities in the United States are multigenerational, there are at least three existing communities (and several more in the planning stages) specifically for persons aged 50 and older: ElderSpirit Community in Abington, Virginia (www.elderspirit.net); Glacier Circle in Davis, California (www.abrahampaiss.com/ElderCohousing/ GlacierCircle. htm); and Silver Sage Village in Boulder, Colorado (www.silversagevillage.com). Each of these communities incorporates universal design elements and accessible common areas. Residents define their collective approach to aging in community, including the limits of co-care that they are willing to provide to one another. Residents, of which a high proportion are never married, divorced, or childless; have identified mutual support as a driving reason to move into cohousing; and have emphasized the centrality of community "fictive kin" support in their lives (A. P. Glass, 2009).

Although lesbian, gay, bisexual, and transgender (LGBT) retirement and long-term care communities are still very few, this is a burgeoning field that will be fueled by the issues LGBT seniors have voiced about current housing and healthcare options (Adelman, Gurevitich, de Vries, & Blando, 2006; Stein, Beckerman, & Sherman, 2010). Projects such as Services and Advocacy for Gay, Lesbian and Transgender Elders (SAGE: http://www.sageusa.org/about/ index.cfm) are helping service professionals and LGBT seniors realize the possibilities for more inclusive housing options in late life. One of the earliest LGBT-friendly retirement community efforts was Openhouse, established in San Francisco in 1998 to provide housing and offer a full range of care for residents of all income levels, and operate as a community "hub" offering a variety of LGBT-sensitive services, programs, and events to both residents and nonresidents (Adelman et al., 2006). Although actual housing units specifically for LGBT seniors were not available through Openhouse until 2008, this organization has educated LGBT seniors about their rights and the LGBT-friendly policies of existing housing options. To learn more about this pioneering community, visit their website (http://openhouse-sf.org).

Best Practice: Supportive Services Program— Public–Private Partnerships

Some elderly residents of public and federally subsidized multifamily housing receive supportive services through partnerships between property owners and local organizations, and through programs provided by USDHHS. For example, property owners can establish relationships with local nonprofit organizations, including churches, to ensure that residents have access to the services they need. At their discretion, property owners may establish relationships that give older adults access to meals, transportation, and housekeeping and personal care services. Examples of such partnerships include the following:

- In Greensboro, North Carolina, Dolan Manor, a Section 202 housing development, has established a relationship with a volunteer group from a local church. The volunteer group provides a variety of services for the residents, such as transportation.

- In Plain City, Ohio, residents of Pleasant Valley Garden, a Section 515 property, receive meals five times a week at the community's senior center (a $2.50 donation is suggested). A local hospital donates a large portion of the food and volunteers, including residents, serve the meals. Any funds collected from the lunch go directly back into the senior center food program. The United Way, several other local businesses and organizations, private donors, and some funds from neighboring counties provide additional support for both the food program and other senior center activities.

- In, Philadelphia, Pennsylvania, with the support of HUD, a public–private partnership between the Pennsylvania Housing Finance Agency, dmhFund, and Penrose Properties formed to develop LGBT-friendly housing. The partnership between government and private entities has laid the groundwork for building a $19 million, 56-bedroom housing establishment for LGBT seniors 62 and older who earn less than 60% of the Philadelphia median income.

Source: HUD (2012) and U.S. General Accounting Office (2005).

Single-Room Occupancy Hotels

Single-room occupancy hotels (SROs) are "cheap hotels and rooming houses located in areas adjacent to the downtown business districts" (Erickson & Eckert, 1977, p. 440). They can be remodeled hotels, tenements, school buildings, hotels that have always served as SROs, or newer buildings built specifically as SROs. Typically, SROs provide inner-city residents with a private room and a shared kitchen, bath, and common area. Some SROs have been built as micro-efficiency units that include a small kitchenette and a bathroom with a shower (Regnier & Culver, 1994). Services provided to tenants range from nothing to highly managed care. Sometimes, SROs will offer limited security, light housekeeping, or an errand service (Rollinson, 1991a). Although perceived to be at the bottom rung of the housing ladder, SROs provide emergency, transitional, and permanent housing for single low-income persons of all ages (Regnier & Culver, 1994).

Most research on older adults living in SROs was published before the mid-1990s. In studies of SROs located in Chicago and New York, the percentage of tenants who were older adults ranged from 15% to 33%. Most of these individuals indicated not only that they were lifelong residents of the city but also that many had lived in the same neighborhood during their childhood (Crystal & Beck, 1992; Rollinson, 1991b).

In contrast to the image of the SRO tenant as primarily male and alcoholic, older adults who live in SROs represent a diverse group with regard to gender, age, health status, marital status, race, and education (Crystal & Beck, 1992; Rollinson, 1990). Approximately 40% of older tenants are women. The age and health profile of tenants creates a picture of an older adult, usually in his or her 70s, coping with chronic conditions such as arthritis and other musculoskeletal problems, diabetes, heart conditions, and sensory losses. Few older SRO residents reported a past or current drinking problem. Almost one half of the older SRO tenants reported never being married; most others were widowed, divorced, or separated. Approximately one third of the tenants had less than a ninth-grade education, whereas almost one fourth reported that they had attended or graduated from college. Researchers also report a diverse picture with regard to race of the tenants with the percentage of White residents ranging from 54% to 97% (Bild & Havingurst, 1976; Community Emergency Shelter Organizations, cited in Rollinson, 1991b; Crystal & Beck, 1992). Residents live on small incomes from Supplemental Security Income (SSI) and Social Security. The majority of older tenants reported average incomes falling below current poverty levels, with their housing costs (i.e., rent and utilities) taking up as much as half of their monthly income. For example, monthly rents at the Ellis Hotel in Los Angeles range from $180 for General Relief recipients to $240 for Social Security recipients ("Single Room Occupancy Housing Corporation," 2012).

Researchers and service providers characterize residents of SROs as fiercely independent individuals who are protective of their autonomy and who receive little assistance from relatives, friends, or neighbors (Rollinson, 1990). Rollinson quotes one resident, confined to a wheelchair, as saying, "Some people say, 'Can I help you do this and help you do that,' and being bullheaded as hell I tell them no, except to go to the [grocery] store" (p. 201).

CHALLENGES FOR INDEPENDENT LIVING PROGRAMS

As discussed at the outset of the chapter, the majority of older adults reside in independent living settings and desire to do so for as long as possible. Many issues need to be addressed, however, to promote independent living in the community.

Removing Barriers to Shared Housing

Several barriers can impede the use of shared housing in later life (Mantell & Gildea, 1989). The most frequently cited barrier is a lack of financial support for programs that help match older individuals with prospective housemates. Limited federal, state, or local support is available for these programs, and the clients served are often unable to pay the actual cost of providing the service. Second, restrictive zoning regulations and building and fire codes prohibit shared housing in many residential neighborhoods (Liebig, Koenig, & Pynoos, 2006). A third barrier is older adults' fear that their income from SSI, food stamps, or fuel subsidies will be reduced if regulatory agencies base decisions on the income of the household. In addition, older adults may be hesitant to share their homes with a stranger. Such attitudes, no doubt, are tied to deep-rooted values of privacy and independence.

Serving Older Adults Living in Public Housing

Several challenges have emerged for older adults living in public housing. While public housing units are adequate for the majority of low-income older residents, the units do not provide the flexibility to allow residents to age in place, nor do they necessarily provide the range of housing options needed to serve the increasing share of frail seniors. In addition, a significant portion of public housing for older adults is rapidly becoming physically and functionally obsolete. Most developments are simply not equipped to meet the residential and supportive service needs of their increasingly frail and diverse residents (Milbank Memorial Fund, 2006). Furthermore, there are lengthy waiting lists to get into public housing. In some cities, 28 older persons apply for every vacancy that occurs in newer units. The lengthy waiting lists are due in part to the lack of available units and a low turnover rate. Yet, in FY 2012, Congress did not appropriate any money for new construction. As the low turnover rate suggests, many older tenants who move into public housing stay there until they are no longer able to live independently, creating a tremendous need for supportive services to help them age in place. About one third of Section 202 properties have a service coordinator available to assess residents' needs, identify and link residents to services, and monitor the delivery of services (National Low Income Housing Coalition [NLIHC], 2006). In addition, in 2004, HUD completed conversion of seven existing 202 housing units into assisted living facilities. This was one of the first attempts to develop an affordable continuum of care within public housing complexes for low-income seniors.

Promoting Communities for Older Adults

The future of planned retirement communities is uncertain because many of the original residents are aging in place. In addition, some older individuals who move to a planned community find that they miss interacting with children and younger adults, who typically live within traditional community neighborhoods.

Because NORCs typically emerge within traditional residential environments, health and other supportive services are not usually available within or close to the immediate neighborhood. Residents therefore must be able to seek out and obtain these services on their own. NORCs that develop within structured environments, such as an apartment complex, are likely to have some form of building management and may also have resident councils or recreation committees. How successful NORC supportive services programs are depends on how successful service providers are in establishing strong relationships with the NORC organizational structure and its residents (Bedney et al., 2010; Ormond et al., 2004).

Will cohousing options for the older adult be the wave of the future for the aging boomers? Current developments and neighborhoods have had initial success, but their long-term growth and viability is yet to be determined. It takes a significant amount of time and work to establish such communities, and the downturn of the real estate market makes the process, particularly financing, a difficult challenge. On the resident side, not everyone is suited to consensus decision making or the responsibilities of community life. As residents of cohousing developments "age in place," members will face choices about adapting the buildings and units for safety and security, making accommodations for their oldest residents, and caring long-term for members in the community.

Enhancing SROs

Although SROs offer the most vulnerable persons in society a place to live, they provide little in the way of comfort, security, or support. They often are in deteriorating condition and poorly maintained. Faced with no other viable options for affordable or senior housing, however, many SRO residents, particularly those in the most economically and socially vulnerable groups of elders, are aging in place and in need of services such as case management, healthcare, and food access (D. Kelly, 2009; National Resource Center on LGBT Aging, 2011).

Many SROs in large cities such as New York, San Francisco, and Los Angeles were built before or at the turn of the century (Ovrebo, Minkler, & Liljestrand, 1991). The rooms are sparse and small; most cannot easily accommodate wheelchairs. Kitchenettes often consist of a nonworking stove (Rollinson, 1990). Elevators frequently break down, leaving frail residents stranded in their rooms. Lack of adequate heating in the winter and extreme heat in the summer, steep stairs, unsteady banisters, torn tiles, holes in the wall, bedbug-infested mattresses, mold covering bathtubs, drug paraphernalia litter, and rodents are problems reported by residents (D. Kelly, 2009; Knight & Lee, 2011).

Urban renewal has eliminated many SROs (Harahan, Sanders, & Stone, 2006). The media has captured some particularly prolonged conflicts between property owners or developers and SRO tenants in New York City, where battles have raged regarding whether conversions of SROs to tourist hotels have followed legal guidelines (Kamping-Carder, 2011; Segan, 2006). Some SRO projects have moved in the direction of providing better supports for older residents rather than pushing them out. For example, Project Hotel Alert in Los Angeles, California, received funds from the city aging department to offer older SRO residents a wide range of services including case management, information and referral, transportation, meals, and medical screening; one SRO was even renovated with wheelchair-accessible bathrooms through this initiative (Harahan et al., 2006).

Best Practice: Communities for a Lifetime

Communities for a Lifetime is a statewide initiative started by former Florida Governor Jeb Bush to assist Florida cities, towns, and counties in planning and implementing improvements benefiting the lives of all residents, youthful or senior. This initiative recognizes the diverse needs of residents and the unique contributions individuals can make to their communities. Participating communities use existing resources and state technical assistance to make crucial civic improvements in such areas as housing, health care, transportation, accessibility, business partnerships, community education, efficient use of natural resources, and volunteer opportunities to the betterment of their communities.

A Community for a Lifetime values individuals of all ages and engages communities in a process of continuous self-assessment and improvement. Through this process, communities enhance opportunities for people to age in place, or continue living in their own communities for a lifetime, while also benefiting people of all ages. Once a community commits to creating a Community for a Lifetime, they assemble a team of community partners to gather information about the opportunities, programs, and services that are available to older adults. The information is used by community planners to develop work plan strategies for incorporating universal design for housing accessibility, health care, transportation, and efficient use of natural resources. As of October 2010, more than 100 Florida cities, towns, and counties had committed themselves to creating a better place for older adults to live, providing all residents with the opportunity to achieve their full potential and contribute to the betterment of their communities.

For more information, go to http://www.communitiesforalifetime.org/highlights.php.

Although SROs are fraught with serious problems, they provide housing to a group of older persons who are at risk of being homeless. However, the SRO as a housing option for low-income older persons is diminishing. Since the 1970s, the number of SRO units has rapidly declined. An estimated 1,111,000 SRO units were eliminated from 1970 to 1980 (Hooper & Hamberg, 1986). The major forces behind the loss of SROs include downtown revitalization, gentrification, and lack of funding to rehabilitate deteriorating buildings (Ovrebo et al., 1991). This loss of housing represents a serious problem for older SRO residents, many of whom reported that they did not know what they would do if they had to move.

SUPPORTIVE LIVING ENVIRONMENTS

Supportive living environments are designed to help older adults who are self-sufficient and are capable of self-care to some extent, but who need some assistance with ADLs. Generally, supportive environments provide older adults varying degrees of assistance and oversight.

Accessory Dwelling Units

Accessory Dwelling Units (ADUs) are residential units that provide independent living facilities for one or more persons, with designated areas for cooking and sanitation, plus space for living, sleeping, and eating (Antoninetti, 2008; Liebig et al., 2006). Between 65,000 and 300,000 units are created legally each year (Cobb & Dvorak, 2000); the number of annually built illegal ADUs (e.g., home additions or garage conversions completed without permits) is estimated at between 60,000 and 300,000 units nationwide. Depending on their location relative to the primary dwelling unit, ADUs are categorized as interior units, attached units, or detached units (HUD, 2008a). Regardless of type, ADUs contribute to a community's housing supply and provide an affordable housing option for many low- and middle-income older adults.

Elder Cottage Housing Opportunity (ECHO) housing units (also known as *granny flats* or *garden suites*) are small, self-contained, movable housing units located next to the home of a family member. The units also may fit into the space of an attached garage or be connected directly to the main house. They have their own electrical system, temperature controls, and plumbing. Meters can be attached to the unit to keep utility costs separate from the main house. Configurations of the units vary; most have a living room, kitchen, bedroom, and bath. ECHO senior housing units can cost far less to purchase or lease than traditional homes—companies in California and Pennsylvania offer 500-square-foot one-bedroom units, completely installed, for around $25,000 (Senior Living, 2012). In other areas, ECHO senior housing may cost more, but leasing a unit could be an option. Once no longer needed, the units are removed.

To create an accessory or mother-in-law apartment, families remodel an existing room or basement into a living area in which a frail older adult can live. An accessory cottage, also known as *guest cottage* or *carriage house*, is a permanent separate structure placed on the same parcel or lot as the single-family dwelling. Garage or barn apartments are similar to accessory cottages because they are not part of the primary dwelling; the latter is more popular in rural areas (Liebig et al., 2006). As with ECHO housing, accessory apartments and cottages provide the same benefits of privacy and support, although the construction is more permanent.

Both ECHO housing and accessory apartments/cottages allow older adults to live with or near their families. They offer families a way to assist older family members yet allow privacy and independent living. Other benefits include lower living costs, increased intergenerational interaction, a possible delay of institutionalization, and enhanced quality of life. For example, in comparison to older adults on a waiting list for a cottage, residents of elder cottages reported significantly greater satisfaction with their housing, increased independence, more telephone contacts with friends and family, improved relationships with family members living in the main house, and less formal service use (Altus, Xaverius, Mathews, & Kosloski, 2002). However, zoning requirements, policy barriers, and low consumer acceptance have severely limited the growth of ADUs in the United States (Koebel, Beamish, & Danielson, 2003; Wardrip, 2010b).

Congregate Housing

Although public housing often is referred to as *congregate housing*, many congregate facilities are privately owned. Most congregate housing facilities have separate apartments for each resident plus common, shared areas for meals and recreation, including "congregate dining, social lounges, laundry facilities, recreation spaces, and a secure barrier free environment" (Heumann, 1990, p. 46; Monk & Kaye, 1991). These facilities provide services in a residential setting for persons who can no longer independently manage the tasks of everyday living. The typical onsite staff includes a building manager, janitorial services, and social/activity organizer. Medical personnel are not usually onsite in a congregate facility.

Residents in congregate housing receive at least one major group meal per day and have the option of receiving assistance with additional meals, housekeeping, personal care, transportation, and other support services if needed. Residents typically have some limitation that precludes independent living, but that does not require continuous medical or nursing care or full-time personal care.

Continuing Care Retirement Communities

Continuing care retirement communities (CCRCs) provide a full range of housing options for retired adults, from independent living through nursing home care. There are more than 1,861 CCRCs in 48 states and the District of Columbia with more than 745,000 residents (U.S. Senate Special Committee on Aging, 2012). Pennsylvania, Ohio, California, Illinois, Florida, Texas, Kansas, Indiana, Iowa, and North Carolina have the largest number of CCRCs. Eighty-two percent of CCRCs are not-for-profit, and approximately one half of are affiliated with faith-based organizations. The majority of CCRCs are part of a multi-site system with the typical CCRC having fewer than 300 units (Zarem, 2010).

CCRCs offer incoming residents a contract that remains in effect for the balance of their lifetime. There are three basic types of CCRC agreements (Zarem, 2010).

A *life-care, extensive,* or *all-inclusive contract* includes shelter, residential services, and amenities, as well as long-term nursing care for little or no substantial increase in monthly payments, except for normal operating costs and inflation. They provide for the prepayment of medical expenses, similar to an insurance arrangement. About 29% of CCRCs offer extensive/all-inclusive contracts (McCarthy & Rutledge, 2012).

A *modified contract* also includes shelter, residential services, and amenities, but offers only a specified amount of long-term nursing care for little or no substantial increase in monthly payments, except for normal operating costs and inflation adjustments. After using the specified amount of nursing care, residents pay either partial or full per-diem rates for the care they require. About 19% of CCRCs offer modified agreements (McCarthy & Rutledge, 2012).

A *fee-for-service contract* includes shelter, residential services, amenities, and emergency and infirmary nursing care, but does not include any discounted health care or assisted living services. Residents receive priority or guaranteed admission for these services, as needed, but must pay full per-diem rates. About 20% of CCRCs offer fee-for-service agreements (McCarthy & Rutledge, 2012).

Basic continuing care agreements typically require a lump-sum entrance fee, paid on moving into the community, and monthly payments thereafter. Still other CCRCs have periodic fee-only agreements where there is no entry fee and the costs of the living unit, service, and care are covered solely by a monthly fee. Rental CCRC contracts, like the fee-for-service, entrance-fee contract, include no coverage for the cost of assisted living or nursing services, but offer the resident the lowest level of upfront expense (Zarem, 2010). Least common are CCRCs with equity agreements that involve the actual purchase of real estate or membership; service and health care package transactions are generally separate from the purchase transaction.

Entry fees and monthly fees vary greatly from one CCRC to another. Entrance fees can range from about $20,000 to more than $500,000 (AARP, 2012b); nationally, the average CCRC entrance fee in 2010 was $248,000. The majority of CCRCs offer some type of entrance-fee refund. Refundable entrance-fee contracts may include a declining-scale feature where the refund declines over time, a partial refund, or a full refund. Many CCRCs offer contracts that refund a specific percentage of the entrance fee (e.g., 50%, 75%, 90%, 100%) regardless of the length of residency (Zarem, 2010).

As one might expect from the high entry fees, which make CCRCs the most expensive of all long-term care options, CCRCs typically attract an affluent older population. In addition to required entrance fees, residents pay monthly charges that may range from $3,000 to $5,000 (AARP, 2012b). The typical CCRC resident is a White, widowed woman in her mid-80s (Zarem, 2010). They tend to have higher incomes and educational attainments than the general population of older adults. Krout, Moen, Holmes, Oggins, and Bowen (2002) found that a decline in the health of one's spouse or in one's own health and freedom from the burden of home maintenance were motivating factors for those who recently moved to a not-for-profit CCRC designed for people older than age 65 in good physical and mental health. Enticing features of the CCRC included: the quality of the management of the facility; the size, design, and choice of units; climate; and location near cultural activities.

Attitudes toward CCRCs have changed since the emergence of this type of retirement housing in the 1960s. Current and future generations of older adults are looking for retirement communities where they can enjoy an active life, rather than simply shopping for quality health care they hope never to need (High, 2000). CCRCs have responded by adding new housing, health care, and amenities options to their current structures. Examples include fitness centers, casual dining programs, business centers, computer labs, putting greens, expanded libraries, and indoor pool/fitness complexes.

Assisted Living

Assisted living has emerged as a popular choice for people who need supportive and health-related services and help with unscheduled ADLs. According to a 2007 survey, there are about 38,000 assisted living facilities (ALFs) accommodating about 975,000 residents in the United States (National Center for Assisted Living, 2012). Although definitions of assisted living vary across states, the term is generally defined as a residential setting that provides or coordinates personal care services, 24-hour supervision, scheduled and unscheduled assistance, social activities, and some health-related services. These settings may include personal care boarding homes with additional services, residential care units owned by and adjacent to nursing homes, congregate housing settings that have added services, purpose-built assisted living programs, or the middle level of CCRCs. Ownership of these facilities may be either nonprofit or for-profit (Wright, 2004).

The average assisted living community has 54 units (National Center for Assisted Living, 2012). Whereas studios used to be the most common type of assisted living apartment, one-bedroom units are now more preferable as they allow residents to keep more of their furniture and personal belongings. Most facilities offer private occupancy units with at least: full bathrooms, kitchenettes with refrigerators and cooking capacity, and lockable doors; three meals a day in a group dining room; general housekeeping and maintenance services; personal care according to individual needs; onsite delivery or coordination of nursing, health, and social services; and supervision and oversight for persons with cognitive limitations. Facilities use fewer medical staff than nonmedical staff, and the majority of facilities contract services from a variety of consultants, ranging from beauticians to physicians (Wright, 2004).

In 2011, the national average, private-pay monthly rate for a private room with a private bath in an assisted living facility was $3,477, with average rents ranging from $2,156 a month to $5,757 a month (Metlife Mature Market Institute, 2011a). Most facilities charge higher rates for added services. Most of the rates, even at the high end, are substantially less than nursing home care for private-paying residents. Insurance companies are increasingly allowing holders of long-term care policies to use their benefits for assisted living if the services are cost-effective. Public payment for assisted living includes: supplemental payments to the facility for services for SSI clients; reimbursement by Medicaid, Medicaid waiver, or state long-term care programs; or some combination of these sources.

According to the National Center for Assisted Living (2009), the typical assisted living resident is an 86-year-old woman who is mobile but needs assistance with two activities of daily living such as bathing (64%), dressing (39%), or toileting (26%). About 87% of residents also need help with meal preparation, and 81% need help managing their medications. Residents come to assisted living facilities from a variety of settings, including a private home or apartment (70%), a retirement or independent living community (9%), a nursing facility (9%), a family residence (such as living with adult children; 7%), or another assisted living residence or group home (5%). Most facilities admit and retain residents with a variety of disabling conditions and physical health care needs, but few residents typically need moderate or heavy care. The average length of stay of residency in an assisted living facility is about 28.3 months. Fifty-nine percent of residents will move into a nursing care facility, 33% will pass away, and the remainder will move home or to another location.

Personal Care Boarding Homes

Board and care homes are "non-medical community-based living arrangements that provide shelter (room), board (food), and 24-hour supervision or protective oversight and personal care services to residents" (Hawes, Wildfire, & Lux, 1993, p. 3). The names used to identify board and care homes, and the nature of the homes, vary considerably. Small homes may provide for as few as two residents, whereas some institutions may designate all or a large percentage of their beds for board and care residents. All states license board and care homes, although licensing requirements differ. The variability of the names used to classify board and care homes makes it difficult to get an exact count of the number of these facilities nationwide. Unlicensed homes include facilities excluded from mandatory licensure because of size or service criteria established by the state in which they operate as well as homes that meet a state's criteria for obtaining an operating license but avoid securing one.

We know little about the characteristics of board and care residents except that persons seeking this type of housing alternative are likely to need some supervision and personal care. Most residents are physically or cognitively frail and at risk for further health and functional declines (Hopp, 1999; Morgan, Gruber-Baldini, & Magaziner, 2001; M. E. Quinn, Hohnson, Andress, McGinnis, & Ramesh, 1999). Compared to larger facilities, smaller board and care homes (five to six residents) have a higher proportion of Black residents, residents with lower incomes and educational levels, and residents with higher physical dependency and cognitive impairments (Carder, Morgan, & Eckert, 2006).

The cost of living in a board and care residence is modest compared with other assisted living or nursing home options, but can vary widely depending on its location, the size of living space, the amount of privacy, and the amenities provided. Price can range from several hundred dollars a month to several thousand (Katz, 2009). Some residents rely on assistance from federal and state programs to pay at least part of the cost of living in a board and care home. For example, the monthly check of an SSI recipient may go toward the payment of the home's charges. Most states also provide some form of additional payment to supplement an older person's SSI payment. In some states, payment for board and care homes comes from Medicaid waiver program funds, block grants, or county funds.

Across the Globe: Old Age Homes

In India, Old Age Homes are available for older adults who are unable to stay with their families or who are poor and have very few resources. These homes are either government supported or funded by human service organizations and strive to create a family-like atmosphere for the residents. Although the quality and range of services available through the more than 1,000 government-run homes vary considerably, they may provide free accomodations, special medical facilities, mobile health care systems, nursing care, well-balanced meals, access to communication services, and yoga classes. HelpAge India assists the government in addressing the increasing need for age-friendly housing for poor older adults who have no family support by building integrated housing and care facilities. This organization is working to transform Old Age Homes into "composite shelters which go beyond providing simply a roof and meeting the basic needs of the elderly," envisioning residential complexes for elders offering a broader range of services and comfort.

Source: http://www.helpageindia.org/about-us/57.html.

Foster Care

Adult foster care (AFC) "serves people who, because of physical, mental, or emotional limitations, are unable to continue independent functioning in the community and who need and desire the support and security of family living" (U.S. Department of Health, Education, and Welfare, 1964, p. 2). Foster care includes support services, supervision, and personal care provided by a private host family or an individual who takes in a small number of older adults and encourages them to participate in the lives of the family and in the community (Sherman & Newman, 1988). Foster care homes operate under a social care model in contrast to the medical model of nursing homes. Individuals needing only supervision and assistance, but not continuous medical attention, can benefit from foster care. Elders generally go into foster care because they do not have family who can take care of them or because their family is unable or unwilling to provide daily care.

Research on foster care for older adults is scant. The landmark study of Sherman and Newman (1988) provided an extensive examination of three populations of foster care residents: residents with mental illness, residents with mental retardation, and frail elders. The elder residents in foster care are likely to have one of three histories: they may have been in foster care for many years, they may have been residents of institutions (e.g., a psychiatric hospital) for many years and only recently been placed in foster care, or they may recently have been placed with a foster family from the community. Many elders in foster care will remain with their foster family until their death. Others will leave AFC for a more specialized care center, such as a nursing home, psychiatric hospital, or residence for persons with mental retardation. In Carder et al.'s (2006) comparison of small care facilities for older adults, they describe Oregon's adult foster care program, which began in the early 1980s. The program requires that facilities provide residents with three meals daily, assistance with personal care, assessment, and care planning. Oregon uses the Medicaid 1915(c) waiver to help finance adult foster care and requires training of both managers and staff, including successful completion of a competency examination. Surveys of resident and family members suggest the family-like, home-style setting and the interpersonal relationship between the resident and the provider heavily influenced ratings of satisfaction and quality of care.

In 2008, the AARP Public Policy Institute conducted a national survey of state AFC regulations or standards, focused on homes that provided care to older adults and adults with physical disabilities (Mollica et al., 2009). States reported that 18,901 licensed and certified facilities were operating, with a capacity to serve 64,189 residents. AFC falls into three categories: (a) single-home, owner-occupied "mom and pop" residences—a person or household has become an AFC provider for a small number of residents; (b) corporate chains—a company, for-profit or nonprofit, owns or rents the property and is responsible for all business operations, and services are delivered by staff who live onsite; and (c) agency-sponsored homes—the home owner/operator is in residence but relies on an agency for referrals, training, oversight, and some business functions. Family-owned and -operated homes are the dominant provider type. AFC homes provide a range of services, including social activities, assistance with personal care and money management, transportation, housekeeping services, and oversight of or help with medications. States tend to require that providers have sufficient staff available to provide 24-hour supervision and to meet the needs of residents.

The Department of Veterans Affairs (VA) recently began implementing a Medical Foster Home (MFH) program designed for veterans with disabling chronic disease or terminal illness who need assistance and supervision, and who are no longer able to live safely at home because of functional, cognitive, or psychiatric impairments and have no caregiver able to meet their needs. Foster care providers take dependent veterans into their private homes and serve as MFH caregivers, providing daily supervision and personal assistance. The VA's home-based primary care staff members provide comprehensive medical care, management, and caregiver education support for the providers. As of 2010, there were 32 MFH programs operating in 21 states, with 35 additional sites in various phases of development (Edes, 2010).

Best Practice: Mary Sandoe House

The Mary Sandoe House assisted living project in Boulder, Colorado, has been operational since 1988. Its multiple sponsors include the City of Boulder Housing Authority, the Boulder County Community Action Program, the Boulder Gray Panthers Service Project, Inc., and an interfaith housing group. Funding for the project was leveraged through the Community Development Block Grant program, Colorado Housing and Finance Authority low-interest loans, and local fundraising. Juniper Partners, Inc. provides day-to-day oversight of management and conducts board development training and technical assistance.

A small project built in an existing neighborhood, the Mary Sandoe House accommodates elders in 24 private bedrooms adjacent to shared living and dining areas. Many of the residents have mobility limitations because of a stroke or arthritis, and some suffer from mild dementia. A unique aspect of the Mary Sandoe House is that for private pay residents, all services are included in a flat fee of $3,500 a month. Support services include some bathing assistance, supervision of medications, personal laundry, social activities, and arrangements for special transit. Rooms are also available for Medicaid-eligible residents.

Two words sum up the underlying philosophy that influenced the design of the house and continues to influence its day-to-day management: good neighbor. Residents of Mary Sandoe House

(Continued)

(Continued)

are part of the community. Neighbors attend outdoor barbecues, and neighbor children are encouraged to visit the residents. Typical residential activities, such as tending a garden, picking up the mail, and socializing on the patio, are part of the daily routine of the residents. Persons associated with Mary Sandoe House believe it has been successful, in part because many sectors of the community—public and private—were committed to the concept of a small residential program that could blend in with the day-to-day activities of an existing neighborhood.

For more information, contact Mary Sandoe House, 1244 Gillaspie Drive, Boulder, CO 80305; phone: 303-494-7317; http://www.themarysandoehouse.com.

Long-Term Care Facilities

At the most dependent end of the housing continuum are long-term care facilities, known more commonly as nursing homes. In 2009, 7.1% of the 3.3 million Americans 65 years of age and older had a nursing home stay, some as long-term nursing home residents, and some for shorter-term rehabilitation after an acute hospitalization. By contrast, 21.5% of those individuals 85 and older had a nursing home stay in the same year (Centers for Medicare and Medicaid Services [CMS], 2010f). Although the population of nursing home residents continued to become more ethnically diverse and the proportion of male nursing home residents is rising, the typical nursing home resident is still female, non-Hispanic White, not married, over the age of 75, and in need of assistance with several activities of daily living (Centers for Disease Control and Prevention, 2009a; CMS, 2010f). The person requires skilled, 24-hour care because of severe physical or cognitive limitations. Given the unique role of nursing homes in the continuum of care, and the broad range of issues to consider, we will consider them separately in Chapter 19.

CHALLENGES FOR SUPPORTIVE LIVING ENVIRONMENTS

Supportive living environments make it possible for many frail elders to continue living in the community. A wide range of supportive living options, including long-term care facilities, is needed to address the physical, psychological, and social needs of older adults. Exhibit 15.3 displays a summary of the different housing options discussed in this chapter and the level of assistance appropriate in each option. We now turn to the concerns that will need to be addressed in the future regarding supportive living arrangements for older adults.

Removing Barriers

Although ADUs promise many benefits, there are several barriers facing elders and their families interested in this housing option. In some jurisdictions, zoning laws prohibit the addition of such units, and neighbors often are concerned about ADUs becoming permanent rentals, thereby changing the neighborhoods from single-family to multifamily dwellings and negatively impacting property values, parking, and community services (Cobb & Dvorak, 2000; Liebig et al., 2006). In addition, few manufacturers of ECHO housing exist,

Exhibit 15.3 Spectrum of Housing Options

Housing Option	Little or No Assistance	Moderate Assistance	Cannot Perform Without Assistance
Single-family dwelling	▓		
Public housing	▓		
NORCs—Naturally occurring retirement communities	▓		
House sharing	▓	▓	
Home with	▓	▓	
Chore services	▓	▓	
Nutrition services	▓	▓	
Home repair	▓	▓	
Home equity conversion	▓	▓	
Low-income energy assistance	▓	▓	
Congregate housing	▓	▓	
ECHO housing accessory apartments		▓	
Home with		▓	
Delivered meals		▓	
Homemaker		▓	
Home health aide		▓	
Telephone reassurance		▓	
Visiting programs		▓	
Home with adult day services		▓	
Assisted living/personal care		▓	
Boarding homes		▓	
Foster care		▓	
Long-term care facilities		▓	▓
Continuing care retirement communities		▓	▓

Source: Adapted from AARP (1985).

limiting the purchasing opportunities for families who are looking for solutions for immediate care needs. A viable alternative may be a mobile version of an ADU used in Canada, Homecare Suite, which can quickly be installed in a garage space (Chapman & Howe, 2001).

Enhancing Services

Almost all the research shows cost savings with congregate housing compared with long-term care facilities. Congregate housing, however, relies on the availability of community-provided services to assist residents in meeting their care needs. Where such services are not readily available, staff at the congregate facility must carefully monitor residents and coordinate their care to appropriately support the residents' independence. Although older adults may prefer to "age in place" with assistance from community programs, the successful linking of housing with services requires a competent, stable, and committed workforce, the absence of which currently plagues the long-term care system (R. Stone, 2006).

Protecting Residents

In the mid-1980s, reform advocates called for increased regulation among CCRCs to protect elderly consumers (Saunders, 1997). In an effort to prevent strong government involvement in the industry and maintain security for older adults without the negative side effects of regulation, CCRCs formed their own regulating agency, the Continuing Care Accreditation Commission (CCAC). Acquired by the Commission on Accreditation of Rehabilitation Facilities (CARF) in 2003, CARF-CCAC has adopted basic standards that cover critical areas such as the organization's governance structure, financial status, and quality of services provided to residents. To qualify for accreditation, CCRCs must perform self-evaluations that focus on these aspects of operation, as well as undergo inspections from the CARF-CCAC; CCRCs go through recertification every five years. CARF-CCAC accredits approximately 15% of the CCRC market (S. Matthiesen, personal communication, December 15, 2011).

In the past, the financial stability of the CCRC industry was a serious concern, resulting from a number of bankruptcies among various CCRCs. Today, fears are alleviated somewhat as the industry has gained more experience in management and as regulation has taken hold in many states (Saunders, 1997). However, concern over possible bankruptcy, particularly during economic turndowns, still exists (U.S. Senate Special Committee on Aging, 2012). Opinions on exactly how much of a threat financial failure is vary among those monitoring the industry.

Although there are federal laws that impact assisted living, oversight of assisted living occurs primarily at the state level. The varying laws and regulations affecting these settings have created a diverse and fluid operating environment for providers and a mix of terminology, settings, and available services for consumers (National Center for Assisted Living, 2006). States vary significantly in their licensing requirements, quality standards, and monitoring and enforcement activities to help ensure quality care of residents (Morgan et al., 2011).

States face a variety of issues in deciding whether and how to regulate board-and-care settings, including resources, affordability, local culture, quality standards, and consumer demand (Carder et al., 2006). Some states require a license for every residential setting that houses people who need personal care or supervision; most states require licensure only if the home actually provides such services or advertises that it provides care and supervision. Licensure requirements also may depend on the size of the facility and the number of persons receiving care. The content of the licensure standards also varies from state to state, as do minimum staffing levels and training requirements. Needless to say, evaluating the quality of board and care homes is an ongoing challenge.

Enhancing Opportunities for Foster Care Residents

Adult foster care will be most successful if older adults understand how the setting and services operate, and if they are good matches with the provider (Mollica et al., 2009). More consumer education is needed to inform older adults about the potential of foster care as a viable housing option. In addition, there is a need for more research to characterize older adult foster care residents and assess the benefits and challenges of living in this type of housing environment.

Developing Housing Options for Marginalized Older Adults

The issues and needs of the aging LGBT population is gaining attention in the gerontology research (Herdt & de Vries, 2004). Housing and supportive services is a critical issue, as older LGBTs often find that they must conceal their sexual identity when they begin to require supportive services (Brotman, Ryan, & Cormier, 2003). De Vries (2006) describes several housing communities designed to openly address the needs of this growing population of elders. For example, RainbowVision, located in Sante Fe, New Mexico (www.rainbowvisionprop.com), is said to be the first retirement and care community developed specifically for LGBT older adults. It offers a range of options from condominiums for purchase to independent living in leased residences to assisted living with access to health care and supportive services.

Expanding Housing Options for Older Adults

In closing, although older adults have a myriad of options regarding their living arrangements, problems in housing availability and affordability continue to exist. As boomers age, the tension between the issues of person–environment fit will become apparent for many more older adults, and a variety of housing options and programs will continue to be in demand. Enhancing the affordability and availability of housing for older Americans was among the top 50 resolutions put forth by delegates of the 2005 White House Conference on Aging (2006). In addition, delegates put forth resolutions encouraging community designs to promote livable communities that enable aging in place, and expanding opportunities for developing innovative housing designs for seniors' needs.

CASE STUDY

Finding a New Home

Ellen, an active 77-year-old widow, had resided in a triplex rental for eight years. Ellen was happy with her living arrangement and said that she planned to "live here the rest of my life." An outgoing person, she became well acquainted with her neighbors and enjoyed the convenient

(Continued)

(Continued)

location of her home. She spent many hours out of doors tending her roses and helping with other yard duties voluntarily. Because she had established herself as an excellent renter, the owner considered Ellen's fixed income of $1,000 per month and in eight years had increased her rent by only $75, bringing it to $350 per month. She could cover her living expenses and enjoy recreational activities at a local senior center.

In 1994, the owner notified Ellen that he had turned over his property to his daughter and that she would raise the rent to $700 per month. Ellen reported that "the rent increase devastated" her and that for days she "cried at the drop of a hat" because she had no idea what she was going to do. Ellen did not want to depend on her two children, who lived nearby. She wanted to be independent. If she found another rental, the same thing could happen to her again. Where would she find affordable rent now that this midsized community was growing rapidly and rentals were in great demand?

Ultimately, a friend advised her to contact the manager of a small mobile home park in a nearby community of 7,500. Ellen knew nothing about mobile homes and was skeptical but open-minded. She had heard that the manager was "very strict" about whom he accepted into the park. Initially, the manager told her that nothing was available. As the conversation progressed, Ellen won him over with her pleasing personality. He offered that she could look at one unit that was available. Ellen was more than impressed with the well-kept home that was for sale by an older couple.

Her next problem was financial. Her banker advised her to use a certificate of deposit of $35,000, her entire savings, for collateral. This would more than cover the full cost of the mobile home at $28,000 and generate enough interest to pay the interest of the loan. The lot fee was $175 per month and included water and trash rates. Ellen pays on the principal each month in an amount that varies depending on her monthly finances. Ellen has settled into her two-bedroom mobile home with an attached garage and "more storage space" than she has "ever had." Her children like her new home and visit often. Ellen's grandson says, "Grandma, you do not live in a mobile home, you live in a home." Ellen tells her friends, "I love it. I have never been happier in my life. Please, God, don't do anything to my little house."

Case Study Questions

1. Citing research, explain Ellen's emotional reaction to having to move from her apartment home of many years.

2. What factors does Ellen have working in her favor in this situation? What circumstances could be working against her?

3. Ellen has advanced arthritis in her hips and knees. What bearing does this condition have on her future housing choices?

4. On the basis of the person–environment fit model, what housing options would be appropriate for Ellen? Why?

5. Where might Ellen go to find out more about housing options in her community?

LEARNING ACTIVITIES

1. Investigate the housing opportunities available for older adults in your community. What types of services, if any, are offered? Do the residents reflect what you have learned about senior housing in this chapter?

2. Interview someone from the public housing authority. What does the person see as the primary challenges for providing housing for older adults? What policy changes are needed to address these challenges?

3. Conduct a review of recent housing legislation (federal, state, and local) that deals with housing for older adults. What is the focus of legislation or policy? What are its strengths and weaknesses?

4. Interview older residents who reside in public or residential housing facility. What do they like about the facility? What are their primary concerns? What do they like about living in an age-specific environment? What don't they like about it? What do you perceive to be the advantages and disadvantages for residents living there? Would you encourage a family member to live in age-specific housing? Would you consider it as an alternative for yourself?

FOR MORE INFORMATION

International Resources

1. World Health Organization Global Network of Age-Friendly Cities: http://www.who.int/ageing/age_friendly_cities_network/en/index.html

   This is an online network designed to support a common global understanding of "age-friendly" city. The goals of the network are to provide technical support and training; link cities to the WHO and each other; facilitate the exchange of information and best practices; and ensure that interventions taken to improve the lives of older people are appropriate, sustainable, and cost-effective.

2. Changing Housing Schemes for an Ageing Society: Emerging Issues and Design Solutions (Biocca & Morini, 2011): http://www.enhr2011.com/sites/default/files/paper%20Biocca-Morini WS15.pdf

   This paper, from the 23rd European Network for Housing Research Conference in Toulouse, France, examines relevant trends and future consideration in the European Union regarding housing for aging populations.

3. Lifetime Homes, Lifetime Neighborhoods: A National Strategy for an Ageing Society: http://webarchive.nationalarchives.gov.uk/20120919132719/http://www.communities.gov.uk/documents/housing/pdf/lifetimehomes.pdf

   The United Kingdom was first country in the world to set out a national strategy to address comprehensively the unique housing needs of an ageing society. This report outlines the country's plans "for making sure that there is enough appropriate housing available in the future to relieve the forecasted unsustainable pressures on homes, health and social care services."

4. Canadian Senior Years: Housing http://www.senioryears.com/residences.html

   Our friends up north have put together a great page that explains all the types of living accommodations available to older adults. Take a look at the different housing options available for older adults in Canada.

National Resources

1. National Resource Center on Supportive Housing and Home Modification, Andrus Gerontology Center, 3715 McClintock Avenue, University of Southern California, Los Angeles, CA 90089–0191; phone: 213-740-1364; www.homemods.org; e-mail: homemods@usc.edu

   The purpose of the Center is to promote supportive housing that encourages healthy, independent living. The Center conducts applied research, evaluation and policy analysis, training and education, policy updates, and national teleconferences. The Center also provides reports, guidebooks, newsletters, and fact sheets to make available objective information about housing.

2. National Council on the Aging, 1901 L Street NW, 4th Floor, Washington, DC 20036; phone: 202-479-1200; www.ncoa.org

   The National Council on the Aging has resource materials on a wide variety of topics, including senior housing and supportive services available to older adults living in their own homes.

3. National Council of Senior Citizens, 8403 Colesville Road, Suite 1200, Silver Spring, MD 20910; phone: 301-578-8800

   The Council is an advocacy organization of older adults whose primary purpose is to work for legislation to benefit older adults. It is one of the major sponsors of housing for older adults— its Housing Management Corporation manages buildings across the country.

4. Assisted Living Federation of America, 1650 King Street, Suite 602, Alexandria, VA 22314-2747; phone: 703-894-1805; www.alfa.org

   This is the largest national association exclusively dedicated to professionally operated assisted living communities for seniors. ALFA's member-driven programs promote business and operational excellence through national conferences, research, publications, and executive networks. ALFA works to influence public policy by advocating for informed choice, quality care, and accessibility for all Americans seeking assistance with long-term care. ALFA produces numerous publications and reports on the business of assisted living, including its flagship magazine, *Assisted Living Executive.*

5. LeadingAge (formerly American Association of Homes and Services for the Aging), 2519 Connecticut Avenue NW, Washington, DC 20008; phone: 202-783-2242; http://www.leadingage .org/About_LeadingAge.aspx

   This national association of nonprofit organizations represents 6,000 nonprofit nursing homes, continuing care retirement communities, assisted living residences, senior housing facilities, and community service organizations for older adults. This group also sponsors the Continuing Care Accreditation Commission that accredits continuing care retirement communities. Free information on long-term care and housing for older adults is available on its website, along with links that explore different housing options.

6. *Journal of Housing for the Elderly*, Taylor & Francis, Inc., 325 Chestnut Street, Suite 800, Philadelphia, PA 19106, phone: 800-354-1420; http://www.tandfonline.com/loi/wjhe20

This journal covers the latest efforts of housing researchers and policy experts—from research on energy conservation or privacy needs to policy implications of home equity conversion. It also examines management issues, housing-related service delivery innovations, case histories of successful housing alternatives, and financing strategies.

Web Resources

1. U.S. Department of Housing and Urban Development (HUD): www.hud.gov

This is the place to start to look for information about housing policies or programs. Visitors can search HUD's database and gain access to housing reports, program information, and a variety of housing data. The site also has consumer information about housing.

2. HomeStore.com—Senior Living: www.springstreet.com/seniors/index.jhtml?source=a1rnftjt597

This website displays buildings, grounds, and interiors of retirement communities, assisted living facilities, and nursing homes in color photographs. Detailed information on each property may also be found, as well as names of moving companies, self-storage facilities, financing, and retirement-planning books.

3. Mature Market Resource Center: www.seniorprograms.com

The Mature Market Resource Center has two web-based organizations. First, the Association of Marketing and Sales Executives in Senior Housing is a web-based national membership organization dedicated exclusively to the needs of marketing, sales, and communications executives in senior housing. Second, the National Association of Senior Health Professionals is a web-based membership organization specifically designed to address the unique needs and special interests of professionals in the rapidly growing field of senior health.

4. Center for Excellence in Assisted Living (CEAL): www.theceal.org/about.php

CEAL's website provides information about assisted living including research findings and outcomes, best practices, consumer materials, training and education materials, and links to other relevant websites.

5. Consumer Consortium on Assisted Living (CCAL): www.ccal.org

The Consumer Consortium on Assisted Living is the only national consumer education and advocacy organization focused on the needs, rights, and protection of assisted living consumers and their caregivers. CCAL educates consumers, trains professionals, and advocates for assisted living issues.

6. Center for Housing Policy: www.nhc.org

The Center for Housing Policy is the research affiliate of the National Housing Conference (NHC), an organization dedicated to ensuring that all Americans have access to safe, decent, and affordable housing. In partnership with NHC and its members, the Center combines research with practical expertise to broaden understanding of the nation's housing challenges and to examine the impact of policies and programs developed to address these needs.

CHAPTER 16

Care Management

Ruby, 86, suffers from Parkinson's disease. Widowed for five years, Ruby lives in a small house one block from the main street of the town in which she has lived for 25 years. Ruby is becoming quite frail and must always use a walker. She has wonderful neighbors who are helpful, a 76-year-old sister-in-law who lives five miles away, and two nieces who are caring and attentive but live out of state. To help her remain independent and to enable her to continue living in her own home, Ruby's care manager recommended a variety of service options, including Meals on Wheels, home health care, and the use of the senior bus for visits to the doctor when her neighbors are not available to take her.

Care management is central to the integrative delivery of services for older adults. Without it, many older adults such as Ruby become frustrated when seeking help from an often fragmented, complex, and costly service system. Care managers serve as navigators, guiding older persons in their pursuit of services that will foster their independence. The National Advisory Committee of Long-Term Care Case Management defines *care management* as "coordinating services that helps frail elders and others with functional impairments and their families identify and secure cost-effectively administered services appropriate to the consumers' needs" (Connecticut Community Care, 1994, p. 5). This dual mission of planning and individualizing services to promote client independence while controlling costs makes care management a cornerstone of community-based service provision for older adults (Rife, 1992).

Known by a variety of names (e.g., case management, case coordination, service management), care management occurs in a diverse range of long-term care programs for older adults. Although programs differ in how they implement, access, and monitor their services, they do agree on the core elements of care management (Cress, 2012b; National Chronic Care Consortium, 2000; S. K. Powell & Tahan, 2007)

The care management process begins with *case finding* (see Exhibit 16.1). The purpose of case finding is to locate individuals who might benefit from services. Care managers often rely on referrals from other professional service providers to help them in identifying viable clients. Gatekeepers, or individuals who by the nature of their day-to-day work come into routine contact with many people, can be trained to successfully identify isolated older individuals with functional limitations and refer them to care management programs (Emlet & Hall, 1991). Once these individuals are identified, care managers begin the *intake and prescreening* process by obtaining basic information about them (e.g., presenting problem, age, income, living arrangements, current level of both formal and informal service use, type of disability). Care managers also evaluate potential clients according to program criteria (e.g., income, level of frailty) to determine eligibility for particular services.

After a client is accepted via the pre-screening, the care manager continues the process by conducting a more *comprehensive client assessment*. Using a multidimensional assessment tool (see Exhibit 16.2), the care manager gathers in-depth information about the person's physical well-being and medical history, psychological and mental functioning, functional ability (i.e., activities of daily living [ADLs] and instrumental activities of daily living [IADLs]), social activities, formal and informal service use, economic and financial status, in-home safety, and family relationships (Krout, 1993a; Morano & Morano, 2012; Newquist, Rosenberg, & Barber, 2012; Quinn, 1993). From the assessment, the *development of the care plan* occurs. The care plan describes the type of problem the client has and the planned outcomes of the services. The care manager describes the needs of the individual in conjunction with the client's values and preferences to set desired outcome goals and to design a care plan of informal and formal services to best meet the needs of the individual. The care manager then identifies, coordinates, and negotiates service provision and funding (Cress, 2012a). How the care manager handles the *acquisition and implementation of services* depends on which care management model is being used (the different models will be described later in the chapter).

Monitoring is also a function of the care manager. After arranging for services, the care manager continues to periodically monitor client satisfaction with the care plan and the appropriateness and implementation of the plan (e.g., quality, timeliness, duration). After a specified time, the care manager conducts a *reassessment* of the client and care plan to detect changes in the client's needs and to evaluate the effectiveness of the care plan in meeting the client's goals. Based on this evaluation, the care manager revises or adjusts the care plan as appropriate to reflect the client's current needs, or the client may be discharged from the program.

Exhibit 16.1 Care Management: Process

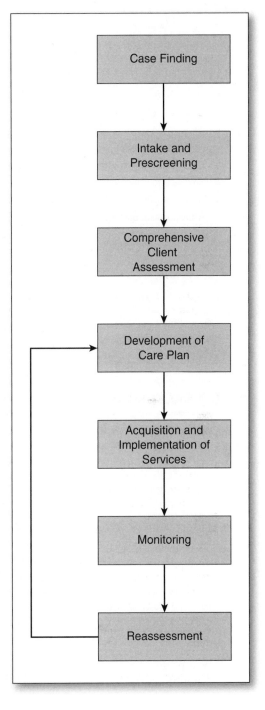

Exhibit 16.2   Care Management—Comprehensive Assessment

When the care manager determines that a client is eligible for care management services, he or she conducts a multidimensional assessment that profiles details of the client's needs and support systems. Although the specific assessment tool used varies across programs, during the assessment process, care managers typically address the following questions:

- What are the present state and history of the client's illness?
- What medications are being taken?
- What is the client's perception of his or her health?
- How is the client coping with the situation?
- How good is the client's short- and long-term memory?
- How well is the client able to dress, feed, bathe, walk, toilet him- or herself?
- Who, if anyone, helps support the client among family, friends, church, neighbors?
- What physical barriers in the client's dwelling help or hinder her or his mobility?
- What financial resources are available to the client to pay for services?

Source: Quinn (1993).

In the remainder of this chapter, we focus our attention on the rapidly developing field of care management. We begin by examining the political influence on and support for care management services. This section is followed by a profile of care management users and providers. We end the narrative portion of the chapter with a discussion of the challenges facing care management programs now and in the future.

POLICY BACKGROUND

Federal support has been critical to the development of care management programs serving older adults. With the passing of the Comprehensive Health Planning and Public Health Service Amendments of 1966, care management began to surface as a method for helping individuals overcome the federal bureaucracy and improve their access to federal health care programs (Spitz & Abramson, 1987). In the 1970s, when the government began to allocate significant dollars for the development of community-based services, many programs incorporated care management as a key service (Quinn, 1993). By 1979, 333 care management programs for older adults existed throughout the United States (Downing, 1985).

Federal initiatives supporting the development of community-based services continued through the 1980s, but with greater focus on cost containment. With the Omnibus Budget Reconciliation Act of 1981, Congress attempted to reform the Medicaid program by allowing states to modify Medicaid regulations. States could apply for waivers that limited the services offered by a statewide program, allowed reimbursements to provider organizations for services not ordinarily part of the state's Medicaid plan, or allowed modifications of the existing eligibility criteria for the client applying to the Medicaid program. This was a significant policy change because public programs could now include a range of both health and personal care services and care management services through one funding source (Quinn, 1993). Although an optional service in all state waiver program plans, the majority of states allow reimbursement for care management as part of their specialized home and community-based services.

The Older Americans Act (OAA) began supporting care management demonstration and research projects with the Act's 1978 revisions. The 1985 reauthorization of the OAA identified care management as a basic service. This legislation authorized Area Agencies on Aging (AAAs) to "support services designed to avoid institutionalization including care management" (§ 321 [5]). The reauthorization of the OAA in 2006 once again directed funding under Title III, Part B for care management services, and identified care management as an important component of in-home services for frail older adults under Title III, Part D.

The Program of All-Inclusive Care (PACE) developed through a combination of private and public funding. PACE programs seek to replicate On Lok, an innovative community-based model of capitated acute and chronic care for nursing home–eligible seniors in San Francisco's Chinatown. The On Lok program emphasizes the use of day health care and reliance on an extensive multidisciplinary team to manage and deliver services for frail, older participants (Wells, 2002). In 1986, federal legislation allowed 10 organizations to replicate On Lok's service delivery and funding model in other parts of the country. Program sites received support from the Centers for Medicare and Medicaid Services (CMS), which provided waivers that allowed capitated contracts using Medicare and Medicaid funds. Private foundations and sponsoring organizations largely support the initial start-up costs (i.e., site support, staff development, and service expansion). In 1997, the Balanced Budget Act (Pub. L. 105- 33) established PACE as a permanent provider under Medicare and allowed states the option to pay for PACE services under Medicaid. Each PACE site operates under its own unique mix of federal, state, and private funds. Participants must be at least 55 years old, live in the PACE service area, currently live safely in the community with assistance, and be certified as eligible for nursing home level of care by the appropriate state agency (Sebelius, 2011). In 2006, the Rural PACE Pilot Grant Program, established under the Deficit Reduction Act of 2005, provided 15 providers in 13 states with start-up funds to develop PACE organizations serving rural elders.

USERS AND PROGRAMS

Public and private care management services have proliferated during the past decade in response to demographic changes, increased concern about the cost of services, and the complexity of the health care and service systems. In this section, we describe the general characteristics of individuals using care management and the persons and programs providing care management services. In addition, we briefly present evaluation outcomes from several long-term care demonstration programs built around the provision of care management.

Characteristics of Care Management Clients

It is difficult to profile the typical care management client because most authors describe the consumers of care management in descriptive (e.g., frail, nursing home eligible) rather than in empirical terms. Typically, publicly funded programs require a predetermined level of client frailty to qualify for care management services (Quinn, 1993). Private care management services often are available to any individual who has the resources to pay for the service. The following examples show the similarity and diversity of clients found among and within care management programs.

Like Ruby, whom we met at the beginning of the chapter, many care management clients are White, older, female, and widowed. A national study of 553 rural, primarily community-based care management providers found that most clients were women, over 75 years of age, and widowed (Krout, 1993a). Most of the clients lived alone and had yearly incomes below $15,000. Approximately one half of the individuals receiving services were Medicaid eligible. The agencies retained the older adults as care management clients for an average of 32 months. The most frequently noted reasons for termination of services were the client's recovery, death, institutionalization, relocation, or need for a higher level of care.

The 864 clients referred to hospital-based care management programs located primarily in urban areas of New Mexico and Arizona ranged in age from 60 to 106, with an average age of 78.7 years (Warrick, Netting, Christianson, & Williams, 1992). Two thirds of all clients were female; the greatest proportion of clients was White (80%), followed by Hispanics (13%). They reported having an average of 11 years of formal education and a yearly income of approximately $9,600. Overall, 41% of the clients said that they had experienced major health deterioration within the previous six months of receiving care management services, and 13% had undergone major surgery. Clients enrolled in the program immediately following hospitalization presented care management needs different from those of individuals referred from other community service programs. Many hospital-referred clients needed intensive, immediate assistance as they exited the hospital. They did not need long-term intensive care management services as required by community-referred clients, who, in comparison, were older, less likely to have informal caregivers, and more likely to be functionally dependent. Approximately 36% of all clients continued in care management for at least one year. Clients terminated from the program because of death, nursing home admission, self-sufficiency, referral to another care management agency, or relocation outside the hospital service area.

Best Practice: Kaiser Permanente's Care Management Institute

Kaiser Permanente's Care Management Institute (CMI) is a unique, pioneering institution with a mandate to drive, fund, and catalyze care management activities throughout its nonprofit HMO. Created in 1997 for the express purpose of helping Kaiser Permanente improve the quality of care and health outcomes for its members, CMI draws on the extensive clinical experience, research, and data of an integrated health care system with more than 8.5 million members. CMI synthesizes knowledge about the best clinical approaches to create, implement, and evaluate effective and efficient care management programs.

To meet the diverse needs of the aging population, care management strategies for elder care are multifaceted and highly flexible. CMI's population-based approach has focused primarily on those with the greatest care needs, emphasizing clinically proven techniques for managing the most serious health challenges. Its integrative approach facilitates awareness of successful practices.

For more information, contact CMI at 1 Kaiser Plaza, 16th Floor, Oakland, CA 94612; phone: 510-271-6424; www.kpcmi.org.

Older clients of the Community Care Services Program (CCSP), a care management program funded through the Medicaid waiver program in Georgia, ranged in age from 60 to over 100 with almost one half (48%) of clients aged 75 and older (CCSP, 2012). Of the persons served in FY11, 77% were over aged 60, 72% were female, and 42% were African American. CCSP services supported consumers living in the community for over four years. Overall, 96% of consumers reported satisfaction with CCSP care coordination. Ninety-five percent of consumers report the CCSP care coordinator assisted them in having a better quality of life. A study of the time spent with CCSP clients identified four variables predictive of higher use of care manager time: problematic client behaviors, greater difficulties in performing activities of daily living, problematic informal support, and problematic formal services (Diwan, 1999). A comparison of high-end users of the care management services with the rest of program's clients revealed that these clients had a higher prevalence of dementia and mental illness, multiple health conditions, and more problematic client, caregiver, and service provider situations.

In the private sector, professional geriatric care managers (PGCMs) serve as consultants for families with dependent older adults or as contracted agent representatives for corporate employee benefit services. Results of a national survey completed by 712 members of the National Association of Professional Geriatric Care Managers suggest that, although the focus of geriatric care managers' work is on the needs of an older person, it is often family members who seek and pay for the PGCM's services (R. Stone, Reinhard, Machemer, & Rudin, 2002). In fact, the primary contact is often not the older person. Only 21% of respondents said they usually communicated with the elderly client. The PGCMs reported serving an average of 17 clients per month. Hourly fees for care management services averaged $74 an hour; they charged an average of $168 to develop a care plan and $175 for initial consultations. The most common services provided by the PGCMs were assessing clients' functional abilities (90%), assessing family and social support (94%), developing a care plan (93%), finding and arranging appropriate services for the client (95%), and providing ongoing management of the care plan (90%). About two thirds of the PGCMs were licensed professionals (e.g., nurses, social workers). Of the 615 PGCMs employed at the time of the survey, slightly more than half (57%) were working full time. More than two thirds (68%) were self-employed, and 28% were working for an organization.

Analysis of in-depth telephone interviews with 19 PGCMs, Kelsey and Laditka (2009) revealed that most persons became a PGCM as a natural progression of their career. More than one third of PGCMs expressed a personal interest in working with older people and had previous experience caring for older parents. The PGMCs indicated that they enjoyed working with older clients and their families in their home (50%), gained satisfaction from crisis management and solving complex problems (42%), and liked being able to make a difference in the quality of the lives of their clients and families (37%).

For Your Files: National Association of Professional Geriatric Care Managers

The National Association of Professional Geriatric Care Managers (GCM) is an organization of practitioners whose goal is the advancement of gentle and dignified care for the elderly and their families. In 2011, the GCM membership comprised approximately 1,900 individuals representing themselves or a company, who were doing business in the field of geriatric care management. GCM members assist older persons and their families to cope with the challenges of aging. Most GCM's members have master's degree–level training in gerontology, social work, nursing, or counseling. Member benefits include quarterly publications, *Inside GCM* and the *GCM Journal*, an annual conference, a membership directory, and professional development opportunities.

For more information, contact GCM at 1604 N. Country Club Road, Tucson, AZ 85716-3102; phone: 520-881-8008; www.caremanager.org.

CARE MANAGEMENT PROGRAMS

Program staff composition, qualifications, and numbers vary depending on the size and mission of the organization providing care management services. Typically, care management programs set minimum qualifications for their care managers, usually expressed in varying combinations of academic and work experience in human services (e.g., gerontology, nursing, social work). Besides the primary care managers, some organizations employ care manager assistants to work with clients, families, service providers, and other internal agency staff to help the assist care manager in the day-to-day management of the client careload (Quinn, 1993; Schraeder, Fraser, Bruno, & Dworak, 1990). A care manager supervisor may also be on staff to assist care managers with clinical and stress management issues (Applebaum & Wilson, 1988). The supervisor typically is responsible for managing program staff and supervising the care managers, negotiating service provider contracts, maintaining and analyzing data for program evaluation, and implementing quality assurance protocol (Schraeder et al., 1990).

Agencies and organizations use various approaches to carrying out care management, ranging from simple referral services to the actual delivery of comprehensive services. Each model varies both organizationally and operationally. The main differences between models are the level of authority directly controlling service use, the types and systems of service provision, and the method of payment. No evaluation data exist demonstrating that any one approach to care management is better than another (National Chronic Care Consortium, 1997).

In the *broker model*, care managers act as brokers for clients and service providers by linking the two through a referral system (Howe, 1994; Quinn, 1993). The purpose of broker care management is to match the target population with appropriate services on the basis of predefined agreements and standards of practice. Under this model, the care manager supplies individuals with objective information from which to make decisions, a care plan with options and recommendations to help guide them, and a neutral party to help with the process of securing services. They have no service dollars to spend on the clients' behalf; thus, they cannot guarantee their clients that services are delivered as prescribed. This model works particularly in "service-rich" communities in which the client has many service options and the care manager has no direct conflict of interest with the various providers. Care management provided under this model is usually a freestanding service provided by both public and private organizations (Milne, 1994).

For Your Files: Connecticut Community Care, Inc.

Connecticut Community Care, Inc. (CCCI) is a statewide, private, nonprofit organization. Since its inception in 1974, CCCI has helped thousands of individuals to stay at home by using care management strategies. Services provided by CCCI include simplifying the health and home care maze, providing professional objectivity, relieving caregiver stress by linking appropriate services and respite support with the individual's needs, identifying cost-effective home care services and solutions, and advocating for the elder's needs. The Case Management Institute (CMI), founded in 1985, provides training, consultation, and education services to CCCI and to organizations and individuals nationwide.

For more information, contact Connecticut Community Care, Inc. at 43 Enterprise Drive, Bristol, CT 06010-7472; phone: 860-589-6226; www.ctcommunitycare.org.

Schraeder et al. (1990) describe four variations of the broker model. *Simple broker models* of care management inform and arrange needed services. Care managers under this model do not authorize or purchase services, nor are they directly responsible for the delivery of services. In the *combined broker model*, the organization providing care management furnishes some services for the client and coordinates the remainder with external agencies. The *complex broker model* authorizes types and levels of services provided with certain financial controls or capped expenditures. The *consolidated broker model* consists of a single or merged provider system delivering a full range of services through directed provisions or contracts. This care management model exists within a prepaid, capitated funding structure housed under one administrative umbrella.

Under the *service management model*, used by many of the Medicaid waiver programs, care managers have funds available for services. The care management agency contracts with area providers to deliver the services authorized in each client's care plan. Most states have policies that limit the total cost of services that can be authorized by care managers. "Cost caps" usually are 60% to 80% of a state's comparable Medicaid nursing home rate (Quinn, 1993). Under this model, the care manager is fiscally accountable, and the care manager's authority to purchase services is constrained by the range of services offered and the supply of those services in the local delivery system (Austin, 1996).

Based on prospective financing, whereby programs receive a specific dollar amount for each client they serve, regardless of whether it costs more or less to deliver the care that is needed, the *managed care model* operates much like a health maintenance organization (Quinn, 1993; U.S. General Accounting Office [GAO], 1993). Clients pay a predetermined fee, and care managers are responsible for providing all needed services to clients. The care managers have control over a pool of funds to purchase services for clients. Providers are prepaid, so that the liability for excess costs is placed on the care managers. Often, the managed care agency will control cost by providing services directly or by selectively contracting with outside providers to offer services to clients at a discounted price.

The *medical group model* provides a direct link between primary care physicians, nurse or social work care managers, and older patients (Shelton, Schraeder, Britt, & Kirby, 1994; M. White, Gundrum, Shearer, & Simmons, 1994). This model emphasizes a collaborative team approach under the leadership of the primary care physician. It stresses patient targeting, comprehensive multidisciplinary office-based and in-home assessment, individualized care planning, arrangement and coordination of needed services, continuing care management, follow-up, monitoring, and patient/caregiver education. The care manager helps facilitate the person's medical care by addressing the psychosocial and environmental influences affecting care. The use of care management in this setting complements and enhances the medical group's practice by providing a direct link between clients/caregivers in their homes and primary care physicians (Schraeder et al., 1990).

Best Practice: Professional Care Management Institute

The Professional Care Management Institute (PCMI) is a nonprofit organization that specializes in designing and delivering training programs to professionals in the field of community-based long-term care. PCMI's mission is to enhance the quality of care management services to clients, support the professional development of care management staff, and promote the use of care management

(Continued)

(Continued)

concepts and skills in the provision of human services. It comprises a core staff, a Board of Directors, Training Advisory Committee, Accreditation Committee, and Independent Consultants/Trainers that all work to help reach PCMI's mission.

Since the institute was founded in 1987, PCMI has provided over 25,000 units of training (1 day of training + 1 person = 1 training unit) to 12,000 professionals from over 250 different organizations in Pennsylvania, New Jersey, Delaware, and Ohio. Offering more than 30 programs ranging from clinical programs for care managers to leadership programs for supervisors, managers, and administrators, PCMI programs combine up-to-date information and current theory with a practice orientation. In addition, PCMI provides a range of consultation services to public and private agencies. The institute works with organizations interested in developing or modifying service delivery programs, strategic planning, executive coaching, managing organizational culture, program evaluation, needs assessments, employment development programs, and a variety of other issues and topics.

Care managers who want to improve their professional status may become certified through PCMI's Care Management Accreditation Program. The certification is verification that the care manager has completed a comprehensive series of training courses and has attained a level of competency and experience in the practice of care management.

For more information, contact Professional Care Management Institute, 2605 Egypt Road, Norristown, PA 19403-2317; phone: 610-650-0496; www.p-c-m-i.org.

Under the auspices of the *acute care hospital-based model*, there is a linking of previously disconnected disciplines and departments within the hospital (e.g., finance, patient care delivery, administration). This model organizes patient care from a team approach, which in turn results in better quality of care for the patient (Cohen & Cesta, 1994). Most hospitals view care management as a cost-effective means of shortening the patient's length of hospital stay while reducing the use of unnecessary tests, treatments, procedures, and other hospital resources ("Rethinking an Old Notion," 1996; Sinnen & Schifalacqua, 1991; Trella, 1993).

Episodic care management occurs only when called for by providers in any of the other models of care management (Howe, 1994). The key feature of this model is that it can only be reactionary. It occurs in reaction to admission, consultation, or a phone call. The objective of this approach is to provide, during periods of stress, specialized diagnostic services and intervention services that are beyond the capabilities of the client and the primary care provider. The suppliers of episodic care management services include hospitals, specialized treatment centers, and health care specialists (e.g., physical therapist).

Evaluation of Care Management Programs

Does care management prevent or delay institutionalization? Is it cost-effective? To answer these questions, the federal government and several private foundations have funded numerous community-based long-term care demonstration projects that have included care management services. The fundamental hypothesis tested by these projects is whether community care can be a cost-effective substitute for institutional care. Some of the evaluations indicate that the use of home- and community-based services is not cost-effective when compared with nursing home costs. The findings also suggest, however, that the use of care management is an effective and successful way to control the total cost of home- and community-based care programs.

The most notable care management demonstration project was the National Long-Term Care Channeling Project. This federally funded program, started in 1980, examined the effects of care-managed, community-based long-term care on increasing older adults' use of home care, reducing their unmet health care needs, increasing their confidence in receipt of care and satisfaction with arrangements for it, and enhancing their satisfaction with life while not resulting in large reductions in informal caregiving (Kemper, 1988). Contrary to its original intent, however, the project increased costs of care. The evaluators suggested that one reason for increased costs was that although the population served was extremely frail, its members were not at high risk for nursing home placement. Thus, the costs of the additional home care were not offset by reductions in nursing home placements.

In 1985, the Social/Health Maintenance Organization demonstration project began at four sites across the country (Abrahams, Nonnenkamp, Dunn, Mehta, & Woodard, 1988) and continues to be evaluated. Each federally funded site has a care management unit responsible for allocation of long-term care services. Individuals enrolled in the organizations pay premiums to receive services. The project sites consolidate services and providers to provide a full range of medical, personal care, and social services. They pool funding resources (e.g., Medicare, Medicaid, private insurance premiums, client out-of-pocket fees) to provide members with acute health care plus expanded long-term care services. The care manager must administer service dollars judiciously because payments for services are capitated and prospective (Quinn, 1993). With the introduction of "provider risk" in the care management process, the project provider organizations can remain financially sound only if they keep their costs below the negotiated capitation rate.

Support from private organizations stimulated hospitals' interest in the use of care management services. The Robert Wood Johnson Foundation provided four-year demonstration grants to 24 hospitals throughout the country under its 1983 program for Hospital Initiatives in Long-Term Care (MacAdam et al., 1989). The purpose of the program was to encourage hospitals to develop new programs to better meet the needs of older persons. The participating public and not-for-profit hospitals set up unique projects. Each program initiated organizational changes; administrative improvements; educational activities for clinicians, staff, and consumers; care management programs; and community-oriented long-term care services. Care management was the only service that the foundation required all grantees to implement. Although most of the hospitals viewed care management as a valuable, relatively low-cost addition to the widening range of services they provided older adults, on completion of the demonstration period, most were unable to document changes in outcomes because of the provision of care management. Twenty-two hospitals reported, however, that they planned to continue some level of care management activities; one hospital ended the service; and one hospital was unable to report the future course of the service.

The Flinn Foundation sponsored the Hospital-Based Coordinated Care demonstration project at six sites in Arizona and New Mexico from 1986 to 1989 (Christianson et al., 1991; Warrick et al., 1992). The purpose of this project was to encourage private, not-for-profit hospitals to provide care management services to older adults at risk of rehospitalization after discharge. The clients and the community network of long-term care service providers had a positive view of the care management program. It delivered quality services to older individuals who met conventional eligibility criteria related to need. In contrast, the care management programs encountered several obstacles when trying to integrate into their own hospitals. For example, top administrators often lacked a strategy for blending long-term care with acute care service delivery in their organizations. Internal conflicts with hospital social workers, discharge planners, and home health agency staff about "ownership" of the patients in the hospital emerged during the implementation period and persisted throughout the project. In addition, most physicians had limited contact with the program care managers. They were not frequent users of, or effective advocates for, the program. After the grant funding ended, most hospital administrators chose not to continue the program primarily because of the inability of care management to pay for itself (Christianson et al., 1991).

In 2001, in response to the landmark Olmstead decision that required state and local governments to administer services, programs, and activities in the most integrated setting appropriate to the needs of qualified individuals with disabilities, CMS began offering "Real Choice Systems Change" grants to encourage states to examine and improve the services provided through waivers and other programs to assist these individuals. In Colorado, for example, all Medicaid clients who receive non-developmental disabilities–related long-term care services are entitled to services from a care manager at one of 23 Single Entry Point (SEP) care management agencies. Responses to a client satisfaction survey from 1,281 randomly selected clients from all SEP agencies revealed that 80% of respondents were "very satisfied" with their current care managers (Colorado Department of Health Care Policy and Financing, 2006). Nearly all SEP clients (93%) said they knew the names of their care managers, and approximately 88% reported that they felt comfortable calling their care managers with questions or concerns. Communication between care managers and clients was generally rated very positively. Most of the respondents indicated that they were always involved in their care planning (71%) and were offered choices among different providers. However, less than half of the respondents reported receiving accurate, useful information about consumer-directed care, and only about one third said that their care managers had discussed consumer directed care with them and encouraged them to participate.

Care management also is an important component of the Aging and Disability Resource Centers (ADRCs), a federally funded initiative launched in 2003. Administered through the Administration on Aging (AoA) and the CMS, ADRCs carry out five key functions: (a) information and referral and awareness; (b) options counseling (OC); (c) streamlined eligibility determination for public programs and streamlined access to services; (d) person-centered transition support; and (e) quality assurance and continuous improvement. Most of these functions are carried out by information specialists, nurses or social workers, a multidisciplinary team, or other trained staff. As of October 2010, 325 ADRC sites were in operation in 45 states and territories (O'Shaughnessy, 2010). Almost $111 million in joint AoA-CMS funding has been devoted to the ADRC initiative. Organizationally, most states have placed ADRCs in AAAs. Although the operational configuration of the ADRCs varies from state to state, all grantees must serve older adults and at least one disability target population. Evaluations thus far have pointed to some ADRC success in helping consumers. The initial evaluation found that the ADRCs provided information and long-term support to more than 750,000 contacts in the first two years of operation. Most ADRCs engaged in short-term care management, characterized as intensive assistance to stabilize a consumer's situation to enable the individual to remain in the community and follow-up to ensure that consumers' needs were met. Forty-seven percent of the programs had care workers on staff (average of 5.8 per program), and 33% had nurse care workers (average of 2.7 per program). These workers are responsible for providing clinical consultation or health promotion services, performing assessments, determining level of care, conducting options counseling, interacting with Medicaid eligibility workers, and confirming eligibility approval for consumers. In a recent multistate study, consumers reported high levels of satisfaction with ADRC operations (ADRC Technical Assistance Exchange, 2010). During the next several years, a federally supported evaluation will be conducted to understand the broad experiences of people who access services through the ADRCs and the community and program characteristics that facilitate access (O'Shaughnessy, 2010). For additional information on the ADRC initiative, visit the ADRC Technical Assistance Exchange website at www.adrctae.org.

As of 2011, there were 82 approved PACE organizations operating in 29 states (National PACE Association, 2012). Multiple evaluations have found PACE to result in fewer hospitalizations and nursing home placements, and improved health status and quality of life (Beauchamp, Cheh, Schmitz, Kemper, & Hall, 2008; Chatterji, Burstein, Kidder, & White, 1998; Wieland et al., 2000) and Medicaid savings (Wieland, Kinosian, Stallard, & Boland, 2012). However, program administrators note that several critical pieces need to be in place for the successful development of a PACE program (R. A. Kane, Illston, & Miller, 1992; Trice, 2006). The first is the necessity for sites to obtain sufficient start-up funds. Without such funds, the financial viability of the program is a constant source of concern. Another issue is the importance of building and maintaining staff with the skills and abilities to work in a multidisciplinary setting. Finally, care managers must develop the right patient mix in both acuity and dementia to accommodate the needs of all clients in a capitated system.

Preliminary evaluations of the rural PACE programs suggest that the programs preserve, enhance, and, in many cases, restore the independence, health, and well-being of its participants and reduces burden among family caregivers. However, initial implementation of these programs did not occur without many challenges. The number one challenge raised by the rural PACE programs was the issue of staffing. The rural areas reported a shortage of skilled clinical professionals (e.g., master's in social work, physical therapists, occupational therapists, speech therapists, primary care and specialty physicians). Another common challenge identified was transportation; most participants traveled long distances to attend the PACE centers. Fourteen of the 15 original rural programs have maintained their program (Maui PACE terminated their contract with CMS; Sebelius, 2011).

The Geriatric Resources for Assessment and Care of Elders (GRACE) model of primary care was developed specifically to improve the quality of care for low-income seniors (Counsell et al., 2007). Features of this model include in-home assessment and care management provided by a nurse practitioner and social worker team; extensive use of specific care protocols for evaluation and management of common geriatric conditions; use of an integrated electronic medical record and a web-based care management tracking tool; and integration with affiliated pharmacy, mental health, home health, and community-based and inpatient geriatric care services. An evaluation of the GRACE model found that the 474 patients enrolled in the GRACE intervention compared with the 477 patients assigned to the usual care protocol received better quality of care and had significant improvements in health-related quality of life measures. In addition, intervention patients experienced a reduction in emergency department visits and hospital readmissions over a two-year evaluation period. However, there were no significant differences between the two groups of patients in their physical health or ability to conduct ADLs. The authors suggested that a longer intervention period or a more intensive intervention may be necessary to alter ADL outcomes.

Guided Care is an interdisciplinary model of health care designed to improve the quality of life and efficiency of resource use for persons with medically complex health conditions (Boult, Giddens, Frey, Reider, & Novak, 2009). A Guided Care nurse works in partnership with the primary care physician, the patient, and the family to provide coordinated, patient-centered, cost-effective care. Guided Care nurses provide care management and perform several other functions (Johns Hopkins Bloomberg School of Public Health, 2012, p. 1):

- Assessing the patient and primary caregiver at home

- Creating an evidence-based comprehensive Care Guide and Action Plan

- Promoting patient self-management
- Monitoring the patient's conditions monthly
- Coordinating the efforts of all the patient's health care providers
- Smoothing the patient's transitions between sites and providers of care
- Educating and supporting family caregivers
- Facilitating access to community resources

Findings from an one-year pilot study suggested that Guided Care improved the quality and efficiency of care, and was feasible and acceptable to physicians, patients, and families caregivers (Boyd et al., 2008; Sylvia et al., 2006). Preliminary data from a randomized controlled trial of Guided Care at eight urban and suburban community primary care practices in the Baltimore–Washington, DC, area showed that Guided Care improved the quality of care of older persons (Boult et al., 2008), decreased family caregiver strain (Wolff et al., 2010), and reduced health care costs (Leff et al., 2009).

Across the Globe: Agency for Integrated Care

In 2009, Singapore's National Ministry of Health and other partners created the Agency for Integrated Care (AIC) as an independent corporate entity designed to smooth the transitions of patients from one care setting to another. Because these transitions disproportionately affect older adults in the country, managing the unique medical needs of aging adults has become a primary focus of the agency. To this end, the AIC has set-up a four-year government funded pilot project involving the Aged Care Transition (ACTION) team. Care coordinators stationed at five acute hospitals and one national center help patients make the important transitions from hospitals to their homes and communities. Care coordinators help with discharge and the arrangement of appropriate community services for older patients and their caregivers at home to optimize the patients' health and functional outcomes throughout an episode of illness. By placing care coordinators at these pivotal pilot sites, the project has established a single contact point at each site to coordinate communications between hospital patients, AIC office care consultants (who specialize in referral management for long-term care facilities/services), and community service providers.

Sources: AIC (n.d.-a, n.d.-b).

CHALLENGES FOR CARE MANAGEMENT PROGRAMS

Care management provides the entry into the community-based long-term care system. It plays a significant role in the coordination of services and resources for many older adults. However, some providers suggest that the scope of geriatric care management must be expanded from the existing primary focus on service coordination to include theoretically driven interventions that hold more promise for influencing long-term change in health-related behaviors and improving outcomes (Enguidanos et al., 2003). We end this chapter by addressing several current and future challenges facing care management programs.

Providing Care Management Services

Considerable debate has emerged about where in the structure of services care management should reside, whether agencies that provide home care services should be allowed also to be care managers, and how care managers should interact with other agencies and individuals who are authorized to bill for services (R. A. Kane & Frytak, 1994). To address these issues, two criteria need to be considered: the client's well-being and the interest of the organization paying for services. As Kane and Frytak (1994) point out, the care provided should meet unmet needs and result in improved or maintained physical, social, and emotional functioning of the individual. Service should be provided in a courteous and respectful manner and should be perceived as satisfactory. From a payer's perspective, the program should make efficient and effective expenditures. Kane and Frytak report that proponents of care managers in the provider role say that using independently employed care managers to authorize and monitor service is inefficient and redundant, and does not lead to allocation in the patient's best interest.

Proponents of nonprovider care management argue that publicly funded long-term care programs are efficient and effective only to the extent that they are under the authority of care managers who are not providers of care. Given these opposing positions, policy makers and researchers must explore more specifically what care management means operationally to home care agencies, nonprovider care management agencies, and state programs that fund both types of programs.

Ensuring the Effectiveness of Care Management Programs

How effective programs are in delivering care management services rests with several critical elements. First, care managers must receive proper training. Interviews with 95 care managers from six states in the GAO (1993) study identified the following as key practices essential for effective care management: the ability and skills to comprehensively assess client needs; time to have adequate contact with clients; knowledge of resources available in the community; and continual training to maintain and improve skills. Second, large care loads limit the ability of care managers to give clients sufficient attention to ensure that clients' needs are met and that services are provided adequately. Other effects of large care load sizes include limited time available to spend with each client and increased risk of burnout for care managers. Third, some barriers to effective care management outcomes are outside the control of local care management agencies. These include a lack of financial resources, inadequate availability of services in the local area, and extensive administrative requirements imposed by state administering agencies. In rural areas, the vast geographical areas for which many rural care managers are responsible often limit their ability to see their more "low-risk" clients regularly (Urv-Wong & McDowell, 1994).

To increase the effectiveness of care management programs, there also is a need for greater evidence-based design of care management programs (Cudney, 2002; J. Jones & Bandos, 2010). However, collecting adequate data is an ongoing challenge for agencies (Schneider, Landon, Tobias, & Epstein, 2004). As noted by Horvath, Silberg, Landerman, Johnson, and Michener (2006), available data do not always measure the goals of the program, or they may capture outcomes but do not allow researchers to link outcomes to program strategies.

Providing Quality Care Management Services

Although most publicly funded care management programs have some requirements concerning qualifications, training, and timely completion of activities (Justice, 1993), there are no uniform state or federal guidelines for the practice of care management. Geron and Chassler (1995) have called for guidelines that reflect changing practice and legislative realities; that promote flexibility in practice according to consumer values, preferences, and needs; that foster the efficient use of resources; and that ensure the equitable provision of quality services to those who are in need.

Diversifying Care Loads

Care managers can increasingly expect to manage a more diverse care load as the number of minority and ethnic elders continues to grow. To successfully work with minority populations, it is vital for care managers to develop cultural competencies (AoA, 2001b, 2004; Arnsberger, 2005; Meyer, 2011). Greater understanding, sensitivity, respect, and appreciation of diverse cultural norms (i.e., history, lifestyles, experiences, and beliefs) will be needed if care managers are to serve all older clients and their families effectively.

Addressing Ethical Issues Facing Care Managers

Sometimes, care managers find their personal and professional ethics in conflict (Galambos, 1997; R. A. Kane & Caplan, 1993; National Chronic Care Consortium, 1997). For example, many care managers have control over the services used by their clients by virtue of the funding for the services and the contracts or agreements that the care management agency has with other organizations to provide services. This controversial issue raises questions about care managers' control of the use of particular services by their older clients. Care management firms that also provide direct services in addition to care management services may restrict client access to a greater variety or less costly selection of services.

The medicalization of aging also jeopardizes the capacity of care managers to provide the social services critical to meeting the needs of older persons and their family caregivers (Binney, Estes, & Ingman, 1990; Clemens, Wetle, Feltes, Crabtree, & Dubitzky, 1994; J. Powell, 2009). The problem stems from public policy decisions that often define long-term care as a need for medical services. This either makes the need for medical services an absolute condition for access to "free" social services or makes the medical services "free" and charges for social services. Consequently, care managers sometimes provide unnecessary medical services to make individuals eligible for social services (Shapiro, 1995).

Promoting Care Management in the Future

Care management services will continue to evolve along with the health care system in this country, and will undoubtedly become even more important as the number of Medicare and Medicaid recipients enrolled in managed care programs increases. Thus, it is critical to continue to evaluate the effectiveness and efficiency of both public and private care management services. Delegates of the 2005 White House Conference on Aging (2006) promoted care management as part of several resolutions made for policy recommendations. For example, they identified care management as a strategy for improving state- and local-based integrated delivery systems, supporting informal caregivers of seniors to enable adequate quality and supply of services, and promoting economic development policies that respond to the unique needs of rural seniors.

CASE STUDY

When Information and Referral Are Not Enough

Five years ago, Helen, 83, was diagnosed with a benign brain tumor that is causing partial memory loss. The tumor also may be the cause of several other physical symptoms such as excessive tearing in one eye, constant postnasal drip, imbalance, and difficulty swallowing. Because Helen no longer drives or arranges appointments, and is unable to keep house or cook, Ross, her husband of 55 years, has taken over most of the household duties. Helen taught high school English for many years and was an avid reader. She continues to read with encouragement, but she loses her concentration quickly. Her math skills are completely intact, and she is an avid cribbage player. Helen's social skills are appropriate but repetitive. She offers visitors coffee and sweets often during the visit and forgets that they previously discussed subjects. She has a keen memory for some aspects of her past and has completely lost her memory of other past events. Within a year of diagnosis, she lost the memory that her parents were killed in an automobile accident when she was 19 years old.

Ross is a retired electrical engineer. An organized person, he keeps lists and has an established routine for everything he does. These habits carry over into his approach to caregiving. He reads constantly, writes letters to the editor and to his elected representatives, and keeps abreast of local, state, and national events. He is interested in the status of the educational system and the future of children. Ross has suffered from periods of depression throughout his life. He has sought professional counseling several times, once within the past year after becoming depressed about Helen's memory loss and overwhelmed with the caregiving responsibilities. Meal preparation was especially worrisome to Ross. He was placed on an antidepressant, but had serious physical and psychological reactions to the drug. As a result, their two daughters, who live 100 miles away, encouraged and helped their parents to move into an alternative care facility. They stayed at the facility for two months. After Ross stabilized, he arranged to return home.

Home is a small, modest house near a midsize university. Although hardly considered wealthy, Ross and Helen receive retirement pensions from their engineering and teaching professions and Social Security totaling $2,225 per month. Ross speaks of investment savings as well. They have excellent health insurance coverage. In short, they can purchase most items that they want, but they want little.

Once, they were moderately involved in the community. Ross volunteered for a congregate meal program and was an advisory board member for several human service agencies. Because of Helen's condition, however, they have withdrawn from all their social activities. They continue to go for daily drives in the country when the weather is pleasant. They no longer go out to eat.

(Continued)

(Continued)

Recently, Helen was hospitalized for a blood clot in her leg. This has added to Ross's worries, and a friend who visits the couple weekly fears that Ross is headed for another bout of depression that could destabilize the couple's situation.

Case Study Questions

1. Care finding—that is, locating individuals who might benefit from care management services—is the first step in the care management process. Who might be possible referral sources for this care? What elements make this care an appropriate referral?

2. What information provided in this case study would be the most critical for a care manager to consider in the prescreening process? Do you believe that Helen or Ross may be in danger of institutionalization? Why or why not?

3. The comprehensive assessment is a detailed step in care management. The following are only a few of the many questions to consider:
   a. Who is the client in this care scenario?
   b. What is the central problem?
   c. What additional information would you want to know about Helen and Ross?
   d. What outcomes would you as a care manager like to see achieved for Helen and Ross?
   e. What strengths or resources do they already have in place?

4. If you were to develop a plan of community services for Helen and Ross, what would you include and why?

5. Considering the outcome(s) and the community resources you have determined for Helen and Ross, what would be considerations in monitoring the progress of this care?

LEARNING ACTIVITIES

1. Interview an AAA director or staff member who works closely with care management. What are perceived to be the benefits of and issues related to care management? Does the staff member want to see amendments to the OAA to address concerns? What type of direction does the agency receive from the AoA and the state Office on Aging?

2. Interview the director of a private care management program or a care manager. What are the requirements (education and experience) to be a care manager? What are the responsibilities of a care manager? What are primary concerns with the program? What does the individual believe are the benefits of care management (to older adults, caregivers, service providers, and the community)?

3. Interview a caregiver or client receiving care management. How has this service affected the lives of the caregiver and client? How would they manage without it? What changes would they like to see in the program?

FOR MORE INFORMATION

International Resources

1. Improving Care for People With Long-Term Conditions: A Review of UK and International Frameworks: http://www.improvingchroniccare.org/downloads/review_of_international_frame works__chris_ham m.pdf

   This report, compiled by the National Health Service Institute for Innovation and Improvement in the UK and University of Birmingham Health Services Management Centre, focuses on both UK and international care management systems to identify ways to improve care for older adults with chronic conditions. Questions addressed include the following: What frameworks for people with long-term conditions have been used internationally? What evidence is there about the impacts of these frameworks? What approaches have been adopted by strategic health authorities?

2. A Systematic Review of Different Models of Home and Community Care Services for Older Persons (Low, Yap, & Brodaty, 2011): http://www.biomedcentral.com/1472-6963/11/93

   The authors of this report examine the outcomes of case-managed, integrated, or consumer-directed home and community care services for older persons in several different countries where research-based evidence was available.

National Resources

1. National Long-Term Care Resource Center, University of Minnesota, Institute for Health Services Research, School of Public Health, 420 Delaware Street SE, Minneapolis, MN 55455; phone: 612-624-5171; www.hpm.umn.edu/ltcresourcecenter

   The resource center has issued reports on care management in long-term care, including *Models for Care Management in Long Term Care: Interactions of Care Managers and Home Care Providers*. Contact the center for a list of publications about care management.

2. National Association of Professional Geriatric Care Managers (GCM), 1604 North Country Club Road, Tucson, AZ 85716; phone: 520-881-8008; www.caremanager.org

   GCM is an organization of practitioners whose goal is the advancement of dignified care for older adults. Association members assist older adults and their families in coping with the challenges of aging. The association publishes a national referral directory as well as the *Geriatric Care Management Journal*, which is published four times a year.

3. Aging Network Services, 4400 East-West Highway, Suite 907, Bethesda, MD 20814; phone: 301-657-4329; www.agingnets.com

   Aging Network Services is a nationwide, for-profit organization of private practice geriatric social workers who serve as care managers for older adults by providing a comprehensive assessment of older adults in their own homes and assisting in arranging the delivery of home care services.

4. *Care Management Journals*, Springer Publishing Company: 11 West 42nd Street, 15th Floor, New York, NY 10036; phone: 877-687-7476; www.springerpub.com/journal.aspx?jid = 1521–0987

Created from two well-established and authoritative journals in the field, this new publication offers a digest of contemporary expertise in the home care field. The *Journal of Care Management* contributes readily applicable professional-style articles about care/care management in many practice settings. It is complemented by the *Journal of Long Term Home Health Care*, which presents a creative, interdisciplinary approach to program and policy analysis as it affects frail homebound older adults.

5. *Professional Case Management*, Lippincott Williams & Wilkins, 530 Walnut Street, Philadelphia, PA 19106-3621; phone: 888-291-4242; http://www.lww.com/webapp/wcs/stores/servlet/product_Professional-Case-Management_11851_-1_12551_Prod-19328087

This journal features best practices and industry benchmarks for the professional case manager. It is focused on coordination of patient care, efficient use of resources, improving the quality of care, data and outcomes analysis, and patient advocacy.

Web Resources

1. Numerous private care management agencies describe their services on the web. Take a look at how this growing field is advertising its services (we do not endorse these programs; we list them only as a source of information):
   - Advanced Senior Solutions: www.advancedseniorsolutions.com
   - Buckley's For Seniors, LLC: www.buckleys4seniors.com
   - Elder Care Solutions: www.eldercaresolutions.com
   - Senior Care Management: www.seniorcaremgt.com
   - South Florida Geriatric Care Managers: http://caremanage.com

2. The American Society on Aging: Healthcare and Aging Network: www.asaging.org/networks/index.cfm?cg = HAN

Multiple articles on managed care for older adults are located within the archives section of this website. One is specifically related to care management and Latino elders; another focuses on Medicare-managed care.

CHAPTER 17

Home Care Services

Margaret, 72 years old, has had multiple sclerosis for 20 years. For approximately 15 of those years, she and her husband, Wilbert, have lived a relatively normal life. The disease, however, has progressed to the point that Margaret needs assistance with most of her daily living activities. Wilbert has been a model caregiver, but the last five years have taken their toll on him. Wilbert never thought that he could afford regular home health care for Margaret. He was relieved to learn that she qualified for home health care under Medicare because her doctor was willing to certify that she was homebound and required skilled nursing care. The home health agency schedules aides early in the morning. This allows Wilbert to attend his weekly Lions Club breakfast meeting. Wilbert would never complain about his caregiving responsibilities, but he does admit that he really enjoys the weekly breakfast outing.

Home care is a continuum of comprehensive care, providing individuals services that allow for maximum health, comfort, function, and independence in a home setting (Harper, 1991). Older adults such as Wilbert and Margaret choose to use home care services for several reasons, including the hope of avoiding institutionalization, familiarity of the home environment and sense of independence associated with this familiarity, lower perceived costs, and the continuity of family life and care (Chen & Thompson, 2010; Mollica, 2003).

In the United States, there are three primary types of home care: skilled home health care, nonmedical home care, and hospice care. More than 33,000 providers deliver home care services to some 12 million individuals who require services because of acute illness, long-term health conditions, permanent disability, or terminal illness. In 2009, annual expenditures for these services were estimated at about $72.2 billion (National Association for Home Care and Hospice [NAHC], 2010). Skilled home health care represents the largest segment of public expenditure for home care. Nonmedical home care services are care services of a nontechnical nature that emphasize the daily needs of individual users. The services include home aides, homemaker services, respite care, and home-delivered meals. The intent of hospice care is to provide supportive and palliative care for persons who are terminally ill and their families but not to treat the underlying conditions.

Research on home care often combines skilled and nonskilled services without specifying which services are being analyzed. This makes it difficult to profile the users and providers of these services. Because specific chapters in this book are devoted to services that fall under the rubric of nonmedical home care (e.g., care management, nutrition services, respite care), our primary focus in this chapter is on home health services and related nonmedical services (i.e., home health aide and homemaker services) that provide personal assistance to older persons confined to their homes. The latter part of the chapter focuses on hospice care.

HOME CARE

Policy Background

The first home care agencies were established in the 1880s to serve individuals who otherwise would not have access to medical care (Arneson, 1994). From that time until the mid-1960s, the industry grew slowly. With the passage of Medicare and Medicaid in 1965, however, the use of formal home care services increased dramatically.

To be eligible for home health coverage under Medicare, a person must meet four qualifying criteria (Centers for Medicare and Medicaid Services [CMS], 2010e). First, a physician must certify the need for services. Second, the individual must remain under the care of a physician. Third, the person must be certified by a physician as homebound, meaning that he or she is unable to leave the home because of illness or injury without the assistance of a person or device and without a considerable and taxing effort. Fourth, the individual must need part-time or intermittent skilled nursing care (defined as up to and including 28 hours of skilled nursing and home health aide services combined provided on a less-than-daily basis)[1]or physical therapy or speech therapy. If the older adult meets these conditions, he or she may also receive occupational therapy, medical social services, and home health aide services.

If a person meets all four of the above qualifying criteria, and acquires services through a Medicare-certified provider, then Medicare will pay for the types and amounts of home health services covered if the services are "medically reasonable and necessary." Services are covered in full with no deductible or co-payment from the beneficiary. The passage of the 1980 Omnibus Budget Reconciliation Act (OBRA) greatly expanded Medicare's home care benefit. Specifically, it removed the 100-visit limit, and an acute care hospitalization was no longer necessary to receive home care services. Because one must need skilled nursing or therapeutic care to obtain home care services from Medicare, typical coverage averages two to three months. Thus, services normally do not address chronic needs for home care.

The introduction of Medicare's prospective payment system in 1983 also contributed to the growth of the home care industry, particularly with respect to home health care services. The cost-containment strategy promoted earlier hospital discharges, thereby sending patients home "quicker and sicker" with initiation and maintenance of treatments formerly performed only within the hospital now provided in the home. As a result, the acuity of illness, types of therapeutic care administered, and the amount of direct care to persons in their homes increased dramatically. The Balanced Budget Act (BBA) of 1997 reduced growth in Medicare home health expenditures by introducing a new per-beneficiary limit, requiring reimbursement limits to be held to a below-inflation rate of growth, and

---

[1]Additional hours and days of services may be provided subject to review by fiscal intermediaries on a case-by-case basis, with proper documentation justifying the need for and reasonableness of such additional care.

restricting agency payments to the lowest of its allowable costs, per-visit cost limits, or per-beneficiary costs limits. As a result, home health care payments declined from about 9% of total Medicare spending in 1997 to 4.2% in 2009 (NAHC, 2010). Initially BBA implementation seemed to have resulted in the closing of a considerable number of home health care agencies, but as agencies adjusted to changes in the Medicare payment system and regained financial stability under the prospective payment system, there has been renewed growth in the home health care industry (S. Choi & Davitt, 2009).

States may also provide home care services under three provisions of the federal Medicaid statute: state plan home health services, state plan optional services, and 1915c waiver programs. In 2008, all states and the District of Columbia (DC) operated the Medicaid home health benefit while 48 states and DC operated multiple home and community-based services (HCBS) waivers; 32 states offered the optional state plan (Kaiser Commission on Medicaid and the Uninsured, 2011a). Federal law sets forth minimum mandated benefits and allows states the option of providing other services. States must provide the following home health services for all individuals eligible for Medicaid and entitled to nursing facility placement: part-time or intermittent nursing, home health aide, and medical equipment and supplies. Although all states require the provision of these particular home health services, federal law does not set the amount of service provided. The optional home care services that states may provide to individuals include personal care services, home- and community-based care for older adults with functional disabilities, private-duty nursing, and respiratory therapy for ventilator-dependent individuals. Both mandatory and optional services offered under the Medicaid state plan must meet the following federal requirements: (a) services must be uniformly offered throughout the state, (b) the recipient must have free choice of providers, (c) comparable services must be available to all individuals, and (d) any limits placed on the amount of services must be sufficient in amount, duration, and scope to achieve the purposes of the Medicaid program.

In 2002, the CMS developed the Independence Plus waiver to promote the use of consumer-directed (CD) care in Medicaid. These waivers encourage person-centered planning, individualized budgeting, and self-directed services and supports (Kassner, 2006). Under this program, persons eligible for services can hire family members, friends, or neighbors to provide home care. According to Kassner, not only does CD HCBS meet consumers' preferences, but it also helps address worker shortages, the need for culturally appropriate workers, and the availability of services in rural and other hard-to-reach areas, by expanding the pool of available workers. In 2010, waivers in 39 states allowed some form of CD, while eight states required CD for all or some services within the waivers programs serving older adults (Kaiser Commission on Medicaid and the Uninsured, 2011b).

If states want to provide services without complying with mandated and optional state plan requirements, they may obtain a waiver for one or more of them under certain federal provisions (Rosenzwieg, 1995). OBRA 1981 revised Medicaid's funding to allow states to cover HCBSs for individuals who would otherwise require institutional care. The Section 2176 waiver program permits states to provide a comprehensive range of HCBSs to individuals who, but for the provisions of such services, would be institutionalized. Services that states may cover include care management, homemaker, home health aide, personal care, adult day care, health care, habilitation, respite care, and other services approved by the state Medicaid agency and CMS as cost-effective. Section 1396 legislation, enacted in 1987, waives the same rules but applies only to persons aged 65 and older. As of 1999, all 50 states and DC had waiver programs serving older adults (Harrington, Carrillo, Wellin, Miller, & LeBlanc, 2000).

Money Follows the Person (MFP) was established by the Deficit Reduction Act of 2005 as a demonstration grant program to assist states in their efforts to reduce their reliance on institutional care while developing community-based long-term care opportunities, enabling older adults and people with disabilities to fully participate in their communities. Over a three-year time span (August 2008–2011), 44 states engaged in MFP to transition nearly 17,000 older adults and individuals with disabilities out of institutions and back home into the community. Older adults (average age 71) were more likely than other MFP participants to transition back to their own or a family member's home rather than relying on small group homes (Kaiser Commission on Medicaid and the Uninsured, 2011c). Pre-transition and one-year post-transition surveys of 803 of the earliest MFP participants, including 138 respondents 65 and older, provided found that MFP participants experienced significant quality of life improvements after transition to community settings (Simon & Hodges, 2011). For older adult respondents, the percentage of MFP participants reporting overall satisfaction with life increased 26% (from 53% to 79%) one year post-transition. Other improvements for older adults included (a) reduction in unmet care need (16% to 6%), (b) increase in reporting treatment with respect and dignity (69% to 94%), (c) increase satisfaction with living situation (53% to 94%), (d) reduction in number of older respondents reporting barriers to community integration (55% to 35%), and (e) modest gains in perceived choice and control related to their care (Simon & Hodges, 2011).

The 2010 Patient Protection and Affordable Care Act (ACA) put forth by the Obama administration created two new Medicaid options for states to cover HCBS—Community First Choice and the Balancing Incentive Program—and amended two existing Medicaid HCBS options—the 1915(i) state plan option and MAP program (United States Government Accountability Office [GAO], 2012). These program additions and adjustments provide states with new incentives and flexibilities to help increase the availability of home-based services for Medicaid beneficiaries. The Community Choice First, Balancing Incentive, and modified MFP programs provide states with enhancement to the Medicaid matching rate that determines the federal share of program costs. Community First Choice covers personal care and other services for eligible individuals. The Balancing Incentive Program offers incentives for states to increase the proportion of their long term care services offered through home- and community-based providers. The ACA also relaxed some of the eligibility requirements for the MFP program and added revisions to the 1915(i) state plan that provide flexibility to offer an expanded range of HCBS for specific target populations. Since the enactment of ACA, 13 states have applied for new MFP grants.

Although home care options may expand under the ACA for poor older adults who qualify for Medicaid, some groups have raised concerns that the Act could potentially restrict services for those who rely solely on Medicare for reimbursement (Eck, 2010). According to the American Health Lawyers Association, the Act makes substantial cuts in Medicare payments for home care. It also tightens regulations on health provider referrals of patients to both home and hospice care. Physicians and nurse practitioners will be bound to more stringent rules regarding face-to-face contact and reduced timelines when wanting to certify the need for home health or hospice for Medicare recipients. There is an exception to some of the anticipated budget cuts for rural home health providers, but the majority of home care agencies relying on Medicare payments will "be forced to adapt to an even leaner payment environment than previously, and will face challenges to become more efficient in continuing to deliver quality care to Medicare beneficiaries" (p. 20). From the perspective of the CMS, however, this tightening of payments and regulations could be a positive for consumers. According to a U.S. Department of Health and Human Services (2012e) report to Congress, the CMS has developed a plan for a home health value-based purchasing program to revamp how Medicare pays for health care services, creating a system that rewards better value, outcomes, and patient-focused care.

Three other federal programs also authorize home-based services: Title III of the Older Americans Act (OAA), the Social Services Block Grant Program under Title XX of the Social Security Act, and the U.S. Department of Veterans Affairs (VA). Area Agencies on Aging have the option of funding home health care services under Title III-B. In 1987, legislators added Title III-D to the OAA, which provided additional financial support for nonmedical in-home services for frail older persons (e.g., case management, lifeline systems, deep cleaning). The intent was that they provide new and additional services, not just increase already existing services. Although states have broad authority to spend their Title XX allocations on a wide array of social services, most states use some portion of their funds to support home services (e.g., homemaker, chore aide) for frail elders.

The VA provides a wide range of home- and community-based care options to qualifying veterans including home based primary care, homemaker and home aide care, hospice and palliative care, respite care, skilled home health care, telehealth care, and veteran-directed HCBS (U.S. Department of Veterans Affairs, 2012). Services vary, however, based on proximity to VA health centers and state policy decisions. Each program has its own eligibility and payment requirements; some services are provided directly through VA health services, and others are offered by independent agencies that contract with the VA (U.S. Department of Veterans Affairs, 2012). (For more information about specific programs and eligibility requirements, go to www.va.gov/GERIATRICS/Guide/LongTermCare/Home_and_Community_Based_Services.asp.)

Funding of home care can also come from private sources. Ten percent of home care services are covered through out-of-pocket payments (NAHC, 2010). Private insurance also constitutes about 8% of home care payments. Most policies cover skilled nursing and therapist services; fewer cover the costs of nonmedical home care services such as home health aides or homemakers.

Users and Programs

Characteristics of Home Health Care Clients

According to the 2007 National Home and Hospice Care Survey, of the nearly 1.5 million Americans receiving formal home health services each day, 68.7% were 65 years of age and older (Caffrey, Sengupta, Moss, Harris-Kojetin, & Valverde, 2011). Among these older home health care users, 18% were aged 65 to 74, 29% were aged 75 to 84, and 22% were aged 85 and older. Sixty-four percent of home health care users were women. Approximately 82% of the users were White, 16% were Black, and about 8% were of Hispanic or Latino origin.

One consistent predictor of home health care service use is functional disability. Of all home health care users, 84% reported receiving help with at least one activity of daily living (ADL)—bathing, dressing, transferring, toileting, and eating. Of users with ADL limitations, 50.5% had four to five limitations (see Exhibit 17.1). The mean length of service for home health care patients was 315 days, with a median of 70 days (Caffrey et al., 2011). Persons in remote rural communities use fewer provider days than patients in urban areas (McAuley, Spector, & Van Nostrand, 2009).

In 2007, the average length of service among older patients was 315 days; the median length of services was 70 days (Caffrey et al., 2011). As shown in Exhibit 17.2, the most common types of services received by older home health care clients were skilled nursing services (84%), physical therapy (40%), and assistance with ADLs (37%; A. L. Jones, Harris-Kojetin, & Valverde, 2012). A greater percentage of older women than older men

Exhibit 17.1   Home Health Clients Aged 65+ With ADL Limitations (percentage)

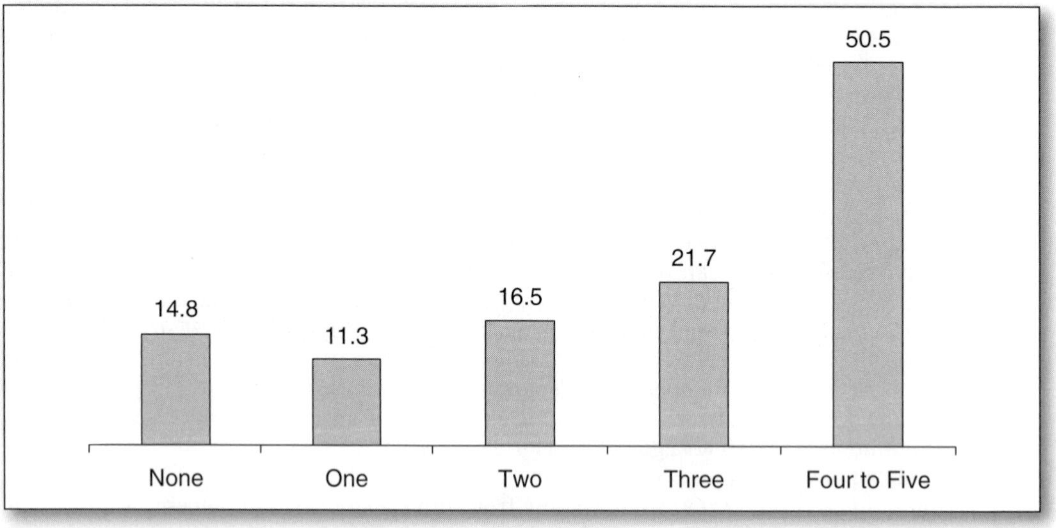

Source: Caffrey et al. (2011).

received homemaker services (19% vs. 11%) whereas a greater percentage of older men than older women received wound care (18% vs. 12%).

Mixed evidence exists regarding the relationship between personal background characteristics and the use of home care by older adults (Alkema, Reyes, & Wilber, 2006). One such variable is cognitive status. Some researchers suggest that individuals with fewer cognitive limitations are more likely to be using home care services (Borrayo, Salmon, Polivka, & Dunlap, 2002), whereas others report no relationship between cognitive abilities and home care use (Grabbe et al., 1995). Still others report higher use of home care among older adults with cognitive impairments than those without such problems. For example, a study of the effect of cognitive status on the use of in-home services (i.e., homemaking, nursing, personal care, and home-delivered meals) by 380 caregivers and care receivers in Canada found that care recipients with dementia were more likely to use personal care services and use two or more in-home services than caregivers and their care recipients with no cognitive impairment and those with cognitive impairment but no dementia (Hawranik, 2002). Part of this confusion in usage patterns comes from the use of different definitions of home care in these studies.

Race rarely is a significant predictor of the use of home care, although White older adults are the predominant users of home care services (Caffrey et al., 2011). For example, Peng, Navaie-Waliser, and Feldman (2003) reported minimal differences in the type of home health care use among older adults from racial and ethnic groups and their White counterparts. On average, all home health care recipients received at least two different types of home health services. White and Asian recipients had a greater variety of services and were more likely to have received multiple services than Black or Hispanic recipients. Regardless of race or ethnicity, having a greater number of comorbid conditions was the strongest predictor of increased use of home health services. Other

Exhibit 17.2   Type of Services Received by Home Health Clients Aged 65 by Sex (percentage)

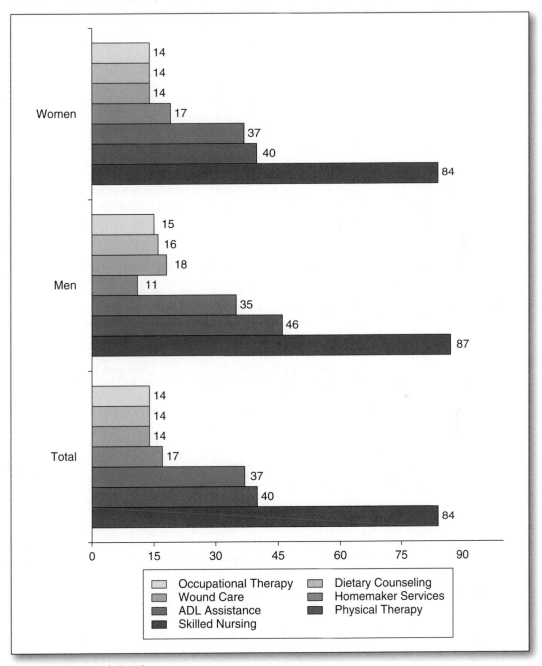

Source: A. L. Jones et al. (2012).

variables associated with higher service use included pain, more ADL dependencies, being female, and being eligible for both Medicare and Medicaid (i.e., dually eligible). Kirby and Lau (2010) also found little evidence for differences in home health care use by race. However, they did find that non-Hispanic Asians and Hispanic elders living in communities where 25% or more of residents were of the same race/ethnicity were more likely to use informal but not formal home health care than their counterparts in mixed ethnic/racial neighborhoods. The researchers concluded that policy makers promoting home health care require a better understanding of how care is typically provided in different racial, ethnic, and cultural communities.

Differences in home health service use between rural and urban residents are often attributed to access issues rather than individual characteristics of users. Rural areas are less likely to have a home health agency; when they do, the agency is likely to be smaller and to provide fewer services than agencies in urban areas. McAuley and colleagues (2009) found that older adults living in rural and metropolitan areas were just as likely to use home-based care. However, they discovered that residents in remote rural areas received fewer provider days on average than in metropolitan and other more populous communities, suggesting a possible access problem for adults in certain rural areas.

Home Health Care Programs

In 2007, there were 12,200 agencies in the United States providing home health care (10,600) or home health care and hospice (1,600) services (Park-Lee & Decker, 2010). Of these, 81% were certified by Medicare or Medicaid. Approximately 70% of the agencies were proprietary, 23% were nonprofit, and 7% were government and some other type of ownership. About one third of the agencies (35%) cared for 50 patients or less, 28% cared for between 51 and 100 patients, 11% cared for between 101 and 150 patients, and 25% cared for more than 150 patients. Eleven states had over 200 Medicare-certified home health agencies: California, Florida, Indiana, Illinois, Louisiana, Michigan, Minnesota, Ohio, Oklahoma, Pennsylvania, and Texas. Texas, with 2,190 home health agencies, had the highest number of Medicare-certified agencies, whereas Vermont reported the fewest such agencies, with 12 (CMS, 2009). Approximately 14% of the agencies were located in nonmetropolitan areas of between 10,000 to 49,999 persons.

It is relatively easy for new home care agencies to establish themselves, especially if they are not providing Medicare-certified home health care. Nonmedical home care services are not subject to federal regulation. States put forth their own definitions of and regulations for home care; both vary from state to state (Arneson, 1994). Although most states require state licensure for nonmedical home care services, standards are minimal and not difficult for most agencies to meet.

According to the U.S. Department of Labor, in 2008, there were 958,000 home health workers employed by private, freestanding home care organizations (this figure excluded hospital-based and public home care agency employees; NAHC, 2010). Home care staff consisted of both skilled professionals (e.g., doctors, nurses, physical, occupational, and speech therapists, lab technicians, and social workers) and paraprofessional members (e.g., homemakers, home health aides, and companions). The largest numbers of employees were home care aides (324,400) and nurses (132,400 registered nurses; 62,100 licensed practical nurses). Licensed practical and licensed vocational nurses provided a greater mean number of home health visits per eight-hour day than any other group of staff members (NAHC, 2010).

For Your Files: National Association for Home Care and Hospice

The NAHC is the nation's largest trade association representing the interests of home care agencies, hospices, home care aide organizations, and medical equipment suppliers. NAHC is the premier clearinghouse for home care and hospice information. Its research department compiles and reports the data for use in policy analysis and educational campaigns to policy makers and the general public. Publications include *Caring Magazine* and other information and newsletters, and periodic reports providing basic statistics about home care and hospice.

For more information, call 202-547-7424; or visit www.nahc.org.

Source: NAHC (2012).

The 2007 National Home Health Aide Survey estimated that 60,700 home health aides are employed by agencies providing home health and hospice care (Bercovitz et al., 2011). The majority of home health aides are women, at least 35 years of age, and disproportionately minority (35% African American). Their average pay is $10.88 per hour; two thirds of aides report an annual family income of less than $40,000. Most agencies offer aides a variety of benefits, including health insurance and paid time off (e.g., paid vacation or personal days, paid holidays, sick leave). The most common benefit aides reported was health insurance. The majority of home health aides are satisfied with their job overall, would definitely become an aide again, and feel the work they do is valuable and rewarding. About 50% of aides have worked as an aide for at least 10 years, and 15% have worked as an aide for more than 20 years.

For Your Files: Caring for Lesbian and Gay Older Adults

The Center for Applied Gerontology at the Council for Jewish Elderly (CJE) in Chicago has produced *Understanding and Caring for Lesbian and Gay Older Adults: Frontline Worker Sensitivity Training System,* an interactive one-hour curriculum tailored to direct-care staff who work with elders living at home and in institutional settings. It consists of a 76-page trainer's guide and a CD-ROM with PowerPoint slides and masters of handouts. The materials equip providers to offer their own in-service training to enhance cultural competence regarding lesbian and gay older adults.

For more information or to order a copy of the curriculum, contact CJE at 777-508-1006 or visit their website at www.cje.net.

Source: ASA Connection: The Monthly e-Newsletter of the American Society on Aging (June 2005).

Challenges for Home Health Care

As the health care delivery system continues its evolution, receiving health and supportive care at home will be part of the normal pathway of care. For many older adults, receiving medical care and nonmedical services in their home is less expensive than institutional care. It is the most preferred care modality among older adults. We end our discussion of home health care by addressing several current and future challenges facing home health care agencies.

Working With New Clients

The majority of new home health care clients are recent hospital discharges (NAHC, 2010) who are likely to be in a state of partial recovery from the conditions that first precipitated their acute care stay. These older individuals may encounter overwhelming stress as they attempt to adapt not only to the illness and hospitalization but also to the continuing need for physical care and emotional support. In addition, cognitive limitations are prevalent in new admissions, which can seriously impair the older person's ability to absorb and retain discharge information or acclimate to the home environment (Dellasega & Stricklin, 1993; Ellenbecker, Samia, Cushman, & Alster, 2008). Four major types of stressors face the home care patient: (a) inadequate patient teaching and insufficient discharge planning; (b) acute illness at discharge, resulting in having home care demands, high use of complex and sophisticated technology in providing care, and client dependency; (c) a home setting poorly adapted for client care, resulting in an unsafe environment; and (d) inadequate or inappropriate resources, including informal caregivers, insufficient finances, and inability to access the service system (Ellenbecker et al., 2008; Wagnild & Grupp, 1991). Agencies need to work with older patients to reduce the impact of these stressors because older persons unable to manage them will not achieve optimal care outcomes.

Serving Older Adults in Rural Communities

Although home health care is largely available in rural areas, low population density, long travel distances, and other overhead costs may make it particularly difficult for small, rural agencies to deliver home-based services to more remote parts of their communities (Hartman, Jarosek, Virnig, & Durham, 2007). In addition, many rural communities have a greater need for in-home medical and nonmedical services than they can meet. Nearly 24% of rural residents received home health care services from an urban agency or a branch office of an urban agency (Franco, 2004). These home health care users tended to be younger and less frail than those receiving care in agencies in rural areas, suggesting that the limited supply of home care services are targeted to those most in need. In addition, rural Medicare beneficiaries are less likely than urban beneficiaries to obtain specialty services such as therapy services or medical social services (Kenney, 1993). For example, rural residents consistently face more limited access to, and have to travel much greater distances for, specialty care such as dialysis or cancer treatment (Chan, Hart, & Goodman, 2006; Medicare Payment Advisory Commission, 2012b). More research is needed to further explore the home care needs of rural elders and the degree to which the more limited supply of specialized in-home services impact their health and overall well-being. Federal health and human services policies also need further scrutiny to ensure their viability for promoting and supporting adequate and effective programs for rural older adults.

Financing and Paying for Services

Although public funds pay for a large amount of home care, many older adults also must pay for some of their care. According to data from leading insurers, 8 million Americans have long-term care insurance provided through individual plans purchased directly from insurance companies (excludes those with government or employer-supplied long-term care insurance; American Association for Long Term Care Insurance, 2008). The cost of long-term care insurance varies widely depending on the options selected. Insurance prices have been steadily rising in recent years—for people aged 55 to 65, they are up an average of 30% to 50% compared to 5 years ago. At the same time, however, the range of companies offering long-term care insurance has expanded considerably. For a policy with mid-range benefits, an individual 55 and in "standard" health would expect to pay about $2,000 a year, and a couple aged 65 years old can expect to pay an average of $5,000 a year (J. B. Quinn, 2012). As new strategies are considered to improve the financing available for home care services, a key policy decision that legislators must address is determining an appropriate balance between public- and private-sector financing that meets the needs of frail older adults, does not undermine the efforts of informal caregivers, and is equitable and politically viable (D. Stone, 2000).

Recruiting and Retaining Staff

Given the growth and diversity in the health care system, there often is competition for employees among home care agencies, hospitals, and nursing homes as well as from other service sectors (e.g., discount stores). This competition, along with minimal wages and benefits, the lack of job security, and limited opportunity for career development, contributes to high turnover rates, particularly among nonmedical health care staff (Hewitt et al., 2008). In addition, as the aging population expands, the health care workforce will be too small and unprepared to meet their healthcare needs (Institute of Medicine [IOM], 2008). This is due, in part, to fewer young workers entering the health care workforce, the aging of the nursing workforce, increased options for women, and increased dissatisfaction with the health care workplace (Kimball & O'Neill, 2002). In addition, few health care providers of any type receive adequate training in geriatric care; this is particularly true for primary care providers such as nurse aides, home health aides, and personal care aides (IOM, 2008). With the predicted future increase in the demand for home health care services, the home health industry will need to enhance geriatric training of all providers as well as improve health aide monetary compensation and develop more creative strategies for the recruitment and retention of all of its employees.

Ensuring Quality Care

Home health care agencies must continually address the issue of quality assurance. The CMS (2003) developed and published a set of home health quality measures on every Medicare-certified home health agency in the United States. The quality measures are intended to help consumers compare the quality of care provided by home health agencies as well as to motivate home health agencies to improve care and to inform discussions about quality between consumers and clinicians. The challenge for communities is to continually promote consumers' use of these measures when making decisions about home care. More information about the measures is available at http://www.medicare.gov/home healthcompare/%28S%28jmt45eaivhqutwlnkjoauajk%29%29/Data/Quality-Measures/Data-Sources.aspx.

A staple of state quality assurance systems has been the consumer satisfaction survey (Folkemer, 2006). Consumers typically are asked whether they are satisfied with their case workers, their care plans, and their personal care workers. These surveys have often failed, however, to provide any depth of information about consumer preferences in service delivery or desired outcomes, as there is a well-known reluctance of many older people to criticize those providing care, both because of inherent courtesy and because of dependence on providers. Clearly, alternative approaches to assessing client satisfaction need to be developed. There also is a lack of consistency in home care research as to the definition of client outcomes, which makes it difficult to generalize the findings beyond the specific study population. The lack of use of a consistent set of measures makes it difficult for state officials to examine the association between various programs, practices, and outcomes (R. A. Kane, 2000).

In the wake of health care reform, enrollment in Medicare HMOs has increased (see Chapter 11). The outcomes for HMO patients compared with fee-for-service patients, however, have come into question. Schlenker, Shaughnessy, and Crisler (1995) suggest that HMOs provide too few home health care visits to patients and attribute the difference in care, in part, to the capitation payments provided to HMOs by Medicare. Conversely, Porell and Miltiades (2001) found that, among older people who were functionally impaired, neither HMO enrollment nor having private supplementary insurance affected the risk of further functional decline or functional improvement. With changes in health care delivery and regulations, agencies must continually evaluate their services as related to client outcomes.

Supporting the Future of Home Health Care

Several of the top 50 resolutions put forth by delegates of the 2005 White House Conference on Aging (2006) gave support for home health care services by proposing resolutions that expand and enhance delivery and payment for these services. These include

- developing a coordinated, comprehensive, long-term care strategy by supporting public and private sector initiatives that address financing, choice, quality, service delivery, and the paid and unpaid workforce;
- promoting innovative models of noninstitutional long-term care; and
- fostering innovations in financing long-term care to increase options available to consumers.

Whether the federal government and the private sector are able to meet the challenges facing home health care remains to be seen.

Best Practice: Visiting Nurse Association of the Treasure Coast

Health Care on Wheels, operated by the Visiting Nurse Association (VNA) of the Treasure Coast in Indian River County, Florida, is a unique program addressing the needs of residents who do not have a primary care physician or who cannot afford health insurance or the services of a physician. A mobile medical unit, staffed with a nurse practitioner and basic screening and testing equipment, operates approximately 50 hours per week in neighborhoods with high concentrations of residents lacking access to primary health care. Practitioners on board the mobile unit can examine, diagnose, and prescribe medications for minor, nonurgent illnesses such as upper respiratory infections, sore throats, earaches, and minor cuts. The van also carries a computer that allows staff to quickly and easily manage demographic data associated with the program. Services include screening for issues such as blood pressure and blood sugar, physicals, flu shots, and a few diagnostic activities. In 2011, VNA made 4,200 mobile unit visits.

For further information, contact Program Director for Health Services, VNA of the Treasure Coast, 1110 35th Street, Vero Beach, FL 32960; phone: 772-567-5551 or 800-749-5760; www .vnatc.com.

HOSPICE

Hospice is a philosophy of caring for individuals who are terminally ill and their family members. It is a comprehensive approach providing palliative medical, social, emotional, and spiritual support. As of 2010, there were over 5,000 hospice programs in the United States, and more than 3,500 of these programs were Medicare certified (National Hospice and Palliative Care Organization [NHPCO], 2012). Although most hospice patients are older adults, persons of any age may receive hospice care.

Policy Background

The Tax Equity and Fiscal Responsibility Act enacted in 1982 created the Medicare hospice program. Originally, reimbursement for coverage was limited to 210 days. The passing of OBRA (1990) removed this limitation. Medicare now provides for unlimited days of coverage for hospice care when provided by a Medicare-certified hospice program for as long as the doctor certifies that there is a need. To be eligible for hospice care, a person must be certified as terminally ill, with only about six months to live, by the patient's physician or a hospice staff physician, and the hospice care must be part of the written plan of treatment established by the attending professionals.

Medicare entitles the person to the following hospice services: physician services; nursing care; medical social services; home health aides; counseling for the patient, family, and other caregivers; short-term inpatient care; physical, speech, and occupational therapy; homemaker services; and medical supplies, appliances, and equipment. When a patient receives these services from a Medicare-certified hospice, Medicare pays providers one of four fixed prospective per-diem rates, based on service level and setting, for every day of hospice benefit coverage. Medicare hospital insurance (Part A) pays almost the entire cost of care. Hospice can charge the patient $5 for each prescription drug or other similar products for pain relief and symptom control provided on an outpatient basis by the hospice program (Hospice Association of America, 2010). Hospice also can charge 5% of the Medicare payment amount for inpatient respite care (about $151.67 per day in FY 2011). Patients can stay in a Medicare-approved hospital or nursing home for up to five days each time they get respite care. There is no limit to the number of times patients can get respite care (CMS, 2010a). In 2009, Medicare expenditures for hospice services were approximately 12 billion (Hospice Association of America, 2010).

Although Medicare is the most common source of funding for hospice services, other entities also cover the cost of participation in hospice. Medicaid provides hospice coverage in 48 states plus DC. Medicaid hospice expenditures totaled $1,639 million in 2006 (Hospice Association of America, 2010). Hospices also receive reimbursement from private health insurance, HMOs, preferred provider organizations, and private pay, and to a lesser extent from local (e.g., United Way), state, and federal sources. More than 80% of employees in medium and large businesses have coverage for hospice services, and 82% of managed care plans offer hospice services (NHPCO, 2001).

There is currently no mandatory nationwide accreditation or "seal of approval" for hospice programs. To be eligible for Medicare or Medicaid reimbursement, programs undergo a certification process to ensure that appropriate care is provided to clients and that all employee and clinical records are in compliance with licensure requirements (Hospice Association of America, 2006). Some hospices voluntarily seek accreditation from the Joint Commission on Accreditation of Healthcare Organizations or the Community Health Accreditation Program. Less is known about hospices that do not participate in Medicare or Medicaid or national accreditation programs, as rules and regulations for licensure vary by state.

Users and Programs

Characteristics of Hospice Clients

Data from the 2007 National Home and Hospice Care Survey (Caffrey et al., 2011) suggest that almost 1.1 million patients receive hospice care in the United States. The majority of hospice patients (83%) were aged 65 or older; 15% were aged 65 to 74, 29% were aged 75 to 84, and 33% were at least 85 years of age. Of the older patients, 58% were women. Approximately 77% of hospice patients were White, 9% were Black, and 6% were of Hispanic or Latino origin (NHPCO, 2012).

The balance between hospice patients with cancer diagnoses and those with non-cancer diagnoses has shifted dramatically in recent years. In 1992, 75% of hospice patients had a primary diagnosis of cancer; in 2007, 43% of hospice patients had a cancer diagnosis. Non-cancer patients typically had heart disease (11.1%), dementia (6.6%) chronic obstructive pulmonary disease and allied conditions (4.7%), or cerebrovascular disease (4.5%).

Although the average length of stay in hospice was 86 days in 2010, the median length of stay has held steady since 2000 at 17 or 18 days (Medicare Payment Advisory Commission, 2012a). Most hospice patients died at their place of residence (67%); 41.1% died at a private residence; 25% died at a nursing home or other residential facility; 22% died in a hospice in-patient facility; and 11.4% died at an acute care hospital (NHPCO, 2012).

Across the Globe: Hospice Malta

The Malta Hospice Movement, founded in 1989, drew inspiration from the work of Dame Cicely Saunders, the visionary founder of the modern hospice movement, who set the highest standards in care for the dying. Today, Hospice Malta cares for over 750 patients and their families from all over the Maltese Islands. Most of the program's patients have cancer, but a small number have motor neuron disease or respiratory disease. Although most clients are older adults and their families, the program provides services to all in need regardless of race, religion, or lifestyle. Services provided by a multidisciplinary professional team and trained volunteers include: home care, day care (comprehensive day therapy and medical treatment facility), hospital support, respite care, social work support, physiotherapy, complementary therapy (reflexology, aromatherapy, massage), occupational therapy, bereavement support, family support, equipment loans, and library resources. All services are free and available to all patients.

Sources: http://hospicemalta.org/about-us; http://hospicemalta.org/services.

Hospice Programs

Approximately 94% of the hospice programs in the United States are certified by Medicare and Medicaid (Caffrey et al., 2011). A variety of organizations provide hospice services. Approximately 40% of hospices are independent community-based organizations; 44% are part of a group or chain, 25% are divisions of hospitals, and 4% are operated by a health maintenance organization. Freestanding hospices serve the majority of hospice patients; skilled nursing facility-based hospices served the fewest number of patients. Approximately 67% of hospices are nonprofit, 31% are for-profit, and 2% are government or other organizations. The majority of hospices are located in metropolitan areas (87%).

The numbers of Medicare-certified hospices in 2008 ranged from just three in DC and five in Arkansas, to 222 in California and 298 in Texas (Hospice Association of America, 2010). The majority of states (96%) provide hospice care for more than 1,000 Medicare recipients annually; only two states served fewer than 1,000 patients in 2008; Florida alone served 96,262 patients through hospice.

Hospice patients receive individualized services, depending on their personal needs. In 2009, Medicare-certified hospices employed more than 102,058 full-time equivalent paid professionals (Hospice Association of America, 2010). These individuals included medical personnel such as physicians and nurses, home health aides, social workers, clergy, and pastoral counselors. The largest numbers of employees were registered nurses (31,548) and home health aides (21,386). In addition, 48,571 volunteers provided assistance and support to patients and their caregivers. The largest numbers of volunteers were homemakers (2,079) and counselors (1,447). All Medicare hospice volunteers must participate in intensive volunteer training programs.

Hospices also offer bereavement groups and services for families and caregivers to help them with their grief. Most hospices offer these programs and services to the community at large, not just those families served directly by hospices. Bereavement services include follow-up phone calls and visits, information regarding meetings or group offerings, and literature and material on grief. A survey completed by 260 hospice providers indicated that either nurses or individuals with human services backgrounds (e.g., social work, clergy, counseling) coordinate bereavement services (Demmer, 2003). Because of a lack of time and too few bereavement staff, programs tend to focus on less time-intensive services such as mailing of letters and literature on grief versus phone calls and home visits.

For Your Files: Hospice of the Florida Suncoast

The Hospice of the Florida Suncoast, located in Largo, Florida, is a not-for-profit organization committed to serving those living with chronic and or terminal illnesses, nearing the end of life, or experiencing grief. Suncoast Hospice is community based, offering comprehensive hospice and palliative care, caregiver education, individual and group counseling, spiritual support, and many other programs to those it serves regardless of race, age, faith, diagnosis, or financial circumstances. Hospice services are provide both in-home and at hospice houses. The organization also maintains an online resource center that has a wealth of easily accessible information for patients and caregivers.

For more information, visit their website: https://www.thehospice.org.

Challenges for Hospice

Hospice programs in the United States focus on home care and dehospitalization (Mor & Allen, 1995). Family members, along with the hospice staff, provide care to their terminally ill loved ones. Hospice, along with other health care providers, will be affected by the ever-changing nature of health care and the graying of the population. We end this section with a discussion of the challenges facing hospice programs now and in the future.

Serving a Greater Diversity of Patients

White, middle-class patients are the predominant users of hospice programs. For hospices to respond to the needs of ethnic minority patients, workers need to be sensitive to culture-specific issues and practices. Challenges to overcome in providing hospice services across cultures include language differences, family values, lack of trust, and the hospice patient's feelings of discrimination or inequality (Casey, Moscovies, Virnig, & Durham, 2005; Cort, 2004; K. S. Johnson, Kuchibhatla, & Tulsky, 2008). To successfully expand services into minority communities, hospices must establish a pattern of education and communication appropriate to consumers, volunteers, and professionals of all races, ethnicities, and cultural groups (Carrion, Park, & Lee, 2012; Harding, Epiphaniou, & Chidgey-Clark, 2012; Haxton & Boelk, 2010).

Supporting Patients Without Families

By design, the hospice home care model supports the efforts of families caring for terminally ill relatives at home. An increasing number of hospice candidates, however, do not have home support available, or the support that is available is inadequate or unreliable (MacDonald, 1992). Thus, hospice programs face either not serving this group of individuals or providing care for patients whose needs far exceed available resources. To address this issue, hospices need to develop creative approaches to serving patients without primary caregivers, such as at a hospice house (Hrehocik, 2008). Without strong community support (e.g., donations, volunteers) and supportive legislative action, most hospices will continue to struggle with how to provide care to individuals who are for the most part alone.

Assessing Hospice Care

Hospices vary considerably in their performance and in the services they provide. Although the NHPCO developed and promotes standards of care for hospice programs, there is no means of enforcement; thus, a problem in the U.S. hospice community is the lack of consistency among hospices as to compliance with standards (Connor, Tecca, LundPerson, & Teno, 2004). To address this issue, the NHPCO established a national database to be used to establish benchmarks for hospice practice throughout the country. This database provides a critical tool for furthering the use of consistent operations and performance measurement in hospice.

Enhancing Bereavement Programs

Bereavement programs are often the most underdeveloped component of the hospice program. Program staff indicate a desire to provide more group and educational programs, as well as more home visits to families, but cite lack of sufficient staff time, lack of personnel, and funding pressures as barriers to increasing the delivery of bereavement services (Demmer, 2003). Language and cultural barriers also are challenges when offering and delivering bereavement services (Arriaza, Martin, & Csikai, 2011). Thus, the lack of resources for bereavement services is an issue facing most hospice programs.

Educating Americans on End-of-Life Issues

Delegates to the 2005 White House Conference on Aging (2006) listed educating Americans on end-of-life issues as one of their top 50 resolutions. Strategies proposed to implement this resolution included educating people about hospice and palliative care, and developing health care and community collaborations with faith-based communities, aging service, and other community providers to promote advance care planning and completion of advance directives for all individuals.

CASE STUDY

Will Home Health Care Work for Harriet?

Harriet is a 79-year-old woman who has never married. She lives in a small mobile home situated on land several miles from a rural town of 2,500 persons. Until three years ago, she lived with her bachelor brother who had been at the center of her life. His sudden death left Harriet confused and depressed because her life had revolved around the companionship and care of her brother. Her health has deteriorated steadily since his death. People in her community describe Harriet as a colorful character. She dropped out of school when she was 16 years old and took a job as a ranch cook's assistant. Her interest in ranching led to several years of traveling the rodeo circuit, assisting well-known bronco riders. Eventually, Harriet ended up owning a small grocery store in the town where she now lives. Her independent spirit became well known by her customers and business acquaintances. Harriet made no time for other social contacts beyond work and her brother. Harriet is not a religious woman and has little patience for "frivolous" socializing. Until recently, she devoted her spare time to raising and showing an exotic breed of house cat.

(Continued)

(Continued)

Although she accumulated considerable savings, she spent most of it supporting her brother, who had an alcohol problem. She does receive a monthly Social Security check of $524. Because she owns her mobile home and the acre of land on which it is situated, her monthly expenses average only $225. She has Medicare and a small supplemental health insurance policy. Harriet has a history of diabetes and high blood pressure, which have gone untreated. She has fallen several times, and it is becoming difficult for her to get in and out of her bathtub. This, combined with some incontinence, has made it difficult for her to maintain her personal hygiene. She recently was discharged from the hospital after gallbladder surgery. Her wound is not healing quickly.

Case Study Questions

1. The chapter discusses several predictors of use for home health services. Describe these predictors. Which apply to Harriet?

2. What are the social and environmental dynamics of Harriet's situation that a home health agency would take into consideration when assigning a worker to this case?

3. What criteria would Harriet have to meet to qualify for Medicare home health services? What other payment sources might be available to Harriet?

4. Harriet is likely to resist the idea of home health care. What arguments could best make the case to Harriet that this is a good option for her?

LEARNING ACTIVITIES

1. Review current Medicare, Medicaid, or OAA legislation that pertains to home care services. What do the various laws mandate? How do they differ, and where do they overlap? What areas do you believe legislation needs to address in preparation for future growth of the aging population?

2. Interview a home health care provider or hospice staff member. What situations does the provider encounter? What types of on-the-job or in-service training do workers receive? What are the education and experience requirements for staff positions? What are some of the obstacles as well as benefits of the service? What changes would the staff like to see?

3. Interview someone who receives or is the caregiver of someone who receives home health or home care services. What does the recipient or caregiver feel are the benefits of the program? Where are the gaps? How would the individual change the program or services, if at all? What would the individual do without the program or services? How did the household find out about the program and select the provider?

4. Check local newspapers, television, radio, and magazines for home care service and hospice services. Whom are they trying to reach? How would you respond to the ads?

5. Design a new home care or hospice program. What elements would be primary? Whom would you serve? How would you market your program?

6. Use the Glenworth Financial online interactive map at the webpage below to compare the cost of long-term care in your state to that of two different states in other regions of the United States (http://www.genworth.com/content/non_navigable/corporate/about_genworth/indus try_expertise/cost_of_care.html). How would these cost differences interact with other factors (e.g., climate, proximity to family) to affect your decisions about where to retire? How do these differences in long-term care costs impact the lives of older adults in these regions?

FOR MORE INFORMATION

International Resources

1. International Association for Hospice and Palliative Care: http://www.hospicecare.com

   This not-for-profit organization is dedicated to increasing and optimizing the availability of and access to hospice and palliative care for patients and their families throughout the world. They also offer palliative care education and training opportunities to care providers, provide information for professionals and policy makers, and develop collaborative strategies for hospice and palliative care providers, organizations, institutions, and individuals.

2. Worldwide Palliative Care Alliance (WPCA): http://www.thewpca.org

   The WPCA is a global action network focused exclusively on hospice and palliative care development worldwide. With main offices based in both the United Kingdom and the United States, they operate through work groups based in different national hospice and palliative care organizations around the world to promote the development of expanded hospice and palliative care, support members to achieve high-quality standards and organizational structure, and address international barriers to hospice care through advocacy and policy work.

3. Palliative Care: A Public Health Priority in Developing Countries (Webster, Lacey & Quine, 2007): http://www.nhpco.org/files/public/Statistics_Research/Webster.pdf

   This article in the *Journal of Public Health Policy* highlights the discrepancies between advancement of hospice care in developed versus developing countries where high incidences of cancer and AIDS characterize the health care landscape.

National Resources

1. National Association for Home Care, 228 7th Street SE, Washington, DC 20003; phone: 202-547-7424; www.nahc.org

   The National Association for Home Care represents home health agencies, hospice programs, and homemaker/home health aid agencies. *Caring Magazine* and *Home Care News* are published by the association. Contact it for a list of publications.

2. National Hospice Organization, 1700 Diagonal Road, Suite 625, Alexandria, VA 22314; phone: 703-837-1500 or 800-646-6460; www.nhpco.org

   The national office offers technical assistance and training to local hospice organizations. It operates a toll-free referral line to local hospice programs. Numerous free publications are available.

3. Visiting Nurse Association of America, 8403 Colesville Road, Suite 1550, Silver Spring, MD 20910-6374; phone: 240-485-1856; www.vnaa.org

The VNA is the parent organization of local VNAs that provide personal care; speech, physical, and occupational therapies; and nutritional counseling. A fact sheet is available.

4. National Hospice Foundation, 1700 Diagonal Road, Suite 300, Alexandria, VA 22314; phone: 703-243-5900 or 800-854-3402; www.hospicefoundation.org

   The foundation promotes home care and hospice care through the establishment of standards of care, educational programs, and research. Free consumer guides about home care and hospice are available.

5. *Home Health Care Services Quarterly*, Taylor & Francis Group, 4 Park Square, Milton Park, Abingdon, Oxfordshire, OX14 4RN, UK; phone: 44-0-20-7017-6000; http://www.tandfonline.com/toc/whhc20/31/2

   The journal publishes creative and scholarly articles that provide new insights into the delivery and management of home health and related community services. It is aimed toward service providers and health care specialists involved with health care financing, evaluation of services, organization of services, and public policy issues.

6. *American Journal of Hospice and Palliative Medicine*, Sage Publications, 2455 Teller Road, Thousand Oaks, CA 91320; phone: 805-410-7763; www.sagepub.com/journalsProdDesc.nav?prodId=Journa1201797

   Provides physicians, nurses, psychologists/psychiatrists, pastoral care professionals, hospice administrators, and related health care professionals with high-quality, practical, and multidisciplinary information on the medical, administrative, and psychosocial aspects of hospice and palliative care.

Web Resources

1. GriefNet: www.griefnet.org

   GriefNet is a webpage that can connect visitors with a variety of resources related to death, dying, bereavement, and major emotional and physical losses. It offers interactive discussion and support groups—all for bereaved persons and those working with the bereaved, both professional and laypersons. The support and discussion groups are accessed by e-mail. Groups include grief-chat, a general discussion list for any topic related to death, dying, bereavement, or other major loss; and grief-widowed, a support group for anyone who has lost a partner or a spouse at any age, at any time, of any sexual orientation. This is a great site. Be sure to stop by for a visit.

2. National Hospice and Palliative Care Organization: www.nhpco.org/templates/1/homepage.cfm

   The NHPCO site offers a wide range of links, including How to Find a Hospice, Basics of Hospice, Discussion Groups, Publications and Resources, and Specific Diseases. This well-designed site furnishes much useful information.

3. HomeCare On Line: http://www.nahc.org

   This website of the National Association for Home Care offers information about state associations, consumer information, news updates, and legislative information. Visitors can search the database for information.

4. ElderCare Locator: www.eldercare.gov/Eldercare/Public/Home.asp

   ElderCare Locator is a free national service of the Administration on Aging. Just one phone call or website visit provides an instant connection to resources that enable older persons to live independently in their communities. Support services for caregivers are also available.

Respite Services

William, 78 years old, was at the end of his rope when he called the Area Agency on Aging. He had resisted making the call for months, but a close friend urged him to get help. William had watched his wife's memory fade year by year, but he could not completely accept that she had Alzheimer's disease. His doctor was advising him that the stress and continuous physical exertion were aggravating his arthritis. The case manager suggested that William consider having a trained respite worker come into his home twice a week. Reluctantly, William agreed. After a month of respite help, he is beginning to appreciate the six hours per week when he can concentrate on other things.

Respite care is temporary, short-term supervisory, personal, and nursing care provided to older adults with physical or mental impairments (Montgomery, 1996). Programs provide services in the older person's home or at a specific site in the community (e.g., adult day services, nursing home, hospital). Although older adults are the recipients of care, these dual-purpose programs also provide temporary periods of relief or rest for caregivers. Like William, the primary caregiver tends to be a spouse who has assumed the role of caregiver because of the failing physical or mental health of his or her partner. The role of spousal caregiver often comes at a time in the couple's lives when they may be experiencing health problems or the reduction of functional capacities associated with aging. When a spouse is not available or is unable to provide care, adult children assume the caregiving responsibilities for their aging parents. It is usually a daughter or daughter-in-law who takes on the major responsibility. These women often face the competing demands of caring for an aging parent, managing a household, parenting their own children, and working outside the home (Aumann, Galinsky, Sakai, Brown, & Bond, 2010; MetLife Mature Market Institute, 2011c; National Alliance for Caregiving & AARP, 2009).

Although family caregivers experience a sense of pride and emotional gratification when they perceive themselves as successfully fulfilling their caregiving responsibilities (R. Robertson, Zarit, Duncan, Rovine, & Femia, 2007; Roff et al., 2004), the demands of providing daily care for an older family member are not without physical, psychological, and social liabilities. Caregivers often experience poor physical health and emotional distress (R. Schulz & Sherwood, 2008). Fulfilling the role of primary caregiver often restricts the use of personal time, interferes with employment responsibilities and obligations, and strains family relationships (Blieszner, Roberto, Wilcox, Barham, & Winston, 2007; C. Quinn, Clare, Pearce, & van Dijkhuizen, 2008; Roberto & Jarrott, 2008). To help alleviate the burden and stress of caregiving, respite services have become an integral part of the continuum of support services for older adults. They provide relief for caregivers from the constant responsibilities of caring for dependent older adults and allow both the caregivers and care receivers time for independent relationships and activities (Gaugler et al., 2003; Salin, Kaunonen, & Astedt-Kurki 2009).

In this chapter, we present information about the types of respite programs available for older adults and their caregivers. The chapter begins with an overview of federal support for respite services, followed by a presentation of the general characteristics of older adults who participate in respite programs and a description of the primary types of respite services. We end the chapter with a discussion of the challenges facing providers of respite services now and in the future.

POLICY BACKGROUND

Some of the first support for respite care for older adults came from the Older Women's League. In the early 1980s, the league sponsored model legislation in several states to encourage the development of statewide respite programs for caregivers of frail older adults. As a result, several states mandated respite care as part of their state-sponsored programs for older adults and their families (e.g., Illinois's Alzheimer's Disease Program, New York State's Expanded In-Home Services for the Elderly Program, California's Alzheimer's Disease Institute; Petty, 1990).

In its 1987 report, *Losing a Million Minds*, the U.S. Congress, Office of Technology Assessment (OTA) firmly established the need for respite care, particularly for persons with dementia. Of the top 10 services rated by caregivers of persons with dementia as essential or most important, six related to respite care: (a) a paid companion who can come to the home for a few hours each week to give caregivers a rest, (b) a paid companion for overnight care, (c) personal care for the older person, (d) short-term respite outside the home in nursing homes or hospitals, (e) adult day care, and (f) nursing visits at home. In addition, the OTA report suggested that the provision of respite services postpones the need for nursing home placement.

Despite these findings and other research documenting the need for and effectiveness of respite services, the federal government provides limited financial support for respite services. Because the government defines respite care for the older individual as "personal care," it is not a reimbursable service under Medicare. Medicaid allows for such care through its waiver programs and can cover both in-home respite and adult day services (ADS). ADS centers typically are supported by a "patchwork" of private and public funding, with a little more than one half of funding coming through publicly paid participant fees. Recent increases in these publicly available funds could reflect success of efforts to augment such home- and community-based respite programs with public funding, but could also indicate that ADS is serving clients with fewer resources (Metlife Mature Market Institute, 2010c). State reimbursement through Medicaid ranges from less than $50 per six-hour ADS day in 13 states including Texas, Alabama, and Idaho, to more than $70 per six-hour day in 10 states such as Missouri, New Jersey, and Vermont (LeadingAge, 2011). In addition, most states provide scaled funding based on acuity level of the client (e.g. basic/specialized).

Some respite programs receive support through Older Americans Act (OAA) funds under Title III-D, which authorizes the support of in-home services, including in-home respite and adult day care. In addition, the Act provides funds for educational programs that teach caregivers about Alzheimer's disease, how to cope with the disease process, and how to use behavior management techniques. As part of the OAA amendments of 2000, Congress created the National Family Caregiver Support Program (NFCSP), representing the largest new support program under the OAA since 1972. NFCSP funds may be used to support services that provide information about services, assist with access to services, provide individual counseling or organize support groups and caregiver training, provide respite care, and provide supplemental services. States and Area Agencies on Aging have the flexibility to determine the funding allocated to these services. In FY 2010, over 700,000 caregivers received services through the NFCSP, including 64,000 caregivers who received 6.8 million hours of temporary relief—either at home or in an adult day care or institutional setting—from their caregiving responsibilities (Administration on Aging [AoA], 2012g). Although slightly reduced from previous years, Congress appropriated almost $154 million in support of caregivers through the NFCSP in FY 2011.

In December 2006, Congress passed legislation establishing new respite care programs to help families who are taking care of persons with serious illnesses. The Lifespan Respite Care Act (S 1283/HR 3248) provides grants to state agencies, public and private nonprofit groups, and other organizations to make respite care available and accessible to family caregivers, regardless of age, condition, or special need. Individuals with Alzheimer's disease, including those with early onset Alzheimer's, are eligible for services. The Bill directs the Secretary to work in cooperation with the NFCSP, the AoA, and other respite care programs within the Department of Health and Human Services to ensure coordination of respite care services. The Bill also establishes a National Respite Resource Center to maintain a national database on lifespan respite care, provide training and technical assistance, and provide information, referral, and educational programs to the public on lifespan respite care. Since FY 2009, Congress has appropriated approximately $2.5 million per year for grants to eligible state agencies to implement the program. As of 2011, 30 states have been award grants to improve the availability and quality of respite across the lifespan (AoA, 2011f).

Family caregivers who work and must pay for respite services for their care receivers may benefit from federal and state dependent care assistance plans (B. Coleman, 2000; National Governors' Association, 2004). If employers offer this benefit option, authorized under Section 129 of the Internal Revenue Code, dependent care assistance plans provide reimbursement of up to $5,000 per year for out-of-the-home dependent care expenses. Qualifying individuals include spouses or dependents who are unable to care for themselves, regardless of age, and who regularly spend at least eight hours each day in the employee's household. This time requirement makes such plans less useful for adult children and other individuals with elder care responsibilities because many of these employees do not share a household with the older person whom they are helping (R. W. Johnson & Weiner, 2006). In addition to dependent care assistance plans, the dependent care tax credit (DCTC) assists families in meeting the cost of care by allowing taxpayers to offset a portion of their employment-related dependent care expenses against their federal income tax liability. An expense is "employment related" for the purpose of claiming the DCTC if it is a dependent care expense that is necessary to enable the family member to be gainfully employed. The federal DCTC reduces the amount of income tax the employee owes by a percentage of the expenses the employee has incurred because of dependent care responsibilities. The maximum amount the DCTC can reduce the taxpayer's overall taxes is from $600 to $1,050 depending on the amount of the individual's adjusted gross income. The maximum amount of work-related dependent care expenses that can be applied toward the tax credit is $3,000. The amount ranges from 20% to 35% of qualified expenses, depending on a taxpayer's adjusted gross income (American Elder Care Research Organization, 2011a). Individuals eligible to receive care and the types of expenditures allowed are the same as those that apply to the dependent care assistance plan. Thus, employees with children are the primary users of federal DCTCs. State tax credit programs build on the federal tax credit, using the federal eligibility rules, and defining the state credit as a percentage of the federal credit. Twenty-eight states and the District of Columbia provide tax deductions or tax credits that provide some financial relief to caregivers (American Elder Care Research Organization, 2011b). Most states allow tax filers to deduct a percentage of their federal tax credit from their state tax returns, with maximum tax credits for elder care ranging from $173 (Virginia) to $1,155 (New York). Unlike deductions, tax credits generally benefit lower income taxpayers and often are viewed as a more equitable way of providing tax incentives to family caregivers.

Across the Globe: Elder Care in Sweden

In Sweden, overall responsibility for the care of elderly adults rests with the state. The country has a comprehensive range of community- and facility-based programs, including adult day care centers in most municipalities. Activities of these units originally targeted the needs of individuals with dementia or mental disabilities and their caregivers, but in recent decades, day cares have also begun serving older adults with somatic diseases. Dependent older adults in Sweden most often live at home and are cared for by their families. Thus, adult day care programs play an important role in providing supervised care for the elders while family caregivers have some respite. The number of older adults in these centers at any one time is limited and specialized medical and social support staff members provide care.

Sources: National Board of Health and Welfare (2009) and Swedish Institute (2012).

USERS AND PROGRAMS

Respite programs typically provide care for older adults with a wide range of physical and mental disabilities. Some programs, however, provide services for specific subgroups of older adults such as persons with Alzheimer's disease (Alzheimer's Association, 2012b; ARCH National Respite Network and Resource Center, 2012) or developmental disabilities (AoA, 2009b; ARCH National Respite Network and Resource Center, 2011; Washko, Campbell, & Tilly, 2012). The small number of reports that include data on client and family characteristics makes it difficult to develop an accurate profile of respite care users. Thus, we begin this section by providing a general profile of older adults who use respite services. We then focus our attention on the three most common types of respite programs: in-home respite care, adult day care, and institutional respite care. Where data are available, we provide information about the older adults and caregivers using each type of respite care.

Characteristics of Older Adults Using Respite Services

Drawing on the limited research literature, Montgomery (1992) profiled older adults participating in respite programs. Typically, these elders are around 80 years of age. Male participants tend to be younger than their female counterparts. They also are overrepresented in the client population in comparison with the gender distribution of this age group in the general population—about 40% of the clients are male and 60% are female. More than 85% of the older adults live with their caregivers, who are either spouses or adult children. Most older respite users have multiple impairments that limit their ability to perform activities of daily living. Among caregivers who use respite services, African Americans, as a group, used day care for a longer period of time than any other race or ethnic group. However, they used fewer hours of service each week (Montgomery, Marquis, Schaefer, & Kosloski, 2002). In contrast, Hispanic caregivers used greater amounts of respite services to assist with the care of a relative with Alzheimer's disease than did White and African American caregivers, even after controlling for a variety of caregiver attitudes and beliefs about families, help, religion, and service (Kosloski, Schaefer, Allwardt, Montgomery, & Karner, 2002).

Respite Programs

A variety of agencies, including both for-profit and nonprofit organizations, operate respite programs. Programs differ with respect to their definitions of respite, target populations, eligibility criteria, and the amount and type of respite offered. Costs for respite services vary, depending on the type and level of care provided to the participants. Most programs rely on contributions from their clients, who either pay a preset amount or contribute on a sliding scale according to their financial resources.

In-Home Respite Care

In-home respite care takes place in the home in which the older person lives. Depending on the needs of the caregiver, in-home respite can occur on a regular or occasional basis and can take place during the day or evening hours. Some programs provide personal and instrumental care for the older person, whereas others provide only companionship or supervisory services (Mensie & Stephen, 2011; Montgomery et al., 2002; Noelker & Browdie, 2012). Professionals and nonprofessionals employed by community-based agencies that offer respite services (e.g., home health agencies, senior support programs, church-affiliated organizations) typically provide the care. Several communities have developed programs that rely on family members, friends, and trained volunteers to provide in-home respite care (AoA, 2011a, 2012g). For example, North Carolina's Project C.A.R.E. (Caregiver Alternatives to Running on Empty) uses a family consultant model to provide consumer-directed respite care and comprehensive support to caregivers. Family consultants with expertise in Alzheimer's disease and other types of dementia visit the homes of referred or self-referred dementia caregivers in crisis and offer individualized services with the aim of matching families with the most appropriate and preferred local respite and community services (North Carolina Division of Aging and Adult Services, 2012). In Minnesota, the Normandale Center for Healing and Wholeness uses a Care Team Model, matching caregivers with a team of two to three trained volunteers who provide in-home respite and other care-related services as needed; they strive to support older adults and their families in "body, mind, and spirit" (Normandale Center for Healing and Wholeness, 2012).

Data from a seven-state study of respite care (Montgomery et al., 2002) that included 1,143 in-home term respite users suggest that the typical older adult using in-home respite care is 80 years old, White (63.8%), female (64.5%), married (49.3%), lives in a rural area (62.3%), has been diagnosed with Alzheimer's disease, and has an average of 4.7 activity of daily living (ADL) limitations and 13.2 instrumental ADL limitations. Caregivers of in-home respite users have a mean age of 63.6 years. Most are female (70.0%), either a spouse (42.1%) or adult child/child-in-law (41.7%), married (71.2%), and either working at least part time (30.6%) or retired (41.2%). They have been providing care for an average of 44.5 months.

For Your Files: Alzheimer's Association

The Alzheimer's Association, the world leader in Alzheimer's research and support, is the first and largest voluntary health organization dedicated to finding prevention methods, treatments, and an eventual cure for Alzheimer's disease. The Association offers a wide range of materials containing information and advice for persons afflicted with Alzheimer's disease, caregivers, and professionals. Its 24/7 Helpline provides reliable information, referrals, and support in 140 languages. Alzheimer's Association chapters are located nationwide; chapter programs are tailored to the communities they serve, so the range and type of programs varies from chapter to chapter. The national office of the Alzheimer's Association is located at 225 N. Michigan Ave., Fl. 17, Chicago, IL 60601-7633; phone: 800-272-3900; www.alz.org.

Older adults who receive in-home care typically exhibit more frequent social and behavioral problems than do participants in other types of respite programs (Cox, 1997; Gaugler et al., 2003). Their caregivers report a higher degree of burden and provide more intense care compared with caregivers using other types of respite. Caregivers using in-home respite services also spend fewer hours per day away from their care receivers than those using adult day services (Berry, Zarit, & Rabatin, 1991). These caregivers, however, spend less time on caregiving activities on days on which they use in-home services compared with caregivers using adult day programs, perhaps because of the amount of time consumed preparing the older adult for the out-of-home program.

An alternative type of in-home respite is called Video Respite (Caserta & Lund, 2002; Lund, Hill, Caserta, & Wright, 1995). This series of 20 to 50 minute videotapes was designed to capture and maintain the attention of persons with dementia. While the person with dementia watches and participates with the visitor on television, caregivers have opportunities for respite breaks in their own homes. Others implementing this program in long-term care settings report that watching the video increased positive behaviors among the residents (Hall & Hare, 1997).

In-home respite is the type of respite most acceptable to family caregivers (Conlin, Caranasos, & Davidson, 1992; Lawton, Brody, & Saperstein, 1991). It typically is more flexible than other forms of respite because it most easily accommodates to the specific day and time that the caregiver wants. Caregivers also view in-home respite as more acceptable than other types of programs because they do not have to take the older adult out of the environment in which he or she is most comfortable. Having access to quality, trustworthy, and familiar respite care providers also positively influences caregivers' beliefs about the value of home-based respite services (Phillipson & Jones, 2011a). But in-home respite has its limitations because in-home respite services can be expensive, particularly if frequently used for several hours per day. Families also may be reluctant to use in-home respite services because they have complex feelings of guilt or abandonment regarding having strangers in their homes or taking care of their loved ones (Noelker & Browdie, 2012).

Adult Day Service Centers

The National Adult Day Services Association (NADSA, 2011) defines ADS as a coordinated program of professional and compassionate services for adults in a community-based group setting. It is a structured, comprehensive program that provides a variety of health, social, and related support services in a protective setting during any part of a day but less than 24-hour care. The use of ADS also affords family members respite from the demanding responsibilities of caregiving.

Since 1974, the number of adult day care centers operating nationwide has grown from 18 (Weissert, 1977) to more than 4,600 (Metlife Mature Market Institute, 2010c). The ADS industry promotes three models of care: the social model, the medical/health model, and specialized care model. Most ADS programs typically follow a social model, focusing on the socialization needs of the participants through the provision of individual and group activities, meals, and health maintenance programs. In addition to meeting the socialization and support needs of participants, Adult Day Health Care (ADHC) programs offer intensive health and therapeutic services prescribed in individual plans for each participant (Lucas, Scotto, Andrew, & Howell-White, 2002). It is difficult to identify any given center as falling into either category, however, because all centers provide varying degrees of social programs and health services. A national survey of 3,407 ADS centers conducted in 2001–2002 found that 21% of centers are based on the medical model of care, 37% are based on the social model of care, and 42% are a combination of the two (Wake Forest University School of Medicine, 2002). In addition, there are some specialized centers that provide services only to specific care recipients, such as those with dementia or developmental disabilities (NADSA, 2011). The distinctions among centers tend to be based on the intensity of services and activities provided rather than on the philosophical orientation of the centers. Whatever a program's primary emphasis, NADSA (2006) recommends that all adult day care programs provide eight essential services: personal care, nursing services, social services, therapeutic activities, nutrition and therapeutic diets, transportation, emergency care for participants, and family education.

Approximately three fourths of all ADS centers are in urban settings (Wake Forest University School of Medicine, 2002). About 39% of ADS centers are freestanding agencies; the others are affiliated with larger organizations, such as churches, senior centers, nursing homes, medical centers, or the Veterans Administration (Metlife Mature Market Institute, 2010c). Most centers are private not-for-profit (56%) or affiliated with public or government agencies (16%); 27% are private for-profit agencies. Regardless of the hosting agency, typical staff members for adult day centers include an administrator (or executive director), a program director, and one or more of the following: program assistants/aides, nurse and nurse aides, therapist, social workers, custodial workers, van drivers, and office staff. The average day care worker–participant ratio is approximately one direct care worker for every six participants. Volunteers, including students, also play an essential role in the staffing of many ADS programs. The average daily fee for adult day care is $61.71, but this can vary depending upon the services provided. Funding comes from participant fees, third-party payers as well as public and charitable sources.

According to the Metlife study (2010c), programs served over 260,000 participants in 2010. The average number of participants served per day was 34. The majority of day care participants are aged 65 and older (69%) and female (58%). Approximately 61% of participants were White, 16% African American, 9% Asian, and 9% Hispanic. Some 80% of participants live with a spouse, adult children, or other family and friends. About one half (52%) of the day care participants suffer from dementia (see Exhibit 18.1); many participants also need assistance with at least one ADL (See Exhibit 18.2). Most participants (81%) attend full days (at least five hours per day), and approximately 46% of participants attend five days per week. The typical length of participant enrollment is 24 months. Participants leave adult day services due to nursing home placement, a significant health decline, or death.

Caregivers of ADS participants were primarily adult children (36%), spouses (23%), and paid professionals (19%; Metlife Mature Market Institute, 2010c). Early studies reported that the majority of caregivers of ADS users are female (73.0%), married (66.4%), and working at least part time (44.2%). They have been providing care for an average of 39.1 months (NADSA, 2006). ADS centers also provide programs and services specifically for the caregivers of their participants, including educational programs (70%), support groups (58%), and individual counseling (40%; Metlife Mature Market Institute, 2010c).

Exhibit 18.1 Conditions and Diagnoses of Older Adults Attending Adult Day Services

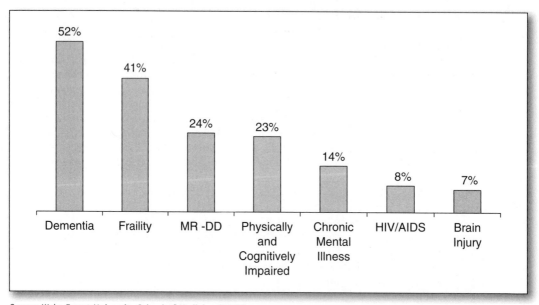

Source: Wake Forest University School of Medicine (2002).

Exhibit 18.2 Adult Day Services Participants Needing Assistance With Activities of Daily Living

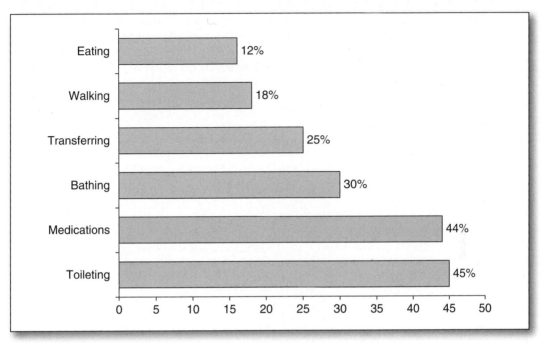

Source: Metlife Mature Market Institute, 2010c.

Best Practice: Parker Jewish Institute for Health Care and Rehabilitation

The Parker Jewish Institute for Health Care and Rehabilitation in New Hyde Park, New York, offers short-term rehabilitation/subacute care, long-term care/skilled nursing, adult day health care, Alzheimer's day care, home health care, and hospice care. The extensive network of inpatient and outpatient/community health care and rehabilitation services for older adults serves more than 7,000 patients each year. Parker has been successful due to flexible hours, a drop-in service, and a six-day-a-week operation. With the center open from 7:00 a.m. to 7:00 p.m. Monday through Friday, and on Saturdays and holidays from 9:00 a.m. to 5:00 p.m., families have greater flexibility in arranging their schedules.

Another customer-driven service that has been popular with caregivers is an à la carte approach to purchasing services. Instead of one daily or hourly rate, caregivers may purchase meals, shaves, bathing, transportation, and other special services separately. This type of customer choice is unique in the adult day care business.

(Continued)

(Continued)

According to a 2010 survey of Parker's caregivers, 96% believed the program benefited them personally by giving them the chance to complete tasks, socialize with friends, and rest, and 62% said that having their loved one attend the program helped them to be better caregivers. Most caregivers (96%) also indicated that the participant benefited by attending the program by giving them opportunities to socialize with peers and pursue previous leisure activities. About 35% of the caregivers believed the program had delayed the need for nursing home care.

The center also provides fieldwork for students in gerontology and recreation therapy. For more information, contact Parker Jewish Institute, 271-11 76th Avenue, New Hyde Park, NY 11040-1433; phone: 718-289-2100 or 516-247-6500; www.parkerinstitute.org.

An advantage of day care over in-home respite care for the care receiver is that it provides important peer group support and greater opportunities for social interaction. For the caregiver, adult day care offers freedom from caregiving responsibilities for potentially long, continuous blocks of time at a lesser cost than in-home services (Metlife Mature Market Institute, 2010c). A disadvantage of using adult day care is the physical and emotional effort required to prepare care receivers to attend a day program. For example, transportation to and from the center is a major issue that caregivers and programs must resolve (Wake Forest University School of Medicine, 2002). Caregivers often view getting the care receiver ready to leave home as more time-consuming and exhausting than providing the usual care.

Institutional Respite Care

Institutional settings such as nursing homes, Veterans Administration hospital-based nursing homes, and hospitals provide temporary institutional respite (TIR) services. In most situations, caregivers pay out of pocket for institutional respite care. This type of respite care differs from in-home and day programs in that it provides overnight and extended services. Beds may be available for both emergency respite care (e.g., illness of a caregiver) and planned respite stays, such as when a caregiver plans an extended vacation or a short weekend of relaxation (Adler, Kuskowksi, & Mortimer, 1995; Lawton et al., 1991). They also may use this type of respite service on a trial basis before permanent nursing home placement (J. P. Larkin & Hopcroft, 1993; Miller & Goldman, 1989; Scharlach & Frenzel, 1986). Caregivers often have negative views or misconceptions about TIR. They often believe that (a) temporary residential respite is only appropriate when care responsibilities become overwhelming or they encounter an emergency situation; (b) TIR may exacerbate negative behaviors of the care recipient; (c) use of institutional respite is equivalent to betrayal of family responsibility for care; (d) residential respite is cost prohibitive; and (e) care received in an institution is always inferior to the care provided in a familiar home environment (Phillipson & Jones, 2011b). Caregivers who have used residential respite have expressed that they are attempting to delay long-term residential placement or, conversely, trying to better facilitate transition into long-term care. Although these are contrasting objectives, they both place institutional respite use "toward the end of the caring trajectory" (p. 703).

A comparative study of 1,911 TIR users and nonusers (Gräsell, 1997) revealed that more TIR users were likely to be females (75.8%) and had more ADL limitations (M = 6.0) than nonusers (65.6%, M= 5.5, respectively). Both TIR users and nonusers were approximately 80 years of age and had had a diagnosis of Alzheimer's disease for five years. The caregivers of TIR users compared to nonusers were more likely to be female (90.9% vs. 83.3%) and to have significantly higher levels of subjective burden (44.5 vs. 41.0). No differences were found between caregivers of TIR users and nonusers with respect to average age (56.4 vs. 58.1), employment status (21.4% vs. 27.0%), average number of hours per day they provided care (6.0 vs. 6.0), and the average length of time they had provided care (4.0 vs. 3.0).

Institutional respite programs have their advantages and disadvantages with respect to cost, caregivers' perceptions of care, beliefs about the facility's ability to provide care, and the additional burden of preparation required of the caregiver (de la Cuesta-Benjumea, 2010; Lawton et al., 1991; Rosenheimer & Francis, 1992; Shaw et al., 2009; J. Tang, Ryburn, Doyle, & Wells, 2011). Although institutional programs offer respite care at the cost of comparable amounts of in-home respite, caregivers still view it as a costly care alternative. Nursing homes and hospitals usually provide a supervised, professional setting equipped to handle emergencies, which seems to alleviate family anxiety about care. Caregivers, however, often try so hard to avoid nursing home placements that even a temporary placement evokes fear and guilt about future placement possibilities. In addition, although institutions typically can accept older individuals with a range of behavioral problems and functional disabilities, caregivers often fear that their elders will not receive proper, individual attention and care. The preparation required for a nursing home or hospital stay (e.g., filling out forms, preparing personal effects, explaining the situation to the care receiver, transportation to and from the facility) and limitations on the number of days a person can stay in the program also discourage some caregivers from using this type of respite care.

Best Practice: Social Day Care and Respite Program

The Georgia Mobile Day Care Program provides social day care and respite services in rural Georgia. Program staff travel up to 50 miles one way each day to a program site—generally a senior center in the community. Program staffing varies but typically includes a registered nurse supervising the program, an activity director, an aide, and community volunteers. With a staff-to-client ratio of one to four, most sites maintain a capacity of up to eight clients per site. On a typical day, clients participate in exercises, cognitive activities, movies, crafts, and reminiscing. Lunch and snacks are provided at each site. One-on-one time is set aside at the start and end of each day to allow caregivers and the staff to discuss concerns regarding the client. Caregivers indicated that the program provides them with relief and peace of mind.

For more information, contact the Georgia Division of Aging Services, Two Peachtree Street N.W., Suite 9.398, Atlanta, GA 30303-3142; phone: 404-657-5336; www.aging.dhr.georgia.gov.

CHALLENGES FOR RESPITE PROGRAMS

Respite programs play an important role in maintaining and enhancing the psychological and physical well-being of older adults and their caregivers. We discuss a number of policy and programmatic challenges that must be addressed in the future.

Increasing the Use of Respite Services

Researchers report that, as a result of using respite services, caregivers enhance their well-being (Gaugler et al., 2003; Gitlin, Reever, Dennis, Mathieu, & Hauck, 2006; Salin et al., 2009), reduce their feelings of burden and stress (Conlin et al., 1992; Kosloski & Montgomery, 1993), and delay placing their loved one in a nursing home (Kosloski & Montgomery, 1995; Lawton et al., 1991). In addition, most caregivers who use respite services report being highly satisfied with the program and the care their family member receives (Henry & Capitman, 1995; Jarrott, Zarit, Stephens, Townsend, & Greene, 1999; Nicoll, Ashworth, McNally, & Newman, 2002). Yet, despite the potential for positive outcomes, and the growing availability of respite programs throughout the United States, caregivers are still reluctant to use any type of respite service (Cox, 1997; Kosloski, Montgomery, & Youngbauer, 2001). When caregivers do seek respite services, it is often at a time of crisis; their family situation escalates to a point at which they cannot continue providing care without some assistance. Even then, caregivers use respite services only in modest amounts.

To increase program use by family caregivers, providers must address both family- and system-related variables. Family-related variables include caregivers' lack of awareness, apprehension, and attitudes about using respite services and the reactions of care receivers (Stockwell-Smith, Kellett, & Moyle, 2010). Many caregiving families have little or no contact with formal services, and thus are often unaware of the availability of respite care in their communities. Even when caregivers are aware of such services, their fierce independence and personal beliefs about caregiving may hinder their use. It is common to hear caregivers say such things as, "She's my mother, I am responsible for her care," or "No one can care for my wife better than I can." Just like William, whom we introduced at the beginning of the chapter, caregivers often feel guilty about leaving their care receivers and believe that using formal services is a sign of failure. They may be even more reluctant to use respite services if they see it as benefiting themselves rather than their care receivers. In addition, some care receivers respond negatively to and resist respite care, thus reinforcing feelings of guilt often harbored by many caregivers. Karner and Hall (2002) note the importance of describing and emphasizing to caregivers—particularly those from minority and rural communities where family values and traditions are strong influences on service use—that community care programs are designed to complement and supplement, not replace, family care.

System barriers related to the use of respite care services include lack of service availability when wanted or needed most and lack of control over who provides services (MaloneBeach, Zarit, & Shore, 1992; Stockwell-Smith et al., 2010; J. Tang et al., 2011; Townsend & Kosloski, 2002). For in-home respite users, having different workers every time they request help is a deterrent to the use of such services. Caregivers generally want to have more control over which respite care workers provide care for their loved ones. The limited availability (e.g., only weekdays) and time schedules (e.g., 8:00 a.m. to 5:00 p.m.) of many respite programs prohibit their use by some caregivers, particularly those who are working outside the home. Transportation is another major barrier to the use of respite services, particularly for adult day care. Many family caregivers find it difficult to get their care receivers to a center, and many centers have limited means of providing transportation for their participants. Finally, the lack of reimbursement from Medicare and most private insurance carriers for respite care also is a significant barrier for many families who may otherwise wish to use this service.

The recent movement toward more consumer-directed care, particularly community-based models that allow caregivers to hire and supervise their own in-home care aides, may facilitate the use of respite care. These programs provide families with a better sense of control, choice, consistency in providers, and flexibility—including the option of hiring family members or friends to provide care (Whitlatch & Feinberg, 2006). Although overall demographic characteristics, mental health indicators, and level of distress are similar among those who hire family and friends to provide care versus caregivers participating in less consumer-directed models, there are some important differences. Not only do caregivers who are able to hire family and friends express a greater sense of control and satisfaction with respite services, but they also consistently report both cost savings and receipt of more hours of relief from the stress of care responsibilities.

Expanding Community Awareness and Education

The limited use experienced by some respite programs suggests the need for agencies and organizations to continually inform and educate people about their services. Caregivers are often unaware that respite services exist and do not understand the concept. They often see respite programs as a "last resort" or "end of the road" solution, rather than a preventive service. Respite services will be more effective in alleviating the stress and strains of caregiving if providers can get caregivers to enroll in their programs earlier in their caregiving career. Strategies for increasing program awareness and use include identifying key members within the community who can work as liaisons for the programs, actively recruiting families through personal contacts with programs already serving majority and minority families, and having bilingual and culturally competent staff members delivering the programs (Gallagher-Thompson et al., 2000).

Providing Flexible and Alternate Formats

Greater flexibility and expanded hours and days are needed for all types of respite programs. Successful programs will adapt to the time needs of caregivers, particularly those who work outside the home. In recent years, the idea of the adult day center as the hub for an all-inclusive system of respite (e.g., weekend programs, overnight services) has emerged. Support for more inclusive programming has received strong endorsement, as evidenced by programs such as the Robert Wood Johnson Foundation's Dementia/Respite Services Program (1988–1992) and Partners in Caregiving Program (1993–1995). Advocates for providers of these programs assert the effectiveness and efficiency of delivering more comprehensive day programs ("Extra Mile," 1996).

The idea of intergenerational day services centers deserves further consideration (Steinig & Simon, 2005). For example, TLC Health Network in New York has operated an intergenerational child and adult day care program for employees and members of the surrounding community at its Lake Shore campus since 1990. Virginia Tech's *Neighbors Growing Together* program is the oldest university-based shared site intergenerational program in the United States (www.intergenerational.clahs.vt.edu/neighbors). This nationally recognized, award-winning program, co-located since 1994, consists of the ADS and Child Development Center for Learning and Research (CDCLR). Affiliated ADS and CDCLR faculty and staff have worked to craft an intergenerational community that takes a strengths-based approach to supporting the well-being of its members (participants, families, staff, and students) through positive intergenerational contact (Jarrott, Gigliotti, & Smock, 2006). Although there are several intuitively positive sociocultural, organizational, and delivery aspects of providing care across generations, researchers need to evaluate the outcomes for both the children and older adults (Jarrott, 2008, 2011).

Reaching Underserved Populations

A frequent criticism of respite services is the lack of programs targeted to minority families. Cultural and attitudinal influences and preferences of agency care workers determining eligibility for respite services can significantly sway the prescription of respite services (Chumbler, Dobbs-Kepper, Beverly, & Beck, 2000; Degenholtz, Kane, & Kivnick, 1997). Senior programs must be marketed to all groups of individuals. They must employ professionals and volunteers who speak languages other than English and have knowledge of and experience working with individuals from diverse backgrounds.

Providing respite services in rural areas can be especially challenging. The primary sources of support available to elders in more metropolitan areas—adult children—may be absent due to out-migration of younger populations from rural settings (D. L. Wagner & Niles-Yokum, 2006). Rural areas also have fewer home- and community-based services, meaning that the more preferred modes of respite relief may be absent. Higher rates of institutionalization among rural elders suggest that community-based and consumer-directed care options, including respite models, either are lacking or have not been appropriately adapted to rural settings. Distance is a major factor in rural communities, not only with adult children living further from elders, but also greater distances separating neighbors and separating residents from existing services. Traveling distance for in-home respite providers and transportation for participants to attend out-of-home programs can prohibit the use of services in sparsely populated areas. Programs must consider nontraditional means of program delivery such as expanded consumer-direction and outreach, take into account the cultural context of rural communities, and develop public–private and formal-informal linkages to help expand services.

Enhancing the Quality of Care

Few systematic studies reported in the literature evaluate the outcomes of respite services. We have derived most of what we know about effectiveness of respite services from anecdotal or descriptive reports of small programs. In addition, few studies provide a comparison of respite users with nonusers, or include baseline measures of caregivers' and care receivers' physical and emotional status before using respite care. Researchers need to consider these limitations and work with respite service providers in the development of more rigorous program evaluations (Kennet, Burgio, & Schulz, 2000; Sörenson, Pinquart, & Duberstein, 2002).

Anticipating Industry Challenges

Given U.S. policy efforts to divert older adults from institutional care to more home- and community-based options, ADS programs and other respite initiatives will become an even more crucial and used component of the long-term care spectrum. However, "the preparedness of the ADS industry to address these projected demographic changes remains unclear" (Anderson, Dsabelko-Schoeny, & Tarrant, 2012, p. 132). In a national sample of ADS centers, funding was by far the most pressing concern for all centers, both now and projected into the future. Fiscal challenges generated many other obstacles for ADS managers including inadequate staffing, inability to effectively market services, physical space limitations, and limited ability to address complex care needs. As ADS centers and other respite providers serve elders with increasingly complex care needs, face rising costs, and anticipate increase in demand for services, policy makers must come up with creative policy adaptations and public-private partnerships that can keep facilities adequately funded for continued operation; otherwise these services might be disappearing right at the time when they are in peak demand (Anderson, Dsabelko-Schoeny, & Tarrant, 2012; LeadingAge, 2011).

Supporting the Future of Respite Programs

The 2005 White House Conference on Aging (2006) gave specific support for caregivers by passing resolutions to promote innovative models of noninstitutional long-term care and develop a national strategy for supporting informal caregivers of seniors to enable adequate quality and supply of services. As with home care services discussed in the previous chapter, there will be an increased demand for respite services in the next 20 years. Sheer numbers of older adults, especially those over 85 years of age, will force the public and private sector to respond to the respite needs of older adults and their families.

CASE STUDY

Respite for a Devoted Caregiver

Ben and Ethel have been married for 60 years. Both are 85 years old. They reside in a small apartment that is about the size of an average high school classroom. They partially subsidize their rent through a Section 8 rental voucher program. Ben was a tenant farmer all his adult life. Ethel worked in the home. Both worked hard, but Ben's income was low, and he and Ethel were not able to accumulate any savings. Their only income is Ben's Social Security check of $475 per month. They can barely make ends meet.

Ben has some hearing loss and suffers from gout, which interferes with his mobility. Ethel is bedridden with Parkinson's disease. She is totally incontinent, and someone must turn her three times per day to keep her from getting bedsores. Ethel communicates only by using eye signals and is on a liquid diet. Her condition warrants full-time, skilled nursing care. Ben's devotion to his wife of 60 years prohibits him from placing her in a nursing home. One of his few happy moments is when he is showing off their wedding picture.

Ben and Ethel have one daughter who is employed full time. Their daughter does help her father prepare meals when she has time. The daughter is concerned about the tremendous caregiving load her father has assumed. Ben used to frequent the local senior center a couple days per week to play pool with "the guys." Occasionally, he would take a day trip on the senior center van. The daughter would like her father to "give in" and place Ethel in a nursing home so that he can have some time to himself. Her father simply will not consider it.

Case Study Questions

1. On the basis of the information provided, what barriers are presented that would make it difficult to work with Ben to develop a respite care plan?

2. Despite the barriers that you have identified in the first question, what aspects of this situation lend itself to convincing Ben that respite care is an option for him to consider?

(Continued)

(Continued)

3. Given the financial situation of this couple, what type of respite options would you be looking for in this community?

4. Short of skilled nursing home care, what other community-based services might be appropriate for this couple to improve their quality of life?

5. Do you think the daughter should use legal means to force her father to place her mother in a nursing home? Why or why not?

LEARNING ACTIVITIES

1. Interview a director or staff member of a respite program. What services does the program provide and to whom? What is the cost of the services? What does the individual perceive to be the primary obstacles for caregivers in requesting or receiving respite services? What changes would the staff member like to make to the legislative policy as it relates to respite care and to the program?

2. Interview someone who has received or is receiving respite services. How did the caregiver find out about the service? Why did the caregiver decide to use it? What does the caregiver see as the benefits to the service as well as what type of changes would be desirable? How has respite care affected the person's life? How has it affected the life of the care receiver?

3. Design a respite program that includes services you believe is necessary for an effective program. Include to whom the program would be directed and how you would fund it.

4. Search YouTube for two different respite programs for older adults and draw a comparison between the approaches. Consider program strengths and weaknesses in terms of issues such as appropriateness and creativity of design for the target client group, accessibility of care, and long-term sustainability. Choose YouTube clips that provide specific details about how these programs have affected individual participants and provide program benefits or drawbacks using examples of client experiences.

FOR MORE INFORMATION

International Resources

1. Policies to Support Family Carers: http://www.oecd.org/dataoecd/52/30/47884889.pdf

   This fourth chapter in the Organization for Economic Co-operation and Development's book, *Help Wanted? Providing and Paying for Long Term Care*, provides an overview and assessment of the current set of policies among OECD countries targeted at family caregivers in relation to three themes: caring and the labor market; caregivers' well-being, and financial recognition of caregivers. The authors discuss the effectiveness of policies that help caregivers combine care with paid work, reduce burnout and stress of care providers, and recognize additional costs associated with caring.

2. Systematic Review of Respite Care in the Frail Elderly (Shaw et al., 2009): http://www.hta.nhs .uk/fullmono/mon1320.pdf

   In this comprehensive review of the literature, the authors examine the effectiveness of various international respite models for improving the well-being of informal caregivers of frail and disabled older adults. They also identify unmet needs of care providers and barriers to uptake of respite services.

3. Australian Respite Care Services (Australian Institute of Health and Welfare, 2011): http://www .aihw.gov.au/respite-care/

   Many consider Australia a pioneer of comprehensive respite services for older adults. This webpage provides access to a description of their full spectrum of government-supported respite initiatives.

National Resources

1. Alzheimer's Disease and Education and Referral Center (ADEAR), P.O. Box 8250, Silver Spring, MD 20907-8250; phone: 800-438-4380; www.nia.nih.gov/Alzheimers

   This center, a service of the National Institute on Aging, offers information about diagnosis and treatment, research, and services available to patients and their families.

2. American Health Assistance Foundation, 22512 Gateway Center Drive, Clarksburg, MD 20871; phone: 301-948-3244 or 800-437-2423; www.ahaf.org

   The American Health Assistance Foundation's Alzheimer's Family Relief Program was created to help ease the often-unbearable financial burdens faced by Alzheimer's patients and their families. Since 1988, the program has given more than $2.3 million in emergency financial assistance to families in need.

3. National Adult Day Services Association, Inc., 2519 Connecticut Ave NW, Washington, DC 20008; phone: 800-558-5301; www.nadsa.org

   The National Adult Day Services Association (NADSA) is the leading voice of the rapidly growing ADS industry in the United States. NADSA is an independent national organization dedicated to raising public and government awareness of the value of ADS. ADS provide community-based care for frail elders as well as persons of all ages with multiple and special needs associated with conditions such as Alzheimer's disease, developmental disabilities, traumatic brain injury, mental illness, HIV/AIDS, vision and hearing impairments, and more.

Web Resources

1. Administration on Aging, Family Caregiver Options: www.aoa.gov/eldfam/For_Caregivers/For_ Caregivers.asp

   This is a great place to start when looking for information about respite and caregiver support services. The Family Caregiver Options page is continually updated with links to national resources. Definitely worth a visit.

2. *Caregiver's Handbook*: www.acsu.buffalo.edu/ ~ drstall/hndbk0.html

   This site contains a complete version of a handbook for caregivers originally published by the San Diego County Mental Health Services. In addition to 47 chapters that cover every aspect of caregiving, there is also a guide for choosing a residential facility.

3. Eldercare WEB: www.elderweb.com/home

   This was one of the first sites on caregiving to be established in the United States. It has lots of great information of value to caregivers and older adults. There are links to a library, a forum, and information about health (nutrition was the highlight topic when we visited last), aging, legal, and social issues.

4. Family Caregiver Alliance: www.caregiver.org/caregiver/jsp/home.jsp

   The Family Caregiver Alliance, a nonprofit organization with caregiver centers throughout California, provides assistance to caregivers of individuals with Alzheimer's, Parkinson's, and other brain disorders. The home page has links to resource centers, information about work and family, a newsletter published by the alliance, publications and fact sheets, and information on events.

5. Inclusive Services for LGBT Older Adults: A Practical Guide to Creating Welcoming Agencies: http://www.lgbtagingcenter.org/resources/pdfs/NRCInclusiveServicesGuide2012.pdf

   This guide, developed by the National Resource Center on Lesbian, Gay, Bisexual, and Transgender (LGBT) Aging, provides an overview of how respite programs and other aging services providers can adapt their models to accommodate the unique needs of LGBT elders. The guide covers everything from first impressions and intake to the hiring of LGBT staff. Other related resources to improve the inclusive atmosphere of respite programming, including such topics as homophobia and HIV in late life, are available through the Resource Center website at www.lgbtagingcenter.org.

Long-Term Care Services

As she approached her mother's room at Prairie View Manor, Sharon thought about the day she had had to come to grips with the reality that Eleanor, then 84 years old, needed nursing home care. She had promised her mother that she would never put her in a nursing home. This promise would nearly break Sharon mentally and physically, jeopardize her marriage, and drive a wedge between her and her children. At first, the extra work cleaning Grandma's house, caring for the yard, and taking her shopping and to the doctor was welcomed. The whole family pitched in to make it work. Eleanor went to the adult day program every day where the family knew she was safe while they were at work and at school. When Eleanor became frailer, her falls more frequent, and the incontinency too difficult to manage, Sharon brought her mother to live with her. Even with a leave of absence from her job, Sharon became exhausted trying to manage her mother's care. Her husband became more and more angry about all the time Sharon was spending caring for her mother, and her children resented having to give up some of their activities to help care for Grandma. Why, thought Sharon, had it taken her so long to seek nursing home care? Eleanor was content. She loved her room with a view across the countryside. Most happily for Sharon, her mother was still able to participate in limited activities and enjoy the company of a few new friends.

The words *nursing home* conjure up negative images, and most older adults and their families dread the thought of moving to one. Sharon, like many other family members, goes to great lengths to avoid nursing home placement—even when such placement would be physically and psychologically beneficial for everyone. Despite the negative image nursing homes have, they are a critical part of the long-term care continuum in our communities and provide a wide range of vital services to those who live there. Because nursing homes are a part of the long-term care continuum, many refer to nursing homes as *long-term care facilities*. Indeed, these facilities have evolved into more than "nursing" homes—they are places in which a wide range of restorative, rehabilitative, and medical services are delivered. The term *nursing home*, however, is still frequently used in the literature. Therefore, we will use the terms *long-term care facilities* and *nursing homes* interchangeably in our discussion. In this chapter, we review policies that have been instrumental in creating the existence of and oversight for long-term care facilities and present a profile of users and programs. The chapter ends with a presentation of the many challenges that lie ahead for long-term care facilities.

POLICY BACKGROUND

The growth of the nursing home industry parallels the passage of federal policy that evolved in the first half of the twentieth century (Waldman, 1985). Prior to the enactment of Social Security, Medicare, and Medicaid, many older adults had few options if they needed medical and personal care. In some communities, older adults were boarded out to families that agreed to provide care in their homes; many of these were the homes of retired nurses—thus, the basis for the term *nursing home* (Crandall, 1991). In the early part of the century, almshouses or "poor farms" cared for many frail older adults, persons with mental illnesses, and those who were chronically ill. An estimated 60% to 90% of the persons living in almshouses were over the age of 65 (D. L. Fischer, 1978). Almshouses were deplorable places, and the few states that had old age assistance payments and, later, Social Security would not send payments to almshouse residents (Small, 1988). Older adults who were financially well off had the option of living in old age homes run by ethnic or religious groups: German and Scandinavian immigrants built Lutheran Homes, and Jews and Methodists built their own facilities (Waldman, 1985). The 1950 amendments to the Social Security Act of 1935, allowing residents of institutions to receive benefits and health providers to directly receive payments for services, helped expand the creation of nursing homes. But the real impetus to the creation of the nursing home industry came with the enactment of Medicare and Medicaid. Both Medicare and Medicaid provide payments to nursing homes—Medicare for acute care, and Medicaid for long-term care for those with low incomes (Crandall, 1991; Small, 1988). Since the enactment of Medicare and Medicaid, the percentage of adults aged 65 and older living in nursing homes doubled from 2.5% in 1963 to 5.1% in 1990 and 4.5% in 2000 (Hetzel & Smith, 2001; Hooyman & Kiyak, 2002; Small, 1988). The most recent data from 2010 indicate that 3.3% ($\sim$ 1.25 million) of adults over the age of 65 live in one of the 15,682 nursing homes in the country (American Health Care Association, 2011; U.S. Census Bureau, 2012b).

PAYMENT FOR NURSING HOME CARE

The median cost of nursing home care in 2012 was $73,000 per year ($200 per day) for a semi-private room, and $81,030 ($222 per day) a year for a private room (Genworth Financial, 2012). Thus, because of the high cost of nursing home care, many older adults and their families are concerned about having the resources to pay for care or are concerned about becoming impoverished while paying for care. Currently, there are four sources of payment of nursing home costs: Medicaid, Medicare, out of pocket, and long-term care insurance.

Most nursing homes are certified by the Centers for Medicare and Medicaid Services (formally known as Health Care Financing Administration, or HCFA) and are eligible to receive reimbursement for their services to persons qualified for Medicaid and Medicare. Annually, Medicaid pays approximately 41%, or $47.7 billion, of nursing home care for eligible individuals (Klees et al., 2011). Medicaid offers nursing home coverage to low-income individuals who meet income, asset, and medical guidelines. Medicare plays a limited role in covering nursing home costs because it pays only for skilled nursing services that are needed following a hospitalization (24-hour care provided by a registered nurse, under a physician's supervision) and does not cover custodial care. Medicare pays 17% of nursing home costs (Congressional Budget Office [CBO], 2004; Kaye, Harrington, & LaPlante, 2010).

Out-of-pocket payments made by older adults and their families amount to approximately 41% of nursing home care expenses (CBO, 2004). Because of the limited sources that help pay for long-term nursing home care costs, a small but growing number of adults have purchased long-term care insurance policies. Long-term care insurance policy sales have risen steadily since 1987, and currently between 7 and 9 million people have purchased private long-term care insurance (America's Health Insurance Plans [AHIP], 2012). Private health and long-term care insurance pays between 3% and 7% of nursing home costs (CBO, 2004; Georgetown University Long-Term Care Financing Project, 2007). Older adults have been slow to purchase such policies because of the availability, the cost, the limited benefits, and a belief that Medicare or Medicaid will cover long-term care costs; however, recent data show that the age at which people purchase long-term care insurance has decreased slightly over the last 10 years (AHIP, 2012). A recent policy change enacted by Congress in 2006 may help increase the purchase of long-term care insurance. Congress passed legislation giving states the permission to coordinate the purchase and payment of long-term care insurance with Medicaid. The law permits Medicaid to cover long-term care needs beyond the terms of the policy, and policyholders would not be required to "spend down" their assets to meet the Medicaid eligibility guidelines (Capretta, 2007). The extent to which long-term care insurance will play a role in paying for long-term care costs in the future is unknown (see R. W. Johnson & Uccello, 2005; Zedlewski, Barnes, Burt, McBride, & Meyer, 1990), and it appears that most of the coverage is for home care or assisted living, and only 27% of claims against long-term care insurance policies are for nursing home care (Ujvari, 2012).

USERS AND PROGRAMS

Resident Characteristics

The decision to permanently move into in a nursing home is a difficult one for the elder and his or her family and friends. Contrary to popular perception, families do not "dump" their older members in nursing homes at the first available opportunity. Like Sharon at the beginning of the chapter, they go to great lengths exploring other alternatives and often insist on providing caregiving activities at the expense of their personal wellbeing (Brody, 1985; Smallegan, 1985). Families provide an estimated 80% to 90% of long-term care to older adults while they are living in the community and continue providing assistance even after nursing home placement (Bowers, 1988; R. Stone et al., 1987). Nursing home placement is a community resource that is most often the last alternative used by families.

Because of increased longevity and the increase in the number of baby boomers entering later life, the nursing home population is projected to increase considerably over the next 20 years (Sahyoun, Pratt, Lentzner, Dey, & Robinson, 2001; Spillman & Lubitz, 2002). Spillman and Lubitz (2002) estimate that 44% of those turning 65 in the year 2000 will use nursing home care at some point in their lifetimes. Moreover, the number of 65-year-olds who will use nursing home care in their lifetimes will more than double in the next 20 years, and 37% of men turning 65 in 2000 and 50% of women turning 65 in 2000 are projected to receive nursing home care. R. W. Johnson, Toohey, and Wiener (2007) projected the need for nursing home care using three different models of future rates of disability in the older adult population: low disability, intermediate disability, and high disability. Their analyses indicate that by 2040, the number of older adults needing nursing home services will rise to 2.0 million or 2.7 million in the low to intermediate scenario. Under the high disability scenario, the number of older adults in nursing homes would be 3.1 million, which would be double the current number of users.

For Your Files: Long-Term Care Insurance

The America's Health Insurance Plans (AHIP) is an organization representing companies that provide health insurance. AHIP has posted on its website a consumers' *Guide to Long-Term Care Insurance*. Here is a summary of some key points. Visit their site (www.ahip.org) to read the entire guide. Most long-term care insurance policies are indemnity policies that pay a fixed amount for each day of care received, once the individual reaches specified disability levels. Fixed amounts range from $50 to $300 per day, depending on the terms of the policy. Good policies will adjust the benefit amount each year (about 5%) to keep up with inflation. The cost of long-term care insurance depends on the age of the beneficiary and the level of benefits and deductibles. For example, a policy offering $150 per day for four years, with a 90-day waiting period, costs a 40-year-old approximately $1,831 per year, a 55-year-old about $2,261 per year, a 65-year-old $2,781, and a 70-year-old $3,421. Therefore, the younger the age at purchase, the lower the cost.

Most policies cover skilled, intermediate, and custodial care as well as skilled and nonskilled home care, physical therapy, and care provided by homemaker home health aides. Some policies also cover adult day care and respite care. There are, however, exclusions for pre-existing conditions and some types of disorders. Policies generally limit benefits to a maximum dollar amount or days of care, and some pay benefits for a limited number of years.

Those interested in purchasing long-term care insurance should compare policies before they buy. Also check out *Consumer Reports*, which regularly conducts in-depth reviews of long-term care insurance policies.

The length of stay in a nursing home has varied little over the past 20 years, as approximately 30% of residents stay three or more years, and 30% stay one year to less than three years (Decker, 2005). However, length of stay does vary among different subpopulations. For example, length of stay for persons aged 65 years of age and older is longer for women than for men—30 months and 25 months, respectively (Gabrel, 2000). The most common reasons for discharge from a nursing home are admission to a hospital, death, and stabilized health status. Researchers have discovered several personal characteristics associated with the likelihood of living in a nursing home.

Age

Not surprisingly, the majority of nursing home residents are over age 75. In 2010, 28.2% of nursing home residents were between the ages of 75 and 84; 41.6%% were over the age of 85 (U.S. Census Bureau, 2012a). The median age of a nursing home resident is 82.7.

Sex

Mirroring the demographic characteristics of the older adult population, more nursing home residents are women. In 2005, approximately two thirds of residents were women; in 2010, 70.6% of persons living in nursing homes were women over 65 (Centers for Medicare and Medicaid Services [CMS], 2006; Gabrel, 2000; U.S. Census Bureau, 2012a). As shown in Exhibit 19.1, there are more long-term care residents who are women than are men at every age category over the age of 65 (National Center for Health Statistics, 2008).

Race

Older adults who are non-White are underrepresented in nursing homes. As shown in Exhibit 19.2, smaller percentages of Blacks, Hispanics, Asian American, and American Indians aged 65 and older live in nursing homes compared with White elders. Although these percentages have stayed relatively constant over the years, the increase in the sheer number of older adults means that there have been a growing number of non-White nursing home residents. Feng, Fennell, Tyler, Clark, and Mor (2011) found that among Blacks, Hispanics, and Asians, there was an annual increase in nursing home residents of 1.2%, 5.0% and 4.9% from 1999 to 2008.

Exhibit 19.1 Long-Term Care Facility Residents by Age and Gender (residents per 1,000 population)

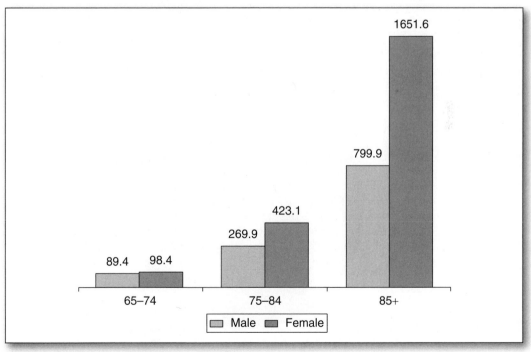

Source: National Center for Health Statistics (2008).

Overall, this differential use in nursing home care has been attributed to cost, discrimination, personal choice, social and cultural differences, and access issues (Feng et al., 2011). From testimony given by family members and professionals, Moss and Halamandaris (in Yeo, 1993) conclude that all four reasons may be operating to different degrees in keeping older adults of color from receiving nursing home care. For example, among Pacific Asian elders, language differences and cultural differences were the most predominant explanations; among older Blacks, cost and discrimination were the most important factors; Native American elders cited cost and personal choice as the most important; and older Hispanic adults identified more barriers to use than other groups—language and cultural differences, discrimination, and cost.

Marital Status and the Availability of a Caregiver

Widowed older adults represent the majority of those who live in nursing homes, followed by those who have never married. Not surprisingly, the lack of an available caregiver, such as a spouse, adult child, or other relative, increases the likelihood of nursing home placement (Wingard, Jones, & Kaplan, 1987).

Functional Status

A majority of residents of nursing homes have multiple impairments in activities of daily living (ADLs) for which they need assistance. Exhibit 19.3 shows the percentage of nursing

Exhibit 19.2 Long-Term Care Facility Residents Aged 65 and Older by Race (percentage)

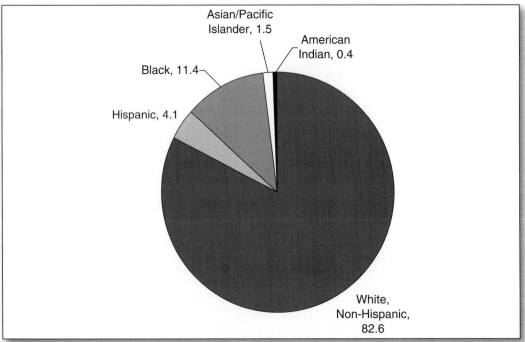

Source: CMS (2010f).

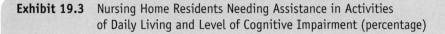

Exhibit 19.3   Nursing Home Residents Needing Assistance in Activities
of Daily Living and Level of Cognitive Impairment (percentage)

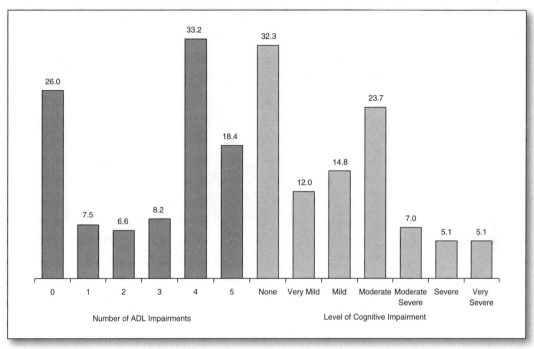

Source: CMS (2010f).

home residents who have ADL and cognitive impairments. Fifty-one percent of residents have impairments in four or more ADLs, and 40.9% are reported to have a moderate or more severe level of cognitive impairment. Exhibit 19.4 presents the percentage of residents who have difficulty with their mobility, continence, eating, and bathing. Mobility, incontinence, and bathing are the most problematic activities for all residents regardless of age. The percentage of residents needing assistance with these ADLs increases slightly with age. Those aged 85 + are more likely than younger residents to need assistance with all four activities. Thus, the majority of nursing home residents are quite old and in need of personal care assistance in a number of ADLs.

LONG-TERM CARE FACILITIES

Nursing home care is provided predominantly by for-profit enterprises; some 69% are identified as a for-profit nursing. Nonprofit nursing homes have an average of 101 beds, and for-profit homes average 87 beds; occupancy rates are, on average, around 87% (American Health Care Association, 2012). The LeadingAge (formally known as American Association of Homes and Services for the Aging) reported that 2,108 of the more than 4,000 member agencies are associated with ethnic or denominational organizations

Exhibit 19.4 Nursing Home Residents Who Need Assistance, by Age and Activity

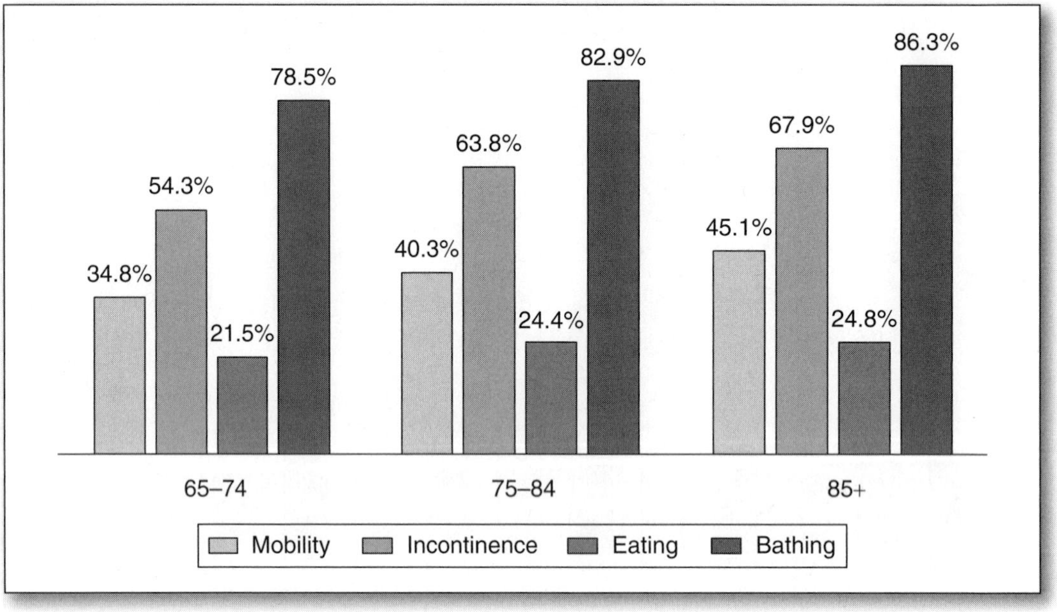

Source: National Center for Health Statistics (2008).

(American Association of Homes and Services for the Aging, 1988). Such homes are sponsored by religious organizations, including those that are Baptist, Catholic, Mennonite, Jewish, and United Church of Christ. Others are under national sponsorships, such as the British American Home; a few are racially specific, such as the Eliza Bryant Center in Cleveland, which serves only older Blacks (Kaplan & Shore, 1993).

Levels of Care

Prior to federal legislation passed in 1987, nursing homes had two levels of care on which reimbursement was based. Nursing homes were categorized as skilled nursing facilities or as intermediate care facilities. Skilled nursing facilities were designed to care for residents who needed skilled nursing care that was more medically oriented. Residents in intermediate care facilities required custodial, rather than skilled nursing, care. These classifications were based on Medicare and Medicaid payment criteria for nursing home care. Because the two levels of classification did not accurately reflect the variations in the functional abilities of nursing home residents, the federal government replaced the dichotomous classification with one designation: the nursing facility (Boondas, 1991). CMS, which administers Medicare and Medicaid, designed a different classification system in 1998 called the Resource Utilization Groups: Version III (RUG-III). Instead of paying facilities retrospectively after services were delivered based on "reasonable costs," facilities are now paid prospectively based on a patient's care needs and classification. Under the 1998 RUG- III classification system, nursing homes began to use seven major classification groups for cost reimbursement: rehabilitation, extensive services, special care, clinically complex, impaired cognition, behavior problems, and reduced physical functions (Zbylot, Job, McCormick, Boulter, & Moore, 1995). The seven major groups were further divided into 44 case mix groups based on intensity of ADL needs. Such classification reflected the many types of residents in need of nursing home care. However, recent changes enacted in 2006 refined the 44 RUGS-III groups by adding nine new Rehabilitation Plus Extensive Services, thus increasing the classification types to 53 RUGs (Leavitt, 2006). The RUGS-IV update added 13 more classifications in 2010, bringing the current total to 66 (Spector, Limcangco, Ladd, & Mukamel, 2011). Changes in the RUGS were driven in part by of the increase in the number of residents with diverse health care needs, and the fact that nursing homes are expanding the range of services they offer.

Post-Acute Care

When patients need medical and rehabilitative care services after a hospitalization of at least three days, the care patients receive is referred to as *post-acute care*. Older adults needing medical or rehabilitative care provided in an institution are frequently discharged to either an Inpatient Rehabilitation Facility (IRF) or a Skilled Nursing Facility (SNF). Patients in IRFs must be able to withstand a more intensive rehabilitation care schedule (e.g., tolerate a minimum of three hours of rehabilitation per day) and show consistent functional improvement (Kramer, 2006). In contrast, patients who receive post-acute care (often referred to as *subacute care*) in SNFs have different guidelines that allow for a less intensive rehabilitative protocol to occur over a longer time frame (Gage et al., 2007).

Many long-term care facilities now offer a wide range of rehabilitative services that cater to a specific target population. For example, they may specialize in serving rehabilitation patients who need help recovering from hip replacement or spinal cord injuries. Other subacute units are considered to be "medical subacute" units and serve patients who need intensive medical care, such as ventilator care, wound care, or IV therapy. Typically, subacute units require staff to be more highly trained, require more physician involvement, and use interdisciplinary teams to plan and monitor care. The growth of subacute care has been encouraged by Medicare's prospective payment system, which pays hospitals a flat rate for care, resulting in a shorter length of stay (see Chapter 11). A shorter length of stay, in turn, encourages patient care in these "stepdown" or subacute units. Studies of the effectiveness and efficiency of subacute care units are being conducted; it is generally thought that postacute care is a cost-effective alternative to inpatient acute hospital care (Office of the Assistant Secretary for Planning and Evaluation, 1995).

For Your Files: Special Care Unit in Lynden, Washington

The Christian Health Care Center (previously known as the Christian Rest Home), a 150-bed nursing home in Lynden, Washington, has had a special care unit since 1988. The 15-bed special care unit was established because of staff concerns about the safety and well-being of residents with dementia who wander or have other behavioral symptoms that cannot be handled in the facility's regular units.

(Continued)

(Continued)

The special care unit, called Cedar Cove, consists of resident bedrooms, an activity/dining area, and an enclosed outdoor courtyard. Physical changes were made to the building to create the unit: (a) A set of doors was installed in an existing partition off the resident bedrooms and the activity/dining area, (b) a door was made in an exterior wall to give the residents access to the enclosed courtyard, and (c) keypad-operated locks were installed on the exit doors; the doors open when a number code is punched in on the keypad, and the doors open automatically when the alarm goes off. These physical changes cost less than $5,000.

Some residents of the special care unit have been transferred to the unit from other parts of the nursing home; other residents have been admitted directly from home. Although all the special care unit residents have dementia in the opinion of the facility staff, a few have not had a diagnosis of dementia in their medical records.

The objectives of the unit are to ensure the residents' safety, to reduce agitation and behavioral symptoms, to maintain independent functioning, and to improve the residents' quality of life. The staff members perceive resident agitation and behavioral symptoms as significant expressions of feelings and unmet needs. They attempt to understand and respond to those feelings and needs in the belief that, by doing so, they will reduce agitation and behavioral symptoms and improve the residents' quality of life. Although many of the residents exhibited severe behavioral symptoms before coming to the unit, the unit staff report that these symptoms are relatively easily managed in the special care unit.

Formal and informal activity programs are conducted in the unit. Each afternoon, there is a formal activity program, such as a weekly Bible study and music group, a weekly reminiscence group, a weekly "validation" group, and "high tea"—a Monday afternoon event with real china and lace tablecloths. Other activities, such as food preparation and singing, take place informally in the unit. One resident who likes to fold laundry is encouraged to do so. Family members are welcome in the unit at any time. Staff members know the residents' families and involve them in decisions about the residents' care. Staff members report that family members often thank them for the help they give the residents and the emotional support they give the family members. During the day, the staff in the special care unit consist of one registered nurse, who functions as the unit coordinator, and two nurse aides. A licensed practical nurse and two other nurse aides take over for the evening shift. Because staff consistency is considered important for the unit, the unit staff members generally are not rotated to other units. Special care unit residents are discharged from the unit when staff believe that the residents can no longer benefit from the unit. Several spouses of former special care unit residents have created an informal support group that meets almost daily in the facility, presumably to replace the emotional support they previously received from the unit staff.

Source: U.S. Congress, Office of Technology Assessment (1992).

Specialized Alzheimer's Unit

In the past decade, increasing numbers of nursing homes have created specialized services to care for persons with Alzheimer's disease and other dementias. Included in these efforts are cluster settings, in which persons with dementia are grouped together on a floor or unit, and special care units (SCUs) that are housed in separate wings or buildings. In a national review of nursing homes, 19.2% facilities had at least one distinct SCU, and 65.7% of these units were for Alzheimer's disease (Freiman & Brown, 1999). SCUs have increased in part because of the special care needs of persons with various types of dementias. For example, persons with dementia are more likely to need assistance with ADLs, to need help remaining continent, to have psychiatric symptoms (delusions and hallucinations), and to have behavioral problems (e.g., wandering, physically hurting self or others) than those without dementia (U.S. Congress, Office of Technology Assessment [OTA], 1992; U.S. Department of Health and Human Services [USDHHS], 1991). In response to a congressional request, the OTA conducted a comprehensive review of the available research on SCUs. Their best estimate, based on national data, was that 8% to 10% of nursing homes had SCUs for persons with Alzheimer's disease or dementia, and that more facilities reported having plans to create such units. Not surprisingly, larger nursing homes were more likely than smaller ones to have SCUs, and nursing homes in the West were more likely to report having SCUs than were homes located in other geographical areas. The majority of nursing homes indicated that residents of SCUs were charged more for their care than were residents of non-SCUs. Descriptive studies showed that units varied greatly in their patient-care philosophy, number of residents, physical design, staffing patterns and ratios, activity programs, and patient-care practices. Patient-care philosophies included goals such as to provide a safe, secure, and supportive environment for residents; reduce feelings of anxiety; maintain optimal levels of physical and cognitive functioning; and provide holistic care. The number of residents living in SCUs ranged from less than 10 to more than 40. Studies showed that, on average, SCU residents were younger, White, and male, and were more likely to have a specific diagnosis, such as Alzheimer's disease, than other residents with or without dementia. SCU residents also were less likely than other nursing home residents with dementia to have impairments in ADLs but were more likely to exhibit behavioral problems.

According to the OTA (1992) report, most SCUs had some special environmental adaptations for residents, including alarm or locking systems, secured areas for wandering, and color-coding of rooms and personal markers to help residents find their way around the unit. Many of the SCUs provided some type of specialized training for staff; these units had a higher staff-to-resident ratio than did non-SCUs. In addition, studies indicated that SCUs had activities designed to increase stimulation and reduce resident stress. Activities offered to residents in SCUs included singing, exercises, games, painting, field trips, and reminiscence therapy.

Some argue that segregating persons with dementias from other nursing home residents improves resident well-being, enhances family interaction and satisfaction, increases staff satisfaction, and improves the nursing home experience for residents who do not have dementia (Maas, 1988; Ronch, 1987). For example, Buchanan, Choi, Wang, Hysunsu, and Graber (2005) examined national data of all Medicaid- and Medicare-certified nursing homes to examine the differences between residents with Alzheimer's disease in SCUs and those residents with Alzheimer's who were not in SCUs. They found that SCU residents had more structured activities and received better management of mood, behavioral problems, and cognitive losses. Others argue that there are no discernible differences in resident outcomes for those living in SCUs (Rabins, 1986; Ronch, 1987). Slone, Lindeman, Phillips, Moritz, and Koch (1995) evaluated studies of effectiveness of SCUs and concluded that existing studies were inconclusive because some investigators reported improvements in residents' ADL performance, mood, behavior, and cognition, whereas others found no differences in these outcomes. Chappell and Reid (2000) conducted one of the most comprehensive examinations to date of resident outcomes in SCU and non-SCUs in Canadian nursing homes. When examining changes in resident outcomes in six different areas (e.g., physical functioning, social skills, agitation) over a one-year period, they found that residing in a SCU was unrelated to any of the changes in these areas. They concluded that many non-SCUs were implementing a similar quality of care to SCUs. These seemingly contradictory findings are due to the difficulty in controlling for sampling variations and the differences in SCU care delivery, treatment, and outcome measurement.

Across the Globe: Special Care for Persons With Dementia in the United Kingdom

The Russets is a dementia care home that was awarded the most innovative new dementia care project in the United Kingdom in 2009. The Russets is a 73-bed care home specially designed for people living with dementia and is a part of the Sandford Station Retirement Village, which has a 108 retirement homes, consisting of cottages and apartments for independent living. The care provided at the Russets is guided by six areas of well-being:

- control and choice,
- dignity and respect,
- health and comfort,
- peace of mind,
- positive living environment, and
- social life.

The Russets has individual 15-bed "bungalows" that offer a homely environment among familiar people, and each house is designed to foster a high level of intimacy by naturally dividing shared areas so that small groups of individuals are more closely involved with one another. Each bungalow offers easy access to a secure garden and clubhouse at the center of the home, and each is decorated in different colors (on the inside and outside) so that residents are more readily able to find their own way around. Bedrooms open straight into the shared spaces so that residents are immediately able to determine where they are, and a flexible approach to daily living allows individuals make their own choices about each day.

For more information, check out their website: http://www.stmonicatrust.org.uk/what-we-do/dementia-care.

STAFFING PATTERNS

Nursing homes have a variety of professionals and paraprofessionals who provide care to their residents. The number of staff in each area depends on the number of beds; those certified by Medicare and Medicaid have to meet certain staffing requirements. Nursing homes generally have departments that are responsible for resident or social services, administrative services, rehabilitation, nursing, supportive services, and dietary services. Social services staff work with residents and their families to assist them in adjusting to the social and emotional aspects of living in the facility. In addition, social service staff offer medically related social and psychological treatment goals for residents. Nursing homes with 120 beds or more must employ a director of social services; smaller homes may employ a social service director on a consultancy basis (Allen, 2011).

Mental health services may be provided by staff or contracted out with mental health professionals in the community. Facilities are also required to offer residents an activities program that enhances their physical, social, and psychological well-being. Staff in the activities department usually have training in recreational or therapeutic programming and are responsible for developing and implementing social and recreational activities for all residents. Activities staff also are responsible for recruiting, training, and using volunteers to assist with activities. Administrative services staff are responsible for processing admissions and financial accounting. Rehabilitation services such as physical, occupational, and speech therapies can be provided by qualified staff or contracted with outside companies. The goal of various therapies is to help the resident achieve the desired level of functioning in ADLs (Allen, 2011).

Support services staff tend to the cleanliness of the facility, laundry, and maintenance of the physical systems in the nursing home. Staff in the dietary department are responsible for the nutritional needs of the residents. Nursing departments are in charge of the delivery of nursing and personal care services to its residents. Nursing homes employ registered nurses and licensed practical nurses to deliver and oversee medical care, whereas certified nurse aides (CNAs) provide much of the direct personal care of the residents.

Staff retention has been a problem in many nursing homes across the country, in part because of the stressful nature of the work and the low wages (Foner, 1994). Especially problematic are the turnover rates of CNAs. CNAs are responsible for approximately 80% of direct resident care, yet turnover rates in some facilities have ranged from 64% to 78% in a given year (Castle, 2008; Decker et al., 2003; Donoghue, 2010; Harrington, 1991). Factors associated with job satisfaction and turnover rates of CNAs include wage levels, job characteristics, interpersonal relationships with nursing staff, lack of involvement in care planning and assessment of residents, lack of advancement opportunities, working in for-profit nursing homes, higher top-management turnover, working in larger facilities, and lower facility quality (Banaszak-Holl & Hines, 1994; Castle & Engberg, 2006; Castle, Engberg, Anderson, & Men, 2007; Donoghue, 2010; Donoghue & Castle, 2007; Foner, 1994; Harrington & Swan, 2003; Wacker, 1996).

Best Practice: Intergenerational Programs at St. John Lutheran Nursing Home

In 1988, the management at St. John Lutheran Nursing Home in Springfield, Minnesota, began two programs designed to meet the need for childcare in the community and for the children of staff of the skilled nursing home. Two programs—St. John's GrandKids, a childcare center; and the Very Important Kids (VIK) Club offering a summer daycare, full-year Kindergarten Readiness, and after-school program for school-age children—were created on the campus of St. John Lutheran Home.

(Continued)

(Continued)

St. John's Grandkids/VIK Club is a place that cherishes wisdom, builds self-esteem, offers intergenerational opportunities, and values learning at all ages. The intergenerational program includes all of the St. John's Circle of Care—skilled nursing home, Alzheimer/dementia care unit, memory care facility, senior congregate housing complex, and senior housing. The infants and toddlers take daily buggy rides to visit nursing home residents. The three-year-old class visits twice weekly with the tenants in Vista Ridge, the memory care facility. The four-year-old class does a daily station visit with each station in the nursing home and eats daily in the dining room with the residents of St. John's Lutheran Home, seated at the same table as the residents. Monthly activities are planned such as Chinese New Year, Beach Day, Rubber Ducky's B-day, and Valentines Fun. The tenants in the Vista Ridge memory suites love to recall nursery rhymes and familiar childhood songs with the children on their visits, as do the residents of Riverhaven, the dementia care unit. The facility serves and supports whole families; there are two four-generation families at St. John, where great-grandmas, grandmas, and moms who work there have their small children in care. All staff is trained at orientation on the benefits and the expectations of intergenerational care. The Chaplin, Therapeutic Recreation Director, and the Childcare Director meet monthly to evaluate the previous month and to plan for the coming month. The Director of the Childcare Program documents all intergenerational activities so they may be replicated each year. Recently, an employee survey was conducted as to the importance of the intergenerational programs at St. John's, and out of 120 returned surveys, they had a 99% positive response in relation to intergenerational programming.

For more information, contact St. John Lutheran Home, 201 S. County Road 5, Springfield, MN 56087; www.sjlhome.com.

Source: Generations United (2010).

ACTIVITY PROGRAMS

As mentioned above, nursing homes are required to provide activity programs that enhance residents' physical and mental well-being. Indeed, researchers have shown that participation in activities is important to residents' quality of life (Lawton, 1989; Riddick & Keller, 1991). Nursing homes frequently offer a wide variety of programs and have expanded the scope and type of activities available to residents. Activities include discussion groups, religious groups and services, music programs, raised garden beds, pet visitation, exercise programs, oil painting and other arts-and-crafts activities, and, of course, bingo. One activity that fosters a helping relationship between nursing home residents and young adults is intergenerational learning programs. The purpose of these programs is to bring young people and older adults together in a way that allows both older and younger adults to assist one another. For example, an intergenerational learning program between one Illinois nursing home and a local elementary school provided both residents and students with positive interactions (Angelis, 1990). Students helped residents with letter writing and other activities, while residents often read to students and engaged in playing games. Students and residents exchanged cards and presents on birthdays and participated in intergenerational group activities. In addition, several residents attended classes at the elementary school, and a school activity newsletter was sent to the residents every month. Intergenerational programs involving students and residents offer students an educational experience and improve resident well-being.

Residents' Rights and the Ombudsman Program

As we discussed earlier in the chapter, older adults living in nursing homes suffer from multiple physical or cognitive impairments. By its very nature, institutional living tends to compromise individual choices. Thus, long-term care ombudsman programs were created to act as advocates for older adults living in nursing homes and board-and-care homes. In response to concerns raised about the quality of care provided in nursing homes, the federal government funded seven nursing home ombudsman demonstration projects in the early 1970s to establish a mechanism for receiving and resolving complaints regarding the delivery of nursing home care, to document problems in nursing homes, and to test the effectiveness of using volunteer ombudsmen (U.S. Senate Special Committee on Aging, 1993). By 1975, the Administration on Aging (AoA) funded small residents' rights programs in all 50 states, and in 1978, the ombudsman program was incorporated into the Older Americans Act (OAA). Later revisions to the OAA expanded the scope of ombudsmen to persons living in board and care homes and assisted living facilities. In 2010, there were 1,167 staff and 8,800 certified volunteer ombudsmen in 578 local or regional ombudsman programs located in every state in the United States, and in 2010, they resolved 211,937 complaints and opened 143,062 new cases (AoA, n.d.-a, 2010b). Congress established separate authorization of $20 million for the ombudsman program in 1988; in 1992, Congress appropriated $8.3 million for ombudsman and elder abuse programs. In the reauthorization of the OAA in 2000, ombudsman services are authorized under Title VII; and the budget enacted for 2012 was $16.7 million (AoA, 2012e).

Under the OAA as amended, each state must establish and operate a long-term care ombudsman program. Under the direction of a full-time state ombudsman, programs are directed to

- identify, investigate, and resolve complaints made by or on behalf of residents;
- provide information to residents about long-term care services;
- represent the interests of residents before governmental agencies and seek administrative, legal, and other remedies to protect residents;
- seek administrative, legal and other remedies to protect residents;
- analyze, comment on, and recommend changes in laws and regulations pertaining to the health, safety, welfare, and rights of residents;
- educate and inform consumers and the general public regarding issues and concerns related to long-term care and facilitate public comment on laws, regulations, policies, and actions;
- promote the development of citizen organizations to participate in the program;
- provide technical support for the development of resident and family councils to protect the wellbeing and rights of residents; and
- advocate for changes to improve residents' quality of life. (AoA, n.d.-a)

Of course, one primary responsibility of ombudsmen is to protect the rights of residents. Resident rights are based on federal and state laws that are designed to protect the basic liberties of nursing home residents (see Exhibit 19.5). For example, resident rights legislation includes the rights to receive information; participate in planning all types of care; make choices and independent personal decisions; enjoy privacy in care and confidentiality regarding medical, personal, and financial matters; be treated with dignity and respect; have personal possessions that are kept safe and secure; and have advance notice of transfer or change of rooms or roommates (Burger, Fraser, Hunt, & Frank, 1996; National Consumer Voice for Quality Long-Term Care, 2011).

Exhibit 19.5   Summary of Nursing Home Residents' Rights

1. The right to be fully informed about
   - all services available and all charges;
   - the facility's rules and regulations;
   - how to contact the state ombudsman, the other advocacy organizations; and
   - the state survey reports on the facility.

2. The right to participate in their own care and to
   - receive adequate or appropriate health care;
   - be informed of their medical condition and to participate in treatment planning and be invited to participate in care planning;
   - refuse medication and treatment;
   - participate in discharge planning and review their medical records;
   - have daily communication in their own language; and
   - have assistance if there is sensory impairment.

3. The right to make independent choices, including the right to
   - know that choices are available;
   - make independent personal decisions;
   - choose a physician;
   - participate in activities of the community inside and outside the facility, and participate in a Resident Council; and
   - vote.

4. The right to privacy and confidentiality, including the right to
   - private and unrestricted communication with any person of their choice, including privacy for telephone calls, unopened mail, privacy for meetings with family and friends and other residents;
   - privacy in treatment and care for personal needs;
   - have reasonable access to any entity or individual that provides health, social, legal, or other services; and
   - confidentiality regarding medical, personal or financial affairs.

5. The right to security for possessions, including the right to
   - manage financial affairs; and
   - file a complaint with the state agencies for abuse, neglect, or misappropriation of their property.

6. The right to dignity, respect, and freedom, including the right to
   - be treated with consideration, respect, and dignity;
   - be free from mental and physical abuse;
   - be free from physical and chemical restraints; and
   - have self-determination.

7. The right to remain in the facility, including the right to
   - be transferred or discharged only for medical reasons, if needs cannot be met in the facility, if the health and safety of other residents is endangered, or for nonpayment of stay;
   - receive notice of transfer—a 30-day notice for transfer out of the facility is required, and the notice must include (a) reason for transfer, (b) effective date, (c) location to which the resident is discharged, (d) a statement of right to appeal, and (e) the name, address, and telephone number of the state long-term care ombudsman; and
   - have sufficient preparation to ensure a safe transfer or discharge.

8. The right to raise concerns or complaints including the right to
   - present grievances to the staff of the nursing home, or to any other person, without fear of reprisal; and
   - prompt efforts by the facility to resolve grievances.

9. The facility must maintain identical policies and practices regarding transfer, discharge, and provision of services for all residents regardless of payment source.

Source: Adapted from Burger et al. (1996).

For Your Files: The National Consumer Voice for Quality Long-Term Care

The National Consumer Voice for Quality Long-Term Care (formerly known as the National Citizens' Coalition for Nursing Home Reform), founded in 1975, is a nonprofit consumer advocacy group whose mission is to ensure quality of care for people in the long-term care system. There are more than 200 state and local member groups and approximately 2,000 members in nearly all 50 states. The coalition reviews and distributes information on legislative and regulatory issues, develops training and resource materials for those who act as advocates for nursing home residents, and connects local, state, and national organizations with long-term care experts and resources. The coalition also publishes a variety of resource materials and books, and members can receive a weekly newsletter, *The Gazette*, which summarizes the latest developments in long-term care, and books such as *Nursing Homes: Getting Good Care There*.

   For more information, contact the National Consumer Voice for Quality Long Term Care, 1001 Connecticut Avenue NW, Suite 425, Washington, DC 20036, 202-332-2275 or info@theconsumervoice.org; http://www.theconsumervoice.org.

Ombudsmen also deal with a wide range of other issues, including resolving problems that residents might have with their public benefits or guardianship procedures. Netting, Paton, and Huber (1992) examined ombudsman program reports sent to the AoA in 1990 to determine the nature of complaints received by long-term care ombudsman programs. They found that the largest number of complaints were related to resident care, and included such things as not being dressed, physical abuse, neglect, and poorly trained staff. The next most frequent category of complaints comprised administrative complaints about understaffing, roommate conflict, and laundry procedures, followed by resident rights. In 1995, the complaints most frequently received by ombudsmen from residents in board and care homes were about menu quality, building disrepair, administration of medication, and staff respect and attitude (AoA, 1995b). Ten years later, the top five complaints made to ombudsmen in 2005 regarding care provided in board and care homes were (a) menu—quantity, quality, variation, choice; (b) medications—administration, organization; (c) discharge/eviction—planning, notice, procedure; (d) equipment/building—disrepair, hazards, poor lighting, fire safety; and (e) dignity, respect—staff attitudes. These five represented 22% of all complaints in both nursing homes and board and care homes (AoA, 2005). Interestingly, the top five complaints made to ombudsmen about nursing home care in 2010 were (a) unanswered requests for assistance; (b) inadequate or no discharge/eviction notice or planning; (c) lack of respect for residents, poor staff attitudes; (d) medications—administration, organization; and (e) resident conflict, including roommate to roommate (AoA, 2010c). Although the top five complaints have changed somewhat over the last 25 years, one complaint that remains constant is staff attitudes.

In their study of ombudsman programs, Monk, Kaye, and Litwin (1984) identified two models of ombudsman activities. The *patient rights model* is perceived as a watchdog approach designed to create systemic change in long-term care services. The *quality-of-life model* is based on resolving resident difficulties with staff on a more informal level. Of course, many programs may use both elements in delivering services. Regardless of the model selected by local programs, they all rely on well-trained staff to deliver program services. Some programs use paid staff, volunteers, certified volunteers, or a combination of these to deliver their services. As mentioned above, in 2010, there were 8,800 certified ombudsmen volunteers across the country used to investigate nursing home complaints; 37 states reported using certified volunteer ombudsmen at the regional or local level (AoA, 2010c). Although using volunteer ombudsmen has some drawbacks (see Monk et al., 1984), some programs have successfully relied on volunteers to provide services. For example, the East Tennessee Advocates for Elders Program has successfully used volunteer ombudsmen since 1978, and in 1989 had 94 volunteers who were trained or being trained as ombudsmen (Netting & Hinds, 1989). The program covers a 16-county area and serves 60 nursing homes and 160 assisted living care facilities and serve an average of 100 residents each month (East Tennessee Human Resource Agency, n.d.). However, the heavy reliance on volunteer ombudsmen requires that trainers must examine personal characteristics and motivations of volunteers in order to better prepare volunteers for the difficult work they do (Keith, 2003).

In an attempt to give residents input in the quality of care that they receive, resident councils have emerged as a vehicle to voice residents' concerns. Meyer (1991) collected data about the activities of resident councils through participant observations and interviews with residents as well as statewide resident council members and staff. Resident councils usually meet once a month with the activities director facilitating the meetings; meetings are usually attended by 15 to 30 residents. On the basis of her observations, Meyer concluded that resident councils have at least four functions. First, they make modest changes in the care they receive and condition of the home. For example, specific items discussed at council meetings included acquiring shower chairs for frail residents, more frequent adjustment of window blinds by staff, and parking of carts and wheelchairs on only one side of the hallway. Their success in accomplishing these and other goals was mixed. Resident councils were more successful in obtaining products than they were in changing procedures or services. Second, resident councils provide services to residents and the needy living in their communities. Residents make and sell handcrafted items; the funds are used to assist residents who have experienced a financial crisis or are given to charitable organizations. Third, they broaden the scope of social activities available to residents. These activities include feeding birds, planning ethnic and cultural menus and activities, and arranging social outings to nearby restaurants, zoos, and theaters. Finally, resident councils cooperate with resident councils at other nursing homes to lobby for improvements in quality of care.

Although the resident councils studied by Meyer were unsuccessful in changing procedures, participation in resident councils gave residents a sense of having some control over their lives and a chance to participate in beneficial activities. Meyer also identified barriers to participation in resident councils. Many residents have difficulty hearing, are entering nursing homes with more functional limitations, and have shorter average length of stays. Some residents did not participate because they felt that councils were ineffective in creating change, and others feared retaliation for voicing complaints. Overall, resident councils play an important role in improving the lives of nursing home residents. More research is needed, however, to determine ways to improve participation and outcomes.

IMPROVING QUALITY OF LIFE IN NURSING HOMES

The issue of quality of care has been a concern since nursing homes were formally established decades ago. Indeed, substandard resident care and resident abuse have led to nursing homes being one of the most regulated enterprises in the country. Quality of care includes a wide variety of indicators from the small details of accommodating personal preference to the delivery of personal and medical care. The challenge for nursing homes is that they are at once a place where medical care is provided and where people live their lives (Wiener, 2003).

Stop and consider for a moment how you begin a typical day. You get yourself up, shower and dress, and grab a bite to eat before you go on your way. You decide when to get up, what to wear, and what to eat. You also probably have routines built into your morning—perhaps enjoying a cup of coffee and checking out the latest news online or postings on your favorite social media site while having breakfast. The mere fact of residing in an institution, where hundreds of residents need assistance with daily needs such as eating and bathing, compromises these types of personal freedoms to some extent. Higher-quality homes attempt to accommodate personal differences, employ well-trained staff, and deliver high-quality medical care.

A landmark work, *Improving the Quality of Care in Nursing Homes* (Institute of Medicine, 1986), was instrumental in identifying key indicators of quality of care in nursing homes. Specific indicators that measured resident outcome and care process were identified. Negative indicators included excessive use of psychotropic drugs, high incidence of avoidable decubitus ulcers and urinary tract infections, dehydration, and considerable weight loss. Personal care indicators included whether residents' hair was neat and clean, whether they were dressed in their own clothing, whether they received daily oral care, and whether they received prompt responses to resident call lights. Nutritional and dietary indicators included assisting residents who needed help eating, serving food while it was still warm, and giving residents some choice in menu selections. Finally, overall quality-of-care indicators included living in a clean environment in which residents were allowed to have personal possessions and furnishings in their rooms, opportunities for personal choice, participation in social activities, and treatment by staff with dignity. As a result of this work, the Omnibus Budget and Reconciliation Act of 1987 (OBRA-87) was passed by Congress, instituting 47 recommended changes and this act is largely responsible for improvements in nursing home quality (Castle & Ferguson, 2010).

For Your Files: The Eden Alternative in Nursing Homes

In 1991, Dr. Bill Thomas, his wife Judy, and the administrative team at Chase Memorial Nursing Home in New York sought an alternative to caring for the residents of this rural nursing home to address what they identified as the three plagues of nursing homes—loneliness, helplessness, and boredom. They incorporated pets (100 birds, to be exact, as well as dogs, cats, and rabbits), plants and gardens, and visiting children, and changed the way in which care was organized and provided. Pets were designed to get people talking, and involved in their environment; helping children care for pets and plants was designed to assist elders to overcome feelings of helplessness; and an environment with all this "diversity" was expected to provide the unexpected. Residents also bring their own furniture and their favorite pictures, and their rooms are painted in their favorite colors. In addition to introducing the changes in the environment, Eden Alternative homes create nursing care teams where each team is responsible for a small number of residents, and the staff (considered to be anyone who comes into contact with the residents) work together to prepare their own schedules and daily assignments. They dubbed this new approach the Eden Alternative, which is guided by the following ten principles.

1. The three plagues of loneliness, helplessness, and boredom account for the bulk of suffering among our elders.
2. An elder-centered community commits to creating a human habitat where life revolves around close and continuing contact with plants, animals, and children. It is these relationships that provide the young and old alike with a pathway to a life worth living.
3. Loving companionship is the antidote to loneliness. Elders deserve easy access to human and animal companionship.
4. An elder-centered community creates opportunity to give as well as receive care. This is the antidote to helplessness.
5. An elder-centered community imbues daily life with variety and spontaneity by creating an environment in which unexpected and unpredictable interactions and happenings can take place. This is the antidote to boredom.

6. Meaningless activity corrodes the human spirit. The opportunity to do things that we find meaningful is essential to human health.

7. Medical treatment should be the servant of genuine human caring, never its master.

8. An elder-centered community honors its elders by de-emphasizing top-down bureaucratic authority, seeking instead to place the maximum possible decision-making authority into the hands of the elders or into the hands of those closest to them.

9. Creating an elder-centered community is a never-ending process. Human growth must never be separated from human life.

10. Wise leadership is the lifeblood of any struggle against the three plagues. For it, there can be no substitute.

Persons interested in the Eden Alternative can complete an Associate Training class to learn about the process. One empirical study that compared resident outcomes of an Eden Alternative and a non–Eden Alternative nursing home found no beneficial effects in terms of cognitive function or functional status; however, qualitative data revealed the Eden Alternative nursing home had psycho-social changes that were positive for both staff and residents (M. T. Coleman et al., 2002).

For more information, contact Eden Alternative, P.O. Box 18369; 1900 S. Clinton Avenue, Rochester, NY 14618; phone: 585-461-3951; www.edenalt.org.

Source: Adapted from the National Center on Accessibility (n.d.) and Eden Alternative (n.d.).

The extent to which nursing homes fail to provide good quality of care has been well documented. For example, in a survey of nursing home staff, Pillemer and Moore (1989) found that 36 % of nursing home staff had seen at least one resident physically abused in the past year, and 10 % admitted to physically abusing residents. Eighty-one percent reported seeing residents psychologically abused—most often in the form of being yelled at. In addition, treatment of residents has been found to be related to personal characteristics. Residents who had higher incomes, had more personal possessions, had visitors at least once a month, and were White received better overall quality of care (Pillemer, 1988). More recent data from the Ombudsman Annual Report for 2010 indicated that, of the 157,962 nursing home complaints made to long-term care ombudsmen across the country, some 7,150 complaints were made regarding resident abuse, neglect, or exploitation (AoA, n.d.-a, 2010c). Of all the various types of complaints reported (e.g., residents' rights, resident care, quality of life, administration), physical abuse, verbal/mental abuse, and gross neglect represented 2.0 %, 1.4 %, and 1.0 %, respectively. As quality of care in nursing homes continues to be a concern among gerontologists, policy makers, families, and those working in the long-term care field, the effort to identify, measure, and advocate quality care continues. Current quality of care indicators are related to structure measures (e.g., organizational characteristics such as staffing levels and qualifications), process measures (e.g., things done to and for the resident), and outcomes (e.g., desired states to be achieved for the resident), or SPO (Castle & Ferguson, 2010). Castle and Ferguson (2010), in their comprehensive review of nursing home quality measurement, note that determining how many of the SPO measures are needed to reflect quality is still being debated and actually collecting the data on quality indicators in a consistent and accurate manner can also be a challenge in accurately determining which facilities provide quality care. There have, however, been two recent efforts by the government and the private sector to bring the issue of quality into the public's consciousness. The Nursing Home Compare (NHC) program was developed by the Centers for Medicare and Medicaid Services (CMS). NHC is an interactive web-based program that uses a five-star system to report how well Medicare and Medicaid certified nursing homes across the country perform on quality measures (CMS, 2012c).Another program, Advancing Excellence, is a voluntary coalition of nursing home providers, health care providers, and consumers that works to help nursing homes achieve quality care focused on eight goals and provides resources designed to help providers improve their quality care (Advancing Excellence, n.d.). Over the last four years, there has been a marked increase in a movement generally defined as *person-centered care*. The focus of the person-centered care movement is on changing the culture of nursing home care so that it reflects a living experience where residents experience enhanced quality of care in environments that are more homelike and reflect the "voice" of the resident in all matters (Rahman & Schnelle, 2008). Leaders and organizations in the nursing home culture change movement include the Pioneer Network, the Eden Alternative, the Wellspring model, and CMS's help in launching the Advancing Excellence (mentioned above) and creating a 79-item questionnaire to assess progress toward person-center care called the Artifacts of Culture Change Tool. As Rahman and Schnelle point out, many of the person-centered care interventions now being implemented have yet to be evaluated to determine what effect they have on quality care, and more research is needed to determine the outcomes of these interventions.

Although much of what is reported in the popular press and to some extent in professional publications focuses on poor-quality care provided in some homes, researchers have identified positive outcomes for residents and family members after nursing home placement. For example, K. F. Smith and Bengston (1979) found in their two-year study of nursing home residents and their families that 70 % reported that the consequences of nursing home placement were positive. Families reported a renewed or continued closeness among family members as well as a reduction in caregiving stress, which in turn resulted in more time to focus on the emotional aspects of the relationship. Families can also see improvements in residents' physical and mental health, and see residents developing new relationships with other residents. When the AARP (1990) conducted interviews of nursing home residents, it found that many residents talked about the positive aspects of residing in a nursing home. For example, one resident stated, "I learned to walk when I got here." Another commented, "I've gained weight. You better believe it. I was going downhill rather rapidly before [moving into the nursing home]" (p. 13). Other researchers found that, after nursing home placement, health and financial stresses were reduced for spouses and that caregivers' quality of life and health improved compared with caregivers who kept their loved one at home (S. King & Collins, 1991; S. Pushkar, Gold, & Reis, 1995). Although there is some indication that nursing home placement can reduce some aspects of family stress, other researchers found that the emotional strain of being a caregiver does not decrease (Lieberman & Fisher, 2001).

CHALLENGES FOR NURSING HOMES IN THE FUTURE

For most of the general public, the nursing home stands as a symbol of all that is dreaded about old age—its residents are physically and mentally impaired, they have become dependent on others to accomplish the most basic tasks of daily living, and they appear lonely and discarded by society. Every so often, popular news programs report the abuses that occur within a nursing home's confines. These images are embedded in our collective consciousness. Nursing homes do care for those who are among the most frail and debilitated in our society; some facilities are better than others. But rather than view nursing homes with contempt, we must embrace them as necessary places within the continuum of care and work to enhance the quality of care provided to their residents. Improving quality of care is like putting together the pieces of a puzzle. No one piece will solve the problems that exist in nursing homes because many pieces need to be addressed.

Reforming Reimbursement and Payment of Long-Term Care Facility Services

Having Medicaid as the largest third-party payer of nursing home care causes a number of problems. First, many have observed that Medicaid reimbursement rates are terribly inadequate, especially for those with high care needs (Swan & Benjamin, 1990). For example, the Medicaid long-term care expenditure in states ranges from $4.2 billion in New York to $833 million in Arizona, and Medicaid reimbursement rates for nursing home care are approximately 70% to 80% of private-pay rates (Harrington-Meyer, 2001; Kaiser Family Foundation, 2012d; R. L. Kane, Kane, Ladd, & Veazie, 1998). In turn, this has led, according to some scholars, to structural discrimination toward Medicaid residents in the form of long waiting lists and preferential treatment toward private-pay residents (Abend-Wein, 1991; Estes, Swan, & Associates, 1993; Grimaldi, 1982). Second, for middle-class families, the only alternative to paying for nursing home costs has been to impoverish themselves to qualify for nursing home care. About one third of nursing home residents who are ineligible for Medicaid when they are admitted deplete enough of their assets to meet the eligibility guides for Medicaid (Wiener, Sullivan, & Skaggs, 1996). How many older families—or their children, for that matter—who need to secure extended long-term care services can afford $200 per day—more than $73,000 per year for multiple years—for nursing home care? Many health scholars have called for developing a more rational system for financing nursing home care—one that combines both public and private financing (Aiken, 1989; Estes et al., 1993). In 2010, the Community Living Assistance Services and Supports (CLASS) Act was enacted as Title VIII of the Patient Protection and Affordable Care Act (ACA; P.L. 111-148) as an attempt to address this policy gap in long-term care access and affordability (USDHHS, 2011d). CLASS was designed to establish a voluntary, national insurance program for workers to help pay for long-term services and support and the program was to be administered by the AoA. The CLASS program would have offered lifetime benefits and availability of a cash benefit to help enrollees live independently in the community and to give them the choice to determine the necessary services and supports they purchase with their coverage. CLASS benefits were to be funded entirely through enrollee premiums with no taxpayer subsidy to support the program and the law required that the program be solvent over a 75-year period. However, in October 2011, Kathy Greenlee, Assistant Secretary for Aging, announced after conducting an actuarial analyses of the program concluded that the program, as currently structured, may not be able to achieve actuarially solvency over the next 75 years, and therefore recommended that the program should be suspended (USDHHS, 2011b).

An increase in public support, either directly or through taxation, is needed, along with efforts such as permitting the integration of Medicaid and long-term care insurance mentioned earlier in this chapter to increase the use of private sector insurance to help spread the risk of long-term care across different sectors of society and thus making nursing home care more affordable.

Attracting Qualified Staff and Improving Working Conditions

To increase the number of qualified staff applying for positions and working in nursing homes, we must work to reduce the stigma associated with working in a nursing home among all professional and certified staff. Anecdotal evidence suggests that nursing homes are often the last employment choice of newly graduated nurses. Nursing programs can work to encourage the placement of their students into long-term care. Just as initiatives have been developed to increase the number of nurses placed in rural areas, so too should initiatives be implemented to increase the number of nurses placed in long-term care facilities. A recent change in nursing program credentialing may help encourage more nurses to choose to work in long-term care facilities. Nursing schools will now award Advance Practice Registered Nurses (APRNs) with certifications as an adult-gerontology acute care practitioner, adult-gerontology primary care nurse practitioner, or adult-gerontology clinical nurse specialist (Gerontological Society of America, 2012). Of course, chances of attracting qualified staff are improved if working conditions and benefits are competitive. Salary and benefits must be competitive with both the medical and nonmedical employment sectors, opportunities for professional advancement must exist, and the organizational climate must convey a sense of respect and appreciation for its employees.

Increasing Family and Community Involvement

Researchers have discovered a link between increased volunteer and family visits and improved quality of care. Staff and those in the aging network must work together to improve the amount of community involvement in nursing homes. Something as simple as having the Area Agency on Aging advisory board meet every month in the nursing home's conference room could increase the amount of contact between "outsiders" and the nursing home community. Kansas Advocates for Better Care documented community-based intergenerational programs in over 100 nursing homes in Kansas. For example, the Generation Bridge program brings the sixth-grade class from Goessel Elementary School to Bethesda Nursing Home every Tuesday to play spelling bingo, bake cookies, make crafts, and visit with residents (Kansas Advocates for Better Care, 2002).

Meeting the Care Needs of a Diverse Group of Residents

The changing nature of the health care delivery system means that the type of care provided in nursing homes will have to change as well. As more community-based alternatives emerge for persons who need custodial care, nursing homes will no doubt emerge as primary places for more therapeutic and rehabilitative care. Furthermore, the increased number of persons with AIDS who will need long-term nursing may have a hand in shaping the future of nursing homes (Aiken, 1989). The changing demographics of the older adult population includes an increasing number of ethnically and racially diverse elders who will be in need of long-term care. Cultural competence is a relatively new concept in health care delivery. A culturally competent organization is "committed to serving diverse clients, hiring diverse staff, and establishing programs that address the needs of different client populations" (Management Sciences for Health, n.d., para. 1). The Office of Minority Health identifies national standards for culturally and linguistically appropriate care that includes care where patients "receive from all staff members effective understandable, and respectful care that is provided in a manner compatible with their cultural health beliefs and practices and preferred language" (USDHHS, 2001, p. 7). Culturally competent training must be incorporated in curriculum and ongoing training provided by long-term care facilities.

Finally, the 2005 White House Conference on Aging (2006) delegates passed two resolutions aimed at improving long-term care. They supported policies that

- establish and foster innovations in financing long-term care to increase options available to consumers; and

- develop a coordinated, comprehensive long-term care strategy by supporting public and private sector initiatives that address financing, choice, quality, service delivery, and the paid and unpaid workforce.

As the population ages and becomes more diverse in the coming decades, long-term care facilities will be faced with a myriad of social and organizational challenges.

CASE STUDY

Defending Individual Rights—A Nursing Home's Dilemma

Edna, an 83-year-old with mild dementia, has lived in a nursing home for the past three years. Her only remaining family is an estranged daughter. Although she can walk with assistance, she prefers to use a wheelchair. Edna has formed a strong attachment to George, a 90-year-old with moderate to severe dementia, depending on the day and his stress level. George's chart also documents a diagnosis of transient ischemic attacks. George is quite handsome and is "the catch of the nursing home." Edna feels important when George is pushing her around in her wheelchair. Being with George has become a status symbol for Edna. George's roommate, Bud, has complained that he does not have any privacy. Edna and George neglect to pull the privacy curtain when they are lying in George's bed. Bud's family also has complained about how embarrassing it is, especially for younger family members, to find Edna and George in bed together when they visit. Edna's daughter called the nursing home and told the head nurse that the facility should stop this relationship because Edna and George were too old to have sex. She demanded that something be done immediately and indicated that if some measures were not taken, she would move her mother to another facility.

The staff of the facility have offered Edna and George the opportunity to room together. Some staff members are uncomfortable with this relationship because George is more confused than Edna, and they feel that she dominates the relationship. They suspect that she can be physically abusive to George if he refuses to spend time with her. They have observed such jealous behavior during group activities and in the dining room when other women try to sit next to George. Other staff members believe that to try to separate the couple would be a violation of their rights to choose their own companions. George's two sons are not adamantly opposed to George's being with Edna. They find it amusing and have joked about it in front of the staff.

Edna and George decide to be roommates. After three days together, George has many bruises on his arms and face. Staff members notice that he is attempting to avoid Edna. They ask George if

(Continued)

(Continued)

he wants to move back into his old room, and he replies that he does. Staff members move George back to his room. Within a day, George is seeking Edna out and refuses to leave her. Staff decide to call the local long-term care ombudsman for technical assistance.

Case Study Questions

1. As the long-term care ombudsman, what additional information would you like to know?

2. What resident rights are in question in this case scenario?

3. Whose interests must be considered? Do any of these interests take precedence over any of the others?

4. Do you believe it is a violation of George's and Edna's rights to keep them separated? Why or why not?

5. Can you think of a creative compromise that would mostly satisfy all parties in this case? Are there any other community resources or agencies that could be called on to assist staff? Family members? George or Edna? Bud?

LEARNING ACTIVITIES

1. Visit a resident council meeting at a local nursing home. What issues were discussed at the meeting? How many residents and staff attended? Interview the chair of the resident council. Have the chair reflect on the council's accomplishments during the past year.

2. Join the Gerinet Listserv discussion group (http://listserv.buffalo.edu/cgi-bin/wa?A0=GERINET). Monitor the discussion during a two-week period. What issuess are discussed by the group?

3. Obtain a map of your city and mark on the map the locations of the nursing homes in your community. On the same map, draw a line around what you believe are low-income or minority neighborhoods. Where are the nursing homes located in relation to these neighborhoods? If you live in a rural area, determine how far away these facilities are from smaller rural towns. What are the implications of the geographic location of these nursing homes?

FOR MORE INFORMATION

International Resources

1. WeDO Partnership: www.wedo-partnership.eu

   WeDO (Wellbeing and Dignity of Older people) is a European project involving 18 partners from 12 countries. The objective of WeDO is to promote the wellbeing and dignity of vulnerable and disabled older people in all settings through the promotion of quality long-term care. Check out their "European quality framework for long-term care services" publication.

2. European Association for Directors and Providers of Long-Term Care Services (E.D.E.) for the Elderly: www.ede-eu.org

The E.D.E. is an international umbrella organization representing national associations for directors and providers of long-term care services in Europe. One of its major tasks is to promote the exchange of information and experience among its members and facilitate mutual learning about long-term care best practices and training.

3. Ontario Family Councils' Program: www.familycouncilmembers.net/

The Ontario Family Councils' Program is an organized, self-led, self-determining, democratic group composed of family and friends of the residents of Long-Term Care Homes. The Council produces and distributes a manual on "Starting and Maintaining Your Family Council", factsheets, toolkits, a video, and a semi-annual newsletter.

National Resources

1. LeadingAge (formally known as the American Association of Homes and Services for the Aging), 2519 Connecticut Avenue NW, Washington, DC 20008; Phone: 202-783-2242; www .leadingage.org

LeadingAge is an organization whose members include not-for-profit organizations in the United States, state partners, businesses, research partners, consumer organizations, foundations, and a broad global network of aging services organizations from other countries. The work of LeadingAge is focused on advocacy, leadership development, and applied research and promotion of effective services, home health, hospice, community services, senior housing, assisted living residences, continuing care communities, and nursing homes.

2. American Health Care Association, 1201 L Street NW, Washington, DC 20005; phone: 202-842-4444; www.ahca.org

AHCA is the nation's largest association of long-term and post-acute care providers, and in that role AHCA advocates for quality care and services for frail, elderly, and disabled Americans. AHCA represents the long-term care community to the nation at large—to government, business leaders, and the general public. They serve as a voice for change, providing information, education, and administrative tools that enhance quality care.

3. The National Consumer Voice for Quality Long-Term Care (formerly known as the National Citizens' Coalition for Nursing Home Reform), 1828 L Street NW, Suite 801 Washington, DC 20036; phone: 202-332-2276; www.nccnhr.org

The National Consumer Voice for Quality Long-Term Care is a nonprofit organization that represents the consumer voice at the national level for quality long-term care, services, and supports. The National Consumer Voice advocates for public policies that support quality care and quality of life responsive to consumers' needs in all long-term care settings; empowering and educating consumers and families with the knowledge and tools they need to advocate for themselves; training and supporting individuals and groups that empower and advocate for consumers of long-term care; and promoting the critical role of direct-care workers and best practices in quality care delivery. It also operates the National Long-Term Care Ombudsman Resource Center.

Web Resources

1. The Provider's Guide to Quality and Culture: http://erc.msh.org/mainpage.cfm?file=1.0.htm& module=provider&language=English

   The Provider's Guide to Quality and Culture is a website designed to provide information to health care organizations to assist them in providing culturally competent care to multi-ethnic populations. This website is a joint project of Management Sciences for Health (MSH), HHS, Health Resources and Services Administration, and the Bureau of Primary Health Care. The site explains cultural competence and provides information on how to create culturally competent organizations and how to improve the quality of provider/client interaction. It also provides an extensive list of resources.

2. America's Health Insurance Plans: www.hiaa.org

   The Health Insurance Association of America has a number of consumer guides online, including one on long-term care insurance. The information about long-term care insurance is comprehensive and covers such topics as "Are you likely to need long-term care?" "What kind of insurance is available?" "What do policies cost?" and "What do long-term care insurance policies cover?" It is a good primer on long-term care insurance.

3. Care Conversations—The American Health Care Association and the National Center for Assisted Living: www.careconversations.org

   This is a website for consumers interested in information about nursing homes, assisted living/residential care, and other types of long-term care.

4. New York State Office of the Long Term Care Ombudsman: http://www.ltcombudsman.ny.gov

   This website does a good job of explaining what an ombudsman is and does and how to use one. The site also has links to other related resources.

5. Pioneer Network: http://www.pioneernetwork.net

   Pioneer Network was formed in 1997 by a small group of prominent professionals in long-term care to advocate for person-directed care and a more humane consumer-driven models that embrace flexibility and self-determination. Pioneer Network partners and audience are primarily engaged in some aspect of long-term care including long-term care CEOs and administrators, consumers and family caregivers, doctors and nurses, direct care providers, and others who care about, and care for, the aging.

6. National Clearinghouse for Long-Term Care Information: http://www.longtermcare.gov

   The HHS created the National Clearinghouse for Long-Term Care Information website that helps consumers understand the coverage and costs of LTC insurance in their state.

PART III

Preparing for the Future

CHAPTER 20

Programs and Services in an Era of Change

In the previous chapters of this book, we described the wide array of programs and services that exist to assist older adults. Yet to end without describing the important issues facing the nation with regard to service delivery of programs would present an incomplete picture. The programs and services we have described throughout this book exist within a social and political context that influences their existence, the nature of what they offer, and those to whom they offer services. In this final chapter, we discuss the social forces that have brought us to a crossroads of aging policy and service delivery. We then discuss some key issues that will need to be addressed with subsequent reauthorizations of the Older Americans Act (OAA). We conclude with some thoughts about the changing nature of U.S. society and its implications for aging professionals.

SOCIAL AND POLITICAL INFLUENCES ON AGING POLICIES AND PROGRAMS

Two key social and political factors that have emerged in the past decade are forcing a re-examination of aging policies and, in turn, the programs and services they fund. First, the number of people 65 and older is steadily increasing and, concomitantly, there has been a steady increase in the percentage of the federal budget spent on older adults. Second, society's current image of older adults commonly portrays them as healthy, wealthy, and self-consumed. Such an image drives the opinion that programs and services for older adults are no longer needed. Thus these social forces have influenced a discussion regarding possible solutions to "fix" Medicare, to stabilize Social Security in the twenty-first century, and to "protect" society from buckling under the weight of its burdensome older population. Many scholars have argued against the assumptions that older adults are a burden to society and that all older adults are financially and socially comfortable and have voiced the need for society to acknowledge the benefits, both direct and indirect, that everyone experiences when society cares for its elders (see Kingston, Hirshorn, & Cornman, 1986; Marmor, Mashaw, & Harvey, 1990).

Because the OAA is the one of the key social policies created to serve older adults, it too has been the focus of much debate. What role should the OAA play, and whom should its programs serve? We will examine some of the issues currently being debated that will shape the future of the OAA.

CHALLENGES FOR THE OLDER AMERICANS ACT

Policy makers and advocates of older adults are currently re-examining a number of issues associated with the OAA. The reauthorization of the Act in 2006 has given professionals in the field of aging an opportunity to debate the role of the OAA, to think about new ways of increasing linkages with the private sector, and to re-examine who should be eligible for services. The OAA was scheduled to be reauthorized in 2011. Because Congress has yet to reauthorize the Act, uncertainty remains about what changes will be made to the OAA and the scope of services available in the coming years.

The Role of the Older Americans Act

The purpose of the OAA is to provide the policy foundation and nationwide infrastructure to advance advocacy, planning, program design, and implementation for older adults (Takamura, 1999). Funding for the OAA direct service programs has not keep pace with the growth of the older adult population for many years, and new amendments expanding the role of the aging network have been added in recent years without an increase in overall funding. For example, in 1980, when there were 35 million older adults over the age of 60, OAA funding was, in 2007 dollars, $2.5 billion; in 2007, with 53 million older adults over the age of 60, OAA funding was $1.8 billion (Burgess & Applebaum, 2009). In addition, the economic collapse begun in 2008–2009 dubbed *the Great Recession* has made it even more difficult for professionals in the aging network to serve an increasing number of older adults. As Area Agencies on Aging (AAA) funding from all sources is being cut, the demand for assistance has increased as many older adults have experienced economic and social hardships caused by the economic downturn (U.S. Government Accountability Office, 2011). Moreover, we know that many of the participants who receive support through the aging network are low-income older adults who are not eligible for services under Medicaid. OAA funding provides a critical role in enhancing low-income older adults' well-being and helping them remain living in the community (Burgess & Applebaum, 2009). Until the economy turns around, it is unlikely that an increase in funding—federal, state, or through philanthropy—will be forthcoming. Given the historically inadequate funding, some have called for a re-examination of the role of the OAA. Kutza (1991) has suggested that the OAA be restructured to reflect its strengths (e.g., advocacy, meeting the nutritional needs of older adults, providing information and referral services) that would allow AAAs to concentrate their efforts on fewer services, rather than the multitude that they now cover. There is evidence to support, however, that rather than a narrowing of roles for AAAs as suggested by Kutza, the AAA role has expanded. Many AAAs are responsible for implementing Medicaid's Home and Community Based Waiver programs, and partner with a variety of federal, state, private, and nonprofit entities to deliver services. Another possible change in the Act could be to allow local AAAs more flexibility in determining what programs their communities need and which are funded to better calibrate funding with service delivery expectations.

At the most recent White House Conference on Aging (WHCOA) in 2005, the delegates recommended (a) expanding the role of the OAA, (b) that Congress establish set authorization levels for all OAA programs throughout the authorization period of the Act by increasing authorization levels for all of the Titles in the OAA by a minimum of 25%, (c) allowing flexibility and capability for local autonomy, (d) ensuring necessary resources to adequately serve the projected growth in the number of older Americans, and (e) taking into consideration the growing ethnic and cultural diversity, and particularly the growing ranks of the "old-old"—those age 85 and over—who are the most frail, vulnerable, and in the greatest need of aging support services (2006, p. 31).

Related to how programs are structured and delivered, the WHCOA (2006) recommended that programs serving older adults

> proactively realign and modernize . . . to be more efficient and effective in their performance, so as to free-up resources for unmet needs . . . such support has greatly served to enhance the quality of their lives. That support should be continued using more modern and integrated approaches. (p. 22)

In 2010, just prior to when OAA was due to be reauthorized in 2011, the Administration on Aging (AoA) sought feedback from professionals working in the aging network about changes in the OAA. During this process, AoA (2012b) consistently heard the following themes about the OAA:

- It's "not broken" and it works well.
- It's helpful, flexible, and responsive to individual/community needs whether the person lives in a very rural/frontier area or an urban center.
- Its national aging services network structure is the "glue" that holds everything together and is effective in coordinating services from multiple sources to build a seamless delivery system.
- It meets the goals established by Congress in providing assistance to help people maintain their health, independence, dignity, and avoid premature institutionalization. In addition, it is effective in targeting the poor, near poor, and those who are frail and at risk of nursing home admission.
- It only needs minor enhancements designed to strengthen the capacity of the network to meet the increasing needs and diversity of the older population.

Using input from stakeholders, the AoA (2012b) developed the following list of targeted changes to the OAA that are focused on a more efficient and effective of program delivery. The recommendations are summarized below:

1. National Family Caregiver Support Program
   - Add "parent caregiver" to the National Family Caregiver Support Program in order to provide much needed services to older individuals providing care to their adult children (ages 19 to 59).
2. Consolidated Funding for Congregate and Home-Delivered Nutrition Programs
   - Consolidate the funding for Title III congregate and home-delivered meal programs, in a way that ensures no state receives less from AoA in consolidated funding than the state's total C1 and C2 allocations for FY 2011.

   – Require AAA, provider, and community input in allocation determination to allow States more flexibility to direct services to identified needs, and allow more local input into funding allocations.

3. Consumer Contributions

   – Expand the range of Title III services for which cost-sharing is permitted, but require states to request a waiver to test cost-sharing for nutrition and case management, or to deny service to an individual for failure to pay cost-sharing. Require states to demonstrate that there is no negative impact from implementing cost-sharing, prior to waiver approval. Low-income individuals will continue to be excluded from payments under OAA cost-sharing programs. The proposed changes would allow states to expand services.

4. Incentive Payments to Enhance the Capability of the Aging Network

   – Provide additional funds to states as an incentive for high performance in achieving program goals, and give authority to the Assistant Secretary for Aging to develop performance standards that support the aging network as a critical vehicle for administration/delivery of home- and community-based services and supports for seniors and other long-term care populations.

5. Expanded Eligibility for Long-term Care Ombudsman Services and Abuse Reporting

   – Allow Long-Term Care Ombudsmen (LTCO) to serve all residents of nursing facilities regardless of age, and to report abuse without consent where the resident is unable to give consent and where the legal representative is the suspected perpetrator of abuse, neglect, or exploitation of the resident.

6. Supplemental Funding and Expansion of State Legal Assistance Development Program

   – Establish a minimum amount of Title III funds that may be used for implementing the currently unfunded State Legal Assistance Development Program, and add direct legal assistance services as an option. States would be permitted to retain any portion of the amount reserved for legal assistance for the most effective means of responding to legal assistance needs—including allocating funds to some or all AAAs and legal assistance providers, or funding a legal assistance developer.

7. Transformation of Title IV

   – Add an emphasis on timely evaluation and dissemination of projects that inform core programs, for example, under Titles III, VI, and VII. This is designed to focus the authority in Title IV on the ability to respond to current and future needs in the field of aging.

8. Transfer of Older American Community Service Employment (OACSE) to Department of Health and Human Services

   – Transfer the OACSE program under Title V, along with the authority to administer the program, from the Secretary of Labor to the Secretary of Health and Human Services, acting through the Assistant Secretary.

9. Establishment of Senior Medicare Patrol as a Permanent Program
   - Add a new Chapter 5 to Title VII ("Elder Rights Protection") that creates express statutory authority for the Senior Medicare Patrol (SMP) program.

10. Evidence-Based Disease Prevention and Health Promotion Services
    - Allow states to provide for Title III-D Disease Prevention and Health Promotion services directly or by grant/contract, with a requirement that such services be evidence based.

Finally, the U.S. Department of Health and Human Services' restructuring of the AoA under the office of the Administration for Community Living has raised concerns from professionals in the aging network. During a webinar with the Assistant Secretary of Aging, Kathy Greenlee, some in attendance worried that aligning the AoA alongside offices that focus on disabilities meant that the AoA would change its focus and funding toward serving older adults with disabilities, or that placing the AoA under another layer of bureaucracy would cause the AoA to lose its visibility in the federal landscape (K. Greenlee, *Recent Changes at the Administration on Aging: Impact on the Aging and Disability Networks* webinar, July 17, 2012). Assistant Secretary Greenlee indicated that it was not the intent of the restructuring to change the focus of the OAA. She also noted that by law, the head of the ACL will always be the Assistant Secretary of Aging, thus ensuring visibility for the aging network. It is hoped that the restricting will provide opportunities for collaboration and efficiencies in serving all persons with disabilities, regardless of age. Although no one knows how the restructure will affect the AoA operations and effectiveness, it is likely that changes in the operation and direction will ensue in the coming years.

Reaching Out to the Private Sector

In the era of smaller budgets and greater needs, there has been a call for the aging network to expand its effort to work with the private sector to help meet the needs of older adults. A strong private sector presence currently exists in many areas of service delivery to older adults, including housing, long-term care, case management, transportation services, and recreational opportunities. With the increase in the number of older adults and an increase in the number of older adults who have adequate income, the role of the private sector in service delivery will become even greater. This increase in private sector involvement has several implications. First, the AAAs have been and must continue to increase their role in forging public–private partnerships to create employment opportunities and to create additional housing options (McConnel & Beitler, 1991). AAAs can also occupy leadership positions coordinating the services and programs offered by both the public and private sectors. Second, with the increase in the service options available because of private sector involvement, a central role of AAAs may be to act as a broker of services on behalf of older adults. As the choices for housing, health care, and other services become increasingly more complex, AAAs might become more actively involved in assisting older adults to make lifestyle choices that best fit their needs.

Who Should Be Eligible for Services?

There has been considerable debate about the universality of the OAA programs and services. As we discussed in Chapter 2, until recently, OAA eligibility was determined to be adults 60 years of age and older regardless of their income, but specifically targeting low-income older adults and racial and ethnic minority elders. Again, because of the reduction in OAA funding and the need to extend its limited dollars to reach more people, the questions of who should be targeted to receive services and what cost, if any, participants should pay for those services have been posed and have influenced recent amendments to the Act.

Targeting Services

Through the years, the OAA has been amended so that it targets its services to those deemed to be most in need. The idea of redefining who should be targeted to receive services has once again emerged. Should the Act be revised to raise the age of eligibility? Should additional classes of individuals be targeted, such as those living in public-assisted housing, those living alone, or those who are at risk when discharged from the hospital (AoA, 1997). Ideally, identifying and targeting services to those most in need make programs more effective in assisting the most needy. The recent clarification of the definition of *greatest social need* by the AoA, which now may include religious minorities, GLBT elders, and other special populations, helps provide additional clarification about populations deemed to be at risk. The effect on program service and delivery outcomes due to the expansion of the number of targeted groups that can be served by AAA is unclear. More research is needed to determine the effectiveness of such expansion.

It also has been proposed that the OAA should simply target its services to low-income individuals by developing financial eligibility standards for participation in its programs (see Gelfand & Bechill, 1991). Under the current provisions of the Act, programs and services are meant to serve those who have both economic and social needs, but the Act does not yet use means-test cutoffs for programs and services (e.g., 150% poverty-level income). At first glance, establishing specific income-eligibility guidelines seems to be a reasonable solution to shrinking funding levels. There are, however, many issues to consider. Using income as a criterion for eligibility undermines the "social insurance" principle that has provided broad-based support for universal programs from a wide variety of constituencies (Hudson & Kingson, 1991). The inclusion of the middle class along with the lower class broadens the power base that helps protect the program from complete elimination. Moreover, the exclusion of older adults who have more social and financial resources than their less well-off counterparts might have a negative impact on program delivery. Many of these older adults play a key role in volunteering and assisting their less well-off counterparts. In addition, a means-based program might keep older adults from attending to avoid the social stigma attached to "welfare" programs. More important, the development of the definition of need requires a great deal of thought. Clearly, the most convenient definition of need is based on income or asset level. Aside from the concern that collecting financial information from its participants would create an additional level of bureaucracy and a paperwork nightmare, how will programs measure "social need"? How will programs measure the social need of persons for whom attending a congregate meal is the only source of social interaction? If they do not meet the income guidelines developed, are they any less needy?

On the other hand, there are some arguments for implementing income-eligibility criteria. First, insufficient resources force the need to target service to those least able to afford those services. Second, the collective plight of older adults was much worse when the OAA was enacted in 1965 than it is today. Thus, as social and economic conditions of older cohorts change, the OAA must respond in kind. Clearly, any change in the constituency the OAA serves would have to be carefully weighed against the advantages and disadvantages of changing the eligibility criteria.

Cost-Sharing

Mandating cost-sharing is another option that has been proposed as a way to make program dollars go farther. The 2006 amendments to the OAA included language that permitted the expansion of cost-sharing for selected programs (see Chapter 2) and as mentioned above, aging network professionals would like to have the option to expand cost-sharing in certain circumstances. Requiring cost-sharing also has some advantages and disadvantages. In addition to covering program costs, cost-sharing might promote a sense of equity among participants (see Chapter 3) and reduce their feelings of dependency. Evidence shows that cost-sharing can be successful. Participants at congregate meal sites are asked to make a suggested donation that helps cover programmatic expenses. As we discussed in Chapter 10, participant contributions play an important role in supporting the congregate meal program. On the other hand, if programs are required to implement cost-sharing as a condition of participation, they will spend a great deal of time and money on the task of collecting and managing paperwork, determining the cost-sharing amount, and collecting the fee from participants. A cost-sharing requirement also may keep the most needy from receiving services.

The discussion about creating financial eligibility guidelines or cost-sharing provisions would benefit from research that collects demographic characteristics of all OAA participants, including measures of income and social support, as well as the impact of cost-sharing on service use and delivery. If most OAA programs serve primarily older adults with middle to low incomes or those with minimal social support networks, as data suggest the congregate meal programs do, to what extent would eligibility criteria be needed? How much could participants contribute before the contribution became a barrier? The debate about providing services based on need rather than age will no doubt continue.

SERVING A NEW GENERATION OF OLDER ADULTS: PLANNING FOR TWENTY-FIRST-CENTURY AGING

We have attempted to illustrate in this text that policy is inextricably linked to the creation of programs that, in turn, directly support the physical, social, and psychological well-being of older adults. By thinking first about social policy at the federal, state, or local level, those working with older adults can advocate for positive changes in the way our communities can be transformed into Livable Communities that are "good places to grow up and grow old" (WHCOA, 2006, p. 58). The WHCOA recommended a new Title within the OAA called "Community Preparedness for an Aging Population" that would fund programs that help communities address the needs of an aging population. Specifically, it recommended that the new Title would create and fund programs that promote "community preparedness" for today and tomorrow's aging population. The new Title would support AAAs to be the liaison to help cities, counties, and tribal councils as well as the private/nonprofit sectors to address the needs of older adults in the areas of housing and transportation, health, human services, public safety, recreation, and workforce development. This is needed since every aspect of a community will be directly and dramatically impacted by an aging population. The goal is to ensure that America's communities are good places to grow up and grow old (p. 58). Aging network professionals can play a leadership role in promoting and participating in initiatives that support the Livable Community movement. Collaborative partnerships across federal, state, and local entities will be critical in creating communities that are "livable" for persons of all ages (National Association of Area Agencies on Aging, 2011b).

Although the suggestion to create a new Title within the OAA that would support livable community initiatives was not included in the 2006 amendments to the OAA, it is reflective of the importance of the connections between policy, programs, and serving the daily needs of older adults. At the program delivery level, the challenge that aging professionals have always faced, and will continue to face, is how to change the way services are delivered to meet the needs of a new cohort in a new era. As we discussed in Chapter 1, the new cohort—the baby boomers—is different in a number of ways. But what about the new era that will emerge in the next century? We will experience societal changes related to the way we interact with one another and the way we do business. Consider the influence technology has had on our lives and will have in the future. Technology of all types holds great promise in helping people of all ages with various functional limitations to live more independently in our communities. The central role that technology now occupies in our lives will challenge professionals to consider ways to use technology in meeting the social, psychological, and physical needs of older adults. How can technology—from smart-phones to automated robots—be used to deliver information or services? To provide information and referral? To reach those who are socially isolated?

A new era will also bring about changes in how we define and redefine what it means to be old. Former president George Bush, at age 73, jumped from an airplane (with a parachute, of course!). Dorothy Custer, 100 years old, was a guest on the Tonight Show with Jay Leno (Vickers, 2012). These are not the activities that come to mind when thinking about the normative behaviors of older adults! Although these activities are not reflective of the behaviors of most older adults, perhaps the importance of these behaviors lies in their symbolism. They make us rethink what we can and cannot do in our old age.

A new era will also give us an opportunity to redefine the timing of our entry into life course transitions (Atchley, 1997). For example, the timing of entering and leaving the workforce, of entering into lifelong partnerships and having children, and of pursuing educational opportunities is changing. How will the aging network respond to these changes? Our challenge will be to make sure that the programs and services we offer to older adults will evolve along with the social changes we encounter in the coming years.

> We should not approach the challenge of aging with fear and apprehension, but rather with creative foresight, optimism, and a sense of determination. (WHCOA, 2006, p. 23)

References

AARP. (1985). *The right place at the right time: A guide to long-term care choices.* Washington, DC: Author.

AARP. (1990). *Nursing home life: A guide for residents and family.* Washington, DC: Author.

AARP. (2003). *Time and money: An in-depth look at 45+ volunteers and donors.* Retrieved December 19, 2006 from http://assets.aarp.org/rgcenter/general/multic_2003.pdf

AARP. (2005). *Beyond 50.05: A report to the nation on livable communities creating environments for successful aging.* Retrieved August 11, 2006 from http://assets.aarp.org/rgcenter/il/beyond_50_communities.pdf

AARP. (2006). *We can do better: Lessons learned from protecting older persons in disasters.* Retrieved March 3, 2007 from http://assets.aarp.org/rgcenter/il/better.pdf

AARP. (2008a). *Legal needs of older Ohioans: A 2008 survey.* Washington, DC: AARP, Knowledge Management and Pro Seniors.

AARP. (2008b). *National Rural Electric Cooperative Association. Winner: 2008 AARP best employers for workers over 50.* Retrieved from http://www.aarp.org/work/employee-benefits/info-09-2008/national_rural_electric_2008.html

AARP. (2012a). *Continuing care retirement communities: What they are and how they work.* Retrieved from http://www.aarp.org/relationships/caregiving-resource-center/info-09-2010/ho_continuing_care_retirement_communities.html

AARP. (2012b). *GrandFacts: National fact sheet for grandparents and other relatives raising children.* Retrieved from http://www.aarp.org/content/dam/aarp/relationships/friends-family/grandfacts/grandfacts-national.pdf

AARP Foundation. (2006). *Senior legal hotlines annual report 2005.* Retrieved from http://www.legalhotlines.org/standards/files/senior_hotline_annual_report_2005.doc

AARP Public Policy Institute. (2010). *Fact sheet. Social Security: A key retirement income source for minorities.* Retrieved from http://assets.aarp.org/rgcenter/ppi/econ-sec/fs201-economic.pdf

AARP Public Policy Institute. (2011). *State housing profiles 2011: United States.* Retrieved from http://assets.aarp.org/rgcenter/ppi/liv-com/AARP-HouProf_2011-USs.pdf

Abend-Wein, M. (1991). Medicaid's effect on the elderly: How reimbursement policy affects priority in the nursing home. *Journal of Applied Gerontology, 10*(1), 71–87.

Abrahams, R., Nonnenkamp, L., Dunn, S., Mehta, S., & Woodard, P. (1988). Case management in the social/health maintenance organization. *Generations, 12*(5), 39–43.

Abramson, T. A., Trejo, L., & Lai, D. W. L. (2002). Culture and mental health: Providing appropriate services for a diverse older population. *Generations, 16*(1), 21–27.

Acierno, R., Rheingold, A. A., Resnick, H. S., & Kilpatrick, D. G. (2004). Predictors of fear of crime in older adults. *Journal of Anxiety Disorders, 18*(3), 385–396. doi:10.1016/s0887-6185(03)00012-4

ACTION. (1990a). *Foster Grandparent Program 25th anniversary 1965–1990: Bridging the generations of need.* Washington, DC: Author.

ACTION. (1990b). *Senior Companion Program: Serving with compassion, caring as friends.* Washington, DC: Author.

ACTION. (1992). *Retired Senior Volunteer Program: A part of ACTION.* Washington, DC: Author.

Adams, J. S. (1965). Inequity in social exchange. In L. Berkowitz (Ed.), *Advances in experimental social psychology* (Vol. 2, pp. 267–300). New York, NY: Academic Press.

Aday, R. H. (2003). *Identifying important linkages between successful aging and senior center participa-tion*. Retrieved June 18, 2006 from http://www.aoa.gov/prof/agingnet/Seniorcenters/NISC.pdf

Aday, R. H., Kehoe, G. C., & Farney, L. A. (2006). Impact of senior center friendships on aging women who live alone. *Journal of Women & Aging, 18*(1), 57–73.

Adelman, M., Gurevitch, J., de Vries, B., & Blando, J. A. (2006). Openhouse: Community building and research in the LGBT aging population. In D. Kimmel, T. Rose, & S. David (Eds.), *Lesbian, gay, bisexual, and transgender aging: Research and clinical perspectives* (pp. 247–264). New York, NY: Columbia University Press.

Adler, G., & Hilber, D. (2008). Will the types of jobs being created enable older workers to keep work-ing? *Journal of Workplace Behavioral Health, 23*(1–2), 71–87.

Adler, G., Kuskowski, M. A., & Mortimer, J. (1995). Respite use in dementia patients. *Clinical Gerontologist, 15*(3), 17–30.

Administration for Children and Families. (2011a). *Administration for Children and Families: All-purpose Table: FY 2010–2012: Low income home energy assistance program*. Retrieved from http://www.acf.hhs.gov/sites/default/files/assets/fy2012apt.pdf

Administration for Children and Families. (2011b). *Low income home energy assistance program: Fact sheet*. Retrieved from http://www.acf.hhs.gov/programs/ocs/liheap/about/factsheet.html

Administration on Aging. (1983). *An evaluation of the nutritional services for the elderly: Vol. 3. Descriptive report* (OHDS Pub. No. 83–20917). Washington, DC: Government Printing Office.

Administration on Aging. (1995a). *Elder facts: The Administration on Aging*. Washington, DC: Author.

Administration on Aging. (1995b). *Long-term care ombudsman annual report: Fiscal year 1995*. Washington, DC: Author.

Administration on Aging. (1995c). *Title III state and community programs*. Retrieved July 30, 2001 from http://www.aoa.dhhs.gov/aoa/pages/titleiii.html

Administration on Aging. (1997). *Targeting of Older Americans Act services: Issues for reauthorization*. Washington, DC: Author.

Administration on Aging. (1998). *The national elder abuse incidence study: Final report*. Retrieved July 15, 2001 from http://www.aoa.gov/AoARoot/AoA_Programs/Elder_Rights/Elder_Abuse/docs/ABuse Report_Full.pdf

Administration on Aging. (2000). *AoA awards $1 million to help end health disparities among older racial and ethnic minority populations*. Retrieved September 16, 2001 from www.aoa.dhhs.gov/ pr/ Pr2000/healthdisparities.html

Administration on Aging. (2001a). *1998 state performance reports*. Retrieved August 1, 2001 from http://www.aoa.dhhs.gov/napis/98spr/tables/tables1.html

Administration on Aging. (2001b). *Achieving cultural competence: A guidebook for providers of services to older Americans and their families*. Retrieved January 22, 2007 from http://archive.org/stream/ achievingcultura00admi#page/n1/mode/2up

Administration on Aging. (2003). *Administration on Aging Nutrition Services Incentive Program fre-quently asked questions*. Retrieved January 1, 2007 from http://www.aoa.gov/eldfam/Nutrition/ NSIP%20FreqAskedQs%20fb%2007%2003rev.pdf

Administration on Aging. (2004). *Guidelines for culturally and/or linguistically competent agencies*. Retrieved January 22, 2007, from http://www.aoa.gov/prof/adddiv/progmod/addiv_progmod_ section_two.asp

Administration on Aging. (2005). *2005 National Ombudsman Reporting System Data Tables, Top 20 complaints by category for board and care facilities (FFY 1996–2005)*. Retrieved February 13, 2007 from http://www.aoa.gov/AoA_programs/Elder_Rights/Ombudsman/National_State_Data/2005/ Index.aspx

Administration on Aging. (2006a). *Administration on Aging Reauthorization of the Older Americans Act technical clarifying amendments*. Retrieved February 13, 2007 from http://www.aoa.gov/about/ legbudg/oaa/eNews_Technical_Amendments.doc

Administration on Aging. (2006b). *Evidence based disease prevention grants program*. Retrieved January 23, 2007 from http://www.aoa.gov/AoA_programs/HPW/Evidence_Based/index.aspx

Administration on Aging. (2006c). *Older Americans Act cost sharing provisions OAA Section 315(a)*. Retrieved February 13, 2007 from http://www.aoa.gov/about/legbudg/oaa/Cost%20Sharing%20statute.doc

Administration on Aging. (2007). *Justification of estimates for appropriations committees*. Retrieved February 25, 2007 from http://www.aoa.gov/aoaroot/about/Budget/DOCS/FY_2013_AoA_CJ_Feb_2012.pdf

Administration on Aging. (2009a). AoA expands volunteer opportunities for older Americans. *AoA News*. Retrieved from http://www.epa.gov/aging/press/othernews/2009/2009_0605_ons_1.htm

Administration on Aging. (2009b). *Facts: The Lifespan Respite Care Program*. Retrieved from http://www.aoa.gov/aoaroot/Press_Room/Products_Materials/fact/pdf/Lifespan_Respite_Care_Program.pdf

Administration on Aging. (2010a). *Compendium of AoA discretionary grants completed in FY2010*. Retrieved from http://www.aoa.gov/aoaroot/grants/Compendium/docs/FY2010_AoA__Grant_Compendium.pdf

Administration on Aging. (2010b). *Fiscal year 2010 ombudsman, Table a-8: Staff and volunteers for FY 2010*. Retrieved from http://www.aoa.gov/AoA_programs/Elder_Rights/Ombudsman/National_State_Data/2010/docs/2010ATables.xls

Administration on Aging. (2010c). *Fiscal year 2010 ombudsman, Table b-3: Complaint categories for nursing facilities FY 2010*. Retrieved from http://www.aoa.gov/AoA_programs/Elder_Rights/Ombudsman/National_State_Data/2010/docs/2010BTables.xls

Administration on Aging. (2010d). *A profile of older Americans: 2010*. Retrieved from http://www.aoa.gov/aoaroot/aging_statistics/Profile/2010/docs/2010profile.pdf

Administration on Aging. (2010e). *A toolkit for serving diverse communities*. Retrieved from http://www.aoa.gov/AoA_programs/Tools_Resources/DOCS/AoA_DiversityToolkit_Full.pdf

Administration on Aging. (2011a). *Alzheimer's disease demonstration grants to states: Volunteer respite programs: Resources to establish and sustain volunteer respite programs*. Retrieved from http://www.aoa.gov/AoARoot/AoA_Programs/HPW/Alz_Grants/docs/VolunteerRespitePrograms.pdf

Administration on Aging. (2011b). *A profile of older Americans: 2011*. Retrieved from http://www.aoa.gov/aoaroot/aging_statistics/Profile/2011/docs/2011profile.pdf

Administration on Aging. (2011c). *Civic engagement initiative*. Retrieved from http://www.aoa.gov/AoARoot/AoA_Programs/Special_Projects/Civic_Engagement/index.aspx

Administration on Aging. (2011d). *FY 2009 profile of state Older Americans Act programs: US: Part F. Service profile: Table 10. Focal points and senior centers*. Retrieved from http://www.aoa.gov/AoARoot/Program_Results/SPR/2009/index.aspx#national

Administration on Aging. (2011e). *Historical evolution of programs for older Americans*. Retrieved August 6, 2012, from http://www.aoa.gov/AoARoot/AoA_Programs/OAA/resources/History.aspx

Administration on Aging. (2011f). *Lifespan Respite Care Program*. Retrieved from http://aoa.gov/AoARoot/AoA_Programs/HCLTC/LRCP/index.aspx

Administration on Aging. (2011g). *Table 6a. Title III service expenditures for selected services: FY 2010*. Retrieved from http://aoa.gov/AoARoot/Program_Results/SPR/2010/Index.aspx

Administration on Aging (2012a). *AoA funded resource centers: Information for professionals*. Retrieved Jun 12, 2012 from http://www.aoa.gov/AoARoot/Resource_Centers/Professionals.aspx

Administration on Aging (2012b). *AoA reauthorization targeted changes*. Retrieved from http://www.aoa.gov/AoAroot/AoA_Programs/OAA/Reauthorization/Target_Change.aspx

Administration on Aging. (2012c). *Disease prevention and health promotion services (OAA Title IIID)*. Retrieved from http://www.aoa.gov/AoARoot/AoA_Programs/HPW/Title_IIID/index.aspx

Administration on Aging. (2012d). *Frequently asked questions: Targeting*. Retrieved from http://www.aoa.gov/AoARoot/AoA_Programs/OAA/resources/Faqs.aspx#English

Administration on Aging. (2012e). *FY 2012 AoA budget statement*. Retrieved from http://aoa.gov/AoARoot/About/Budget/DOCS/FY2012_AoA_Budget_508.xls

Administration on Aging. (2012f). *Health, prevention, and wellness programs*. Retrieved September 1, 2012, from http://www.aoa.gov/AoARoot/AoA_Programs/HPW/index.aspx

Administration on Aging. (2012g). *National family caregiver support program (OAA Title IIIE)*. Retrieved from http://aoa.gov/AoARoot/AoA_Programs/HCLTC/Caregiver/index.aspx

Administration on Aging (2012h). *Nutrition services (OAA Title IIIC)*. Retrieved from http://www.aoa.gov/AoA_programs/HCLTC/Nutrition_Services/index.aspx

Administration on Aging. (2012i). *Services for Native Americans (OAA Title VI)*. Retrieved from http://aoa.gov/AoARoot/AoA_Programs/HCLTC/Native_Americans/index.aspx

Administration on Aging. (n.d.-a). *Facts: Long-Term Care Ombudsman Program*. Retrieved from http://www.aoa.gov/aoaroot/Press_Room/Products_Materials/fact/pdf/LTC_Ombudsman_Program_2011.pdf

Administration on Aging. (n.d.-b). *FY 2004 profile of United States OAA Program*. Retrieved January 1, 2007 from http://www.aoa.gov/prof/agingnet/NAPIS/SPR/2004SPR/profiles/US.pdf

Administration on Aging. (n.d.-c). *FY 2010 profile of state OAA Programs: United States: Part F service profile*. Retrieved May 1, 2012 from http://aoa.gov/AoARoot/Program_Results/SPR/2010/Index.aspx

Administration on Aging. (n.d.-d). *Latest news: President's council on physical fitness and sports 50th anniversary partner invitation to get America moving*. Retrieved January 29, 2007 from http://www.aoa.gov/youcan/news/news_pf.asp

Administration on Aging. (n.d.-e). *State program reports 2010, client totals: All services* [Data file]. Retrieved from http://www.agidnet.org/DataGlance/SPR/

Administration on Aging. (n.d.-f). *State program reports 2010, client totals: Ethnicity and race* [Data file]. Retrieved from http://www.agidnet.org/DataGlance/SPR/

Administration on Aging. (n.d.-g). *State program reports 2010, counts by registered service total: All services*. [Data file]. Retrieved from http://www.agidnet.org/DataGlance/SPR/

Administration on Aging. (n.d.-h). *State program reports 2010, unit totals: Title III services* [Data file]. Retrieved from http://www.agidnet.org/DataGlance/SPR/

Administration on Aging. (n.d.-i). *Table 4a. Clusters 1 and 2—Service units provided for selected services under Title III of OAA: Fiscal year: 10/01/2009–09/30/2010*. Retrieved May 1, 2012 from http://aoa.gov/AoARoot/Program_Results/SPR/2010/Index.aspx

Administration on Aging. (n.d.-j). *Table 4b. Clusters 3—Service units provided for selected services under Title III of OAA: Fiscal year: 10/01/2009–09/30/2010*. Retrieved May 1, 2012 from http://aoa.gov/AoARoot/Program_Results/SPR/2010/Index.aspx

Administration on Aging. (n.d.-k). *Title VI services by tribal organization* [Data file]. Retrieved August 11, 2012 http://www.agidnet.org/CustomTables/NA/Results/

Adopt-a-Native-Elder Program. (n.d.). *Elder support activities*. Retrieved from http://www.anelder.org/index.php?ID = 885&XID = 885:917:0:0:0

Advancing Excellence. (n.d). *Advancing excellence in Americas' nursing homes*. Retrieved from http://www.nhqualitycampaign.org

Age Discrimination in Employment Act of 1967, 29 U.S.C. § 621 et seq. (1967), as amended 1986.

Agency for Integrated Care. (n.d.-a). *Aged Care TransiTION (ACTION) Project*. Retrieved from http://www.aic.sg/page.aspx?id = 721

Agency for Integrated Care. (n.d.-b). *Mission & core values*. Retrieved from http://www.aic.sg/page.aspx?id = 127

Aging and Disability Resource Center Technical Assistance Exchange. (2010). *Summary findings from selected Aging and Disability Resource Center (ADRC) evaluations*. Retrieved from http://www.adrc-tae.org/tiki-index.php?page = GranteeEfforts

Aiken, L. H. (1989). An agenda for the year 2000. In M. D. Mezey, J. E. Lynaugh, & M. M. Cartier (Eds.), *Nursing homes and nursing care: Lessons from the teaching nursing homes* (pp. 145–156). New York, NY: Springer.

Akkerman, R. L., & Ostwald, S. K. (2004). Reducing anxiety in Alzheimer's disease family caregivers: The effectiveness of a nine-week cognitive-behavioral intervention. *American Journal of Alzheimer's Disease and Other Dementias, 19,* 117–123.

Alameda County Library. (2009). *Library services for older adults*. Retrieved from http://www.aclibrary.org/services/seniorServices/pdf/Ext10_SOS_Rev9_09.pdf

Alexander, G. J. (1991). Time for a new law on health care advanced directives. *Hastings Law Journal, 42,* 755–778.

Alkema, G. E., Reyes, J. Y., & Wilber, K. H. (2006). Characteristics associated with home- and community-based service utilization for Medicare managed care consumers. *The Gerontologist, 46*(2), 173–182.

Allen, J. E. (2011). *Nursing home administration* (6th ed.). New York, NY: Springer.

Alliance of Information and Referral Systems. (2005). *Standards for professional information and referral* (5th ed.). Seattle, WA: Author. Retrieved January 15, 2007 from http://www.airs.org/documents/StandardsFifthEdition.pdf

Alliance of Information and Referral Systems. (2012). *Nationwide status.* Retrieved from http://211us.org/status.htm

Altus, D. E., Xaverius, P. K., Mathews, R. M., & Kosloski, K. D. (2002). Evaluating the impact of elder cottage housing on residents and their hosts. *Journal of Clinical Geropsychology, 8,* 117–137.

Alzheimer's Association. (2011). Alzheimer's disease facts and figures. *Alzheimer's & Dementia, 7*(2), 208–244.

Alzheimer's Association. (2012a). *Alzheimer's and dementia caregiver center: Care options.* Retrieved from http://www.alz.org/care/alzheimers-dementia-care-housing.asp

Alzheimer's Association. (2012b). 2012 *Alzheimer's disease facts and figures.* Retrieved from http://www.alz.org/downloads/Facts_Figures_2012.pdf

Alzheimer's Association. (n.d.). *About us.* Retrieved June 16, 2011 from http://www.alz.org/about_us_about_us_.asp

Amborgi, D. M., & Leonard, F. (1988). The impact of nursing home admission agreements on resident autonomy. *The Gerontologist, 28*(Suppl.), 82–89.

American Association for Long Term Care Insurance. (2008). *Long-term care insurance facts—Statistics.* Retrieved from http://www.aaltci.org/long-term-care-insurance/learning-center/fast-facts.php

American Association of Homes and Services for the Aging. (1988). *Directory of members.* Washington, DC: Author.

American Elder Care Research Organization. (2011a). *Federal tax credit for elderly dependent care.* Retrieved form http://www.payingforseniorcare.com/longtermcare/resources/dependent_care_tax_credit.html

American Elder Care Research Organization. (2011b). *State tax credits for dependent care expenses.* Retrieved form http://www.payingforseniorcare.com/longtermcare/resources/dependent_care_tax_credit.html

American Health Care Association. (2011). *The state long-term health care sector: Characteristics, utilization, and government funding: 2011 update.* Retrieved from http://www.ahcancal.org/research_data/trends_statistics/Documents/ST_rpt_STStats2011_20110906_FINAL_web.pdf

American Health Care Association. (2012). *LTC stats: Nursing facility operational characteristics report.* Retrieved from http://www.ahcancal.org/research_data/oscar_data/Nursing%20Facility%20Operational%20Characteristics/OperationalCharacteristicsReport_Mar2012.pdf

American Institutes for Research. (2010). *Characteristics of English literacy participants in adult education.* Retrieved from http://www.nrsweb.org/docs/ESL_Fastfacts_CEL_Tagged.pdf

American Psychological Association. (2002). *Guidelines on multi-cultural education, training, research, practice, and organizational change for psychologists.* Washington, DC: Author.

American Public Human Services Association. (1998). *The national elder abuse incidence study, 1998: Final report.* Washington, DC: The National Center on Elder Abuse at The American Public Human Services Association. Retrieved from http://www.aoa.gov/eldfam/Elder_Rights/Elder_Abuse/AbuseReport_Full.pdf

American Public Transportation Association. (2003). *Mobility for the aging population.* Retrieved October 15, 2006 from http://www.apta.com/resources/reportsandpublications/Documents/seniors.pdf

American Public Transportation Association. (2005). *Safe, accountable, flexible, efficient transportation equity act—A legacy for users.* Retrieved October 9, 2006 from http://www.apta.com/government_ affairs/ safetea_lu/documents/brochure/pdf

American Public Transportation Association. (2011). *APTA primer on transit funding: The Safe, Accountable, Flexible, Efficient Transportation Equity Act: A legacy for users, extensions, and other related laws, FY 2004 Through FY 2011.* Retrieved from http://www.apta.com/gap/policyresearch/ Documents/Primer_SAFETEA_LU_Funding.pdf

Americans With Disabilities Act, 42 U.S.C. § 12101 et seq. (1990).

America's Health Insurance Plans. (2004a). *Guide to long-term care insurance.* Retrieved from http:// www.pueblo.gsa.gov/cic_text/health/ltc/guide.pdf

America's Health Insurance Plans. (2004b). *Research findings: Long-term care insurance in 2002.* Retrieved from http://www.ahipresearch.org/pdfs/18_LTC2002.pdf

America's Health Insurance Plans. (2012). *Who buys long-term care insurance in 2010–2011?* Retrieved from http://www.ahip.org/Issues/Long-Term-Care-Insurance.aspx

Amparano, G., & Morena, D. A. (2006, July–August). Senior mobility series: Article 4—Marking the way to greater safety. *Public Roads, 70*(1). Retrieved from http://www.fhwa.dot.gov/publications/ publicroads/index.cfm

Andersen, R. (1995). Revisiting the behavioral model and access to medical care: Does it matter? *Journal of Health and Social Behavior, 36,* 1–10.

Andersen, R., & Newman, J. (1973). Societal and individual determinants of medical care utilization in the United States. *Milbank Memorial Fund Quarterly, 51,* 95–124.

Andersen, R., & Newman, J. F. (2005). Societal and individual determinants of medical care utilization in the United States. *Milbank Quarterly, 83*(4), 1–28.

Anderson, K. A., Dabelko-Schoeny, H., & Johnson, T. D. (2012). The state of adult day services: Findings and implications from the MetLife national study of adult day services. *Journal of Applied Gerontology.* Advance online publication. doi:10.1177/0733464812447284

Anderson, K. A., Dabelko-Schoeny, H. I., & Tarrant, S. D. (2012). A constellation of concerns: Exploring the present and the future challenges for adult day services. *Home Health Care Management & Practice, 24*(3), 132–139. doi:10.1177/1084822311424595

Angelis, J. (1990). *Intergenerational service learning: Strategies for the future.* Carbondale, IL: Author.

Antoninetti, M. (2008). The difficult history of ancillary units: The obstacles and potential opportunities to increase the heterogeneity of neighborhoods and the flexibility of households in the United States. *Journal of Housing for the Elderly, 22,* 348–375.

Applebaum, R., & Wilson, N. (1988). Training needs for providing case management for the long-term care client: Lessons learned from the National Channeling Demonstration. *The Gerontologist, 28,* 172–176.

ARCH National Respite Network and Resource Center. (2011). *ARCH state respite coalitions: A compendium of fact sheets 2011 update.* Retrieved from http://www.lifespanrespite.memberlodge.org/ Resources/Documents/ARCH_State_Respite_Coalitions2011web.pdf

ARCH National Respite Network and Resource Center. (2012). *ABCs of respite: A consumer guide for family caregivers.* Retrieved from http://archrespite.org/images/ARCH/ABCsofRespite_ Updated5_12.pdf

Area Agency on Aging of Northwest Arkansas. (2012). *Transportation services.* Retrieved from http:// www.aaanwar.org/resources/show/49

Argyle, M. (1992). Receiving and giving support: Effects on relationships and well-being. *Counseling Psychology Quarterly, 5*(2), 123–133.

Arneson, B. (1994). State and federal legislation: Nonmedical homecare services. In J. Handy & C. Schuerman (Eds.), *Challenges and innovations in homecare* (pp. 53–55). San Francisco, CA: American Society on Aging.

Arnsberger, P. (2005). Best practices in care management for Asian American elders: The care of Alzheimer's disease. *Care Management Journals, 6,* 171–177.

Arriaza, P., Martin, S. S., & Csikai, E. L. (2011). An assessment of hospice bereavement programs for Hispanics. *Journal of Social Work in End-Of-Life & Palliative Care, 7*(2–3), 121–138.

Ashford, N., Bell, W. G., & Rich, T. A. (1982). *Mobility and transport for elderly and handicapped persons: Proceedings of a conference held at Churchill College, Cambridge, UK, July 1981*. New York, NY: Gordon & Breach Science.

Atchley, R. C. (1971). Retirement and leisure participation: Continuity or crisis? *The Gerontologist, 11*, 13–17.

Atchley, R. C. (1989). A continuity theory of normal aging. *The Gerontologist, 29*, 183–190.

Atchley, R. C. (1997). *Social forces and aging: An introduction to social gerontology* (8th ed.). Belmont, CA: Wadsworth.

Atchley, R. C. (1999). *Continuity and adaptation in aging: Creating positive experiences*. Baltimore, MD: Johns Hopkins University Press.

Aumann, K., Galinsky, E., Sakai, K., Brown, M., & Bond, J.T. (2010). *The elder care study: Everyday realities and wishes for change* (Families and Work Institute 2008 National study of the changing workforce). Retrieved from http://familiesandwork.org/site/research/reports/elder_care.pdf

Austin, C. (1996). Aging and long-term care. In C. Austin & R. McClelland (Eds.), *Perspectives on case management practice* (pp. 73–98). Milwaukee, WI: Families International.

Australian Institute of Health and Welfare. (2011). *Respite care*. Retrieved from http://www.aihw.gov.au/respite-care/

Baer, D. (1998). *Awareness and popularity of property tax relief programs* (AARP Public Policy Institute Research Report). Retrieved January 1, 2007 from http://assets.aarp.org/rgcenter/econ/ 9803_tax.pdf

Bailey, L. (2004). *Aging Americans: Stranded without options* (Surface Transportation Policy Project). Retrieved October 23, 2006 from http://www.apta.com/resources/reportsandpublications/ Documents/aging_stranded.pdf

Balsam, A., & Osteraas, G. (1987). Instituting a continuum of community nutrition services: Massachusetts elderly nutrition programs. *Journal of Nutrition for the Elderly, 6*(4), 51–67.

Balsam, A. L., & Rogers, B. L. (1988). *Service innovations in the elderly nutrition program: Strategies for meeting unmet needs*. Medford, MA: Tufts University School of Nutrition.

Balsam, A. L., & Rogers, B. L. (1991). Serving elders in greatest social and economic need: The challenge to the elderly nutrition program. *Journal of Aging and Social Policy, 3*(1–2), 41–55.

Banaszak-Holl, J., & Hines, M. A. (1994, November). *Organizational antecedents of nursing home staff turnover*. Paper presented at the annual meeting of the Gerontological Society of America, Atlanta, GA.

Bane, S. D., Rathbone-McCuan, E., & Galliher, J. (1994). Mental health services for the elderly in rural America. In J. Krout (Ed.), *Providing community-based services to the rural elderly* (pp. 243–266). Thousand Oaks, CA: Sage.

Barker, J. C. (2002). Neighbors, friends, and other nonkin caregivers of community-living dependent elders. *The Journals of Gerontology Series B: Psychological Sciences and Social Sciences, 57*(3), S158–S167. doi:10.1093/geronb/57.3.S158

Barocas, V. (1994). *Rethinking retirement income*. New York, NY: Conference Board.

Barrett, A. (2006, September). *Characteristics of food stamp household: Fiscal year 2005. Report submitted to the U.S. Department of Agriculture, Food and Nutrition Service* (Report No. FSP-06-CHAR). Retrieved January 7, 2007 from http://www.fns.usda.gov/ora/MENU/Published/snap/FILES/Particip ation/2005Characteristics.pdf

Barrett, A., & Schimmel, J. (2010). *Multiple service use among OAA Title III Program participants* (Mathematica Policy Research Issue Brief 3). Princeton, NJ: Mathematica Policy Research. Retrieved from http://www.nanasp.org/pdf/vulnerableseniors_ib3.pdf

Barrett, D. L., Secic, M., & Borowske, D. (2010). The Gatekeeper Program: Proactive identification and case management of at-risk older adults prevents nursing home placement, saving healthcare dollars program evaluation. *Home Healthcare Nurse, 28*, 191–197.

Barrio, C., Palinkas, L. A., Yamada, A. M., Fuentes, D., Criado, V., Garcia, P., & Jeste, D. V. (2008). Unmet needs for mental health services for Latino older adults: Perspectives from consumers, family members, advocates, and service providers. *Community Mental Health Journal, 44*, 57–74.

Bartels, S. J., Blow, F. C., Brockmann, L. M., & Van Citters, A. D. (2005). *Substance abuse and mental health among older Americans: The state of the knowledge and future directions*. Retrieved from http://gsa-alcohol.fmhi.usf.edu/Substance % 20Abuse % 20and % 20Mental % 20Health % 20 Among % 20Older % 20Adults- % 20The % 20State % 20of % 20Knowledge % 20and % 20Future % 20 Directions.pdf

Bauer, J. M., Kaiser, M. J., Anthony, P., Guigoz, Y., & Sieber, C. C. (2008). The Mini Nutritional Assessment—Its history, today's practice, and future perspectives. *Nutrition in Clinical Practice, 23*(4), 388–396. doi:10.1177/0884533608321132

Bazelon Center. (2000). *Older mental health consumers create new advocacy group.* Retrieved January 25, 2002 from http://www.webcom.com/bazelon/ourownvoice.html

Beauchamp, J., Cheh, V., Schmitz, R., Kemper, P., & Hall, J. (2008). *The effect of the Program of All-Inclusive Care for the Elderly (PACE) on quality: Final report.* Princeton, NJ: Mathematica Policy Research. Retrieved from http://www.cms.gov/Research-Statistics-Data-and-Systems/Statistics-Trends-and-Reports/Reports/downloads/Beauchamp_2008.pdf

Bechill, W. (1992). At age 27, the Older Americans Act needs spirited advocacy, understanding. *Perspective on Aging, 21,* 9–11.

Bedford, V. H. (1989). Understanding the value of siblings in old age: A proposed model. *American Behavioral Scientist, 33,* 33–44.

Bedney, B. J., Goldberg, R. B., & Josephson, K. (2010). Aging in place in naturally occurring retirement communities: Transforming aging through supportive service programs. *Journal of Housing for the Elderly, 24,* 304–321.

Behrman, J. R., Mitchell, O. S., Soo, C., & Bravo, D. (2010). *Financial literacy, schooling, and wealth accumulation* (NBER Working Paper No. 16452). Cambridge, MA: National Bureau of Economic Research. Retrieved from http://www.nber.org/papers/w16452.pdf

Belloc, N., & Breslow, L. (1972). Relationship of physical health status and health practices. *Preventive Medicine, 1,* 409–421.

Belza, B., Shumway-Cook, A., Phelan, E., Williams, B., Snyder, S., & LoGerfo, J. P. (2006). The effects of a community-based exercise program on function and health in older adults: The EnhanceFitness Program. *Journal of Applied Gerontology, 25*(4), 291–306.

Bercovitz, A., Moss, A., Sengupta, M., Park-Lee, E. Y., Jones, A., Harris-Kojetin, L. D., & Squillace, M. R. (2011). *An overview of home health aides: United States, 2007* (National Health Statistics Report No. 34). Hyattsville, MD: National Center for Health Statistics.

Berger, J., & Yang. R. (2010, April). *2009 national energy assistance survey: Final report.* Retrieved February 28, 2011, from http://www.neada.org/communications/surveys/2010-04-19NEADA_2009_ Survey_Report.pdf

Berry, G., Zarit, S., & Rabatin, V. (1991). Caregiver activity on respite and nonrespite days: A comparison of two service approaches. *The Gerontologist, 31,* 830–835.

Biegel, D., Sales, E., & Schultz, R. (1991). *Family caregiving in chronic illness.* Newbury Park, CA: Sage.

Bild, B. R., & Havingurst, R. J. (1976). Senior citizens in great cities: The case of Chicago. *The Gerontologist, 16*(1, Pt. 2), 3–88.

Binney, E., Estes, C., & Ingman, S. (1990). Medicalization, public policy and the elderly: Social services in jeopardy? *Social Science and Medicine, 30,* 761–771.

Biocca, L., & Morini, A. (2010). *The ageing population and the housing issue: An overview of trends, living patterns, and policies in the EU.* Paper presented at the 22nd International Housing Research Conference, Istanbul, Turkey. Retrieved from http://enhr2010.com/fileadmin/templates/ ENHR2010_papers_web/papers_web/WS15/WS15_530_Biocca.pdf

Biocca, L., & Morini, A. (2011). *Changing housing schemes for an ageing society: Emerging issues and design solutions.* Paper presented at the 23rd European Network for Housing Research Conference in Toulouse, France. Retrieved from http://www.enhr2011.com/sites/default/files/paper % 20 Biocca-MoriniWS15.pdf

Black, B. S., Rabins, P. V., German, P., McGuire, M., & Roca, R. (1997). Need and unmet need for mental health care among elderly public housing residents. *The Gerontologist, 37,* 717–728.

Blando, J. A. (2006). Openhouse: Community building and research in the LGBT population. In D.C. Kimmel, T. Rose, & S. David (Eds.), *Lesbian, gay, bisexual and transgender aging: Research and clinical perspectives* (pp. 247–264). New York, NY: Columbia University Press.

Blieszner, R., Roberto, K. A., Wilcox, K. L., Barham, E. J., & Winston, B. L. (2007). Dimensions of ambiguous loss in couples coping with mild cognitive impairment. *Family Relations, 56,* 196–209.

B'nai B'rith. (2012). *Senior services & housing.* Retrieved from http://www.bnaibrith.org/senior-services--housing.html

Boards of Trustees of the Federal Hospital Insurance Trust Fund and the Federal Supplementary Medical Insurance Trust Fund. (2012). *2012 annual report of the Boards of Trustees of the Federal Hospital Insurance Trust Fund and the Federal Supplementary Medical Insurance Trust Fund.* Retrieved from http://www.cms.gov/Research-Statistics-Data-and-Systems/Statistics-Trends-and-Reports/ReportsTrustFunds/Downloads/TR2012.pdf

Bond, J. T., Thompson, C., Galinsky, E., & Prottas, D. (2002). *The national study of the changing workforce.* Families and Work Institute. Retrieved January 25, 2007 from http://www.familiesandwork.org/ site/ work/workforce/2002nscw.html

Bonsang, E. (2009). Does informal care from children to their elderly parents substitute for formal care in Europe? *Journal of Health Economics, 28*(1), 143–154. doi:10.1016/j.jhealeco.2008.09.002

Boondas, J. (1991). Nursing home resident assessment classification and focused care. *Nursing and Health Care, 12,* 308–312.

Borrayo, E. A., Salmon, J. R., Polivka, L., & Dunlap, B. D. (2002). Utilization across the continuum of long-term care services. *The Gerontologist, 42,* 603–612.

Borson S., Loebel, P., Kitchell. M., Domoto, S., & Hyde, T. (1997). Psychiatric assessments of nursing home residents under OBRA-87: Should PASARR be reformed? *Journal of the American Geriatrics Society, 45,* 1173–1181.

Boult, C., Giddens, J., Frey, K., Reider, L., & Novak, T. (2009). *Guided care: A new nurse-physician partnership in chronic care.* New York, NY: Springer.

Boult, C., Reider, L., Frey, K., Leff, B., Boyd, C. M., Wolff, J. L., . . . Sharfstein, D. (2008). Early effects of "Guided Care" on the quality of health care for multimorbid older persons: A cluster-randomized controlled trial. *Journal of Gerontology: Medical Sciences, Series A, 63,* 321–327.

Bourgeois, M. S., Schulz, R., & Burgio, L. (1996). Interventions for caregivers of patients with Alzheimer's disease: A review and analysis of content, process, and outcomes. *International Journal of Aging and Human Development, 43,* 35–92.

Bowen, D. J., Andersen, M. R., & Urban, N. (2000). Volunteerism in a community-based sample of women aged 50 to 80 years. *Journal of Applied Social Psychology, 30,* 1829–1842.

Bowers, B. J. (1988). Family perceptions of care in a nursing home. *The Gerontologist, 27,* 4–8.

Bowman, S. (2007). Low economic status is associated with suboptimal intakes of nutritious foods by adults in the National Health and Nutrition Examination Survey 1999–2002. *Nutrition Research, 27*(9), 515–523. doi:10.1016/j.nutres.2007.06.010

Boyd, C. M., Shadmi, E., Conwell, L. J., Griswold, M., Leff, B., Brager, R., . . . Boult, C. (2008). A pilot test of the effect of guided care on the quality of primary care experiences for multi-morbid older adults. *Journal of General Internal Medicine, 23*(5), 536–542.

Brabazon, K., & Disch, R. (Eds.). (1997). *Intergenerational approaches in aging: Implications for education, policy and practice.* New York, NY: Haworth.

Brandon, E. (2009). Forget tuition: How retirees can attend college for free. *U.S. News & World Report.* Retrieved from http://money.usnews.com/money/articles/2009/04/20/forget-tuition-how-retirees-can-attend-college-for-free

Bratter, B., & Freeman, E. (1990). The maturing of peer counseling. *Generations, 14*(1), 49–52.

Brawley, L. R., Rejeski, W. J., & King, A. C. (2003). Promoting physical activity for older adults: The challenges for changing behavior. *American Journal of Preventive Medicine, 25*(3Sii), 172–183.

Brehm, J. W. (1966). *A theory of psychological reactance.* New York, NY: Academic Press.

Brehm, S. S., & Brehm, J. W. (1981). *Psychological reactance: A theory of freedom and control.* New York, NY: Academic Press.

Briggs, E. (1992). *Nutrition and the black elderly.* San Diego, CA: San Diego State University, National Resource Center on Minority Aging Populations.

Brigl, B. (2001). *Testimony to the Commission on Affordable Housing and Health Facility Needs for Seniors in the 21st century.* Retrieved January 11, 2007 from http://govinfo.library.unt.edu/ seniorscommission/pages/hearings/011107/brignl.html

Brody, E. M. (1981). Women in the middle and family help to older people. *The Gerontologist, 21,* 471–480.

Brody, E. M. (1985). Parent care as a normative family stress. *The Gerontologist, 25,* 19–29.

Brossoie, N., Roberto, K. A., Willis-Walton, S., & Reynolds, S. (2010). *Report on baby boomers and older adults: Information and service needs.* Retrieved from http://www.gerontology.vt.edu/docs/n4a%20Report.pdf

Brotman, S., Ryan, B., & Cormier, R. (2003). The health and service needs of gay and lesbian elders and their families in Canada. *The Gerontologist, 43,* 192–202.

Brown, C. A., McGuire, F. A., & Voelkl, J. (2008). The link between successful aging and serious leisure. *International Journal of Aging and Human Development, 66*(1), 73–95. doi:10.2190/AG.66.1.d

Brown, G. (2011). Lifelong learning with no tuition. *AARP Bulletin.* Retrieved from http://www.aarp.org/personal-growth/life-long-learning/info-12-2011/lifelong-learning-with-no-tuition-oh.print.html

Brown, J., Hassett, K., & Smetters, K. (2005). *Top ten myths of social security reform.* Retrieved January 26, 2007 from http://crr.bc.edu/working-papers/top-ten-myths-of-social-security-reform/

Brown, K. E. (2010). *Older Americans Act: Preliminary observations on services requested by seniors and challenges in providing assistance* (GAO-10-1024T). Washington, DC: U.S. Government Accountability Office. Retrieved from http://www.gao.gov/new.items/d101024t.pdf

Brown, R. (1989). *The rights of older persons* (2nd ed.). Carbondale: Southern Illinois University Press.

Brown, T. H., & Warner, D. F. (2008). Divergent pathways? Racial/ethnic differences in older women's labor force withdrawal. *Journal of Gerontology: Social Sciences, 63B,* 122–134.

Brubaker, T., & Roberto, K. A. (1993). Family life education for the later years. *Family Relations, 42,* 212–221.

Bryant, L. L, Altpeter, M., & Whitelaw, N. A. (2006). Evaluation of health promotion programs for older adults: An introduction. *Journal of Applied Gerontology, 25*(3), 197–213.

Buchanan, R. J., Choi, M., Wang, S., Hysunsu, J., & Graber, D. (2005). Nursing home residents with Alzheimer's disease in special care units compare to other residents with Alzheimer's disease. *Dementia, 4*(2), 249–267.

Buchner, D. M., Cress, M. E., de Lateur, B. J., Esselman, P. C., Margherita, A. J., Price, R., & Wagner, E. H. (1997). The effect of strength and endurance training on gait, balance, fall risk, and health services use in community-living older adults. *Journal of Gerontology: Medical Sciences, 52A,* M218–224.

Buchner, D. M., & Pearson, D. C. (1989). Factors associated with participation in a community senior health promotion program: A pilot study. *American Journal of Public Health, 79,* 775–777.

Bureau of Labor Statistics. (2010a). *Labor force statistics from the Current Population Survey. Table 14. Employed persons in nonagricultural industries by age, sex, race, and Hispanic or Latino ethnicity.* Retrieved from ftp://ftp.bls.gov/pub/special.requests/lf/aa2010/pdf/cpsaat14.pdf

Bureau of Labor Statistics. (2010b). *Labor force statistics from the Current Population Survey. Table 15. Employed persons in agriculture and related and in nonagricultural industries by age, sex, and class of worker.* Retrieved from ftp://ftp.bls.gov/pub/special.requests/lf/aa2010/pdf/cpsaat14.pdf

Bureau of Labor Statistics. (2010c). *Labor force statistics from the Current Population Survey. Table 22. Persons at work in nonagricultural industries by age, sex, race, Hispanic or Latino ethnicity, marital status, and usual full- or part-time status.* Retrieved from ftp://ftp.bls.gov/pub/special.requests/lf/aa2010/pdf/cpsaat22.pdf

Bureau of Labor Statistics. (2010d). *Retirement benefits. March 2010: Private industry. Retirement benefits: Access, participation, and take-up rates data table.* Retrieved from http://www.bls.gov/ncs/ebs/benefits/2010/ownership/private/table02a.htm

Bureau of Labor Statistics. (2011a). *Employee benefits in the United States: March 2011.* Retrieved from http://www.bls.gov/ncs/ebs/sp/ebnr0017.txt

Bureau of Labor Statistics. (2011b). *Persons not in the labor force by desire and availability for work, age, and sex.* Retrieved from http://www.bls.gov/web/empsit/cpseea38.htm

Burger, S. G., Fraser, V., Hunt, S., & Frank, B. (1996). *Nursing homes: Getting good care there.* San Luis Obispo, CA: Impact.

Burgess, M. A. R., & Applebaum, R. (2009). The aging network in today's economy. *Generations, 33*(3), 40–46.

Burkhardt, J. (2005). *Seniors benefit from transportation coordination partnerships—A toolbox: Promising practices from the aging network.* Washington, DC. Retrieved October 23, 2006 from http://www.aoa.gov/prof/ transportation/transportation.asp

Burnette, D. (1999). Custodial grandparents in Latino families: Patterns of service use and predictors of unmet needs. *Social Work, 44*(1), 22–34.

Burtless G. (2006). Social norms, rules of thumb, and retirement: Evidence for rationality in retirement planning. In: K. W. Schaie & L. L. Carstensen (Eds.), *Social structures, self-regulation, and aging* (pp. 123–160). New York: Springer.

Butler, S. S. (2006). Evaluating the senior companion program. *Journal of Gerontological Social Work, 47*(1–2), 45–70. doi:10.1300/J083v47n01_05

Butrica, B. A., Johnson, E. W., & Zedlewski, S. R. (2009).Volunteer dynamics of older Americans. *The Journals of Gerontology Series B: Psychological Sciences and Social Sciences, 64,* 644–655. doi:10.1093/geronb/gbn042

Caffrey, C., Sengupta, M., Moss, A., Harris-Kojetin, L., & Valverde, R. (2011). *Home health care and discharged hospice care patients: United States, 2000 and 2007* (National Health Statistics Report No. 38). Hyattsville, MD: National Center for Health Statistics.

Cahill, S., South, K., & Spade, J. (2000). *Outing age: Public policy issues affecting gay, lesbian, bisexual and transgender elders.* National Gay and Lesbian Task Force. Retrieved November 1, 2006 from http://www.aarp.org/content/dam/aarp/livable-communities/act/transportation/NCST-Seniors-Benefit-from-Transportation-Coordination-Partnerships-Toolbox-AARP.pdf

Cain, M. (1996). Health maintenance organizations. In L. A. Vitt, J. K. Siegenthaler, N. E. Culter, & S. Golant (Eds.), *Encyclopedia of financial gerontology* (pp. 243–248). Westport, CT: Greenwood.

Calsyn, R. J., Burger, G. K., & Roades, L. A. (1996). Cross-validation of differences between users and non-users of senior centers. *Journal of Social Service Research, 21*(3), 39–56.

Calsyn, R. J., & Winter, J. P. (1999). Who attends senior centers? *Journal of Social Service Research, 26*(2), 53–69.

Calsyn, R. J., & Winter, J. P. (2001). Predicting four types of service needs in older adults. *Evaluation and Program Planning, 24,* 157–166.

Campus Y UNC Chapel Hill. (n.d.). *Youth for elderly service.* Retrieved from http://campus-y.unc.edu/committees/elderly-care/youth-elderly-service

Cantor, M. H. (1979). Neighbors and friends: An overlooked resource in the informal support system. *Research on Aging, 1,* 434–463.

Cantor, M. H. (1983). Strain among caregivers: A study of experience in the United States. *The Gerontologist, 23,* 597–604.

Cantor, M. H. (1991). Family and community: Changing roles in an aging society. *The Gerontologist, 31,* 337–346.

Cappelli, P., & Novelli, W. (2010). *Managing the older worker: How to prepare for the new organizational order.* Boston, MA: Harvard Business Review Press.

Capretta, J. (2007). *Long-term care insurance partnerships: New choices for consumers—Potential savings for federal and state government.* AHIP Center for Policy and Research. Retrieved February 2, 2007 from http://www.ahipresearch.org/PDFs/IssueBriefSavingsfromExpandedLTC Partnerships1-24-2007.pdf

Carder, P., Morgan, L. A., & Eckert, K. J. (2006). Small board-and-care homes in the age of assisted living. *Generations, 29*(4), 24–31.

Caregiver Connection. (2010). *Caregivers in the workplace: Best practices for workers with elder caregiving responsibilities.* Retrieved from http://www.whocaresforyou.org/Libraries/Downloads/Caregivers_in_the_Workplace_FINAL_1.sflb.ashx

Carlton-LaNey, I. (1991). Some considerations of the rural elderly blacks' underuse of social services. *Journal of Gerontological Social Work, 16,* 3–16.

Carrion, I. V., Park, N. S., & Lee, B. S. (2012). Hospice use among African Americans, Asians, Hispanics, and Whites: Implications for practice. *American Journal of Hospice and Palliative Care, 29,* 116–121.

Carter, W. B., Elward, E., Malmgren, J., Martin, M., & Larson, E. (1991). Participation in health promotion programs and research: A critical review of the literature. *The Gerontologist, 31,* 584–592.

Casado, B. L., van Vulpen, K. S., & Davis, S. L. (2011). Unmet needs for home and community-based services among frail older Americans and their caregivers. *Journal of Aging and Health, 23*(3), 529–553. doi:10.1177/0898264310387132

Caserta, M. S., & Lund D. A. (2002). Video Respite in an Alzheimer's care center: Group versus solitary viewing. *Activities, Adaptation, & Aging, 27,* 13–28.

Casey, M. M., Moscovies, I. S., Virnig, B. A., & Durham, S. B. (2005). Providing hospice care in rural areas: Challenges and strategies. *American Journal of Hospice and Palliative Care, 22,* 363–368.

Castle, N. G. (2008). State differences and facility differences in nursing home staff turnover. *Journal of Applied Gerontology, 27*(5), 609–630. doi:10.1177/0733464808319711

Castle, N. G., & Engberg, J. (2006). Organizational characteristics associated with staff turnover in nursing homes. *The Gerontologist, 46,* 62–73.

Castle, N. G., Engberg, J., Anderson, R., & Men, A. (2007). Job satisfaction of nurse aides in nursing homes: intent to leave and turnover. *The Gerontologist, 47*(2), 193–204. doi:10.1093/geront/47.2.193

Castle, N. G., & Ferguson, J. C. (2010). What is nursing home quality and how is it measured? *The Gerontologist, 50*(4), 426–442. doi:10.1093/geront/gnq052

Castle, N. G, & Myers, S. (2006). Mental health care deficiency citations in nursing homes and caregiver staffing. *Administration and Policy in Mental Health, 33,* 215–225.

Catalano, S. M. (2006). Criminal victimization, 2005. *Bureau of Justice Statistics Bulletin.* Retrieved from http://bjs.ojp.usdoj.gov/content/pub/pdf/cv05.pdf

Centaur Associates. (1986). *Report on the 502(e) experimental projects funded under Title V of the Older Americans Act.* Washington, DC: Author.

Center for Mental Health Services. (2004). *Community integration for older adults with mental illnesses: Overcoming barriers and seizing opportunities* (DHHS Pub. No. (SMA) 05-4018). Retrieved March 1, 2007 from http://www.mentalhealth.samhsa.gov/media/ken/pdf/SMA05-4018/OlderAdults.pdf

Center for Mental Health Services. (2007). *2005 CMHS Uniform Reporting System (URS) tables: Mental health national outcome measures.* Retrieved from http://download.ncadi.samhsa.gov/ken/pdf/URS_Data05/VA.pdf

Center on an Aging Society. (2004). *Cultural competence in health care.* Retrieved January 19, 2007 from http://hpi.georgetown.edu/agingsociety/pdfs/cultural.pdf

Centers for Disease Control and Prevention. (2007). *Web-based injury statistics query and reporting system.* Retrieved from http://www.cdc.gov/injury/wisqars/index.html

Centers for Disease Control and Prevention. (2009a). *The national nursing home survey: 2004 overview.* Retrieved from http://www.cdc.gov/nchs/data/series/sr_13/sr13_167.pdf

Centers for Disease Control and Prevention. (2009b). *Underlying cause of death 1999–2009. National Center for Health Statistics.* Retrieved from http://wonder.cdc.gov/ucd-icd10.html

Centers for Disease Control and Prevention. (2011). *HIV surveillance report: Diagnoses of HIV infection and AIDS in the United States and dependent areas, 2009* (HIV Surveillance Report Vol. 21). Retrieved from http://www.cdc.gov/hiv/surveillance/resources/reports/2009report/index.htm

Centers for Disease Control and Prevention. (2012a). *Health data interactive: Health and functional status.* Retrieved from http://www.cdc.gov/nchs/hdi.htm

Centers for Disease Control and Prevention. (2012b). *Health data interactive: Incontinence by gender and race.* Retrieved from http://www.cdc.gov/nchs/hdi.htm

Centers for Disease Control and Prevention. (2012c). *Health data interactive: Needing help with routine needs, ages 18+: US, 1997–2010.* Retrieved from http://www.cdc.gov/nchs/hdi.htm

Centers for Disease Control and Prevention. (2012d). *Health, United States, 2011: With special feature on socioeconomic status and health.* Retrieved from http://www.cdc.gov/nchs/hus.htm

Centers for Disease Control and Prevention. (2012e). *Underlying cause of death, 1999–2009 results.* Retrieved from http://wonder.cdc.gov/wonder/help/ucd.html

Centers for Disease Control and Prevention & Merck Company Foundation. (2007). *The state of aging and health in America.* Whitehouse Station, NJ: Merck Company Foundation. Retrieved from http://www.cdc.gov/Aging/pdf/saha_2007.pdf

Centers for Medicare and Medicaid Services. (2003). *Home health quality initiative*. Retrieved January 2, 2007 from http://www.cms.hhs.gov/HomeHealthQualityInits/downloads/HHQIOverview.pdf

Centers for Medicare and Medicaid Services. (2006). *Nursing home data compendium*. Retrieved February 7, 2007 from http://www.cms.hhs.gov/CertificationandComplianc/12_NHs.asp

Centers for Medicare and Medicaid Services. (2009). *Medicare & Medicaid statistical supplement, 2009 edition*. Retrieved from https://www.cms.gov/Research-Statistics-Data-and-Systems/Statistics-Trends-and-Reports/MedicareMedicaidStatSupp/2009.html

Centers for Medicare and Medicaid Services. (2010a). *Hospice payment system: Payment system fact sheet series*. Retrieved from http://www.cms.gov/Outreach-and-Education/Medicare-Learning-Network-MLN/MLNProducts/downloads/hospice_pay_sys_fs.pdf

Centers for Medicare and Medicaid Services. (2010b). *Medicaid managed care enrollment report*. Retrieved from http://www.cms.gov/Research-Statistics-Data-and-Systems/Computer-Data-and-Systems/MedicaidDataSourcesGenInfo/MdManCrEnrllRep.html

Centers for Medicare and Medicaid Services. (2010c). *Medicaid managed care enrollment report: Managed care trends*. Retrieved from http://www.cms.gov/Research-Statistics-Data-and-Systems/Computer-Data-and-Systems/MedicaidDataSourcesGenInfo/Downloads/2010Trends.pdf

Centers for Medicare and Medicaid Services. (2010d). *Medicaid managed care enrollment report: Medicaid managed care enrollment as of July 1, 2010*. Retrieved from http://www.cms.gov/Research-Statistics-Data-and-Systems/Computer-Data-and-Systems/MedicaidDataSourcesGenInfo/Downloads/2010July1.pdf

Centers for Medicare and Medicaid Services. (2010e). *Medicare and home health care*. Retrieved from http://www.medicare.gov/publications/pubs/pdf/10969.pdf

Centers for Medicare and Medicaid Services. (2010f). *Nursing home data compendium 2010 edition*. Retrieved from https://www.cms.gov/Medicare/Provider-Enrollment-and-Certification/CertificationandComplianc/downloads/nursinghomedatacompendium_508.pdf

Centers for Medicare and Medicaid Services. (2011). *Medicare and you*. Washington, DC: U.S. Department of Health and Human Services. Retrieved from http://www.medicare.gov/publications/pubs/pdf/10050.pdf

Centers for Medicare and Medicaid Services. (2012a). *2012 poverty guidelines*. Retrieved from http://www.medicaid.gov/Medicaid-CHIP-Program-Information/By-Topics/Eligibility/Downloads/FederalPovertyLevelRates.pdf

Centers for Medicare and Medicaid Services. (2012b). *CMS fast facts*. Retrieved from http://cms.gov/Research-Statistics-Data-and-Systems/Statistics-Trends-and-Reports/CMS-Fast-Facts/index.html

Centers for Medicare and Medicaid Services. (2012c). *Nursing home compare*. Retrieved May 1, 2012 from http://www.medicare.gov/NursingHomeCompare/search.aspx?bhcp = 1

Centers for Medicare and Medicaid Services. (n.d.-a). *Free preventive services for people in Medicare: 5.5 million Americans on Medicare have used preventive benefits*. Retrieved from http://downloads.cms.gov/files/preventionreport.pdf

Centers for Medicare and Medicaid Services. (n.d.-b). *Medicare enrollment: National trends 1966–2008*. Retrieved February 21, 2007 from http://www.cms.gov/Research-Statistics-Data-and-Systems/Statistics-Trends-and-Reports/MedicareEnrpts/downloads/HISMI08.pdf

Centers for Medicare and Medicaid Services. (n.d.-c). *Part A costs*. Retrieved from http://www.medicare.gov/your-medicare-costs/part-a-costs/part-a-costs.html

Centers for Medicare and Medicaid Services. (n.d.-d). *Part B costs*. Retrieved from http://www.medicare.gov/your-medicare-costs/part-b-costs/part-b-costs.html

Chadee, D. (2011). Toward freedom: Reactance Theory revisited. In D. Chadee (Ed.), *Theories in social psychology* (pp. 13–43). London, UK: Blackwell.

Chalifoux, Z., Neese, J. B., Buckwalter, K. C., Liltwak, E., & Abraham, I. L. (1996). Mental health services for rural elderly: Innovative service strategies. *Community Mental Health Journal, 32*, 463–471.

Chan, L., Hart, G., & Goodman, D. C. (2006). Geographic access to health care for rural Medicare beneficiaries. *Journal of Rural Health, 22*(2), 140–146. doi:10.1111/j.1748-0361.2006.00022.x

Chandra, R. K. (1992). Effect of vitamin and trace-element supplementation on immune responses and infection in elderly subjects. *Lancet, 340*, 1124–1127.

Chapman, N. J., & Howe, D. A. (2001). Accessory apartments: Are they a realistic alternative for ageing in place. *Housing Studies, 16,* 637–650.

Chappell, N. L., & Blandford, A. A. (1987). Health service utilization by elderly persons. *Canadian Journal of Sociology, 12*(3), 195–215.

Chappell, N. L., & Reid, R. C. (2000). Dimensions of care of dementia sufferers in long-term care institutions: Are they related to outcomes? *Journal of Gerontology: Social Sciences, 55B*(4), S234–S244.

Charlotte Department of Transportation. (2012*). East Boulevard resurfacing project (Dilworth Road West to Scott Avenue).* Retrieved from http://charmeck.org/city/charlotte/Transportation/PlansProjects/Pages/East_Blvd.aspx

Charney, P. (2008). Nutrition screening vs. nutrition assessment: How do they differ? *Nutrition in Clinical Practice, 23*(4), 366–372. doi:10.1177/0884533608321131

Chatterji, P., Burstein, N. R., Kidder, D., & White, A. (1998). *Evaluation of the program of All-Inclusive Care for the Elderly (PACE) demonstration: The impact of PACE on participant outcomes.* Retrieved from http://www.npaonline.org/website/download.asp?id = 1933

Chelimsky, E. (1991). *Older Americans Act: Promising practice in information and referral services.* Washington, DC: Government Printing Office.

Chen, Y.-M., & Thompson, E. A. (2010). Understanding factors that influence success of home- and community-based services in keeping older adults in community settings. *Journal of Aging and Health, 22*(3), 267–291. doi:10.1177/0898264309356593

Chernoff, R. (2001). Nutrition and health promotion in older adults. *Journals of Gerontology, 56A,* 47–53.

Cherry, R., Prebis, J., & Pick, V. (1995). Service directories: Reinvigorating community resource for self-care. *The Gerontologist, 35,* 560–563.

Chervin, S. (2007). *Property tax reduction and relief programs.* Retrieved from http://www.tn.gov/tacir/PDF_FILES/Taxes/property%20tax%20reduction.pdf

Chicago Department on Aging, National Council on the Aging, & Washington Business Group on Health. (1992). *Public/private partnerships: Examples from the aging network.* Washington, DC: National Eldercare Institute on Business and Aging.

Choi, N. G. (1999). Determinants of frail elders' length of stay in Meals on Wheels. *The Gerontologist, 39*(4), 397–404.

Choi S., & Davitt, J.K. (2009). Changes in the Medicare home health care market: The impact of reimbursement policy. *Medical Care, 47,* 302–309.

Choi-Allum, L. (2007). *2007 Money management outcomes study: Executive summary.* Washington, DC: AARP, Knowledge Management.

Christianson, J. B., Warrick, L. H., Netting, F. E., Williams, F. G., Read, W., & Murphy, J. (1991). Hospital case management: Bridging acute and long-term care. *Health Affairs, 10*(2), 173–184.

Chumbler, N. R., Cody, M., Booth, B. M., & Beck, C. K. (2001). Rural–urban differences in service use for memory-related problems in older adults. *Journal of Behavioral Health Services & Research, 28,* 212–221.

Chumbler, N. R., Dobbs-Kepper, D., Beverly, C., & Beck, C. (2000). Eligibility for in-home respite care: Ethnic status and rural residence. *Journal of Applied Gerontology, 19*(2), 151–169.

Chwalisz, K., Clancy Dollinger, S. M., O'Neill Zerth, E., & Tamkin, V. (2011). Education, training, and support for rural caregivers. In R. C. Talley, K. Chwalisz, & K. C. Buckwalter (Eds.), *Rural caregiving in the United States: Research, practice, policy* (pp. 181–196). New York, NY: Springer.

Citymeals-on-Wheels. (2012). *About us.* Retrieved from http://www.citymeals.org/about-us

Civic Ventures. (2006). *Fact sheet on older Americans.* Retrieved January 3, 2007, from http://www.civicventures.org/publications/articles/fact_sheet_on older_americans.cfm

Civic Ventures. (2008). *Americans seek meaningful work in the second half of life* (A MetLife Foundation/Civic Ventures Encore Career Survey). Retrieved from http://www.civicventures.org/publications/surveys/encore_career_survey/Encore_Survey.pdf

Civil Rights Act of 1964, Pub. L. No. 88–352, 78 Stat. 241.

Civil Service Retirement Act of 1920, 5 U.S.C. § 8331 et seq. (1990).

Clark, R. L., & Quinn, J. F. (2002). Patterns of work and retirement for a new century. *Generations, 16,* 17–24.

Clemens, E., Wetle, T., Feltes, M., Crabtree, B., & Dubitzky, D. (1994). Contradictions in case management client-centered theory and directive practice with frail elderly. *Journal of Aging and Health, 6,* 70–88.

Cobb, R. L., & Dvorak, S. (2000). *Accessory dwelling units: Model state acts and local ordinances.* Retrieved from http://assets.aarp.org/rgcenter/consume/d17158_dwell.pdf

Coe, M., & Neufeld, A. (1999). Male caregivers' use of formal support. *Western Journal of Nursing Research, 21*(4), 568–588. doi:10.1177/01939459922044045

Cohen, E., & Cesta, T. (1994). Case management in the acute care setting: A model for health care reform. *Journal of Case Management, 3,* 110–116.

Cohen-Mansfield, J., & Frank, J. (2008). Relationship between perceived needs and assessed needs for services in community-dwelling older persons. *The Gerontologist, 48*(4), 505–516. doi:10.1093/geront/48.4.505

Cohn, D., & Taylor, P. (2010). *Baby boomers approach age 65—glumly.* Washington, DC: Pew Research Center Publications. Retrieved from http://pewresearch.org/pubs/1834/baby-boomers-old-age-downbeat-pessimism

Colello, K. J. (2007). *CRS report for Congress: Where do older Americans live? Geographic distribution of the older population* (Order Code RL33897). Washington, DC: Congressional Research Service. Retrieved from http://aging.senate.gov/crs/aging5.pdf

Colello, K. J. (2011). *Older Americans Act: Title III nutrition services program.* Retrieved from http://nationalaglawcenter.org/assets/crs/RS21202.pdf

Coleman, B. (1989). *Primer on Employee Retirement Income Security Act* (3rd ed.). Washington, DC: Bureau of National Affairs.

Coleman, B. (2000). *Helping the helpers: State-supported services for family caregivers* (AARP Public Policy Institute Issue Paper No. 2000–07). Washington, DC: American Association of Retired Persons.

Coleman, D., & Iso-Ahola, S. (1993). The role of social support and self-determination. *Journal of Leisure Research, 25,* 111–128.

Coleman, M. T., Looney, S., O'Brien, J., Ziegler, C., Pastorino, C. A., & Turner, C. (2002). The Eden Alternative: Findings after 1 year of implementation. *Journals of Gerontology, Series A: Biological Sciences and Medical Sciences, 57,* M422–M427.

Coleman-Jensen, A., Nord, M., Andrews, M., & Carlson, S. (2011). *Household food security in the United States in 2010* (Economic Research Report No. 125). Retrieved from http://www.ers.usda.gov/media/121076/err125_2_.pdf

Colorado Department of Health Care Policy and Financing. (2006). *Care management client satisfaction survey project: Final report and recommendations.* Retrieved December 22, 2006, from http://www.hcbs.org/moreInfo.php/nb/doc/1761/Care_Management_Client_Satisfaction_Survey

Committee for the Study on Improving Mobility and Safety for Older Persons. (1988). *Transportation in an aging society: Improving mobility and safety for older persons* (Vol. 1). Washington, DC: National Research Council, Transportation Research Board.

Commonwealth Fund. (1993). *The untapped resource: The final report of the Americans Over 55 at Work Program.* New York, NY: Author.

Community Care Services Program. (2012). *Annual statewide report: State fiscal year (SFY) 2011.* Retrieved from http://aging.dhs.georgia.gov/sites/aging.dhs.georgia.gov/files/STATEWIDE SFY2011ANNUALREPORT.pdf

Community Mental Health Act of 1963, 42 U.S.C. § 2689 et seq., as amended.

Community service is key. (1994). *Community Transportation Reporter, 13*(4), 5.

Community Transportation Association of America. (2001). *Status of rural public transportation—2000. Report submitted to the U.S. Department of Transportation, Federal Transit Administration, April 2001.* Retrieved October 28, 2006 from http://www.ctaa.org/ntrc/rtap/pubs/status2000

Community Transportation Association of America. (2012). *MAP-21: An analysis.* Retrieved from http://web1.ctaa.org/webmodules/webarticles/articlefiles/MAP21analysis.pdf

Comprehensive Health Planning and Public Health Service Amendments of 1966, 42 U.S.C. §§ 243, 246.

Congressional Budget Office. (2004). *Financing long-term care for the elderly*. Washington, DC: Author. Retrieved February 2, 2007 from http://www.cbo.gov/sites/default/files/cbofiles/ftpdocs/54xx/doc5400/04-26-longtermcare.pdf

Conlin, M., Caranasos, G., & Davidson, R. (1992). Reduction of caregiver stress by respite care: A pilot study. *Southern Medical Journal, 85,* 1096–1100.

Connecticut Community Care. (1994). *Guidelines for case management practices across the long-term care continuum*. Bristol, CT: Author.

Connor, S. R., Tecca, M., LundPerson, J., & Teno, J. (2004). Measuring hospice care: The National Hospice and Palliative Care Organization National Hospice Data Set. *Journal of Pain and Symptom Management, 28,* 316–328.

Cooke, D. D., McNally, L., Mulligan, K. T., Harrison, M. J. G., & Newman, S. P. (2001). Psychosocial interventions for caregivers of people with dementia: A systematic review. *Aging and Mental Health, 5,* 120–135.

Copeland, C. (2011). *Employment-based retirement plan participation: Geographic differences and trends, 2010* (Employee Benefit Research Institute Issue Brief No. 363). Retrieved from http://www.ebri.org/pdf/briefspdf/EBRI_IB_10-2011_No363_RetPart.pdf

Corporation for Enterprise Development. (2010). *Asset limit reform in the Supplemental Security Income (SSI) program: Remove the penalty for saving*. Retrieved from http://www.realeconomicimpact.org/UploadedDocs/Documents/SSI_Asset_Limits_One_Pager_HR_4937.pdf

Corporation for National and Community Service. (2006). *Volunteer growth in America: A review of trends since 1974*. Retrieved January 18, 2007 from http://www.nationalservice.gov/pdf/06_1203_volunteer_growth.pdf

Corporation for National and Community Service. (2007). *Keeping baby boomers volunteering: A research brief on volunteer retention and turnover*. Retrieved from http://www.nationalservice.gov/pdf/07_0307_boomer_report.pdf

Corporation for National and Community Service. (2010). *What is the National Service-Learning Clearinghouse?* Retrieved from https://questions.nationalservice.gov/app/answers/detail/a_id/324/ ~ /what-is-the-national-service-learning-clearinghouse%3F

Corporation for National and Community Service. (2011a). *Civic life in America*. Retrieved from http://civic.serve.gov/export.cfm

Corporation for National and Community Service. (2011b). *Edward M. Kennedy Serve America Act of 2009*. Retrieved from http://www.nationalservice.gov/about/serveamerica/index.asp

Corporation for National and Community Service. (2012). *Senior Corps fact sheet*. Retrieved from http://www.seniorcorps.gov/pdf/factsheet_seniorcorps.pdf

Cort, M. A. (2004). Cultural mistrust and use of hospice care: Challenges and remedies. *Journal of Palliative Medicine, 7*(1), 63–71. doi:10.1089/109662104322737269

Costo, S. L. (2006). Trends in retirement plan coverage over the last decade. *Monthly Labor Review, 129,* 58–64.

Coulton, C., & Frost, A. K. (1982). Use of social and health services by the elderly. *Journal of Health and Social Behavior, 23,* 330–339.

Council for Adult Experiential Learning. (2011). *Lifelong learning accounts: Helping to build a more competitive workforce*. Retrieved from http://www.lifelonglearningaccounts.org/pdf/LiLA_Policy_Overview0211.pdf

Counsell, S. R., Callahan, C. M., Clark, D., Tu, W., Buttar, A. B., Stump, T. E., & Ricketts, G. D. (2007). Geriatric care management for low-income seniors. *Journal of the American Medical Association, 2988,* 2223–2633.

Courtenay, B. (1990). Community education for older adults. In M. Galbraith (Ed.), *Education through community organizations* (pp. 37–44). San Francisco, CA: Jossey-Bass.

Covey, H. C., & Menard, S. (1988). Trends in elderly criminal victimization from 1973 to 1984. *Research on Aging, 10,* 329–341.

Cox, C. (1997). Findings from a statewide program of respite care: A comparison of service users, stoppers, and nonusers. *The Gerontologist, 37,* 511–517.

Cox, C., & Monk, A. (1990). Integrating the frail and well elderly: The experience of senior centers. *Journal of Gerontological Social Work, 15,* 131–147.

Coyne, A. C. (1991). Information and referral service usage among caregivers for dementia patients. *The Gerontologist, 31,* 384–388.

Craik, F. I. M., & Salthouse, T. A. (Eds.). (2008). *Handbook of aging and cognition* (3rd ed.). New York, NY: Psychology Press.

Crandall, R. C. (1991). *Gerontology: A behavioral science approach.* New York, NY: McGraw-Hill.

Craver, R. (2007). Winston-Salem company hires mostly older workers. *The Associated Press.* Retrieved January 17, 2007 from http://www.digtriad.com/news/local/story.aspx?storyid = 67889

Cress, C. J. (2012a). Care planning and geriatric assessment. In C. J. Cress (Ed.), *Handbook of geriatric care management* (pp. 73–100). Sudbury, MA: Jones & Bartlett Learning.

Cress, C. J. (2012b). Overview and history of geriatric care management. In C. J. Cress (Ed.), *Handbook of geriatric care management* (pp. 3–12). Sudbury, MA: Jones & Bartlett Learning.

Cruzan v. Harmon, 760 S.W.2d 408 (1988).

Crystal, S., & Beck, P. (1992). A room of one's own: The SRO and the single elderly. *The Gerontologist, 32,* 684–692.

Cudney, A. (2002). Case management: A serious solution for serious issues. *Journal of Healthcare Management, 47*(3), 149–152.

Cuellar, J. (1990). Hispanic American aging: Geriatric education curriculum development for selected health professions. In M. S. Harper (Ed.), *Minority aging* (DHHS Pub. No. HRS P-DV-90–4; pp. 365–414). Washington, DC: Government Printing Office.

Cunnyngham, K. (2004). *Trends in food stamp program participation rates: 1999 to 2002.* Princeton, NJ: Mathematica Policy Research.

Cushing, M., & Long, N. (1974). *Information and referral services: Reaching out* (DHEW Pub. No. OHD 75–110). Washington, DC: Government Printing Office.

Davis, M. A., Murphy, S. P., Neuhaus, J. M., Gee, L., & Quiroga, S. S. (2000). Living arrangements affect dietary quality for U.S. adults aged 50 years and older: NHANES III 1988–1994. *Journal of Nutrition, 130*(9), 2256–2264.

Davis, M. A., Randall, E., Forthofer, R. N., Lee, E. S., & Margen, S. (1985). Living arrangements and dietary patterns of older adults in the United States. *Journal of Gerontology, 40,* 434–442.

de la Cuesta-Benjumea, C. (2010). The legitimacy of rest: Conditions for the relief of burden in advanced dementia care-giving. *Journal of advanced Nursing, 66*(5), 988–998. doi:10.1111/j.1365-2648.2010.05261.x

de Vries, B. (2006). Home at the end of the rainbow. *Generations, 39*(4), 64–69.

Decker, F. H. (2005). *Nursing homes, 1977–1999: What has changed, what has not?* Hyattsville, MD: National Center for Health Statistics. Retrieved February 4, 2007 from http://www.cdc.gov/nchs/data/nnhsd/NursingHomes1977_99.pdf

Decker, F. H., Gruhn, P., Matthews-Martin, L., Dollard, K. J., Tucker, A. M., & Bizette, L. (2003). *Results of the 2002 AHCA survey of nursing staff vacancy and turnover in nursing homes.* Washington, DC: Health Services Research and Evaluation, American Health Care Association. Retrieved February 12, 2007 from http://www.ahca.org/research/rpt_vts2002_final.pdf

Degenholtz, H., Kane, R. A., & Kivnick, H. Q. (1997). Care-related preferences and values of elderly community-based LTC consumers: Can case managers learn what's important to clients? *The Gerontologist, 37,* 767–776.

DeGood, K. (2011). *Aging in place, stuck without options: Fixing the mobility crisis threatening the baby boom generation.* Washington, DC: Transportation for America.

Dellasega, C., & Stricklin, M. L. (1993). Cognitive impairment in elderly home health clients. *Home Health Care Services Quarterly, 14,* 81–92.

DeLong, D., & Associates. (2006). *Living longer, working longer: The changing landscape of the aging workforce.* New York, NY: MetLife Mature Market Institute. Retrieved January 16, 2007 from http://www.metlife.com/assets/cao/mmi/publications/studies/mmi-studies-living-longer.pdf

Demmer, C. (2003). A national survey of hospice bereavement services. *OMEGA: The Journal of Death and Dying, 47*(4), 327–341.

Democratic Policy Committee. (2008, June 26). H.R. 6331, the Medicare Improvements for Patients and Provider Act. *Legislative Bulletin.* Retrieved from http://dpc.senate.gov/dpcdoc.cfm?doc_name=lb-110-2-114

Dennis, H., & Thomas, K. (2007). Ageism in the workplace. *Generations, 31*(1), 84–89.

Denton, M., Ploeg, J., Tindale, J., Hutchison, B., Brazil, K., Akhtar-Danesh, N., & Plenderleith, J. M. (2010). Would older adults turn to community support services for help to maintain their independence? *Journal of Applied Gerontology, 29*(5), 554–578. doi:10.1177/0733464809345495

DePaulo, B. M. (1978). Help seeking from the recipient's point of view. *JSAS Catalogue of Selected Documents in Psychology, 8,* 62 (Ms. No. 1721b).

DePaulo, B. M., & Fisher, J. D. (1980). The cost of asking for help. *Basic and Applied Social Psychology, 1,* 23–35.

Di, J., & Berman, J. (2000). Older New Yorkers' use of senior center services: Effect of family support networks. *The Gerontologist, 40,* 390.

Diebert, L. (1996). *Options for funding rural transit programs: A community transit funding primer.* Boulder: Boulder County Colorado Transit.

Dillard, J. P., & Shen, L. (2005). On the nature of reactance and its role in persuasive health. *Communication Monographs, 72*(2), 144–168.

Dilworth-Anderson, P., Williams, I. C., & Gibson, B. E. (2002). Issues of race, ethnicity, and culture in caregiving research: A 20-year review (1980–2000). *The Gerontologist, 42,* 237–272.

DiMaria-Ghalili, R. A., & Amella, E. (2005). Nutrition in older adults: Intervention and assessment can help curb the growing threat of malnutrition. *American Journal of Nursing, 105*(3), 40–50.

DiPietro, L. (2001). Physical activity in aging: Changes in patterns and their relationship to health and function. *Journal of Gerontology, 56A* (Special Issue II), 13–22.

Diwan, S. (1999). Allocation of case management resources in long-term care: Predicting high use of case management of time. *The Gerontologist, 39,* 580–590.

Donoghue, C. (2010). Nursing home staff turnover and retention. *Journal of Applied Gerontology, 29*(1), 89–106. doi:10.1177/0733464809334899

Donoghue, C., & Castle, N. G. (2007). Organizational and environmental effects on voluntary and involuntary turnover. *Health Care Management Review, 32*(4), 360–369. doi:10.1097/01.HMR.0000296791.16257.44

Doolin, J. (1985). America's untouchables: The elderly homeless. *Perspective on Aging, 9*(2), 8–12.

Doty, P. (1986). Family care of the elderly: The role of public policy. *Milbank Memorial Fund Quarterly, 64,* 34–75.

Downing, R. (1985). The elderly and their families. In M. Weil, J. Karls, & Associates (Eds.), *Case management in human service practice: A systematic approach to mobilizing resources for clients* (pp. 145–169). San Francisco, CA: Jossey-Bass.

Duay, D. L., & Bryan, V. C. (2008). Learning in later life: What seniors want in a learning experience. *Educational Gerontology, 34,* 1070–1086.

Duesing, A., & Pace Maxwell, M. (2007). Teens teaching Alzheimer's caregivers to become tech-savvy: The power of community and intergenerational partnerships. *Age in Action, 22*(3). Retrieved from http://www.sahp.vcu.edu/vcoa/newsletter/

Dumazadier, J. (1967). *Towards a society of leisure.* New York, NY: Free Press.

Duquin, M., McCrea, J., Fetterman, D., & Nash, S. (2004). A faith-based intergenerational health and wellness program. *Journal of Intergenerational Relationships: Programs, Policy, and Research, 2,* 105–118.

Dwyer, J. (1991). *Screening older Americans' nutritional health: Current practices and future possibilities.* Washington, DC: Nutrition Screening Initiative.

East Tennessee Human Resource Agency. (n.d.). *Long term care ombudsman.* Retrieved February 13, 2007 from http://www.ethra.org/services/aging-disability/ombudsman

Eaton, J., & Salari, S. (2005). Environments for lifelong learning in senior centers. *Educational Gerontology, 31,* 461–480.

Eck, W. B. (2010, November). Home care, hospice care, and the Affordable Care Act. *AHLA Connections,* 16–21. Retrieved from http://publish.healthlawyers.org/News/Connections/Pages/default.aspx

Eckerd College. (n.d.). *The Academy of Senior Professionals: Intergenerational learning opportunities.* Retrieved from http://www.eckerd.edu/aspec/about/intergenerational.php

Edelstein, S. (1996). *Legal issues and resources: An introduction for professionals in aging.* Unpublished manuscript.

Edelstein, S. (2004). Partnerships in Law and Aging Program awards mini-grants. *Bifocal, 25.*

Eden Alternative. (n.d.). *Welcome to the Eden Alternative.* Retrieved February 18, 2007 from http://www.edenalt.com

Edes, T. (2010). The VA's Medical Foster Home program. *Generations, 34*(2), 99–101.

Einolf, C. J. (2009). Will the boomers volunteer during retirement? Comparing the baby boom, silent, and long civic cohorts. *Nonprofit & Voluntary Sector Quarterly, 38*(2), 181–199. doi:10.1177/0899764008315182

Eisner, D., Grimm, R. T., Jr., Maynard, S., & Washburn, S. (2009, Winter). The new volunteer workforce. *Stanford Social Innovation Review.* Retrieved from http://www.volunteeringinamerica.gov/assets/resources/TheNewVolunteerWorkforce.pdf

Eldeman, T. S. (1990). The nursing home reform law: Issues for litigation. *Clearinghouse Review, 24,* 545–550.

Elder Justice Act of 2009—Title VI, Subtitle H, of Pub. L. 111-148, Patient Protection and Affordable Care Act (2009).

Elder Justice Coalition. (n.d.). *Elder Justice Act summary.* Retrieved from http://www.elderjusticecoalition.com/docs/EJA-Summary-772010.pdf

Elderhostel Institute Network. (2012a). *History of the Elderhostel Institute Network.* Retrieved from http://www.roadscholar.org/ein/history.asp

Elderhostel Institute Network. (2012b). *The learning and retirement movement.* Retrieved from http://www.roadscholar.org/ein/learning_na.asp

ElderSource. (n.d.). *The National Association of Area Agencies on Aging honors innovative and successful programs serving older adults* [Press release]. Retrieved from http://www.myeldersource.org/reports/press_release_es_award.pdf

Electronic Code of Federal Regulations. (2011a). *Part 2551—Senior Companion Program.* Retrieved from http://ecfr.gpoaccess.gov/cgi/t/text/text-idx?c = ecfr&sid = 99f8e15d953a2684bc6267b117b9713a&rgn = div5&view = text&node = 45:4.1.9.11.33&idno = 45

Electronic Code of Federal Regulations. (2011b). *Part 2552—Foster Grandparent Program.* Retrieved from http://ecfr.gpoaccess.gov/cgi/t/text/text-idx?c = ecfr&sid = b4e30f583e4062c5dd3f97517034712f&rgn = div5&view = text&node = 45:4.1.9.11.34&idno = 45

Electronic Code of Federal Regulations. (2011c). *Part 2553—The Retired and Senior Volunteer Program.* Retrieved from http://ecfr.gpoaccess.gov/cgi/t/text/text-idx?c = ecfr&sid = 6f5657419b5c37b20320abd528e2dcb9&rgn = div5&view = text&node = 45:4.1.9.11.35&idno = 45

Ellenbecker, C. H., Samia, L., Cushman, M. J., & Alster, K. (2008). Patient safety and quality in home health care. In R. G. Hughes (Ed.), *Patient safety and quality: An evidence-based handbook for nurses.* Rockville, MD: Agency for Healthcare Research and Quality. Retrieved from http://internet.ahrq.gov/qual/nurseshdbk/docs/EllenbeckerC_PSQHC.pdf

Elliott, A. F., Burgio, L. D., & DeCoster, J. (2010). Enhancing caregiver health: Findings from the Resources for Enhancing Alzheimer's Caregiver Health II Intervention. *Journal of the American Geriatrics Society, 58*(1), 30–37. doi:10.1111/j.1532-5415.2009.02631.x

Emlet, C., & Hall, A. M. (1991). Integrating the community into geriatric case management: Public health interventions. *The Gerontologist, 31,* 556–560.

Employee Benefit Research Institute). (2011a). *The 2011 retirement confidence survey: Confidence drops to record lows, reflecting "the new normal."* Retrieved from http://www.ebri.org/pdf/briefspdf/EBRI_03-2011_No355_RCS-2011.pdf

Employee Benefit Research Institute. (2011b). Income statistics of the population aged 55 and over. In *EBRI Databook on Employee Benefits.* Retrieved from http://www.ebri.org/pdf/publications/books/databook/DB.Chapter%2006.pdf

Employee Benefit Research Institute. (2011c). Participation in Employee Benefit Programs. In *EBRI Databook on Employee Benefits.* Washington, DC: Author.

Employee Retirement Income Security Act of 1974, 29 U.S.C. §§ 1001–1461 (1974), as amended.

Enguidanos, S. M., Gibbs, N. E., Simmons, W. J., Savoni, K. J., Jamison, P. M., Hackstaff, L., & Cherin, D. A. (2003). Kaiser Permanente Community Partners Project: Improving geriatric care management practices. *Journal of the American Geriatrics Society, 51,* 710–714.

Environmental Protection Agency. (2008). *Senior Environmental Employment (SEE) Program: About SEE Program.* Retrieved from http://www.epa.gov/ohr/see/brochure/backgr.htm

Erickson, R., & Eckert, J. K. (1977). The elderly poor in downtown San Diego hotels. *The Gerontologist, 17,* 440–446.

Eschtruth, A. (2006). *Myths and realities about retirement preparedness.* Retrieved January 12, 2007 from http://crr.bc.edu/wp-content/uploads/2011/09/nrrimyths_realities1.pdf

Eslami, E., Filion, K., & Strayer, M. (2011). *Characteristics of Supplemental Nutrition Assistance Program households: Fiscal Year 2010* (Report No. SNAP-11-CHAR). Alexandria, VA: U.S. Department of Agriculture. Retrieved from http://www.fns.usda.gov/ora/MENU/Published/snap/FILES/Participation/2010Characteristics.pdf

Estes, C. (1979). *The aging enterprise.* San Francisco, CA: Jossey-Bass.

Estes, C. L., Swan, J. H., & Associates. (1993). *The long term care crisis: Elders trapped in the no-care zone.* Newbury Park, CA: Sage.

Ettinger, W. H., Jr., Burns, R., Messier, S. P., Applegate, W., Rejeski, W. J., Morgan, T., & Craven, T. (1997). A randomized trial comparing aerobic exercise and resistance exercise with a health education program in older adults with knee osteoarthritis: The Fitness Arthritis and Senior Trial (FAST). *Journal of the American Medical Association, 277,* 25–31.

Experience Works. (2009). *2008 annual report.* Retrieved from http://www.experienceworks.org/site/DocServer/2007AR-WEB.pdf?docID=2881

Experience Works. (2011). *What we do.* Retrieved from http://www.experienceworks.org/site/PageServer?pagename=WhatWeDo_Main

Extra Mile: Overnight and weekend care. (1996, Fall–Winter). *Respite Report, 1–2,* 6.

FallCreek, S. J., Allen, B. P., & Halls, D. M. (1986). *Health promotion and aging: A national directory of selected programs* (DHHS Pub. No. OHDS 86–950). Washington, DC: U.S. Department of Health and Human Services, Office of Human Development Services, Administration on Aging.

FallCreek, S. J., & Franks, P. (1984). *Health promotion and aging: Strategies for action* (DHHS Pub. No. OHDS 84–818). Washington, DC: U.S. Department of Health and Human Services, Office of Human Development Services, Administration on Aging.

FallCreek, S. J., & Mettler, M. (1982). *A healthy old age: A sourcebook for health promotion with older adults* (DHHS Pub. No. 447-a-1). Washington, DC: U.S. Department of Health and Human Services, Office of Human Development Services, Administration on Aging.

Family and Medical Leave Act of 1993, 5 U.S.C. § 6381 et seq., 29 U.S.C. §§ 2601 et seq., 2631 et seq. (1993).

Family Caregiver Alliance. (2006). Caregivers online: Using support groups on the Internet. *Family Caregiver Alliance Newsletter, 23*(3). Retrieved from http://www.caregiver.org/caregiver/jsp/content_node.jsp?nodeid=1754

Family Caregiver Alliance. (2011). *Family caregiving 2010 year in review.* Retrieved from http://caregiver.org/caregiver/jsp/content/pdfs/2010-Caregiver-Guide.pdf

Farber, N., Shinkle, D., Lynott, J., Fox-Grage, W., & Harrell, R. (2011). *Aging in place: A state survey of livability policies and practices.* Washington, DC: AARP Public Policy Institute. Retrieved from http://assets.aarp.org/rgcenter/ppi/liv-com/aging-in-place-2011-full.pdf

Federal Bureau of Investigation. (2005). *Financial crimes report to the public.* Washington, DC: U.S. Department of Justice. Retrieved from http://www.fbi.gov/publications/financial/fcs_report052005/fcs_ report052005.htm

Federal Highway Administration. (2007). *Highway statistics 2007: Fatalities by 100 Mil VMT by age.* Retrieved from http://www.fhwa.dot.gov/policyinformation/statistics/2007/nhts1231.cfm

Federal Highway Administration. (2009). *Distribution of licensed drivers—2009 by sex and percentage in each age group and relation to population:* Washington, DC: U.S. Department of Transportation.

Federal Interagency Forum on Aging-Related Statistics. (2000). *Older Americans 2000: Key indicators of well-being*. Hyattsville, MD: Author.

Federal Interagency Forum on Aging-Related Statistics. (2010). *Older Americans 2010: Key indicators of well-being*. Retrieved from http://www.agingstats.gov/agingstatsdotnet/Main_Site/Data/2010_Documents/Docs/OA_2010.pdf

Federal Transit Administration. (n.d.). *FY 2012 apportionment, allocations, and program information*. Retrieved from http://www.fta.dot.gov/12308_14615.html

Feinberg, L., & Reamy, A. M. (2011). *Health reform law creates new opportunities to better recognize and support family caregivers*. Washington, DC: AARP Public Policy Institute. Retrieved from http://assets.aarp.org/rgcenter/ppi/ltc/fs239.pdf

Feinberg, L., Reinhard, S. C., Houser, A., & Choula, R. (2011). *Valuing the invaluable: 2011 update the growing contributions and costs of family caregiving*. Washington, DC: AARP Policy Institute. Retrieved from http://assets.aarp.org/rgcenter/ppi/ltc/i51-caregiving.pdf

Feldman, N. S. (1991). Lifelong education: The challenge of change. *Lifelong Education, Resourceful Aging: Today and Tomorrow, 5*, 17–31.

Fellin, P., & Powell, T. (1988). Mental health services and older adult minorities: An assessment. *The Gerontologist, 28*, 442–447.

Feng, Z., Fennell, M. L., Tyler, D. A., Clark, M., & Mor, V. (2011). Growth of racial and ethnic minorities in US nursing homes driven by demographics and possible disparities in options. *Health Affairs, 30*(7), 1358–1365. doi:10.1377/hlthaff.2011.0126

Ficke, S. C. (1985). *Older Americans Act 1965–1985: 20th anniversary: An orientation to the Older Americans Act*. Washington, DC: National Association of State Units on Aging.

Fields, J., O'Connell, M. O., & Downs, B. (2001). *Grandparents in the United States, 2001*. Washington, DC: U.S. Census Bureau. Retrieved from https://www.census.gov/population/www/socdemo/grandparents2001SIPP.pdf

Fischer, D. L. (1978). *Growing old in America*. New York, NY: Oxford University Press.

Fischer, L. R., & Schaffer, K. B. (1993). *Older volunteers: A guide to research and practice*. Newbury Park, CA: Sage.

Fischer, R. (1992). Post-retirement learning. In R. Fischer, M. Blazey, & H. Lipman (Eds.), *Students of the third age* (pp. 13–21). New York, NY: Macmillan.

Fisher, J. D., & Nadler, A. (1976). The effect of donor resources on recipient self-esteem and self-help. *Journal of Experimental Social Psychology, 12*, 139–150.

Fisher, J. D., Nadler, A., & Whitcher-Alagna, S. (1983). Four conceptualizations of reactions to aid. In J. D. Fisher, A. Nadler, & B. M. DePaulo (Eds.), *New directions in helping* (Vol. 1, pp. 51–84). New York, NY: Academic Press.

Fiske, S. T., & Taylor, S. E. (1991). *Social cognition* (2nd ed.). New York, NY: McGraw-Hill.

Flegal, K., Carroll, M. D., Ogden, C. L., & Curtin, L. R. (2010). Prevalence and trends in obesity among us adults, 1999–2008. *The Journal of the American Medical Association, 303*(3), 235–241. doi:10.1001/jama.2009.2014

Flora, P. K., & Faulkner, G. E. J. (2006): Physical activity: An innovative context for intergenerational programming, *Journal of Intergenerational Relationships, 4*, 63–74. doi:10.1300/J194v04n04_05

Folkemer, D. (2006). *Home care quality: Emerging state strategies to deliver person-centered services*. Retrieved January 2, 2007 from http://www.cms.hhs.gov/HomeHealthQualityInits/downloads/HHQIOverview.pdf

Foner, N. (1994). *The caregiving dilemma*. Los Angeles: University of California Press.

Food Stamp Act of 1964, 7 U.S.C. § 2011 et seq. (1995).

Fox, P. J., Breuer, W., & Wright, J. A. (1997). Effects of a health promotion program on sustaining health behaviors in older adults. *American Journal of Preventive Medicine, 13*(4), 257–264.

Franco, S. J. (2004). *Medicare home health care in rural America*. Chicago, IL: NORC Walsh Center for Rural Health Analysis. Retrieved December 18, 2006 from http://www.norc.org/issues/NseriesJan04v1.pdf

Fredriksen-Goldsen, K. I., & Muraco, A. (2010). Aging and sexual orientation: A 25-year review of the literature. *Research on Aging, 32*, 372–413.

Freedman, M. (1994). *Seniors in national and community service: A report prepared for the Commonwealth Fund's Americans Over 55 at Work Program*. Philadelphia, PA: Public/Private Ventures.

Freedman, M. (2007). *Encore: Finding work that matters in the second half of life*. New York, NY: Public Affairs.

Freiman, M., & Brown, E. (1999). *Special care units in nursing homes: Selected characteristics, 1996*. Retrieved December 1, 2000 from http://www.meps.ahrq.gov/mepsweb/data_files/publications/ rf6/rf6.pdf

Friedman, B. M., & Godfrey, F. (2007). Intergenerational exercise addresses the public health issue of obesity. *Journal of Intergenerational Relationships, 5*, 79–94. doi:10.1300/J194v05n01_06

Fuller-Thomson, E., & Redmond, M. (2008). Falling through the social safety net: Food stamp use and nonuse among older impoverished Americans. *The Gerontologist, 48*(2), 235–244. doi:10.1093/geront/48.2.235

Fyrand, L. (2010). Reciprocity: A predictor of mental health and continuity in elderly people's relationships. A review. *Current Gerontology and Geriatrics Research, 2010*. doi:10.1155/2010/340161

Gabrel, C. S. (2000). *Characteristics of elderly nursing home current residents and discharges: Data from the 1997 National Nursing Home Survey* (Advance Data From Vital and Health Statistics No. 312). Hyattsville, MD: National Center for Health Statistics.

Gage, B., Pilkauskas, N., Dalton, K., Constantine, R., Leung, M., Hoover, S., & Green, J. (2007). *Long-Term Care Hospital (LTCH) payment system monitoring and evaluation PHASE II REPORT: January 2007*. Waltham, MA: RTI International Health, Social, and Economics Research. Retrieved from http://www.cms.hhs.gov/LongTermCareHospitalPPS/Downloads/RTI_LTCHPPS_Final_Rpt.pdf

Galambos, C. M. (1997). Resolving ethical conflicts in providing case management services to the elderly. *Journal of Gerontological Social Work, 27*(4), 57–67.

Gale, W. G., Orszag, P. R., Burman, L. E., & Hall, M. (2004). Distributional effects of defined contribution plans and individual retirement arrangements. *National Tax Journal, 57*(3), 1–39. Retrieved January 26, 2007 from http://ssrn.com/abstract = 1754638

Gallagher, D. (n.d.). *Creating great streets & great places—"It wasn't easy but it was worth it." The Charlotte Experience*. Retrieved from http://www.atlantaregional.com/File%20Library/Land%20Use/LCI/lu_lci_sponsors_mtg_12_14_2012_charlotte_dot_presentation.pdf

Gallagher-Thompson, D., Arean, P., Coon, D., Menéndez, A., Tagaki, K., Haley, W. E., . . . Szapocznik, J. (2000). Development and implementation of intervention strategies for culturally diverse caregiving populations. In R. Schulz (Ed.), *Handbook on dementia caregiving* (pp. 151–186). New York, NY: Springer.

Gallagher-Thompson, D., Arean, P., Rivera, P., & Thompson, L. W. (2001). Reducing distress in Hispanic caregivers using a psychoeducational intervention. *Clinical Gerontologist, 23*, 17–32.

Gamm, L., Hutchison, L., Bellamy, G., & Dabney, B. J. (2002). Rural healthy people 2010: Identifying rural health priorities and models for practice. *Journal of Rural Health, 18*(1), 9–14. doi:10.1111/j.1748-0361.2002.tb00869.x

Garden Mosaics. (n.d.). *About us*. Retrieved from http://communitygardennews.org/gardenmosaics/pgs/aboutus/mainaboutus.htm

Garfield, R. L. (2011). *Mental health financing in the United States: A primer*. Washington, DC: Kaiser Commission on Medicaid and the Uninsured. Retrieved from http://www.kff.org/medicaid/upload/8182.pdf

Garson, A. (1994, September). RSVP International: Putting seniors to work as volunteers. *Transitions Abroad, 18*, 53.

Gaugler, J. E., Jarrott, S. E., Zarit, S. H., Stephens, M. A. P., Townsend, A., & Greene, R. (2003). Respite for dementia caregivers: The effects of adult day service use on caregiving hours and care demands. *International Psychogeriatrics, 15*, 37–58.

Gelfand, D. E., & Bechill, W. (1991). The evolution of the Older Americans Act: A 25-year review of the legislative changes. *Generations, 15*(3), 19–22.

Generations United. (2010). *The 2010 MetLife Foundation/Generations United Intergenerational Shared Site Excellence Awards*. Retrieved from http://www.gu.org/LinkClick.aspx?fileticket = mUVVX8cwc-E%3D&tabid = 157&mid = 606

Generations United. (2011a). *LEGACY*. Retrieved from http://www.gu.org/OURWORK/PublicPolicy/GrandfamiliesPolicy/LEGACY.aspx

Generational United. (2011b). *Shared spaces policy*. Retrieved from http://www2.gu.org/OURWORK/PublicPolicy/SharedSpacesPolicy.aspx

Genworth Financial. (2012). *Genworth 2012 cost of care survey: Home care providers, adult day health care facilities, assisted living facilities and nursing homes.* Retrieved from https://www.genworth.com/dam/Americas/US/PDFs/Consumer/corporate/coc_12.pdf

Georgetown University Long-Term Care Financing Project. (2007). *National spending for long-term care fact sheet.* Retrieved from http://ltc.georgetown.edu/pdfs/medicare0207.pdf

Gerber, I. (1969). Bereavement and the acceptance of professional service. *Community Mental Health Journal, 5,* 487–495.

Gergen, K. J., Morse, S. J., & Kristeller, J. L. (1973). The manner of giving: Crossnational continuities in reactions to aid. *Psychologia, 16,* 121–131.

Geron, S., & Chassler, D. (1995). Advancing the state of the art: Establishing guidelines for long-term care case management. *Journal of Case Management, 4,* 9–13.

Gerontological Society of America. (2012, July). Nursing programs undergo nationwide transformation. *Gerontology News.* Retrieved from http://www.geron.org/images/stories/newsletters/gerontology_news/July_2012.pdf

Ghilarducci, T., & Turner, J. (Eds.). (2007). *Work options for older Americans.* Notre Dame, IN: University of Notre Dame Press.

Gigliotti, C. M., Jarrott, S. E., & Yorgason, J. (2004). Harvesting health: Effects of three types of horticultural therapy for persons with dementia. *Dementia, 3,* 161–180.

Gitlin, L., Reever, K., Dennis, M., Mathieu, E., & Hauck, W. (2006). Enhancing quality of life of families who use adult day services: Short- and long-term effects of the adult day services plus program. *The Gerontologist, 46*(5), 630–639.

Given, B. A., & Given, C. W. (2001). Health promotion for older adults in a managed care environment. In E. A. Swason, T. Tripp-Reimer, & K. Buckwalter (Eds.), *Health promotion and disease prevention in the older Adult: Interventions and recommendations.* New York, NY: Springer.

Glass, A. P. (2009). Aging in a community of mutual support: The emergence of an elder international cohousing community in the United States. *Journal of Housing for the Elderly, 23*(4), 283–303. doi:10.1080/02763890903326970

Glass, T. A. (2006). Disasters and older adults: Bringing a policy blind spot into the light. *Public Policy and Aging Report, 16*(2), 1–7.

Godfrey, D., & Weber, C. (2007). *Kentucky model approaches to legal service development legal delivery systems assessment.* Lexington, KY: Access to Justice Foundation.

Goggin, J., & Ronan, B. (2004). Our next chapter: Community colleges and the aging baby boomers. *Leadership Abstracts, 17,* 11–15. Retrieved December 18, 2006 from http://www.civicventures.org/articles.cfm

Goins, R. T., Mitchell, J., & Wu, B. (2006). Service issues among rural racial and ethnic minority elders. In R. T. Goins & J. A. Krout (Eds.), *Service delivery to rural older adults: Research, policy, and practice* (pp. 55–78). New York, NY: Springer.

Gold, M., Hudson M. C., & Davis, S. (2006). *Medicare Advantage benefits and premiums.* Princeton, NJ: Mathematica Policy Research. Retrieved January 17, 2007 from http://assets.aarp.org/rgcenter/health/2006_23_medicare.pdf

Gold, M., Jacobson, G., Damico, A., & Neuman, T. (2010). *Medicare Advantage 2011 data spotlight: Plan availability and premiums.* Menlo Park, CA: Henry J. Kaiser Family Foundation. Retrieved from http://www.kff.org/medicare/upload/8117.pdf

Gold, M., Jacobson, G., Damico, A., & Neuman, T. (2011). *Medicare Advantage enrollment market update.* Menlo Park, CA: Henry J. Kaiser Family Foundation. Retrieved from http://www.kff.org/medicare/upload/8228.pdf

Goldberg, N. G. (2009). *The Impact of inequality for same-sex partners in employer-sponsored retirement plans.* Los Angeles: The Williams Institute, UCLA School of Law. Retrieved from http://escholarship.org/uc/item/0pn9c1h4

Goodwin, J. S. (1989). Social, psychological and physical factors affecting the nutritional status of elderly subjects: Separating cause and effect. *American Journal of Clinical Nutrition, 50,* 1201–1209.

Goodwin, R., Costa, P., & Adonu, J. (2004). Social support and its consequences: "Positive" and "deficiency" values and their implications for support and self-esteem. *British Journal of Social Psychology, 4*(3), 465–474.

Gordon, R. A., & Arvey, R. D. (2004.). Age bias in laboratory and field settings: A meta-analytic investigation. *Journal of Applied Psychology, 34,* 468–492. doi:10.1111/j.1559-1816.2004.tb02557.x

Government of Western Australia, Department of Health. (n.d.). *Older Adult Mental Health Services (OAMHS).* Retrieved from http://www.nmahsmh.health.wa.gov.au/services/oamhs.cfm

Grabbe, L., Demi, A., Whittington, F., Jones, J., Branch, L., & Lambert, R. (1995). Functional status and the use of formal home care in the year before death. *Journal of Aging and Health, 7,* 339–364.

Grant, J. M. (2010). *Outing age 2010: Public policy issues affecting lesbian, gay, bisexual and transgender (LGBT) elders.* Washington, DC: National Gay and Lesbian Task Force. Retrieved from http://www.thetaskforce.org/downloads/reports/reports/outingage_final.pdf

Grant, M., Rue, H., Trainor, S., Bauer, J., Parks, J., Raulerson, M., . . . Souter, S. (2012). *The role of transportation systems management & operations in supporting livability and sustainability.* (FHWA-HOP-12-004). Washington, DC: U.S. Department of Transportation. Retrieved from http://www.ops.fhwa.dot.gov/publications/fhwahop12004/fhwahop12004.pdf

Gräsell, E. (1997). Temporary institutional respite in dementia cases: Who utilizes this form of respite care and what effect does it have? *International Psychogeriatrics, 9,* 437–448.

Greater Boston Food Bank. (2012). *Brown Bag program.* Retrieved from http://gbfb.org/our-mission/brown-bag-program.php

Greater Kansas City Community Foundation. (2012). *Shepherd's Centers of America.* Retrieved from http://gkccf.guidestar.org/NonprofitProfile.aspx?OrgId = 1064387

Green, L., Fitzhugh, E., Wang, M. Q., Perko, J., Eddy, J., & Westerfield, C. (1993). Influence of living arrangements on dietary adequacy for U.S. elderly: 1987–1988 nationwide food consumption survey. *Wellness Perspectives: Research, Theory and Practice, 10*(1), 32–40.

Greenberg, M. S., & Shapiro, S. P. (1971). Indebtedness: An adverse aspect of asking for and receiving help. *Sociometry, 34,* 290–301.

Greenberg, M. S., & Westcott, D. R. (1983). Indebtedness as a mediator of reactions to aid. In J. D. Fisher, A. Nadler, & B. M. DePaulo (Eds.), *New directions in helping* (Vol. 1, pp. 85–112). New York, NY: Academic Press.

Green Thumb, Inc. (2001). *Green Thumb, Inc.* Retrieved May 9, 2001 from www.experience works.org.

Grimaldi, P. L. (1982). *Medicaid reimbursement of nursing home care.* Washington, DC: American Enterprise Institute.

Grinstead, L., Leder, S., Jensen, S., & Bond, L. (2003). Review of the research on the health of caregiving grandparents. *Journal of Advanced Nursing, 44,* 318–326.

Gross, D. (1998). *Different needs, different strategies: A manual for training low-income, older workers.* Retrieved May 9, 2001 from http://www.doleta.gov/seniors/html_docs/docs/dnds.cfm

Grove, N. C., & Spier, B. E. (1999). Motivating the well elderly to exercise. *Journal of Community Health Nursing, 16*(3), 179–189.

Guess, A. (2007). Geography emerges in distance ed. *Inside Higher Education.* Retrieved from http://www.insidehighered.com/news/2007/11/28/online

Guigoz, Z. Y. (2006). The Mini Nutritional Assessment (MNA) Review of the literature—What does it tell us? *Journal of Nutrition, Health & Aging, 10*(6), 466–487.

Gum, A. M., King-Kallimanis, B., & Kohn, R. (2009). Prevalence of mood, anxiety, and substance-abuse disorders for older Americans in the national comorbidity survey-replication. *American Journal of Geriatric Psychiatry, 17,* 769–781.

Gunther, J., & Ormsby, A. (2004). *Planning for the legal needs of Utah's seniors: Final report.* Ann Arbor, MI: The Center for Social Gerontology. Retrieved from http://www.tcsg.org/finalreport1018_04.pdf

Guttman, D. (1980). *Perspective on equitable shares in public benefits by minority elderly: Executive summary.* Washington, DC: Catholic University of America.

Hale, N. (1990). *The older worker.* San Francisco, CA: Jossey-Bass.

Haley, B. A., & Gray, R. W. (2008). *Section 202 supportive housing for the elderly: Program status and performance measurement.* Washington, DC: Office of Policy Development and Research, U.S. Department of Housing and Urban Development. Retrieved from http://www.huduser.org/portal/publications/sec_202_1.pdf

Hall, L., & Hare, J. (1997). Video Respite for cognitively impaired persons in nursing homes. *American Journal of Alzheimer's Disease & Other Dementias, 12*(3), 117–121.

Halpern, D. (2005). *Social capital.* Malden, MA: Polity.

Hanssen, A., Meima, N., Buckspan, L., Henderson, B., Helbig, T., & Zarit, S. (1978). Correlates of senior center participation. *The Gerontologist, 18,* 193–199.

Harahan, M. F., Sanders, A., & Stone, R. (2006). *Creating new long-term care choices for older adults: A synthesis of findings from a study of affordable housing plus service linkages.* Washington, DC: Institute for the Future of Aging Services. Retrieved from http://www.leadingage.org/uploadedFiles/Content/About/Center_for_Applied_Research/Expanding_Affordable_Housing_Plus_Services/Creating_New_Long_Term_Care_Choices.pdf

Hardin, J., Tucker, L., & Callejas, L. (2001). *Assessment of operational barriers and impediments to transit use: Transit information and scheduling for major activity centers.* Retrieved October 28, 2006 from http://ntl.bts.gov/lib/12000/12000/12049/392-11.pdf

Harding, R., Epiphaniou, E., & Chidgey-Clark, J. (2012). Needs, experiences, and preferences of sexual minorities for end-of-life care and palliative care: A systematic review. *Journal of Palliative Medicine, 15,* 602–611. doi:10.1089/jpm.2011.0279

Harper, M. S. (1991). Delivery of mental health services in the home, and other community-based health services. In M. S. Harper (Ed.), *Management and care of the elderly* (pp. 320–331). Newbury Park, CA: Sage.

Harrell, R., & Houser, A. (2011). *State housing profiles: Housing conditions and affordability for the older population* (3rd ed.). Washington, DC: AARP Public Policy Institute. Retrieved from http://assets.aarp.org/rgcenter/ppi/liv-com/AARP_Housing2011_Full.pdf

Harrington, C. (1991). The nursing home industry: A structural analysis. In M. Minkler & C. L. Estes (Eds.), *Critical perspectives on aging: The political and moral economy of growing old* (pp. 153–172). Amityville, MD: Baywood.

Harrington, C., Carrillo, H., Wellin, V., Miller, N., & LeBlanc, A. (2000). Predicting state Medicaid home and community expenditures, 1992–1997. *The Gerontologist, 40,* 673–686.

Harrington, C., & Swan, J. H. (2003). Nursing home staffing, turnover, and case mix. *Medical Care Research and Review, 60*(3), 366–392. doi:10.1177/1077558703254692

Harrington-Meyer, M. (2001). Medicaid reimbursement rates and access to nursing homes: Implications for gender, race, and marital status. *Research on Aging, 23,* 532–539.

Harris & Associates. (1975). *The myth and reality of aging in America.* Washington, DC: National Council on the Aging.

Hartman, L., Jarosek, S. L.,Virnig, B. A., & Durham, S. (2007). Medicare-certified home health care: Urban-rural differences in utilization. *Journal of Rural Health, 23,* 254–257.

Harvard School of Public Health. (2004). *Reinventing aging: Baby boomers and civic engagement* (Harvard School of Public Health–MetLife Foundation Initiative on Retirement and Civic Engagement Report). Boston, MA: Author.

Hatfield, E., & Sprecher, S. (1983). Equity theory and recipient reactions to aid. In J. D. Fisher, A. Nadler, & B. M. DePaulo (Eds.), *New directions in helping* (Vol. 1, pp. 113–141). New York, NY: Academic Press.

Hawes, C., Wildfire, J. B., & Lux, L. J. (1993). *The regulation of board and care homes: Results of a survey in the 50 states and the District of Columbia: National summary.* Washington, DC: American Association of Retired Persons.

Hawranik, P. (2002). In home service use by caregivers and their elders: Does cognitive status make a difference? *Canadian Journal on Aging, 21,* 257–271.

Haxton, J. E., & Boelk, A. Z. (2010). Serving families on the frontline: Challenges and creative solutions in rural hospice social work. *Social Work in Health Care, 49,* 526–550.

He, W., Sengupta, M., Velkoff, V. A., & DeBarros, K. A. (2005). *65+ in the United States.* Retrieved January 9, 2007, from http://www.census.gov/prod/2006pubs/p23-209.pdf

Health Care Financing Administration. (2001a). *Medicaid eligibility.* Retrieved September 1, 2001 from http://www.hcfa.gov/medicaid/meligib.htm

Health Care Financing Administration. (2001b). *Medicare+Choice Program in 2001 and 2002.* Retrieved September 15, 2001 from http://www.hcfa.gov/facts/fs010829.htm

Health Care Financing Administration. (2001c). *Your Medicare benefits*. Retrieved September 15, 2001 from http://www.medicare.gov/Publications/Pubs/pdf/yourmb.pdf

Heath, A. (1993). *ElderTransit facts: Increasing minority participation in transportation programs* [Brochure]. Washington, DC: National Eldercare Institute on Transportation.

Hedge, J. W., Borman, W. C., & Lammlein, S. E. (2006). *The aging workforce: Realities, myths, and implications for organizations*. Washington, DC: American Psychological Association.

Helen Andrus Benedict Foundation. (2011). *Selected grants*. Retrieved from http://foundationcenter.org/grantmaker/benedict/selgrants.html

Henry, M. E., & Capitman, J. (1995). Finding satisfaction in adult day care: Analysis of a national demonstration of dementia care and respite services. *Journal of Applied Gerontology, 14,* 302–320.

Herdt, G., & de Vries, B. (2004). *Gay and lesbian aging: Research and future directions.* New York, NY: Springer.

Herman, C. J., & Wadsworth, N. (1992). *Action for health: Older women's project.* Cleveland, OH: Case Western Reserve University School of Medicine.

Hershey, C., Clark, S., Day, J. R., & Thatcher, R. H. (2010, June). *Accessible public transportation in the United States: Twenty years after passage of the ADA.* Paper presented at the TRANSED 2010: 12th International Conference on Mobility and Transport for Elderly and Disabled Persons, Hong Kong, China.

Hetzel, L., & Smith, A. (2001). *The 65 years and over population: 2000.* Washington, DC: U.S. Census Bureau. Retrieved February 4, 2007 from http://www.census.gov/prod/2001pubs/c2kbr01-10.pdf

Heumann, L. F. (1990). The housing and support costs of elderly with comparable support needs living in long-term care and congregate housing. *Journal of Housing for the Elderly, 6*(1–2), 45–71.

Hewitt, A., Larson, S., Edelstein, S., Seavey, D., Hoge, M. A., & Morris, J. A. (2008). *A synthesis of direct service workforce demographics and challenges across intellectual/developmental disabilities, aging, physical disabilities, and behavioral health.* Retrieved from http://www.hcbs.org/files/152/7561/DSW_RC_Cross-Disability_Synthesis.pdf

Hibbard, J., Greene, J., & Tusler, M. (2006). *An assessment of beneficiary knowledge of Medicare coverage options and the prescription drug benefit.* Washington, DC: AARP Public Policy Institute. Retrieved January 28, 2007 from http://assets.aarp.org/rgcenter/health/2006_12_medicare.pdf

Hickey, T., & Stilwell, D. L. (1991). Health promotion for older people: All is not well. *The Gerontologist, 31,* 822–829.

High, L. (2000). CCRCs: Surviving the evolving landscape. *Assisted Living Today, 7*(8), 61–63.

Higher Education Act, 20 U.S.C. § 1001 et seq. (1965).

Hinrichsen, G. A. (2010). Public policy and the provision of psychological services to older adults. *Professional Psychology: Research and Practice, 41,* 97–103.

Hodgson, L. G. (1995). Adult grandchildren and their grandparents: The enduring bond. *International Journal of Aging and Human Development, 34,* 209–225.

Hoffman, E. D., Klees, B. S., & Curtis, C. A. (2006). *Brief summaries of Medicare and Medicaid Title XVIII and Title XIX of the Social Security Act.* Retrieved from http://www.cms.hhs.gov/Medicare ProgramRatesStats/downloads/MedicareMedicaidSummaries2006.pdf

Hooper, K., & Hamberg, J. (1986). The making of America's homeless: From skid row to the new poor, 1945–1984. In R. Bratt, C. Hartman, & A. Meyerson (Eds.), *Critical perspectives in housing.* Philadelphia, PA: Temple University Press.

Hooyman, N. R., & Kiyak, H. A. (2002). *Social gerontology: A multidisciplinary perspective* (6th ed.). Needham Heights, MA: Simon & Schuster.

Hopp, F. P. (1999). Patterns and predictors of formal and informal care among elderly persons living in board and care homes. *The Gerontologist, 39*(2), 167–176.

Hopp, F. P. (2000). Preferences for surrogate decision makers, informal communication, and advance directives among community-dwelling elders: Results from a national study. *The Gerontologist, 40*(4), 449–457.

Hornillos, C., & Crespo, M. (2012). Support groups for caregivers of Alzheimer's patients: A historical review. *Dementia, 11,* 155–169.

Horowitz, A. (1985). Family caregiving to the frail elderly. In C. Eisdorfer (Ed.), *Annual review of gerontology and geriatrics* (Vol. 5, pp. 194–246). New York, NY: Springer.

Horvath, B., Silberg, M., Landerman, L. R., Johnson, F. S., & Michener, J. L. (2006). Dynamics of patient targeting for care management in Medicaid: A case study of the Durham Community Health Network. *Care Management Journals, 7,* 107–114.

Hospice Association of America. (2006). *Hospice facts and statistics.* Retrieved December 18, 2006 from http://www.nahc.org/hospicefs06.pdf

Hospice Association of America. (2010). *Hospice facts and statistics.* Retrieved from http://www.nahc.org/facts/HospiceStats10.pdf

Hostetler, A. J. (2011). Senior centers in the era of the "Third Age": Country clubs, community centers, or something else? *Journal of Aging Studies, 25*(2), 166–176. doi:10.1016/j.jaging.2010.08.021

Howe, R. (1994). A framework for case management. In R. Howe (Ed.), *Case management for health care professionals* (pp. 3–12). Chicago, IL: Precept.

Hoyert, D. L., Heron, M. P., Murphy, S. L., & Kung, H. (2006). Deaths: Final data for 2003. *National Vital Statistics Reports, 54*(13). Retrieved January 27, 2007 from http://www.cdc.gov/nchs/data/nvsr/nvsr54/nvsr54_13.pdf

Hrehocik, M. (2008). Group effort makes hospice house a reality. *Long-Term Living, 57*(6), 38–40.

Hudson, R. B. (2010). The Older Americans Act and the Aging Services Network. In R. B. Hudson (Ed.), *The new politics of old age policy* (2nd ed.). Baltimore, MD: Johns Hopkins University Press.

Hudson, R. B., & Kingson, E. R. (1991). Inclusive and fair: The case for universality in social programs. *Generations, 15*(3), 51–56.

Hunt, M. (1998). Naturally occurring retirement communities. In N. L. Shumsky (Ed.), *Encyclopedia of urban America: The cities and suburbs* (pp. 517–518). New York, NY: Garland.

Hushbeck, J. (1990). American business, public policy, and the older worker. *Virginia Journal of Science, 41,* 169–181.

Huttman, E. D. (1985). *Social services for the elderly.* New York, NY: Free Press.

Independent Sector. (2012). *National value of volunteer time.* Retrieved from http://independentsector.org/volunteer_time

Institute of Medicine. (1986). *Improving the quality of care in nursing homes.* Washington, DC: National Academy Press.

Institute of Medicine. (1991). *Disability in America: Toward a national agenda for prevention.* Washington, DC: Author.

Institute of Medicine. (2008). *Retooling for an aging America: Building the health care workforce.* Washington, DC: National Academies Press. Retrieved from http://www.iom.edu/Reports/2008/Retooling-for-an-Aging-America-Building-the-Health-Care-Workforce.aspx

Institute of Medicine. (2012). *The mental health and substance use workforce for older adults: In whose hands?* Washington, DC: National Academies Press.

Intermodal Surface Transportation Efficiency Act of 1991, Pub. L. No. 102–240, 105 Stat. 1914.

Issa, P., & Zedlewski, S. R. (2011). *Poverty among older Americans, 2009* (Retirement Security Data Brief No. 1). Washington, DC: Urban Institute. Retrieved from http://www.urban.org/UploadedPDF/412296-Poverty-Among-Older-Americans.pdf

Ivery, J. M., & Akstein-Kahan, D. (2010). The naturally occurring retirement community (NORC) initiative in Georgia: Developing and managing collaborative partnerships to support older adults. *Administration in Social Work, 3,* 329–343.

Jackson, A. M. (2011). *The Low Income Home Energy Assistance Program: A critical resource for low-income households.* Washington, DC: AARP Policy Institute. Retrieved from http://assets.aarp.org/rgcenter/consume/fs138_liheap.pdf

Jaffe, D. J., & Howe, E. (1988). Agency-assisted shared housing: The nature of programs and matches. *The Gerontologist, 28,* 318–324.

Janke, M., Davey, A., & Kleiber, D. (2006). Modeling change in older adults' leisure activities. *Leisure Sciences, 28,* 285–303.

Jarrott, S. E. (2005). Evaluation. In S. Steinig (Ed.), *Under one roof: A guide to starting and strengthening intergenerational shared site programs* (pp. 85–97). Washington, DC: Generations United.

Jarrott, S. E. (2008). Shared site intergenerational programs: Obstacles and opportunities. *Journal of Intergenerational Relationships, 6,* 384–388.

Jarrott, S. E. (2011). Where have we been and where are we going? Content analysis of evaluation research of intergenerational programs. *Journal of Intergenerational Relationships, 9,* 37–52. doi:10.1080/15350770.2011.544594

Jarrott, S. E., Gigliotti, C. M., & Smock, S. A. (2006). Where do we stand? Testing the foundation of a shared site intergenerational program. *Journal of Intergenerational Relationships, 4*(2), 73–92.

Jarrott, S. E., Zarit, S. H., Stephens, M. A. P., Townsend, A., & Greene, R. (1999). Caregiver satisfaction with adult day service programs. *American Journal of Alzheimer's Disease, 14,* 233–244.

Jellinek, I., Pardasani, M., & Sackman, B. (2010a). *21st century senior centers: Changing the conversation: A study of New York City's senior centers.* New York. NY: Council of Senior Centers and Services of New York City. Retrieved from http://cscs-ny.org/files/FINAL-WHOLE-REPORT.pdf

Jellinek, I., Pardasani, M., & Sackman, B. (2010b). *21st century senior centers: Changing the conversation: A study of New York City's senior centers. Technical report: Methodology, literature review and references.* New York, NY: Council of Senior Centers and Services of New York City. Retrieved from http://www.cscs-ny.org/files/Technical-Report.pdf

Jimenez, D. E., Alegria, M., Chen, C., Chan, D., & Laderman, M. (2010). Prevalence of psychiatric illnesses among ethnic minority elderly. *Journal of the American Geriatric Society, 58,* 256–264.

Jirovec, R. L., Erich, J. A., & Sanders, L. J. (1989). Patterns of senior center participation among low income urban elderly. *Journal of Gerontological Social Work, 13,* 115–132.

Job Training Partnership Act of 1982, Pub. L. No. 97–300, 96 Stat. 1322 (1982).

Johns Hopkins Bloomberg School of Public Health. (2012). *Frequently asked questions about guided care.* Retrieved from http://www.guidedcare.org/pdf/Guided%20Care%20FAQs.pdf

Johnson, K., & Wilson, K. (2010). *Current economic status of older adults in the United States: A demographic analysis.* Washington, DC: National Council on Aging. Retrieved from http://www.ncoa.org/assets/files/pdf/Economic-Security-Trends-for-Older-Adults-65-and-Older_March-2010.pdf

Johnson, K. S., Kuchibhatla, M., & Tulsky, J.A. (2008). What explains racial differences in the use of advance directives and attitudes toward hospice care? *Journal of the American Geriatrics Society, 56,* 1953–1958.

Johnson, R. W., Haaga, O., & Simms, M. (2011). *50+ African American workers: A status report, implications, and recommendations.* Washington, DC: Urban Institute. Retrieved from http://assets.aarp.org/rgcenter/econ/aa-workers-11.pdf

Johnson, R. W., & Schaner, S. G. (2005). *Value of unpaid activities by older Americans tops $160 billion per year* (Perspectives on Productive Aging Brief No. 4). Washington, DC: Urban Institute. Retrieved from http://www.urban.org/publications/311227.html

Johnson, R. W., Toohey, D., & Wiener, J. M. (2007). *Meeting the long-term care needs of the baby boomers: How changing families will affect paid helpers and institutions* (The Retirement Project Discussion Paper 07-04). Washington, DC: Urban Institute.

Johnson, R. W., & Uccello, C.E. (2005). Is private long-term care insurance the answer? *An Issue in Brief, 29.* Retrieved from http://www.urban.org/UploadedPDF/1000795.pdf

Johnson, R. W., & Weiner, J. M. (2006). *A profile of frail older Americans and their caregivers.* Washington, DC: Urban Institute. Retrieved March 9, 2006 from http://www.urban.org/publications/311284.html

Johnston, D., Smith, M., Beard-Byrd, K., Albert, A., Legault, C., McCall, W. V., . . . Reifler, B. (2010). A new home-based mental health program for older adults: Description of the first 100 cases. *American Journal of Geriatric Psychiatry, 18,* 1141–1145.

Jones, A. L., Harris-Kojetin, L., & Valverde, R. (2012, April 18). Characteristics and use of home health care by men and women aged 65 and over. *National Health Statistics Report, 52,* 1–8. Retrieved from http://www.cdc.gov/nchs/data/nhsr/nhsr052.pdf

Jones, D. C., & Vaughan, K. (1990). Close friendships among senior adults. *Psychology and Aging, 3,* 451–457.

Jones, J., & Bandos, B. (2010, April). *Knowledge engineering for health care managers.* Paper presented at the 34th Annual Midwest Nursing Research Society, Kansas City, MO. Retrieved from http://www.nursinglibrary.org/vhl/handle/10755/158370

Joung, H.-W., Kim, H.-S., Yuan, J. J., & Huffman, L. (2011). Service quality, satisfaction, and behavioral intention in home delivered meals program. *Nutrition Research and Practice, 5*(2), 163–168.

Jung, J. (1990). The role of reciprocity in social support. *Basic & Applied Social Psychology, 11*(3), 243–253.

Justice, D. (1993). *Case management standards in state community based long-term care programs.* Washington, DC: Congressional Research Service.

Kaiser Commission on Medicaid and the Uninsured. (2010). *Medicaid, a primer: Key information on our nation's health coverage program for low-income people.* Washington, DC: Henry J. Kaiser Family Foundation. Retrieved from http://www.kff.org/medicaid/upload/7334-04.pdf

Kaiser Commission on Medicaid and the Uninsured. (2011a). *Medicaid home and community-based services programs: Data updated.* Washington, DC: Henry J. Kaiser Family Foundation. Retrieved from http://www.kff.org/medicaid/upload/7720-05.pdf

Kaiser Commission on Medicaid and the Uninsured. (2011b). *Money follows the person: A 2010 snapshot.* Washington, DC: Henry J. Kaiser Family Foundation. Retrieved from http://www.kff.org/medicaid/8142.pdf

Kaiser Commission on Medicaid and the Uninsured. (2011c). *Money follows the person: A 2011 survey of transitions, services, and costs.* Washington, DC: Henry J. Kaiser Family Foundation. Retrieved from http://www.kff.org/medicaid/upload/8142-02-2.pdf

Kaiser Family Foundation. (2010a). *Explaining Health Reform: Key changes in Medicare Advantage program.* Retrieved from http://www.kff.org/healthreform/upload/8071.pdf

Kaiser Family Foundation. (2010b). *Medicaid long-term services and supports: Key changes in the health reform law.* Retrieved from http://www.kff.org/healthreform/upload/8079.pdf

Kaiser Family Foundation. (2011a). *Medicare policy: The Medicare Prescription Drug Benefit.* Retrieved from http://www.kff.org/medicare/upload/7044-12.pdf

Kaiser Family Foundation. (2011b). *Summary of the new health reform law.* Retrieved from http://www.kff.org/healthreform/upload/8061.pdf

Kaiser Family Foundation. (2012a). *5 key questions and answers about Medicaid.* Washington, DC: Kaiser Commission on Medicaid and the Uninsured. Retrieved from http://www.kff.org/medicaid/upload/8139-02.pdf

Kaiser Family Foundation. (2012b). *A guide to the Supreme Court's Affordable Care Act decision.* Retrieved from http://www.kff.org/healthreform/upload/8332.pdf

Kaiser Family Foundation. (2012c). *Medicaid health homes for beneficiaries with chronic conditions.* Retrieved from http://www.kff.org/medicaid/upload/8340.pdf

Kaiser Family Foundation. (2012d). *State health facts: Distribution of Medicaid spending on long term care, FY 2010.* Retrieved from http://www.statehealthfacts.org/comparetable.jsp?typ = 4&ind = 180 &cat = 4&sub = 47&print = 1

Kaiser Family Foundation. (n.d.). *Health reform source: Implementation timeline.* Retrieved from http://healthreform.kff.org/timeline.aspx

Kamp, B. J., Wellman, N. S., & Russell, C. (2010). Position of the American Dietetic Association, American Society for Nutrition, and Society for Nutrition Education: Food and nutrition programs for community-residing older adults. *Journal of Nutrition Education and Behavior, 42*(2), 72–82. doi:10.1016/j.jneb.2009.12.001

Kamping-Carder, L. (2011, November 29). SRO owners to pay $600K for renting Upper West Side units to tourists. *The Real Deal.* Retrieved from http://therealdeal.com/blog/2011/11/29/sro-owners-to-pay-600k-for-renting-units-to-tourists-settlement-resolves-2007-lawsuit-that-gave-rise-to-illegal-hotel-law/

Kane, R. A. (2000). *Assuring quality in care at home.* New York, NY: Springer.

Kane, R. A., & Caplan, A. (Eds.). (1993). *Ethical conflict in the management of home care: Case manager's dilemma.* New York, NY: Springer.

Kane, R. A., & Frytak, J. (1994). *Models for case management in long-term care: Interactions of case managers and home care providers.* Minneapolis, MN: National Long-Term Care Resource Center.

Kane, R. A., Illston, L., & Miller, N. (1992). Qualitative analysis of the program of all-inclusive care for the elderly (PACE). *The Gerontologist, 32,* 771–780.

Kane, R. A., & Kane, R. L. (1981). *Assessing the elderly: A practical guide for measurement.* Lexington, MA: Lexington.

Kane, R. L., Kane, R. A., Kaye, N., Mollica, R., Riley, T., Saucier, P., . . . Starr, L. (1996). *Managed care: Handbook for the aging network.* Minneapolis, MN: National Long-Term Care Resource Center.

Kane, R. L., Kane, R. A., Ladd, R. C., & Veazie, W. (1998). Variations in state spending for long-term care: Factors associated with more balanced systems. *Journal of Health Politics, Policy, and Law, 23,* 363–390.

Kannel, W. B. (1986). Nutritional contributors to cardiovascular disease in the elderly. *Journal of the American Geriatrics Society, 34,* 27–36.

Kansas Advocates for Better Care. (2002). *Intergenerational initiatives in Kansas nursing homes.* Retrieved from http://www.kabc.org/pdfs/intergenerational-initiatives-in-kansas-nursing-homes.pdf

Kansas State Research and Extension. (2011). *Sage advice: Programs.* Retrieved from http://www.aging.ksu.edu/p.aspx?tabid = 72

Kaplan, J., & Shore, H. (1993). The Jewish nursing home: Innovations in practice and policy. In C. M. Barresi & D. E. Stull (Eds.), *Ethnic elderly and long-term care* (pp. 115–129). New York, NY: Springer.

Karel, M. J., Gatz, M., & Smyers, M. A. (2012). Aging and mental health in the decade ahead: What psychologists need to know. *American Psychologist, 67,* 184–198.

Karlin, B. E., Duffy, M., & Gleaves, D. H. (2008). Patterns and predictors of mental health service use and mental illness among older and younger adults in the United States. *Psychological Services, 5,* 275–294.

Karlin, B. E., & Norris, M. B. (2006). Public mental health care utilization by older adults. *Administration and Policy in Mental Health and Mental Health Services Research, 33,* 730–735.

Karner, T., & Hall, L. C. (2002). Successful strategies for serving diverse populations. *Home Health Care Services Quarterly, 21*(3–4), 107–131.

Kart, C. S. (1997). *The realities of aging: An introduction to gerontology* (5th ed.). Needham Heights, MA: Allyn & Bacon.

Kassner, E. (2006). *Consumer-directed home and community-based services: Fact sheet.* Washington, DC: AARP Public Policy Institute. Retrieved from http://assets.aarp.org/rgcenter/il/fs128_cons_dir.pdf

Katz, P. (2009). Board-and-care facilities. In *The Merck manual home health handbook for patients and caregivers.* Retrieved from http://www.merckmanuals.com/home/older_peoples_health_issues/long-term_care/board-and-care_facilities.html

Kaufman, A. V., Scogin, F. R., MaloneBeach, E. E., Baumhover, L. A., & McKendree-Smith, N. (2000). Home-delivered mental health services for aged rural home health care recipients. *Journal of Applied Gerontology, 19,* 460–475.

Kaye, H. S., Harrington, C., & LaPlante, M. P. (2010). Long-term care: Who gets it, who provides it, who pays, and how much? *Health Affairs, 29*(1), 11–21. doi:10.1377/hlthaff.2009.0535

Keith, P. M. (2003). Interests and skills of volunteers in an ombudsman program: Opportunities for participation. *International Journal of Aging and Human Development, 57*(1), 1–20.

Keith, P. M., & Wacker, R. R. (1994). *Older wards and their guardians.* New York, NY: Praeger.

Keller, H. H. (1993). Malnutrition in institutionalized elderly—How and why. *Journal of the American Geriatrics Society, 41*(11), 1212–1218.

Kelley, H. H. (1967). Attribution theory in social psychology. In D. Levin (Ed.), *Nebraska Symposium on Motivation* (pp. 151–174). Lincoln: University of Nebraska Press.

Kelly, D. (2009). *Fiscal and policy implications for single room occupancy hotels.* San Francisco, CA: Department of Aging and Adult Services. Retrieved from http://www.sf-planning.org/ftp/files/legislative_changes/HSA_Report_on_SROs_2009.pdf

Kelly, J. R., Steinkamp, M. W., & Kelly, J. R. (1986). Later life leisure: How they play in Peoria. *The Gerontologist, 26,* 531–537.

Kelly, J. R., Steinkamp, M. W., & Kelly, J. R. (1987). Later life satisfaction: Does leisure contribute? *Leisure Sciences, 9,* 189–200.

Kelsey, S. G., & Laditka, S. B. (2009). Evaluating the roles of professional geriatric care managers in maintaining the quality of life for older Americans. *Journal of Gerontological Social Work, 52,* 261–276.

Kemper, P. (1988). The evaluation of the National Long Term Care Demonstration: Overview of the findings. *Health Services Research, 23,* 161–174.

Kendal at Oberlin. (2005). *Kendal at Oberlin—Oberlin at Kendal.* Retrieved from http://kao.kendal.org/living/TheCollegeConnection.aspx

Kennedy, A. M., & Krasny, M. (2005). Garden Mosaics: Students learn about cultural heritage and develop scientific investigation skills in a unique garden program. *The Science Teacher, 72*(3), 44–48.

Kennet, J., Burgio, L., & Schulz, R. (2000). Interventions for in-home caregivers: A review of research 1990 to present. In R. Schulz (Ed.), *Handbook of dementia caregiving* (pp. 61–125). New York, NY: Springer.

Kenney, G. M. (1993). Is access to home health care a problem in rural areas? *American Journal of Public Health, 83*(3), 412–414.

Kenney, G. M., Zuckerman, S., Dubay, L., Huntress, M., Lynch, V., Haley, J., & Anderson, N. (2012). *Opting in to the Medicaid expansion under the ACA: Who are the uninsured adults who could gain health insurance coverage.* Washington, DC: Urban Institute. Retrieved from http://www.urban.org/UploadedPDF/412630-opting-in-medicaid.pdf

Kent, D. (1978, May–June). The how and why of senior centers. *Aging,* 2–6.

Kim, E., Kleiber, D. A., & Kropf, N. (2001). Leisure activity, ethnic preservation, and cultural integration of older Korean Americans. *Journal of Gerontological Social Work, 36*(1–2), 107–129.

Kim, S. (2011). Assessing mobility in an aging society: Personal and built environment factors associated with older people's subjective transportation deficiency in the US. *Transportation Research Part F: Traffic Psychology and Behaviour, 14*(5), 422–429. doi:10.1016/j.trf.2011.04.011

Kimball, B., & O'Neill, E. (2002). *Health care's human crisis: The American nursing shortage.* Princeton, NJ: Robert Wood Johnson Foundation.

King, A. C., Haskell, W. L., Taylor, C. B., Kraemer, H. C., & DeBusk, R. F. (1991). Group versus home-based exercise training in healthy older men and women: A community-based clinical trial. *Journal of the American Medical Association, 266,* 1535–1542.

King, A. C., Rejeski, J., & Buchner, D. M. (1998). Physical activity interventions targeting older adults: A critical review and recommendations. *American Journal of Preventive Medicine, 15*(4), 316–333.

King, S., & Collins, C. (1991). Institutionalization of an elderly family member: Reactions of spouse and nonspouse caregivers. *Archives of Psychiatric Nursing, 5,* 323–330.

Kingston, E. R., Hirshorn, B. A., & Cornman, J. M. (1986). *Ties that bind: The interdependence of generations.* Cabin John, MD: Seven Locks.

Kirby, J. B., & Lau, D. T. (2010). Community and individual race/ethnicity and home health care use among elderly persons in the United States. *Health Services Research, 45,* 1251–1267. doi:10.1111/j.1475-6773.2010.01135.x

Kirschner Associates. (1983). A*n evaluation of the nutritional services for the elderly* (Vols. 1–5). Washington, DC: U.S. Department of Health and Human Services, Administration on Aging.

Klees, B. S., Wolfe, C. J., & Curtis, C. A. (2011). *Brief summaries of Medicare and Medicaid: Title XVIII and Title XIX of the Social Security Act.* Washington, DC: U.S. Department of Health and Human Services. Retrieved from https://www.cms.gov/Research-Statistics-Data-and-Systems/Statistics-Trends-and-Reports/MedicareProgramRatesStats/Downloads/MedicareMedicaidSummaries2011.pdf

Kleiber, D. A., Hutchinson, S. L., & Williams, R. (2002). Leisure as a resource in transcending negative life events: Self-protection, self-restoration and personal transformation. *Leisure Sciences, 24,* 219–235. doi:10.1080/01490400252900167

Knight, H., & Lee, S. (2011, November 22). Supervisors hear about bleakness of living conditions at SRO hotels. *San Francisco Chronicle.* Retrieved from http://www.sfgate.com/bayarea/article/Supervisors-hear-about-bleakness-of-living-2289698.php

Kochanek, K. D., Xu, J. Q., Murphy, S. L., Miniño, A. M., & Kung, H. (2011). Deaths: Final data for 2009. *National Vital Statistics Reports, 60*(3). Hyattsville, MD. Retrieved from http://www.cdc.gov/nchs/data/nvsr/nvsr60/nvsr60_03.pdf

Kochera, A., Straight, A. & Guterbock, T. (2005). *Beyond 50.05: A report to the nation on livable communities: Creating environments for successful aging.* Washington, DC: AARP Public Policy Institute. Retrieved from http://assets.aarp.org/rgcenter/il/beyond_50_communities.pdf

Koebel, C. T., Beamish, J., & Danielson, K. A. (2003). *Evaluation of the HUD Elder Cottage Housing Opportunity (ECHO) program* (Faculty Publications (SEPA), Paper 351). Retrieved from http://digitalscholarship.unlv.edu/cgi/viewcontent.cgi?article = 1350&context = sea_fac_articles

Koffman, D., Raphael, D., & Weiner, R. (2004). *The impact of federal programs on transportation for older adults.* San Francisco, CA: Nelson/Nygaard Consulting Associates. Retrieved January 15, 2006 from http://assets.aarp.org/rgcenter/post-import/2004_17_transport.pdf

Korim, A. (1974). *Older Americans and community colleges: A guide for program implementation.* Washington, DC: American Association of Community and Junior Colleges.

Kosloski, K., & Montgomery, R. (1993). The effects of respite on caregivers of Alzheimer's patients: One-year evaluation of the Michigan model of respite programs. *Journal of Applied Gerontology, 12,* 4–17.

Kosloski, K., & Montgomery, R. (1995). The impact of respite use on nursing home placement. *The Gerontologist, 35,* 67–74.

Kosloski, K., Montgomery, R. J. V., & Youngbauer, J. G. (2001). Utilization of respite services: A comparison of users, seekers, and nonseekers. *Journal of Applied Gerontology, 20*(1), 111–132.

Kosloski, K., Schaefer, J., Allwardt, D., Montgomery, R., & Karner, T. (2002). The role of cultural factors on clients' attitudes toward caregiving, perception of service delivery, and service utilization. *Home Health Care Services Quarterly, 21,* 65–88.

Kramer, A. (2006). *Uniform patient assessment for post-acute care: Final report.* Aurora, CO: Division of Health Care Policy and Research, University of Colorado at Denver and Health Sciences Center. Retrieved February 5, 2007 from http://www.cms.gov/Medicare/Quality-Initiatives-Patient-Assessment-Instruments/QualityInitiativesGenInfo/downloads/QualityPACFullReport.pdf

Krause, K. (2009). Church-based volunteering, Providing informal support at church, and self-rated health in late life. *Journal of Aging and Health, 21,* 63–84. doi:10.1177/0898264308328638

Kreider, R. M., & Ellis, R. (2011). *Living arrangements of children: 2009* (Current Population Reports, P70–126). Washington, DC: U.S. Census Bureau. Retrieved from http://www.census.gov/prod/2011pubs/p70-126.pdf

Krout, J. (1981). *Service utilization patterns of the rural elderly: Final report to the Administration on Aging.* Fredonia, NY: Author.

Krout, J. (1982). *Determinants of service use by the aged: Final report to the AARP Andrus Foundation.* Fredonia, NY: Author.

Krout, J. (1983). Knowledge and use of services by the elderly: A critical review of the literature. *International Journal of Aging and Human Development, 17,* 153–167.

Krout, J. (1984). Knowledge of senior center activities among the elderly. *Journal of Applied Gerontology, 3,* 71–81.

Krout, J. (1985a). Senior center activities and services. *Research on Aging, 7,* 455–471.

Krout, J. (1985b). Service awareness among the elderly. *Journal of Gerontological Social Work, 9,* 7–19.

Krout, J. (1987a). Rural versus urban differences in senior center activities and services. *The Gerontologist, 27,* 92–97.

Krout, J. (1987b). *Senior center linkages and the provision of services to the elderly: Final report to the AARP Andrus Foundation.* Fredonia, NY: Author.

Krout, J. (1988). *The frequency, duration, stability, and discontinuation of senior center participation: Causes and consequences: Final report to the AARP Andrus Foundation.* Fredonia, NY: Author.

Krout, J. (1989). *Senior centers in America.* Westport, CT: Greenwood.

Krout, J. (1990). *The organization, operation, and programming of senior centers in America: A seven-year follow-up: Final report to the AARP Andrus Foundation.* Fredonia, NY: AARP Andrus Foundation.

Krout, J. (1991). Senior center participation: Finds from a multidimensional analysis. *Journal of Applied Gerontology, 10*(3), 244–257.

Krout, J. (1993a). Case management activities for the rural elderly: Findings from a national study. *Journal of Case Management, 2,* 137–146.

Krout, J. (1993b). *Senior centers and at-risk older persons: A national agenda.* Washington, DC: National Institute on the Aging.

Krout, J. (1995). Senior centers and services for the frail elderly. *Journal of Aging and Social Policy, 7*(2), 59–76.

Krout, J., Cutler, S. J., & Coward, R. T. (1990). Correlates of senior center participation: A national analysis. *The Gerontologist, 30,* 72–79.

Krout, J., Moen, P., Holmes, H. H., Oggins, J., & Bowen, N. (2002). Reasons for relocation to a continuing care retirement community. *Journal of Applied Gerontology, 21,* 236–256.

Kuehne, V. S. (2000). *Intergenerational programs: Understanding what we have created.* New York, NY: Haworth.

Kuhn, B. A., Dunn, P. A., Smallwood, D., Hanson, K., Blaylock, J., & Vogel, S. (1996). Policy watch: The food stamp program and welfare reform. *Journal of Economic Perspectives, 10*(2), 189–198.

Kuiken, D. (2004). *A systems integration of mental health services for older adults in community based long term care.* White House Conference on Aging: Listening session. Retrieved January 23, 2007 from http://www.whcoa.gov/about/policy/meetings/summary/ILkuikentestimony.pdf

Kutner, M., Greenberg, E., & Baer, J. (2005). *A first look at the literacy of America's adults in the 21st century.* Washington, DC: National Center for Education Statistics. Retrieved January 22, 2007 from http://nces.ed.gov/NAAL/PDF/2006470.PDF

Kutner, M., Greenberg, E., Jin,Y., Boyle, B., Hsu,Y., & Dunleavy, E. (2007). *Literacy in everyday life: Results from the 2003 National Assessment of Adult Literacy* (NCES 2007–480). Washington, DC: U.S. Department of Education. Retrieved from http://nces.ed.gov/Pubs2007/2007480.pdf

Kutza, E. A. (1991). The Older Americans Act of 2000: What should it be? *Generations, 15*(3), 65–68.

Lachs, M. S., & Pillemer, K. (2004). Elder abuse. *The Lancet, 364,* 1192–1263.

Laditka, S. B. (1998). Modeling lifetime nursing home use under assumptions of better health. *The Journals of Gerontology Series B: Psychological Sciences and Social Sciences, 53B*(4), S177–S187. doi:10.1093/geronb/53B.4.S177

Lakin, M. B., Mullane, L., & Robinson, S. P. (2007). *Framing new terrain: Older adults and higher education.* Washington, DC: American Council on Education. Retrieved from http://www.acenet.edu/Content/NavigationMenu/ProgramsServices/CLLL/Reinvesting/Reinvestingfinal.pdf

Lakin, M. B., Mullane, L., & Robinson, S. P. (2008). *Mapping new directions: Higher education for older adults.* Washington, DC: American Council on Education. Retrieved from http://www.acenet.edu/Content/NavigationMenu/ProgramsServices/CLLL/Reinvesting/MapDirections.pdf

Lalonde, B., Hooyman, N., & Blumhagen, J. (1988). Long-term outcome effectiveness of a health promotion program for the elderly: The Wallingford Wellness Project. *Journal of Gerontological Social Work, 13,* 95–112.

Lamb, W. E., & Morgan, J. C. (2010). *Assessment of the legal needs of older adults in North Carolina.* Retrieved from http://elderlaw.ncbar.org/media/8774049/report_legalNeedsOfOlderAdultsInNC_10012010.pdf

Larkin, E. (1998–1999). The intergenerational response to childcare and after-school care. *Generations, 22*(4), 33–36.

Larkin, J. P., & Hopcroft, B. M. (1993). In-hospital respite as a moderator of caregiver stress. *Health and Social Work, 18,* 132–138.

Lawton, M. P. (1980). Housing elderly: Residential quality and residential satisfaction. *Research on Aging, 2,* 309–328.

Lawton, M. P. (1982). Competence, environmental press, and the adaptation of older people. In M. P. Lawton, P. G. Windley, & T. O. Byerts (Eds.), *Aging and the environment: Theoretical approaches* (pp. 33–59). New York, NY: Springer.

Lawton, M. P. (1989). Three functions of the residential environment. In L. A. Pastalan & M. E. Cowart (Eds.), *Lifestyles and housing of older adults* (pp. 35–50). New York, NY: Haworth.

Lawton, M. P., Brody, E., & Saperstein, A. (1991). *Respite for caregivers of Alzheimer's patients: Research and practice.* New York, NY: Springer.

Lawton, M. P., & Nahemow, L. (1973). Ecology and the aging process. In C. Eisdorfer & M. P. Lawton (Eds.), *Psychology of adult development and aging* (pp. 619–674). Washington, DC: American Psychological Association.

LeadingAge. (2011). *Adult day services/adult day health: Financial viability and scope of services provided under Medicaid waivers.* Washington, DC: Author. Retrieved from http://www.wvpel.org/downloads/MAP/Adult_Day_Services-Adult_Day_Health.pdf

Leanse, J., Tiven, M., & Robb, T. B. (1977). *Senior center operation.* Washington, DC: National Council on the Aging.

Leanse, J., & Wagner, L. (1975). *Senior centers: A report of senior group programs in America.* Washington, DC: National Council on the Aging.

Learning for Action Group. (2010). *Plus 50: Impact report.* Retrieved from http://plus50.aacc.nche.edu/Documents/Impact_Report.pdf

Leavitt, M. O. (2006). *Report to Congress: Patient classification under Medicare's prospective payment system for skilled nursing facilities.* Washington, DC: U.S. Department of Health and Human Services. Retrieved February 8, 2007 from http://www.cms.hhs.gov/SNFPPS/Downloads/RC_2006_PC-PPSSNF.pdf

Lee, G. R. (1983). Social integration and fear of crime among older persons. *Journal of Gerontology, 38,* 745–750.

Lee, J. (1993). *ElderTransit facts: Analysis of area agency on aging transportation survey* [Brochure]. Washington, DC: National Eldercare Institute on Transportation.

Lee, J.-J. (1991). *Development, delivery, and utilization of services under the Older Americans Act: A perspective of Asian American elderly.* New York, NY: Garland.

Lee, J. S., & Frongillo, E. A., Jr. (2001). Nutritional and health consequences are associated with food insecurity among U.S. elderly persons *Journal of Nutrition, 131*(5), 1503–1509.

Lee, J. S., Sinnett, S., Bengle, R., Johnson, M. A., & Brown, A. (2011). Unmet Needs for the Older Americans Act Nutrition Program. *Journal of Applied Gerontology, 30*(5), 587–606. doi:10.1177/0733464810376512

Lee, R. E., & King, A. C. (2003). Discretionary time among older adults: How do physical activity promotion interventions affect sedentary and active behaviors? *Annals of Behavioral Medicine, 25*(2), 112–119.

Lee, Y. (2010). Work incentive and labor force participation after the Senior Citizens Freedom to Work Act of 2000. *Journal of Human Behavior in the Social Environment, 20*(6), 778–790. doi:10.1080/10911351003751843

Lefebvre, R. C., Harden, E. A., Rawkowski, W., Lasater, T. M., & Careton, R. A. (1987). Characteristics of participants in community health programs: Four-year results. *American Journal of Public Health, 77,* 1342–1344.

Leff, B., Reider, L., Frick, K. D., Scharfstein, D. O., Boyd, C. M., Frey, K., . . . Boult, C. (2009). Guided care and the cost of complex healthcare: A preliminary report. *American Journal of Managed Care, 15,* 555–559.

Leftin, J. (2010). *Trends in supplemental nutrition assistance program participation rates: 2001 to 2008.* Princeton, NJ: Mathematica Policy Research.

Legal Services Corporation. (2006). *Legal Services Corporation fact book 2005.* Retrieved from http://grants.lsc.gov/sites/default/files/Grants/RIN/Grantee_Data/fb05010101.pdf

Legal Services Corporation. (2009). *Documenting the justice gap in America: The current unmet civil legal needs of low-income Americans.* Washington, DC: Author.

Legal Services Corporation. (2010). *2010 annual report.* Washington, DC: Author.

Legal Services Corporation Act, 42 U.S.C. § 2996 et seq. (1974).

Legal Services of Northern California Senior Legal Hotline. (n.d.). *About us.* Retrieved from http://slh.lsnc.net/about-us/

Legislative Analyst's Office. (2011). *Overview on poverty.* Retrieved from http://www.lao.ca.gov/handouts/socservices/2011/Poverty_Overview_05_10_11.pdf

Levinson, R. W. (1988). *Information and referral networks.* New York, NY: Springer.

Lewis, S. L., Miner-Williams, D., Novian, A., Escamilla, M. I., Blackwell, P. H., Kretzschmar, J. H., . . . Bonner, P. N. (2009). A stress-busting program for family caregivers. *Rehabilitation Nursing, 34,* 151–159.

Li, H. (2006). Rural older adults' access barriers to in-home and community-based services. *Social Work Research, 30*(2), 109–118. doi:10.1093/swr/30.2.109

Lichtenberg, P. (1994). *A guide to psychological practice in geriatric long-term care*. New York, NY: Haworth.

Lichtenstein, J. H., & Verma, S. (2003). *Older workers' pension plan and IRA coverage*. Washington, DC: Public Policy Institute, American Association of Retired Persons. Retrieved from http://assets .aarp.org/rgcenter/econ/dd91_retire.pdf

Lieberman, M. A., & Fisher, L. (2001). The effects of nursing home placement on family caregivers of patients with Alzheimer's disease. *The Gerontologist, 41,* 819–826.

Liebig, P. S., Koenig, T., & Pynoos, J. (2006). Zoning, accessory dwelling units, and family caregiving: Issues, trends, and recommendations. *Journal of Aging and Social Policy, 18*(3–4), 155–172.

Lifelong Learning Act, Pub. L. No. 94–482 (1976).

Lifespan Respite Care Act, Pub. L. No. 109-442, 120 Stat. 3291 (42 U.S.C. 300ii et seq.) (2006).

Lin, I.-F., & Brown, S. L. (2012). Unmarried boomers confront old age: A national portrait. *The Gerontologist. Special Issue: Baby Boomers, 52*(2), 153–165. doi:10.1093/geront/gnr141

Lincoln Area Agency on Aging. (2006). *Senior centers*. Retrieved from http://www.lincoln.ne.gov/city/ mayor/aging/centers.htm

Linkins, K., Robinson, G., Karp, J., Cooper, S., Liu, J., & Bush, S. (2001). *Screening for mental illness in nursing facility applicants: Understanding federal requirements* (SAMHSA Publication No. (SMA) 01-3543). Washington, DC: U.S. Department of Health and Human Services. Retrieved from http:// store.samhsa.gov/shin/content/SMA01-3543/SMA01-3543.pdf

Lipman, A., & Longino, C. F., Jr. (1982). Formal and informal support: A conceptual clarification. *Journal of Applied Gerontology, 1,* 141–146.

Lipman, A., & Sterne, R. (1962). Aging in the United States: Ascription of a terminal sick role. *Sociology and Social Research, 53,* 194–203.

Lipman, B., Lubell, J., & Salomon, E. (2010). *Housing an aging population: Are we prepared?* Washington, DC: Center for Housing Policy. Retrieved from http://www.nhc.org/media/files/ AgingReport2012.pdf

Lipsky, M., & Thibodeau, M. A. (1990). Domestic food policy in the United States. *Journal of Health Politics, Policy and Law, 15*(2), 319–339.

Litwak, E. (1985). *Helping the elderly: The complementary roles of informal networks and formal systems*. New York, NY: Guilford.

Litwak, E., & Misseri, P. (1989). Organizational theory, social supports, and mortality rates: A theoretical convergence. *American Sociological Review, 54,* 49–66.

Livingston, G., & Parker, K. (2010). *Since the start of the great recession, more children raised by grandparent*. Washington, DC: Pew Research Center. Retrieved from http://www.pewsocialtrends.org/ files/2010/10/764-children-raised-by-grandparents.pdf

Locher, J. L., Ritchie, C. S., Roth, D. L., Baker, P. S., Bodner, E. V., & Allman, R. M. (2005). Social isolation, support, and capital and nutritional risk in an older sample: ethnic and gender differences. *Social Science & Medicine, 60*(4), 747–761. doi:10.1016/j.socscimed.2004.06.023

Long, N. (1975). *Information and referral services: Research findings* (DHEW Pub. No. OHDS 77–410). Washington, DC: Government Printing Office.

Long, N., Anderson, J., Burd, R., Mathis, M. E., & Todd, S. P. (1971). *Information and referral centers: A functional analysis* (DHEW Pub. No. OHDS 75–235). Washington, DC: Government Printing Office.

Low, L.-F., Yap, M., & Brodaty, H. (2011). A systematic review of different models of home and community care services for older persons. *BMC Health Services Research, 11*(93). Retrieved from http://www.biomedcentral.com/1472-6963/11/93

Lowy, L. (1980). *Social policies and programs on aging*. Lexington, MA: Lexington Books.

Lowy, L., & Doolin, J. (1985). Multipurpose and senior centers. In A. Monk (Ed.), *Handbook of gerontological services* (pp. 342–376). New York, NY: Van Nostrand Reinhold.

Lu, L. (1997). Social support, reciprocity, and well-being. *Journal of Social Psychology, 137*(5), 618–628.

Lucas, J. A., Scotto, R. N., Andrew, L. J., & Howell-White, S. (2002). *Review of adult day health services: A review of the literature*. New Brunswick, NJ: Rutgers Center for Health Policy. Retrieved September 28, 2006, from http://www.cshp.rutgers.edu/PDF/AdultDaycareLitRev.pdf

Lund, D. A., Hill, R. D., Caserta, M. S., & Wright, S. D. (1995). Video Respite: An innovative resource for family, professional caregivers, and person with dementia. *The Gerontologist, 35,* 683–687.

Lusardi, A., & Mitchell, O. S. (2011). *Financial literacy and planning: Implications for retirement wellbeing* (NBER Working Paper No. 17078). Cambridge, MA: National Bureau of Economic Research. Retrieved from http://www.nber.org/papers/w17078.pdf

Lynott, J., & Figueiredo, C. (2011). *How the travel patterns of older adults are changing: Highlights from the 2009 National Household Travel Survey*. Washington, DC: AARP Public Policy Institute. Retrieved from http://assets.aarp.org/rgcenter/ppi/liv-com/fs218-transportation.pdf

Maas, M. (1988). Management of patients with Alzheimer's disease in long-term care facilities. *Nursing Clinics of North America, 23,* 57–68.

Mabli, J., Cohen, R., Potter, F., & Zhao, Z. (2010). *Hunger in America 2010*. Princeton, NJ: Feeding America. Retrieved from http://feedingamerica.org/hunger-in-america/hunger-studies/hunger-study-2010.aspx/

MacAdam, M., Capitman, J., Yee, D., Prottas, J., Leutz, W., & Westwater, D. (1989). Case management for frail elders: The Robert Wood Johnson Foundation's program for hospital initiatives in long-term care. *The Gerontologist, 29,* 737–744.

MacArthur Foundation Research Network on an Aging Society. (2008). *Project issues and themes*. Retrieved from http://www.agingsocietynetwork.org/research

MacDonald, D. (1992). Hospice patients without primary caregivers: A critique of prevailing intervention strategies. *Home Healthcare Nurse, 10,* 24–26.

MacNeil, R. D. (2001). Bob Dylan and the baby boom generation: The times they are a-changin'—again. *Activities, Adaptation & Aging, 25*(3–4), 45–58.

Mahoney, S. (2007, July). The new housemates. *AARP The Magazine*. Retrieved from http://www.aarp.org/home-garden/housing/info-2007/the_new_housemates.html

Maine Senior Environmental Leadership Corps. (2011). *Quarterly report*. Retrieved from http://www.epa.gov/aging/pdfs/2011_0407_encorps_final_report.pdf

Majmundar, M. (2010). *Assessing the impact of severe economic recession on the elderly: Summary of a workshop*. National Research Council of the National Academies. Washington, DC: National Academies Press. Retrieved from http://www.nap.edu/openbook.php?record_id=13118&page=R1

MaloneBeach, E., Zarit, S., & Shore, D. (1992). Caregivers' perceptions of case management and community-based services: Barriers to service use. *Journal of Applied Gerontology, 11,* 145–159.

Management Sciences for Health. (n.d.). *Provider's guide to quality and culture*. Retrieved February 2, 2007 from http://erc.msh.org/mainpage.cfm?file=9.0.htm&module=provider&language=English&ggroup=&mgroup=

Manheimer, R. J. (1992). Creative retirement in an aging society. In R. Fischer, M. Blazey, & H. Lipman (Eds.), *Students of the third age* (pp. 122–131). New York, NY: Macmillan.

Manheimer, R. J. (2002). *Older adult education in the United States: Trends and predictions*. Asheville: North Carolina Center for Creative Retirement. Retrieved on January 13, 2007 from http://www.s185927841.onlinehome.us/campusvillages/research_files/Older%20Adult%20Education%20in%20the%20United%20States%20Trends%20and.pdf

Manheimer, R. J., Snodgrass, D., & Moskow-McKenzie, D. (1995). *Older adult education: A guide to research, programs, and policies*. Westport, CT: Greenwood.

Mantell, J., & Gildea, M. (1989). Elderly shared housing in the United States. In D. J. Jaffe (Ed.), *Shared housing for the elderly* (pp. 13–23). New York, NY: Greenwood.

Manton, K. I. (1987). Patterns and psychological correlates of material support within a religious setting: The bidirectional support hypothesis. *American Journal of Community Psychology, 15,* 185–207.

Mark Battle Associates. (1977). *Evaluation of information and referral services for the elderly: Final report* (DHEW Pub. No. OHDS 77–20109). Washington, DC: Government Printing Office.

Marken, D. M. (2005). One step ahead: Preparing the senior center for 2030. *Activities, Adaptation & Aging, 29,* 4, 69–84.

Marmor, T. R., Mashaw, J. L., & Harvey, P. L. (1990). *American's misunderstood welfare state: Persistent myths, enduring realities*. New York, NY: Basic Books.

Martinko, M. J., & Thomson, N. F. (1998). A synthesis and extension of the Weiner and Kelley attribution models. *Basic & Applied Social Psychology, 20*(4), 271–284.

Martinson, B. C., Crain, A. L., Sherwood, N. E., Hayes, M., Pronk, N. P., & O'Connor, P. J. (2010). Population reach and recruitment bias in a maintenance RCT in physically active older adults. *Journal of Physical Activity and Health, 7*(1), 127–135.

Martinson, B. C., Sherwood, N. E., Crain, A. L., Hayes, M. G., King, A. C., Pronk, N. P., & O'Connor, P. J. (2010). Maintaining physical activity among older adults: 24-month outcomes of the Keep Active Minnesota randomized controlled trial. *Preventive Medicine, 51*(1), 37–44. doi:10.1016/j.ypmed.2010.04.002

Matthews, D. H., & Sprey, J. (1984). The impact of divorce on grandparenthood: An exploratory study. *The Gerontologist, 24,* 41–47.

Matthews, J. L., & Berman, D. M. (2012). *Social Security, Medicare and government pensions: Get the most out of your retirement and medical menefits* (17th ed.). Berkeley, CA: Nolo Press.

Matthews, S. H., & Rosner, T. T. (1988). Shared filial responsibility: The family as the primary caregiver. *Journal of Marriage and the Family, 50,* 185–195.

Mauser, T. (1994). *Colorado transit overview*. Denver: Colorado Department of Transportation.

Maxwell, J. (1962). *Centers for older people: Guide for programs and facilities.* Washington, DC: National Council on the Aging.

McAuley, W. J., Spector, W., & Van Nostrand, J. (2009). Formal home care utilization patterns by rural–urban community residence. *Journal of Gerontology: Social Sciences, 64B*(2), 258–268. doi:10.1093/geronb/gbn003

McCarthy, R., & Rutledge, C. (2012). *Improving occupancy: Entrance fee vs. rental contract options.* Madison: LeadingAge Wisconsin. Retrieved from http://www.wahsa.org/resources/12spring/handouts/f36.pdf

McCaslin, R. (1981). Next steps in information and referral for the elderly. *The Gerontologist, 21,* 184–193.

McCaslin, R. (1989). Service utilization by the elderly: The importance of orientation to the formal system. *Journal of Gerontological Social Work, 14,* 153–174.

McClusky, H. (1974). Education for aging: The scope of the field and perspectives for the future. In S. M. Grabowski & W. D. Mason (Eds.), *Learning for aging* (pp. 324–355). Washington, DC: Adult Education Association of the USA.

McConnel, S., & Beitler, D. (1991). The Older Americans Act after 25 years: An overview. *Generations, 15*(3), 5–10.

McConnell, S., & Ponza, M. (1999). *The reaching the working poor and poor elderly study: What we learned and recommendations for future research.* Princeton, NJ: Mathematica Policy Research.

McCormick, S., Underwood, S., & Wang, S. (2012). The changing car: New vehicle technologies. In J. F. Coughlin, L. A. D'Ambrosio, & National Older Driver Safety Advisory (Eds.), *Aging America and transportation: Personal choices and public policy* (pp. 57–76). New York, NY: Springer.

McCrea, J. M., Nichols, A., & Newman, S. (Eds.). (1998–2000). *Intergenerational service learning in gerontology: A compendium* (Vols. 1–3). Washington, DC: Association for Gerontology in Higher Education.

McDonnell, K. (2010). Retirement annuity and employment-based pension income among individuals age 50 and over: 2008. *EBRI Notes, 31*(5), 12–20. Retrieved from http://www.ebri.org/publications/notes/

McGinnis, J. (1988). *Year 2000 health objectives for the nation: Proceedings of the Surgeon General's Workshop: Health Promotion and Aging.* Washington, DC: Government Printing Office.

McGuire, M. (2002). *Food donation initiatives assessment and food recovery infrastructure evaluation: Revised final report.* Portland, OR: Metro Regional Environmental Management. Retrieved on January 7, 2007 from http://www.metrovancouver.org/zwc/themes/ResourceDocs/food_assess_rpt_0402.pdf

McKinsey & Company. (2009). *Restoring Americans' retirement security: A shared responsibility* Washington, DC: Author. Retrieved from http://www.mckinsey.com/clientservice/Financial_Services/Knowledge_Highlights/Recent_Reports/ ~ /media/Reports/Financial_Services/Retirement_Security.ashx

McNickle, L. (2007). Service coordinators and public housing: An essential link for seniors to age in place. *Journal of Housing & Community Development, 64*(4), 40–47.

McPherson, B. D., & Wister, A. (2008). *Aging as a social process: Canadian perspectives.* Don Mills, ON: Oxford University Press.

Meals on Wheels of San Francisco. (2010). *2010 annual report.* Retrieved from http://www.mowsf.org/PDF/MOW2010_AnnualReport.pdf

Medelson, M., Larson, C. E., & Greenwood, H. (2011). Intergenerational shared sites in Hawaii. *Journal of Intergenerational Relationships, 9,* 445–451. doi:10.1080/15350770.2011.619911

Medicaid.gov. (2012). *Waivers*. Retrieved from http://www.medicaid.gov/Medicaid-CHIP-Program-Information/By-Topics/Waivers/Waivers.html

Medical Learning Networks. (2011). *Mental health services*. Washington, DC: U.S. Department of Health and Human Services. Retrieved from http://www.cms.gov/MLNProducts/downloads/Mental_Health_Services_ICN903195.pdf

Medicare Payment Advisory Commission. (2012a). Hospice services. In *Report to the Congress: Medicare payment policy*. Washington, DC: Medpac. Retrieved from http://www.medpac.gov/chapters/Mar12_Ch11.pdf

Medicare Payment Advisory Commission. (2012b). *Report to the Congress: Medicare and the health care delivery system*. Washington, DC: Medpac. Retrieved from http://www.medpac.gov/documents/Jun12_EntireReport.pdf

Menec, V. H. (2003). The relation between everyday activities and successful aging: A 6-year longitudinal study. *Journal of Gerontology, 58B*(2), S74–S82.

Mensie, L. C., & Stephen, A. M. (2011). Predicting in-home respite utilization by family caregivers of older adults: Results of a community study. *Home Health Care Management Practice, 23*(2), 109–117. doi:10.1177/1084822310384694

Mercy Housing. (2011, Summer). Volunteers, community members celebrate opening of Roseland Place apartments. *Community Matters*. Retrieved from https://www.mercyhousing.org/document.doc?id = 151

Meschede, T., Sullivan, L., & Shapiro, T. (2011). *The crisis of economic insecurity for African-American and Latino seniors* (Research and Policy Brief). Waltham, MA: Brandeis University, Institute on Assets and Social Policy. Retrieved from http://iasp.brandeis.edu/pdfs/Author/meschede-tatjana/The%20Crisis%20of%20Economic%20Insecurity.pdf

Messick, D. M., & Cook, K. S. (Eds.). (1983). *Equity theory: Psychological and sociological perspectives*. New York, NY: Praeger.

MetLife Mature Market Institute. (2010a). *Demographic profile: America's older boomers*. Retrieved from http://www.metlife.com/assets/cao/mmi/publications/Profiles/mmi-older-boomer-demographic-profile.pdf

MetLife Mature Market Institute. (2010b). *Demographic profile: America's younger boomers*. Retrieved from http://www.metlife.com/assets/cao/mmi/publications/Profiles/mmi-younger-boomer-demographic-profile.pdf

MetLife Mature Market Institute. (2010c). *The MetLife national study of adult day services: Providing support to individuals and their family caregivers*. Retrieved from http://www.metlife.com/assets/cao/mmi/publications/studies/2010/mmi-adult-day-services.pdf

MetLife Foundation. (2007). *Great expectations: Boomers and the future of volunteering*. Retrieved from http://cdn.volunteermatch.org/www/nonprofits/resources/greatexpectations/GreatExpectations_FullReport.pdf

MetLife Mature Market Institute. (2011a). *The 2011 MetLife market survey of nursing home, assisted living, adult day services, and home care costs*. Retrieved from http://www.metlife.com/assets/cao/mmi/publications/studies/2011/mmi-market-survey-nursing-home-assisted-living-adult-day-services-costs.pdf

Metlife Mature Market Institute. (2011b). *Housing trends update for the 55+ market: New insights from the American Housing Survey*. Retrieved from http://www.metlife.com/assets/cao/mmi/publications/studies/2011/mmi-housing-trends-55-update.pdf

MetLife Mature Market Institute. (2011c). *The MetLife study of caregiving costs to working caregivers: Double jeopardy for baby boomers caring for their parents*. Retrieved from http://www.metlife.com/assets/cao/mmi/publications/studies/2011/mmi-caregiving-costs-working-caregivers.pdf

Meyer, M. D. (1991). Assuring quality of care: Nursing home resident councils. *Journal of Applied Gerontology, 10*(1), 103–116.

Myer, H. (2011). Safe spaces? The need for LGBT cultural competency in aging services. *Public Policy & Aging Report, 21*(3), 24–27.

Michaud, P.-C., & Van Soest, A. (2008). How did the elimination of the US earnings test above the normal retirement age affect labour supply expectations? *Fiscal Studies, 29*(2), 197–231. doi:10.1111/j.1475-5890.2008.00073.x

Michigan Office of Services to the Aging & Elder Law of Michigan. (2008). *A survey of older adults in Michigan: A report on the findings*. Retrieved from http://wiki.elderrightssummit .org/erc/images/8/80/Survey.pdf

Milbank Memorial Fund. (2006). *Public housing and supportive services for the frail elderly: A guide for housing authorities and their collaborators*. Retrieved January 2, 2007 from http://www.milbank.org/ reports/0609publichousing/0609publichousing.pdf

Millen, B. E., Ohls, J. C., Ponza, M., & McCool, A. C. (2002). The Elderly Nutrition Program: An effective national framework for preventive nutrition interventions. *Journal of the American Dietetic Association, 102*(2), 234–240. doi:10.1016/s0002-8223(02)90055-6

Miller, D., & Goldman, L. (1989). Perceptions of caregivers about special respite services for the elderly. *The Gerontologist, 29,* 408–410.

Milne, K. (1994). The evolution of case management to care management. In R. Howe (Ed.), *Case management for health care professionals* (pp. 179–190). Chicago, IL: Precept.

Miner, S., Logan, J. R., & Spitz, G. (1993). Predicting the frequency of senior center attendance. *The Gerontologist, 33,* 650–657.

Minkler, M., & Pasick, R. J. (1985). Health promotion and the elderly: A critical perspective on the past and future. In K. Dychtwald (Ed.), *Wellness and health promotion for the elderly* (pp. 39–51). Rockville, MD: Aspen.

Minkler, M., & Roe, K. M. (1996). Grandparents as surrogate parents. *Generations, 20*(1), 34–37.

Mirel, L. B., Wheatcroft, G., Parker, J. D., & Makuc, D. M. (2012, May 3). Health characteristics of Medicare traditional fee-for-service and Medicare Advantage enrollees: 1999–2004. *National Health Statistics Report, 53,* 1–12.

Mitchell, E. T. (2011). The Child Resiliency Program at Hope Meadows. *Journal of Intergenerational Relationships, 9,* 452–457. doi:10.1080/15350770.2011.619412

Mitchell, J. (1995). Service awareness and use among older North Carolinians. *Journal of Applied Gerontology, 14*(2), 193–209.

Mittler, J. N., Landon, B. E., Zaslavsky, A. M., & Cleary, P. D. (2011). Market characteristics and awareness of managed care options among elderly beneficiaries enrolled in traditional Medicare. *Medicare & Medicaid Research Review, 1*(3), 1–17. doi:10.5600/mmrr.001.03.a03

Moen, E. (1978). The reluctance of the elderly to accept help. *Social Problems, 25,* 293–303.

Mollica, R. (2003). Coordinating services across the continuum of health, housing, and supportive services. *Journal of Aging and Health, 15,* 165–188.

Mollica, R. L., Simms-Kastelein, K., Cheek, M., Farnham, J., Reinhard, S., & Accius, J. (2009). *Building adult foster care: What states can do*. Washington, DC: AARP Public Policy Institute. Retrieved from http://assets.aarp.org/rgcenter/ppi/ltc/2009_13_building_adult_foster_care.pdf

Monk, A., & Kaye, L. W. (1991). Congregate housing for the elderly: Its need, function, and perspective. *Journal of Housing for the Elderly, 9*(1–2), 5–20.

Monk, A., Kaye, L. W., & Litwin, H. (1984). *Resolving grievances in the nursing home: A study of the ombudsman program*. New York, NY: Columbia University Press.

Montgomery, R. J. V. (1992). Examining respite: Its promise and limits. In M. Ory & A. Dunker (Eds.), *In-home care for older people: Health and supportive services* (pp. 75–96). Newbury Park, CA: Sage.

Montgomery, R. J. V. (1996). Examining respite care: Promises and limitations. In R. Kane & J. Dobrof Penrod (Eds.), *Family caregiving in a caring society: Policy perceptions* (pp. 29–45). Thousand Oaks, CA: Sage.

Montgomery, R. J. V., & Kamo, Y. (1989). Parent care by sons and daughters. In J. A. Mancini (Ed.), *Aging parents and adult children* (pp. 213–228). Lexington, MA: Lexington Books.

Montgomery, R. J. V., Marquis, J., Schaefer, J. P., & Kosloski, K. (2002). Profile of respite users. *Home Health Care Services Quarterly, 21*(3–4), 33–63.

Moody, H. R. (1976). Philosophical presuppositions of education for older adults. *Educational Gerontology, 2,* 1–16.

Moody, H. R. (1988). *Abundance of life: Human development policies for an aging society*. New York, NY: Columbia University Press.

Moon, M., & Ruggles, P. (1994). The needy or the greedy? Assessing the income support of an aging population. In T. Marmor, T. Smeeding, & V. Greene (Eds.), *Economic security and intergenerational justice: A look at North America* (pp. 207–226). Washington, DC: Urban Institute.

Moore, M., & Piland, W. (1994). Impact of campus physical environment on older adult learners. *Community College Journal of Research and Practice, 18,* 307–317.

Moore, W. (1989). Assessing the unmet legal needs of older persons: What will it cost to meet that need? *Elder Law Forum, 1*(2), 4.

Moore, W. (1992). Improving the delivery of legal services for the elderly: A comprehensive approach. *Emory Law Journal, 41,* 805–861.

Mor, V., & Allen, S. (1995). Hospice. In G. Maddox (Ed.), *The encyclopedia of aging* (2nd ed., pp. 475–477). New York, NY: Springer.

Morano, C. L., & Morano, B. (2012). Psychosocial assessment. In C. J. Cress (Ed). *Handbook of geriatric care management* (pp. 27–40). Sudbury, MA: Jones & Bartlett.

Morgan, L. A., Frankowski, A. C., Roth, E. G., Keimig, L., Zimmerman, S., & Eckert, J. K. (2011). *Quality assisted living: Informing practice through research.* New York, NY: Springer.

Morgan, L. A., Gurber-Baldini, A. L., & Magaziner, J. (2001). Resident characteristics. In S. I. Zimmerman, P. D. Sloane, & J. K. Eckert (Eds.), *Assisted living: Residential care in transition* (pp. 144–172). Baltimore, MD: Johns Hopkins University Press.

Morley, J. E. (2001). Decreased food intake with aging. *The Journals of Gerontology Series A: Biological Sciences and Medical Sciences, 56*(Suppl. 2), 81–88. doi:10.1093/gerona/56.suppl_2.81

Moulton, P., McDonald, L., Muus, K., Knudson, A., Wakefield, M., & Ludtke, R. (2005). *Prevalence of chronic disease among American Indian and Alaska Native elders.* Grand Forks: Center for Rural Health, University of North Dakota, School of Medicine & Health Sciences. Retrieved January 27, 2007 from http://ruralhealth.und.edu/projects/nrcnaa/pdf/chronic_disease1005.pdf

Mount Sinai Medical Center. (2011). *Family and Friends program.* Retrieved from http://www.mountsinai.org/patient-care/service-areas/children/areas-of-care/family-and-friends-program

Moving Ahead for Progress in the 21st Century Act, Pub. L. No. 112-141, H.R. 4348 Stat. (2012).

Mower, M. T. (2008). Designing and implementing ethnic congregate nutrition programs for older Americans. *Journal of Nutrition For the Elderly, 27*(3–4), 417–430. doi:10.1080/01639360802265954

Mullins, L. C., Cook, C., Mushel, M., Machin, G., & Georgas, J. (1993). A comparative examination of the characteristics of participants of a senior citizens nutrition and activities program. *Activities, Adaptation, and Aging, 17*(3), 15–37.

Munnell, A. H. (2011). *What is the average retirement age?* Chestnut Hill, MA: Center for Retirement Research at Boston College. Retrieved from http://crr.bc.edu/briefs/what-is-the-average-retirement-age/

Musick, M. A., & Wilson, J. (2003). Volunteering and depression: The role of psychological and social resources in different age groups. *Social Science and Medicine, 56*(2), 259–269.

Nadler, A. (1987). Determinants of help-seeking behaviour: The effects of helpers' similarity, task centrality and recipient's self esteem. *European Journal of Social Psychology, 17*(1), 57–67.

Nadler, A., Fisher, J. D., & Streufest, S. (1976). The donor's dilemma: Recipients' reactions to aid from friend or foe. *Journal of Personality, 44,* 392–409.

Nadler, A., & Mayseless, O. (1983). Recipient self-esteem and reactions to help. In J. D. Fisher, A. Nadler, & B. M. DePaulo (Eds.), *New directions in helping* (Vol. 1, pp. 167–188). New York, NY: Academic Press.

Nadler, A., Sheinberg, L., & Jaffe, Y. (1981). Coping with stress by help seeking: Help seeking and receiving behavior in male paraplegics. In C. Spielberger, I. Sarason, & N. Milgram (Eds.), *Stress and anxiety* (Vol. 8, pp. 375–386). Washington, DC: Hemisphere.

Napili, A., & Colello, K. J. (2010). *Older Americans Act: Funding* (CRS Report No. RL33880). Washington, DC: Library of Congress, Congressional Research Service. Retrieved from http://aging.senate.gov/crs/aging18.pdf

National Academy of Social Insurance. (2011). *Social Security benefits, finances, and policy options: A primer.* Retrieved from http://www.nasi.org/research/2012/social-security-benefits-finances-policy-options-primer

National Adult Day Services Association. (2006). *Trends in ADS.* Retrieved December 28, 2006 from http://www.nadsa.org/adsfacts/default.asp

National Adult Day Services Association. (2011). *Overview and facts.* Retrieved from http://www.nadsa.org/?page_id = 80

National Aging I&R/A Support Center. (2002). *Aging Specialty Information and Referral Certification Program. Competencies.* Retrieved January 15, 2007 from http://www.nasuad.org/documentation/I_R/AgingSpecialityIRCertProgram_Competencies.pdf

National Alliance for Caregiving. (2011). *e-connected family caregivers: Bringing caregiving into the 21st century.* Retrieved from http://www.unitedhealthgroup.com/news/rel2011/econnected_family_caregiver_study_jan_2011.pdf

National Alliance for Caregiving & AARP. (2009). *Caregiving in the U.S.* Retrieved from http://www.caregiving.org/data/Caregiving_in_the_US_2009_full_report.pdf

National and Community Service Trust Act of 1993, 42 U.S.C. § 12571 et seq. (1996).

National Association for Home Care and Hospice. (2010). *Basic statistics about home care.* Retrieved from http://www.nahc.org/facts/10HC_Stats.pdf

National Association for Home Care and Hospice. (2012). *About NAHC.* Retrieved from http://www.nahc.org/about/home.html

National Association of Area Agencies on Aging. (1996). *Legislative briefing: Advocate's guide to 1996 national policy priorities.* Washington, DC: Author.

National Association of Area Agencies on Aging. (2009). *n4a aging innovations and achievement awards.* Retrieved from http://www.n4a.org/pdf/09_Awards_Book_Final.pdf

National Association of Area Agencies on Aging. (2011a). *Fast facts about the Eldercare Locator.* Retrieved from http://www.n4a.org/programs/eldercare-locator/?fa = fast-facts

National Association of Area Agencies on Aging. (2011b). *The maturing of America: Communities moving forward for an aging population.* Retrieved from http://www.n4a.org/files/MOA_FINAL_Rpt.pdf

National Association of Area Agencies on Aging. (2012). *FY 2013 Labor-HHS-Education appropriations.* Retrieved from http://n4a.org/files/advocacy/campaigns/FY_2013_Appropriations_6_15_12.pdf

National Association of Home Builders Research Center. (2002). *National older adult housing survey report 2002: Summary of findings.* Retrieved January 9, 2007 from http://nahbrc.info/bookstore/sh0303w_noahssummary.pdf

National Association of Mental Health Planning and Advisory Councils. (2007). *Older adults and mental health: A time for reform.* Rockville, MD: Center for Mental Health Services, Substance Abuse and Mental Health Administration. Retrieved from http://www.namhpac.org/PDFs/01/olderadults.pdf

National Association of State Units on Aging. (2000). *Vision 2010: Toward a comprehensive aging information resource system for the 21st century.* Retrieved January 23, 2007 from http://www.nasuad.org/documentation/I_R/IB_vision2010_towardacomprehensiveagingIRsystem.pdf

National Association of State Units on Aging. (2006). *Medicare Empowerment Program. Part I: Overview of n4a and NASUA role.* Retrieved January 23, 2007 from http://www.nasua.org/informationandreferral/pdf/medicareempowerment.pdf

National Association of State Units on Aging. (n.d.). *Eldercare Locator.* Retrieved January 16, 2007 from http://www.nasuad.org/documentation/I_R/Developing_Aging_Competency/Eldercare_Locator_presentation2010.pdf

National Board of Health and Welfare. (2009). *Care of older people in Sweden 2008.* Retrieved from http://www.socialstyrelsen.se/Lists/Artikelkatalog/Attachments/17857/2009-12-6.pdf

National Center for Assisted Living. (2006). *Assisted living state regulatory review 2006.* Retrieved January 9, 2007 from http://www.ncal.org/about/2006_reg_review.pdf

National Center for Assisted Living. (2009). *Resident profile.* Retrieved from http://www.ahcancal.org/NCAL/RESOURCES/PAGES/RESIDENTPROFILE.ASPX

National Center for Assisted Living. (2012). *Assisted living facility profile.* Retrieved from http://www.ahcancal.org/ncal/resources/Pages/ALFacilityProfile.aspx

National Center for Benefits Outreach and Enrollment. (2010). *Person-centered benefits access: Lessons learned from the benefits enrollment centers' first year.* Washington, DC: National Council on Aging. Retrieved from http://www.ncoa.org/assets/files/pdf/center-for-benefits/becs-lessons-learned.pdf

National Center for Education Statistics. (2010a). *Digest of educational statistics: Table 200. Total fall enrollment in degree-granting institutions, by level of enrollment, sex, age, and attendance status of student: 2007 and 2009*. Retrieved from http://nces.ed.gov/programs/digest/d10/tables/dt10_200.asp

National Center for Education Statistics. (2010b). *Digest of educational statistics: Table 201. Total fall enrollment in degree-granting institutions, by control and type of institution, age, and attendance status of student: 2009*. Retrieved from http://nces.ed.gov/programs/digest/d10/tables/dt10_201.asp

National Center for Education Statistics. (2011). *Digest of educational statistics: 2010*. Retrieved from http://nces.ed.gov/programs/digest/d10/tables/dt10_009.asp?referrer = list

National Center for Health Statistics. (2005). *Health, United States, 2005. Nursing homes, beds, occupancy, and residents, according to geographic division and state: United States, 1995–2003, Table 116*. Retrieved February 4, 2007 from http://www.cdc.gov/nchs/data/hus/hus05.pdf#116

National Center for Health Statistics. (2008). *National nursing home survey 2004 current resident Tables 15 and 16*. Retrieved from http://www.cdc.gov/nchs/nnhs/resident_tables.htm

National Center on Accessibility. (n.d.). *The Eden alternative—Renewing life in nursing homes*. Retrieved February 18, 2007 from http://www.indiana.edu/ ~ nca/ncpad/eden.shtml

National Center on Senior Transportation. (2009). *Everyone rides: Transportation access for culturally and ethnically diverse elders*. Washington, DC: Author.

National Chronic Care Consortium. (1997). *Case management for the frail elderly: A literature review on selected topics*. Retrieved December 22, 2006 from http://www.nccconline.org/pdf/CaseManagement.pdf

National Chronic Care Consortium. (2000, May). *Case management: Methods and issues*. A Technical Assistance Paper of the Robert Wood Johnson Foundation Medicare/Medicaid Integration Program. Retrieved from http://www.nccconline.org/pdf/CaseManagement.pdf

National Citizens' Coalition for Nursing Home Reform. (2003). *Residents' rights: An overview* (Consumer Fact Sheet No. 2). Retrieved February 13, 2007 from http://www.nccnhr.org/uploads/ ResRights03.pdf

National Conference of State Legislatures. (2011). *Facts on state and local government pensions*. Retrieved from http://www.ncsl.org/documents/press/jppfactsheet.pdf

National Consumer Voice for Quality Long-Term Care. (2011). *Residents' rights: An overview*. Retrieved from http://www.theconsumervoice.org/sites/default/files/resident/nursing-home/resident-rights-an-overview.pdf

National Cooperative Highway Research Program. (2006). *Estimating the impacts of the aging population on transit ridership*. Fairfax, VA: ICF Consulting.

National Council on Aging. (1998). *National quality standards for nation's 16,000 senior centers get boost from new accreditation process*. Retrieved August 25, 2001 from http://www.ncoa.org/news/archives/national_quality.htm

National Council on Aging. (2005). *Fact sheets—Senior centers: Background/history*. Retrieved on June 18, 2006 from http://www.ncoa.org/content.cfm?sectionID = 103&detail = 1177

National Council on Aging. (2006). *Special report—Tomorrow's senior center: Dynamic, accessible, and perhaps not even called senior*. Retrieved June 19, 2006 from http://www.ncoa.org/content.cfm?sectionID = 134&detail = 1308

National Council on Aging. (2007). *Congress passes Older Americans Act reauthorization*. Retrieved February 24, 2007 from http://www.ncoa.org/content.cfm?sectionID = 2&detail = 1712

National Council on Aging. (2010a). Innovations: Exploring significant developments and trends in aging. *Innovations, 39*(3). Retrieved from http://www.ncoa.org/news-ncoa-publications/publications/

National Council on Aging. (2010b). *Person-centered benefits access: Lessons learned from the benefits enrollment centers' first year*. Retrieved from http://www.ncoa.org/assets/files/pdf/center-for-benefits/becs-lessons-learned.pdf

National Council on Aging. (2011a). *CFPB's Office of Financial Protection for older Americans: Partnering with the aging network to safeguard seniors*. Retrieved from http://www.ncoa.org/calendar-of-events/cfpbs-office-of-financial.html

National Council on Aging. (2011b). *NCOA awards grants to 10 organizations to help seniors, people with disabilities access benefit* [Press release]. Retrieved July 2, 2011 from http://www.ncoa.org/press-room/press-release/ncoa-awards-grants-to-10.html

National Council on Aging. (2011c). *Standards and accreditation*. Retrieved from http://www.ncoa.org/national-institute-of-senior-centers/standards-accreditation/

National Council on Aging. (2011d). *Senior center fact sheet*. Retrieved from http://www.ncoa.org/assets/files/pdf/FactSheet_SeniorCenters.pdf

National Council on Aging. (n.d.). *The Elder Justice Act* (NCOA Issue Brief). Retrieved on March 3, 2012 from http://www.ncoa.org/assets/files/pdf/IB10-EJA.pdf

National Eldercare Institute on Health Promotion. (1995). Telephone links reduce isolation. *Perspectives in Health Promotion and Aging, 10*(1), 2.

National Eldercare Institute on Transportation. (1992). *Focus group report*. Washington, DC: Author.

National Eldercare Institute on Transportation. (1994). *Meeting the challenge: Mobility for elders*. Washington, DC: Author.

National Gay and Lesbian Task Force. (2009). *Outing age 2010: Public policy issues affecting lesbian, gay, bisexual and transgender (LGBT) elders*. Retrieved from http://www.thetaskforce.org/reports_and_research/outing_age_2010

National Governors' Association. (2004). *State support for family caregivers and paid home-care workers*. Retrieved January 2, 2007 from http://www.subnet.nga.org/ci/assets/4-caregivers.pdf

National Hospice and Palliative Care Organization. (2001). *Facts and figures on hospice care in America*. Retrieved January 25, 2002 from http://www.nhpco.org

National Hospice and Palliative Care Organization. (2012). *2011 edition NHPCO facts and figures: Hospice care in America*. Retrieved from http://www.nhpco.org/files/public/Statistics_Research/2011_Facts_Figures.pdf

National Household Transportation Survey. (2001). Cited in L. Bailey, L. (2004). *Aging Americans: Stranded without transportation. Surface Transportation Policy Project*. Retrieved October 23, 2006 from www.apta.com/resources/reportsandpublications/Documents/aging_stranded.pdf

National Institute of Senior Centers. (1978). *Senior center standards: Guidelines for practice*. Washington, DC: National Council on the Aging.

National Institute on Aging. (2011). *About the ADEAR center*. Retrieved August 21, 2011 from http://www.nia.nih.gov/alzheimers/about-adear-center

National Low Income Housing Coalition. (2006). *Section 202 Supportive Housing for the Elderly*. Retrieved January 9, 2007 from http://www.nlihc.org/detail/article.cfm?article_id=2803&id=46

National Older Worker Career Center. (2012a). *About the SEE program*. Retrieved from http://seeprogram.org/About.aspx

National Older Worker Career Center. (2012b). *Our programs*. Retrieved from http://www.nowcc.org/applicants/programs.home

National PACE Association. (2012). *What is PACE?* Retrieved from http://www.npaonline.org/website/article.asp?id=12

National Policy and Resource Center on Nutrition and Aging. (1996). *Use of medical food and food for special dietary uses in elderly nutrition programs*. Miami: Florida International University.

National Resource Center on LGBT Aging. (2011). *Housing and services: A critical combination—Provisions in LGBT-specific housing*. Retrieved from http://www.lgbtagingcenter.org/resources/print.cfm?r=402

National Service-Learning Clearinghouse. (2012). *About NSLC*. Retrieved from http://www.servicelearning.org/about-nslc

Neese, J. B., Abraham, I. L., & Buckwalter, K. C. (1999). Utilization of mental health services among rural elderly. *Archives of Psychiatric Nursing, 13*(1), 30–40.

Nestlé Nutrition Institute. (n.d.). *MNA Mini Nutritional Assessment*. Retrieved from http://www.mna-elderly.com/mna_forms.html

Netting, F. E., & Hinds, H. (1989). Rural volunteer ombudsman programs. *Journal of Applied Gerontology, 8,* 419–427.

Netting, F. E., Paton, R. N., & Huber, R. (1992). The long-term care ombudsman program: What does the complaint reporting system tell us? *The Gerontologist, 32,* 843–848.

Neumark, D. (2009). The Age Discrimination in Employment Act and the challenge of population aging. *Research on Aging, 31,* 41–68.

Newman, S., & Riess, J. (1992). Older workers in intergenerational child care settings. *Journal of Gerontological Social Work, 19,* 45–66.

Newman, S., Ward, C., Smith, T., Wilson, J., & McCrea, J. (Eds.). (1997). *Intergenerational programs: Past, present, and future.* Bristol, PA: Taylor & Francis.

Newquist, D., Rosenberg, C., & Barber, C. (2012). Functional assessment. In C. J. Cress (Ed.), *Handbook of geriatric care management* (pp. 41–71). Sudbury, MA: Jones & Bartlett.

Newsom, J. T. (1999). Another side to caregiving: Negative reactions to being helped. *Current Directions in Psychological Science, 8*(6), 183–187.

Nicoll, M., Ashworth, M., McNally, L., & Newman, S. (2002). Satisfaction with respite care: A pilot study. *Health and Social Care in the Community, 10,* 479–484.

Noelker, L., & Browdie, R. (2012). Caring for the caregivers: Developing models that work. *Generations, 36*(1), 103–106.

Normandale Center for Healing and Wholeness. (2012). *Who we are.* Retrieved from http://www .normluth.org/healing/about_us/healing_wholeness_who_we_are.html

North Carolina Cooperative Extension. (2011). *AARP's taking care of you: Powerful tools for caregiving.* Retrieved from http://iredell.ces.ncsu.edu/content/a+program+for+people+taking+care+of+ elderly+in+our+community

North Carolina Division of Aging and Adult Services. (2011). *North Carolina Aging Services Plan, 2011–2015.* Raleigh: North Carolina Department of Health and Human Services. Retrieved October 1, 2011 from http://www.ncdhhs.gov/aging/stplan/NC_Aging_Services_Plan_2011-2015.pdf

North Carolina Division of Aging and Adult Services. (2012). *Project C.A.R.E.: Caregiving alternatives to running on empty.* Raleigh: North Carolina Department of Health and Human Services. Retrieved from http://www.ncdhhs.gov/aging/ncprojectcare.htm

NSW Ministry of Health. (n.d.). *Specialist Mental Health Services for Older People (SMHSOP).* Retrieved from http://www0.health.nsw.gov.au/mhdao/SMHSOP.asp

Nuschler, D. (2010). *Social Security reform: Current issues and legislation* (CRS Report No. RL33544). Washington, DC: Library of Congress Congressional Research Service. Retrieved from http:// aging.senate.gov/crs/ss6.pdf

Oak Hammock at the University of Florida. (n.d.). *Lifelong learning: The Institute for Learning in Retirement.* Retrieved from http://www.oakhammock.org/living-at-oak-hammock/lifelong-learning

Office of the Assistant Secretary for Planning and Evaluation. (1995). *Subacute care: Policy synthesis and market area analysis.* Retrieved January 27, 2002 from http://aspe.hhs.gov/daltcp/reports/ xsubacut.htm

Older Adult Service and Information System. (2011a). *Our community impact.* Retrieved from http:// www.oasisnet.org/AboutUs/Impact.aspx

Older Adult Service and Information System. (2011b). *The OASIS Institute 2010 annual report.* Retrieved from http://www.oasisnet.org/LinkClick.aspx?fileticket = skjm-0aSIiA = &tabid = 88

Older Americans Act of 1965, Pub. L. No. 89–73, 42 U.S.C. § 3001 et seq., as amended or reauthorized 1967, 1968, 1972, 1973, 1974, 1975, 1977, 1978, 1984, 1987, 1992, 1997, 2000, 2006.

Older Workers Benefit Protection Act of 1990, 29 U.S.C. §§ 623, 626, 630 (1990).

Omnibus Budget Reconciliation Act of 1980, 5 U.S.C. § 8340 et seq., as amended.

Omnibus Budget Reconciliation Act of 1981, Pub. L. No. 97–35, 95 Stat. 357, 5 U.S.C. § 8340 et seq., as amended.

Omnibus Budget Reconciliation Act of 1987, 5 U.S.C. § 8340 et seq., as amended.

Omnibus Budget Reconciliation Act of 1989, 5 U.S.C. § 8340 et seq., as amended.

Omnibus Budget Reconciliation Act of 1990, 5 U.S.C. § 8340 et seq., as amended.

Omran, M. L., & Morley, J. E. (2000). Assessment of protein energy malnutrition in older persons, part I: History, examination, body composition, and screening tools. *Nutrition, 16*(1), 50–63. doi:10.1016/s0899-9007(99)00224-5

O'Neill, G., Wilson, S. F., & Morrow-Howell, N. (2010). The civic enterprise: A new network for civic engagement in later life. In G. O'Neill & S. F. Fisher (Eds.), *Civic engagement in an older America* (pp. 1–5). Washington, DC: Gerontological Society of America.

Ong, P. M., & Haselhoff, K. (2005). Barriers to transit use. *SCS Fact Sheet, 1*(11). Retrieved from http:// respositories.cdlib.org/lewis/scs/V011_N011

Ormond, B. A., Black, K. J., Tilly, J., & Thomas, S. (2004). *Supportive services programs in naturally occurring retirement communities*. Retrieved January 2, 2007 from http://aspe.hhs.gov/daltcp/reports/NORCssp.pdf

O'Shaughnessy, C. V. (2004). *Older Americans Act: History of appropriations, FY1966–FY2004* (CRS Report No. RL32437). Washington, DC: Library of Congress, Congressional Research Service. Retrieved from http://assets.opencrs.com/rpts/RL32437_20040618.pdf

O'Shaughnessy, C. V. (2010). *Aging and disability resource centers (ADRCs): Federal and state efforts to guide consumers through the long-term services and supports maze*. Washington, DC: National Health Policy Forum. Retrieved from http://www.nhpf.org/library/background-papers/BP81_ADRCs_11-19-10.pdf

Osher Lifelong Learning Institute. (2010). *About us: The National Resource Center for the Osher Lifelong Learning Institutes*. Retrieved from http://usm.maine.edu/olli/national/about.jsp

Ovrebo, B., Minkler, M., & Liljestrand, P. (1991). No room in the inn: The disappearance of SRO housing in the United States. *Journal of Housing for the Elderly, 8*(1), 77–92.

Paillard-Borg, S., Wang, H., Winblad, B., & Fratiglioni, L. (2009). Pattern of participation in leisure activities among older people in relation to their health conditions and contextual factors: A survey in a Swedish urban area. *Ageing & Society, 29*, 803–821. doi:10.1017/S0144686X08008337

Palley, H. A., & Oktay, J. S. (1983). *The chronically limited elderly: The case for a national policy for in-home and supportive community based services*. New York, NY: Haworth.

Pardasani, M. P. (2004a). Senior centers: Increasing minority participation through diversification. *Journal of Gerontological Social Work, 43*(2–3), 41–56.

Pardasani, M. (2004b). *Senior centers: Patterns of programs and services*. Retrieved December 1, 2006 from http://www.ncoa.org/attachments/Senior_Center_Services.pdf

Pardasani, M., Sporre, K., & Thompson, P. (2009). *New models taskforce: Final report*. National Institute of Senior Centers. Retrieved September 2, 2011 from http://www.ncoa.org

Pardasani, M., & Thompson, P. (2010). Senior centers: Innovative and emerging models. *Journal of Applied Gerontology, 31*(1), 52–77. doi:10.1177/0733464810380545

Park-Lee, E. Y., & Decker, F. H. (2010). *Comparison of home and hospice care agencies by organizational characteristics and services provided: United States, 2007* (National Health Statistics Reports No. 30). Hyattsville, MD: National Center for Health Statistics.

Parmelee, P. A., & Lawton, M. P. (1990). The design of special environments for the aged. In J. E. Birren & K. W. Schaie (Eds.), *Handbook of the psychology of aging* (3rd ed., pp. 464–487). San Diego, CA: Academic Press.

Partnership for Public Service. (2008). *A golden opportunity: Recruiting baby boomers into government*. Retrieved from http://www.ourpublicservice.org/OPS/publications/viewcontentdetails.php?id = 122

Partnership for Public Service. (2011). *FedExperience pilot program*. Retrieved from http://www.ourpublicservice.org/OPS/programs/fedexperience/

Partnerships for Sustainable Communities. (n.d.). *An interagency partnership HUD, DOT, EPA*. Retrieved August 12, 2012 from http://www.sustainablecommunities.gov/pdf/FactSheet.pdf

Pascucci, M. (1992). Measuring incentives to health promotion in older adults: Understanding neglected health promotion in older adults. *Journal of Gerontological Nursing, 18*, 16–23.

Patient Protection and Affordable Care Act, Pub. L. 111-152 (2010).

Payette, H., & Shatenstein, B. (2005). Determinants of healthy eating in community-dwelling elderly people. *Canadian Journal of Public Health, 96*(00084263), S27–S31.

Pearson, K. C. (2004). The responsible thing to do about "responsible party" provisions in nursing home agreements: A proposal for change on three fronts. *University of Michigan Journal of Law Reform, 37*(3), 757–790.

Pecchioni, L. L., & Croghan, J. M. (2002). Young adults' stereotypes of older adults with their grandparents as the targets. *Journal of Communication, 52*(4), 715–730. doi:10.1111/j.1460-2466.2002.tb02570.x

Peck, M. D. (2010). *Barriers to using fixed-route public transit for older adults*. San Jose, CA: Mineta Transportation Institute, College of Business.

Peikes, D., Brown, R., Chen, A., & Schore, J. (2008). *Third report to Congress on the evaluation of the Medicare Coordinated Care Demonstration*. Princeton, NJ: Mathematica Policy Research. Retrieved from http://www.policyarchive.org/handle/10207/bitstreams/15737.pdf

Peng, T. R., Navaie-Waliser, M., & Feldman, P. H. (2003). Social support, home health service use, and outcomes among four racial-ethnic groups. *The Gerontologist, 43,* 503–513.

Pension Benefit Guaranty Corporation. (2006). *Pension insurance data book 2005.* Retrieved January 12, 2007 from http://www.pbgc.gov/docs/2005databook.pdf

Perl, L. (2010). *Section 202 and other HUD rental housing programs for low-income elderly residents* (CRS Report No. RL33508). Washington, DC: Library of Congress, Congressional Research Service. Retrieved from http://aging.senate.gov/crs/aging17.pdf

Perlman, B., Kenneally, K., & Boivie, I. (2011). *Pension and retirement security 2011: A roadmap for policy makers.* Washington, DC: National Institute on Retirement Security. Retrieved from http://www.mnpera.org/vertical/Sites/%7BCB6D4845-437C-4F52-969E-51305385F40B%7D/uploads/%7B7ADAFFC9-707C-4C28-81A9-BA047F210B23%7D.pdf

Perron, R. (2010). *African American experiences in the economy: Recession effects more strongly felt.* Washington, DC: AARP. Retrieved from http://assets.aarp.org/rgcenter/econ/economyaa.pdf

Personal Responsibility and Work Opportunity Reconciliation Act of 1996, Pub. L. No. 104–193, H.R. 3734, 104th Cong., 1st Sess., Cong. Rec. H8831 (1996).

Perspective on Aging. (1993). The first half-century of senior centers charts the way for decades to come. *Perspective on Aging, 22*(3), 16–25.

Peterson, D. (1985). A history of education for older learners. In D. Lumsden (Ed.), *The older adult as learner* (pp. 1–23). New York, NY: Hemisphere.

Peterson, D. (1990). A history of the education of older learners. In R. Sherron & D. Lumsden (Eds.), *Introduction to educational gerontology* (3rd ed., pp. 1–21). New York, NY: Hemisphere.

Peterson, J. (1995). The faces of community transportation. *Community Transportation Reporter, 13*(3), 10–12.

Peterson, S. A. (1989). Elderly women and program encounters: A rural study. *Journal of Women and Aging, 1*(4), 41–56.

Peterson, S. A., & Maiden, R. (1991). Older Americans' use of nutrition programs. *Journal of Nutrition for the Elderly, 11*(1–2), 49–67.

Petty, D. (1990). Respite care: A flexible response to service fragmentation. In N. Mace (Ed.), *Dementia care: Patient, family, and community* (pp. 243–269). Baltimore, MD: Johns Hopkins University Press.

Phillips, K. A., Morrison, K. R., Andersen, R., & Aday, L. A. (1998). Understanding the context of healthcare utilization: Assessing environmental and provider-related variables in the behavioral model of utilization. *Health Services Research, 33*(3), 571–596.

Phillipson, L. Y. N., & Jones, S. C. (2011a). "Between the devil and the deep blue sea": The beliefs of caregivers of people with dementia regarding the use of in-home respite services. *Home Health Care Services Quarterly, 30,* 43–62.

Phillipson, L. Y. N., & Jones, S. C. (2011b). Residential respite care: The caregiver's last resort. *Journal of Gerontological social Work, 54*(7), 691–711. doi:10.1080/01634372.2011.593613

Philpotts, J. (2010). ABA Commission and Borchard Foundation celebrate a decade of partnerships in law and aging. *Bifocal, 31*(4). Retrieved from http://www.americanbar.org/content/dam/aba/migrated/aging/PublicDocuments/marapr_10_aba_bifocal_j.authcheckdam.pdf

Pillemer, K. (1988). Maltreatment of patients in nursing homes: Overview and research agenda. *Journal of Health and Social Behavior, 29,* 227–238.

Pillemer, K., & Finkelhor, D. (1989). The prevalence of elder abuse: A random sample survey. *The Gerontologist, 28,* 51–57.

Pillemer, K., & Moore, D. W. (1989). Abuse of patients in nursing homes: Findings from a survey of staff. *The Gerontologist, 29,* 132–135.

Pincas, A. (2007). How do mature learners learn? *Quality in Ageing, 8*(4), 28–32.

Pirie, P. L., Elias, W. S., Wackman, D. B., Jacobs, D. R., Murray, D. M., Mittelmark, M. B., . . . Blackburn, H. (1986). Characteristics of participants and non-participants in a community cardiovascular disease risk factor screening: The Minnesota Heart Health Program. *American Journal of Preventive Medicine, 2,* 20–25.

Ponza, M., Ohls, J. C., & Millen, B. E. (1996). *Serving elders at risk: The Older Americans Act Nutrition Program's national evaluation of the Elderly Nutrition Program, 1993–1995.* Washington, DC: U.S. Department of Health and Human Services.

Ponza, M., Ohls, J. C., Millen, B. E., McCool, A. M., Needels, K. E., Rosenberg, K. et al. (1996). *Serving elders at risk: The Older Americans Act Nutrition Programs: National evaluation of the Elderly Nutrition Program 1993–1995.* Princeton, NJ: Mathematica Policy Research. Retrieved January 5, 2007 from http://www.aoa.gov/aoaroot/program_results/Nutrition_Report/eval_report.aspx

Population Reference Bureau. (2011). *Today's research on aging. Volunteering and health for aging populations.* Retrieved from http://www.prb.org/pdf11/TodaysResearchAging21.pdf

Porell, F. W., & Miltiades, H. B. (2001). Disability outcomes of older Medicare HMO enrollees and fee-for-service Medicare beneficiaries. *Journal of the American Geriatrics Society, 49,* 615–631.

Posner, B. M. (1979). *Nutrition and the elderly.* Lexington, MA: Lexington Books.

Posthuma, R. A., & Campion, M. A. (2009). Age stereotypes in the workplace: Common stereotypes, moderators, and future research directions. *Journal of Management, 35*(1), 158–188. doi:10.1177/0149206308318617

Powell, J. (2009). Social theory, aging, and health and welfare professionals: A Foucauldian "toolkit." *Journal of Applied Gerontology, 28,* 669–682.

Powell, S. K., & Tahan, H. A. (2007). *CMSA core curriculum for case management* (2nd ed.). Philadelphia, PA: Lippincott Williams & Wilkins.

Powers, E., & Bultena, G. (1974). Correspondence between anticipated and actual uses of public services by the aged. *Social Service Review, 48,* 245–254.

Predny, M. L. (2004). Horticulture therapy activities for preschool children, elderly adults, and inter-generational groups. *Activities, Adaptation and Aging, 28*(3), 1–18. doi:10.1300/J016v28n03_01

Prohaska, T., Belansky, E., Belza, B., Buchner, D., Marshall, V., McTigue, K., . . . Wilcox, S. (2006). Physical activity, public health, and aging: Critical issues and research priorities. *Journals of Gerontology, 61B*(5), S267–S273.

Public Health Service Act (42 U.S.C. 201 et seq.) (2006).

Purcell, P. J. (2000). Older workers: Employment and retirement trends. *Monthly Labor Review, 123*(10), 19–30.

Pushkar, D., Chaikelson, J., Conway, M., Etezadi, M., Giannopoulus, J., Li, K., & Wrosch, C. (2010). Testing continuity and activity variables as predictors of positive and negative affect in retirement, *Journal of Gerontology, 65B*(1): 42–49.

Pushkar, S., Gold, D., & Reis, M. (1995). When home caregiving ends: A longitudinal study of outcomes for caregivers of relatives with dementia. *Journal of the American Geriatrics Society, 43,* 10–16.

Putnam, R. (1993). *Making democracy work: Civic traditions in modern Italy.* Princeton, NJ: Princeton University Press.

Putnam, R. (2000). *Bowling alone: The collapse and revival of American community.* New York, NY: Simon & Schuster.

Qualls, S. H., & Noecker, T. L. (2009). Caregiver family therapy for conflicted families. In S. H. Qualls & S. H. Zarit (Eds.), *Aging families and caregiving* (pp. 155-187). Hoboken, NJ: John Wiley & Sons.

Qualls, S. H., & Roberto, K. A. (2006). Diversity and caregiving support interventions: Lessons from elder care research. In B. Hayslip & J. Hicks Patrick (Eds.), *Custodial grandparents: Individual, cultural, and ethnic diversity* (pp. 37–54). New York, NY: Springer.

Quandt, S. A., & Rao, P. (1999). Hunger and food security among older adults in a rural community. *Human Organization, 58*(1), 28–35.

Quinn, C., Clare, L., Pearce, A., & van Dijkhuizen, M. (2008). The experience of providing care in the early stages of dementia: An interpretative phenomenological analysis. *Aging & Mental Health, 12,* 769–778.

Quinn, J. (1993). *Successful case management in long-term care.* New York, NY: Springer.

Quinn, J. B. (2012, June 6). Prices rise for long-term care insurance: But without it, families face extremely high bills. *AARP Bulletin.* Retrieved from http://www.aarp.org/work/retirement-planning/info-06-2012/long-term-care-hikes.html

Quinn, M. E., Hohnson, M. A., Andress, E. L., McGinnis, P., & Ramesh, M. (1999). Health characteristics of elderly personal care home residents. *Journal of Advanced Nursing, 30,* 410–417.

Rabins, P. V. (1986). Establishing Alzheimer's units in nursing homes: Pros and cons. *Hospital and Community Psychiatry, 37,* 120–121.

Rafter, M. V. (2011, September 9). SecondAct asks: Will Obama jobs plan help older workers? *SecondAct.* Retrieved from http://www.secondact.com/2011/09/obamas-american-jobs-act-would-assist-older-workers/

Rahman, A. N., & Schnelle, J. F. (2008). The nursing home culture-change Movement: Recent past, present, and future directions for research. *The Gerontologist, 48*(2), 142–148. doi:10.1093/geront/48.2.142

Railroad Retirement Act of 1937, 45 U.S.C. § 201 et seq. (1995).

Ralston, P. (1982). Perceptions of senior centers by the black elderly: A comparative study. *Journal of Gerontological Social Work, 4,* 127–137.

Ralston, P. (1991). Senior centers and minority elderly: A critical review. *The Gerontologist, 31,* 325–331.

Ralston, P. (1993). Health promotion for rural black elderly: A comprehensive review. *Journal of Gerontological Social Work, 20,* 53–78.

Ralston, P., & Cohen, N. L. (1994). Nutrition and the rural elderly. In J. Krout (Ed.), *Providing community-based services to the rural elderly* (pp. 202–220). Thousand Oaks, CA: Sage.

Raphael, D. (2001). *Medicaid transportation: Assuring access to health care. A primer for states, health plans, providers and advocates.* Washington, DC: Community Transportation Association of America. Retrieved October 23, 2006 from http://trid.trb.org/view.aspx?id = 772398

Rappaport, A. M. (2007). Improving the financial status of elderly women: Issues in savings, pension plans and social security. *Benefits Quarterly, 23*(1), 34–45.

Redfoot, D. L. (2011). *How recent changes in reverse mortgages impact older homeowners.* Washington, DC: AARP Policy Institute. Retrieved from http://assets.aarp.org/rgcenter/ppi/ltc/fs211-economic.pdf

Region VIII Office, Administration on Aging. (n.d.). *Title IV research and development: History of making a difference.* Denver, CO: Author.

Regnier, V., & Culver, J. (1994, February). Single room occupancy: SRO-type housing for older people. *Supportive Housing Connection, 1–3.*

Rehabilitation Act of 1973, Pub.L. 93-112; 29 U.S.C. § 701 e.

Reichman, W. E., Coyne, A. C., Borson, S., Negron, A. E., Rovner, B. W., Pelchat, R. J., . . . Hamer, R. M. (1998). Psychiatric consultation in the nursing home: A survey of six states. *American Journal of Geriatric Psychiatry, 8,* 320–327.

Rejecki, W., & Brawley, L. R. (1997). Shaping active lifestyles in older adults: A group-facilitated behavior change intervention. *Annals of Behavioral Medicine, 19*(Suppl.), S106.

Reno, V. P., Lamme, E., & Walker, E. A. (2011). *Social Security finances: Findings of the 2011 Trustee Report.* Washington, DC: National Academy of Social Insurance. Retrieved from http://www.nasi.org/sites/default/files/research/Social_Security_Finances_Findings_of_the_2011_Trustees_Report.pdf

Research and Training Center on Disability in Rural Communities. (2007). *Models of rural transportation for people with disabilities: Rural practice guideline.* Retrieved May 28, 2012, from http://rtc.ruralinstitute.umt.edu/Trn/models.htm

Rethinking an old notion. (1996). *Hospital Care Management, 4,* 29–30.

Retired Senior and Volunteer Program International. (2010a). *Global connections.* Retrieved from http://www.sph.umd.edu/hlsa/aging/rsvpi/connections.html

Retired Senior and Volunteer Program International. (2010b). *History of RSVPI.* Retrieved from http://www.sph.umd.edu/hlsa/aging/rsvpi/history.html

Retired Senior and Volunteer Program International. (2010c). *Objectives.* Retrieved from http://www.sph.umd.edu/hlsa/aging/rsvpi/objectives.html

Revenue Act of 1921, Pub. L. No. 136, 42 Stat. 227 (1921).

Rich, B. M., & Baum, M. (1984). *The aging: A guide to public policy.* Pittsburgh, PA: University of Pittsburgh Press.

Ricker, M. (2011). Easter Seals' Intentional and integrated intergenerational center: Creating a community that embraces the integration and inclusion of all generations and abilities. *Journal of Intergenerational Relationships, 9,* 466–472. doi:10.1080/15350770.2011.619927

Riddick, C., & Keller, J. (1991). The benefits of therapeutic recreation in gerontology. In C. P. Coyle, W. B. Kinney, B. Riley, & J. Shank (Eds.), *Benefits of therapeutic recreation: A consensus view* (pp. 151–204). Philadelphia, PA: Temple University Press.

Riddick, C. C., & Stewart, D. G. (1994). An examination of the life satisfaction and importance of leisure in the lives of older female retirees: A comparison of blacks to whites. *Journal of Leisure Research, 26*(1), 75–87.

Rife, J. (1992). Case managers' perceptions of case management practice: Implications for educational preparation. *Journal of Applied Social Sciences, 16,* 161–176.

Rix, S. E. (1994). *Older workers: How do they measure up? An overview of age differences in employee cost and performance.* Washington, DC: American Association of Retired Persons.

Rix, S. E. (2011). *The employment situation, July 2011: Little improvement for older workers.* Washington, DC: AARP Public Policy Institute. Retrieved from http://assets.aarp.org/rgcenter/ppi/econ-sec/fs234-employment.pdf

Rizzuto, T. E., & Mohammed, S. (2005, April). *Workplace technology and the myth about older workers.* Paper presented at the Society for Industrial and Organizational Psychology conference, Los Angeles, CA.

Road Scholar. (2011). *2010 annual report.* Retrieved from http://www.roadscholar.org/support/EH_AnnualReport_Feb11_NoDonors.pdf

Road Scholar. (2012a). *Financial aid for Road Scholar Programs.* Retrieved from http://www.roadscholar.org/about/scholarship.asp

Road Scholar. (2012b). *The history of Elderhostel, Inc. and Road Scholar.* Retrieved from http://www.roadscholar.org/about/history.asp

Roberto, K. A., Dolbin-MacNab, M. L., & Finney, J. W. (2008). Promoting the health of grandmothers parenting young grandchildren. In B. Hayslip & P. Kaminski (Eds.), *Parenting the custodial grandchild* (pp. 75–89). New York, NY: Springer.

Roberto, K. A., & Jarrott, S. E. (2008). Caregiving in late life: A life-span human development perspective. *Family Relations, 57,* 100–111.

Roberto, K. A., & Scott, J. (1986). Equity considerations in the friendships of older adults. *Journal of Gerontology, 41,* 241–247.

Roberto, K. A., & Stroes, J. (1992). Grandchildren and grandparents: Roles, influences, and relationships. *International Journal of Aging and Human Development, 34,* 227–239.

Roberts, S. B., Hajduk, C. L., Howarth, N. C., Russell, R., & McCrory, M. A. (2005). Dietary variety predicts low body mass index and inadequate macronutrient and micronutrient intakes in community-dwelling older adults. *The Journals of Gerontology Series A: Biological Sciences and Medical Sciences, 60*(5), 613–621. doi:10.1093/gerona/60.5.613

Robertson, S. M., Zarit, S. H., Duncan, L. G., Rovine, M. J., & Femia, E. E. (2007). Family caregivers' patterns of positive and negative affect. *Family Relations, 56,* 12–23.

Roff, L. L., Burgio, L. D., Gitlin, L., Nichols, L., Chaplin, W., & Hardin, J. M. (2004). Positive aspects of caregiving: The role of race. *Journal of Gerontology: Psychological Sciences, 59,* P185–P190.

Rollinson, P. A. (1990). The story of Edward: The everyday geography of elderly single room occupancy (SRO) hotel tenants. *Journal of Contemporary Ethnography, 19*(2), 188–206.

Rollinson, P. A. (1991a). Elderly single room occupancy (SRO) hotel tenants: Still alone. *Social Work, 36,* 303–308.

Rollinson, P. A. (1991b). The spatial isolation of elderly single-room-occupancy hotel tenants. *Professional Geographer, 43,* 457–464.

Ronch, J. (1987). Specialized Alzheimer's units in nursing homes: Pros and cons. *American Journal of Alzheimer's Care and Research, 2,* 10–19.

Rook, K. S. (1987). Reciprocity of social exchange and social satisfaction among older women. *Journal of Personality and Social Psychology, 52,* 145–154.

Roots and Branches Theatre. (2001). *Roots and Branches: New York's intergenerational theater.* Retrieved May 5, 2001 from http://www.rootsandbranches.org

Rosenbloom, S. (2003). *The mobility needs of older Americans: Implications for transportation reauthorization* (Transportation Reform Series). Washington, DC: Brookings Institution, Center on Urban and Metropolitan Policy. Retrieved from http://www.brookings.edu/ ~ /media/Files/rc/ reports/2003/07transportation_rosenbloom/20030807_Rosenbloom.pdf

Rosenbloom, S., & Waldorf, B. (1999). Older travelers: Does place or race make a difference? In *U.S. Department of Transportation, Conference Proceedings, Personal travel: The long and short of it*. Retrieved August 1, 2001, from http://onlinepubs.trb.org/onlinepubs/circulars/ec026/01_ rosenbloom.pdf

Rosenheimer, L., & Francis, E. (1992). Feasible with subsidy: Overnight respite for Alzheimer's. *Journal of Gerontological Nursing, 18,* 21–29.

Rosenzwieg, E. (1995). Trends in home care entitlements and benefits. *Journal of Gerontological Social Work, 24,* 9–29.

Rosso, R. (2001). *Trends in food stamp program participation rates: 1994 to 1999*. Princeton, NJ: Mathematica Policy Research.

Rothwell, W. J., Sterns, H., Spokus, D., & Reaser, J. (2008). *Working longer: New strategies for managing, training, and retaining older employees*. New York, NY: American Management Association.

Rucker, G. (1995). *ElderTransit facts: Legislation of interest to community transportation: Intermodal Surface Transportation Efficiency Act (ISTEA)* [Brochure]. Washington, DC: National Eldercare Institute on Transportation.

Rupp, K., Strand, A., Davies, P., & Sears, J. (2007). Benefit adequacy among elderly Social Security retired-worker beneficiaries and the SSI federal benefit rate. *Social Security Bulletin, 67*(3). Retrieved from http://www.ssa.gov/policy/docs/ssb/index.html

Ryan, L. H., Smith, J., Anotucci, T. C., & Jackson, J. S. (2012). Cohort differences in the availability of informal caregivers: Are the boomers at risk? *The Gerontologist, 52*(2), 177–188. doi:10.1093/ geront/gnr142

Ryan, V. C., & Bower, M. E. (1989). Relationship of socioeconomic status and living arrangements to nutritional intake of the older persons. *Journal of the American Dietetic Association, 89,* 1805–1807.

Sahyoun, N. R., Pratt, L. A., Lentzner, H., Dey, A., & Robinson, K. N. (2001). *The changing profile of nursing home residents: 1985–1997* (Aging Trends No. 4). Hyattsville, MD: National Center for Health Statistics. Retrieved August 15, 2001 from http://www.cdc.gov/nchs/data/ahcd/agingtrends/04nursin.pdf

Saitz, G. (2009, November). Growing great teachers. *neaToday: This Active Life*. Retrieved from http:// www.nea.org/home/37001.htm#

Salihu, H. M., Bonnema, S. M., & Alio, A. P. (2009). Obesity: What is an elderly population growing into? *Maturitas, 63*(1), 7–12. doi:10.1016/j.maturitas.2009.02.010

Salin, S., Kaunonen, M., & Åstedt-Kurki, P. (2009). Informal carers of older family members: How they manage and what support they receive from respite care. *Journal of Clinical Nursing, 18,* 492–501.

Samuelson, R. J. (2005, April 9). The debate we're not having. *Newsweek*.

San Francisco Senior Center. (2010). *Inspiring stories*. Retrieved from http://www.sfsenior.com/inspir ing_stories.htm

Sanders, G. F., Fitzgerald, M. A., & Bratteli, M. (2008). Mental health services for older adults in rural areas: An ecological systems approach. *Journal of Applied Gerontology, 27,* 252–266.

Sangl, J. (1985). The family support system of the elderly. In R. J. Vogel & H. C. Palmer (Eds.), *Long-term care: Perspectives from research and demonstration* (pp. 307–336). Rockville, MD: Aspen.

Saunders, J. (1997). *Continuing care retirement communities: A background and summary of current issues*. Washington, DC: Department of Health and Human Services. Retrieved January 14, 2007 from http://aspe.hhs.gov/daltcp/reports/ccrcrpt.htm

Save Service in America. (2011). *Why save service?* Retrieved from http://www.saveservice.org/pages/ why-save-service/

Saxon, S. V., Etten, M. J., & Perkins, E. A. (2010). *Physical change and aging: A guide for the helping professions* (5th ed.). New York, NY: Springer.

Saxon-Harrold, S. K. E., & Weitzman, M. (2000). *Giving and volunteering in the United States: 1999 edition*. Washington, DC: Independent Sector.

Schafer, R. B., & Keith, P. M. (1982). Social-psychological factors in the dietary quality of married and single elderly. *Journal of the American Dietetic Association, 81,* 30–34.

Scharlach, A., & Boyd, S. C. (1989). Caregiving and employment: Results of an employee survey. *The Gerontologist, 29,* 382–387.

Scharlach, A., & Frenzel, C. (1986). An evaluation of institutional-based respite care. *The Gerontologist, 26,* 77–82.

Scharlach, A. E., Kellam, R., Ong, N., Baskin, A., Goldstein, C., & Fox, P. J. (2006). Cultural attitudes and caregiver service use. *Journal of Gerontological Social Work, 47*(1–2), 133–156. doi:10.1300/J083v47n01_09

Schlenker, R. E., Shaughnessy, P. W., & Crisler, K. S. (1995). Outcome-based continuous quality of improvement as a financial strategy for home health care agencies. *Journal of Home Health Care, 7*(4), 1–15.

Schneider, F., Landon, B., Tobias, C., & Epstein, A. (2004). Quality oversight in Medicaid primary care case management programs. *Health Affairs, 23,* 235–242.

Schoeffler, R. W. (1995). Senior centers as brokers of home and community-based long term care. In D. Shollenberger (Ed.), *Senior centers in America: A blueprint for the future: Outcomes of a national meeting convened to develop recommendations for programs, policies, and funding of senior center programs of the future.* Washington, DC: National Council on the Aging.

Schraeder, C., Fraser, C., Bruno, C., & Dworak, D. (1990). *Case management in primary care: A manual.* Englewood, CO: Center for Research in Ambulatory Health Care Administration.

Schultz, J. (2001). *The economics of aging* (7th ed.). Westport, CT: Auburn House.

Schulz, J. H., & Binstock, R. H. (2006). *Aging nation: The economics and politics of growing older in America.* Westport, CT: Praeger.

Schulz, R., Belle, S. H., Czaja, S. J., Gitlin, L. N., Wisniewski, S. T., & Ory, M. G. (2003). Introduction to the special section on Resources for Enhancing Alzheimer's Caregiver Health (REACH). *Psychology and Aging, 18,* 357–360.

Schulz, R., Lustig, A., Handler, S., & Martire, L. M. (2002). Technology-based caregiver intervention research: Current status and future directions. *Gerontological Technology Journal, 2,* 15–47.

Schulz, R., & Martire, L. (2004). Family caregiving of persons with dementia: Prevalence, health effects, and support strategies. *American Journal of Geriatric Psychiatry, 12,* 240–249.

Schulz, R., & Sherwood, P. R. (2008). Physical and mental health effects of family caregiving. *American Journal of Nursing, 108*(Suppl. 9), 23–27.

Schütz, A. (1998). Coping with threats to self-esteem: The differing patterns of subjects with high versus low trait self-esteem in first-person accounts. *European Journal of Personality, 12*(3), 169–186.

Schwenk, F. N. (1992). Economic status of rural older adults. *Agriculture Outlook, 92*(4), 3–14.

SCORE. (2010). *About SCORE.* Retrieved from http://www.score.org/about-score

SCORE. (2011). *Our impact.* Retrieved from http://www.score.org/our-impact

SCORE Foundation. (2011). *2010 small business economic impact and 2011 projections.* Retrieved from http://www.score.org/sites/default/files/SCORE%20Overall%202010%20Survey%20Results.pdf

Sebelius, K. (2011). *Report to Congress: Evaluation of the rural PACE provider grant program.* Washington, DC: Centers for Medicare & Medicaid Services' Office of Research, Development, and Information. Retrieved from http://www.npaonline.org/website/download.asp?id=3841

Seekins, T., & Spas, S. (1998). *Ruralfacts: Rural transportation.* Retrieved from http://rtc.ruralinstitute.umt.edu/trn/TrnFact.htm

Segan, S. (2006, August 25). Is your New York hotel legal? *Frommer's.* Retrieved from http://www.frommers.com/articles/3846.html

Senior Citizens' Freedom to Work Act, Pub. L. No. 106–182 (2000).

Senior Corps. (2008). *2005-2006 Senior Corps performance survey findings.* Retrieved from http://www.nationalservice.gov/pdf/08_0530_sc_performance.pdf

Senior Corps. (2009). *RSVP national overview 2008.* Retrieved from http://www.seniorcorps.gov/pdf/overview_rsvp.pdf

Senior Corps—Foster Grandparents. (2005). *Accomplishments of Foster Grandparents Program.* Retrieved December 18, 2006 from http://www.seniorcorps.gov/pdf/06_0327_SC_FGP.pdf

Senior Corps—RSVP. (2005). *Accomplishments of RSVP.* Retrieved December 18, 2006, from http://www.seniorcorps.gov/pdf/06_0327_SC_RSVP.pdf

Senior Corps—Senior Companions. (2005). *Accomplishments of the Senior Companion Program.* Retrieved December 18, 2006 from http://www.seniorcorps.gov/pdf/06_0327_SC_SCP.pdf

Senior Living. (2012). *ECHO: Unique housing option for seniors.* Retrieved from http://seniorliving.about.com/od/housingoptions/a/echo.htm

Senior Service America. (2010). *The Senior Environmental Employment Program*. Retrieved from http://www.seniorserviceamerica.org/site/our-programs/see/

SeniorNet. (2011). *Enrollment information*. Retrieved from http://webcampus.seniornet.org/enrollment-information

Service Canada. (2012). *Guaranteed income supplement*. Retrieved from http://www.servicecanada.gc.ca/eng/sc/oas/gis/guaranteeddincomesupplement.shtml

Shagrin, S. S. (2000). Retirement saving and financial planning: Different from a decade ago. *Generations, 16*, 40–44.

Shanas, E. (1979). Older people and their families: The new pioneers. *Journal of Marriage and the Family, 42*, 9–15.

Shapiro, E. (1983). Embarrassment and help-seeking. In J. D. Fisher, A. Nadler, & B. M. DePaulo (Eds.), *New directions in helping* (Vol. 2, pp. 143-163). New York, NY: Academic Press.

Shapiro, E. (1995). Case management in long-term care: Exploring its status, trends, and issues. *Journal of Case Management, 4*, 43–47.

Sharkey, J. R., & Haines, P. S. (2002). Use of telephone-administered survey for identifying nutritional risk indicators among community-living older adults in rural areas. *Journal of Applied Gerontology, 21*(3), 385–403.

Shaw, C., McNamara, R., Abrams, K., Cannings-John, R., Hood, K., Longo, M., . . . Williams, K. (2009). Systematic review of respite care for the frail elderly. *Health Technology Assessment, 13*(20), 1–224. doi:10.3310/hta13200

Shea, D., Russo, P. A., & Smyer, M. A. (2000). Use of mental health services by persons with a mental illness in nursing facilities: Initial impacts of OBRA87. *Journal of Aging and Health, 12*, 560–578.

Shelton, P., Schraeder, C., Britt, T., & Kirby, R. (1994). A generalist physician-based model for a rural geriatric collaborative practice. *Journal of Case Management, 3*, 98–104.

Shepherd's Center of America. (2012). *SCA programs & services*. Retrieved from http://www.shepherdcenters.org/programs.html

Sherman, S. R., & Newman, E. S. (1988). *Foster families for adults: A community alternative in long-term care*. New York, NY: Columbia University Press.

Shumway-Cook, A., Ciol, M. A., Yorkston, K. M., Hoffman, J. M., & Chan, L. (2005). Mobility limitations in the Medicare population: Prevalence and sociodemographic and clinical correlates. *Journal of the American Geriatrics Society, 53*(7), 1217–1221. doi:10.1111/j.1532-5415.2005.53372.x

Silveira, M. J., Kim, S. Y. H., & Langa, K. M. (2010). Advance directives and outcomes of surrogate decision making before death. *New England Journal of Medicine, 362*(13), 1211–1218. doi:doi:10.1056/NEJMsa0907901

Silvey, R. (1962). Participation in a senior citizen day center. In J. Kaplan & G. J. Aldridge (Eds.), *Social welfare of the aging*. New York, NY: Columbia University Press.

Simon, S. E., & Hodges, M. R. (2011). *Money follows the person: Change in participant experience during the first year of community living* (The National Evaluation of the MFP Demonstration Grant Program, Reports from the Field No. 6). Princeton, NJ: Mathematica Policy Research. Retrieved from http://www.hcbs.org/files/206/10261/mfpfieldrpt6.pdf

Sing, M., Cody, S., Sinclair, M., Cohen, R., & Ohls, J. (2005). *The Food Stamp program's elderly nutrition pilot demonstration: Initial evaluation design*. Princeton, NJ: Mathematica Policy Research. Retrieved January 7, 2007 from http://naldc.nal.usda.gov/download/32803/PDF

Singer, N. (2011, February 5). In a graying population, business opportunity. *The New York Times*. Retrieved from http://www.nytimes.com/

Single room occupancy housing corporation. (2012). *LA4Seniors.com*. Retrieved from http://www.la4seniors.com/single_room_corp.htm

Singleton, J. F., Forbes, W. F., & Agwani, N. (1993). Stability of activity across the lifespan. *Activities, Adaptation & Aging, 18*(1), 19–26.

Sinnen, M., & Schifalacqua, M. (1991). Coordinated care in a community hospital. *Nursing Administration, 22*, 38–42.

Skilton-Sylvester, E., & Garcia, A. (1998–1999). Intergenerational programs to address the challenge of immigration. *Generations, 22*(4), 58–63.

Sloan Center on Aging and Work. (2009). *Factors affecting older women in the work force.* Retrieved from http://www.bc.edu/content/dam/files/research_sites/agingandwork/pdf/publications/FS22_OlderWomen_in_Workforce.pdf

Sloan Work and Family Research Network. (2009). *Questions and answers about older workers: A Sloan Work and Family Research Network fact sheet.* Retrieved from https://workfamily.sas.upenn.edu/sites/workfamily.sas.upenn.edu/files/imported/pdfs/olderworkers.pdf

Slone, P. D., Lindeman, D. A., Phillips, C., Moritz, D. J., & Koch, G. (1995). Evaluating Alzheimer's special care units: Reviewing the evidence and identifying potential sources of study bias. *The Gerontologist, 35,* 103–111.

Small, N. R. (1988). Evolution of nursing homes. In N. R. Small & M. B. Walsh (Eds.), *Teaching nursing homes: The nursing perspective* (pp. 31–46). Owings Mills, MD: National Health.

Smallegan, M. (1985). There was nothing else to do: Needs for care before nursing home admission. *The Gerontologist, 25,* 364–369.

Smeeding, T., Gao, Q., Saunders, P., & Wing, C. (2008). *Elder poverty in an ageing world: Conditions of social vulnerability and low income for women in rich and middle-income nations* (Luxembourg Income Study Working Paper No. 497). Luxembourg: LIS. Retrieved from http://www.lisproject.org/publications/liswps/497.pdf

Smith, G., Smith, M., & Toseland, R. (1991). Problems identified by family caregivers in counseling. *The Gerontologist, 31,* 15–22.

Smith, K. (2003). *How will recent patterns of earnings inequality affect future retirement incomes?* (Working Paper No. 2003–06). Washington, DC: AARP. Retrieved January 10, 2007 from http://www.urban.org/UploadedPDF/411164_future_retire_incomes.pdf

Smith, K. F., & Bengston, V. L. (1979). The positive consequences of institutionalization: Solidarity between elderly parents and their middle-aged children. *The Gerontologist, 19,* 438–447.

Smith, T., & Newman, S. (1992). Older adults in Head Start. *National Head Start Association Journal, 10,* 33–35.

Smith, T., & Newman, S. (1993). Older adults in early childhood programs: Why and how. *Young Children, 48,* 32–35.

Smyer, M. A., Shea, D. G., & Streit, A. (1994). The provision and use of mental health services in nursing homes: Results from the National Medical Expenditure Survey. *American Journal of Public Health, 84,* 284–287.

Snowden, M., & Roy-Byrne, P. (1998). Mental illness and nursing home reform: OBRA-87 ten years later. *Psychiatric Services, 49,* 229–233.

Social Security Act of 1935, 42 U.S.C. § 301 et seq. (1935), as amended 1939, 1950, 1956, 1961, 1965, 1972, 1974.

Social Security Administration. (1997). *History of Social Security.* Retrieved March 26, 1997 from http://www.socialsecurity.gov/history/

Social Security Administration. (2006). *2007 Social Security/SSI/Medicare information.* Retrieved January 22, 2007 from http://www.ssa.gov/legislation/2007FactSheet.pdf

Social Security Administration. (2010). *Income of the population 55 and older, 2008.* Washington, DC: Author.

Social Security Administration. (2011a). *Fast facts & figures about Social Security, 2011* (SSA Publication No. 13-11785). Retrieved from http://www.socialsecurity.gov/policy/docs/chartbooks/fast_facts/2011/fast_facts11.pdf

Social Security Administration. (2011b). *A guide to Supplemental Security Income (SSI) for groups and organizations.* Retrieved from http://www.ssa.gov/pubs/11015.pdf

Social Security Administration. (2012a). *Annual statistical supplement to the Social Security Bulletin, 2011* (SSA Publication No. 13-11700). Washington, DC: Office of Retirement and Disability Policy, Evaluation, and Statistics. Retrieved from http://www.ssa.gov/policy/docs/statcomps/supplement/2011/supplement11.pdf

Social Security Administration. (2012b). *Monthly statistical snapshot, January 2012.* Retrieved August 6, 2012 http://www.ssa.gov/policy/docs/quickfacts/stat_snapshot/

Social Security Administration. (2012c). *OASDI and SSI program rates and limits 2012.* Retrieved from http://www.ssa.gov/policy/docs/quickfacts/prog_highlights/RatesLimits2012.pdf

Society of St. Andrew. (n.d.). *Gleaning Network.* Retrieved February 18, 2012, from http://www.endhunger.org/gleaning_network.htm

Solway, E., Estes, C. L., Goldberg, S., & Berry, J. (2010). Access barriers to mental health services for older adults from diverse populations: Perspectives of leaders in mental health and aging. *Journal of Aging & Social Policy, 22,* 360–378.

Song, J. G. (2003–2004). Evaluating the initial impact of eliminating the retirement earnings test. *Social Security Bulletin, 65,* 1–15.

Sörenson, S., Pinquart, M., & Duberstein, P. (2002). How effective are interventions with caregivers? An updated meta-analysis. *The Gerontologist, 42,* 356–372.

Special Committee on Aging. (1963). *A compilation of materials relevant to the message of the president of the United States on our nation's senior citizens.* Washington, DC: Government Printing Office.

Spector, W. D., Limcangco, M. R., Ladd, H., & Mukamel, D. (2011). Incremental cost of postacute care in nursing homes. *Health Services Research, 46*(1p1), 105–119. doi:10.1111/j.1475-6773.2010.01189.x

Spense, S. A. (1992). Use of community-based social services by older rural and urban blacks: An exploratory study. *Human Services in the Rural Environment, 15*(4), 16–19.

Spillman, B. C., & Lubitz, J. (2002). New estimates of lifetime nursing home use: Have patterns of use changed? *Medical Care, 40*(10), 965–975.

Spillman, B. C., & Pezzin, L. (2000). Potential and active family caregivers changing networks and the "sandwich generation." *Milbank Quarterly, 78*(3), 347–374.

Spitz, B., & Abramson, J. (1987). Competition, capitation, and case management: Barriers to strategic reform. *Millbank Quarterly, 65,* 348–370.

Stajkovic, A. D., & Sommer, S. M. (2000). Self-efficacy and causal attributions: Direct and reciprocal links. *Journal of Applied Social Psychology, 30*(4), 707–737.

Stanley, D., & Freysinger, V. J. (1995). The impact of age, health, and sex on the frequency of older adults' leisure activity participation: A longitudinal study. *Activities, Adaptation, and Aging, 19,* 31–42.

Stebbins, R. A. (1992). *Amateurs, professionals, and serious leisure:* McGill-Queen's University Press.

Steele, M. F., & Bryan, J. D. (1986). Dietary intake of homebound elderly recipients and nonrecipients of home-delivered meals. *Journal of Nutrition and the Elderly, 5,* 23–35.

Stein, G. L., Beckerman, N. L., & Sherman, P. A. (2010). Lesbian and gay elders and long-term care: Identifying the unique psychosocial perspectives and challenges. *Journal of Gerontological Social Work, 53*(5), 421–435. 10.1080/01634372.2010.496478

Steinig, S., & Simon, J. (Eds.). (2005). *Under one roof: A guide to starting and strengthening intergenerational shared site programs.* Washington, DC: Generations United.

Stephens, B. W., McCarthy, D. P., Marsiske, M., Shechtman, O., Classen, S., Justiss, M., & Mann, W. C. (2005). International older driver consensus conference on assessment, remediation and counseling for transportation alternatives: Summary and recommendations. *Physical and Occupational Therapy in Geriatrics, 23*(2–3), 103–121.

Sterns, H., & McDaniel, M. (1994). Job performance and the older worker. In S. Rix (Ed.), *Older workers: How do they measure up?* Washington, DC: American Association of Retired Persons.

Stevens, D. A., Grivetti, L. E., & McDonald, R. B. (1992). Nutrient intake of urban and rural elderly receiving home-delivered meals. *Journal of the American Dietetic Association, 92,* 714–718.

Stockwell-Smith, G., Kellett, U., & Moyle, W. (2010). Why carers of frail older people are not using available respite services: An Australian study. *Journal of Clinical Nursing, 19,* 2057–2064. doi:10.1111/j.1365-2702.2009.03139.x

Stoller, E. P. (1989). Formal services and informal helping: The myth of service substitution. *Journal of Applied Gerontology, 8,* 37–52.

Stoller, E. P., & Pugliesi, K. (1988). Informal networks of community based elderly: Changes in composition over time. *Research on Aging, 10,* 499–516.

Stommes, E. S., Brown, D. M., & Houston, C. M. (2002). *Moving rural residents to work: Lessons learned from implementation of eight job access and reverse commute projects.* Washington, DC: U.S. Department of Agriculture. Retrieved from http://www.fta.dot.gov/3630.html

Stone, D. (2000). *Reframing home health care policy.* Cambridge, MA: Radcliffe Institute for Advanced Study. Retrieved January 2, 2007 from http://www.radcliffe.edu/research/pubpol/Reframing_Home_Health_Care.pdf

Stone, R. (2006). Linking services to housing: Who will provide the care? A competent, stable, and committed workforce is in short supply. *Generations, 29*(4), 44–51.

Stone, R., Cafferata, G., & Sangl, J. (1987). Caregivers of the frail elderly: A national profile. *The Gerontologist, 27,* 616–626.

Stone, R., Reinhard, S. C., Machemer, J., & Rudin, D. (2002). *Geriatric care managers: A profile of an emerging profession.* Retrieved January 23, 2007 from http://assets.aarp.org/rgcenter/il/ dd82_care.pdf

Storey, R. (1962). Who attends a senior activity center? A comparison of Little House members with non-members in the same community. *The Gerontologist, 2,* 216–222.

Stowell-Ritter, A., Straight, A., & Evans, E. (2002). *Understanding senior transportation: Report and analysis of a survey of consumers age 50+.* Washington, DC: AARP Public Policy Institute.

Strain, L. A. (2001). Senior centres: Who participates? *Canadian Journal on Aging, 20*(4), 471–491.

Strain, L. A., & Blanford, A. (2002). Community-based services for the taking but few takers: Reasons for nonuse. *Journal of Applied Gerontology, 21*(2), 220–235.

Strauss, L. R. (2009). *Section 515 Rural Rental Housing.* Washington, DC: National Low Income Housing Coalition. Retrieved from http://www.nlihc.org/detail/article.cfm?article_id = 6077&id = 23

Strauss, P. J., Wolf, R., & Schilling, D. (1990). *Aging and the law.* Chicago, IL: Commerce Clearing House.

Strawbridge, W., & Wallhagen, M. (1991). Impact of family conflict on adult child caregivers. *The Gerontologist, 31,* 770–777.

Strum, R., Ringel, J. S., & Andreyeva, T. (2004). Increasing obesity rates and disability trends. *Health Affairs, 23*(2), 199–205.

Substance Abuse and Mental Health Services Administration. (2004). *Community integration for older adults with mental illnesses: Overcoming barriers and seizing opportunities.* Retrieved May 30, 2006, from http://www.taadas.org/publications/prodimages/Community%20Integration% 20for%20Older%20Adults%20with%20Mental%20Illnesses%20Overcoming%20Barriers% 20and%20Seizing%20Opportunities.pdf

Substance Abuse and Mental Health Services Administration. (2005). *Successful strategies for recruiting, training, and utilizing volunteers: A guide for faith- and community-based service providers.* Retrieved December 10, 2006 from http://www.samhsa.gov/fbci/Volunteer_handbook.pdf

Substance Abuse and Mental Health Services Administration. (2012a). *Mental health, United States, 2010* (HHS Publication No. (SMA) 12-4681). Retrieved from http://www.samhsa.gov/data/2k12/ MHUS2010/MHUS-2010.pdf

Substance Abuse and Mental Health Services Administration. (2012b). *Older adult programs: Get connected! Linking older adults with medication, alcohol and mental health resources.* Retrieved from http://www.samhsa.gov/Aging/docs/GetConnectedToolkit.pdf

Suitor, J. J., & Pillemer, K. (1990). Transitions to the status of family caregiver: A new framework for studying social support and well-being. In S. M. Stahl (Ed.), *The legacy of longevity* (pp. 310–320). Newbury Park, CA: Sage.

Sun, F. (2011). Community service use by older adults: The roles of sociocultural factors in rural–urban differences. *Journal of Social Service Research, 37*(2), 124–135. doi:10.1080/01488376.2011.547446

Swan, J. H., & Benjamin, A. E. (1990). Nursing costs of skilled nursing care for AIDS. *AIDS and Public Policy Journal, 5,* 64–67.

Swedish Institute. (2012). *Elderly care: A challenge for our future.* Retrieved from http://www .sweden.se/eng/Home/Society/Elderly-care/Facts/Elderly-care

Sylvia, M. L., Shadmi, E., Hsiao, C. J., Boyd, C. M., Schuster, A. B., & Boult, C. (2006). Clinical features of high-risk older persons identified by predictive modeling. *Disease Management, 9*(1), 56–62.

Taggart, C. (2005, March). Retired nurses to help fill in gaps at KMC. *The Spokane Spokesman Review.* Retrieved January 20, 2007 from http://www.spokesman.com/stories/2005/mar/09/retired-nurses-to-help-fill-in-gaps-at-kmc/

Taietz, P. (1976). Two conceptual models of the senior center. *Journal of Gerontology, 31,* 219–222.

Takamura, J. C. (1999). Getting ready for the 21st Century: The aging of America and the Older Americans Act. *Health and Social Work, 24*(3), 232–238.

Tang, F., & Morrow-Howell, N. (2008). Involvement in voluntary organizations: How older adults access volunteer roles? *Journal of Gerontological Social Work, 51,* 210–227. doi:10.1080/01634370802039494

Tang, F., Morrow-Howell, N., & Choi, E. (2010). Why do older adult volunteers stop volunteering? *Ageing & Society, 30,* 859–878. doi:10.1017/s0144686x10000140

Tang, J., Ryburn, B., Doyle, C., & Wells, Y. (2011). The psychology of respite care for people with dementia in Australia. *Australian Psychologist, 46,* 183–189. doi:10.1111/j.1742-9544.2010.00005.x

Tarlow, B. J., Steven, S. R. W., Belle, H., Rubert, M., Ory, M. O., & Gallagher-Thompson, D. (2004). Positive aspects of caregiving: Contributions of the REACH Project to the development of new measures for Alzheimer's caregiving. *Research on Aging, 26*(4), 429–453. doi:10.1177/0164027504264493

Tavernise, S., & Gebeloff, R. (2011, November 7). New way to tally poor recasts view of poverty. *The New York Times.* Retrieved from http://www.nytimes.com/

Tax Equity and Fiscal Responsibility Act of 1982, Pub. L. No. 97–248, 96 Stat. 324 (1982).

Taylor, D. H., Ezell, M., Kuchibhatla, M., Ostbye, T., & Clipp, E. C. (2008). Identifying the trajectories of depressive symptoms for women caring for their husbands with dementia. *Journal of the American Geriatrics Society, 56,* 322–327.

Teague, M. L. (1987). *Health promotion programs: Achieving high-level wellness in the later years.* Indianapolis, IN: Benchmark.

Teaster, P. B., Dugar, T. A., Mendiondo, M. S., Abner, E. L., & Cecil, K. A. (2006). *The 2004 Survey of state adult protective services: Abuse of adults 60 years of age and older.* Washington, DC: U.S. Department of Health and Human Services, Administration on Aging.

Teno, J. M., Gruneir, A., Schwartz, Z., Nanda, A., & Wetle, T. (2007). Association between advance directives and quality of end-of-life care: A national study. *Journal of the American Geriatrics Society, 55,* 189–194. doi:10.1111/j.1532-5415.2007.01045.x

Tessler, R. C., & Schwartz, S. H. (1972). Help seeking, self-esteem, and achievement motivation: An attributional analysis. *Journal of Personality and Social Psychology, 21,* 318–326.

Thomas, N. K. (2006). *Elderly legal assistance program: Report on the legal needs of seniors in Georgia.* Atlanta, GA: Department of Human Resources, Division of Aging Services. Retrieved from http://www.tcsg.org/GALegalNeedsSurvey.pdf

Thompson, D. (2012, March 26). Gray nation: The very real economic dangers of an aging America. *The Atlantic.* Retrieved from http://www.theatlantic.com/

Tokarek, J. (1996). Keeping frail seniors independent through money management. *Aging, 367,* 84–86.

Tomstam, L. (2005). *Gerotranscendence: A developmental theory of positive aging.* New York, NY: Springer.

Toossi, M. (2012, January). Labor force projections to 2020: A more slowly growing workforce. *Monthly Labor Review.* Retrieved from http://www.bls.gov/opub/mlr/2012/01/art3full.pdf

Topoleski, J. J. (2009). *Pension sponsorship and participation: Summary of recent trends.* (CRS Report No. RL30122). Washington, DC: Library of Congress, Congressional Research Service. Retrieved from http://aging.senate.gov/crs/pension1.pdf

Torti, F. M., Jr., Gwyther, L. P., Reed, S. D., Friedman, J. Y., & Schulman, K. A. (2004). Multinational review of recent trends and reports in dementia caregiver burden. *Alzheimer's Disease and Associated Disorders, 18,* 99–109.

Toseland, R. W., Haigler, D. H., Monahan, D. J. (2011). *Education and support programs for caregivers: Research, practice, policy.* New York, NY: Springer.

Toseland, R. W., Naccarato, T., & Wray, L. O. (2007). Telephone groups for older persons and family caregivers: Key implementation and process issues. *Clinical Gerontologist, 32,* 59–76.

Tourigny, L., & Pulich, M. (2006). Improving retention of older employees through training and development. *The Health Care Manager, 25,* 43–52.

Townsend, D., & Kosloski, K. (2002). Factors related to client satisfaction with community-based respite services. *Health Care Services Quarterly, 21*(3–4), 89–106.

Travis, S. S. (1995). Families and formal networks. In R. Blieszner & V. H. Bedford (Eds.), *Handbook of aging and the family* (pp. 459–473). Westport, CT: Greenwood.

Trella, R. (1993). A multidisciplinary approach to care management of frail, hospitalized older adults. *Journal of Nursing Administration, 23,* 20–26.

Trentacoste, M. F. (2010). Spotlight on senior mobility. *Public Roads, 73*(4). Retrieved from http://www.fhwa.dot.gov/publications/publicroads/index.cfm

Trice, L. (2006). PACE: A model for providing comprehensive healthcare for frail elders. *Generations, 30*(3), 90–92.

TRIP. (2012). *Keeping baby boomers mobile: Preserving the mobility and safety of older Americans.* Washington, DC: American Association of State Highways and Transportation Officials. Retrieved from http://www.tripnet.org/docs/Older_Drivers_TRIP_Report_Feb_2012.pdf

Trivedi, C. M. (2011). *LEGACY revisited: Challenges and opportunities in providing housing for grand-families.* Washington, DC: U.S. Department of Housing and Urban Development. Retrieved from http://www2.gu.org/Portals/0/documents/Conference/11-conf-ppt-Legacy-Trivedi.pdf

Trotman, F. K., & Brody, C. M. (2002). *Psychotherapy and counseling with older women: Cross-cultural, family, and end-of-life issues.* New York, NY: Springer.

Truman, J. L. (2011, September). *Criminal victimization, 2010* (BJS Bulletin). Washington, DC: U.S. Department of Justice. Retrieved from http://www.bjs.gov/content/pub/pdf/cv10.pdf

Turner, K. W. (2004). Senior citizens centers: What they offer, who participates, and what they gain. *Journal of Gerontological Social Work, 43*(1), 37–47.

Ujvari, K. (2012). *Long-term care insurance: 2012 update fact sheet.* Washington, DC: AARP Public Policy Institute. Retrieved from http://www.aarp.org/content/dam/aarp/research/public_policy_institute/ltc/2012/ltc-insurance-2012-update-AARP-ppi-ltc.pdf

United Way of Connecticut. (2001). *A national initiative to link people with community services.* Retrieved June 13, 2001 from http://www.211.org

University of Miami Ethics Programs. (n.d.). *Terry Schiavo case resources.* Retrieved January 13, 2007 from http://www.miami.edu/index.php/ethics/projects/schiavo/

Urban Institute. (2004). *Volunteer management capacity in America's charities and congregations: A briefing report.* Washington, DC: Author.

Urban Institute. (2012). *Supreme Court decision on the Affordable Care Act: What it means for Medicaid.* Retrieved from http://www.urban.org/UploadedPDF/412605-Supreme-Court-Decision-on-the-Affordable-Care-Act.pdf

Urban Mass Transportation Act of 1964, 49 U.S.C. § 1601 et seq. (1964).

Urv-Wong, E., & McDowell, D. (1994). Case management in a rural setting. In J. Krout (Ed.), *Providing community-based services to the rural elderly* (pp. 65–89). Thousand Oaks, CA: Sage.

U.S. Census Bureau. (1996). *Statistical abstract of the United States* (116th ed.). Washington, DC: Author.

U.S. Census Bureau. (2000). *Current population survey, racial and ethnic composition.* Washington, DC: Government Printing Office.

U.S. Census Bureau. (2004a). *Age and sex of all people, family members and unrelated individuals iterated by income-to-poverty ratio and race, 2004.* Retrieved January 23, 2007 from http://www.pubds3.census.gov/macro/032004/pov/toc.htm

U.S. Census Bureau. (2004b). *U.S. Interim projections by age, sex, race, and Hispanic origin.* Washington, DC: Government Printing Office

U. S. Census Bureau. (2005). *American Housing Survey for the U.S.: 2005* (Current Housing Reports, Series H150-05). Washington, DC: U.S. Government Printing Office. Retrieved from http://www.census.gov/prod/2006pubs/h150-05.pdf

U.S. Census Bureau. (2006). Employed and unemployed full- and part-time workers by age, sex, race, and Hispanic or Latino ethnicity. *Current Population Survey.* Retrieved from http://www.bls.gov/cpsaat08.pdf

U.S. Census Bureau. (2008). *2008 national population projections.* Retrieved from http://www.census.gov/population/projections/data/national/2008.html

U.S. Census Bureau. (2010). *Annual statistics, 2010: Homeownership rates by age of household and family status: 1982–2010.* Retrieved from http://www.census.gov/hhes/www/housing/hvs/annual10/ann10ind.html

U.S. Census Bureau. (2011a). *American Housing Survey for the United States: 2009* (Current housing reports, Series H150/09). Washington, DC: U.S. Government Printing Office. Retrieved from http://www.census.gov/prod/2011pubs/h150-09.pdf

U.S. Census Bureau. (2011b). Educational attainment in the United States: 2010—Detailed tables. *Current Population Survey, 2010 Annual Social and Economic Supplement.* Retrieved from http://www.census.gov/hhes/socdemo/education/data/cps/2010/tables.html

U.S. Census Bureau. (2011c). *Grandparents living with own grandchildren under 18 years by responsibility for own grandchildren by length of time responsible for own grandchildren for the population*

30 years and over (American Community Survey 1-Year Estimates). Retrieved March 15, 2012 from http://factfinder2.census.gov/faces/tableservices/jsf/pages/productview.xhtml?pid = ACS_11_1YR_B10050&prodType = table

U.S. Census Bureau. (2011d). *Income, poverty, and health insurance coverage in the United States: 2010* (Current Population Reports No. 06-239). Retrieved from http://www.census.gov/prod/2011pubs/p60-239.pdf

U.S. Census Bureau. (2011e). *Profile America facts for features—Older Americans month: May 2011.* Retrieved from http://www.census.gov/newsroom/releases/archives/facts_for_features_special_editions/cb11-ff08.html

U.S. Census Bureau. (2011f). *Table A1. Marital status of people 15 years and over, by age, sex, personal earnings, race, and Hispanic origin.* Retrieved from http://www.census.gov/population/socdemo/hh-fam/cps2011/tabA1-all.xls

U.S. Census Bureau. (2012a). *Characteristics of the group quarters population by group quarters type—S2601B.* Retrieved from http://factfinder2.census.gov/faces/nav/jsf/pages/index.xhtml

U.S. Census Bureau. (2012b). *Statistical abstract of the United States: 2012. Resident population projections by race, Hispanic-origin status, and age: 2010 and 2015.* Washington, DC: Government Printing Office. Retrieved from http://www.census.gov/compendia/statab/2012/tables/12s0012.pdf

U.S. Congress, Office of Technology Assessment. (1987). *Losing a million minds: Confronting the tragedy of Alzheimer's disease and other dementias.* Washington, DC: Government Printing Office.

U.S. Congress, Office of Technology Assessment. (1992). *Special care units for people with Alzheimer's and other dementias: Consumer education, research, regulatory, and reimbursement issues* (Pub. No. OTA-H-543). Washington, DC: Government Printing Office.

U.S. Department of Agriculture. (2006a). *Cooperative state research, education, and extension service: About us.* Retrieved from http://www.csrees.usda.gov/qlinks/partners/state_partners.html

U.S. Department of Agriculture. (2006b). *The Emergency Food Assistance Program. Food and nutrition service, food distribution fact sheet, August 2006.* Retrieved January 7, 2007 from http://www.fns.usda.gov/fdd/programs/tefap/pfs-tefap.pdf

U.S. Department of Agriculture. (2011a). *Commodity Supplemental Food Program: Nutrition program fact sheet.* Retrieved January 4, 2012, from http://www.fns.usda.gov/fdd/programs/csfp/pfs-csfp.pdf

U.S. Department of Agriculture. (2011b). *Senior Farmers' Market Nutrition Program.* Retrieved from http://www.fns.usda.gov/wic/SFMNP-Fact-Sheet.pdf

U.S. Department of Agriculture. (2012a). *The Emergency Food Assistance Program (TEFAP): Total food costs.* Retrieved March 12, 2012 from http://www.fns.usda.gov/pd/22tefap.htm

U.S. Department of Agriculture (2012b). *Supplemental Nutrition Assistance Program: Eligibility.* Retrieved March 12, 2012, from http://www.fns.usda.gov/snap/applicant_recipients/eligibility.htm

U.S. Department of Agriculture. (n.d.). *Definitions of food security.* Retrieved from http://www.ers.usda.gov/topics/food-nutrition-assistance/food-security-in-the-us/definitions-of-food-security.aspx

U.S. Department of Agriculture, Rural Development Program. (2004). *Rural housing options for elderly people.* Retrieved from http://www.rurdev.usda.gov/rd/pubs/pa1662.htm

U.S. Department of Agriculture, Rural Development Program. (2011). *Rural housing programs.* Retrieved from http://www.rurdev.usda.gov/hi/rural%20housing%20programs.htm

U.S. Department of Defense. (2001). *TRICARE for life.* Retrieved September 16, 2001 from http://www.tricare.mil/tfl

U.S. Department of Education. (1998). *Vocational and adult education.* Retrieved from http://www.ed.gov/offices/OVAE/98age.html

U.S. Department of Energy. (2011a). *Weatherization Assistance Program.* Retrieved from http://www1.eere.energy.gov/wip/wap.html

U.S. Department of Energy. (2011b). *Weatherization Assistance Program allocation formula.* Retrieved from http://www1.eere.energy.gov/wip/wap_allocation.html

U.S. Department of Energy. (2011c). *Weatherization Assistance Program goals and metrics.* Retrieved from http://www1.eere.energy.gov/wip/wap_goals.html

U.S. Department of Health and Human Services. (1991). *Mental illness in nursing homes: United States, 1985* (DHHS Pub. No. PHS 91–1766). Washington, DC: Government Printing Office.

U.S. Department of Health and Human Services. (1993). *Growing older: Healthy Black lifestyles: The health promotion programs in historically Black colleges and universities* (DHHS Pub. No. MF 0447-A-01). Washington, DC: Government Printing Office.

U.S. Department of Health and Human Services. (2001). *National standards for culturally and linguistically appropriate services in health care final report, March 1, 2001*. Washington, DC: U.S. Department of Health and Human Services, Office of Minority Health.

U.S. Department of Health and Human Services. (2010a). *Community living initiative*. Retrieved from http://www.cms.gov/smdl/downloads/SMD10008.pdf

U.S. Department of Health and Human Services. (2010b). *Fiscal year 2011 Administration on Aging: Justification of estimates for appropriations committee*. Retrieved from http://www.aoa.gov/aoaroot/about/Budget/DOCS/AoA_CJ_FY_2011.pdf

U.S. Department of Health and Human Services. (2010c). *Low income home energy assistance program report to Congress for fiscal year 2007*. Retrieved from http://www.acf.hhs.gov/sites/default/files/ocs/liheap07rc_0.pdf

U.S. Department of Health and Human Services. (2011a). *Fiscal year 2012 Administration on Aging: Justification of estimates for Appropriations Committee*. Retrieved from http://www.aoa.gov/aoaroot/about/Budget/DOCS/FY_2012_AoA_CJ_Feb_2011.pdf

U.S. Department of Health and Human Services. (2011b). *Memorandum on the CLASS Program*. Retrieved from http://aspe.hhs.gov/daltcp/reports/2011/class/CLASSmemo.pdf

U.S. Department of Health and Human Services. (2011c). *National healthcare disparities report, 2010*. Rockville, MD: Agency for Healthcare Research and Quality. Retrieved from http://www.ahrq.gov/qual/nhdr10/nhdr10.pdf

U.S. Department of Health and Human Services. (2011d). *A report on the actuarial, marketing, and legal analyses of the CLASS Program*. Retrieved from http://aspe.hhs.gov/daltcp/reports/2011/class/index.pdf

U.S. Department of Health and Human Services. (2012a). *Administration for Community Living: About us*. Retrieved August 1, 2012, from http://www.hhs.gov/acl/about-us/

U.S. Department of Health and Human Services. (2012b). *Administration for Community Living organizational chart*. Retrieved August 6, 2012 from http://www.hhs.gov/acl/organization/

U.S. Department of Health and Human Services. (2012c). *Fiscal year 2013 Administration on Aging: Justification of estimates for Appropriations Committee*. Retrieved from http://www.aoa.gov/AoARoot/About/Budget/DOCS/FY_2013_AoA_CJ_Feb_2012.pdf

U.S. Department of Health and Human Services. (2012d). *National plan to address Alzheimer's disease*. Retrieved from http://aspe.hhs.gov/daltcp/napa/NatlPlan.pdf

U.S. Department of Health and Human Services. (2012e). *Report to Congress: Plan to implement a Medicare home health agency value-based purchasing program*. Retrieved from http://www.cms.gov/Medicare/Medicare-Fee-for-Service-Payment/HomeHealthPPS/Downloads/Stage-2-NPRM.pdf

U.S. Department of Health and Human Services. (2012f, November 13). Statement of organization, functions, and delegations of authority. *Federal Register, 77*(219), 67653–67655. Retrieved from http://www.gpo.gov/fdsys/pkg/FR-2012-11-13/pdf/2012-27524.pdf

U.S. Department of Health, Education, and Welfare. (1964). Foster care. *Aging, 16,* 1–3.

U.S. Department of Health, Education, and Welfare. (1979). *Healthy people: The surgeon general's report on health promotion and disease prevention* (PHS Pub. No. 79–55071). Washington, DC: Government Printing Office.

U.S. Department of Housing and Urban Development. (2008a). *Accessory dwelling units: Case study*. Retrieved from http://www.huduser.org/portal/publications/adu.pdf

U.S. Department of Housing and Urban Development. (2008b). *Characteristics of HUD-assisted renters and their units in 2003*. Retrieved from http://www.huduser.org/portal/publications/pdf/Hud_asst_renters_report_p1.pdf

U.S. Department of Housing and Urban Development. (2008c). *Demonstration program for elderly housing for intergenerational families*. Retrieved from http://www.hud.gov/offices/hsg/mfh/eldfam/announcement.pdf

U.S. Department of Housing and Urban Development. (2010). *Service coordinator program.* Retrieved from http://portal.hud.gov/hudportal/HUD?src = /program_offices/housing/mfh/scp/scphome

U.S. Department of Housing and Urban Development. (2011a). *FHA reverse mortgages (HECMs) for consumers.* Retrieved from http://portal.hud.gov/hudportal/HUD?src = /program_offices/housing/sfh/hecm/hecmabout

U.S. Department of Housing and Urban Development. (2011b). *Housing choice vouchers fact sheet.* Retrieved from http://portal.hud.gov/hudportal/HUD?src = /program_offices/public_indian_housing/programs/hcv/about/fact_sheet

U. S. Department of Housing and Urban Development. (2012). *Public–private partnerships, ingenuity, and $11M tax credit provides innovative housing solutions for Philadelphia's LGBT seniors.* Retrieved from http://www.whitehouse.gov/blog/2012/04/16/public-private-partnerships-ingenuity-and-11m-tax-credit-provides-innovative-housing

U.S. Department of Labor. (2000). *Report of the working group on phased retirement.* Retrieved January 26, 2007 from http://www.dol.gov/ebsa/publications/phasedr1.htm

U.S. Department of Labor. (2011a). *About SCSEP.* Retrieved August 11, 2012 from http://www.doleta.gov/Seniors/html_docs/AboutSCSEP.cfm

U.S. Department of Labor. (2011b). *Employment and training commission: Workforce Investment Act* (20 CFR Part 652, Part 660 et al., RIN 1205-AB20). Retrieved from http://www.doleta.gov/regs/statutes/finalrule.htm

U.S. Department of Labor. (2011c). *Private pension plan bulletin historical tables and graphs.* Retrieved from http://www.dol.gov/ebsa/pdf/historicaltables.pdf

U.S. Department of Labor. (2011d). *Volunteering in the United States—2010.* Retrieved from http://www.bls.gov/news.release/pdf/volun.pdf

U.S. Department of Labor. (2012a). *FY 2013 Budget in brief: Community service employment for older Americans.* Retrieved from http://www.dol.gov/dol/budget/2013/bib.htm#community

U.S. Department of Labor. (2012b). Household data seasonally adjusted: A-6. Employed and unemployed full- and part-time workers by age, sex, race and Hispanic or Latino ethnicity. *Labor Force Statistics From the Current Population Survey.* Washington, DC: U.S. Bureau of Labor Statistics. Retrieved from http://www.bls.gov/web/empsit/cpseea06.pdf

U.S. Department of Labor. (2012c). Household data seasonally adjusted: A-13. Employment status of the civilian noninstitutional population by age, sex, and race. *Labor Force Statistics From the Current Population Survey.* Washington, DC: U.S. Bureau of Labor Statistics. Retrieved from http://www.bls.gov/web/empsit/cpseea13.pdf

U.S. Department of Labor. (n.d.). *Training: One-stop career centers.* Retrieved from http://www.dol.gov/dol/topic/training/onestop.htm

U.S. Department of Transportation. (1997). *Improving transportation for a maturing society* (DOT-P10–97–01). Retrieved June 14, 2001 from http://trid.trb.org/view.aspx?id = 467910

U.S. Department of Transportation. (2005a). *FTA authorization fact sheet: Elderly persons and persons with disabilities programs.* Retrieved November 16, 2007 from http://www.fta.dot.gov/documents/FTA_Elderly_and_Indiv_with_Disab_Fact_Sheet_Sept05.pdf

U.S. Department of Transportation. (2005b). *FTA authorization fact sheet: New Freedom Program.* Retrieved November 16, 2007 from http://www.fta.dot.gov/documents/FTA_New_Freedom_Fact_Sheet_Sept05.pdf

U.S. Department of Transportation. (2005c). *FTA authorization fact sheet other than urbanized area formula programs.* Retrieved November 16, 2007 from http://www.fta.dot.gov/documents/FTA_Rural_Program_Fact_Sheet_Sept05.pdf

U.S. Department of Veterans Affairs. (2012). *Home and community based services.* Retrieved from http://www.va.gov/GERIATRICS/Guide/LongTermCare/Home_and_Community_Based_Services.asp

U.S. Equal Employment Opportunity Commission. (n.d.). *Age Discrimination in Employment Act (includes concurrent charges with Title VII, ADA and EPA) FY 1997–FY 2011.* Retrieved March 3, 2012 from http://www1.eeoc.gov/eeoc/statistics/enforcement/adea.cfm?renderforprint = 1

U.S. General Accounting Office. (1991a). *Longstanding transportation problems need more federal attention* (Pub. No. HRD-91–117). Washington, DC: Government Printing Office.

U.S. General Accounting Office. (1991b). *Older Americans Act: Promising practice in information and referral services* (GAO Pub. No. PEMD 91–31). Washington, DC: Government Printing Office.

U.S. General Accounting Office. (1993). *Long-term care case management: State experiences and implication for federal policy.* Washington, DC: Author.

U.S. General Accounting Office. (2005). *Elderly housing: Federal housing programs that offer assistance for the elderly.* Retrieved January 2, 2007 from http://www.gao.gov/new.items/d05174.pdf

U.S. Government Accountability Office. (2007). *Older driver safety: Knowledge sharing should help states prepare for increase in older driver population.* (GAO-07-413). Retrieved from http://www.gao.gov/assets/260/259070.pdf

U.S. Government Accountability Office. (2010). *Private pensions: Changes needed to better protect multiemployer pension benefits.* Retrieved from http://www.gao.gov/products/GAO-11-79

U.S. Government Accountability Office. (2011). *Income security: Older adults and the 2007–2009 recession.* Retrieved from http://www.gao.gov/new.items/d1276.pdf

U.S. Government Accountability Office. (2012). *Medicaid: States' plans to pursue new and revised options for home- and community-based service* (GAO-12-649). Washington, DC: Author. Retrieved from http://www.gao.gov/assets/600/591560.pdf

U.S. Housing Act of 1937, 42 USCS §§ 1437 et seq.

U.S. Senate Special Committee on Aging. (1991a). *Developments in aging: 1990, Vol. 1.* Washington, DC: Government Printing Office.

U.S. Senate Special Committee on Aging. (1991b). *Lifelong learning for an aging society* (No. 102-J). Washington, DC: Author.

U.S. Senate Special Committee on Aging. (1993). *Developments in aging: 1992, Vol. 1.* Washington, DC: Government Printing Office.

U.S. Senate Special Committee on Aging. (2000). *Developments in aging: 1997 and 1998, Vol. 1* (Report 106–229). Retrieved June 2, 2001 from http://www.gpo.gov/fdsys/pkg/CRPT-106srpt229/html/CRPT-106srpt229-vol1.htm

U.S. Senate Special Committee on Aging. (2012). *Continuing care retirement communities: Risks to seniors. Summary of Committee investigation.* Retrieved from http://aging.senate.gov/events/hr224cr.pdf

van Heuvelen, M. J. G., Hochstenbach, J. B. M., Brouwer, W. H., de Greef, M. H. G., Ziljstra, G. A. R., van Jaarsveld, E., . . . Mulder, T. (2005). Differences between participants and non-participants in an RCT on physical activity and psychological interventions for older persons. *Aging Clinical and Experimental Research, 17*(3), 236–245

Vickers, D. (Writer). (2012). The Tonight Show: 100-year old Dorothy Custer, Part 2 [Television broadcast]. In *The Tonight Show.* New York, NY: National Broadcasting Company.

Villa, V. M., Wallace, S. P., Bagdasaryan, S., & Aranda, M. P. (2012). Hispanic baby boomers: Health inequities likely to persist in old age. *The Gerontologist, 52*(2), 166–176. doi:10.1093/geront/gns002

Vincent, G. K., & Velkoff, V. A. (2010). *The next four decades. The older population in the United States: 2010 to 2050. Population estimates and projections, P25-1138.* Washington, DC: U.S. Census Bureau. Retrieved from http://www.census.gov/prod/2010pubs/p25-1138.pdf

Vincent, H. K., Vincent, K. R., & Lamb, K. M. (2010). Obesity and mobility disability in the older adult. *Obesity Reviews, 11*(8), 568–579. doi:10.1111/j.1467-789X.2009.00703.x

Vitaliano, P. P., Zhang, J., & Scanlan, J. M. (2003). Is caregiving hazardous to one's physical health? A meta-analysis. *Psychological Bulletin, 129*(6), 946–972. doi:10.1037/0033-2909.129.6.946

Vitolins, M. Z., Tooze, J. A., Golden, S. L., Arcury, T. A., Bell, R. A., Davis, C., . . . Quandt, S. A. (2007). Older adults in the rural south are not meeting healthful eating guidelines. *Journal of the American Dietetic Association, 107*(2), 265–272.e263. doi:10.1016/j.jada.2006.11.009

Volunteers of America. (2011). *Boomer bust 2011: Still unprepared and unaware.* Retrieved from http://www.voa.org/Boomer-Bust-2011

Vorenberg, B. L. (2004). [Review of the book *Roots&Branches: Creating intergenerational theatre,* by A. Strimling]. *Theatre Topics, 14*(2), 502–503. Retrieved from http://muse.jhu.edu/login?auth = 0&type = summary&url = /journals/theatre_topics/v014/14.2vorenberg.html

Wachs, M. (1979). *Transportation for the elderly.* Berkeley: University of California Press.

Wacker, R. R. (1985). *Long term care admission agreements in Colorado: A review.* Denver, CO: Advocacy Assistance Program.

Wacker, R. R. (1992). *What do you think? An evaluation of the Weld County senior nutrition program.* Greeley: University of Northern Colorado.

Wacker, R. R. (1996). *Improving quality of care for nursing home residents: An innovative community program to enhance certified nurse aide training: Final report to the Retirement Research Foundation.* Greeley: University of Northern Colorado.

Wacker, R. R., & Blanding, C. (1994). *Comprehensive leisure and aging study: Final report.* Washington, DC: National Recreation and Park Association.

Wagner, D. L. (1995a). Senior center research in America: An overview of what we know. In D. Shollenberger (Ed.), *Senior centers in America: A blueprint for the future: Outcomes of a national meeting convened to develop recommendations for programs, policies, and funding of senior center programs of the future.* Washington, DC: National Council on the Aging.

Wagner, D. L. (1995b). Senior centers and the "new" elderly cohorts of tomorrow. In D. Shollenberger (Ed.), *Senior centers in America: A blueprint for the future: Outcomes of a national meeting convened to develop recommendations for programs, policies, and funding of senior center programs of the future.* Washington, DC: National Council on the Aging.

Wagner, D. L. (2003). *Workplace programs for family caregivers: Good business and good practice.* Retrieved January 12, 2007 from http://www.caregiver.org/caregiver/jsp/content/pdfs/op_2003_workplace_programs.pdf

Wagner, D. L., & Niles-Yokum, K. J. (2006). Caregiving in a rural context. In R. T. Goins & J. A. Krout (Eds.), *Service delivery to rural older adults: Research, policy, and practice* (pp.145–162). New York, NY: Springer.

Wagner, E. H., Grothaus, L. C., Hecht, J. A., & LaCroix, A. Z. (1991). Factors associated with participation in a senior health promotion program. *The Gerontologist, 31,* 598–602.

Wagnild, G., & Grupp, K. (1991). Major stressors among elderly home care clients. *Home Healthcare Nurse, 9,* 15–21.

Wake Forest University School of Medicine. (2002). *National study of adult day services.* Retrieved January 2, 2007 from http://www.rwjf.org/newsroom/featureDetail.jsp?featureID = 183&type = 2

Waldman, S. (1985). A legislative history of nursing home care. In R. J. Vogel & H. C. Palmer (Eds.), *Long-term care: Perspectives from research and demonstrations* (pp. 507–535). Rockville, MD: Aspen.

Waldrop, J., & Stern, S. M. (2003). *Disability Status: 2000 - C2KBR-17.* Washington, DC: Government Printing Office.

Walker, D. A., & Clarke, M. (2001). Cognitive behavioural psychotherapy: A comparison between younger and older adults in two inner city mental health teams. *Aging & Mental Health, 5,* 197–199.

Walker, J., Bisbee, C., Porter, R., & Flanders, J. (2004). Increasing practitioners' knowledge of participation among elderly adults in senior center activities. *Educational Gerontology, 30,* 353–366.

Walker, S. N. (1989). Health promotion for older adults: Directions for research. *American Journal of Health Promotion, 3,* 47–52.

Wallace, S. P., Cochran, S. D., Durazo, E. M., & Ford, C. L. (2011). *The health of aging lesbian, gay and bisexual adults in California.* Los Angeles: UCLA Center for Health Policy Research. Retrieved from http://www.healthpolicy.ucla.edu/pubs/files/aginglgbpb.pdf

Walster, E., Berscheid, E., & Walster, G. W. (1973). New directions in equity research. *Journal of Personality and Social Psychology, 25,* 176–184.

Walter, K. (2011). *The Senior Community Service Employment Program: A primer for state aging and disability directors.* Washington, DC: National Association of States United for Aging and Disabilities. Retrieved from http://www.nasuad.org/documentation/nasuad_materials/SCSEP%20Primer.pdf

Wardrip, K. (2010a). *Cohousing for older adults.* Washington, DC: AARP Public Policy Institute. Retrieved from http://assets.aarp.org/rgcenter/ppi/liv-com/fs175-cohousing.pdf

Wardrip, K. (2010b). *Strategies to meet the housing needs of older adults.* Washington, DC: AARP Public Policy Institute. Retrieved from http://www.housingpolicy.org/assets/AARP/i38-strategies.pdf

Warrick, L., Netting, E., Christianson, J., & Williams, F. (1992). Hospital-based case management: Results from a demonstration. *The Gerontologist, 32,* 781–788.

Warshaw, G. (1988). *Health promotion and aging: Preventive health services.* Washington, DC: Government Printing Office.

Washko, M. M., Campbell, M., & Tilly, J. (2012). Accelerating the translation of research into practice in long term services and supports: A critical need for federal infrastructure at the nexus of aging and disability. *Journal of Gerontological social Work, 55*(2), 112–125. doi:10.1080/01634372.2011.642471

Washko, M. M., Schack, R. W., Goff, B. A., & Pudlin, B. (2011). Title V of the Older Americans Act, the Senior Community Service Employment Program: Participant demographics and service to racially/ethnically diverse populations. *Journal of Aging & Social Policy, 23,* 182–197.

Webber, P. A., Fox, P., & Burnette, D. (1994). Living alone with Alzheimer's disease: Effects on health and social service utilization patterns. *The Gerontologist, 34,* 8–14.

Webster, R., Lacey, J., & Quine, S. (2007). Palliative care: A public health priotity in developing countries. *Journal of Public Health Policy, 28,* 28–39. doi:10.1057/palgrave.jphp.3200097

Wegman, F., & Aarts, L. (2006). *Advancing sustainable safety: National road safety outlook for 2005–2020.* Leidschendam, Netherlands: SWOV. Retrieved from http://www.swov.nl/rapport/DMDV/Advancing_Sustainable_Safety.pdf

Weiner, B. (2000). Intrapersonal and interpersonal theories of motivation from an attributional perspective. *Educational Psychology Review, 12*(1), 1–14.

Weiner, B. (2011). An attribution theory of motivation. In P. A. M. Van Lange, A. W. Bruglanski, & E. T. Higgins (Eds.), *Handbook of theories of social psychology* (Vol. 1, pp. 135–155). Thousand Oaks, CA: Sage.

Weiner, L. (2007). *The role of community colleges in an aging society.* Washington, DC: AARP. Retrieved from http://web.grcc.cc.mi.us/Pr/olc/2007/RoleofCCinAging_Final.pdf

Weinstock, R. (1978). *The graying of the campus.* New York, NY: Educational Facilities Laboratory.

Weiss, R. S., Bass, S. A., Heimovitz, H. K., & Oka, M. (2005). Japan's silver human resource centers and participant well-being. *Journal of Cross-Cultural Gerontology, 20*(1), 47–66.

Weissert, W. (1977). Adult day care programs in the United States: Current research projects and a survey of ten centers. *Public Health Reports, 92,* 49–56.

Wellman, B., & Wortley, S. (1989). Brothers' keepers: Situating kinship relations in broader networks of social support. *Sociological Perspectives, 32,* 273–306.

Wellman, N. S., Rosenzweig, L. Y., & Lloyd, J. L. (2002). Thirty years of the older Americans nutrition program. *Journal of the American Dietetic Association, 102*(3), 348–350.

Wells, J. (2002). *Setting the PACE: Alternative senior care programs keep up with the needs of the nation's elderly, providing participants with a sense of community and independence.* San Francisco: On Lok. Retrieved January 22, 2007 from http://www.nurseweek.com/news/features/02-12/onlok_print.html

Werner, C. (2011). *The older population: 2010.* 2010 Census Briefs, C2010BR-09. Washington, DC: U.S. Census Bureau. Retrieved from http://www.census.gov/prod/cen2010/briefs/c2010br-09.pdf

West, G. E., Delisle, M. A., Simard, C., & Drouin, D. (1996). Leisure activities and service knowledge and use among the rural elderly. *Journal of Aging and Health, 8,* 254–279.

Whaley, J. S., & Hutchinson, A. B. (1993a). *Implementation guide for Older Americans Act information and referral services.* Washington, DC: National Information and Referral Support Center.

Whaley, J. S., & Hutchinson, A. B. (1993b). *National standards for Older Americans Act information and referral services.* Washington, DC: National Information and Referral Support Center.

White, J. V., Ham, R. J., & Lipschitz, D. A. (1991). *Report of nutritional screening: Vol. 1. Toward a common view.* Washington, DC: Nutrition Screening Initiative.

White, M., Gundrum, G., Shearer, S., & Simmons, J. (1994). A role for case managers in the physician office. *Journal of Case Management, 3,* 62–68.

White House. (2011). *The American Jobs Act: President Obama's plan to create jobs now.* Retrieved from http://www.whitehouse.gov/sites/default/files/jobs_act.pdf

White House. (2012a). *An economy built to last and security for seniors.* Retrieved from http://www.whitehouse.gov/omb/factsheet/an-economy-built-to-last-and-security-for-seniors

White House. (2012b). *Seniors and Social Security.* Retrieved from http://www.whitehouse.gov/issues/seniors-and-social-security

White House Conference on Aging. (2006). *The booming dynamics of aging: From awareness to action. Final report of the 2005 White House Conference on Aging.* Retrieved September 20, 2006 from http://nicoa.org/wp-content/uploads/2012/04/2005-WHCOA-Final-Report.pdf

Whitlatch, C. J., & Feinberg, L. S. (2006). Family and friends as respite providers. *Journal of Aging & Social Policy, 18*(3–4), 127–139. doi:10.1300/J031v18n03_09

Wieland, D., Kinosian, B., Stallard, E., & Boland, R. (2012). Does Medicaid pay more to a Program of All-Inclusive Care for the Elderly (PACE) than for fee-for-service long-term care? *The Journals of Gerontology, Series A.* doi:10.1093/gerona/gls13.

Wieland, D., Lamb, V. L., Sutton, S. R., Boland, R., Clark, M., Friedman, S., et al. (2000). Hospitalization in the Program of All-Inclusive Care for the Elderly (PACE): Rates, concomitants, and predictors. *Journal of the American Geriatric Society, 48,* 1373–1380.

Wiencek, T. (1991). How the Older Workers' Benefit Protection Act affects employers. *Practice Lawyer, 37,* 69–76.

Wiener, J. M. (2003). An assessment of strategies for improving quality of care in nursing homes. *The Gerontologist, 43, Special Issue II,* 19–27.

Wiener, J. M., Sullivan, C. M., & Skaggs, J. (1996). *Spending down to Medicaid: New data on the role of Medicaid in paying from nursing home care* (AARP Public Policy Institute Report No. 9607). Washington, DC: AARP Public Policy Institute.

Wilke, H., & Lazette, J. T. (1970). The obligation to help: The effects of amount of prior help on subsequent helping behavior. *Journal of Experimental Social Psychology, 6,* 488–493.

Wilken, C. S., & Stanback, B. M. (2011). Strategies to support rural caregivers: Practice, education and training, research, policy, and advocacy. In R. C. Talley, K. Chwalisz, & K. C. Buckwalter (Eds.), *Rural caregiving in the United States: Research, practice, policy* (pp. 197–211). New York, NY: Springer.

Williams, A. L., Haber, D., Weaver, G. D., & Freeman, J. L. (1998). Altruistic activity: Does it make a difference in the senior center? *Activities, Adaptation & Aging, 22*(4), 31–39.

Williams, M. M. (2011). *SeniorNet enters its 25th year of bringing computers and the Internet to older Americans.* Retrieved from http://seniornet.org/index.php?option = com_content&view = article&id = 683:seniornet-adds-two-new-members-to-its-board-of-directors&catid = 37:press-releases&Itemid = 232

Williamson, J. B. (1974). The stigma of public dependency: A comparison of alternative forms of public aid to the poor. *Social Problems, 22,* 213–238.

Willis, S. (2006). Technology and learning in current and future generations of elders. *Generations, 30*(2), 44–48.

Wilson, L., & Simson, S. P. (1993). Senior volunteerism policies at the local level: Adaptation and leadership in the 21st century. *Journal of Volunteer Administration, 11*(4), 15–23.

Wilson, L., & Simson, S. P. (Eds.). (2006). *Civic engagement and the Baby Boomer generation: Research, policy, and practice perspectives.* New York, NY: Routledge

Wingard, D. L., Jones, D. W., & Kaplan, R. M. (1987). Institutional care utilization by the elderly: A critical review. *The Gerontologist, 27,* 156–163.

Winter, L., & Gitlin, L. N. (2007). Evaluation of a telephone-based support group intervention for female caregivers of community-dwelling individuals with dementia. *American Journal of Alzheimer's Disease and Other Dementias, 21,* 391–397.

Wolf, R. S. (1996). Understanding elder abuse and neglect. *Aging, 367,* 4–9.

Wolfe, M. A., & Brady, E. M. (2010). Adult and continuing education for an aging society. In C. E. Kasworm, A. D. Rose, & J. M. Ross-Gordon (Eds.), *Handbook of adult and continuing education* (pp. 369–378). Thousands Oaks, CA: Sage.

Wolfe, W. S., Olson, C. M., Kendall, A., & Frongillo, E. A. (1998). Hunger and food insecurity in the elderly. *Journal of Aging and Health, 10*(3), 327–350.

Wolff, J. L., Giovannetti, E. R., Boyd, C. M., Reider, L., Palmer, S., Scharfstein, D. O., . . . Boult, C. (2010). Effects of guided care on family caregivers. *The Gerontologist, 50,* 459–470.

Wolinsky, F. D., Coe, R. M., Miller, D. K., Prendergast, J. M., Creel, M. J., & Chavez, M. N. (1983). Health services utilization among the noninstitutionalized elderly. *Journal of Health and Social Behavior, 24,* 325–337.

Woller, K., Buboltz, M. P., Walter, C., & Loveland, J. M. (2007). Psychological reactance: Examination across age, ethnicity, and gender. *American Journal of Psychology, 120*(1), 15–24.

Wong, J. D., & Hardy, M. A. (2009). Women's retirement expectations: How stable are they? *Journal of Gerontology: Social Sciences, 64B,* 77–86. doi:10.1093/geronb/gbn010

Wood, S., & Liossis, P. (2007). Potentially stressful life events and emotional closeness between grandparents and adult grandchildren. *Journal of Family Issues, 28*(3), 380–398. doi:10.1177/0192513x06293893

Woolcock, M. (2001). The place of social capital in understanding social and economic outcomes. *Canadian Journal of Policy Research, 2*(1), 11–17.

Wright, B. (2004). *Assisted living in the United States.* Washington, DC: AARP Public Policy Institute. Retrieved December 28, 2006 from http://assets.aarp.org/rgcenter/post-import/fs62r_assisted.pdf

Wu, K. B. (2011a). *Income, poverty, and health insurance coverage of older Americans, 2010.* Washington, DC: AARP Public Policy Institute. Retrieved from http://www.aarp.org/content/dam/aarp/research/public_policy_institute/econ_sec/2011/fs232v2.pdf

Wu, K. B. (2011b). *Family income sources for older persons, 2009.* Washington, DC: AARP Public Policy Institute. Retrieved from http://assets.aarp.org/rgcenter/ppi/econ-sec/fs224-economic.pdf

Wurtman, J. J., Lieberman, H., Tsay, R., Nader, T., & Chew, B. (1988). Calorie and nutrient intakes of elderly and young subjects measured under identical conditions. *Journal of Gerontology, 79,* 117–131.

Yankelovich, D. (2005, November 25). Ferment and change: Higher education in 2015. *Chronicle of Higher Education.* Retrieved January 13, 2007 from http://www.chronicle.com/

Yee, J. L., & Schulz, R. (2000). Gender differences in psychiatric morbidity among family caregivers: A review and analysis. *The Gerontologist, 40,* 147–164.

Yeo, G. (1993). Ethnicity and nursing homes: Factors affecting use and successful components for culturally sensitive care. In C. M. Barresi & D. E. Stull (Eds.), *Ethnic elderly and long term care* (pp. 161–177). New York, NY: Springer.

Yin, T., Zhou, Q., & Bashford, C. (2002). Burden on family members caring for frail elderly: A meta-analysis of interventions. *Nursing Research, 51,* 199–208.

Young, K. (1992). LIR program and organizational models. In R. Fischer, M. Blazey, & H. Lipman (Eds.), *Students of the third age* (pp. 25–37). New York, NY: Macmillan.

Zarem, J. E. (Ed.). (2010). *Today's Continuing Care Retirement Community (CCRC).* Washington, DC: American Seniors Housing Association. Retrieved from http://www.leadingage.org/uploadedFiles/Content/Consumers/Paying_for_Aging_Services/CCRCcharacteristics_7_2011.pdf

Zarit, S. H. (2006). Assessment of family caregivers: A research perspective. In Family Caregiver Alliance (Ed.), *Caregiver assessment: Voices and views from the field: Report from a National Consensus Development Conference* (Vol. 2, pp. 113–137). San Francisco, CA: Family Caregiver Alliance.

Zarit, S. H. (2008). Empircally supported treatement for family caregivers. In S. H. Qualls & S. H. Zarit (Eds.), *Aging families and caregiving* (pp. 131–154). Hoboken, NJ: John Wiley & Sons.

Zbylot, S., Job, C., McCormick, E., Boulter, C., & Moore, A. (1995). A case-mix classification system for long-term care facilities. *Nursing Management, 26*(4), 49–54.

Zedlewski, S. R., Barnes, R., Burt, M., McBride, T., & Meyer, J. (1990). *The needs of the elderly in the 21st century* (Urban Institute Rep. No. 90–5). Washington, DC: Urban Institute.

Zedlewski, S. R., & Schaner, S. G. (2006). *Older adults engaged as volunteers.* Retrieved January 3, 2007 from http://www.urban.org/publications/311325.html

Zhan, L., Cloutterbuck, J., Keshian, J., & Lombardi, L. (1998). Promoting health: Perspectives from ethnic elderly women. *Journal of Community Health Nursing, 15*(1), 31–44.

Zickuhr, K. (2010). *Generations 2010.* Washington, DC: Pew Research Foundation. Retrieved from http://www.pewinternet.org/~/media//Files/Reports/2010/PIP_Generations_and_Tech10.pdf

Ziliak, J., & Gundersen, C. (2011). *Food insecurity among older adults.* Washington, DC: AARP Foundation. Retrieved from http://www.aarp.org/content/dam/aarp/aarp_foundation/pdf_2011/AARPFoundation_HungerReport_2011.pdf

Zissimopoulos, J. M., & Karoly, L. A. (2007). Transitions to self-employment at older ages: The role of wealth, health, health insurance and other factors. *Labour Economics, 14,* 269–295.

Index

About the Authors

Robbyn R. Wacker, PhD, is the provost and senior vice president and professor of gerontology at the University of Northern Colorado in Greeley, Colorado. Her research interests include international aging social policy and psychosocial predictors of community service use among older adults. Prior to obtaining her doctorate, she provided legal assistance to older adults through the Title III Legal Services program. Along with her administrative duties, she continues to be an active scholar in the field of gerontology. She has published over 65 referred presentations, scholarly articles, and conference proceedings, and is the author of three books. She has earned numerous university and professional awards, including UNC's Academic Leadership Excellence Award, and was selected by the Harvard Graduate School of Education to attend its Management Development Program for leaders in higher education.

Karen A. Roberto, PhD, is the director of the Center for Gerontology; founding director of the Institute of Society, Culture, and Environment; and professor of human development at Virginia Polytechnic Institute and State University. She also holds adjunct appointments in the Departments of Internal Medicine, and Psychiatry and Behavioral Medicine at the Virginia Tech Carilion School of Medicine in Roanoke, Virginia. Her research program focuses on health and social support in late life, and includes studies of the health of rural older women, family relationships and caregiving, and elder abuse and exploitation. She has published over 150 scholarly articles and book chapters and is the editor/author of 10 books. She is a fellow of the Gerontological Society of America, the Association for Gerontology in Higher Education, the National Council on Family Relations, and the World Demographic Association. She is a recipient of the Gordon Streib Academic Gerontologist Award from the Southern Gerontological Society, the Virginia Tech Alumni Award for Excellence in Research, and the Behavioral and Social Sciences Distinguished Mentorship Award from the Gerontological Society of America.